Numerical and Evolutionary Optimization 2020

Numerical and Evolutionary Optimization 2020

Editors

Marcela Quiroz-Castellanos
Juan Gabriel Ruiz Ruiz
Luis Gerardo de la Fraga
Oliver Schütze

MDPI • Basel • Beijing • Wuhan • Barcelona • Belgrade • Manchester • Tokyo • Cluj • Tianjin

Editors

Marcela Quiroz-Castellanos
Universidad Veracruzana
Mexico

Juan Gabriel Ruiz Ruiz
Universidad de la Sierra Juarez
Mexico

Luis Gerardo de la Fraga
CINVESTAV-IPN
Mexico

Oliver Schütze
CINVESTAV-IPN
Mexico

Editorial Office
MDPI
St. Alban-Anlage 66
4052 Basel, Switzerland

This is a reprint of articles from the Special Issue published online in the open access journal *Mathematical and Computational Applications* (ISSN 2297-8747) (available at: https://www.mdpi.com/journal/mca/special_issues/NEO20).

For citation purposes, cite each article independently as indicated on the article page online and as indicated below:

LastName, A.A.; LastName, B.B.; LastName, C.C. Article Title. *Journal Name* **Year**, *Volume Number*, Page Range.

ISBN 978-3-0365-1669-1 (Hbk)
ISBN 978-3-0365-1670-7 (PDF)

© 2021 by the authors. Articles in this book are Open Access and distributed under the Creative Commons Attribution (CC BY) license, which allows users to download, copy and build upon published articles, as long as the author and publisher are properly credited, which ensures maximum dissemination and a wider impact of our publications.

The book as a whole is distributed by MDPI under the terms and conditions of the Creative Commons license CC BY-NC-ND.

Contents

About the Editors vii

Preface to "Numerical and Evolutionary Optimization 2020" ix

Kalyanmoy Deb, Proteek Chandan Roy and Rayan Hussein
Surrogate Modeling Approaches for Multiobjective Optimization: Methods, Taxonomy, and Results
Reprinted from: *Math. Comput. Appl.* 2021, 26, 5, doi:10.3390/mca26010005 1

José-Yaír Guzmán-Gaspar, Efrén Mezura-Montes and Saúl Domínguez-Isidro
Differential Evolution in Robust Optimization Over Time Using a Survival Time Approach
Reprinted from: *Math. Comput. Appl.* 2020, 25, 72, doi:10.3390/mca25040072 29

Xiatong Cai, Abdolmajid Mohammadian and Hamidreza Shirkhani
An Efficient Framework for Multi-Objective Risk-Informed Decision Support Systems for Drainage Rehabilitation
Reprinted from: *Math. Comput. Appl.* 2020, 25, 73, doi:10.3390/mca25040073 45

Perla Rubi Castañeda-Aviña, Esteban Tlelo-Cuautle, and Luis Gerardo de la Fraga
Single-Objective Optimization of a CMOS VCO Considering PVT and Monte Carlo Simulations
Reprinted from: *Math. Comput. Appl.* 2020, 25, 76, doi:10.3390/mca25040076 61

Fernanda Berltrán, Oliver Cuate and Oliver Schütze
The Pareto Tracer for General Inequality Constrained Multi-Objective Optimization Problems
Reprinted from: *Math. Comput. Appl.* 2020, 25, 80, doi:10.3390/mca25040080 75

Iman Bahreini Toussi, Abdolmajid Mohammadian and Reza Kianoush
Prediction of Maximum Pressure at the Roofs of Rectangular Water Tanks Subjected to Harmonic Base Excitation Using the Multi-Gene Genetic Programming Method
Reprinted from: *Math. Comput. Appl.* 2021, 26, 6, doi:10.3390/mca26010006 95

Juan Frausto-Solis, Leonor Hernández-Ramírez, Guadalupe Castilla-Valdez, Juan J. González-Barbosa and Juan P. Sánchez-Hernández
Chaotic Multi-Objective Simulated Annealing and Threshold Accepting for Job Shop Scheduling Problem
Reprinted from: *Math. Comput. Appl.* 2021, 26, 8, doi:10.3390/mca26010008 117

Luis Gerardo de la Fraga
Differential Evolution under Fixed Point Arithmetic and FP16 Numbers
Reprinted from: *Math. Comput. Appl.* 2021, 26, 13, doi:10.3390/mca26010013 151

Alejandro Castellanos-Alvarez, Laura Cruz-Reyes, Eduardo Fer, Nelson Rangel-Valdez, Claudia Gómez-Santillán, Hector Fraire and José Alfredo Brambila-Hernández
A Method for Integration of Preferences to a Multi-Objective Evolutionary Algorithm Using Ordinal Multi-Criteria Classification
Reprinted from: *Math. Comput. Appl.* 2021, 26, 27, doi:10.3390/mca26020027 161

Mercedes Perez-Villafuerte, Laura Cruz-Reyes, Nelson Rangel-Valdez, Claudia Gomez-Santillan and Héctor Fraire-Huacuja
Effect of the Profile of the Decision Maker in the Search for Solutions in the Decision-Making Process
Reprinted from: *Math. Comput. Appl.* 2021, 26, 28, doi:10.3390/mca26020028 175

Juan Frausto-Solís, Lucía J. Hernández-González, Juan J. González-Barbosa,
Juan Paulo Sánchez-Hernández and Edgar Román-Rangel
Convolutional Neural Network–Component Transformation (CNN–CT) for Confirmed
COVID-19 Cases
Reprinted from: *Math. Comput. Appl.* **2021**, *26*, 29, doi:10.3390/mca26020029 197

Manuel Berkemeier and Sebastian Peitz
Derivative-Free Multiobjective Trust Region Descent Method Using Radial Basis Function Surrogate Models
Reprinted from: *Math. Comput. Appl.* **2021**, *26*, 31, doi:10.3390/mca26020031 209

Teodoro Macias-Escobar, Laura Cruz-Reyes, César Medina-Trejo, Claudia Gómez-Santillán, Nelson Rangel-Valdez and Héctor Fraire-Huacuja
An Interactive Recommendation System for Decision Making Based on the Characterization of Cognitive Tasks
Reprinted from: *Math. Comput. Appl.* **2021**, *26*, 35, doi:10.3390/mca26020035 247

**Alejandro Estrada-Padilla, Daniela Lopez-Garcia, Claudia Gómez-Santillán,
Héctor Joaquín Fraire-Huacuja, Laura Cruz-Reyes, Nelson Rangel-Valdez and
María Lucila Morales-Rodríguez**
Modeling and Optimizing the Multi-Objective Portfolio Optimization Problem with
Trapezoidal Fuzzy Parameters
Reprinted from: *Math. Comput. Appl.* **2021**, *26*, 36, doi:10.3390/mca26020036 283

**Juan P. Sánchez-Hernández, Juan Frausto-Solís, Juan J. González-Barbosa,
Diego A. Soto-Monterrubio, Fanny G. Maldonado-Nava and Guadalupe Castilla-Valdez**
A Peptides Prediction Methodology for Tertiary Structure Based on Simulated Annealing
Reprinted from: *Math. Comput. Appl.* **2021**, *26*, 39, doi:10.3390/mca26020039 313

Esmeralda López, René F. Domínguez-Cruz and Iván Salgado-Tránsito
Optimization of Power Generation Grids: A Case of Study in Eastern Mexico
Reprinted from: *Math. Comput. Appl.* **2021**, *26*, 46, doi:10.3390/mca26020046 335

About the Editors

Marcela Quiroz-Castellanos is a full-time researcher with the Artificial Intelligence Research Institute at the Universidad Veracruzana in Xalapa City, Mexico. Her research interests include: Combinatorial Optimization, Metaheuristics, Experimental Algorithms, Characterization and Data Mining. She received her Ph.D. in Computer Science from the Instituto Tecnológico de Tijuana, Mexico. She studied engineering in computer systems and received the master's degree in Computer Science at the Instituto Tecnológico de Ciudad Madero, Mexico. She is a member of the Mexican National Researchers System (SNI), and also a member of the directive committees of the Mexican Computing Academy (AMexComp) and the Mexican Robotics Federation (FMR).

Juan Gabriel Ruiz Ruiz is a Research Professor at the University of the Sierra Juarez (UNSIJ), Oaxaca, Mexico. His areas of interest are related to Evolutionary Computing, Human Factor, People-Centered Design, Semiotics, and Usability in Interactive Systems. In 2020, he served as General Chair of the 8th International Workshop on Numerical and Evolutionary Optimization (NEO). In 2017, he was General Chair of the 2nd Congress of Informatics and Technological Innovation (CIIT-2017) and Guest Editor for the special issue of the IPN Research in Computing Science magazine: Advances in Social Informatics and its Applications.

Luis Gerardo de la Fraga received the BS degree in Electrical Engineering from the Veracruz Institute of Technology (Veracruz, Mexico), in 1992, the MSc degree from the National Institute of Astrophysics, Optics, and Electronics (INAOE), Puebla, Mexico, in 1994, and the PhD degree from the Autonomous University of Madrid, Spain, in 1998. He has developed his predoctoral work in the National Center of Biotechnology (CNB) in Madrid, Spain. Since 2000, he has been with the Computer Science Department at the Center of Research and Advanced Studies (Cinvestav) in Mexico City, Mexico. His research areas include Computer Vision, application of Evolutionary Algorithms, Applied Mathematics, and Network Security. He is very enthusiastic about open software and GNU/Linux systems. Dr. de la Fraga has published more than 35 articles in international journals, 6 book chapters, 2 books, and more than 55 articles in international conferences. He has graduated 28 MSc and 4 PhD students. He is member of the ACM and IEEE societies since 2005.

Oliver Schütze is Full Professor at the Cinvestav—IPN in Mexico City, Mexico. His main research interests are in numerical and evolutionary optimization. He is co-author of more than 160 publications including two monographs, five school textbooks, and 12 edited books. Two of his papers have received the IEEE Transactions on Evolutionary Computation Outstanding Paper Award (in 2010 and 2012). He is founder of the Numerical and Evolutionary Optimization (NEO) workshop series. He is Editor-in-Chief of the journal Mathematical and Computational Applications, and is a member of the Editorial Board of the journals *Engineering Optimization*, *Computational Optimization and Applications*, and *Mathematical Problems in Engineering*.

Preface to "Numerical and Evolutionary Optimization 2020"

This volume was inspired by the 8th International Workshop on Numerical and Evolutionary Optimization (NEO), hosted by the Universidad de la Sierra Juárez, Oaxaca, Mexico, the Universidad Veracruzana, Xalapa, Mexico, and the Cinvestav-IPN, Mexico City, Mexico. The workshop was held on November 18 and 19, 2020, as an online-only event and was attended by a total of around 70 researchers, plus another 130 students from the Research Experience Day of NEO 2020.

Solving scientific and engineering problems from the real world is currently a very complicated task; that is why the development of powerful search and optimization techniques is of great importance. Two well-established fields focus on this duty; they are (i) traditional numerical optimization techniques and (ii) bio-inspired metaheuristic methods. Both general approaches have unique strengths and weaknesses, allowing researchers to solve some challenging problems but still failing in others. The goal of NEO is to gather people from both fields to discuss, compare, and merge these complementary perspectives. Collaborative work allows researchers to maximize strengths and to minimize the weaknesses of both paradigms. NEO also intends to help researchers in these fields to understand and tackle real-world problems such as pattern recognition, routing, energy, lines of production, prediction, and modeling, among others.

This Special Issue consists of 16 research papers. In the first paper, https://doi.org/10.3390/mca26010005, K. Deb et al. survey surrogate modeling approaches for the numerical treatment of multi-objective optimization problems. Moreover, the authors propose an adaptive switching based metamodeling approach yielding results that are highly competitive to state-of-the-art approaches.

The following ten papers are devoted to the design of new algorithms for particular optimization problems. In the second paper, https://doi.org/10.3390/mca26020031, M. Berkemeier and S. Peitz present a local trust region descent algorithm for unconstrained and convexly constrained multi-objective optimization problems. The method targets at problems that have at least one objective function that is computationally expensive. Convergence of the derivative-free method to a Pareto critical point is proven. In the third paper, https://doi.org/10.3390/mca26020028, M. Perez-Villafuerte proposes a new hybrid multi-objective optimization evolutionary algorithm, called P-HMCSGA, that allows to incorporate decision makers preferences already in early stages of the optimization process. The strength of the novel method is illustrated on real-size multi-objective project portfolio problems. In the fourth paper, https://doi.org/10.3390/mca26020027, A. Castellanos-Alvarez et al. propose a method, NSGA-III-P, for the integration of preferences to a multi-objective evolutionary algorithm using ordinal multi-criteria classification. Numerical results show that the new method is capable of identifying the proper region of interest as specified by the decision maker. In the fifth paper, https://doi.org/10.3390/mca26020035, T. Macias-Escobar et al. propose a new interactive recommendation system for the decision making process based on the characterization of cognitive tasks. The system focuses on a user–system interaction that guides the search towards the best solution considering a decision maker's preferences. The developed prototype has been assessed by several test users leading to a satisfying score and most overall acceptance.

In the sixth paper, https://doi.org/10.3390/mca25040072, J.-Y. Guzmán-Gaspar et al. present an empirical comparison of the standard differential evolution (DE) against three random sampling methods to solve particular robust optimization problems in dynamic environments. The findings indicate that DE is a suitable algorithm to deal with this type of dynamic search space when a survival time approach is considered. In the seventh paper, https://doi.org/10.3390/mca26020039, J. P. Sánchez-Hernández et al. address the protein folding problem. To this end, they present the algorithm GRSA-SSP, a hybrid of golden ratio simulated annealing with a secondary structure prediction. Numerical results show that the new algorithm competes to the state-of-the-art in small peptides except when predicting the largest peptides. In the eighth paper, https://doi.org/10.3390/mca26020036, A. Estrada-Padilla et al. propose a new methodology to deal with uncertainties in multi-objective portfolio optimization problems via using fuzzy numbers. The results show a significant difference in performance favoring the proposed steady-state algorithm based on the fuzzy adaptive multi-objective evolutionary (FAME) methodology. In the ninth paper, https://doi.org/10.3390/mca26010008, J. Frausto-Solis et al. propose two multi-objective job shop scheduling metaheuristics based on Simulated Annealing: Chaotic Multi-Objective Simulated Annealing (CMOSA) and Chaotic Multi-Objective Threshold Accepting (CMOTA). Numerical results indicate that the two novel methods are highly competitive to the state-of-the-art. In the tenth paper, https://doi.org/10.3390/mca26010013, L. G. de la Fraga analyzes the use of numbers with 16 bits in the conventional Differential Evolution (DE) algorithm. It is shown that the additional use of fixed point arithmetic can speed up the evaluation time of the objective function. In the eleventh paper, https://doi.org/10.3390/mca25040080, F. Beltrán et al. deal with a continuation method for the numerical treatment of multi-objective optimization problems. More precisely, the Pareto Tracer is extended to treat general inequalities which greatly enhances its applicability.

The last five papers of this Special Issue deal with the numerical treatment of particular applications that arise in the real world. In the twelfth paper, https://doi.org/10.3390/mca26020046, are presented some preliminary results of a study of 17 interconnected power generation plants situated in eastern Mexico. The study shows that fossil fuel plants, besides emitting greenhouse gases that affect human health and the environment, incur maintenance expenses even without operation. In the thirteenth paper, https://doi.org/10.3390/mca26020029, J. Frausto-Solis et al. propose a new method designed to confirm cases of COVID-19 in the United States, Mexico, Brazil, and Colombia, based on Component Transformation and Convolutional Neural Networks. Numerical results show that it consistently achieves highly competitive results in terms of the MAPE metric. In the fourteenth paper, https://doi.org/10.3390/mca25040073, X. Cai et al., propose and analyze a novel framework for the multi-objective risk-informed decision support systems for the drainage rehabilitation problem. This study shows that the conventional framework can be significantly improved in terms of calculation speed and cost-effectiveness by removing the constraint function and adding more objective functions. In the fifteenth paper, https://doi.org/10.3390/mca26010006, I. Bahreini Toussi et al. investigate the impact forces caused by liquid storage tanks which can lead to structural damage as well as economic and environmental losses. To this end, an OpenFOAM numerical model is used to simulate various tank sizes with different liquid heights. The last contribution of this Special Issue is given by the sixteenth paper, https://doi.org/10.3390/mca25040076. P. R. Castañeda-Aviña et al. design an analog circuit, a voltage-controlled oscillator (VCO), optimized using Differential Evolution. It is shown that the suggested approach yields highly robust solutions.

Finally, we thank all participants at NEO 2020 and hope that this book can be a contemporary reference regarding the field of numerical evolutionary optimization and its exciting applications.

Marcela Quiroz-Castellanos, Juan Gabriel Ruiz Ruiz, Luis Gerardo de la Fraga, Oliver Schütze
Editors

Review

Surrogate Modeling Approaches for Multiobjective Optimization: Methods, Taxonomy, and Results

Kalyanmoy Deb *,†, Proteek Chandan Roy † and Rayan Hussein †

Computational Optimization and Innovation (COIN) Laboratory, Michigan State University, East Lansing, MI 48824, USA; royproteekchandan@gmail.com (P.C.R.); husseinr@egr.msu.edu (R.H.)
* Correspondence: kdeb@egr.msu.edu
† These authors contributed equally to this work.

Abstract: Most practical optimization problems are comprised of multiple conflicting objectives and constraints which involve time-consuming simulations. Construction of metamodels of objectives and constraints from a few high-fidelity solutions and a subsequent optimization of metamodels to find in-fill solutions in an iterative manner remain a common metamodeling based optimization strategy. The authors have previously proposed a taxonomy of 10 different metamodeling frameworks for multiobjective optimization problems, each of which constructs metamodels of objectives and constraints independently or in an aggregated manner. Of the 10 frameworks, five follow a generative approach in which a single Pareto-optimal solution is found at a time and other five frameworks were proposed to find multiple Pareto-optimal solutions simultaneously. Of the 10 frameworks, two frameworks (M3-2 and M4-2) are detailed here for the first time involving multimodal optimization methods. In this paper, we also propose an adaptive switching based metamodeling (ASM) approach by switching among all 10 frameworks in successive epochs using a statistical comparison of metamodeling accuracy of all 10 frameworks. On 18 problems from three to five objectives, the ASM approach performs better than the individual frameworks alone. Finally, the ASM approach is compared with three other recently proposed multiobjective metamodeling methods and superior performance of the ASM approach is observed. With growing interest in metamodeling approaches for multiobjective optimization, this paper evaluates existing strategies and proposes a viable adaptive strategy by portraying importance of using an ensemble of metamodeling frameworks for a more reliable multiobjective optimization for a limited budget of solution evaluations.

Keywords: surrogate modeling; multiobjective optimization; evolutionary algorithms; kriging method; ensemble method; adaptive algorithm

1. Introduction

Practical problems often require expensive simulation of accurate high-fidelity models. To get close to the optimum of these models, most multiobjective optimization algorithms need to compute a large number of solution evaluations. However, in practice, only a handful of solution evaluations are allowed due to the overall time constraint available to solve such problems. Researchers usually resort to surrogate models or metamodels constructed from a few high-fidelity solution evaluations to replace computationally expensive models to drive an optimization task [1–3]. For example, Gaussian process model, Kriging, or response surface method is commonly used. The Kriging method is of particular interest, since it is able to provide an approximated function as well as an estimate of uncertainty of the prediction of the function [4].

In extending the metamodeling concept to multiobjective optimization problems, an obvious issue is that multiple objective and constraint functions are required to be metamodeled before proceeding with the optimization algorithm. Despite this challenge of multiple metamodeling efforts, a good number of studies have been made to solve computationally expensive multiobjective optimization problems using metamodeling based evolutionary algorithms [5–10]. However, most of these studies ignored constraints and extending an unconstrained optimization algorithm to constrained optimization is not trivial [11]. In any case, the structure of most of these methods is as follows. Starting an initial archive of solutions obtained by an usual Latin-hypercube sampling, a metamodel for each objective and constraint function is built independently [12,13]. Then, in an *epoch*—one cycle of metamodel development and their use to obtain a set of *in-fill* solutions, an evolutionary multiobjective optimization (EMO) algorithm is used to optimize the metamodeled objectives and constraints to find one or more in-fill points. Thereafter, the in-fill points are evaluated using high-fidelity models and saved into the archive. Next, new metamodels are built using the augmented archive members and the procedure is repeated in several epochs until the allocated number of solution evaluations is consumed [5,14–19]. Many computationally expensive optimization problems involve noisy high-fidelity simulation models. Noise can come from inputs, stochastic processes of the simulation, or the output measurements. In this paper, we do not explicitly discuss the effect of noise in handling metamodeling problems, but we recognize that this is an important matter in solving practical problems.

In a recent taxonomy study [20], authors have categorized different plausible multiobjective metamodeling approaches into 10 frameworks, of which the above-described popular method falls within the first two frameworks—M1-1 or M1-2, depending on whether a single or multiple nondominated in-fill solutions are found in each epoch. The other eight frameworks were not straightforward from a point of view extending single-objective metamodeling approaches to multiobjective optimization and hence were not explored in the past. Moreover, the final two frameworks (M5 and M6) attempt to metamodel an EMO algorithm's implicit overall fitness (or selection) function directly, instead of metamodeling an aggregate or individual objective and constraint functions. There is an advantage of formulating a taxonomy, so that any foreseeable future metamodeling method can also be categorized to fall within one of the 10 frameworks. Moreover, the taxonomy also provides new insights to other currently unexplored ways of handling metamodels within a multiobjective optimization algorithm.

So far, each framework has been applied alone in one complete optimization run to solve a problem, but in a recent study [21], a manual switching of one framework to another after 50% of allocated solution evaluations has produced improved results. An optimization process goes through different features of the multiobjective landscape and it is natural that a different metamodeling framework may be efficient at different phases of a run. These studies are the genesis of this current study, in which we propose an adaptive switching based metamodeling (ASM) approach, which automatically finds one of the 10 best-performing frameworks at the end of each epoch after a detailed statistical study, thereby establishing self-adaptive and efficient overall metamodeling based optimization approach.

In the remainder of the paper, Section 2 briefly describes a summary of recent related works. Section 3 provides a brief description of each of 10 metamodeling frameworks for multiobjective optimization. The proposed ASM approach is described in Section 4. Our extensive results on unconstrained and constrained test problems for each framework alone and the ASM approach are presented in Section 5. A comparative study of the ASM approach with three recent existing algorithms is presented in Section 5.5. We summarize our study of the switching framework based surrogate-assisted optimization with future research directions in Section 6.

2. Past Methods of Metamodeling for Multiobjective Optimization

We consider the following original multi- or many-objective optimization problem (P), involving n real-valued variables ($\mathbf{x}$), J inequality constraints ($\mathbf{g}$) (equality constraints, if any, are assumed to be converted to two inequality constraints), and M objective functions ($\mathbf{f}$):

$$\begin{aligned}
\text{Minimize} \quad & (f_1(\mathbf{x}), f_2(\mathbf{x}), \ldots, f_M(\mathbf{x})), \\
\text{Subject to} \quad & g_j(\mathbf{x}) \leq 0, \quad j = 1, 2, \ldots, J, \\
& x_i^{(L)} \leq x_i \leq x_i^{(U)}, \quad i = 1, 2, \ldots, n.
\end{aligned} \quad (1)$$

In this study, we assume that all objective and constraint functions are *computationally expensive* to compute and that they need to be computed independent to each other for every new solution $\mathbf{x}$. To distinguish from the original functions, the respective metamodeled function is represented with a "tilde" (such as, $\widetilde{f}_i(\mathbf{x})$ or $\widetilde{g}_j(\mathbf{x})$). The resulting metamodeled problem is denoted here as MP, which is formed with developed metamodels of individual objective and constraints or their aggregates. *In-fill* solutions are defined as optimal solutions of problem MP. It is assumed here that constructing the metamodels and their comparisons among each other consume comparatively much less time than evaluating objective and constraints exactly, hence, if the metamodels are close to the original functions, the process can end up with a huge savings in computational time without much sacrifice in solution accuracy. Naturally, in-fill solutions (obtained from metamodels) need to be evaluated using original objective and constraints (termed here as "high-fidelity" evaluations) and can be used to refine the metamodels for their subsequent use within the overall optimization approach.

A number of efficient metamodeling frameworks have been proposed recently for multiobjective optimization [10,22–28], including a parallel implementation concept [29]. These frameworks use different metamodeling methods to approximate objective and constraint functions, such as radial basis functions (RBFs), Kriging, Bayesian neural network, support vector regression, and others [30]. Most of these methods proposed a separate metamodel for each objective and constraint function, akin to our framework M1. Another study have used multiple spatially distributed surrogate models for multiobjective optimization [31]. It is clear that this requires a lot of metamodeling efforts and metamodeling errors from different models can accrue and make the overall optimization to be highly error-prone. As will be clear later, these methods will fall under our M1-2 framework.

Zhang et al. [14] proposed the MOEA/D-EGO algorithm which metamodeled each objective function independently. They constructed multiple expected global optimization (EGO) functions for multiple reference lines of the MOEA/D approach to find a number of trade-off solutions in each optimization task. No constraint handling procedure was suggested. Thus, this method falls under our M1-2 framework.

Chugh et al. [23] proposed a surrogate-assisted adaptive reference vectors guided evolutionary algorithm (K-RVEA) for computationally expensive optimization problems with more than three objectives. Since all objectives and constraints are metamodeled separately, this method also falls under our M1-2 framework. While no constraint handling was proposed with the original study, a later version included constraint handling [32].

Zhao et al. [24] classified the sample data into clusters based on their similarities in the variable space. Then, a local metamodel was built for each cluster of the sample data. A global metamodel is then built using these local metamodels considering their contributions in different regions of the variable space. Due to the construction and optimization of multiple metamodels, one for each cluster, this method belongs to our M-3 framework. The use of a global metamodel by combining all local cluster-wise metamodels qualify this method under the M3-2 framework. No constraint handling method is suggested.

Bhattacharjee et al. [25] used an independent metamodel for each objective and constraint using different metamodeling methods: RBF, Kriging, first and second-order response surface models, and multilayer perceptrons. NSGA-II method is used to optimized metamodeled version of the problem. Clearly, this method falls under our M1-2 category.

Wang et al. [26] used independent metamodeling of objectives but combined them using a weight-sum approach proposed an ensemble-based model management strategy for surrogate-assisted evolutionary algorithm. Thus, due to modeling a combined objective function, this method falls under our M3-1 framework. A global model management strategy inspired from committee-based active learning (CAL) was developed, searching for the best and most uncertain solutions according to a surrogate ensemble using a particle swarm optimization (PSO) algorithm. In addition, a local surrogate model is built around the best solution obtained so far. Then, a PSO algorithm searches on the local surrogate to find its optimum and evaluates it. The evolutionary search using the global model management strategy switches to the local search once no further improvement can be observed and vice versa.

Pan et al. [33] proposed a classification based surrogate-assisted evolutionary algorithm (CSEA) for solving unconstrained optimization problems by using an artificial neural network (ANN) as a surrogate model. The surrogate model aims to learn the dominance relationship between the candidate solutions and a set of selected reference solutions. Due to a single metamodel to find the dominance structure involving all objective functions, this algorithm falls under our M3-2 framework.

Deepti et al. [34] suggested a reduced and simplified model of each objective function in order to reduce the computational efforts.

Recent studies on nonevolutionary optimization methods for multiobjective optimization using trust-region method [35,36] and using decomposition methods [37] are proposed as well.

A recent study [38] reviewed multiobjective metamodeling approaches and suggested a taxonomy of the existing methods based on whether the surrogate assisted values match well the original function values. Three broad categories were suggested: (i) algorithms that do not use any feedback from the original function values, (ii) algorithms that use a fixed number of feedback, and (iii) algorithms that adaptively decide which metamodeled solutions must be checked with the original function values. This extensive review reported that most existing metamodeling approaches used a specific EMO algorithm—NSGA-II [39]. While a check on the accuracy of a metamodel is important for its subsequent use, this is true for both single and multiobjective optimization and no specific issues related to multiobjective optmization were discussed in the review paper.

Besides the algorithmic developments, a number of studies have applied metamodeling methods to practical problems with a limited budget of solution evaluations [40–47], some restricting to a few hundreds [48].

Despite all the above all-around developments, the ideas that most distinguish surrogate modeling in multiobjective optimization from their single-objective counterparts were not addressed well. They are (i) how to fundamentally handle multiple objectives and constraints either through a separate modeling of each or in an aggregated fashion? and (ii) how to make use of the best of different multiple surrogate modeling approaches adaptively within an algorithm? In 2016, Rayan et al. [5] have proposed a taxonomy in which 10 metamodeling frameworks were proposed to address the first question. This paper addresses the second question in a comprehensive manner using the proposed 10 metamodeling frameworks using an ensemble method.

Ensemble methods have been used in surrogate-assisted optimization for solving expensive problems [49–53], but in most of these methods, an ensemble of different metamodeling methods, such as RBF, Kriging, response surfaces, are considered to choose a single suitable method. While such studies are important, depending on the use of objectives and constraints, each such method will fall in one of the first eight frameworks presented in this paper. No effort is made to consider an ensemble of metamodeling frameworks for combining multiple objectives and constraints differently and choosing the most suitable one for optimization. In this paper, we use an ensemble of 10 metamodeling frameworks [5,20] described in the next section and propose an adaptive selection scheme of choosing one in an iterative manner thereafter.

3. A Taxonomy for Multiobjective Metamodeling Frameworks

Having M objective and J constraints to be metamodeled, there exist many plausible ways to develop a metamodeling based multiobjective optimization methods. Thus, there is a need to classify different methods into a few finite clusters so that they can be compared and contrasted with each other. Importantly, such a classification or taxonomy study can provide information about methods which are still unexplored. A recently proposed taxonomy study [20] put forward 10 different frameworks based on the metamodeling objective and constraint functions based on their individual or aggregate modeling, as illustrated in Figure 1.

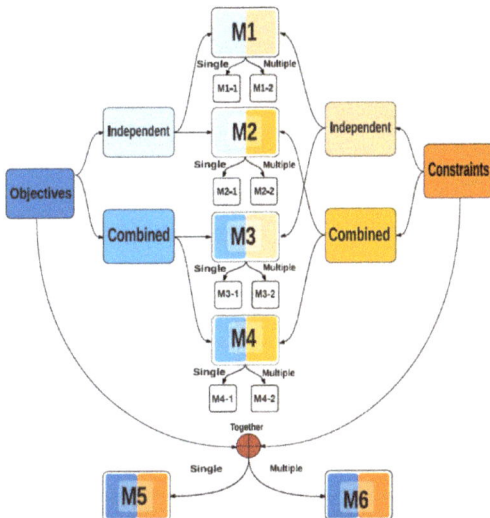

Figure 1. The proposed taxonomy of 10 different metamodeling frameworks for multi- and many-objective optimization. (Taken from [20]).

We believe most ideas of collectively metamodeling all objectives and constraints can be classified into one of these 10 frameworks. We describe each of the 10 frameworks below in details for the first time.

We explain each framework using a two-variable, two-objective SRN problem [54,55] as an example:

$$\begin{aligned}
\text{Minimize} \quad & f_1(\mathbf{x}) = 2 + (x_1 - 2)^2 + (x_2 - 1)^2, \\
\text{Minimize} \quad & f_2(\mathbf{x}) = 9x_1 - (x_2 - 1)^2, \\
\text{Subject to} \quad & g_1(\mathbf{x}) = x_1^2 + x_2^2 - 225 \leq 0, \\
& g_2(\mathbf{x}) = x_1 - 3x_2 + 10 \leq 0, \\
& -20 \leq (x_1, x_2) \leq 20.
\end{aligned} \quad (2)$$

The PO solutions are known to be as follows: $x_1^* = -2.5$ and $x_2^* \in [2.5, 14.79]$. To apply a metamodeling approach, one simple idea is to metamodel all four functions. The functions and the respective PO solutions are marked on f_1 and f_2 plots shown in Figure 2a,b, respectively. The feasible regions for g_1 anf g_2 are shown in Figure 2c,d.

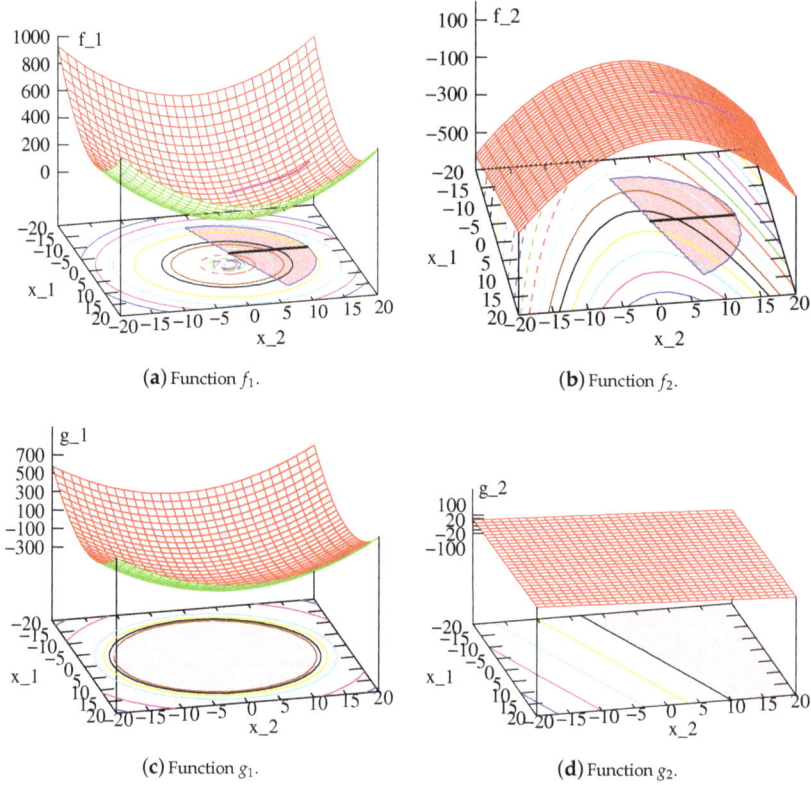

Figure 2. Two objectives and two constraints are shown for SRN problem. The combined feasible region is shown in the contour plot. PO solutions lie on the black line marked inside the feasible region.

3.1. M1-1 and M1-2 Frameworks

Most existing multiobjective metamodeling approaches are found to fall in these two frameworks [20]. In M1-1 and M1-2, a total of $(M + J)$ metamodels (M objectives and J constraints) are constructed. The metamodeling algorithm for M1-1 and M1-2 starts with an archive of initial population ($\mathcal{A}_0$ of size N_0) created using the Latin hypercube sampling (LHS) method on the entire search space, or by using any other heuristics of the problem. Each objective function ($f_i(\mathbf{x})$, for $i = 1, \ldots, M$) is first normalized to obtain a normalized function $\underline{f}_i(\mathbf{x})$ using the minimum ($f_i^{\min}$) and maximum ($f_i^{\max}$) values of all high-fidelity evaluation of archive members, so that the minimum and maximum values of $\underline{f}_i(\mathbf{x})$ is zero and one, respectively:

$$\underline{f}_i(\mathbf{x}) = \frac{f_i(\mathbf{x}) - f_i^{\min}}{f_i^{\max} - f_i^{\min}}. \qquad (3)$$

Then, metamodels are constructed for each of the M normalized objective functions independently: $(\widetilde{\underline{f}}_1(\mathbf{x}), \ldots, \widetilde{\underline{f}}_M(\mathbf{x})), \forall i \in \{1, 2, \ldots, M\}$ using a chosen metamodeling method. For all implementations here, we use the Kriging metamodeling method [56] for all frameworks of this study.

Each constraint function ($g_j(\mathbf{x})$, for $j = 1, \ldots, J$) is first normalized to obtain a normalized constraint function ($\underline{g}_j(\mathbf{x})$) using standard methods [57], and then metamodeled separately to obtain an approximate function ($\tilde{g}_j(\mathbf{x})$) using the same metamodeling method (Kriging method is adopted here) used for metamodeling objective functions.

In M1-1, all metamodeled normalized objectives are combined into a single *aggregated* function and optimized with all separately metamodeled constraints to find a *single* in-fill point using a single-objective evolutionary optimization algorithm (real-coded genetic algorithm (RGA) [54] is used here). In τ generations of RGA (defining an epoch), the following achievement scalarization aggregation function (ASF$_{12}(\mathbf{x}, \mathbf{z})$) [58] is optimized for every $\mathbf{z}$ vector:

$$\text{Problem O1-1:} \atop \text{Solution: } \mathbf{x}^*(\mathbf{z}), \quad \begin{cases} \text{Minimize} & \text{ASF}_{12}(\mathbf{x}, \mathbf{z}) = \max_{j=1}^{M} \left(\underline{\tilde{f}}_j(\mathbf{x}) - z_j \right), \\ \text{Subject to} & \tilde{g}_j(\mathbf{x}) \leq 0, \quad j = 1, 2, \ldots, J, \\ & x_i^{(L)} \leq x_i \leq x_i^{(U)}, \quad i = 1, 2, \ldots, n, \end{cases} \quad (4)$$

where the vector $\mathbf{z}$ is one of the Das and Dennis's [59] point on the unit simplex on the M-dimensional hyperspace (making $\sum_{j=1}^{M} z_j = 1$). Thus, for each of H different $\mathbf{z}$ vectors, one optimization problem (O1-1) is formed with an equi-angled weight vector, and solved one at time to find a total of H in-fill solutions using a real-parameter genetic algorithm (RGA). Figure 3a shows the infill solution for $\mathbf{z} = (0.5, 0.5)$ for the SRN problem. Notice, the ASF$_{12}$ function constitutes a minimum point on the Pareto-optimal (PO) line (black line on the contour plot) for the specific $\mathbf{z}$-vector. If the exact ASF$_{12}$ function can be constructed as a metamodeled function from a few high-fidelity evaluations, one epoch would be enough to find a representative PO set. However, since the metamodeled function is expected to have a difference from the original function, several epochs will be necessary to get close to the true PO set. For a different $\mathbf{z}$-vector, the ASF$_{12}$ function will have a different optimal solution, but it will fall on the PO line. The ASF$_{12}$ model, constructed from metamodeled objective and constraint functions, will produce optimal solutions on the Pareto set for different $\mathbf{z}$-vectors. Multiple applications of a RGA will discover a well-distributed set of multiple in-fill points one at a time.

The RGA procedure uses a *trust-region* concept, which we describe in detail in Section 4.3. The best solution for each $\mathbf{z}$ is sent for a high-fidelity evaluation. The solution is then included in the archive ($\mathcal{A}_1$) of all high-fidelity solutions. After all H solutions are included in the archive, one epoch of the M1-1 framework optimization problem is considered complete. In the next epoch, all high-fidelity solutions are used to normalize and metamodel all $(M + J)$ objective functions and constraints, and the above process is repeated to obtain $\mathcal{A}_2$. The process is continued until all prespecified maximum solution evaluations (SE$_{\max}$) is completed. Nondominated solutions of final archive $\mathcal{A}_t$ is declared as outcome of the whole multiobjective surrogate-assisted approach.

In M1-2, the following M-objective optimization problem,

$$\text{Problem O1-2:} \atop \text{Solutions: } \mathbf{x}^{i,*}, \; i = 1, \ldots, H \quad \begin{cases} \text{Minimize} & \left(\underline{\tilde{f}}_1(\mathbf{x}), \underline{\tilde{f}}_2(\mathbf{x}), \ldots, \underline{\tilde{f}}_M(\mathbf{x}) \right), \\ \text{Subject to} & \tilde{g}_j(\mathbf{x}) \leq 0, \quad j = 1, 2, \ldots, J, \\ & x_i^{(L)} \leq x_i \leq x_i^{(U)}, \quad i = 1, 2, \ldots, n, \end{cases} \quad (5)$$

constructing $(M + J)$ metamodels in each epoch, is solved to find H in-fill solutions in a *single run* with an EMO/EMaO procedure. We use NSGA-II procedure [39] for two-objective problems, and NSGA-III [60] for three or more objective problems here. All H solutions are then evaluated using high-fidelity models and are included in the archive for another round of metamodel construction and optimization for the next epoch. The process is continued until SE$_{\max}$ evaluations are done. Figure 3b shows that when NSGA-II optimizes a well-approximated metamodel to the original problem, the obtained solutions will lie on the true PO front.

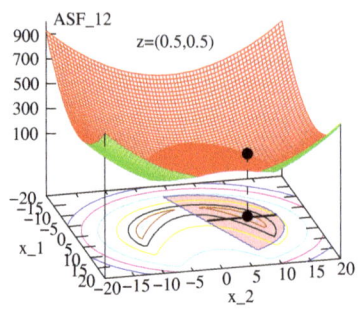
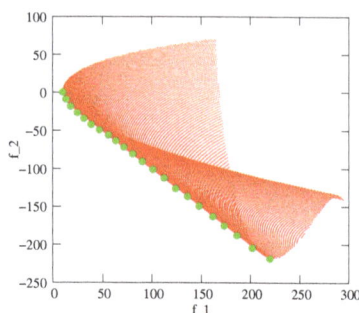

(**a**) The ASF solution with $\mathbf{z} = (0.5, 0.5)$ in M1-1, M2-1, M3-1 and M4-1. The solution lies on the true PO set (black line).

(**b**) Efficient solutions in M1-2 and M2-2. For illustration, a few PO solutions are shown in green circles.

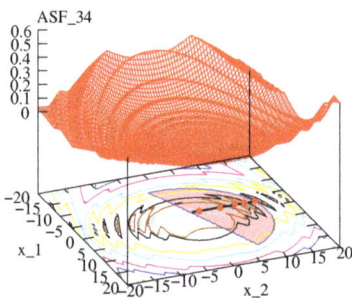

(**c**) minASF$_{34}$ in M3-2 and M4-2. For illustration, five **z**-vectors and their respective PO solutions, found simultaneously, are shown in red circles.

Figure 3. In-fill solutions for different frameworks for SRN problem. True functions are plotted here, however, different metamodeling frameworks use different approximations to find in-fill solutions on the true PO set.

3.2. Frameworks M2-1 and M2-2

For M2-1 and M2-2, a single aggregated constraint violation function (ACV(**x**)) is first constructed using the normalized constraint functions $(\underline{g}_j(\mathbf{x}), j = 1, \ldots, J)$ at high-fidelity solutions from the archive ($\mathbf{x} \in \mathcal{A}_t$), as follows:

$$\text{ACV}(\mathbf{x}) = \begin{cases} \sum_{j=1}^{J} \underline{g}_j(\mathbf{x}), & \text{if } \mathbf{x} \text{ is feasible,} \\ \sum_{j=1}^{J} \langle \underline{g}_j(\mathbf{x}) \rangle, & \text{otherwise,} \end{cases} \quad (6)$$

where the bracket operator $\langle \alpha \rangle$ is α, if $\alpha > 0$; and zero, otherwise. It is clear from the above equation that for high-fidelity solutions, ACV(**x**) takes a negative value for feasible solutions and a positive value for an infeasible solution. In M2-1 and M2-2, the constraint violation function (ACV(**x**)) is then metamodeled to obtain $\widetilde{\text{ACV}}(\mathbf{x})$, instead of every constraint function ($g_j(\mathbf{x})$) metamodeled in M1-1 and M1-2. This requires a total of $(M+1)$ metamodel constructions (M objectives and one constraint violation function) at each epoch. In M2-1, the following problem

$$\begin{array}{c} \text{Problem O2-1:} \\ \text{Solution: } \mathbf{x}^*(\mathbf{z}) \end{array} \begin{cases} \text{Minimize} & \text{ASF}_{12}(\mathbf{x}, \mathbf{z}) = \max_{j=1}^{M}\left(\widetilde{f}_j(\mathbf{x}) - z_j\right), \\ \text{Subject to} & \widetilde{\text{ACV}}(\mathbf{x}) \leq 0, \\ & x_i^{(L)} \leq x_i \leq x_i^{(U)}, \quad i = 1, 2, \ldots, n, \end{cases} \quad (7)$$

is solved to find one in-fill point for each reference line originating from one of the chosen Das-Dennis reference points **z**. Similarly, M2-2 solves the following problem:

$$\text{Problem O2-2:} \quad \begin{cases} \text{Minimize} & \left(\widetilde{\underline{f}}_1(\mathbf{x}), \widetilde{\underline{f}}_2(\mathbf{x}), \ldots, \widetilde{\underline{f}}_M(\mathbf{x})\right), \\ \text{Subject to} & \widetilde{\text{ACV}}(\mathbf{x}) \leq 0, \\ & x_i^{(L)} \leq x_i \leq x_i^{(U)}, \quad i = 1, 2, \ldots, n, \end{cases} \quad (8)$$
Solutions: $\mathbf{x}^{i,*}, i = 1, \ldots, H$

to find H in-fill solutions simultaneously. The rest of the M2-1 and M2-2 procedures are identical to that in M1-1 and M1-2, respectively. RGA is used to solve each optimization problem in M2-1 to find one solution at a time, and NSGA-II or NSGA-III is used in M2-2 depending on number of objectives in the problem. Thus, M2-1 requires an archive to store each solution, whereas M2-2 does not require an archive.

3.3. M3-1 and M3-2 Frameworks

In these two methods, instead of metamodeling each normalized objective function $\underline{f}_i(\mathbf{x})$ for $i = 1, \ldots, M$ independently, we first aggregate them to form the following ASF$_{34}$ function for each high-fidelity solution $\mathbf{x}$:

$$\text{ASF}_{34}(\mathbf{x}, \mathbf{z}) = \max_{j=1}^{M} \left(\underline{f}_j(\mathbf{x}) - z_j\right), \quad (9)$$

where $\mathbf{z}$ is defined as before. Note this formulation is different from ASF$_{12}$ in that the ASF formulation is made with the original normalized objective functions $\widetilde{f}_j$ here. Then, one ASF$_{34}$ function (for a specific $\mathbf{z}$-vector) is metamodeled to obtain $\widetilde{\text{ASF}}_{34}(\mathbf{x}, \mathbf{z})$, along with J separate metamodels for J constraints ($\widetilde{g}_j$) to solve the following problem for M3-1:

$$\text{Problem O3-1:} \quad \begin{cases} \text{Minimize} & \widetilde{\text{ASF}}_{34}(\mathbf{x}, \mathbf{z}), \\ \text{Subject to} & \widetilde{g}_j(\mathbf{x}) \leq 0, \quad j = 1, 2, \ldots, J, \\ & x_i^{(L)} \leq x_i \leq x_i^{(U)}, \quad i = 1, 2, \ldots, n. \end{cases} \quad (10)$$
Solutions: $\mathbf{x}^*(\mathbf{z})$

For every $\mathbf{z}$, a new in-fill point is found by solving the above problem using the same RGA, discussed for M1-1. Every in-fill point is stored in an archive to compare with M∗-2 methods, which creates multiple solutions in one run, thereby not requiring an explicit archive. In M3-2, the following problem is solved:

$$\text{Problem O3-2:} \quad \begin{cases} \text{Minimize} & \min\text{ASF}_{34}(\mathbf{x}) = \min_{\mathbf{z}} \widetilde{\text{ASF}}_{34}(\mathbf{x}, \mathbf{z}), \\ \text{Subject to} & \widetilde{g}_j(\mathbf{x}) \leq 0, \quad j = 1, 2, \ldots, J, \\ & x_i^{(L)} \leq x_i \leq x_i^{(U)}, \quad i = 1, 2, \ldots, n, \end{cases} \quad (11)$$
Solutions: $\mathbf{x}^{i,*}, i = 1, \ldots, H$

in which the objective function of $\mathbf{x}$ is computed as the minimum $\widetilde{\text{ASF}}_{34}$ for all $\mathbf{z}$-vectors at $\mathbf{x}$. Figure 3c shows the multimodal objective function $\min\text{ASF}_{34}(\mathbf{x})$ for the SRN problem, clearly indicating multiple local optima on the PO front. Notice how the $\min\text{ASF}_{34}$ function has ridges and creates multiple optima on the PO set, one for each reference line. Due to the complexity involved in this function, it is clear that a large number of high-fidelity points will be necessary to make a suitable metamodel with a high accuracy. Besides the need of more points, there is another issue that needs a discussion. Both M3-1 and M3-2 requires H, $\widetilde{\text{ASF}}_{34}(\mathbf{x}, \mathbf{z})$ and J constraint functions to be metamodeled, thereby making a total of $(H + J)$ metamodels in each epoch. Since each of multiple optima of the $\min\text{ASF}_{34}$ function will finally lead us to a set of PO solutions, we would need an efficient multimodal optimization algorithm, instead of a RGA, to solve the metamodeled $\min\text{ASF}_{34}$ function.

We use a *multimodal* single-objective evolutionary algorithm to find H multimodal in-fill points of $\min\text{ASF}_{34}$ simultaneously. We propose a multimodal RGA (or MM-RGA) which starts with a random population of size N for this purpose. In each generation, the population (P_t) is modified to a new population (P_{t+1}) by using selection, recombination, and mutation operators. The selection operator emphasizes multiple diverse solutions as follows. First, a *fitness* is assigned to each population member **x** by computing $\widetilde{\text{ASF}}_{34}(\mathbf{x}, \mathbf{z})$ for all H, **z**-vectors and then assigning the smallest value as the fitness. Then, we apply the binary tournament selection to choose a parent using the following selection function:

$$\text{SF}(\mathbf{x}) = \begin{cases} \min\text{ASF}_{34}(\mathbf{x}), & \text{if } \mathbf{x} \text{ is feasible,} \\ \min\text{ASF}_{34}^{\max} + \sum_{j=1}^{J} \langle \widetilde{\underline{g}}_j(\mathbf{x}) \rangle, & \text{otherwise,} \end{cases} \quad (12)$$

where $\min\text{ASF}_{34}^{\max}$ is the maximum $\min\text{ASF}_{34}(\mathbf{x})$ value of all feasible population members of MM-RGA. The above selection function has the following effects. If two solutions are feasible, $\min\text{ASF}_{34}(\mathbf{x})$ is used to select the winner. If one is feasible and the other is infeasible, the former is chosen, and for two infeasible members, the one with smaller constraint violation $\sum_{j=1}^{J} \langle \widetilde{\underline{g}}_j(\mathbf{x}) \rangle$ is chosen. After N offspring population members are thus created, we merge the population to form a combined population of $2N$ members. The best solution to each **z**-vector is then copied to P_{t+1}. In the event of a duplicate, the second best solution for the **z**-vector is chosen. If H is smaller than N, then the process is repeated to select a second population member for as many **z**-vectors as possible. Thus, at the end of the MM-RGA procedure, exactly H in-fill solutions are obtained.

3.4. Frameworks M4-1 and M4-2

In these two frameworks, constraints are first combined to a single constraint violation function ACV(**x**) as in M2-1 (Equation (6)) and then ACV is metamodeled to obtain $\widetilde{\text{ACV}}(\mathbf{x})$. The following problem is then solved:

$$\begin{array}{c} \text{Problem O4-1:} \\ \text{Solution: } \mathbf{x}^*(\mathbf{z}) \end{array} \begin{cases} \text{Minimize} & \widetilde{\text{ASF}}_{34}(\mathbf{x}, \mathbf{z}), \\ \text{Subject to} & \widetilde{\text{ACV}}(\mathbf{x}) \leq 0, \\ & x_i^{(L)} \leq x_i \leq x_i^{(U)}, \quad i = 1, 2, \ldots, n, \end{cases} \quad (13)$$

to find a single in-fill solution for every **z**. An archive is built with in-fill solutions. In M4-2, following problem is solved to find H in-fill solutions simultaneously:

$$\begin{array}{c} \text{Problem O4-2:} \\ \text{Solutions: } \mathbf{x}^{i,*}, \, i = 1, \ldots, H \end{array} \begin{cases} \text{Minimize} & \min\text{ASF}_{34}(\mathbf{x}) = \min_{\mathbf{z}} \widetilde{\text{ASF}}_{34}(\mathbf{x}, \mathbf{z}), \\ \text{Subject to} & \widetilde{\text{ACV}}(\mathbf{x}) \leq 0, \\ & x_i^{(L)} \leq x_i \leq x_i^{(U)}, \quad i = 1, 2, \ldots, n, \end{cases} \quad (14)$$

Both these frameworks require H, $\widetilde{\text{ASF}}_{34}(\mathbf{x}, \mathbf{z})$ and one ACV function to be metamodeled, thereby making a total of $(H+1)$ metamodels in each epoch. The same MM-RGA is used here, but the SF function is modified by replacing $\sum_{j=1}^{J} \langle \widetilde{\underline{g}}_j(\mathbf{x}) \rangle$ term with $\langle \widetilde{\text{ACV}}(\mathbf{x}) \rangle$ in Equation (12). A similar outcome as in Figure 3c occurs here, but the constraints are now handled using one metamodeled $\widetilde{\text{ACV}}(\mathbf{x})$ function. M4-2 does not require an archive to be maintained, as H solutions will be found in one MM-RGA application.

3.5. M5 Framework

The focus of M5 is to use a generative multiobjective optimization approach in which a single PO solution is found at a time for a **z**-vector by using a combined *selection* function involving all objective and constraint functions together. The following *selection* function is first created:

$$S_5(\mathbf{x}, \mathbf{z}) = \begin{cases} \text{ASF}_{34}(\mathbf{x}, \mathbf{z}), & \text{if } \mathbf{x} \text{ is feasible,} \\ \text{ASF}_{34}^{\max}(\mathbf{x}, \mathbf{z}) + \langle \text{ACV}(\mathbf{x}) \rangle, & \text{otherwise.} \end{cases} \quad (15)$$

Here, the parameter $\text{ASF}_{34}^{\max}(\mathbf{x}, \mathbf{z})$ is the worst ASF_{34} function value (described in Equation (9)) of all feasible solutions from the archive. The selection function $\mathcal{S}_5(\mathbf{x}, \mathbf{z})$ is then metamodeled to obtain $\widetilde{\mathcal{S}}_5(\mathbf{x}, \mathbf{z})$, which is then optimized by RGA (described for M1-1) to find one in-fill solution for each $\mathbf{z}$-vector. The unconstrained optimization problem with only variable bounds is given below:

$$\text{Problem O5:} \quad \begin{cases} \text{Minimize} & \widetilde{\mathcal{S}}_5(\mathbf{x}, \mathbf{z}), \\ \text{Subject to} & x_i^{(L)} \leq x_i \leq x_i^{(U)}, \quad i = 1, 2, \ldots, n. \end{cases} \quad \text{Solution: } \mathbf{x}^*(\mathbf{z}) \tag{16}$$

Thus, H metamodels of $\mathcal{S}_5(\mathbf{x}, \mathbf{z})$ need to be constructed for M5 in each epoch. Figure 4a shows the S_5 function with $\mathbf{z} = (0.1, 0.9)$ for SRN problem. Although details are not apparent in this figure, Figure 4b, plotted near the optimum, shows optimum more clearly. The entire surface plot is not shown for clarity, but it is interesting to see how a single function differentiates infeasible from feasible region and also makes the optimum of the function as one of the PO solutions.

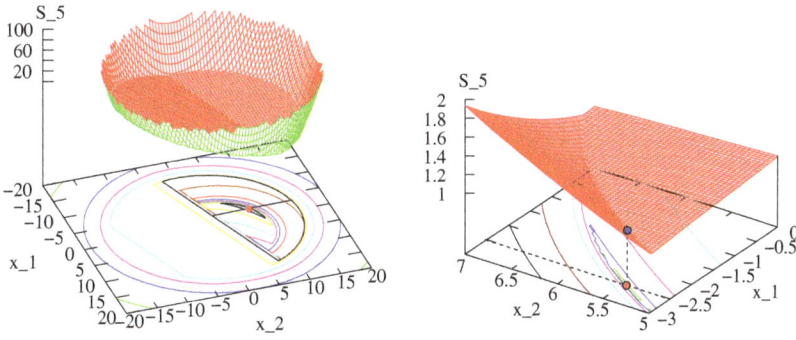

(a) Optimal solution with $\mathbf{z} = (0.1, 0.9)$ in M5. (b) The function S_5 surface is blown up near the optimum.

Figure 4. In-fill solution for a specific $\mathbf{z}$-vector to be obtained by framework M5 for SRN problem.

Clearly, the complexity of the resulting $\mathcal{S}_5(\mathbf{x}, \mathbf{z})$ function will demand a large number of archive points for an accurate identification of the PO solution or a large number of epochs to arrive at the PO solution. However, the concept of metamodeling a selection function, which is not one of the original objective or constraint function, to find an in-fill solution of the problem is intriguing and opens up a new avenue for surrogate-assisted multiobjective optimization studies.

3.6. Framework M6

Finally, M6 framework takes the concept of M5 a bit further and constructs a single metamodel in each epoch by combining all M objectives and J constraints together. A multimodal selection function having each optimum corresponding to a distinct PO solution is formed for this purpose:

$$\text{ASF}_6(\mathbf{x}) = \min_{\mathbf{z} \in \mathbf{Z}} \max_{i=1}^{M} \left(\underline{f}_i(\mathbf{x}) - z_i \right). \tag{17}$$

Then, the following selection function is constructed:

$$\mathcal{S}_6(\mathbf{x}) = \begin{cases} \text{ASF}_6(\mathbf{x}), & \text{if } \mathbf{x} \text{ is feasible,} \\ \text{ASF}_{6,\max} + \text{CV}(\mathbf{x}), & \text{otherwise,} \end{cases} \tag{18}$$

where $ASF_{6,max}$ is the maximum ASF_6 value of all feasible archive members. For each archive member **x**, $\mathcal{S}_6(\mathbf{x})$ is first computed. CV(**x**) is same as ACV(**x**), except that for a feasible **x**, CV is set to zero. Then, the following multimodal unconstrained problem (with variable bounds) is constructed to find H in-fill solutions simultaneously:

$$\begin{array}{c} \text{Problem O6:} \\ \text{Solutions: } \mathbf{x}^{i,*},\ i=1,\ldots,H \end{array} \left\{ \begin{array}{ll} \text{Minimize} & \widetilde{\mathcal{S}}_6(\mathbf{x}), \\ \text{Subject to} & x_i^{(L)} \leq x_i \leq x_i^{(U)}, \quad i=1,2,\ldots,n. \end{array} \right. \quad (19)$$

A single metamodel needs to be constructed in each epoch in M6 framework. Due to the complexity involved in the $\mathcal{S}_6$-function, we employ a neural network $\widetilde{\mathcal{S}}_6(\mathbf{x})$ to metamodel this selection function. A niched RGA [7] similar to that described in Section 3.4 is used here to find H in-fill solutions corresponding to each local optimum of the metamodeled $\widetilde{\mathcal{S}}_6(\mathbf{x})$ function. No explicit archive needs to be maintained to store H solutions. Figure 5a shows $\mathcal{S}_6$ function for SRN function on the entire search space. The detail inside the feasible region and near the optimal solutions shown in Figure 5b makes it clear that this function creates six optima on the PO front, corresponding to six **z**-vectors. Although the function is multimodal, the detail structure from Figure 5a to Figure 5b can be modeled gradually with iterations of a carefully designed optimization algorithm.

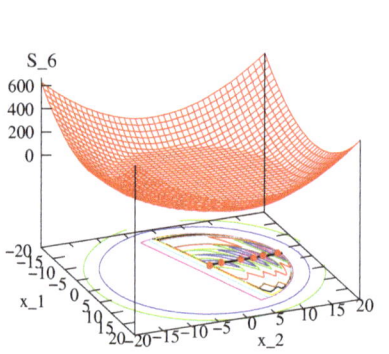 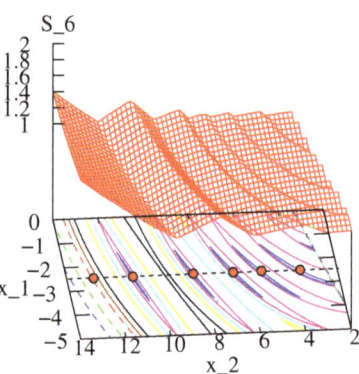

(**a**) Multimodal optimal solutions in M6. For illustration, six **z**-vectors are used in Equation (15).

(**b**) The function $\mathcal{S}_6$ surface is blown up near the optimal region showing six optima.

Figure 5. The function $\mathcal{S}_6$ surface is blown up near the optimal region showing six optima.

3.7. Summary of 10 Frameworks

A summary of metamodeled functions and the optimization algorithms used to optimize them for all 10 frameworks is provided in Table 1. The relative computational cost for each framework can be derived from this table. M3-1 and M3-2 require to construct the maximum number of metamodels (assuming the number of desired PO solutions $H > M$) among all the frameworks, and M6 requires the least, involving only one metamodel in each epoch.

The evolutionary algorithm used to solve each optimization problem is also provided in the table.

Table 1. Summary of metamodeled functions and optimization algorithms needed in each epoch for all 10 frameworks.

Frame-Work	Metamodeling Functions	#Metamodels	Optimization Method	#Opt. Runs
M1-1	$(\underline{f}_1, \ldots, \underline{f}_M)$ $(\underline{g}_1, \ldots, \underline{g}_J)$	$M+J$	RGA	H
M1-2	Same as above	$M+J$	NSGA-II/III	1
M2-1	$(\underline{f}_1, \ldots, \underline{f}_M)$ & ACV	$M+1$	RGA	H
M2-2	Same as above	$M+1$	NSGA-II/III	1
M3-1	ASF_{34} & $(\underline{g}_1, \ldots, \underline{g}_J)$	$H+J$	RGA	H
M3-2	Same as above	$H+J$	MM-RGA	1
M4-1	ASF_{34} & ACV	$H+1$	RGA	H
M4-2	Same as above	$H+1$	MM-RGA	1
M5	S_5	H	RGA	H
M6	S_6	1	N-RGA	1

4. Adaptive Switching Based Metamodeling (ASM) Frameworks

Each metamodeling framework in our proposed taxonomy requires building metamodels for either each objective and constraint or their aggregations. Thus, it is expected that each framework may be most suitable for certain function landscapes that produce a smaller approximation error, but that framework may not be good in other landscapes. During an optimization process, an algorithm usually faces different kinds of landscape complexities from start to finish. Thus, no one framework is expected to perform best during each step of the optimization process. While each framework was applied to different multiobjective optimization problems in another study [6,20] from start to finish, different problems were found to be solved best by different frameworks. To determine the best performing framework for a problem, a simple-minded approach would be to apply each of the 10 frameworks to solve each problem independently using SE_{max} high-fidelity evaluations, and then determine the specific framework which performs the best using an EMO metric, such as hypervolume [61] or inverse generational distance (IGD) [62]. This will be computationally expensive, requiring 10 times more than the prescribed SE_{max}. If each framework is allocated only 1/10-th of SE_{max}, they may be insufficient to find comparatively good solutions. A better approach would be to use an adaptive switching strategy that chooses the most suitable framework at each epoch.

As mentioned in the previous section, in each epoch, exactly H new in-fill solutions are created irrespective of the metamodeling framework used, thereby consuming H high-fidelity SEs. Clearly, the maximum number of epochs allowable is $E_{max} = \lceil \frac{SE_{max} - N_0}{H} \rceil$ with a minor adjustment on the SEs used in the final epoch. At the beginning of each epoch (say, t-th epoch), we have an archive ($\mathcal{A}_t$) of N_t high-fidelity solutions. For the first epoch, these are all N_0 Latin hypercube sampled (LHS) solutions, and in each subsequent epoch, H new in-fill solutions are added to the archive. At the start of t-th epoch, each of the 10 frameworks is used to construct its respective metamodels using all N_t archive members. Then, a 10-fold cross-validation method (described in Section 4.2) is used with a suitable performance metric (described in Section 4.1) to determine the most suitable framework for the next epoch. Thereafter, the best-performing framework is used to find a new set of H in-fill solutions. They are evaluated using high-fidelity evaluations and all 10 frameworks are statistically compared to choose a new best-performing framework for the next epoch. This process is continued until SE_{max} evaluations are made. A pseudocode of the proposed ASM approach is provided in Algorithm 1.

Algorithm 1: Adaptive Swithing Framework

Input : Objectives: $[f_1,\ldots,f_m]^T$, Constraints: $[g_1,\ldots,g_J]^T$, frameworks $\mathcal{M}_i$ with parameter Γ_i for $i \in \{1\ldots,S\}$ where S is number of frameworks, Number of initial samples, allowed high-fidelity solution evaluations, solutions per epoch and cross-validation partitions are N_0, SE_{max}, u and K respectively.

Output: P_T

1 $t, P_t, F_t, G_t, e \leftarrow 0, \emptyset, \emptyset, \emptyset, N_0$;
2 $P_{new} \leftarrow \text{LHS}(\rho)$ // Initial sampling
3 **while** *True* **do**
4    $F_{new} = \{f_i(P_{new}), \forall i \in \{1,\ldots,M\}\}$ // high-fidelity objectives eval.
5    $G_{new} = \{g_j(P_{new}), \forall j \in \{1,\ldots,J\}\}$ // high-fidelity constraints eval.
6    $P_{t+1}, F_{t+1}, G_{t+1} \leftarrow (P_t \cup P_{new}), (F_t \cup F_{new}), (G_t \cup G_{new})$ // merge pop
7    $e \leftarrow e + |P_{new}|$ // number of high-fidelity evaluations
8   **break if** $e \geq SE_{max}$ // termination
9   Calculate $\{ASF(.), ACV(.), S_5, S_6\}$ etc. from P_{t+1}, F_{t+1} & G_{t+1} as per requirements of $\mathcal{M}_i, \forall i$;
10   Create random K partition (training and test set) Q_{t+1}^k from $P_{t+1}, \forall k \in \{1,\ldots,K\}$;
11   **for** $k=1$ *to* K **do**
12   **for** $i=1$ *to* S **do**
13          $m_i \leftarrow$ Build corresponding metamodels for framework $\mathcal{M}_i$ using training set of Q_{t+1}^k;
14          $SEP(k, i) \leftarrow$ Calculate selection-error probability for m_i with test set of Q_{t+1}^k;
15    $\mathcal{M}_B \leftarrow$ Identify best frameworks from SEP;
16    $\mathcal{M}_b \leftarrow$ Randomly choose a framework from $\mathcal{M}_B$;
17    $P_{new} \leftarrow$ Optimize framework $\mathcal{M}_b(m_b, \Gamma_b)$;
18   **if** $|P_{t+1}| + |P_{new}| > SE_{max}$ **then**
19       $P_{new} \leftarrow$ Randomly pick $SE_{max} - |P_{t+1}|$ solutions from P_{new};
20    $t \leftarrow t + 1$;
      // end of epoch
21 **return** $P_T \leftarrow$ filter best solutions from P_{t+1}

4.1. Performance Metric for Framework Selection

To compare the performances among multiple surrogate models, mean squared error (MSE) has been widely used in literature [30]. For optimization algorithms, the regression methods that use MSE are known to be susceptible to outliers. For multiple objectives, different objectives and constraints may have different scaling. Our pilot study shows that even with the normalization of the objectives and constraints, the MSE metric does not always correctly evaluate the metamodels. Here, we introduce a *selection error probability* (SEP) metric which is more appropriate for an optimization task than MSE metric or even other measures, such as, the Kendal rank correlation coefficient [63] metric. The usual metrics may be better for a regression task, but for an optimization task, the proposed SEP makes a more direct evaluation of pair-wise comparisons of solutions.

SEP is defined as the probability of making an error in correctly predicting the better of two solutions compared against each other using the constructed metamodels. Consider Figure 6, which illustrates an minimization task and comparison of three different population members pair-wise. The true function values are shown in solid blue, while the predicted function values are shown in dashed blue. When points x_1 and x_2 are compared based on predicted function, the prediction is correct, since $f((x_1) < f(x_2)$ and also $\tilde{f}(x) < \tilde{f}(x_2)$. However, when points x_1 and x_3 are compared against each other, the prediction is wrong. Out of the three pairwise comparisons, two predictions are correct and one is wrong, thereby making a selection error probability of 1/3 for this case. We argue that in an optimization procedure, it is the SEP which provides a better selection error than the actual function values, as the relative function values are important than the exact function values.

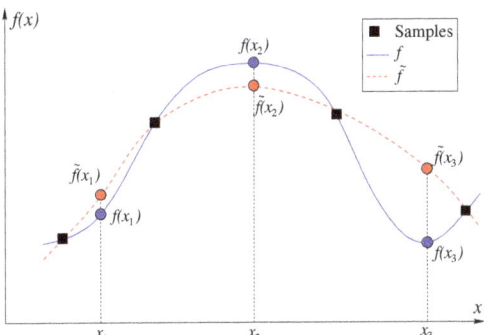

Figure 6. Selection Error Probability (SEP) concept is illustrated.

Mathematically, the SEP metric can be defined for n points as follows. For each of $N = \binom{n}{2}$ pairs of points (p and q), we evaluate the selection error function ($E(p,q)$), which is one, if there is a mismatch between predicted winner and actual winner of p and q; zero, otherwise. Then, SEP is calculated as follows:

$$\text{SEP} = \frac{1}{N} \sum_{p=1}^{n-1} \sum_{q=p+1}^{n} E(p,q). \tag{20}$$

The definition of a "winner" can be easily extended to multiobjective and constrained multiobjective optimization by considering the domination [64] and constraint-domination [54] status of two points p and q.

4.2. Selecting a Framework for an Epoch

Frameworks having least SEP value are considered to be the best for performing the next epoch. We have performed 10-fold cross-validation in order to identify the best frameworks. After each epoch, H new in-fill points are evaluated using high-fidelity evaluations and added to the archive. In each fold of cross-validation, 90% solutions are used for constructing metamodels with respect to the competing frameworks. Then the corresponding frameworks are used to compare every pair (p and q) of the remaining 10% of archive points using the SEP metric. We apply constrained domination checks to identify the relationship between these two solutions. We then compare this relationship with the true relationship given by their high-fidelity values with the same constrained domination check. We calculate the selection error function ($E(p,q)$) for each pair of test archive solutions. The above process is repeated 10 times by using different blocks of 90% points to obtain 10 different SEP values for each framework. This cross-validation procedure does not require any new solution evaluations, as the whole computations are performed based on the already-evaluated archive points and their predicted values from each framework. Thereafter, the best framework is identified based on the median SEP value of frameworks.

Finally, the Wilcoxon rank-sum test is performed between the best framework and all other frameworks. All frameworks within a statistical insignificance (having $p > 0.05$) are identified to obtain the best-performing set $\mathcal{M}_B$. Then a randomly chosen framework ($\mathcal{M}_b$) is selected from $\mathcal{M}_B$ for the next epoch. Since each of these frameworks performs similarly in a sense of median performance, the choice of a random framework makes the ASM approach diverse with the probability of using different metamodeling landscapes in successive epochs. This procedure, in practice, prohibits the overall approach from getting stuck in similar metamodeling frameworks for long, even it is one of the best performing frameworks.

4.3. Trust-Region Based Real-Coded Genetic Algorithms

Before we present the results, we need to discuss one other algorithmic aspect, which is important. Since the metamodels are not error-free, predictions of solutions close to high-fidelity solutions are usually more accurate than predictions far from them. Therefore, we use a trust-region method [65] in which predictions are restricted within a radius R_{trust} from each high-fidelity solution in the variable space. Trust region method is used in nonevolutionary metamodeling studies [35,36]. Another parameter R_{prox} is also introduced which defines the minimum distance with which any new solution should be located from an archive member to provide a diverse set of in-fill solutions. We simulate a feasible search region R_{search} around every high-fidelity solution: $R_{prox} \leq R_{search} \leq R_{trust}$. Using the concepts of trust-region method from the literature [66], we reduce the two radii at every epoch by constant factors: $R_{trust}^{new} = 0.75 R_{trust}^{old}$ and $R_{prox}^{new} = 0.1 R_{trust}^{new}$. A reduction of two radii helps in achieving more trust on closer to high-fidelity solutions with iterations. These factors are found to perform well on a number of trial-and-error studies prior to obtaining the results presented in the next section.

The optimization methods for metamodels are modified as follows. At generation t, parent population P_t is applied by a standard binary constrained tournament selection on two competing population members using the metamodeled objectives, constraints, or selection criteria described before to choose the winner. Standard recombination and mutation operators (without any care for trust region concept) are used to create an offspring population, which is then combined with the parent population P_t and then better half is chosen for the next generation as parent population P_{t+1} using the trust region concept. We first count the number of solutions in the combined population within the two trust regions. If the number is smaller than or equal to N, then they are copied to P_{t+1} and remaining slots are filled with solutions which are closest to the high-fidelity solutions in the variable space. On the other hand, if the number is larger than N, the same binary constrained tournament selection method is applied to pick N solutions from them and copied to P_{t+1}.

5. Results and Discussion

We present the results of the ASM approach on 18 different test and engineering problems. The problems include two to five-objective, constrained, and unconstrained problems. In order to get robust performance, we have included all 10 frameworks as options for switching in our ASM approach. The performance of ASM approach is compared with each framework alone. We then compare ASM's performance with three recently suggested multiobjective metamodeling methods: MOEA/D-EGO [14], K-RVEA [23], and CSEA [33].

5.1. Parameter Settings

For two-objective problems, we use NSGA-II [39] for M1-2 and M2-2 frameworks. For problems with higher number of objectives, we use NSGA-III [60] procedure. Note that, other multiobjective evolutionary algorithms (e.g., MOEA/D [14] or RVEA [23]) can also be used. A population of size ($N = 100$) is used when the number of reference lines (H) is less than 100. Otherwise, the population size is set identical to H. Initial archive size is set according to Table 2. Other parameter settings are as follows: number of generations $\tau = 300$, SBX crossover probability $p_c = 0.95$, polynomial mutation probability $p_m = 1/n$ (where n is the number of variables), distribution indices for SBX and mutation operators are $\eta_c = 20$ and $\eta_m = 20$, respectively. Initial value of R_{trust} is set to be $\sqrt{n}$ for the normalized problems having variable domain $[0,1]^n$. The number of reference points, SE_{max}, resulting epochs for each problem are presented in Table 2.

Table 2. Parameter values for 18 problems.

Problem	n	M	J	N_0	SE_{max}	H	#Epochs
ZDT1	10	2	0	100	500	21	20
ZDT2	10	2	0	100	500	21	20
ZDT3	10	2	0	100	500	21	20
ZDT4	5	2	0	100	1000	21	43
ZDT6	10	2	0	100	500	21	20
OSY	6	2	6	200	800	21	29
TNK	2	2	2	200	800	21	29
SRN	2	2	2	200	800	21	29
BNH	2	2	2	200	800	21	29
WB	4	2	4	300	1000	21	39
DTLZ2	7	3	0	500	1000	91	6
C2DTLZ2	7	3	1	700	1500	91	9
CAR	7	3	10	700	2000	91	15
DTLZ5	7	3	0	500	1000	91	6
DTLZ4	7	3	0	700	2000	91	15
DTLZ7	7	3	0	500	1000	91	6
DTLZ2-5	7	5	0	700	2500	210	9
C2DTLZ2-5	7	5	1	700	2500	210	9

5.2. Two-Objective Unconstrained Problems

First, we apply our proposed methodologies to two-objective unconstrained problems: ZDT1, ZDT2, ZDT3, ZDT4 and ZDT6. Table 3 presents the median IGD values of 11 runs for each framework applied standalone from start to end. In the absence of any constraint or having a single constraint, M1-1 and M2-1 are identical frameworks; so are M1-2 and M2-2, M3-1 and M4-1, M3-2, and M4-2. This is why we keep a blank under M2-1, M2-2, M4-1, M4-2 entries for unconstrained and single-constraint problems in the table. The best performing method is first identified based on the median IGD values and is marked in bold. A *p*-value from an Wilcoxon rank sum test of each other method is then computed for 11 runs with the 11 runs of the best-performing method. If any algorithm produces a *p*-value greater than 0.05, it indicates that the algorithm has produced a statistically similar performance to the best-performing method and its median IGD value is then marked in italics. It is clear from the table that the ASM approach (right-most column), being mostly in bold, performs better or equivalent to all frameworks for all five ZDT problems, whereas M1-1 performs the best in the first four problems. M1-2 and M3-1 performs well in three test problems, whereas M6 performs the best in ZDT6 problem. Obtained nondominated solutions of two-objective constrained and unconstrained problems of the median run are presented in Figure 7. We also show performance of other comparing algorithms: MOEA/D-EGO [14], K-RVEA [23], and CSEA [33] in the figure.

It is apparent that ASM approach is able to find a better distributed and converged set of points than other methods for an identical number of SEs.

The epoch-wise proportion of usage of each framework over 11 runs of the ASM approach is shown in Figure 8 for all five ZDT problems. For ZDT1, standalone M1-1, M2-1, M3-1, and M4-1 perform in a statistically similar manner as shown in Table 3, but the ASM approach mostly restricts its epoch-wise choice on M1-1, M1-2, M2-1, and M2-2 and produces a similar performance in most epochs. Since multiple frameworks can appear with a similar performance in an epoch, the proportions (shown in Figure 8) need not sum up to one at each epoch. For ZDT2, only M1-1 and M1-2 perform well as a standalone framework (Table 3), and the ASM approach is able to pick these two frameworks to produce the best performing result. Notice that since ZDT1 and ZDT2 do not have any constraint, M1-1 and M2-1 are identical frameworks and M1-2 and M2-2 are identical frameworks. Except in ZDT6, M1-1, M1-2, M1-2, and M2-2, for which objectives are independently metamodeled, turn to be dominating frameworks. However, for ZDT6, M3-2, M4-2, and M6 show their dominance. In ZDT4, almost all the frameworks are found to be switching between them early on but settles with M1 and M2 frameworks at the latter part of the optimization runs. Switching among different frameworks performs well on all five problems.

The switching patterns of frameworks for the median performing run for ZDT1, ZDT4, and ZDT6 are shown in Figure 9. Although multiple frameworks may exist at the end of each epoch, the figure shows the specific framework which was chosen for this specific run. For ZDT2, the ASM approach juggles mostly between M1 and M2 variants and produce the best performing result, even better than M1 and M2 alone. In ZDT4, the ASM approach alternates between eight frameworks in the beginning and settles with four of them (M3 and M4 variants) in the middle and then uses M3 variants at the end to produce statistically equivalent result to M1-1 alone. Interestingly, while as a standalone framework from start to end, M1-1 performs the best performance, the ASM approach does not use M1-1 in any of the epochs. The switching of different frameworks from epoch to epoch is clear from these plots.

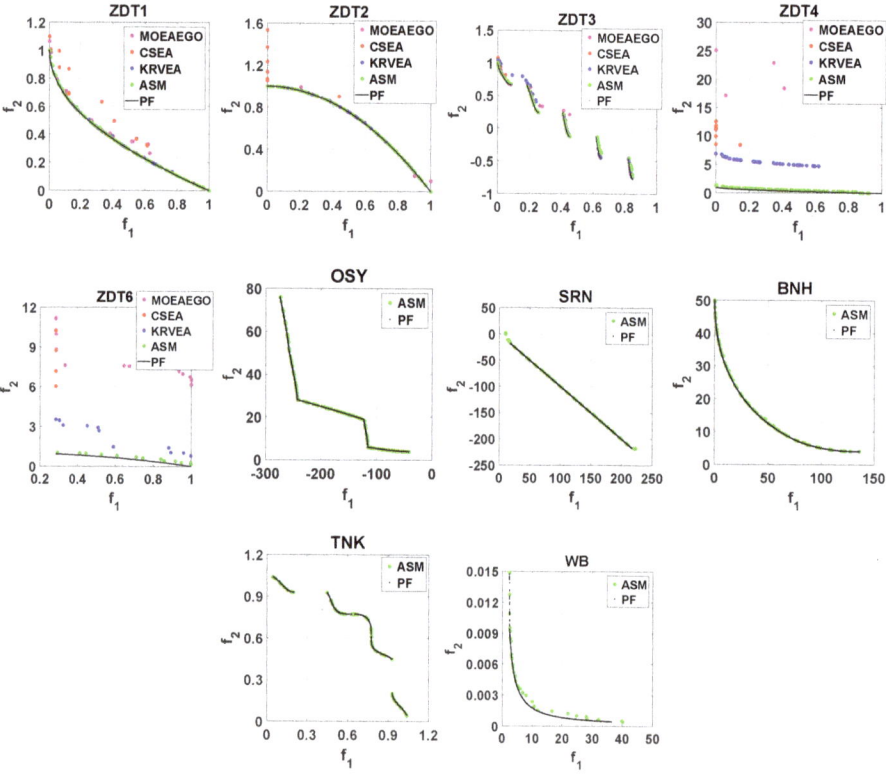

Figure 7. Non-dominated solutions of the final archive for the median run of ASM approach for two-objective ZDT and constrained problems. In all cases, a well-diversified set of near PO solutions is obtained with a limited solution evaluations.

5.3. Two-Objective Constrained Problems

Next, we apply ASM approach and all the frameworks separately to standard two-objective constrained problems: BNH, SRN, TNK, OSY, and the welded beam problem (WB) [54]. The ASM approach performs the best on three of the five problems, followed by M1-1 which performed best in two problems; however, both these methods perform the best statistically on all five problems. Other individual frameworks do not perform so well. Figure 8 shows the epoch-wise utilization of different frameworks for TNK and WB in 11 runs. The plots for TNK shows that ASM almost always chooses M1-1 or M1-2 as the best-performing frameworks as supported by IGD values in Table 3.

However, on WB problem, ASM approach selects M1-1, M5, and M6 in most of the epochs, despite poor performance of the latter two when applied in a stand-alone manner from start to end.

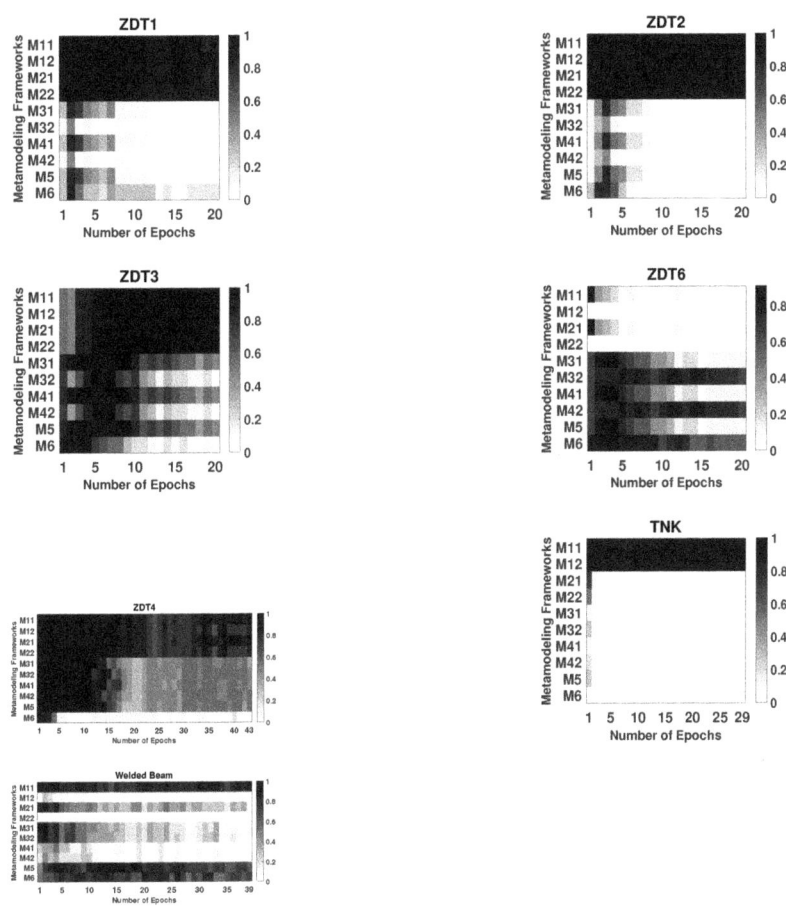

Figure 8. Epoch-wise proportion of appearance of 10 frameworks within M_B in 11 runs of the ASM approach for ZDT problems, TNK, and welded beam design problems indicates the use of multiple frameworks during optimization. Some problems uses some specific frameworks more frequently.

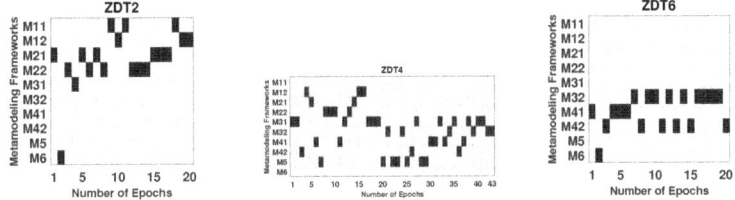

Figure 9. Switching among frameworks for the median IGD run of the ASM approach for ZDT2, ZDT4, and ZDT6 indicates that many frameworks are used during the optimization process.

Table 3. IGD values obtained from all the individual frameworks and proposed switching algorithm on different test problems are presented. The best performing framework and other statistically similar frameworks are marked in bold with their p-values in the second row. For problems without any constraint, the framework Mi-1 is identical to Mi-2, hence a "-" is provided for the latter. For unconstrained problems, M5 and M6 are also identical.

Problem	M1-1	M2-1	M1-2	M2-2	M3-1	M4-1	M3-2	M4-2	M5	M6	ASM
ZDT1	**0.00090** -	- -	**0.00555** $p = 0.4701$	- -	**0.00447** $p = 0.4702$	- -	**0.00537** $p = 0.7928$	- -	- -	0.01337 $p = 8.1 \times 10^{-5}$	**0.00130** $p = 0.091$
ZDT2	**0.00065** $p = 0.2372$	- -	**0.00062** $p = 0.2372$	- -	0.00568 $p = 8.1 \times 10^{-5}$	- -	0.00910 $p = 8.1 \times 10^{-5}$	- -	- -	0.72366 $p = 8.1 \times 10^{-5}$	**0.00055** -
ZDT3	**0.00531** $p = 0.325$	- -	**0.00212** -	- -	0.17123 $p = 8.1 \times 10^{-5}$	- -	0.19050 $p = 8.1 \times 10^{-5}$	- -	- -	0.08315 $p = 8.1 \times 10^{-5}$	**0.00391** $p = 0.369$
ZDT4	**0.28900** -	- -	5.43450 $p = 8.1 \times 10^{-5}$	- -	**0.29300** $p = 0.4307$	- -	0.43450 $p = 0.0126$	- -	- -	6.15510 $p = 8.1 \times 10^{-5}$	**0.39992** $p = 0.1310$
ZDT6	**0.37058** $p = 0.2934$	- -	0.48360 $p = 8.1 \times 10^{-5}$	- -	**0.24192** $p = 0.8438$	- -	0.47159 $p = 0.0013$	- -	- -	0.21327 -	**0.24440** $p = 0.3933$
OSY	0.15323 $p = 0.2301$	24.57940 $p = 8.1 \times 10^{-5}$	0.18806 $p = 8.1 \times 10^{-5}$	22.99990 $p = 8.1 \times 10^{-5}$	6.26550 $p = 8.1 \times 10^{-5}$	18.49200 $p = 8.1 \times 10^{-5}$	4.77670 $p = 8.1 \times 10^{-5}$	18.33760 $p = 8.1 \times 10^{-5}$	45.18110 $p = 8.1 \times 10^{-5}$	57.15870 $p = 8.1 \times 10^{-5}$	**0.12110** -
TNK	**0.00073** -	0.04383 $p = 8.1 \times 10^{-5}$	**0.00082** $p = 0.206$	0.02849 $p = 8.1 \times 10^{-5}$	0.01180 $p = 8.1 \times 10^{-5}$	0.03332 $p = 8.1 \times 10^{-5}$	0.01121 $p = 8.1 \times 10^{-5}$	0.03743 $p = 8.1 \times 10^{-5}$	0.03077 $p = 8.1 \times 10^{-5}$	0.03990 $p = 8.1 \times 10^{-5}$	**0.00080** $p = 0.494$
SRN	**0.13191** -	4.17160 $p = 8.1 \times 10^{-5}$	1.00930 $p = 8.1 \times 10^{-5}$	0.92614 $p = 8.1 \times 10^{-5}$	1.06120 $p = 8.1 \times 10^{-5}$	1.20480 $p = 8.1 \times 10^{-5}$	1.51360 $p = 8.1 \times 10^{-5}$	1.48870 $p = 8.1 \times 10^{-5}$	1.28450 $p = 8.1 \times 10^{-5}$	2.41710 $p = 8.1 \times 10^{-5}$	**0.13406** $p = 0.1891$
BNH	**0.07885** $p = 0.0865$	0.74425 $p = 8.1 \times 10^{-5}$	**0.04630** $p = 0.5114$	**0.04457** $p = 0.5994$	0.23728 $p = 8.1 \times 10^{-5}$	0.23923 $p = 8.1 \times 10^{-5}$	0.32874 $p = 8.1 \times 10^{-5}$	0.36600 $p = 8.1 \times 10^{-5}$	0.23699 $p = 8.1 \times 10^{-5}$	0.71300 $p = 8.1 \times 10^{-5}$	**0.04176** -
WB	**0.13794** $p = 0.2933$	0.55529 $p = 8.1 \times 10^{-5}$	0.23159 $p = 0.0126$	0.84746 $p = 8.1 \times 10^{-5}$	**0.16909** $p = 0.1007$	0.88586 $p = 8.1 \times 10^{-5}$	1.39250 $p = 8.1 \times 10^{-5}$	3.40770 $p = 8.1 \times 10^{-5}$	0.96166 $p = 8.1 \times 10^{-5}$	1.41110 $p = 8.1 \times 10^{-5}$	**0.08960** -

Table 3. Cont.

Problem	M1-1	M2-1	M1-2	M2-2	M3-1	M4-1	M3-2	M4-2	M5	M6	ASM
DTLZ2	0.07870 $p = 8.1\times10^{-5}$	-	0.03340 -	-	0.05377 $p = 8.1\times10^{-5}$	-	0.05040 $p = 8.1\times10^{-5}$	-	-	0.07736 $p = 8.1\times10^{-5}$	*0.03701* $p = 0.562$
C2DTLZ2	0.05130 $p = 8.1\times10^{-5}$	-	*0.03355* $p = 0.115$	-	0.03493 $p = 0.008$	-	*0.03190* $p = 0.148$	-	0.12403 $p = 8.1\times10^{-5}$	0.04410 $p = 8.1\times10^{-5}$	0.03062 -
CAR	0.43510 $p = 8.1\times10^{-5}$	0.43145 $p = 8.1\times10^{-5}$	0.50119 $p = 8.1\times10^{-5}$	**0.29817**	0.39809 $p = 8.1\times10^{-5}$	0.42223 $p = 8.1\times10^{-5}$	0.40494 $p = 8.1\times10^{-5}$	0.44251 $p = 8.1\times10^{-5}$	0.50061 $p = 8.1\times10^{-5}$	0.55569 $p = 8.1\times10^{-5}$	0.40110 $p = 8.1\times10^{-5}$
DTLZ5	0.01960 $p = 8.1\times10^{-5}$	-	**0.00948** -	-	0.01352 $p = 8.1\times10^{-5}$	-	0.01537 $p = 8.1\times10^{-5}$	-	-	0.05421 $p = 8.1\times10^{-5}$	*0.01252* $p = 0.0605$
DTLZ4	**0.05840** -	-	*0.09024* $p = 0.1203$	-	0.20668 $p = 8.1\times10^{-5}$	-	0.12570 $p = 8.1\times10^{-5}$	-	-	*0.08731* $p = 0.3933$	0.07934 $p = 0.425$
DTLZ7	0.11808 $p = 0.0187$	-	*0.07664* $p = 0.2122$	-	0.87172 $p = 8.1\times10^{-5}$	-	1.26300 $p = 8.1\times10^{-5}$	-	-	0.82989 $p = 8.1\times10^{-5}$	0.06529
DTLZ2-5	0.21450 $p = 8.1\times10^{-5}$	-	**0.03981** -	-	0.14401 $p = 8.1\times10^{-5}$	-	0.14403 $p = 8.1\times10^{-5}$	-	-	0.11028 $p = 8.1\times10^{-5}$	*0.04918* $p = 0.595$
C2DTLZ2-5	0.17341 $p = 8.1\times10^{-5}$	-	*0.03676* $p = 0.8541$	-	0.15388 $p = 8.1\times10^{-5}$	-	0.11669 $p = 8.1\times10^{-5}$	-	0.29291 $p = 8.1\times10^{-5}$	0.20842 $p = 8.1\times10^{-5}$	0.03441 -

5.4. Three and More Objective Constrained and Unconstrained Problems

Next, we apply all ten frameworks and ASM approach to three-objective optimization problems (DTLZ2, DTLZ4, DTLZ5, and DTLZ7) and also to two three-objective constrained problem (C2DTLZ2 and the car side impact problem CAR [60]). Table 3 shows that while M2-2 works uniquely the best on CAR, M1-2 and M3-2 on C2-DTLZ2, and M1-1, M1-2, and M6 on DTLZ4, the performance of ASM approach is better or equivalent compared to all 10 problems.

The epoch-wise proportion of utilization of 10 frameworks in 11 runs are shown in Figure 10 for three and five-objective problems. It can be clearly seen that M3-1 to M6 frameworks are not usually chosen by the ASM approach on most of these problems, except for complex problems, such as DTLZ4. Switching has been confined between M1-1 to M2-2 for most problems, except in DTLZ4, in which all generative frameworks are found to be useful in certain stages during the optimization process. DTLZ7 works better with simultaneous frameworks M1-2 and M2-2.

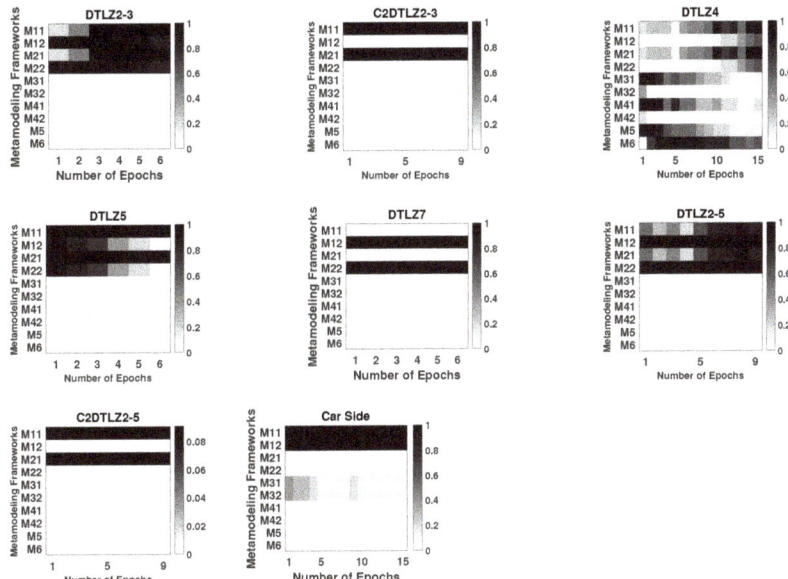

Figure 10. Epoch-wise proportion of usage of 10 frameworks in 11 runs of the ASM approach for three and five-objective problems.

On two five-objective unconstrained DTLZ2 and constrained C2-DTLZ2 problems, M1-2 alone and ASM approach perform the best with statistically significant difference with other frameworks. Constrained C2DTLZ2 problems use similar a switching pattern for three and five-objective version of the problem.

Table 4 calculates the rank of each of the 10 frameworks for solving 18 problems. The table shows that the ASM approach performs the best overall, followed by M1-2, M2-2, and M3-1 respectively. It indicates that overall, metamodeling of objectives independently is a better approach for these problems. M6, although being the most efficient in the number of metamodels, performs the worst.

Table 4. Average rank of 10 frameworks and the ASM approach on 18 problems based on Wilcoxon rank-sum test.

M1-1	M2-1	M1-2	M2-2	M3-1	M4-1	M3-2	M4-2	M5	M6	ASM
3.66	6.16	2.88	3.00	4.55	5.44	6.22	6.94	6.33	8.55	**1.11**

5.5. Comparison with Existing Methods

Next, we examine the performance of our adaptive switching metamodeling (ASM) strategy by comparing them with a few recent algorithms, namely, MOEA/D-EGO [14], K-RVEA [23], and CSEA [33]. Algorithms are implemented in PlatEMO [67]. Since these three competing algorithms can only be applied to unconstrained problems, only ZDT and DTLZ problems are considered here. We plan to compare our constrained approach with existing constraint handling methods [32]. Identical parameters settings as those used with the ASM approach are used for the three competing algorithms. Table 5 presents the mean IGD value of each algorithm. The Wilcoxon rank-sum test results are also shown. It is clearly evident that ASM approach outperforms three competing methods, of which K-RVEA performs well only on two of the nine problems.

Table 5. Median IGD on unconstrained problems using ASM approach, and MOEA/D-EGO, K-RVEA, and CSEA algorithms. DNC is denoted as "Did not converge" within given time.

Problem	MOEA/D-EGO	K-RVEA	CSEA	ASM
ZDT1	0.05611 $p = 8.1 \times 10^{-5}$	0.07964 $p = 8.1 \times 10^{-5}$	0.95330 $p = 8.1 \times 10^{-5}$	**0.00130** $p = 0.0910$
ZDT2	0.04922 $p = 8.1 \times 10^{-5}$	0.03395 $p = 8.1 \times 10^{-5}$	1.01060 $p = 8.1 \times 10^{-5}$	**0.00055** -
ZDT3	0.30380 $p = 8.1 \times 10^{-5}$	0.02481 $p = 8.1 \times 10^{-5}$	0.94840 $p = 8.1 \times 10^{-5}$	**0.00391** -
ZDT4	73.25920 $p = 8.1 \times 10^{-5}$	4.33221 $p = 8.1 \times 10^{-5}$	12.71600 $p = 8.1 \times 10^{-5}$	**0.39992** -
ZDT6	0.51472 $p = 8.1 \times 10^{-5}$	0.65462 $p = 8.1 \times 10^{-5}$	5.42620 $p = 8.1 \times 10^{-5}$	**0.24440** $p = 0.0612$
DTLZ2	0.33170 $p = 8.1 \times 10^{-5}$	0.0548 $p = 8.1 \times 10^{-5}$	0.11420 $p = 8.1 \times 10^{-5}$	**0.03701** $p = 0.157$
DTLZ4	0.64533 $p = 8.1 \times 10^{-5}$	**0.0449** -	0.08110 $p = 0.0022$	0.07934 $p = 0.0380$
DTLZ5	0.26203 $p = 8.1 \times 10^{-5}$	0.0164 $p = 8.1 \times 10^{-5}$	0.03081 $p = 8.1 \times 10^{-5}$	**0.01252** $p = 0.211$
DTLZ7	5.33220 $p = 8.1 \times 10^{-5}$	**0.0531** -	0.70520 $p = 8.1 \times 10^{-5}$	0.06529 $p = 0.1930$
DTLZ2-5	0.31221 $p = 8.1 \times 10^{-5}$	0.23031 $p = 8.1 \times 10^{-5}$	DNC DNC	**0.04918** -

6. Conclusions

In this paper, we have provided a brief review of existing metamodeling methods for multiobjective optimization, since there has been a surge in such studies in the recent past. Since this calls for modeling multiple objectives and constraints in a progressive manner, a recently proposed taxonomy of 10 frameworks involving metamodeling of independent or aggregate functions of objectives and constraints have been argued to cover a wide variety such methods. Each framework has been presented in detail, comparing and contrasting them in terms of the number of metamodeling functions to be constructed, the number of internal optimization problems to be solved, and the type of optimization methods to be employed, etc. We have argued that each metamodeling framework may be ideal at different stages during an optimization run on an arbitrary problem, hence, an ensemble use of all 10 frameworks becomes a natural choice. To propose an efficient multiobjective metamodeling algorithm, we have proposed an adaptive switching based metamodeling (ASM) methodology which automatically chooses the most appropriate framework epoch-wise during the course of an optimization run. In order to choose the best framework in every epoch, we perform statistical tests based on a newly proposed acceptance criterion—selection error probability (SEP), which counts the correct pairwise relationships of objectives between two test solutions in a k-fold cross-validation test, instead of calculating the usual mean-squared error of metamodeled objective values from true values. We have observed that SEP is less sensitive to outliers and is much better suited for multiobjective constrained optimization. In each epoch, the ASM approach switches to an appropriate framework which then creates a prespecified number of in-fill points by using either an evolutionary single or multiobjective algorithm or by using a multimodal or a niche-based real-parameter genetic algorithm. On 18 test and engineering problems having two to five objectives and multiple constraints, the ASM approach has been found to perform much better compared to each framework alone and also to three other existing metamodeling multiobjective algorithms.

It has been observed that in most problems a switching between different M1 and M2 frameworks, in which objectives are independently metamodeled, has performed the best. Metamodeling of constraints in an aggregate manner or independently is not an important matter. However, for more complex problems, such as ZDT3, ZDT6, ZDT4, DTLZ4, and engineering design problems, all 10 frameworks, including M5 and M6, have been involved at different stages of optimization. Interestingly, certain problems have preferred to pick generative frameworks (Mi-1 and M5) only, while some others have preferred simultaneous frameworks (Mi-2 and M6). Clearly, further investigation is needed to decipher a detail problem-wise pattern of selecting frameworks, but this first study on statistics-based adaptive switching has clearly shown its advantage over each framework applied alone.

While in this paper, Kriging metamodeling method has been used for all frameworks, this study can be extended to choose the best metamodeling method from an ensemble of RBF, SVR, or other response surface methods to make the overall approach more computationally efficient. In many practical problems, some functions may be relatively less time-consuming, thereby creating a *heterogeneous* metamodeling scenario [16,68,69]. A simple extension of this study would be to formulate a heterogeneous *MP* (for example, M1-1's objective function for a two-objective problem involving a larger evaluation time for f_1 can be chosen as $\left(\widetilde{f}_1(\mathbf{x}), f_2(\mathbf{x})\right)$, in which the objective f_2 has not been metamodeled at all). However, more involved algorithms can be tried for to handle such pragmatic scenarios. Another practical aspect comes from the fact that a cluster of objectives and constraints can come at the end of a single expensive evaluation procedure (such as, compliance objective and stress constraint comes after an expensive finite element analysis on a mechanical component design problem), whereas other functions come from a different time-scale evaluation procedure. The resulting definition of an epoch and the overall metamodeling approach need to be reconsidered to make the overall approach efficient. Other tricks, such as, the use of a low-fidelity evaluation scheme for expensive objective and constraints early on during the optimization process using a multifidelity scheme and the use of domain-informed heuristics to initialize population and repair offspring solutions must also be considered while developing efficient metamodeling approaches.

Funding: This research received no external funding.

Conflicts of Interest: The authors declare no conflict of interest.

References

1. Cassioli, A.; Schoen, F. Global optimization of expensive black box problems with a known lower bound. *J. Glob. Optim.* **2013**, *57*, 177–190. [CrossRef]
2. Jin, Y. Surrogate-assisted evolutionary computation: Recent advances and future challenge. *Swarm Evol. Comput.* **2011**, *1*, 61–70. [CrossRef]

3. Ponweiser, W.; Wagner, T.; Biermann, D.; Vincze, M. Multiobjective Optimization on a Limited Budget of Evaluations Using Model-Assisted S-Metric Selection. In *Parallel Problem Solving from Nature–PPSN X*; Springer: Berlin/Heidelberg, Germany, 2008; pp. 784–794.
4. Jones, D.R. A taxonomy of global optimization methods based on response surfaces. *J. Glob. Optim.* **2001**, *21*, 345–383. [CrossRef]
5. Hussein, R.; Deb, K. A Generative Kriging Surrogate Model for Constrained and Unconstrained Multi-objective Optimization. In Proceedings of the Genetic and Evolutionary Computation Conference (GECCO '16), Denver, CO, USA, 20–24 July 2016; ACM Press: New York, NY, USA, 2016.
6. Deb, K.; Hussein, R.; Roy, P.; Toscano, G. Classifying Metamodeling Methods for Evolutionary Multi-objective Optimization: First Results. In *Evolutionary Multi-Criterion Optimization EMO*; Springer: Berlin/Heidelberg, Germany, 2017.
7. Roy, P.; Hussein, R.; Deb, K. Metamodeling for multimodal selection functions in evolutionary multi-objective optimization. In Proceedings of the Genetic and Evolutionary Computation Conference (GECCO '17), Berlin, Germany, 15–19 July 2017; ACM Press: New York, NY, USA, 2017.
8. Bhattacharjee, K.S.; Singh, H.K.; Ray, T. Multi-objective optimization with multiple spatially distributed surrogates. *J. Mech. Des.* **2016**, *138*, 091401. [CrossRef]
9. Bhattacharjee, K.S.; Singh, H.K.; Ray, T.; Branke, J. Multiple Surrogate Assisted Multiobjective Optimization Using Improved Pre-Selection. In Proceedings of the 2016 IEEE Congress on Evolutionary Computation (CEC-2016), Vancouver, BC, Canada, 24–29 July 2016.
10. Emmerich, M.T.M.; Giannakoglou, K.C.; Naujoks, B. Single- and multiobjective evolutionary optimization assisted by Gaussian random field metamodels. *IEEE Trans. Evol. Comput.* **2006**, *10*, 421–439. [CrossRef]
11. Byrd, R.H.; Nocedal, J.; Waltz, R.A. Knitro: An Integrated Package for Nonlinear Optimization. In *Large-Scale Nonlinear Optimization*; Springer US: Boston, MA, USA, 2006.
12. Jin, Y.; Oh, S.; Jeon, M. Incremental approximation of nonlinear constraint functions for evolutionary constrained optimization. In Proceedings of the 2010 IEEE Congress on Evolutionary Computation (CEC-2010), Barcelona, Spain, 18–23 July 2010; pp. 1–8.
13. Datta, R.; Regis, R.G. A surrogate-assisted evolution strategy for constrained multi-objective optimization. *Expert Syst. Appl.* **2016**, *57*, 270–284. [CrossRef]
14. Zhang, Q.; Liu, W.; Tsang, E.; Virginas, B. Expensive Multiobjective Optimization by MOEA/D With Gaussian Process Model. *IEEE Trans. Evol. Comput.* **2010**, *14*, 456–474. [CrossRef]
15. Knowles, J. ParEGO: A Hybrid Algorithm with On-line Landscape Approximation for Expensive Multiobjective Optimization Problems. *IEEE Trans. Evol. Comput.* **2006**, *10*, 50–66. [CrossRef]
16. Allmendinger, R.; Emmerich, M.T.; Hakanen, J.; Jin, Y.; Rigoni, E. Surrogate-assisted multicriteria optimization: Complexities, prospective solutions, and business case. *J. Multi-Criteria Decis. Anal.* **2017**, *24*, 5–24. [CrossRef]
17. Roy, P.C.; Deb, K. High Dimensional Model Representation for Solving Expensive Multi-objective Optimization Problems. In Proceedings of the 2016 IEEE Congress on Evolutionary Computation (CEC), Vancouver, BC, Canada, 24–29 July 2016.
18. Rahat, A.A.M.; Everson, R.M.; Fieldsend, J.E. Alternative Infill Strategies for Expensive Multi-objective Optimisation. In Proceedings of the Genetic and Evolutionary Computation Conference (GECCO '17), Berlin, Germany, 15–19 July 2017; ACM: New York, NY, USA, 2017; pp. 873–880. [CrossRef]
19. Gómez, R.H.; Coello, C.A.C. A Hyper-heuristic of Scalarizing Functions. In Proceedings of the Genetic and Evolutionary Computation Conference (GECCO '17), Berlin, Germany, 15–19 July 2017; ACM: New York, NY, USA, 2017; pp. 577–584. [CrossRef]
20. Deb, K.; Hussein, R.; Roy, P.C.; Toscano, G. A Taxonomy for Metamodeling Frameworks for Evolutionary Multi-Objective Optimization. *IEEE Trans. Evol. Comput.* **2018**, *23*, 104–116. [CrossRef]
21. Hussein, R.; Roy, P.C.; Deb, K. Switching between Metamodeling Frameworks for Efficient Multi-Objective Optimization. In Proceedings of the 2018 IEEE Symposium Series on Computational Intelligence (SSCI), Bangalore, India, 18–21 November 2018; pp. 1188–1195.
22. Viana, F.A.C.; Haftka, R.T.; Watson, L.T. Efficient global optimization algorithm assisted by multiple surrogate techniques. *J. Glob. Optim.* **2013**, *56*, 669–689. [CrossRef]
23. Chugh, T.; Jin, Y.; Miettinen, K.; Hakanen, J.; Sindhya, K. A Surrogate-Assisted Reference Vector Guided Evolutionary Algorithm for Computationally Expensive Many-Objective Optimization. *IEEE Trans. Evol. Comput.* **2018**, *22*, 129–142. [CrossRef]
24. Zhao, D.; Xue, D. A multi-surrogate approximation method for metamodeling. *Eng. Comput.* **2011**, *27*, 139–153. [CrossRef]
25. Bhattacharjee, K.; Singh, H.; Ray, T. Multi-Objective Optimization Using an Evolutionary Algorithm Embedded with Multiple Spatially Distributed Surrogates. *Am. Soc. Mech. Eng.* **2016**, *138*, 135–155.
26. Wang, H.; Jin, Y.; Doherty, J. Committee-Based Active Learning for Surrogate-Assisted Particle Swarm Optimization of Expensive Problems. *IEEE Trans. Cybern.* **2017**, *47*, 2664–2677. [CrossRef]
27. Gaspar-Cunha, A.; Vieira, A. A Multi-Objective Evolutionary Algorithm Using Neural Networks to Approximate Fitness Evaluations. *Int. J. Comput. Syst. Signal* **2005**, *6*, 18–36.
28. Rosales-Perez, A.; Coello, C.A.C.; Gonzalez, J.A.; Reyes-Garcia, C.A.; Escalante, H.J. A hybrid surrogate-based approach for evolutionary multi-objective optimization. In Proceedings of the IEEE Congress on Evolutionary Computation (CEC-2013), Cancun, Mexico, 20–23 June 2013; pp. 2548–2555.

29. Akhtar, T.; Shoemaker, C.A. Efficient Multi-Objective Optimization through Population-based Parallel Surrogate Search. *arXiv* **2019**, arXiv:1903.02167v1.
30. Chugh, T.; Sindhya, K.; Hakanen, J.; Miettinen, K. A survey on handling computationally expensive multiobjective optimization problems with evolutionary algorithms. *Soft Comput.* **2019**, *23*, 3137–3166. [CrossRef]
31. Isaacs, A.; Ray, T.; Smith, W. An evolutionary algorithm with spatially distributed surrogates for multiobjective optimization. In Proceedings of the 3rd Australian Conference on Progress in Artificial Life, Gold Coast, Australia, 4–6 December 2007; Springer: Berlin/Heidelberg, Germany, 2007; pp. 257–268.
32. Habib, A.; Singh, H.K.; Chugh, T.; Ray, T.; Miettinen, K. A Multiple Surrogate Assisted Decomposition-Based Evolutionary Algorithm for Expensive Multi/Many-Objective Optimization. *IEEE Trans. Evol. Comput.* **2019**, *23*, 1000–1014. [CrossRef]
33. Pan, L.; He, C.; Tian, Y.; Wang, H.; Zhang, X.; Jin, Y. A Classification Based Surrogate-Assisted Evolutionary Algorithm for Expensive Many-Objective Optimization. *IEEE Trans. Evol. Comput.* **2018**, *23*, 74–88. [CrossRef]
34. Chafekar, D.; Shi, L.; Rasheed, K.; Xuan, J. Multiobjective GA optimization using reduced models. *IEEE Trans. Syst. Man Cybern. Part C Appl. Rev.* **2005**, *35*, 261–265. [CrossRef]
35. Peitz, S.; Dellnitz, M. A Survey of Recent Trends in Multiobjective Optimal Control—Surrogate Models, Feedback Control and Objective Reduction. *Math. Comput. Appl.* **2018**, *23*, 30. [CrossRef]
36. Thoman, J.; Eichfelder, G. Trust-Region Algorithm for Heterogeneous Multiobjective Optimization. *SIAM J. Optim.* **2019**, *29*, 1017–1047. [CrossRef]
37. Banholzer, S.; Beermann, D.; Volkwein, S. POD-Based Error Control for Reduced-Order Bicriterial PDE-Constrained Optimization. *Annu. Rev. Control* **2017**, *44*, 226–237. [CrossRef]
38. Díaz-Manríquez, A.; Toscano, G.; Barron-Zambrano, J.H.; Tello-Leal, E. A Review of Surrogate Assisted Multiobjective Evolutionary Algorithms. *Comput. Intell. Neurosci.* **2016**, *2016*, 9420460. [CrossRef] [PubMed]
39. Deb, K.; Agrawal, S.; Pratap, A.; Meyarivan, T. A fast and Elitist multi-objective Genetic Algorithm: NSGA-II. *IEEE Trans. Evol. Comput.* **2002**, *6*, 182–197. [CrossRef]
40. Singh, P.; Rossi, M.; Couckuyt, I.; Deschrijver, D.; Rogier, H.; Dhaene, T. Constrained multi-objective antenna design optimization using surrogates. *Int. J. Numer. Model.* **2017**, *30*, e2248. [CrossRef]
41. Koziel, S.; Bekasiewicz, A.; Szczepanski, S. Multi-objective design optimization of antennas for reflection, size, and gain variability using Kriging surrogates and generalized domain segmentation. *Int. J. RF Microw. Comput. Eng.* **2018**, *28*, e21253. [CrossRef]
42. Beck, J.; Friedrich, D.; Brandani, S.; Fraga, E.S. Multi-objective optimisation using surrogate models for the design of VPSA systems. *Comput. Chem. Eng.* **2015**, *82*, 318–329. [CrossRef]
43. Liao, X.; Li, Q.; Yang, X.; Zhang, W.; Li, W. Multi-objective optimization for crash safety design of vehicles using stepwise regression model. *Struct. Multidiscip. Optim.* **2008**, *35*, 561–569. [CrossRef]
44. Sreekanth, J.; Datta, B. Multi-objective management of saltwater intrusion in coastal aquifers using genetic programming and modular neural network based surrogate models. *J. Hydrol.* **2010**, *393*, 245–256. [CrossRef]
45. Arias-Montaño, A.; Coello, C.A.C.; Mezura-Montes, E. Multi-objective airfoil shape optimization using a multiple-surrogate approach. In Proceedings of the 2012 IEEE Congress on Evolutionary Computation (CEC-2012), Brisbane, Australia, 10–15 June 2012; pp. 1–8.
46. D'Angelo, S.; Minisci, E.A. Multi-objective evolutionary optimization of subsonic airfoils by Kriging approximation and evolution control. In Proceedings of the IEEE Congress on Evolutionary Computation (CEC-2005), Scotland, UK, 2–5 September 2005; pp. 1262–1267.
47. Alvarado-Iniesta, A.; Cuate, O.; Schütze, O. Multi-objective and many objective design of plastic injection molding process. *Int. J. Adv. Manuf. Technol.* **2019**, *102*, 3165–3180. [CrossRef]
48. Knowles, J.; Hughes, E.J. Multiobjective Optimization on a Budget of 250 Evaluations. In *Evolutionary Multi-Criterion Optimization*; Springer: Berlin/Heidelberg, Germany, 2005; pp. 176–190.
49. Hüsken, M.; Jin, Y.; Sendhoff, B. Structure optimization of neural networks for evolutionary design optimization. *Soft Comput.* **2005**, *9*, 21–28. [CrossRef]
50. Pilát, M.; Neruda, R. Improving many-objective optimizers with aggregate meta-models. In Proceedings of the 2011 11th International Conference on Hybrid Intelligent Systems (HIS), Melacca, Malaysia, 5–8 December 2011; pp. 555–560. [CrossRef]
51. Le, M.N.; Ong, Y.S.; Jin, Y.; Sendhoff, B. A Unified Framework for Symbiosis of Evolutionary Mechanisms with Application to Water Clusters Potential Model Design. *IEEE Comput. Intell. Mag.* **2012**, *7*, 20–35. [CrossRef]
52. Li, F.; Cai, X.; Gao, L. Ensemble of surrogates assisted particle swarm optimization of medium scale expensive problems. *Appl. Soft Comput.* **2019**, *74*, 291–305. [CrossRef]
53. Jin, C.; Qin, A.K.; Tang, K. Local ensemble surrogate assisted crowding differential evolution. In Proceedings of the 2015 IEEE Congress on Evolutionary Computation (CEC-2015), Sendai, Japan, 25–28 May 2015; pp. 433–440.
54. Deb, K. *Multi-Objective Optimization Using Evolutionary Algorithms*; John Wiley & Sons: Hoboken, NJ, USA, 2001.
55. Srinivas, N.; Deb, K. Multi-Objective function optimization using non-dominated sorting genetic algorithms. *Evol. Comput. J.* **1994**, *2*, 221–248. [CrossRef]
56. Jones, D.R.; Schonlau, M.; Welch, W.J. Efficient Global Optimization of Expensive Black-Box Functions. *J. Glob. Optim.* **1998**, *13*, 455–492. [CrossRef]

57. Deb, K. An efficient constraint handling method for genetic algorithms. *Comput. Methods App. Mech. Eng.* **2000**, *186*, 311–338. [CrossRef]
58. Wierzbicki, A.P. The use of reference objectives in multiobjective optimization. In *Multiple Criteria Decision Making Theory and Application*; Springer: Berlin/Heidelberg, Germany, 1980; pp. 468–486.
59. Das, I.; Dennis, J.E. Normal-Boundary Intersection: A New Method for Generating the Pareto Surface in Nonlinear Multicriteria Optimization Problems. *SIAM J. Optim.* **1998**, *8*. [CrossRef]
60. Deb, K.; Jain, H. An evolutionary many-objective optimization algorithm using reference-point-based nondominated sorting approach, part I: Solving problems with box constraints. *IEEE Trans. Evol. Comput.* **2014**, *18*, 577–601. [CrossRef]
61. Zitzler, E.; Thiele, L. Multiobjective optimization using evolutionary algorithms—A comparative case study. In Proceedings of the Conference on Parallel Problem Solving from Nature (PPSN V), Amsterdam, The Netherlands, 27–30 September 1998; pp. 292–301.
62. Coello, C.A.C.; Sierra, M.R. A study of the parallelization of a coevolutionary multi-objective evolutionary algorithm. In *MICAI 2004: Advances in Artificial Intelligence*; Springer: Berlin/Heidelberg, Germany, 2004; pp. 688–697.
63. Kendall, M.G. A new measure of rank correlation. *Biometrika* **1938**, *30*, 81–93. [CrossRef]
64. Miettinen, K. *Nonlinear Multiobjective Optimization*; Kluwer: Dordrecht, The Netherlands, 1999.
65. Roy, P.C.; Blank, J.; Hussein, R.; Deb, K. Trust-region Based Algorithms with Low-budget for Multi-objective Optimization. In Proceedings of the Genetic and Evolutionary Computation Conference Companion (GECCO '18), Kyoto, Japan, 15–19 July 2018; ACM: New York, NY, USA, 2018; pp. 195–196.
66. Alexandrov, N.M.; Dennis, J.E.; Lewis, R.M.; Torczon, V. A trust-region framework for managing the use of approximation models in optimization. *Struct. Optim.* **1998**, *15*, 16–23. [CrossRef]
67. Tian, Y.; Cheng, R.; Zhang, X.; Jin, Y. PlatEMO: A MATLAB Platform for Evolutionary Multi-Objective Optimization. *IEEE Comput. Intell. Mag.* **2017**, *12*, 73–87. [CrossRef]
68. Allmendinger, R.; Knowles, J. 'Hang on a minute': Investigations on the effects of delayed objective functions in multiobjective optimization. In *Evolutionary Multi-Criterion Optimization*; Purshouse, R.C., Fleming, P.J., Fonseca, C.M., Greco, S., Shaw, J., Eds.; Springer: Berlin/Heidelberg, Germany, 2013; pp. 6–20.
69. Blank, J.; Deb, K. *Constrained Bi-objective Surrogate-Assisted Optimization of Problems with Heterogeneous Evaluation Times: Expensive Objectives and Inexpensive Constraints*; Technical Report COIN Report 2020019; COIN Laboratory, Michigan State University: East Lansing, MI, USA, 2020.

Article

Differential Evolution in Robust Optimization Over Time Using a Survival Time Approach

José-Yaír Guzmán-Gaspar [1,*], Efrén Mezura-Montes [1] and Saúl Domínguez-Isidro [2]

[1] Artificial Intelligence Research Center, University of Veracruz, Sebastián Camacho 5, Col. Centro, Xalapa 91000, Veracruz, Mexico; emezura@uv.mx
[2] National Laboratory on Advanced Informatics, Rebsamen 80, Xalapa 91000, Veracruz, Mexico; saul.dominguez@lania.edu.mx
* Correspondence: yairguz@gmail.com

Received: 2 October 2020; Accepted: 23 October 2020; Published: 26 October 2020

Abstract: This study presents an empirical comparison of the standard differential evolution (DE) against three random sampling methods to solve robust optimization over time problems with a survival time approach to analyze its viability and performance capacity of solving problems in dynamic environments. A set of instances with four different dynamics, generated by two different configurations of two well-known benchmarks, are solved. This work also introduces a comparison criterion that allows the algorithm to discriminate among solutions with similar survival times to benefit the selection process. The results show that the standard DE holds a good performance to find ROOT solutions, improving the results reported by state-of-the-art approaches in the studied environments. Finally, it was found that the chaotic dynamic, disregarding the type of peak movement in the search space, is a source of difficulty for the proposed DE algorithm.

Keywords: robust optimization; differential evolution; ROOT

1. Introduction

Optimization is an inherent process in various areas of study and everyday life. The search to improve processes, services, and performances has originated in different solution techniques. However, there are problems in which uncertainty is present over time, given that the solution's environment can change at a specific time. These types of problems are named Dynamic Optimization Problems (DOPs) [1]. This study deals with dynamic problems where the environment of the problem changes over time. Various studies have been carried out to resolve DOPs through tracking moving optima (TMO), which is characterized by the search for and implementation of the global optimal-solution every time the environment changes [2–4].

Evolutionary algorithms, such as Differential Evolution (DE), have shown good performance to solve tracking problems [5–7]. However, the search and implementation of the optimum each time the environment changes may not be feasible due to different circumstances, such as time or cost.

The approach introduced in [8] tries to solve DOPs through a procedure known as robust optimization over time (ROOT). ROOT seeks to solve DOPs by looking for a good solution for multiple environments and preserve it for as long as possible, while its quality does not decrease from a pre-established threshold. The solution found is called Robust Solution Over Time (RSOT).

In this regard, Fu et al. [9] introduced different measures to characterize environmental changes. After that, the authors developed two definitions for robustness [10]. The first one was based on "Survival Time"—when a solution is considered acceptable (an aptitude threshold must be previously defined).

The second definition was based on the "Average Fitness"—the solution's average fitness is maintained during a previously defined time window. The measurements incorporate information on the concepts of robustness and consider the values of error estimators. An algorithm performance measure was suggested to find ROOT solutions. The study was carried out using a modified version of the moving peaks benchmark (mMPB) [10].

Jin et al. [11] proposed a ROOT framework that includes three variants of the Particle Swarm Optimization algorithm (PSO). PSO with a simple restart strategy (sPSO), PSO with memory scheme (memPSO), and a variant that implements the species technique SPSO. The authors applied a radial basis function as an approximation and an autoregressive model as a predictor.

On the other hand, Wang introduced the concept of robustness in a multi-objective environment, where a framework is created to find robust Pareto fronts [12]. The author adopted the dynamic multi-objective evolutionary optimization algorithm in the experiments. At the same time, Huang et al. considered the cost derived from implementing new solutions, thus addressing the ROOT problem by a multi-objective PSO (MOPSO); The Fu metric was applied in that study [13].

Yazdani et al. introduced a new semi-ROOT algorithm that looks for a new solution when the current one is not acceptable, or if the current one is acceptable but the algorithm finds a better solution, whose implementation is preferable even with the cost of change [14].

Novoa-Hernández, Pelta, and Corona analyzed the ROOT behavior using some approximation models [15]. The authors suggested that the radial basis network model with radial basis function works better for problems with a low number of peaks. However, considering all the scenarios, the SVM model with Laplace Kernel shows notably better performance to those compared in the tests carried out.

Novoa-Hernández and Amilkar in [16] reviewed different relevant contributions to ROOT. The authors analyzed papers hosted in the SCOPUS database. Concerning new methods to solve ROOT problems, Yazdani, Nguyen, and Branke proposed a new framework using a multi-population approach where sub-populations track peaks and collect information from them [17]. Adam and Yao introduced three methods to address ROOT (Mesh, Optimal in time, and Robust). The authors mentioned that they significantly improves the results obtained for ROOT in the state-of-the-art [18]. Fox, Yang and Caraffini studied different prediction methods in ROOT, including the Linear and Quadratic Regression methods, an Autoregressive model, and Support Vector Regression [19]. Finally, Liu and Liang mapped a ROOT approach to minimize the electric bus transit center's total cost in the first stage [20].

In different studies, DE has been used to solve ROOT problems using the Average Fitness approach, achieving competitive results [21,22]. However, to the best of the authors' knowledge, there are no studies that determine DE's performance in solving ROOT problems with the Survival Time approach, and this is where this work precisely focuses. This research aims to present an empirical comparison of the standard DE against three random sampling methods to solve robust optimization over time problems with a survival time approach to analyze its viability and performance capacity of solving problems in dynamic environments.

The paper is organized as follows: Section 2 includes ROOT's definition under a survival time approach, while in Section 3 the implemented methods based on random sampling are detailed. Section 4 details the standard differential evolution and the objective function used by the algorithm in the present study. Section 5 specifies the benchmark problems to be solved. After that, Section 6 specifies the experimental settings and Section 7 shows the results obtained. Finally, Section 8 summarizes the conclusions and future work.

2. Survival Time Approach

Under this approach, a threshold is predefined to specify the quality that a solution must have to be considered good or suitable to survive. Once the threshold is defined, the search begins for a solution whose fitness can remain above the threshold in as many environments as possible. In this sense, the solution is maintained until its quality does not meet the predefined expectations, and then new robust solution over time must be sought.

In Equation (1), the function $F^s(\vec{x}, t, V)$ to calculate the survival time fitness of a solution $\vec{x}$ at time t is detailed. It measures the number of environments that a solution remains in above the threshold V.

$$F^s(\vec{x}, t, V) = \begin{cases} 0 & \text{if } f_t(\vec{x}) < V \\ 1 + \max\{l | \forall i \in \{t, t+1, ..., t+l\} : f_i(\vec{x}) \geq V\}, & \text{in other case} \end{cases} \quad (1)$$

3. Random Sampling Methods

In the study presented in [18] the authors proposed three random sampling methods to solve ROOT problems, with a better performance against the state-of-the-art algorithms. The methods are described below.

In all three methods, the best solution should be searched in the current time's solutions space, modifying the solution space when the "Robust method" is used and then using that solution next time according to the approach used (Survival Time or Average Fitness).

3.1. Mesh

This method performs random sampling in the current search space, then uses the sample with the best fitness in the current environment as a robust solution over time, using the solution found in the following times (Figure 1).

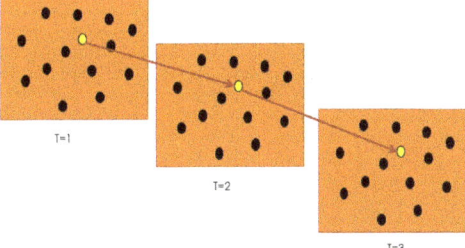

Figure 1. Mesh method. The yellow point is the robust solution found by the method and it is used in the next times.

3.2. Time-Optimal

This method performs a search similar to the "Mesh" method, with the difference that the best solution found being improved using a local search (Figure 2).

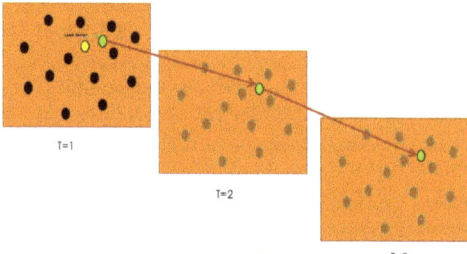

Figure 2. Time-optimal method. The green point is the robust solution found by the method, which is used in the next times.

3.3. Robust

This method performs a search similar to the "Mesh" method, differing in that a smoothing preprocessing of the solution space is performed before the search process. As seen in Figure 3, the solution obtained (green dot) can vary concerning the solution with better suitability in the raw environment (yellow dot).

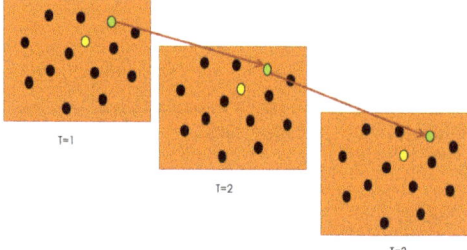

Figure 3. Robust method. The green point is the robust solution found by the method which is used in the next times.

4. Differential Evolution

In 1995, Storm and Price proposed an evolutionary algorithm to solve optimization problems in continuous spaces. DE is based on a population of solutions that, through simple recombination and mutation, evolves, thus improving individuals' fitness [23].

Considering the fact that this work, to the best of the authors' knowledge, is the first attempt to study DE in this type of ROOT problems (i.e., survival time), and also taking into account that the most popular DE variant (DE/rand/1/bin) has provided competitive results in ROOT problems under an average fitness approach [21,22], the algorithm used in this study is precisely the most popular variant known as DE/rand/1/bin, where "rand" (random) refers to the base vector used in the mutation, "bin" (binomial) refers to the crossover type used, and 1 means one vector difference computed.

The algorithm starts by randomly generating a uniformly distributed population $\vec{x}_{i,G} \in i = 1, ..., NP$, where NP is the number of individuals for each generation "G".

After that, the algorithm enters an evolution cycle until the stop condition is reached. We applied the maximum number of evaluations allowed "MAX_{Eval}" as the stop condition.

Subsequently, to adapt individuals, the algorithm performs recombination, mutation, and the replacement of each one in the current generation. One of the most popular mutations is DE/rand/1 in

Equation (2), where $r0 \neq r1 \neq r2 \neq i$ are the indices of individuals randomly chosen from the population, 1 is the number of differences used in the mutation and $F > 0$ is the scale factor.

$$\vec{v}_{i,G} = \vec{x}_{r0,G} + F(\vec{x}_{r1,G} - \vec{x}_{r2,G}) \quad (2)$$

The vector obtained $\vec{v}_{i,G}$ is known as mutant vector, which is recombined with the target (parent) vector by binomial crossover, as detailed in Equation (3).

$$u_{i,j,G} = \begin{cases} v_{j,i,G}, & if\ (rand_j \leq CR)\ or\ (j = j_{rand}) \\ x_{j,i,G}, & otherwise \end{cases} \quad (3)$$

In this study, the elements of the child vector (also called trial) $u_{i,j,G}$ are limited according to the pre-established maximum and minimum limits, also known as boundary constraints. Based on the study in [24], we use the boundary method (see Algorithm 1, line 14). In the selection process, the algorithm determines the vector that will prevail for the next generation between parent (target) and child (trial), as expressed in Equation (4).

$$\vec{x}_{i,G+1} = \begin{cases} \vec{u}_{i,G}, & if\ (f(\vec{u}_{i,G}) \leq f(\vec{x}_{i,G})) \\ \vec{x}_{i,G}, & otherwise \end{cases} \quad (4)$$

Algorithm 1: "DE/rand/1/bin" Algorithm. NP, MAX_{Eval}, CR and F are parameters defined by the user. D is the dimension of the problem.

1. $G \leftarrow 0$
2. Generate an uniform initial random population $\vec{x}_{i,G} \in i = 1, ..., NP$
3. Compute $f(\vec{x}_{i,G}) \forall i, i = 1, ..., NP$
4. $Eval \leftarrow NP$
5. **while** $Eval < MAX_{Eval}$ **do**
6.   **for** $j = 1$ **to** NP **do**
7.   Randomly select $r0 \neq r1 \neq r2 \neq i$:
8. $j_{rand} \leftarrow rand_i([1,D])$
9.   **for** $j = 1$ **to** D **do**
10.   **if** $rand_j([0,1]) < CR\ or\ j = j_{rand}$ **then**
11. $u_{i,j,G} \leftarrow x_{r0,j,G} + F(x_{r1,j,G} - x_{r2,j,G})$
12.   **else**
13. $u_{i,j,G} \leftarrow x_{i,j,G}$
14. $u_{i,G} \leftarrow min(max(u_{i,G}, xmin), xmax)$
15.   **if** $f(\vec{u}_{i,G}) \geq f(\vec{x}_{i,G})$ **then**
16. $\vec{x}_{i,G+1} \leftarrow \vec{u}_{i,G}$
17.   **else**
18. $\vec{x}_{i,G+1} \leftarrow \vec{x}_{i,G}$
19. $Eval \leftarrow Eval + 1$
20.   **if** $Eval >= MAX_{Eval}$ **then**
21.   break
22. $G \leftarrow G + 1$

In Equation (1), the function to obtain an individual's fitness through the survival time approach is shown. However, the fitness obtained is not enough to differentiate similar individuals, i.e., individuals who have survived the same amount of environments. That is why, in the implemented algorithm, we consider an additional calculation to help identify better solutions.

We propose to obtain the average of the solution's quality in the environments that have survived. This average value helps to differentiate solutions with similar survival times. Therefore, the objective function now considers both, the number of surviving environments and the performance achieved by this solution in those environments that it has survived.

Considering the fact that the maximum height of the peaks is defined at 70 (see Table 3), the objective function for the implemented algorithm is given by the result obtained in Equation (1) multiplied by 100 plus the average fitness of the solution throughout the environments it has survived.

5. Benchmark Problems

The problems tackled in this study are based on Moving Peaks Benchmark (MPB) [25] and are configured in a similar way to that used in various specialized literature publications on ROOT, and specifically as used in [18].

Two modified MPBs can be highlighted, which are described in the following subsections. The dynamics used are presented in Table 1, where $\Delta \phi$ is the increment from time t to time $t+1$ of the ϕ parameter.

Table 1. Dynamic Functions.

1. Small Step	$\Delta \phi = \gamma \cdot \|\phi\| \cdot r \cdot \phi_{severity}$
2. Large Step	$\Delta \phi = \|\phi\| \cdot (\gamma * sign(r) + (\gamma_{max} - \gamma) \cdot r) \cdot \phi_{severity}$
3. Random	$\Delta \phi = N(0,1) \cdot \phi_{severity}$
4. Chaotic	$\phi_{t+1} = \phi_{min} + A \cdot (\phi_t - \phi_{min}) \cdot (1 - (\phi_t - \phi_{min})/\|\phi\|)$

5.1. Moving Peaks Benchmark 1 (MPB1)

In this benchmark, environments with conical peaks of height $h(t) \in [h_{min}, h_{max}]$, width $w(t) \in [w_{min}, w_{max}]$ and center $c(t) \in [x_{min}, x_{max}]$ are generated, where the design variable x is bounded in $[x_{min}, x_{max}]$. The function to generate the environment is expressed in Equation (5), where the dynamic function for height and width is given as in Table 1, while the center moves according to Equation (6). r^i follows an uniform distribution of a D-dimensional sphere of radius s^i, and $\lambda \in [0,1]$ is a fixed parameter.

$$f(\vec{x}, \vec{a}(t)) = \max_{i=1}^{i=m} \{h^i(t) - w^i(t)\|\vec{x} - \vec{c}^i(t)\|_{l_2}\} \quad (5)$$

$$\vec{c}^i(t+1) = \vec{c}^i(t) + \vec{v}^i(t+1)$$

$$\vec{v}^i(t+1) = s^i \frac{(1-\lambda)r^i(t+1) + \lambda v^i(t)}{\|(1-\lambda)r^i(t+1) + \lambda v^i(t)\|} \quad (6)$$

In the present study, two problems generated by this benchmark are solved, with $\lambda = 0$ it implies that the movement of the peaks is random, while with $\lambda = 1$ it implies that the movement is constant in the direction $\vec{v}^i(t)$.

5.2. Moving Peaks Benchmark 2 (MPB2)

The set of test functions in this benchmark is described in Equation (7), where $\vec{a}(t)$ is the environment at time step t, $h^i(t), w^i(t), \vec{c}^i(t)$ is the height, width and center of the i-th peak function at time t, respectively;

$\vec{x}$ is the decision variable and m is the total number of peaks. $h^i(t+1)$ and $w^i(t+1)$ vary according to Table 1. An additional technique that uses a rotation matrix is used to rotate the centers [25].

$$f(\vec{x}, \vec{a}(t)) = \frac{1}{d}\sum_{j=1}^{d} max_{i=1}^{i=m}\{h^i(t) - w^i(t)\|\vec{x} - \vec{c}^i(t)\|\} \qquad (7)$$

6. Experimental Settings

Based on the information in Section 5, different environments are generated as test problems and they are summarized in Table 2.

Table 2. Summary of problems.

Benchmark	Abbreviation	Configuration	Dynamic (δ)
MPB1	$B1D\delta - 1$	$\lambda = 0$	{1,2,3,4}
MPB1	$B1D\delta - 2$	$\lambda = 1$	{1,2,3,4}
MPB2	$B2D\delta - a$	uniform start of peak distribution	{1,2,3,4}
MPB2	$B2D\delta - b$	random start of peak distribution	{1,2,3,4}

The parameter settings of the problems are detailed in Table 3.

Table 3. Parameters settings.

Parameter	MPB1	MBP2
Number of peaks m	5	25
Number of dimensions d	2	2
Search range $[x_{min}, x_{max}]$	$[0, 50]$	$[-25, 25]$
Height range $[h_{min}, h_{max}]$	$[30, 70]$	$[30, 70]$
Width range $[w_{min}, w_{max}]$	$[1, 12]$	$[1, 13]$
Angle range $[\theta_{min}, \theta_{max}]$	-	$[-\pi, \pi]$
$height_{severity}$	$U(1, 10)$	5.0
$width_{severity}$	$U(0.1, 1)$	0.5
$angle_{severity}$	-	1.0
Initial h	50	$U(h_{min}, h_{max})$
Initial w	6	$U(w_{min}, w_{max})$
Initial Angle	-	0
λ	$\{0, 1\}$	-
Number of dimensions for rotation l_r	-	2
Computational budget at each step Δe	2500	2500

The height and width of the peaks were randomly initialized in the predefined ranges. The centers were randomly initialized within the solution space.

A survival threshold $V = 50$ is selected, representing the most difficult cases that have been resolved in the literature under the survival approach. The higher the survival threshold, the more difficult it is to find solutions that satisfy multiple scenarios.

The DE parameters were fine-tuned using the iRace tool [26] and they are summarized in Table 4, where NP is the population size, CR is the crossover parameter, and F is the scale factor.

Table 4. Parameter settings of DE.

NP	CR	F
54	0.53	0.73

For each problem, a solution is sought at each time $t \in (2, ..., 100)$.

In order to evaluate an RSOT in a specific time, approximate and predictive methods have been used in the literature so that the performance of an algorithm depends on their accuracy. However, in this study, we want to know the DE behavior when solving the ROOT environments considering they had ideal predictors to evaluate the solutions. In this regard, the process to study the algorithm's ability to find RSOT using DE at each instant of time is as follows:

- A solution is sought according to the algorithm described in Section 4, and the measured solution value by Equation (1) is recorded.
- Subsequently, to obtain the algorithm's performance in the following environment, the search process is performed again using the real-environments; the best solution found is newly measured by Equation (1) and is also recorded.
- The described procedure is carried out at each instant of time that is being recorded. Therefore, in the present study, it is not necessary to detect environmental changes to know at what point in time a solution is no longer considered good. Each time a solution is sought, the algorithm initializes its population randomly, avoiding diversity problems.

7. Results and Discussion

The results for the problems generated with dynamics 1–4 are detailed in Table 7 and graphically shown in Figures 6–9, for each one of the four dynamics. In all four figures, those labeled with (a) and (b) present the results obtained in the MPB1 problems, while those labeled with (c) and (d) refer to the MPB2 problems. In all cases, the average survival values obtained by Mesh, time-optimal and robust approaches are compared against DE.

Non-parametric statistical tests [27] were applied to the corresponding numerical results presented in Table 7. The 95%-confidence Kruskal–Wallis and 95%-confidence Friedman tests were applied and their obtained p-values are reported in Table 5.

Table 5. Results of the 95%-confidence Kruskal–Wallis (KW) and Friedman (F) tests. The symbol (*) after letter "D" in the Problem column refers to the type of dynamic used according to columns Dynamic. A p-value less than 0.05 means that there are significant differences among the compared algorithms in such problems.

Problem Instance	p-Value							
	Dynamic 1		Dynamic 2		Dynamic 3		Dynamic 4	
	KW	F	KW	F	KW	F	KW	F
B1D*-1	<0.0001	<0.0001	<0.0001	<0.0001	<0.0001	<0.0001	<0.0001	<0.0001
B1D*-2	<0.0001	<0.0001	<0.0001	<0.0001	<0.0001	<0.0001	0.0082	<0.0001
B2D*-a	<0.0001	<0.0001	<0.0001	<0.0001	<0.0001	<0.0001	<0.0001	<0.0001
B2D*-b	<0.0001	<0.0001	<0.0001	<0.0001	<0.0001	<0.0001	<0.0001	<0.0001

To further determine differences among the compared algorithms, the 95%-confidence Wilcoxon test was applied to pair-wise comparisons for each problem instance. The obtained p-values are reported in

Table 6, where the significant improvement with a significance level $\alpha = 0.5$ is shown in boldface. We can observe that the Wilcoxon test confirmed significant differences obtained in Kruskal–Wallis and Friedman Tests, most of them comparing DE/rand/1/bin versus random sampling methods, with the exception of four corresponding to problems generated with dynamic 4 (B1D4-1 and B1D4-2 both, in the comparison of DE/rand/1/bin versus Mesh and DE/rand/1/bin versus Time-optimal).

Table 6. Results of the 95%-confidence Wilcoxon signed-rank test. A p-value less than 0.05 means that exists significant differences.

Problem	Algorithm	p-Value			
		Dynamic 1	Dynamic 2	Dynamic 3	Dynamic 4
B1D*-1	DE/rand/1/bin versus Mesh	**<0.0001**	**<0.0001**	**<0.0001**	0.2545
	DE/rand/1/bin versus Time-optimal	**<0.0001**	**<0.0001**	**<0.0001**	0.2881
	DE/rand/1/bin versus Robust	**<0.0001**	**<0.0001**	**<0.0001**	**<0.0001**
	Mesh versus Time-optimal	0.1167	**0.0019**	**0.0483**	0.8758
	Mesh versus Robust	**<0.0001**	**0.0006**	0.1019	**<0.0001**
	Time-optimal versus Robust	**<0.0001**	**<0.0001**	**0.0007**	**<0.0001**
B1D*-2	DE/rand/1/bin versus Mesh	**<0.0001**	**<0.0001**	**<0.0001**	0.7724
	DE/rand/1/bin versus Time-optimal	**<0.0001**	**<0.0001**	**<0.0001**	0.7531
	DE/rand/1/bin versus Robust	**<0.0001**	**<0.0001**	**<0.0001**	**0.0037**
	Mesh versus Time-optimal	0.9602	0.9358	0.8852	0.9984
	Mesh versus Robust	0.0987	0.9078	**0.0087**	**0.0067**
	Time-optimal versus Robust	0.104	0.8558	**0.0126**	**0.0069**
B2D*-a	DE/rand/1/bin versus Mesh	**<0.0001**	**<0.0001**	**<0.0001**	**<0.0001**
	DE/rand/1/bin versus Time-optimal	**<0.0001**	**<0.0001**	**<0.0001**	**<0.0001**
	DE/rand/1/bin versus Robust	**<0.0001**	**<0.0001**	**<0.0001**	**<0.0001**
	Mesh versus Time-optimal	0.8796	0.6044	0.8479	0.9221
	Mesh versus Robust	0.5502	0.9639	**<0.0001**	0.761
	Time-optimal versus Robust	0.4222	0.5658	**<0.0001**	0.7259
B2D*-b	DE/rand/1/bin versus Mesh	**<0.0001**	**<0.0001**	**<0.0001**	**<0.0001**
	DE/rand/1/bin versus Time-optimal	**<0.0001**	**<0.0001**	**<0.0001**	**<0.0001**
	DE/rand/1/bin versus Robust	**<0.0001**	**<0.0001**	**<0.0001**	**<0.0001**
	Mesh versus Time-optimal	0.7937	0.9805	0.6242	0.9028
	Mesh versus Robust	0.7231	0.6922	**0.0001**	0.3679
	Time-optimal versus Robust	0.8786	0.6761	**0.0014**	0.3369

Table 7 summarizes the mean and standard deviation statistical results obtained by the compared algorithms. It can be seen that DE/rand/1/bin obtains the highest average values in all the problems that were solved. Nevertheless, the higher standard deviation values obtained by DE/rand/1/bin in problems B1D4-1 and B1D4-2 confirm those expressed by the non-parametric tests—the differences are not significant with respect to the random sampling methods. Figures 4 and 5 have the box-plots for B1D4-1 and B1D4-2, where all the compared algorithms reach survival times between 1 and 3, with the exception of the Robust approach in B1D4-1, but such a difference was not significant.

Math. Comput. Appl. 2020, 25, 72

Table 7. Statistical Results obtained by each Algorithm in each one of the problem instances. Best statistical results are marked with boldface.

Problem	Algorithm	Dynamic 1		Dynamic 2		Dynamic 3		Dynamic 4	
		Mean	S.D.	Mean	S.D.	Mean	S.D.	Mean	S.D.
B1D*-1	DE/rand/1/bin	**10.1438**	1.5056	**6.1306**	0.6816	**10.6581**	1.4973	**1.5678**	1.7595
	Mesh	4.9337	0.7772	2.9772	0.3448	5.6844	0.8894	0.9429	0.8177
	Time-optimal	5.0527	0.7756	3.0365	0.3503	5.7979	0.8857	0.9569	0.8728
	Robust	4.4819	0.7853	2.8947	0.3577	5.5371	0.9837	0.3176	0.2515
B1D*-2	DE/rand/1/bin	**13.5633**	3.866	**8.623**	2.1388	**13.8394**	3.6942	**1.8219**	1.9531
	Mesh	10.329	4.0575	5.6162	1.8619	10.5887	3.9488	1.7269	1.8693
	Time-optimal	10.3309	4.0328	5.6104	1.8461	10.5731	3.923	1.7235	1.8584
	Robust	10.1437	3.9241	5.6533	1.8166	10.2246	3.7413	1.2843	1.4648
B2D*-a	DE/rand/1/bin	**19.1757**	0.1236	**19.8474**	0.0399	**19.381**	0.0748	**18.0117**	0.3944
	Mesh	6.596	0.7258	6.5154	0.26	6.3956	0.3199	2.7558	0.229
	Time-optimal	6.5914	0.7413	6.5321	0.2713	6.4116	0.3177	2.7593	0.2315
	Robust	6.6709	0.7904	6.5109	0.2611	6.1947	0.2593	2.7411	0.2276
B2D*-b	DE/rand/1/bin	**16.9954**	0.4005	**18.1336**	0.1144	**17.7187**	0.1345	**13.1993**	0.8169
	Mesh	5.5729	0.8528	5.2304	0.3239	4.8788	0.2544	2.2192	0.3461
	Time-optimal	5.5825	0.836	5.233	0.3227	4.868	0.2463	2.2238	0.3472
	Robust	5.6479	0.981	5.215	0.3266	4.7578	0.2359	2.1818	0.334

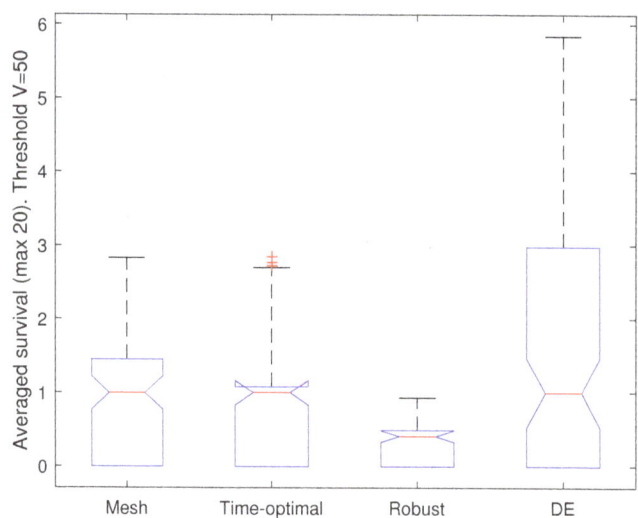

Figure 4. Boxplot of the results obtained in B1D4-1.

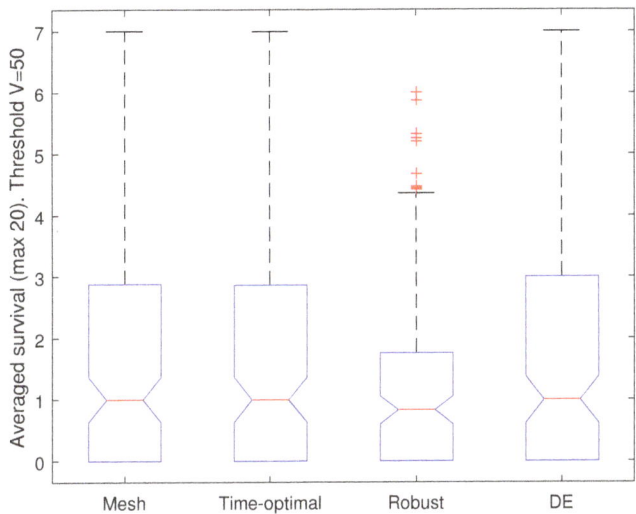

Figure 5. Boxplot of the results obtained in B1D4-2.

With respect to the graphical results, when MPB1 (items (a) and (b)) is compared against MPB2 (items (c) and (d)) in Figures 6–9, it is clear that MPB1 is more difficult to solve by all four approaches. However, in all cases (MPB1 and MPB2 in the four dynamics) DE is able to provide better results against the three other algorithms. Such a performance is more evident in all MPB2 instances.

Regarding MPB1 (items (a) and (b)), it is important to note that it is more difficult to find higher survival times when the peak movement is random (items (a), where $\lambda = 0$).

Another interesting behavior found is that all four compared methods are affected mainly by the random and chaotic dynamics in those MPB1 instances, the latter one being the most complex (chaotic dynamic). However, even in such a case DE was able to match and in some cases improve the survival values of the compared approaches. This source of difficulty now found motivates part of our future research.

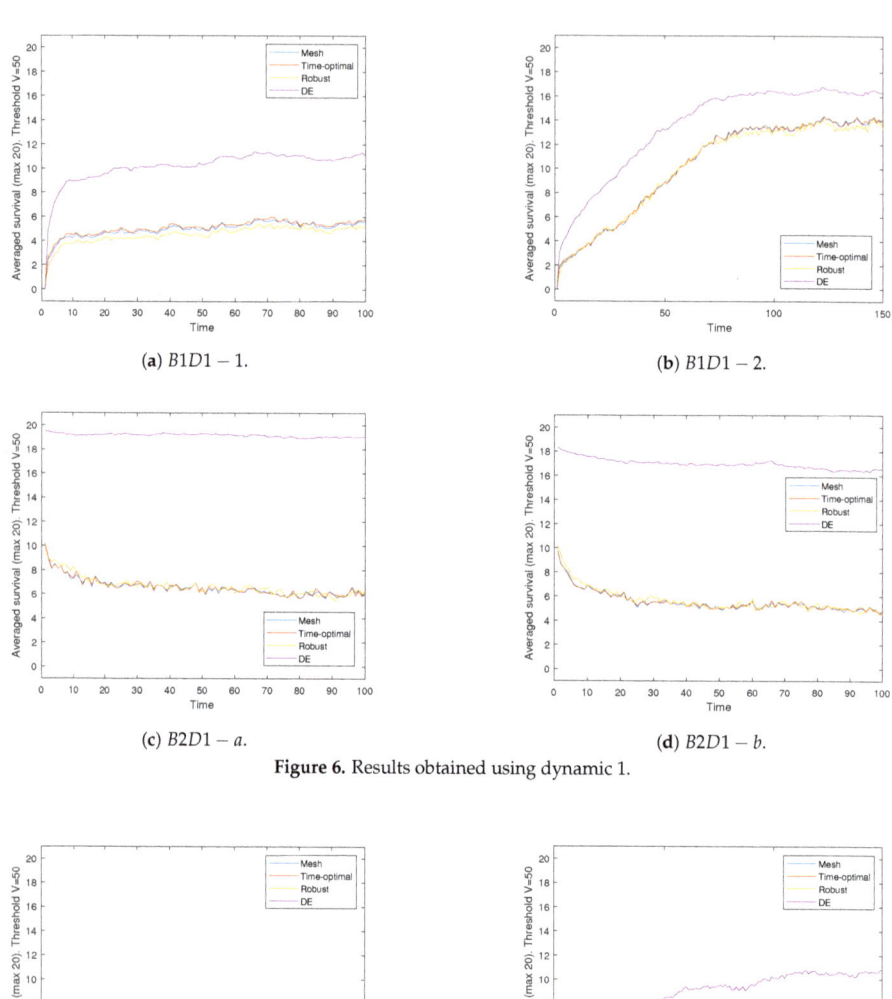

Figure 6. Results obtained using dynamic 1.

Figure 7. Cont.

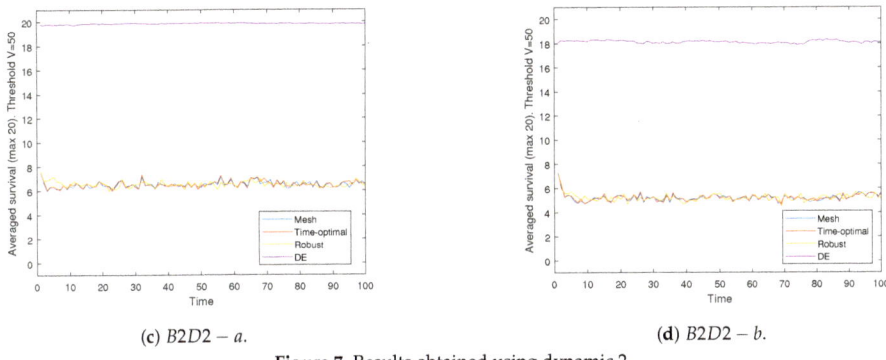

(c) $B2D2-a$. (d) $B2D2-b$.

Figure 7. Results obtained using dynamic 2.

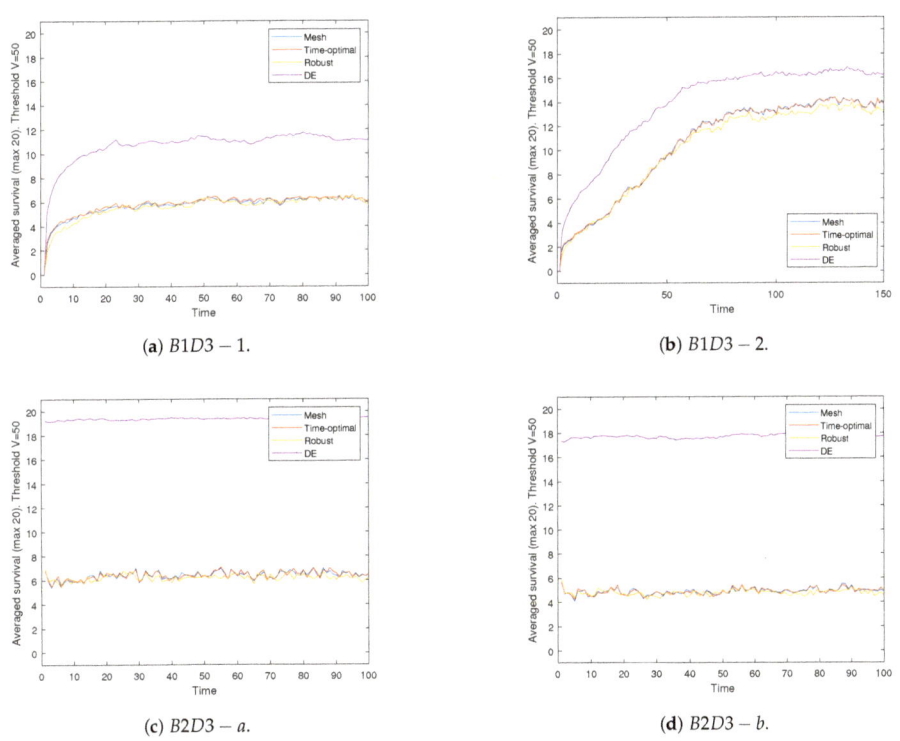

(a) $B1D3-1$. (b) $B1D3-2$.

(c) $B2D3-a$. (d) $B2D3-b$.

Figure 8. Results obtained using dynamic 3.

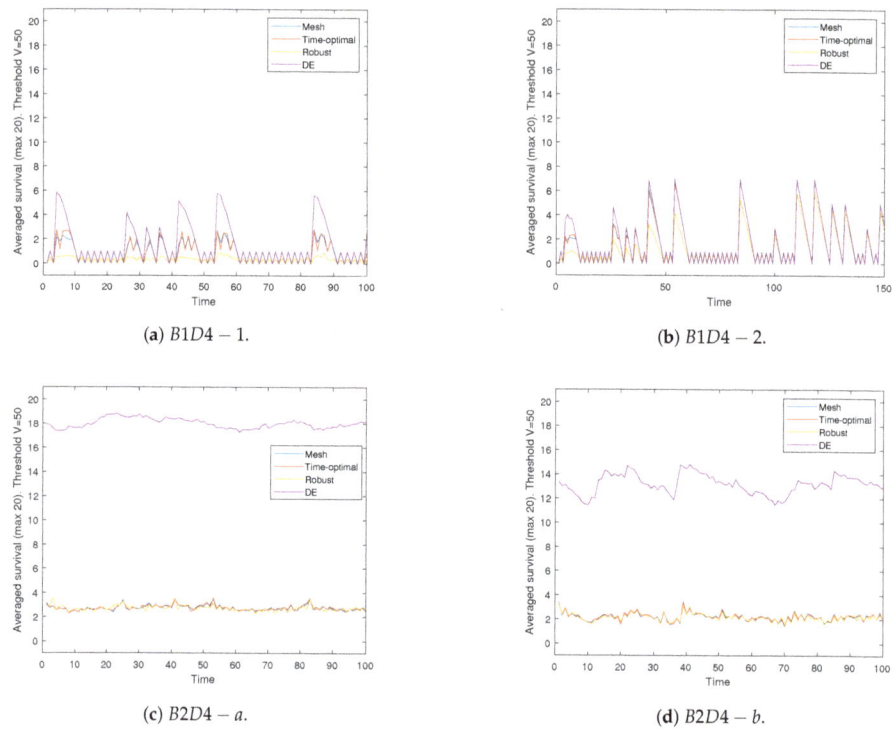

Figure 9. Results obtained using dynamic 4.

8. Conclusions

A performance analysis of the differential evolution algorithm, with one of its original variants, called DE/rand/1/bin, when solving robust optimization over time problems with a survival time approach, was presented in this paper. Three state-of-the-art random sampling methods to solve ROOT problems were used for comparison purposes. Sixteen generated problems by two benchmarks with two configurations and four different dynamics were solved. The solutions generated by the DE were obtained using the real environments without prediction mechanisms with the aim to analyze its behavior in ideal conditions. The findings supported by the obtained results indicate that DE is a suitable algorithm to deal with this type of dynamic search space when a survival time approach is considered. Moreover, the additional criterion that was added to the DE objective function allowed the algorithm to better discriminate between similar solutions in terms of survival time. Furthermore, it was found that the combination of a chaotic dynamic with both, random and constant peak movements, is a source of difficulty that requires further analysis.

This last finding is the starting point of our future research, where more recent DE variants, such as DE/current-to-p-best, will be tested in those complex ROOT instances. Moreover, the effect of predictors in DE-based approaches will be studied.

Author Contributions: Conceptualization, J.-Y.G.-G.; methodology, E.M.-M. and J.-Y.G.-G.; software, J.-Y.G.-G.; data curation, J.-Y.G.-G.; investigation, J.-Y.G.-G.; formal analysis, J.-Y.G.-G. and E.M.-M.; validation, E.M.-M. and S.D.-I.; writing—original draft preparation, J.-Y.G.-G., E.M.-M. and S.D.-I.; writing—review and editing, S.D.-I., E.M.-M. and J.-Y.G.-G. All authors have read and agreed to the published version of the manuscript.

Funding: The first author acknowledges support from the Mexican National Council of Science and Technology (CONACyT) through a scholarship to pursue graduate studies at the University of Veracruz.

Conflicts of Interest: The authors declare no conflict of interest.

Abbreviations

The following abbreviations are used in this manuscript:

DE	Differential Evolution
MPB1	Moving Peaks Benchmark 1
MPB2	Moving Peaks Benchmark 2
ROOT	Robust Optimization over Time
RSOT	Robust Solution over Time
S.D.	Standard deviation

References

1. Nguyen, T.T.; Yang, S.; Branke, J. Evolutionary dynamic optimization: A survey of the state of the art. *Swarm Evolut. Comput.* **2012**, *6*, 1–24. [CrossRef]
2. Dang, D.C.; Jansen, T.; Lehre, P.K. Populations Can Be Essential in Tracking Dynamic Optima. *Algorithmica* **2017**, *78*, 660–680. [CrossRef] [PubMed]
3. Yang, S.; Li, C. A clustering particle swarm optimizer for locating and tracking multiple optima in dynamic environments. *IEEE Trans. Evolut. Comput.* **2010**, *14*, 959–974. [CrossRef]
4. Yang, S.; Yao, X. *Evolutionary Computation for Dynamic Optimization Problems*; Springer: Berlin/Heidelberg, Germany, 2013. [CrossRef]
5. Das, S.; Mullick, S.S.; Suganthan, P. Recent advances in differential evolution—An updated survey. *Swarm Evolut. Comput.* **2016**, *27*, 1–30. [CrossRef]
6. Lin, L.; Zhu, M. Efficient Tracking of Moving Target Based on an Improved Fast Differential Evolution Algorithm. *IEEE Access* **2018**, *6*, 6820–6828. [CrossRef]
7. Zhu, Z.; Chen, L.; Yuan, C.; Xia, C. Global replacement-based differential evolution with neighbor-based memory for dynamic optimization. *Appl. Intell.* **2018**, *48*, 3280–3294. [CrossRef]
8. Yu, X.; Jin, Y.; Tang, K.; Yao, X. Robust optimization over time; A new perspective on dynamic optimization problems. In Proceedings of the IEEE Congress on Evolutionary Computation, Barcelona, Spain, 18–23 July 2010; pp. 1–6. [CrossRef]
9. Fu, H.; Sendhoff, B.; Tang, K.; Yao, X. Characterizing environmental changes in Robust Optimization Over Time. In Proceedings of the IEEE Congress on Evolutionary Computation, Brisbane, QLD, Australia, 10–15 June 2012; pp. 1–8. [CrossRef]
10. Fu, H.; Sendhoff, B.; Tang, K.; Yao, X. Finding Robust Solutions to Dynamic Optimization Problems. In *Applications of Evolutionary Computation*; Esparcia-Alcázar, A.I., Ed.; Springer: Berlin/Heidelberg, Germany, 2013; pp. 616–625.
11. Jin, Y.; Tang, K.; Yu, X.; Sendhoff, B.; Yao, X. A framework for finding robust optimal solutions over time. *Memetic Comput.* **2013**, *5*, 3–18. [CrossRef]
12. Wang, H.L.G.C. The Evolutionary Algorithm to Find Robust Pareto-Optimal Solutions over Time. *Math. Probl. Eng.* **2014**, *2014*, 814210.
13. Huang, Y.; Ding, Y.; Hao, K.; Jin, Y. A multi-objective approach to robust optimization over time considering switching cost. *Inf. Sci.* **2017**, *394–395*, 183–197. [CrossRef]
14. Yazdani, D.; Branke, J.; Omidvar, M.N.; Nguyen, T.T.; Yao, X. Changing or Keeping Solutions in Dynamic Optimization Problems with Switching Costs. In Proceedings of the Genetic and Evolutionary Computation Conference, Kyoto, Japan, 15–19 July 2018; pp. 1095–1102. [CrossRef]

15. Novoa-Hernández, P.; Pelta, D.A.; Corona, C.C. Approximation Models in Robust Optimization Over Time—An Experimental Study. In Proceedings of the 2018 IEEE Congress on Evolutionary Computation (CEC), Rio de Janeiro, Brazil, 8–13 July 2018; pp. 1–6. [CrossRef]
16. Novoa-Hernández, P.; Puris, A. Robust optimization over time: A review of most relevant contributions [Optimización robusta en el tiempo: Una revisión de las contribuciones más relevantes]. *Rev. Iber. Sist. Tecnol. Inf.* **2019**, *2019*, 156–164.
17. Yazdani, D.; Nguyen, T.T.; Branke, J. Robust Optimization Over Time by Learning Problem Space Characteristics. *IEEE Trans. Evolut. Comput.* **2019**, *23*, 143–155. [CrossRef]
18. Adam, L.; Yao, X. A Simple Yet Effective Approach to Robust Optimization Over Time. In Proceedings of the 2019 IEEE Symposium Series on Computational Intelligence (SSCI), Xiamen, China, 6–9 December 2019; pp. 680–688.
19. Fox, M.; Yang, S.; Caraffini, F. An Experimental Study of Prediction Methods in Robust optimization Over Time. In Proceedings of the 2020 IEEE Congress on Evolutionary Computation (CEC), Glasgow, UK, 19–24 July 2020; pp. 1–7.
20. Liu, Y.; Liang, H. A ROOT Approach for Stochastic Energy Management in Electric Bus Transit Center with PV and ESS. In Proceedings of the 2019 IEEE Global Communications Conference (GLOBECOM), Waikoloa, HI, USA, 9–13 December 2019; pp. 1–6.
21. Guzmán-Gaspar, J.; Mezura-Montes, E. Differential Evolution Variants in Robust Optimization Over Time. In Proceedings of the 2019 International Conference on Electronics, Communications and Computers (CONIELECOMP), Cholula, Mexico, 27 February–1 March 2019; pp. 164–169.
22. Guzmán-Gaspar, J.; Mezura-Montes, E. Robust Optimization Over Time with Differential Evolution using an Average Time Approach. In Proceedings of the 2019 IEEE Congress on Evolutionary Computation (CEC), Wellington, New Zealand, 10–13 June 2019; pp. 1548–1555.
23. Price, K.; Storn, R.M.; Lampinen, J.A. *Differential Evolution a Practical Approach to Global Optimization*, 1st ed.; Springer: Berlin/Heidelberg, Germany, 2005.
24. Juárez-Castillo, E.; Acosta-Mesa, H.G.; Mezura-Montes, E. Adaptive boundary constraint-handling scheme for constrained optimization. *Soft Comput.* **2019**, *23*, 8247–8280. [CrossRef]
25. Li, C.; Yang, S.; Nguyen, T.T.; Yu, E.L.; Yao, X.; Jin, Y.; Beyer, H.G.; Suganthan, P.N. Benchmark Generator for CEC 2009 Competition on Dynamic Optimization. Available online: https://bura.brunel.ac.uk/bitstream/2438/5897/2/Fulltext.pdf (accessed on 24 October 2020).
26. López-Ibáñez, M.; Dubois-Lacoste, J.; Pérez Cáceres, L.; Birattari, M.; Stützle, T. The irace package: Iterated racing for automatic algorithm configuration. *Oper. Res. Perspect.* **2016**, *3*, 43–58. [CrossRef]
27. García, S.; Molina, D.; Lozano, M.; Herrera, F. A Study on the Use of Non-Parametric Tests for Analyzing the Evolutionary Algorithms' Behaviour: A Case Study on the CEC'2005 Special Session on Real Parameter Optimization. *J. Heuristics* **2009**, *15*, 617–644. [CrossRef]

Publisher's Note: MDPI stays neutral with regard to jurisdictional claims in published maps and institutional affiliations.

© 2020 by the authors. Licensee MDPI, Basel, Switzerland. This article is an open access article distributed under the terms and conditions of the Creative Commons Attribution (CC BY) license (http://creativecommons.org/licenses/by/4.0/).

Article

An Efficient Framework for Multi-Objective Risk-Informed Decision Support Systems for Drainage Rehabilitation

Xiatong Cai [1,*], Abdolmajid Mohammadian [1] and Hamidreza Shirkhani [1,2]

1. Department of Civil Engineering, University of Ottawa, 161 Louis Pasteur, CBY A114, Ottawa, ON K1N 6N5, Canada; amohamma@uottawa.ca (A.M.); Hamidreza.Shirkhani@uottawa.ca (H.S.)
2. National Research Council Canada (NRCC), 1200 Montreal Road, Ottawa, ON K1A 0R6, Canada
* Correspondence: xiatong.c@uottawa.ca

Received: 6 September 2020; Accepted: 18 October 2020; Published: 2 November 2020

Abstract: Combining multiple modules into one framework is a key step in modelling a complex system. In this study, rather than focusing on modifying a specific model, we studied the performance of different calculation structures in a multi-objective optimization framework. The Hydraulic and Risk Combined Model (HRCM) combines hydraulic performance and pipe breaking risk in a drainage system to provide optimal rehabilitation strategies. We evaluated different framework structures for the HRCM model. The results showed that the conventional framework structure used in engineering optimization research, which includes (1) constraint functions; (2) objective functions; and (3) multi-objective optimization, is inefficient for drainage rehabilitation problem. It was shown that the conventional framework can be significantly improved in terms of calculation speed and cost-effectiveness by removing the constraint function and adding more objective functions. The results indicated that the model performance improved remarkably, while the calculation speed was not changed substantially. In addition, we found that the mixed-integer optimization can decrease the optimization performance compared to using continuous variables and adding a post-processing module at the last stage to remove the unsatisfying results. This study (i) highlights the importance of the framework structure inefficiently solving engineering problems, and (ii) provides a simplified efficient framework for engineering optimization problems.

Keywords: optimization framework; drainage rehabilitation; overflooding; pipe breaking

1. Introduction

Urban flooding happens when the capacity of a municipal sewerage system cannot support the amount of water that emerges in a short period of time [1]. Such a large amount of water could have either resulted from an intensified storm due to climate change [2–4], or freshets that amplify the stress on the sewerage system [5]. In order to release the stress of overflooding in cities, transforming the sewerage system and increasing its resilience to extreme weather can be a priority to increase the resilience of cities.

Computational simulations have been used for urban planning, including underground infrastructure design and pipe rehabilitation in recent years [6,7]. The essential idea is to build an optimization framework and apply it to modify a set of drainage system related variables such as the diameter, slope, and depth of the pipe. The framework requires the users to select applicable objective functions, which can be the system hydraulic performance or system pipe breaking risk [8,9], to maximize the performance of the system. Previous studies have focused on various aspects such as the cost of flooding damage [10], and integrated 1D/2D hydraulic modelling, where the SWMM5 was used as the 1D hydraulic model for sewer system simulations and a 2D model was employed to analyze the overflooding consequences in the drainage basin to obtain more accurate results on the damage of urban flooding [11].

In addition to the surcharge, drainage systems face more challenges, such as ageing due to natural and human impacts [12]. The threat of drainage pipes breaking cannot be ignored at locations across the world [13–15]. Canada's Infrastructure Card [12], reported that nearly one-third of potable water and sewerage pipes underground are imposed to breaking risk. Due to the ageing of the pipe system, the breakage of water supply pipes and sewerage pipes can introduce secondary pollutants into potable water and threaten human health [16].

Accurate predictions of the current and future conditions of a sewerage system using available assessment data are crucial for developing appropriate strategies for ageing pipe maintenance and rehabilitation. Statistical models are used to predict the probability of pipe failure in a drainage system [17]. The advantage of statistical models is that they are easy to apply in a large system to calculate the systematical performance when the random impacts can be ignored. Some statistical models such as the homogeneous Poisson processes model, non-homogeneous Poisson process model, and zero-inflated non-homogeneous Poisson process model, which use the age (time) of a pipe to predict its failure, have good performance in practice [18,19].

Altarabsheh et al. [20,21] conducted research based on whole lifecycle assessment, genetic algorithm, and Monte Carlo simulation to maximize network condition and serviceability while minimizing network risk of failure and total lifecycle cost for the entire planning period. State transition in a Markov chain can simulate the life of a pipe and predict the whole life risk of a pipe [22]. Other methods such as evolutionary polynomial regression [23], ordinal regression model [24], and flexible fuzzy model [25] are promising methods. Researchers have also concentrated on deciding the consequences of failure, such as the analytical hierarchy process [26,27]. However, this line of research has not been applied with drainage surcharge for drainage rehabilitation and design.

Cai et al. [28] combined hydraulic performance and breaking risk via a multi-objective genetic algorithm optimization framework. By building a relationship between rehabilitation and hydraulic performance as well as pipe breaking risk, they provided a novel decision support system for drainage systems rehabilitation. In their methodology, they used the traditional three-element optimization method: (1) set constraint functions to allow the system meet basic requirements; (2) set objective functions to improve the performance of the system; and (3) use a linkage module to link different modules in the system. They used one constraint function to control the overflooding in an urban system, and used a hydraulic performance objective function to optimize the rehabilitation methods. In their paper, they used a breadth-first searching algorithm to separate the problematic system and then optimized the system by a hydraulic diagnostic model [29] from the high impact drainage chain route to the low impact drainage chain route. This method provides good results for various drainage systems. However, there are some limitations in their framework. The overflooding was solved by constraint function, which means they added many logistic judgments in their algorithm, and that will decrease the calculation speed. Second, this hydraulic diagnostic model is designed to search for a narrow pipe in a chain route in a drainage system. Therefore, it can decrease the speed when they apply this method chain by chain to search for all the narrow pipes in the drainage network. In their research, they only discussed the genetic algorithm (GA), which neglected other optimization methods, such as particle swarm optimization (PSO) that has been used in drainage rehabilitation problems [30].

In this research, we improved the three-element optimization framework, which included constraint functions, objective functions, and multi-objective optimization, and created a faster and more accurate framework for urban drainage system. We improved their first-generation rehabilitation methodology from four aspects. (1) Enlighted by a multiple-stage decision support system [31], we improved their framework to get accurate results by adding a new objective function to optimize the budget distribution. (2) We tested whether the constraint function can be removed, and the final results can be selected by a filter to increase the speed. (3) We examined whether it is accurate enough to use the overflooding index in each node for optimization. In this way, the new algorithm does not need to search the network chain by chain. (4) We tested whether particle swarm optimization can have better results than the genetic algorithm in this problem. This is because, in literatures, there is a debate on which method has a better performance in drainage systems.

This paper is organized as follows: first, the structure of our new algorithms is introduced; subsequently, we specify the new algorithms in a computational model, Hydraulics and Risk Combined Model (HRCM). Then, two scenarios are studied to verify those new methods. Finally, we provide a combined methodology to replace/rehabilitate pipes in the drainage system for urban flooding control and pipe breaking precaution.

2. Materials and Methods

2.1. Introduction to the Hydraulics and Risk Combined Model Model

In this research, we used the Hydraulics and Risk Combined Model (HRCM) [28] to calculate the hydraulic performance, risk, and maintenance cost of a drainage system. There are five modules in the HRCM model:

(1) Hydraulic simulation module: In this module, the SWMM5 model calculates hydraulic grade line in the drainage system. Then, the hydraulic diagnostic model is applied to this system to calculate the hydraulic performance index (flooding index) for the drainage.

The GA-HRMC method has a hydraulic diagnostic model [29], which calculates the overflooding impact of a pipe to the system; Equations (1)–(3). According to this model, the hydraulic impacts of a pipe are represented by the sum of the pipe to the system (other pipes). The diagnostic model can have better performance than using the ratio of the hydraulic grade line over the depth of the manhole [32]. The system overflooding objective function N_s is calculated by the weight average value of the overflooding ratio of each pipe weighted by its length; Equation (4).

$$N_i = 100\% \times \frac{H_i^{US}}{G_i} \tag{1}$$

$$N_i^i = N_{min} + (N_{max} - N_{min}) \frac{\left(H_i^{US} - H_i^{DS}\right)}{G_i} \tag{2}$$

$$N_i^{DS} = N_i - N_i^i = (N_{max} - N_{min}) \frac{H_i^{DS}}{G_i} \tag{3}$$

$$N_s = \sum_{j,i} N_i^j l_i \bigg/ \sum_i l_i \tag{4}$$

where H_i^{US} = upstream hydraulic grade line of pipe i; H_i^{DS} = downstream hydraulic grade line of pipe i; G_i = height of the node i; N_i^i = net effect of the surcharge causes by pipe i; N_i = overflooding ratio of node i; N_{min} = minimum overflooding ratio of node i; N_{max} = maximum overflooding ratio of node i; N_s = system overflooding index.

(2) Risk assessment module: In the risk assessment module, the probability of failure for each pipe is calculated according to the age of each pipe. Then, a statistical exponential equation gives the probability of breaking for each pipe. The breaking probability of each pipe multiplies the consequence of failure of that pipe to get the breaking risk of that pipe. We assumed that the probability of failure for each pipe is given in Equation (5):

$$P(t) = a \times e^{b \times (t-c)} \tag{5}$$

where: $P(t)$ = the possibility of failure with time t (year). The a, b, and c are fitting parameters.

In the risk-informed model, Cai et al. [28] assumed a statistical exponential model [33] to calculate the probability of failure; and they used the consequence of failure criteria by Baah et al. [34] to calculate the weighted system pipe breaking risk index. In this study, we kept the same setting in our risk-informed model. The objective function of the system pipe breaking risk R_S is given in Equation (6):

$$R_S = \frac{\sum l_i C_i P^i}{\sum l_i} \tag{6}$$

where R_S = the risk of the system; C_i = the consequence of a failure of pipe i; P^i = the possibility of failure of pipe i; l_i = the length of pipe i.

(3) Rehabilitation module: In this module, different rehabilitation methods are connected to the age and diameter of a pipe. This can change the values of breaking risk index and overflooding index in a drainage system.

Six rehabilitation methods were linked to hydraulic performance (pipe diameter) and breaking risk (pipe age) (Table 1) [20]. In order to make the HRCM model recognize the cost difference among different pipe diameters, Cai et al. [28] added a pipe cost item for pipe replacement. The pipe cost C_p is a function that is related to pipe diameter and pipe length. The cost to rehabilitate one pipe is the sum of the rehabilitation cost, disruption cost, and pipe cost. The cost objective function is the total cost of all the pipes.

Table 1. The rehabilitation matrix [20,28]

Rehabilitation Number	Action	Rehabilitation Cost ($/m)	Disruption Cost ($/m)	Pipe Cost ($/m)	Benefit (Year)
1	Do nothing	0	0	0	-
2	Routine cleaning	16	0	0	10
3	Shotcrete	656	0	0	20
4	Cured-in-place pipe	1558	0	0	50
5	Reinforced fiberglass sliplining	2231	0	0	100
6	Dig and replace with concrete pipe	1148	656	C_p[1]	50

[1] $C_p = f(d_i, l_i)$ pipe cost function. In this research, we assumed $C_p = d \times l$.

(4) Multi-objective optimization module: There are two objective functions in this multi-objective optimization. First, a set of constraint functions on hydraulics performance, breaking risk, and budget limits the minimum requirements for rehabilitation methods. Second, they use a non-dominated sorting genetic algorithm (NSGA-II) to optimize hydraulic performance and decrease breaking risk in this system.

(5) Postprocessing filter (expert system): This module can select results from the Pareto Front according to the cost.

The structure of the HRCM model can be seen in Figure 1.

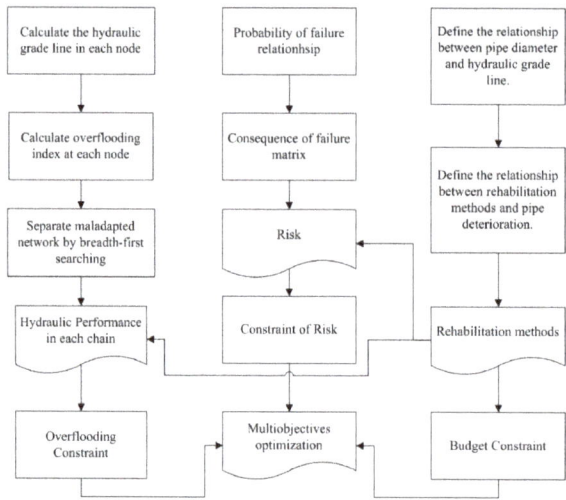

Figure 1. Structure of the HRCM model.

2.2. Algorithm Frameworks

HRCM Model Simulation Frameworks

We considered six alternative methodologies for HRCM calculation to compare with the method by Cai et al. [28], which we named the GA-HRCM method. We used their original framework (GA-HRCM) as our control group to compare with other methods. Explanations of other alternative algorithms, GA-Continuous, GA-Cost, GA-Unconstraint, PSO-Cost, PSO-HRCM, and GA-Network, are given in Figure 2.

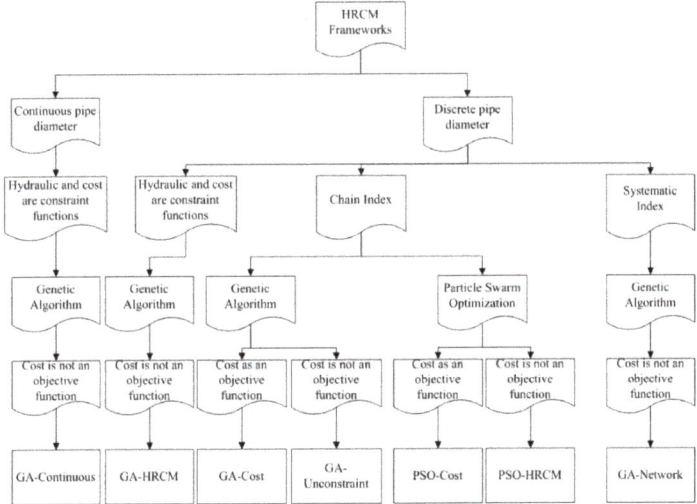

Figure 2. Flowchart of different optimization algorithms.

The GA-HRCM method uses a discrete pipe diameter, which increases the time in each iteration to transform the continuous value to discrete value, which is a process in the GA algorithm itself. The GA-Continuous method uses a continuous diameter for pipes during optimization. In the post-processing section, the continuous pipe diameters were transformed to the nearest discrete pipe diameters, which are used in engineering, and then the overflooding index and the pipe breaking index were calculated (Table 2).

The GA-HRCM method did not use cost as an objective function, because in an engineering project, budget is seen as a constraint. GA-Cost uses rehabilitation cost as another objective function. We use this comparison to evaluate whether this can improve rehabilitation strategy results by increasing cost-effectiveness (Table 2).

The GA-HRCM method has a constraint function for both hydraulic and budget. It did not limit the breaking risk because it uses a stochastic model, so the breaking risk is an objective function rather than a constraint function. The GA-Unconstraint method removes the hydraulic constraint in rehabilitation as well as the budget constraint. The results were filtered and we only kept the results that satisfied our expectations after the optimization process (Table 2).

The particle swarm optimization (PSO) and genetic algorithm (GA) methods have been widely used in sewerage pipe design and rehabilitation [35,36] and have shown good results in predicting hydraulic performance. However, it is still unclear as to which method is suitable for drainage optimization [7,36–38]. We revised the code given by Yarpiz [39] in order to solve the mixed integers problem. We employed two PSO methods, PSO-HRCM and PSO-Cost, to compare their performance with the employed genetic algorithm. The PSO-HRCM method replaces the NSGA-II to non-dominant sorting PSO method. Upon this replacement, the PSO-Cost method adds cost as another objective function to the PSO-HRCM method.

A drainage system has a complex structure [40]. In their research work, Bennis et al. [29] provided a hydraulic diagnostic model. To distinguish it from other indexes, we call it the chain route index in this study. In the model, they recognized narrow pipes by calculating an index to evaluate backwater effects downstream to upstream. Their method can separate the surcharge effect into two categories: (1) surcharge caused by the pipe itself; (2) surcharge caused by the downstream narrow pipes. Therefore, a computational model can detect which pipe affects the system easily. The GA-HRCM method used this hydraulic diagnostic model to optimize the overall overflooding index. The GA-Network method tests whether this strong searching model is unnecessary to find the narrow pipe. Dion and Bennis [32] introduced a global modeling approach to evaluate hydraulic performances in a drainage system. Instead of calculating the chain route index, they directly used the hydraulic grade line in each junction to evaluate the hydraulic performance of the drainage system; Equation (7).

$$N_s = \sum_i N_i l_i / \sum_i l_i \qquad (7)$$

To distinguish this index from the chain route one, it will be called the network index in the present study. The GA-HRCM model uses the chain route index. It has high efficiency when the drainage system is simple, but it is not efficient when the drainage system becomes complex, because this chain route index needs to calculate the index from one branch of the system to another [28]. In this research, we evaluated this speed-accuracy compromise by comparing the GA-HRCM method and the GA-Network method, using the global hydraulic index (Table 2).

Table 2. Parameter setting of different HRCM methods.

Name	Discrete Pipe	Constraint Functions [1]	Diagnostic Model [2]	Network Index [3]	Objective Cost	GA
GA-HRCM	√	√	√			√
GA-Continuous		√	√			√
GA-Cost	√	√	√		√	√
GA-Unconstrainted	√		√			√
GA-Network	√	√		√		√
PSO-HRCM	√		√			
PSO-Cost	√		√		√	
RHRCM				√	√	√

[1] Constraint functions of cost and hydraulic overflooding. [2] The system overflooding index in Equation (4). [3] The system overflooding index in Equation (7).

2.3. Revised HRCM Method (RHRCM)

In previous sections, seven calculation methods were applied to the HRCM model to verify how they affect the framework. On comparing the performance of the seven methods, we revised the HRCM model to improve its efficiency to solve overflooding and pipe breaking combined problems.

The revised framework is presented in Figure 3. In this new framework, we simplified the three-element framework to: (1) optimization; (2) linkage; (3) post-processing. This framework can be applied to other pipe systems and solve similar problems. The method with the fastest convergence speed—GA-Continuous—was selected to improve convergence speed. The GA-Network method was selected to enhance the performance of the HRCM model on the network drainage system and improve efficiency. Besides, the GA-Continuous method and the GA-Network method can offer fewer strategies than the original HRCM method. In order to compensate for the weakness of the original HRCM inefficient budget distribution to rehabilitate each pipe, we selected the GA-Cost method to increase the accuracy of the framework. The new framework removes constraint functions and adds cost as another objective function. It also removes the hydraulic diagnostic and discrete models. Distinguished from other studies that study optimization methods directly without improving the structure of optimization, we propose to study optimization structure in each step for drainage optimization.

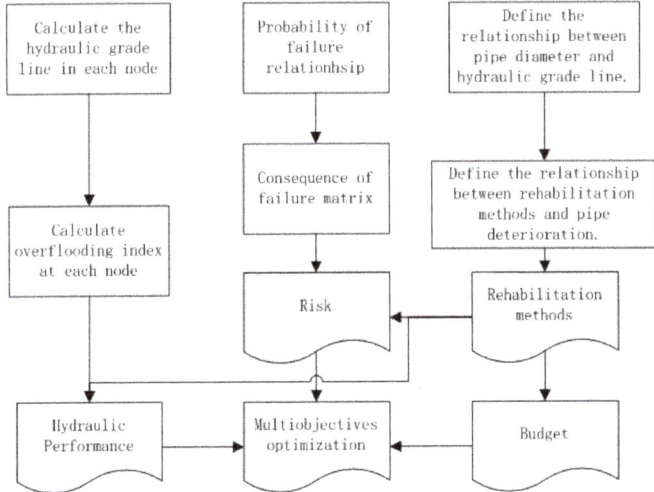

Figure 3. Diagram of the revised framework (RHRCM).

2.4. Case Study

Because the validation of the HRCM model was evaluated by Cai et al. [28] and the objective of this study is to compare the performance of different frameworks, we assumed two idealized scenarios in which it is easy to recognize narrow and aged pipes. Therefore, we can easily evaluate the performance of different frameworks. The configuration of the drainage system used the system proposed by Bennies et al. [29] (Figure 4).

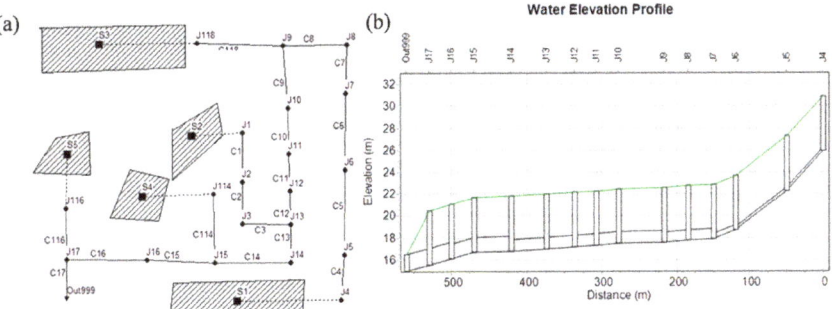

Figure 4. Drainage system configuration: (**a**) structure of the drainage system; (**b**) schematic view of the pipe diameter, length, and depth (Data from Bennis et al. and Cat et al. [28,29]).

In this paper, we considered two scenarios (Table 3) to evaluate the seven methods mentioned in Figure 2. The first scenario represented a narrow pipe scenario, and the second scenario an aged pipe scenario.

Table 3. The simulation scenarios.

Classification	Scenario	Description	Function
Hydraulic	1	A system with one narrow pipe (poor hydraulic performance) at the chain route. The diameter of pipe (C8) is replaced to 0.1 m. The age of all the pipes is zero.	In this simulation, it was tested whether the method can detect the narrow pipe.
Ageing risk	2	A system with a pipe at high risk but there is no hydraulic risk. The diameters of pipes are presented in Figure 4b. The age of pipe C9 was 60, and other pipes ages are zero.	In this simulation, it was tested whether the method can detect an aged pipe.

The first scenario is used to test whether these methods can choose the correct pipe and replace it with a larger one. In the first scenario, three narrow pipes were placed in the system, and all the pipes were of the same age. Among the three narrow pipes, one pipe was extremely narrow, which means that the model must find and replace it; the overflooding constraint can then be satisfied. The other pipes will affect the overflooding index but are not necessary to satisfy requirements. The second scenario includes an aged pipe and two narrow pipes. The aged pipe was severely deteriorated as compared to the other pipes, and the narrow pipes were not severely narrow. The second scenario was used to test whether these methods can find the aged pipe and use a reasonable rehabilitation method to solve the ageing problem. The drainage system was set as in Figure 4a. This is the same as that in the Cai et al. [28] study, for comparison purposes. Chicago designed rainfall is a common case for the simulation of sewerage systems [29,41,42].

2.5. Model Performance Evaluation

Sensitivity Analysis

Result accuracy can increase with an increased population size of the optimization algorithm, but the computational time will also increase. As per the functionality limitation of our computer—Intel® Core™ i7-8750H CPU @2.20GHz, 16.0 GB (RAM), we set the population size to 100, 500, 1000, 1500, 2000, and 2500 for both GA and PSO methods. We evaluated population convergence (i.e., whether the results will converge at our population setting) and time convergence (i.e., the computational time at the convergent population if the convergence exists). The evaluation criteria are: (1) computational time at the population equals to 2500; (2) how many rehabilitation solutions are given by the HRCM model at population size equal to 2500; (3) and the average cost of the total solutions at the 2500 population size (Tables 4 and 5). It should be noted that the word 'convergence' in this research means the number of strategies, the overflooding index, and the pipe breaking index in strategies set for one population size, which does not change at a larger population size.

After postprocessing, the selected output results can solve the overflooding problem. Then, we compared their rehabilitative effectiveness. The cost-effectiveness analysis can quantify the rehabilitation performance of a rehabilitation strategy at per unit cost [43,44]. This method can evaluate the effectiveness of our rehabilitation method, as it provides information on which method can best improve the performance of a system under the unit cost. It is defined as the index in Equation (8) to evaluate the efficiency of each method. The original overflooding index and the risk index of scenario 1 were 29.72 and 16.24, respectively. The overflooding index and risk index of scenario 2 were 5.07 and 22.68, respectively:

$$Ce = \frac{1}{k}\sum_j \left(I_j^p - I_j^a\right)/C_j^r \qquad (8)$$

where Ce = cost-effectiveness index; I_j^p = average of the difference between the original overflooding/risk index; I_j^a = overflooding/risk index after the rehabilitation; C_j^r = cost for rehabilitation; k = the total number of j.

3. Results

3.1. Computational Time Competition

Figure 5 shows the time competition of the seven methods. The computational time increases with an increased population. However, the trend was not monotonic.

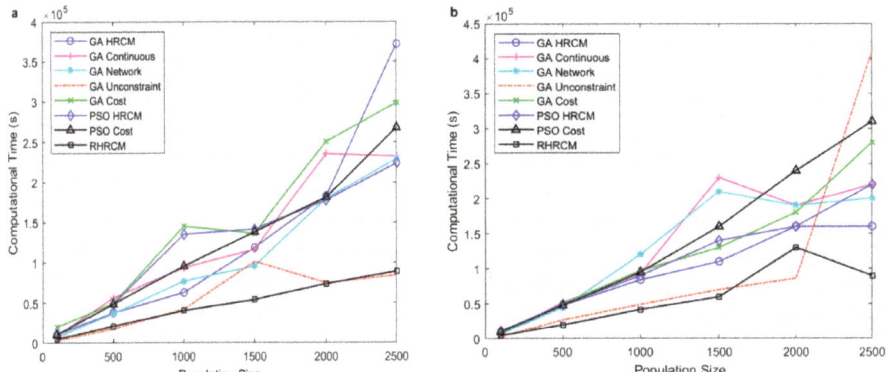

Figure 5. The time competition for seven methods: (**a**) scenario 1; (**b**) scenario 2.

Different methods exhibited discrepancies in calculation speed under the various scenarios. The GA-Unconstraint method had the minimum calculation time in the first scenario. There is a bump up when the population equals 2500 of GA-Unconstraint in the second scenario. We calculated two simulations for the GA-Unconstraint method with the population size being equal to 2200 and 3000, respectively. The computational times were 77,286 s and 89,393 s, respectively. Therefore, we inferred that the high computational time for the GA-Unconstraint method at the population size (equal to 2500) is because of the fluctuations of the program. The GA-Continuous method had a fast convergence speed for both scenarios. It was found that the GA-HRCM method was the slowest method (Figure 5). The computational time comparison between the RHRCM method and the other seven modified methods is presented in Figure 5. The RHRCM method exhibited the fastest speed compared to the other seven methods, and it was stable with respect to the population increase in scenario 1. This property can be also seen from the computational time comparison of scenario 2. The RHRCM method was relatively stable, compared to the GA-Unconstraint method. It showed a significant advantage over other methods in terms of computational speed.

3.2. Methods Evaluation

3.2.1. Scenario 1—Narrow Pipe

We assessed the results by evaluating the converged population, convergence time, number of solutions, and cost-effectiveness at a population of 2500 (Table 4). The cost-effectiveness value was calculated by dividing the difference between the original hydraulic/risk index and the new hydraulic/risk index by cost (million $) (Table 4).

After adding cost as another objective function, the expense of rehabilitation decreased from 0.67 million dollars to 0.3 million dollars. Compared to the GA-HRCM method, we found that it is less likely that the GA-Cost method selects fiberglass reinforcement, which is the most expensive rehabilitation method in our case (Table 1). This can reduce costs on unnecessary rehabilitation.

Table 4. The summarized results of the seven methods with scenario 1.

Method	Convergent Population	Convergent Time (s)	2500 Time (s)	2500 Number of Solutions	2500 Average Cost (million $)	2500 Cost Effectiveness	
						Hydro [1]	Risk [2]
GA-HRCM	2000	182,334	372,035	6	0.67	54.81	31.36
GA-Continuous	1500	116,374	232,122	5	0.44	62.65	33.60
GA-Cost	N/A	N/A	298,599	34	0.30	138.26	73.92
GA-Network	500	36,696	229,006	4	0.70	43.97	23.82
GA-Unconstraint	N/A	N/A	84,157	8	0.78	47.81	24.64
PSO-HRCM	N/A	N/A	223,591	5	1.03	28.16	13.99
PSO-Cost	N/A	N/A	268,340	13	0.61	45.24	22.18
RHRCM	N/A	N/A	89,182	10	0.30	177.29	87.82

[1] Hydro is the cost-effectiveness of the overflooding index. [2] Risk is the cost-effectiveness of the breaking index.

The GA-Network method converged at population size equals to 500, which is faster than the GA-HRCM method converged at a population of 2000 (Table 4). The GA-Network method offered four strategies, which is smaller than the six strategies obtained from the chain route index— the GA-HRCM method (Table 4). The GA-Unconstraint method has the fastest calculation speed for the same population size as the other methods (Figure 5). It was found that GA-Continuous converged at the 1500 population size, and it is faster than GA-HRCM.

PSO-based methods did not offer a significant advantage in cost-effectiveness and computational speed (Table 4), when compared to the GA-based method. Zarbaf et al. [45] compared the PSO method and the GA method for the calculation of cable tension estimate. They found that both methods can evaluate the tensioned cable, but the PSO method was more accurate. Surendar et al. [37] compared the GA and PSO methods in predicting Brazilian tensile strength. They found that even though the two methods can predict the value, PSO had better performance in fitting the result. Vasudevan and Sinha [36] showed that the PSO method had better performance in the distribution system. However, in the sewerage system, one study showed that GA methods can offer similar results as the PSO method [46]. In our research, we find that the PSO method was not as good. The PSO method uses the best values in one generation to guide the algorithm to produce the next generation. This will be efficient when searching for an optimum value in a continuous function. However, to rehabilitate drainage systems, there are many parallel solutions. For example, even though the hydraulic performance is improved when we enlarge the diameter of a pipe, after enlarging the diameter and exceeding a threshold, the results are improved. This means that in one generation, there will be many optimum values, thus impacting the performance of the PSO method in searching for the optimum value.

The RHRCM method can combine the strengths of previous frameworks. We found that the RHRCM method has one advantage offered by the GA-Unconstraint method—it took 89,182 s for the 2500 population; it is also more stable (Figure 5). Besides, the RHRCM achieved maximum cost-effectiveness as compared to the other methods. The cost-effectiveness of overflooding rehabilitation was found to be 177.29, and the pipe breaking rehabilitation cost-effectiveness was 87.82 (Table 4). Besides, the RHRCM offered 10 rehabilitation strategies, which is acceptable (Table 4). These strategies simplified those provided by the GA-Cost method.

3.2.2. Scenario 2—Ageing Pipe

Previous studies, such as Kleiner et al. [47] considered age of the pipe as a Fuzzy variable. Scenario 2 includes an aged pipe; its results are presented in Table 5. Among the seven methods, GA-Cost showed high cost-effectiveness of system overflooding and pipe breaking risk—13.92 and 129.5, respectively. The hydraulic cost-effectiveness value (11.7) is higher than that of the RHRCM method. The RHRCM method gave the highest risk cost-effective of 137.31, which shows that it is compatible with the risk scenario.

Table 5. The summarized results of seven methods with scenario 2.

Method	Convergent Population	Convergent Time (s)	2500 Time (s)	2500 Number of Solutions	2500 Average Cost (million $)	2500 Cost Effectiveness Hydro [1]	2500 Cost Effectiveness Risk [2]
GA-HRCM	N/A	N/A	163,519	6	0.65	4.46	40.77
GA-Continuous	1500	232,415	222,536	6	0.67	3.64	39.66
GA-Cost	N/A	N/A	277,206	40	0.24	13.92	129.50
GA-Network	N/A	N/A	196,281	6	0.66	3.69	41.07
GA-Unconstraint	2000	86,322	406,361	6	0.73	4.40	36.62
PSO-HRCM	N/A	N/A	219,888	5	1.00	3.30	19.87
PSO-Cost	N/A	N/A	309,305	33	0.63	4.29	27.17
RHRCM	N/A	N/A	89,863	30	0.26	11.70	137.31

[1] Hydro is the cost-effectiveness of the overflooding index. [2] Risk is the cost-effectiveness of the breaking index.

4. Discussion

4.1. Advantage and Limitation of RHRCM Method

The refined HRCM model is faster because unnecessary parts in the original HRCM model are removed. We also acquired a higher cost-effectiveness by adding cost as another objective function, as it can remove the parallel solutions.

We believe that there is a convergence of optimum value in an optimum question because the Pareto Front is the set of optimum values. However, are there optimum strategies in a rehabilitation problem? The answer is no. The reason for this is because the two types of situations can result in the same value on the Pareto Front with different strategies. First, if there are two pipes which have the same breaking risk and hydraulic performance in this network, one will have the same result when replacing the first pipe or the second pipe. That means that one will have two solutions offering the same result on the Pareto Front; furthermore, both are optimum solutions. The second type is that if one can replace a pipe to a diameter of 0.305 m to 1 m, it may solve the surcharge problem; however when one changes the dimeter to 2 m, it can get the same surcharge index at that junction. This means that every pipe has a threshold; when the diameter of the pipe goes beyond that threshold, all of the rehabilitation strategies are the same in the optimization program. In the HRCM model, we used a post-processing strategy to select solutions from the set of rehabilitation plans. In the RHRCM model, the new dimension (cost) can help to partly solve the parallel results problem because different diameters have different costs. This can improve the performance of an optimization method. However, this method does not increase the search speed for hydraulic performance and breaking risk. How to solve the parallel solution problem and increase the searching speed can be a topic for future study.

4.2. Discrete Versus Continuous Data

In engineering, certain parameters are not continuous. For example, the diameter of the pipe in a real case should be a discrete value, based on manufacturing standards. Therefore, although the mixed-integer optimization method is widely used in many engineering problems, there should be a discussion on whether mixed-integer is better than continuous optimization. In our research, we found the GA-Continuous has a faster convergence speed in scenario 1 than GA-HRCM. However, GA-Continuous is slower than GA-HRCM in scenario 2. We found that both continuous and discrete methods can solve the problem well. Therefore, mixed-integer optimization is not always better than continuous optimization. In the context of optimization algorithms, the continuous optimization method can have a higher sensitivity to variables that are changed continuously, and they do not have a process to transform a continuous number to an integer. However, it may be easy to obtain the local optimum value. Thus, it is a competition between these two situations, and we should adjust it according to different situations.

4.3. Parallel Results Problem

The slow convergence speed can be attributed to the parallel results problem; in network optimization, it is defined as having multiple solutions with the same performance. For example, consider a case in which there is a pipe in a drainage system leading to a surcharge, such as C8 in Figure 4b, and the critical diameter is δ (which is enough to solve the surcharge). When the model assigns diameter values larger than δ, they can get the same results for the overflooding index. This means that even though there are limited points on the Pareto Front, there are many strategies that can have the exact same values on the Pareto Front. Therefore, this seriously affects the convergence speed of optimization. The parallel results problem may explain this non-convergence in the framework. This motivated us to study how to evaluate the performance of optimization for rehabilitation problems in the future.

In this study, we use the GA and PSO methods because they are the most widely used in engineering. Many kinds of optimization algorithms, such as ant colony optimization algorithm [45], random forest [25], cellular automata [48], hanging gardens algorithm [49], and whale optimization [50] should be tested in the future to see whether they are more suitable for this framework.

We found that when we add the cost into our framework our program can have better results. That provided the initial idea to solve the parallel solution problem. We can add more parameters to this system. The GA-Unconstraint and RHRCM show that there is no significant difference in the calculation speed when we have two or three objective functions. The GA-Cost and GA-HRCM showed that the case of three objective functions needs more time for calculation. This means that when we remove the constraint function, the calculation time will not increase significantly even though we add more objective functions. Therefore, we can add more parameters to this framework to make it more resistant to the parallel solutions. Besides, we believe, this framework can have a higher calculation speed when we use parallel computing.

4.4. Framework

Distinguishing our research from other studies, and improving the performance of an optimization model by using different optimization methods, we studied whether the simplified calculation framework can improve performance. In our research, we found that with our new framework, the calculation speed and cost-effectiveness of the HRCM model were significantly improved. The computational speed of RHRCM was increased four times, and cost-effectiveness increased three times as compared to the GA-HRCM method, by changing the computational framework. This emphasizes the importance of studying how to improve the calculation methodology of an optimization question. A multi-objective optimization model is a complex system, because it has a multifaceted calculation structure and involves many modules to solve one question. Therefore, current optimization methods should be simplified to achieve a higher performance. Research on framework structure thus needs to be paid more attention.

5. Conclusions

Developing rehabilitation strategies in order to obtain maximum benefit for solving urban flooding and reducing pipe breaking risk at the same time is an important issue in urban drainage systems. In this paper, seven potential frameworks were compared. The results showed that calculation speed and accuracy were improved when continuous variables are used and constraint functions are removed. A post-processing filter was added at the end to transform pipe diameter to a discrete value and remove the unsatisfying strategies that result in a high overflooding index or breaking risk index. Multi-objective optimization was found to be adequate in finding a solution. Furthermore, calculation accuracy can increase when cost is selected as an objective function. We also found that the GA algorithm had a better performance than the PSO method in drainage optimization problems. Simulation results showed that these methods can significantly improve the decision support system for drainage rehabilitation. A new method was proposed (RHRCM), which exhibited a remarkably higher computational speed (four times faster than the original HRCM model) and was able to obtain results with a higher cost-effectiveness (three times higher than the original HRCM model). We found that a simplified framework can significantly improve the calculation performance of the original model; therefore, further research should focus on study of the framework structure.

Author Contributions: Conceptualization, A.M., H.S. and X.C.; methodology, X.C. and H.S.; software, X.C.; investigation, X.C. and H.S.; resources, A.M. and H.S.; writing—original draft preparation, X.C.; writing—review and editing, A.M., H.S. and X.C.; supervision, A.M. and H.S. All authors have read and agreed to the published version of the manuscript.

Funding: This research received no external funding.

Acknowledgments: We extend our acknowledgements to Colin Rennie, Hossein Bonakdari, and Chengxi Li.

Conflicts of Interest: The authors declare no conflict of interest.

References

1. Jegatheesan, V. *Urban Stormwater and Flood Management: Enhancing the Liveability of Cities*; Springer: New York, NY, USA, 2019; ISBN 978-3-030-11817-4.
2. Adamowski, J.; Adamowski, K.; Bougadis, J. Influence of Trend on Short Duration Design Storms. *Water Resour. Manag.* **2010**, *24*, 401–413. [CrossRef]
3. Buttle, J.M.; Allen, D.M.; Caissie, D.; Davison, B.; Hayashi, M.; Peters, D.L.; Pomeroy, J.W.; Simonovic, S.; St-Hilaire, A.; Whitfield, P.H. Flood processes in Canada: Regional and special aspects. *Can. Water Resour. J. Rev. Can. Ressour. Hydr.* **2016**, *41*, 7–30. [CrossRef]
4. Buttle, J.M.; Lafleur, P.M. Anatomy of an Extreme Event: The July 14–15, 2004 Peterborough Rainstorm. *Can. Water Resour. J.* **2007**, *32*, 59–74. [CrossRef]
5. Government of Canada. Causes of Flooding. 2013. Available online: https://www.canada.ca/en/environment-climate-change/services/water-overview/quantity/causes-of-flooding.html (accessed on 19 October 2020).
6. Ogidan, O.; Giacomoni, M. Multiobjective Genetic Optimization Approach to Identify Pipe Segment Replacements and Inline Storages to Reduce Sanitary Sewer Overflows. *Water Resour. Manag.* **2016**, *30*, 3707–3722. [CrossRef]
7. Yazdi, J.; Sadollah, A.; Lee, E.H.; Yoo, D.G.; Kim, J.H. Application of multi-objective evolutionary algorithms for the rehabilitation of storm sewer pipe networks: Comparison of MOEAs. *J. Flood Risk Manag.* **2017**, *10*, 326–338. [CrossRef]
8. Moussavi, A.; Samani, H.M.V.; Haghighi, A. A framework for optimal reliability-based storm sewer network design in flat areas. *Can. J. Civ. Eng.* **2017**, *44*, 139–150. [CrossRef]
9. Shao, Z.; Zhang, X.; Li, S.; Deng, S.; Chai, H. A Novel SWMM Based Algorithm Application to Storm Sewer Network Design. *Water* **2017**, *9*, 747. [CrossRef]
10. Barreto, W.; Vojinovic, Z.; Price, R.; Solomatine, D. Multiobjective Evolutionary Approach to Rehabilitation of Urban Drainage Systems. *J. Water Resour. Plan. Manag.* **2010**, *136*, 547–554. [CrossRef]
11. Vojinovic, Z.; Sahlu, S.; Torres, A.S.; Seyoum, S.D.; Anvarifar, F.; Matungulu, H.; Barreto, W.; Savic, D.; Kapelan, Z. Multi-objective rehabilitation of urban drainage systems under uncertainties. *J. Hydroinf.* **2014**, *16*, 1044–1061. [CrossRef]
12. CIRC. Canada Infrastructure Report Card. 2019. Available online: http://canadianinfrastructure.ca/en/index.html (accessed on 19 October 2020).
13. Dawson, R.J.; Speight, L.; Hall, J.W.; Djordjevic, S.; Savic, D.; Leandro, J. Attribution of flood risk in urban areas. *J. Hydroinf.* **2008**, *10*, 275–288. [CrossRef]
14. Elsawah, H.; Bakry, I.; Moselhi, O. Decision Support Model for Integrated Risk Assessment and Prioritization of Intervention Plans of Municipal Infrastructure. *J. Pipeline Syst. Eng. Pract.* **2016**, *7*, 04016010. [CrossRef]
15. Huang, D.; Liu, X.; Jiang, S.; Wang, H.; Wang, J.; Zhang, Y. Current state and future perspectives of sewer networks in urban China. *Front. Environ. Sci. Eng.* **2018**, *12*, 2. [CrossRef]
16. Haller, L.; Hutton, G.; Bartram, J. Estimating the costs and health benefits of water and sanitation improvements at global level. *J. Water Health* **2007**, *5*, 467–480. [CrossRef] [PubMed]

17. Del Giudice, G.; Padulano, R.; Siciliano, D. Multivariate probability distribution for sewer system vulnerability assessment under data-limited conditions. *Water Sci. Technol.* **2016**, *73*, 751–760. [CrossRef] [PubMed]
18. Santos, P.; Amado, C.; Coelho, S.T.; Leitão, J.P. Stochastic data mining tools for pipe blockage failure prediction. *Urban Water J.* **2017**, *14*, 343–353. [CrossRef]
19. Ana, E.V.; Bauwens, W. Modeling the structural deterioration of urban drainage pipes: The state-of-the-art in statistical methods. *Urban Water J.* **2010**, *7*, 47–59. [CrossRef]
20. Altarabsheh, A.; Kandil, A.; Ventresca, M. New Multiobjective Optimization Approach to Rehabilitate and Maintain Sewer Networks Based on Whole Lifecycle Behavior. *J. Comput. Civil. Eng.* **2018**, *32*, 04017069. [CrossRef]
21. Altarabsheh, A.; Ventresca, M.; Kandil, A. New Approach for Critical Pipe Prioritization in Wastewater Asset Management Planning. *J. Comput. Civil. Eng.* **2018**, *32*, 04018044. [CrossRef]
22. Baik, H.-S.; Jeong, H.S.; Abraham, D.M.; Director, A. Estimating Transition Probabilities in Markov Chain-Based Deterioration Models for Management of Wastewater Systems. *J. Water Resour. Plan. Manag.* **2006**, *123*, 15–24. [CrossRef]
23. Berardi, L.; Giustolisi, O.; Kapelan, Z.; Savic, D.A. Development of pipe deterioration models for water distribution systems using EPR. *J. Hydroinf.* **2008**, *14*, 113–126. [CrossRef]
24. Younis, R.; Knight, M.A. Continuation ratio model for the performance behavior of wastewater collection networks. *Tunn. Undergr. Sp. Technol.* **2010**, *25*, 660–669. [CrossRef]
25. Hosseini, S.M.; Ghasemi, A. Hydraulic performance analysis of sewer systems with uncertain parameters. *J. Hydroinf.* **2012**, *14*, 682–696. [CrossRef]
26. Rudiono, J. Priority Scale of Drainage Rehabilitation of Cilacap City. *IOP Conf. Ser. Mater. Sci. Eng.* **2018**, *333*, 012111. [CrossRef]
27. Tarigan, A.P.M.; Rahmad, D.; Sembiring, R.A.; Iskandar, R. An application of the AHP in water resources management: A case study on urban drainage rehabilitation in Medan City. *IOP Conf. Ser. Mater. Sci. Eng.* **2018**, *309*, 012096. [CrossRef]
28. Cai, X.; Shirkhani, H.; Mohammadian, A. Risk-Informed Framework for Sewerage Flooding and Ageing Rehabilitation Management. *J. Pipeline Syst. Eng. Pract.* **2020**. Accepted.
29. Bennis, S.; Bengassem, J.; Lamarre, P. Hydraulic Performance Index of a Sewer Network. *J. Hydraul. Eng.* **2003**, *129*, 504–510. [CrossRef]
30. Sabzkouhi, A.M.; Haghighi, A. Uncertainty Analysis of Pipe-Network Hydraulics Using a Many-Objective Particle Swarm Optimization. *J. Hydraul. Eng.* **2016**, *142*, 04016030. [CrossRef]
31. Amador, L.; Mohammadi, A.; Abu-Samra, S.; Maghsoudi, R. Resilient storm pipes: A multi-stage decision support system. *Struct. Infrastruct. Eng.* **2020**, *16*, 847–859. [CrossRef]
32. Dion, Y.; Bennis, S. A global modeling approach to the hydraulic performance evaluation of a sewer network. *Can. J. Civ. Eng.* **2010**, *37*, 1432–1436. [CrossRef]
33. Duchesne, S.; Beardsell, G.; Villeneuve, J.-P.; Toumbou, B.; Bouchard, K. A Survival Analysis Model for Sewer Pipe Structural Deterioration: A sewer deterioration model. *Comput. Aided Civil. Infrastruct. Eng.* **2013**, *28*, 146–160. [CrossRef]
34. Baah, K.; Dubey, B.; Harvey, R.; McBean, E. A risk-based approach to sanitary sewer pipe asset management. *Sci. Total Environ.* **2015**, *505*, 1011–1017. [CrossRef]
35. Afshar, M.H.; Afshar, A.; Mariño, M.A.; Darbandi, A.A.S. Hydrograph-based storm sewer design optimization by genetic algorithm. *Can. J. Civ. Eng.* **2006**, *33*, 319–325. [CrossRef]
36. Vasudevan, B.; Sinha, A.K. Reliability improvement of reconfigurable distribution system using GA and PSO. *Electr. Eng.* **2018**, *100*, 1263–1275. [CrossRef]
37. Surendar, A.; Kuzichkin, O.R.; Kanagarajan, S.; Hashemi, M.H.; Khorami, M. Applying two optimization techniques in evaluating tensile strength of granitic samples. *Eng. Comput.* **2019**, *35*, 985–992. [CrossRef]
38. Yazdi, J.; Yoo, D.G.; Kim, J.H. Comparative study of multi-objective evolutionary algorithms for hydraulic rehabilitation of urban drainage networks. *Urban Water J.* **2017**, *14*, 483–492. [CrossRef]
39. Yarpiz. Multi-Objective Particle Swarm Optimization. Available online: https://yarpiz.com/59/ypea121-mopso (accessed on 18 October 2020).
40. Haghighi, A. Loop-by-Loop Cutting Algorithm to Generate Layouts for Urban Drainage Systems. *J. Water Resour. Plan. Manag.* **2013**, *139*, 693–703. [CrossRef]

41. Akan, A.O.; Houghtalen, R.J. *Urban Hydrology, Hydraulics, and Stormwater Quality*; Wiley: Hoboken, NJ, USA, 2003.
42. Watt, E.; Marsalek, J. Critical review of the evolution of the design storm event concept. *Can. J. Civ. Eng.* **2013**, *40*, 105–113. [CrossRef]
43. Irfan, M.; Khurshid, M.B.; Labi, S.; Flora, W. Evaluating the Cost Effectiveness of Flexible Rehabilitation Treatments Using Different Performance Criteria. *J. Transp. Eng.* **2009**, *135*, 753–763. [CrossRef]
44. Yao, L.; Dong, Q.; Ni, F.; Jiang, J.; Lu, X.; Du, Y. Effectiveness and Cost-Effectiveness Evaluation of Pavement Treatments Using Life-Cycle Cost Analysis. *J. Transp. Eng. Part B Pavements* **2019**, *145*, 04019006. [CrossRef]
45. Haji Agha Mohammad Zarbaf, S.E.; Norouzi, M.; Allemang, R.J.; Hunt, V.J.; Helmicki, A. Stay Cable Tension Estimation of Cable-Stayed Bridges Using Genetic Algorithm and Particle Swarm Optimization. *J. Bridge Eng.* **2017**, *22*, 05017008. [CrossRef]
46. Kumar, S.; Kaushal, D.R.; Gosain, A.K. Evaluation of evolutionary algorithms for the optimization of storm water drainage network for an urbanized area. *Acta Geophys.* **2019**, *67*, 149–165. [CrossRef]
47. Kleiner, Y.; Sadiq, R.; Rajani, B. Modelling the deterioration of buried infrastructure as a fuzzy Markov process. *J. Water Supply Res.Technol. Aqua.* **2006**, *55*, 67–80. [CrossRef]
48. Afshar, M.H.; Shahidi, M.; Rohani, M.; Sargolzaei, M. Application of cellular automata to sewer network optimization problems. *Sci. Iran.* **2011**, *18*, 304–312. [CrossRef]
49. Bakhshipour, A.E.; Bakhshizadeh, M.; Dittmer, U.; Haghighi, A.; Nowak, W. Hanging Gardens Algorithm to Generate Decentralized Layouts for the Optimization of Urban Drainage Systems. *J. Water Resour. Plan. Manag.* **2019**, *145*, 04019034. [CrossRef]
50. Mirjalili, S.; Lewis, A. The Whale Optimization Algorithm. *Adv. Eng. Softw.* **2016**, *95*, 51–67. [CrossRef]

Publisher's Note: MDPI stays neutral with regard to jurisdictional claims in published maps and institutional affiliations.

© 2020 by the authors. Licensee MDPI, Basel, Switzerland. This article is an open access article distributed under the terms and conditions of the Creative Commons Attribution (CC BY) license (http://creativecommons.org/licenses/by/4.0/).

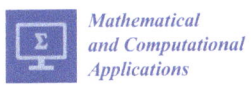 *Mathematical and Computational Applications*

Article

Single-Objective Optimization of a CMOS VCO Considering PVT and Monte Carlo Simulations

Perla Rubi Castañeda-Aviña [1,†], Esteban Tlelo-Cuautle [1,*,†] and Luis Gerardo de la Fraga [2,†]

1. Department of Electronics, INAOE, Tonantzintla, Puebla 72840, Mexico; perlacastaneda@inaoep.mx
2. Computer Science Department, Center for Research and Advanced Studies of the National Polytechnic Institute (CINVESTAV), Ciudad de Mexico 07360, Mexico; fraga@cs.cinvestav.mx
* Correspondence: etlelo@inaoep.mx; Tel.: +52-222-266-3100
† These authors contributed equally to this work.

Received: 23 September 2020; Accepted: 30 November 2020; Published: 3 December 2020

Abstract: The optimization of analog integrated circuits requires to take into account a number of considerations and trade-offs that are specific to each circuit, meaning that each case of design may be subject to different constraints to accomplish target specifications. This paper shows the single-objective optimization of a complementary metal-oxide-semiconductor (CMOS) four-stage voltage-controlled oscillator (VCO) to maximize the oscillation frequency. The stages are designed by using CMOS current-mode logic or differential pairs and are connected in a ring structure. The optimization is performed by applying differential evolution (DE) algorithm, in which the design variables are the control voltage and the transistors' widths and lengths. The objective is maximizing the oscillation frequency under the constraints so that the CMOS VCO be robust to Monte Carlo simulations and to process-voltage-temperature (PVT) variations. The optimization results show that DE provides feasible solutions oscillating at 5 GHz with a wide control voltage range and robust to both Monte Carlo and PVT analyses.

Keywords: VCO; differential evolution; CMOS differential pair; PVT variations; Monte Carlo analysis

1. Introduction

The voltage-controlled oscillator (VCO) is quite useful in applications such as: analog-to-digital converters [1–3], phase-locked loops [4], and so on. The VCO can be implemented by using complementary metal-oxide-semiconductor (CMOS) technology of integrated circuits, as already shown in [5], and also by using LC-tank structures. Several CMOS VCO designs can be classified by using single-ended stages [6,7], differential stages [8,9] and pseudo-differential stages [10]. Among the currently available VCO topologies, the one consisting of a ring structure [11], and using CMOS differential stages has the advantage of providing great immunity to supply disturbances [12]. Other desired features in designing a VCO are associated to accomplish low-power consumption, minimum layout area, high-frequency and wide control voltage range. These target specifications become difficult to achieve due to the continuous down scaling of silicon CMOS technologies. Besides, designing a VCO in a ring topology is frequently a more attractive alternative because it allows accomplishing a wide tuning (control voltage) range, small layout area, high gain, low cost, robustness to variations, simplicity and scalability in nanoscale CMOS processes [13,14]. The three principal causes of alteration on the performace for a circuit are the variations in the fabrication process, power supply and operation temperature, these constitute PVT variations and their impact is increased with the devices' downscaling [15]. Process variations include wafer defects or may be produced by certain chemical procedures causing some circuit's paremeters to change, voltage fluctuations in the circuit take place for a variety of reasons such as supply noise and can be compensated with a voltage regulator to prevent the transistor's operating point from being affected, last but not least temperature variations can be caused by external sources or by the circuit's own power dissipation. These PVT variations can be minimized by a proper design and layout placement and routing. Among the currently available designs, the authors in [5] introduced a wide-band VCO implemented by CMOS differential stages connected in a ring topology. Other design guidelines to improve the VCO's performance can be found in [16–19].

The oscillation frequency f_{osc} of a VCO can be evaluated by (1), where N indicates the number of stages and τ is a time constant that depends on the associated resistance of the active load and the value of the capacitor load. f_{osc} varies in a range determined by a control voltage V_{ctrl} [14], and depends on the number of CMOS differential stages N, but decreasing N yields a reduction in gain, which may result in the oscillation mitigation. This trade-off can be improved by applying metaheuristics to maximize f_{osc} under a wide range of V_{ctrl}, and low silicon area or number of CMOS differential stages N. Different metaheuristics have been applied to the optimization of CMOS integrated circuits in previous works due to the complexity involved in the design processes [7,20–22]. In this manner, the differential evolution (DE) algorithm is applied herein to vary the sizes of the transistors in the CMOS differential stages to maximize the oscillation frequency of a CMOS VCO f_{osc}. The electrical characteristics of the VCO are evaluated by linking the simulation program with integrated circuit emphasis (SPICE).

$$f_{osc} = \frac{1}{2N \cdot \tau} \qquad (1)$$

The rest of the paper is organized as follows: Section 2 describes the considerations taken for the design of both the CMOS differential pair stage and the VCO in a ring topology. The DE algorithm is detailed in Section 4. The single-objective optimization is described in Section 5. Section 6 describes a brief disscussion about this work. Finally, Section 7 summarizes the conclusions.

2. Ring VCO-Based on CMOS Differential Stages

In this paper, the main objective in designing a CMOS differential stage as the one shown in Figure 1, which will be used to implement a ring VCO, is oriented to achieve the highest oscillation frequency f_{osc} given in (1), which is inversely proportional to both the number of CMOS stages N and the propagation delay τ. Supposing N constant, then the delay generated by the differential pair must be minimized [14,23]. Some authors recommend that the delay can be reduced by augmenting the output transconductance g_{ds} of the active MOS transistor and by reducing the equivalent capacitance, where the load capacitance C_L could be the dominant one [13,23,24]. The trade-off here is that augmenting g_{ds} leads to increase the sizes of the MOS transistors and this generates larger parasitic capacitance values. Therefore, this problem is quite suitable for applying metaheuristics, like the DE algorithm.

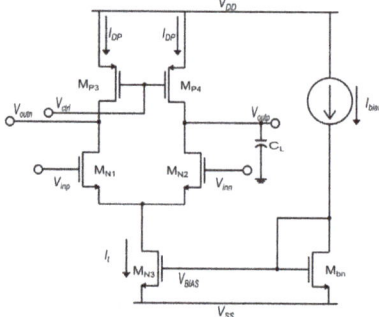

Figure 1. CMOS differential stage with active load and control voltage V_{ctrl}.

If the MOS transistors M_{N1} and M_{N2} operate in their saturation region, then they must accomplish $|V_{DS}| > (|V_{GS}| - |V_{TH}|)$ and $|V_{GS}| > |V_{TH}|$, where the voltages are associated to the drain (D), gate (G) and source (S) terminals of the MOS transistors, and its associated threshold voltage V_{TH}. The width (W) and length (L) sizes of the MOS transistors can be evaluated by (2), where I_D is the drain current, and $\mu_n C_{ox}$ are parameters provided by the CMOS technology foundry. In this work the sizing is performed by using 180 nanometers (nm) from United Microelectronics Corporation (UMC).

$$\frac{W}{L} = \frac{2I_D}{\mu_n C_{ox}(|V_{GS}| - |V_{TH}|)^2} \quad (2)$$

As already shown in [5], the active loads are implemented by P-type MOS transistors (M_{P3} and M_{P4}) operating in the triode region, and their sizing accomplish $|V_{DS}| < (|V_{GS}| - |V_{TH}|)$ and (3) [25]. The equivalent resistance is tuned by the control voltage V_{ctrl} at the gates of the PMOS transistors [14,26], and the output conductance of the PMOS transistor can be approached as $1/g_o = 1/g_{ds} = 1/\mu C_{ox}(|V_{ctrl} - V_s| - |V_{th}|)$.

$$I_D = \mu C_{ox} \frac{W}{L} \left[|V_{GS} - V_{TH}| \; |V_{DS}| - \frac{1}{2}|V_{DS}|^2 \right] \quad (3)$$

The propagation delay τ is directly related to the dominant pole, and it has been approximated as in (4), which depends on C_L, the transconductance g_m of the CMOS differential pair, and g_{ds} of the active load [27], so that the reduction of the transistors' sizes leads to an increase of the dominant pole ω_p.

$$\omega_p = \frac{3.29 \cdot 10^{54}(C_D + C_{db2} + C_{db4} + C_L) + 2.43 \cdot 10^{44}(g_{ds2} + g_{ds4}) + 1.46 \cdot 10^{56} g_{m2}(C_D + C_L) + 3.86 \cdot 10^{45}(g_{ds4} g_{m2}) + 2.51 \cdot 10^{58}(C_L g_{ds4} g_{m2})}{3.29 \cdot 10^{54}(g_{ds2} + g_{ds4}) + 1.46 \cdot 10^{56}(g_{ds4} g_{m2} + g_{ds2} g_{ds4} + g_{ds4} g_{mb2})} \quad (4)$$

The delay cell shown in Figure 1 can therefore be characterized by measuring the open-loop gain A_{OL} and the dominant pole ω_p. For instance, the gain-bandwidth product (GBW) of the delay cell, is the frequency at which A_{OL} becomes 0 dB [28]. Its design including process, voltage and temperature (PVT) variations is given in [5], and in this paper the delay cell is optimized to provide the smallest propagation delay τ to increase f_{osc}. The CMOS differential stage with active load is used to design the four-stages ($N = 4$) VCO shown in Figure 2.

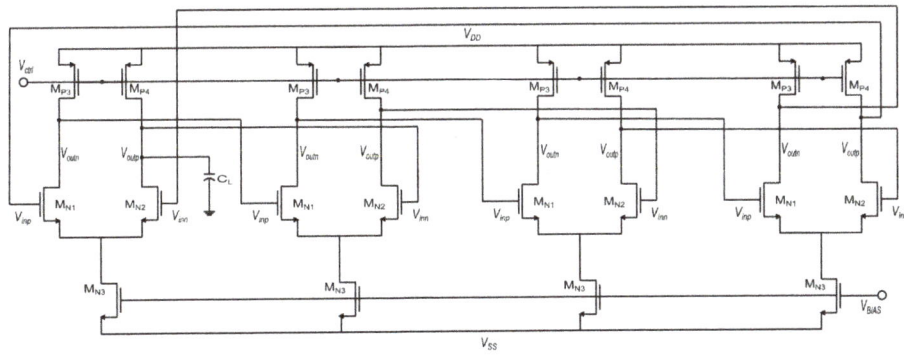

Figure 2. VCO consisting of four CMOS differential stages with active loads, in a ring topology.

3. VCO Optimization Methods

The VCO optimization has been carried out through different approaches, such as metaheuristics [7,22]. In [7], a ring VCO's operation improvement is performed through particle swam optimization (PSO) and non-dominated sorting genetic algorithm (NSGA-II), to minimize both the phase noise and the power consumption. This is carried out through the use of symbolic modeling techniques to obtain the total output noise density and VCO's phase noise expressions by doing this the run time is reduced and the noise expression is simplified. Achieving also an improvement in tuning range without being an objective and also performing both Monte Carlo and process corners analyses to the final design. Similarly, in [22] the optimal sizing of a differential ring VCO is carried out through multi-objective particle swam optimization (MOPSO) and infeasibility-driven evolutionary algorithm (IDEA) to improve its performances by minimizing both the phase noise and the power consumption while maintaining a given oscillation frequency. Noise modeling is also carried out, to obtain the simplified noise expressions and solve the equations' system the determinate decision diagram (DDD) symbolic technique is used. Furthermore, Monte Carlo and PVT variations analyses were performed to guarantee the design robustness.

In [29], an algorithm that performs RF circuits sizing by using evolutionary strategies and simulating annealing in the search and selection parts, respectively, is implemented in Matlab. The optimization is carried out taking into account the parasitics caused by the passive elements' layout through physical based equivalent parasitic models, by doing this the number of iterations between circuit sizing and layout generation is reduced (reducing the synthesis time) since the difference between synthesis and post-layout results is decreased. The use of simplified models through RF circuit synthesis to approximate layout-induced parasitics lead to unrealistic outcomes. An LC cross-coupled oscillator was optimized using this approach, where the restrictions are: oscillation frequency, phase noise, power consumption, and oscillation amplitude.

In [30], the circuit optimization tool AIDA-C is used to carry out a multi-objective optimization and perform the sizing of an LC-tank VCO with the aim to minimize two compromised objectives, which are phase noise and power consumption. This optimization process achieves a good balance between the two objectives, since there is a trade-off between them, the optimization execution takes several hours to run. In [31], two design tools AIDA and SIDe-O to design a robust LC-tank VCO are introduced. SIDe-O is employed to face the problems relative to the passive elements and through AIDA a robust design is assured due to its corner-aware approach and NSGA-II is employed for the phase noise, power consumption and area minimization, as in the previous case the algorithm takes several hours to run, in both algorithms none of the objectives are focused on achieving a higher oscillation frequency.

4. Problem Formulation for the Optimization of the VCO by Applying DE

The single-objective function $g(x)$ is formulated by (5), where μ is a constant established to one and $r(x)$ stands for the constraints. One can see that when all the constraints are fulfilled then the second term of the function is equal to 0 and the objective function is the oscillating-period of the ring VCO $g(x) = f(x)$. Therefore, the sizing optimization problem can be defined by (6).

$$g(x) = f(x) + \mu \sum r^2(x) \tag{5}$$

$$\begin{aligned}
&\text{Search}: x = [W_1, W_3, L_1, L_3, V_{ctrl}] \\
&\text{Minimize}: g(x) \\
&\text{Subject to}: 5 > A_{OL} > 1, \\
&V_{DS} \leq V_{GS} - V_{TH} \quad \text{for} \quad M_{P3} \text{ and } M_{P4}, \\
&V_{DS} \geq V_{GS} - V_{TH} \quad \text{otherwise}, \\
&W_{min} < W < W_{max}, \\
&L_{min} < L < L_{max}, \\
&V_{SS} < V_{ctrl} < V_{DD}
\end{aligned} \tag{6}$$

By applying the DE algorithm, which is described below, the sizing optimization process requires a population of I_n individuals, a maximum number of generations $maxGen$, and the objective function

$g(x)$. Two of the main factors guaranteeing that global optimality is achievable by a metaheuristic like DE are the selection of the best solutions and randomization, where the former ensures that the solution converges to an optimum value while the later keeps the solution from getting halted at local optima [32]. To maximize f_{osc}, this paper minimizes the oscillating period of the ring VCO, which is subject to the constraints of maintaining the load MOS transistors M_{P3} and M_{P4} operating in the triode region and the rest N-type MOS transistors operating in the saturation region. The SPICE simulator is linked within the optimization loop to evaluate the delay cell's gain A_{OL} to be maintained within 1 and 5 dB.

The DE algorithm is a metaheuristic that performs an iterative optimization based on the evolution of a population of individuals under the concept of competition. The initial population is randomly generated where each individual represents a tentative solution that is associated to a fitness value through an objective function to point out the individual's suitability to a particular problem. The individuals with better fitness are more likely to be selected as parents, the chosen ones are reproduced using genetic operators (crossover, mutation) to produce new offsprings, which will also be evaluated to determine its survival. This represents a generation and this process is repeated until a stop criteria is met [33–36]. The DE algorithm is suitable for continuous optimization problems, like sizing analog CMOS integrated circuits as the VCO. In the DE algorithm, a vector population is altered through a vector of differences, which translates to a two operators: the first one being a recombination operator of two or more solutions and the second one coming as a self-referential mutation operator that conducts the algorithm unto finding acceptable solutions. Each individual is encoded as a vector of real numbers that are within the limits defined for each design variable (as the widths (W) and lengths (L) of the MOS transistors). The crossover operator defines the offspring-associated variable to be a a linear combination of three randomly selected individuals or an inheritance of its parents value while guaranteeing that at least one of the offspring's variable will be different from its parent. A scaling factor is employed to prevent stagnation of the search process [33,37].

In the DE algorithm, if a variable's magnitude is out of range, the recombination and mutation operators can be employed to reset the value. For instance the value can be established to the limit it exceeds, however this diminish the population's diversity. Other approaches reset it to a random value or initializing this value to a mid point between its previous value and the violated bound. In the latter the limits are approached asymptotically leading to diminish the amount of disruption [33]. In our current DE implementation, the individual is reset randomly within the search bounds. Other guidelines to design a DE algorithm may include to set the population number to ten times the amount of decision variables and initialize the weighting factor, P_f to 0.8 and the crossover constant, P_c to 0.9. If no convergence is achieved an increase in population may be necessary, however frequently the weighting factor is the one that has to be modified to be a little lower or higher than 0.8. The relation between convergence speed and robustness features is a trade-off, if the amount of population increments and the weighting factor decrements then convergence is more likely to occur but within a longer period of time. The performance of DE is more sensitive to the value of the weighting factor than the value of the crossover constant, and the range of both is generally in [0.5, 1]. A faster convergence may occur with higher values of the crossover constant [33].

The usefulness of the DE algorithm in sizing CMOS integrated circuits has been proved in [38–40]. Algorithm 1 describes its adaptation to maximize the oscillation frequency of the ring VCO shown in Figure 2. As mentioned above, herein the objective function is associated to minimize the propagation delay τ that is accomplished by measuring the oscillating period by using SPICE.

Algorithm 1 DE pseudocode.

1: **procedure** DE(I_n, $maxGen$, $g(x)$)
2:     Generate the SPICE netlist of the ring VCO
3:     **for** $i = 1 : I_n$ **do**
4:         Initialize the population randomly and replace the initial individuals (Ws, Ls, V_{ctrl}) into the netlist
5:         Evaluate the VCO's delay cell and check the constraints
6:         **if** $constraints = 0$ **then**
7:             Simulate the VCO and evaluate the objective function
8:         **end if**
9:     **end for**
10:     **while** $j < maxGen$ **do**
11:         **for** $i = 1 : I_n$ **do**
12:             Create a trial solution from three randomly selected parents using (7)
13:             Apply crossover using (8)
14:             Replace the new individual into the netlist
15:             Simulate the VCO's delay cell and count the constraints
16:             **if** $constraints = 0$ **then**
17:                 Simulate the VCO and evaluate the objective function
18:             **end if**
19:             **if** the individual's objective function is lower than that of the parent **then**
20:                 The new individual replaces the parent using (9)
21:             **end if**
22:         **end for**
23:     **end while**
24: **end procedure**

In the optimization process the individuals I_n of the population generated by the DE algorithm are replaced into the netlist file of the VCO's delay cell and each individual is simulated in SPICE. The electrical characteristics are obtained from the (.lis) output SPICE-file to verify that all the MOS transistors are working in the appropriate region of operation and that the gain is within the range of $5 > A_{OL} > 1$. A flag assigns 0 to a fulfilled constraint and 1 to a not fulfilled one. The period of the sinusoidal wave is associated to the function $f(x)$. If the VCO is not oscillating then a high value is assigned to $f(x)$. In the DE algorithm each individual is mutated to generate an adaptive solution v_{ij} from three randomly selected parents, as given in (7). Afterwards, the crossover takes place creating a trial solution, through the recombination of a mutated solution v_{ij} with an individual x_{ij}, given by (8). Finally, the replacement is carried out employing an elitist selection, where the new individual will replace its parent if its objective function value is better than the parent, as given in (9) [33].

$$v_{ij} = x_{r3j} + P_f(x_{r1j} - x_{r2j}) \qquad (7)$$

$$u_{ij} = \begin{cases} v_{ij} & \text{if } rand_j[0,1] < P_c \text{ or } j = j_{rand} \\ x_{ij} & \text{otherwise} \end{cases} \qquad (8)$$

$$x_i(t+1) = \begin{cases} u_i(t+1) & \text{if } f(u_i(t+1)) < f(x_i(t)) \\ x_i(t) & \text{otherwise} \end{cases} \qquad (9)$$

5. Optimizing the CMOS VCO by Applying DE Algorithm

The sizing optimization problem defined by (6), requires the sizes of the design variables (widths W and lengths L) of the MOS transistors, but one must determine the search space ranges. For instance, the limits of the sizes are set to: $2\lambda \leq W \leq 1000\lambda$ and $2\lambda \leq L \leq 10\lambda$, respectively, where $\lambda = 90$ nm for the UMC CMOS technology of 180 nm. Another design variable is the control voltage, which bounds are set to $V_{SS} \leq V_{ctrl} \leq V_{DD}$, and where $V_{SS} = -0.9$ V is the lower supply voltage and $V_{DD} = 0.9$ V the higher supply voltage.

The DE algorithm was calibrated by adjusting P_c, P_f and I_n to 0.7, 0.6 and 50, respectively. The maximum number of generations is set to 50. In total, 30 runs of DE were performed. The best feasible solution provided an oscillation frequency of 5 GHz, as shown in Figure 3. In such a case the obtained parameter values are: $I_{bias} = I_{MN3} = 4$ mA, $W_{MN1} = W_{MN2} = 40$ µm, $W_{MN3} = 500$ µm, $W_{MP3} = W_{MP4} = 17$ µm, $L_{MN1} = L_{MN2} = L_{MN3} = L_{MP3} = L_{MP4} = 0.18$ µm, $V_{ctrl} = -0.8$ V and $C_L = 31.39$ fF. The V_{BIAS} is created from Figure 1, in which the CMOS differential stage with active load is biased with $I_{bias} = 2$ mA, and the sizes of M_{bn} are $W = 200$ µm and $L = 180$ µm.

The SPICE simulation result of the best solution of the DE algorithm is shown in Figure 3.

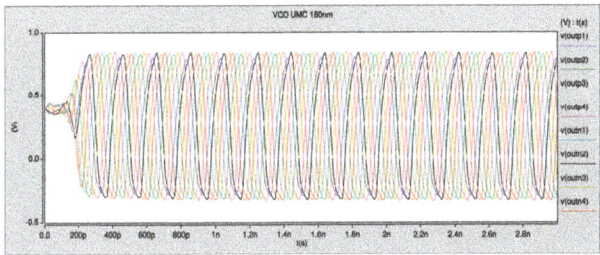

Figure 3. VCO's oscillation frequency provided by the best solution of the DE algorithm.

Monte Carlo is an integrated circuits' statistical analysis in which a circuit devices' parameters and mismatch are varied randomly. Monte Carlo simulation allows the designer to consider the possible effects of a random variation of certain circuit's parameter over its performance. Monte Carlo analysis is carried out through the variation of W and L for each one of the 30 feasible solutions over 1000 runs, and considering a Gaussian distribution with 10% deviation. The outcome of the Monte Carlo simulations is employed to compute the mean and the standard deviation of the objetive function value, those results are sketched in Figure 4.

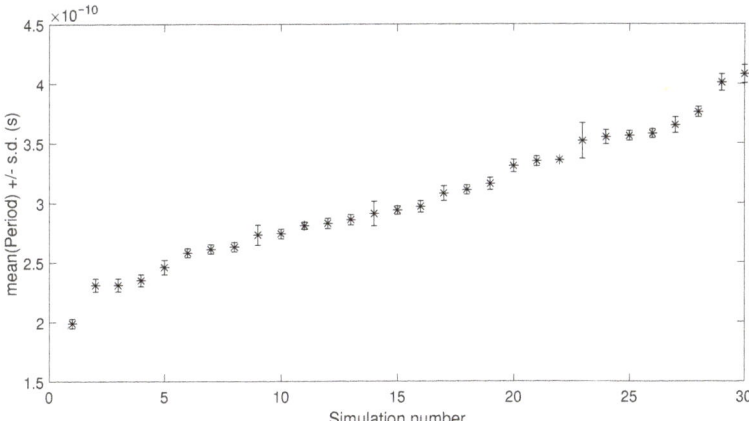

Figure 4. Mean and standard deviation of the Monte Carlo analysis for 30 feasible sized solutions of the DE algorithm. The best solution is the one with the lowest period (corresponding to a greater oscillation frequency).

The feasible sized solutions that accomplished the lower time delay τ of the CMOS differential stages are analyzed and their statistics related to the mean and standard deviation of the period of the sinusoidal wave are summarized in Table 1. From this table, the Monte Carlo simulation of the best solution of the DE algorithm is shown in Figure 5.

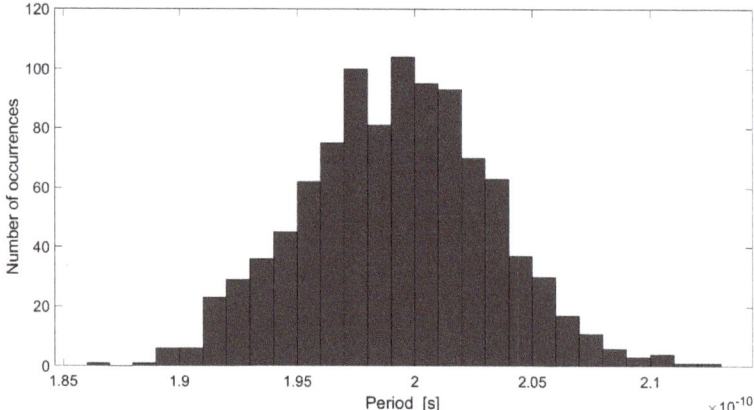

Figure 5. Monte Carlo simulation of the best feasible sized solution of the DE algorithm.

Table 1. Statistics of the Monte Carlo analysis of the best 5 feasible sized solutions provided by the DE algorithm.

Solution	Minimum (ns)	Maximum (ns)	Mean (ns)	Variance	Standard Deviation
1	0.187	0.213	0.199	1.55×10^{-23}	3.94×10^{-12}
2	0.214	0.248	0.231	2.86×10^{-23}	5.35×10^{-12}
3	0.214	0.249	0.231	2.93×10^{-23}	5.41×10^{-12}
4	0.219	0.251	0.235	2.39×10^{-23}	4.89×10^{-12}
5	0.226	0.265	0.246	3.59×10^{-23}	5.99×10^{-12}

The parameters of each one of the five best feasible sized solutions and the simulated period, frequency and gain of the VCO and the CMOS delay cell, respectively, are summarized in Table 2.

Table 2. Best 5 feasible sized solution design parameters provided by the DE algorithm.

Solution	W_{MN1} (µm)	W_{MP3} (µm)	L_{MN1} (µm)	L_{MP3} (µm)	V_{ctrl} (V)	C_L (fF)	Period (ns)	Frequency (GHz)	A_{OL} (dB)
1	40	17	0.18	0.18	−0.80	31.39	0.199	5.02	1.89
2	45	20	0.18	0.18	−0.56	35.22	0.232	4.32	3.39
3	61	26	0.18	0.18	−0.56	54.69	0.232	4.30	1.78
4	69	22	0.18	0.18	−0.79	96.17	0.235	4.25	2.26
5	46	20	0.18	0.18	−0.51	36.19	0.246	4.07	4.41

A PVT simulation of the ten best feasible sized solutions was also performed to assure that the CMOS VCO is robust to variations. The PVT variations are simulated by setting $V_{ctrl} = -0.8$ V. Considering five process corners (typical-typical (TT), slow-slow (SS), slow N-type MOS transistor and fast P-type MOS transistor (SNFP), fast N-type MOS transistor and slow P-type MOS transistor (FNSP), and fast-fast (FF)), three voltage variations (±10% of $\pm V_{supply} = 0.9$ V), and three temperature variations ($T- = -20\,°C$, $T = 60\,°C$ and $T+ = 120\,°C$) [41], Figure 6 shows the higher and lower gain and oscillation frequency values provided by the DE algorithm. Table 3 summarizes PVT simulation results, where the five corners (TT, SS, SNFP, FNSP and FF) correspond to the MOS transistor models provided by the UMC foundry.

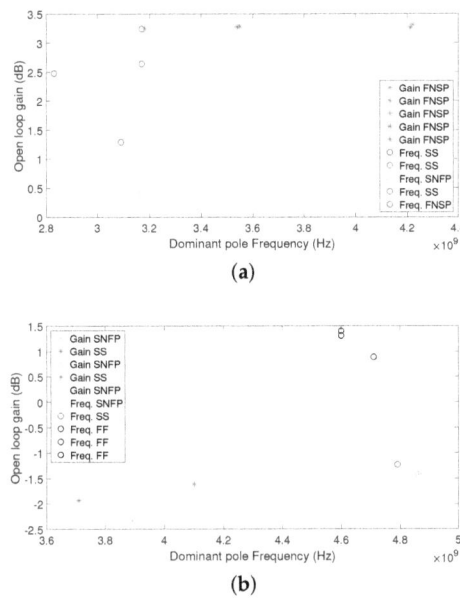

Figure 6. (**a**) Higher and (**b**) lower gains and dominant pole frequencies, for the solution 1 CMOS delay cell designed with United Microelectronics Corporation (UMC) technology of 180 nm by applying DE algorithm.

Table 3. Open-loop gain and dominant pole frequency over PVT variations with $V_{ctrl} = -0.8$ V.

Solution	Corners	Temperature	T−			T			T+		
		Voltage	V−	V	V+	V−	V	V+	V−	V	V+
1	TT	A_{OL} (dB)	0.82	1.88	2.06	0.55	1.74	1.89	0.24	1.61	1.78
		ω_p (GHz)	4.54	4.24	4.21	3.90	3.58	3.56	3.58	3.22	3.19
	SS	A_{OL} (dB)	−1.23	2.17	2.81	−1.61	1.76	2.64	−1.93	1.29	2.48
		ω_p (GHz)	4.79	3.92	3.77	4.10	3.37	3.17	3.71	3.09	2.83
	SNFP	A_{OL} (dB)	−1.42	0.51	0.88	−1.92	0.20	0.60	−2.33	−0.085	0.41
		ω_p (GHz)	4.86	4.25	4.16	4.23	3.61	3.52	3.89	3.28	3.15
	FNSP	A_{OL} (dB)	2.66	3.26	3.31	2.64	3.27	3.28	2.49	3.24	3.24
		ω_p (GHz)	4.35	4.21	4.22	3.68	3.54	3.55	3.34	3.17	3.18
	FF	A_{OL} (dB)	0.89	1.31	1.40	0.77	1.15	1.20	0.64	1.05	1.08
		ω_p (GHz)	4.71	4.60	4.60	4.00	3.91	3.91	3.63	3.52	3.53
2	TT	A_{OL} (dB)	2.75	3.22	3.02	2.77	3.31	3.06	2.61	3.3	3.07
		ω_p (GHz)	4.21	4.1	4.17	3.51	3.43	3.49	3.23	3.06	3.12
	SS	A_{OL} (dB)	1.62	4.23	4.25	1.49	4.24	4.38	1.21	4.01	4.4
		ω_p (GHz)	4.16	3.62	3.63	3.53	3.04	3.01	3.21	2.75	2.67
	SNFP	A_{OL} (dB)	0.42	1.67	1.68	0.16	1.57	1.57	−0.16	1.43	1.49
		ω_p (GHz)	4.51	4.16	4.17	3.86	3.5	3.5	3.53	3.15	3.13
	FNSP	A_{OL} (dB)	4.93	4.91	4.51	5.27	5.21	4.74	5.29	5.34	4.86
		ω_p (GHz)	3.97	3.99	4.11	3.3	3.31	3.42	2.96	2.94	3.04
	FF	A_{OL} (dB)	2.23	2.27	2.08	2.29	2.28	2.05	2.26	2.28	2.03
		ω_p (GHz)	4.55	4.56	4.64	3.84	3.85	3.92	3.45	3.45	3.52

Table 3. Cont.

Solution	Corners	Temperature	T−			T			T+		
		Voltage	V−	V	V+	V−	V	V+	V−	V	V+
3	TT	A_{OL} (dB)	1.57	1.7	1.52	1.63	1.69	1.45	1.64	1.7	1.43
		ω_p (GHz)	4.6	4.66	4.8	3.85	3.91	4.04	3.47	3.51	3.62
	SS	A_{OL} (dB)	1.52	2.65	2.5	1.5	2.65	2.47	1.36	2.62	2.45
		ω_p (GHz)	4.22	4.06	4.17	3.54	3.38	3.47	3.2	3.02	3.09
	SNFP	A_{OL} (dB)	−0.1	0.42	0.35	−0.18	0.3	0.18	−0.28	0.24	0.1
		ω_p (GHz)	4.73	4.68	4.78	3.99	3.93	4.02	3.61	3.52	3.61
	FNSP	A_{OL} (dB)	3.19	3.07	2.77	3.39	3.18	2.82	3.49	3.26	2.87
		ω_p (GHz)	4.45	4.58	4.76	3.72	3.84	3.99	3.33	3.44	3.58
	FF	A_{OL} (dB)	0.89	0.87	0.72	0.91	0.81	0.61	0.93	0.82	0.59
		ω_p (GHz)	5.11	5.22	5.37	4.32	4.43	4.55	3.9	3.99	4.11
4	TT	A_{OL} (dB)	1.9	2.25	2.3	1.91	2.16	2.13	1.94	2.15	2.08
		ω_p (GHz)	4.77	4.81	4.93	4	4.05	4.16	3.6	3.64	3.74
	SS	A_{OL} (dB)	1.82	2.94	3.06	1.79	2.87	2.92	1.72	2.85	2.87
		ω_p (GHz)	4.37	4.23	4.31	3.66	3.52	3.6	3.29	3.15	3.21
	SNFP	A_{OL} (dB)	5.2	1.15	1.27	0.43	0.97	1.02	0.39	0.91	0.91
		ω_p (GHz)	4.83	4.79	4.88	4.07	4.04	4.12	3.67	3.62	3.7
	FNSP	A_{OL} (dB)	3.21	3.4	3.4	3.32	3.41	3.32	3.41	3.46	3.33
		ω_p (GHz)	4.69	4.78	4.91	3.93	4.02	4.14	3.53	3.61	3.73
	FF	A_{OL} (dB)	1.42	1.62	1.68	1.37	1.48	1.47	1.4	1.47	1.41
		ω_p (GHz)	5.28	5.36	5.49	4.47	4.56	4.67	4.04	4.12	4.23
5	TT	A_{OL} (dB)	3.89	4.17	3.82	4	4.34	3.94	3.86	4.38	3.98
		ω_p (GHz)	4.02	3.96	4.07	3.38	3.3	3.39	3.06	2.94	3.02
	SS	A_{OL} (dB)	3.05	5.53	5.3	3.04	5.71	5.57	2.77	5.55	5.67
		ω_p (GHz)	3.89	3.44	3.49	3.29	2.85	2.87	3	2.57	2.53
	SNFP	A_{OL} (dB)	1.39	2.5	2.38	1.19	2.45	2.33	0.88	2.34	2.28
		ω_p (GHz)	4.34	4.05	4.09	3.7	3.4	3.43	3.38	3.05	3.06
	FNSP	A_{OL} (dB)	6.37	6.07	5.45	6.9	6.53	5.8	6.94	6.72	5.98
		ω_p (GHz)	3.73	3.81	3.97	3.06	3.13	3.28	2.73	2.76	2.9
	FF	A_{OL} (dB)	3.14	3.04	2.74	3.25	3.11	2.76	3.24	3.12	2.77
		ω_p (GHz)	4.41	4.45	4.56	3.7	3.74	3.84	3.33	3.35	3.44

As one can see from Table 3 solution number 4 is the most robust to PVT. This solution has the greater frequency with all the gains been positive. Figure 6 depicts the higher and lower gains and dominant pole frequencies for solution number 1 since this is the one that provides the higher oscillation frequency, as one can see the greater gains occur at the FNSP process-corner (in Figure 6a) while the lower gains for the most part occur at SNFP process-corner (see Figure 6b. Furthermore, the greater ω_p takes place mostly at FF process-corner, while the lower ω_p mostly takes place at SS process-corner.

Figure 7 depicts the higher and lower gains and dominant pole frequencies for solution number 4 since is the most robust one. As one can see in Figure 7a the greater gains occur mostly at the FNSP process-corner, while the lower gains, in Figure 7b, for the most part occur at SNFP process-corner. The greater ω_p takes place mostly at the FF process-corner (in Figure 7b), while the lower ω_p mostly takes place at the SS process-corner (in Figure 7a).

Table 4 shows the oscillation frequency and power dissipation corresponding to each control voltage V_{ctrl} value for the best 5 feasible sized solutions.

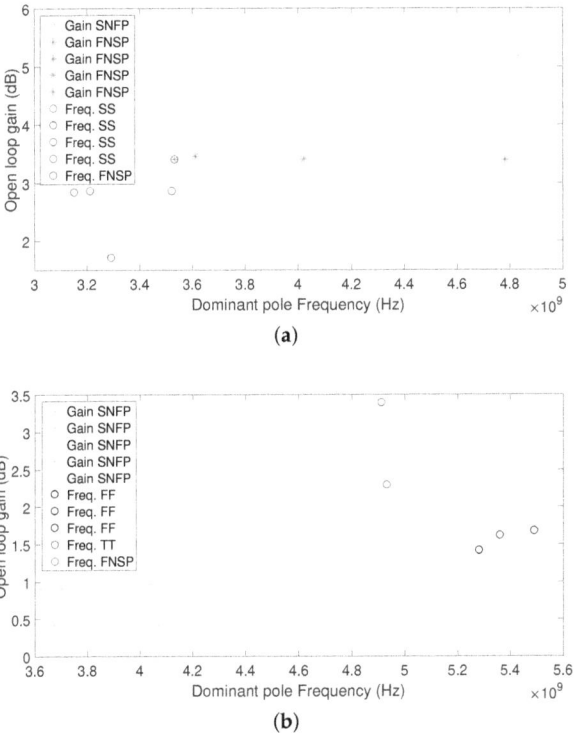

Figure 7. (a) Higher and (b) lower gains and dominant pole frequencies, for the solution 4 CMOS delay cell designed with UMC technology of 180 nm by applying DE algorithm.

Table 4. Oscillation frequency and power dissipation to the corresponding V_{ctrl}.

Solution	Parameter	Measured Oscillation Frequency and Power Dissipation							
1	V_{ctrl} (V)	−0.53	−0.55	−0.6	−0.65	−0.7	−0.75	−0.8	−0.85	−0.9
	f_{osc} (GHz)	4.03	4.08	4.27	4.48	4.69	4.83	5	5.15	5.32
	P_{cons} (mW)	30.6	31	32.1	33.1	33.9	34.6	35.3	35.8	36.3
2	V_{ctrl} (V)	−0.41	−0.5	−0.6	−0.65	−0.7	−0.75	−0.8	−0.85	−0.9
	f_{osc} (GHz)	3.56	4.02	4.46	4.65	4.83	5	5.18	5.29	5.35
	P_{cons} (mW)	30.8	33.1	35.1	35.9	36.6	37.2	37.7	38.1	38.4
3	V_{ctrl} (V)	−0.27	−0.3	−0.4	−0.5	−0.56	−0.6	−0.7	−0.8	−0.9
	f_{osc} (GHz)	2.91	3.07	3.61	4.05	4.3	4.37	4.78	5.1	5.38
	P_{cons} (mW)	31.9	33	35.9	38	38.9	39.4	40.3	40.9	41.2
4	V_{ctrl} (V)	−0.36	−0.4	−0.5	−0.6	−0.7	−0.75	−0.8	−0.85	−0.9
	f_{osc} (GHz)	2.72	2.88	3.25	3.6	3.98	4.08	4.26	4.33	4.44
	P_{cons} (mW)	32	33.2	35.7	37.5	38.9	39.4	39.8	40.2	40.5
5	V_{ctrl} (V)	−0.41	−0.5	−0.6	−0.65	−0.7	−0.75	−0.8	−0.85	−0.9
	f_{osc} (GHz)	3.56	3.97	4.39	4.57	4.74	4.93	5.1	5.21	5.38
	P_{cons} (mW)	30.8	33.1	35.2	36	36.7	37.2	37.7	38.1	38.5

6. Discussion

The proposed methodology to circuit design here is: (1) apply DE at least 30 times. This give us 30 solutions to our design problem, considering only the best solutions according to the objective function. (2) From the best 10 solutions, apply the Monte Carlo (MT) analysis. (3) From the best 10 solutions of the MC analysis apply the PVT analysis. Finally, (4) select the best solution according to the showed variations in the PVT analysis.

We apply the MC analysis to vary the dimension for all the circuit's transistors up to 10% of their value. As shown in Figure 5, these variations are not too high to move the operating point of the MOS transistors, and still the order of the obtained solution according to the objective function is kept after the MC analysis.

Then we apply the PVT analysis: The five process corners employed for this simulation are the ones provided by the foundry which are typical-typical (TT), slow NMOS transistor and fast PMOS transistor (SNFP), fast NMOS transistor and slow PMOS transistor (FNSP), slow-slow (SS) and fast-fast (FF), these account for the variation of fabrication parameters. A circuit can also be subject to temperature (considering three temperatures $-20°$, $60°$ and $120°$) and voltage variations (considering a variation of $\pm 10\%$) in its operation environment therefore each corner is simulated with each temperature and voltage variation.

The chosen solution is the one with lower time period (or higher operation frequency) while all the gains are positive, within the gain constraint of $1 < A_{OL} < 5$.

In Table 3 are shown only the first five solutions, although 10 analyses were performed.

We use a DE version programmed in C language. One single run (50 individuals, and 50 generations) took around 32 min.

The MC and PVT analyses could be incorporated within the optimization loop, as another set of constraints. This idea also will increase the simulation time to several hours. We are going to analyse this idea as a future work.

7. Conclusions

The application of the DE algorithm has proven to be effective in the minimization of the time period of a CMOS VCO designed with CMOS differential delay cells in a ring topology. We use the Monte Carlo analysis over the sized transistor dimensions to rank the obtained DE solutions. Then we apply the PVT analyses to the 10 best solutions according to the Monte Carlo analysis. The most robust solution to PVT, provides an oscillation frequency up to 4.25 GHz (corresponding to a time period of 0.235 ns), and it has a wider tunning range, of 2.72–4.44 GHz, corresponding to V_{ctrl} of -0.36 to -0.9V.

Author Contributions: Investigation, P.R.C.-A., E.T.-C., and L.G.d.l.F.; and Writing—review and editing, P.R.C.-A., E.T.-C., and L.G.d.l.F. All authors have read and agreed to the published version of the manuscript.

Funding: This research received no external funding.

Conflicts of Interest: The authors declare no conflict of interest. The founding sponsors had no role in the design of the study; in the collection, analyses, or interpretation of data; in the writing of the manuscript, or in the decision to publish the results.

References

1. Al-Tamimi, K.M.; El-Sankary, K.; Fouzar, Y. VCO-Based ADC With Built-In Supply Noise Immunity Using Injection-Locked Ring Oscillators. *IEEE Trans. Circuits Syst. Express Briefs* **2019**, *66*, 1089–1093. [CrossRef]
2. Ding, Z.; Zhou, X.; Li, Q. A 0.5-1.1-V Adaptive Bypassing SAR ADC Utilizing the Oscillation-Cycle Information of a VCO-Based Comparator. *IEEE J. Solid State Circuits* **2019**, *54*, 968–977. [CrossRef]
3. Danesh, M.; Sanyal, A. 0.13 pW/Hz Ring VCO-Based Continuous-Time Read-Out ADC for Bio-Impedance Measurement. *IEEE Trans. Circuits Syst. II Express Briefs* **2020**. [CrossRef]
4. Sharma, J.; Krishnaswamy, H. A 2.4-GHz Reference-Sampling Phase-Locked Loop That Simultaneously Achieves Low-Noise and Low-Spur Performance. *IEEE J. Solid State Circuits* **2019**, *54*, 1407–1424. [CrossRef]

5. Tlelo-Cuautle, E.; Castañeda-Aviña, P.R.; Trejo-Guerra, R.; Carbajal-Gómez, V.H. Design of a Wide-Band Voltage-Controlled Ring Oscillator Implemented in 180 nm CMOS Technology. *Electronics* **2019**, *8*, 1156. [CrossRef]
6. Lee, I.Y.; Im, D. Low phase noise ring VCO employing input-coupled dynamic current source. *Electron. Lett.* **2019**, *56*, 76–78. [CrossRef]
7. Panda, M.; Patnaik, S.K.; Mal, A.K. Performance enhancement of a VCO using symbolic modelling and optimisation. *IET Circuits Devices Syst.* **2017**, *12*, 196–202. [CrossRef]
8. Gui, X.; Tang, R.; Zhang, Y.; Li, D.; Geng, L. A Voltage-Controlled Ring Oscillator With VCO-Gain Variation Compensation. *IEEE Microw. Wirel. Components Lett.* **2020**, *30*, 288–291. [CrossRef]
9. Jung, O.Y.; Seok, H.G.; Dissanayake, A.; Lee, S.G. A 45-μ W, 162.1-dBc/Hz FoM, 490-MHz Two-Stage Differential Ring VCO Without a Cross-Coupled Latch. *IEEE Trans. Circuits Syst. II Express Briefs* **2017**, *65*, 1579–1583. [CrossRef]
10. Jiang, T.; Yin, J.; Mak, P.I.; Martins, R.P. A 0.5-V 0.4-to-1.6-GHz 8-phase bootstrap ring-VCO using inherent non-overlapping clocks achieving a 162.2-dBc/Hz FoM. *IEEE Trans. Circuits Syst. II Express Briefs* **2018**, *66*, 157–161. [CrossRef]
11. Sun, I.F.; Yin, J.; Mak, P.I.; Martins, R.P. A Comparative Study of 8-Phase Feedforward-Coupling Ring VCOs. *IEEE Trans. Circuits Syst. II Express Briefs* **2019**, *66*, 527–531. [CrossRef]
12. Abidi, A.A. Phase noise and jitter in CMOS ring oscillators. *IEEE J. Solid State Circuits* **2006**, *41*, 1803–1816. [CrossRef]
13. Gui, X.; Green, M.M. Design of CML ring oscillators with low supply sensitivity. *IEEE Trans. Circuits Syst. Regul. Pap.* **2013**, *60*, 1753–1763. [CrossRef]
14. Zhang, Z.; Chen, L.; Djahanshahi, H. A SEE Insensitive CML Voltage Controlled Oscillator in 65 nm CMOS. In Proceedings of the 2018 IEEE Canadian Conference on Electrical & Computer Engineering (CCECE), Quebec City, QC, Canada, 13–16 May 2018; pp. 1–4. [CrossRef]
15. Amaya, A.; Villota, F.; Espinosa, G. A robust to PVT fully-differential amplifier in 45 nm SOI-CMOS technology. In Proceedings of the 2013 IEEE 4th Latin American Symposium on Circuits and Systems (LASCAS), Cusco, Peru, 27 February–1 March 2013; pp. 1–4.
16. Hsieh, J.Y.; Lin, K.Y. A 0.7-mW LC Voltage-Controlled Oscillator Leveraging Switched Biasing Technique for Low Phase Noise. *IEEE Trans. Circuits Syst. II Express Briefs* **2019**, *66*, 1307–1310. [CrossRef]
17. Basaligheh, A.; Saffari, P.; Winkler, W.; Moez, K. A Wide Tuning Range, Low Phase Noise, and Area Efficient Dual-Band Millimeter-Wave CMOS VCO Based on Switching Cores. *IEEE Trans. Circuits Syst. I Regul. Pap.* **2019**, *66*, 2888–2897. [CrossRef]
18. Poor, M.A.; Esmaeeli, O.; Sheikhaei, S. A low phase noise quadrature VCO using superharmonic injection, current reuse, and negative resistance techniques in CMOS technology. *Analog. Integr. Circuits Signal Process.* **2019**, *99*, 633–644. [CrossRef]
19. Ghorbel, I.; Haddad, F.; Rahajandraibe, W.; Loulou, M. Design Methodology of Ultra-Low-Power LC-VCOs for IoT Applications. *J. Circuits Syst. Comput.* **2019**, *28*. [CrossRef]
20. de Melo, J.L.; Pereira, N.; Leitão, P.V.; Paulino, N.; Goes, J. A Systematic Design Methodology for Optimization of Sigma-Delta Modulators Based on an Evolutionary Algorithm. *IEEE Trans. Circuits Syst. I Regul. Pap.* **2019**, *66*, 3544–3556. [CrossRef]
21. Vural, R.A.; Yildirim, T.; Kadioglu, T.; Basargan, A. Performance evaluation of evolutionary algorithms for optimal filter design. *IEEE Trans. Evol. Comput.* **2011**, *16*, 135–147. [CrossRef]
22. Panda, M.; Patnaik, S.K.; Mal, A.K.; Ghosh, S. Fast and optimised design of a differential VCO using symbolic technique and multi objective algorithms. *IET Circuits Devices Syst.* **2019**, *13*, 1187–1195. [CrossRef]
23. Heydari, P.; Mohanavelu, R. Design of ultrahigh-speed low-voltage CMOS CML buffers and latches. *IEEE Trans. Very Large Scale Integr. (VLSI) Syst.* **2004**, *12*, 1081–1093. [CrossRef]
24. Kumar, M. Design of Linear Low-Power Voltage-Controlled Oscillator with I-MOS Varactor and Back-Gate Tuning. *Circuits Syst. Signal Process.* **2018**, 1–17. [CrossRef]
25. Sedra, A.S.; Smith, K.C. *Microelectronic Circuits*; Holt, Rinehart and Winston: New York, NY, USA, 1982.
26. Jyotsna, K.; Kumar, P.S.; Madhavi, B. Implementation of 8 Bit Microprocessor Using Current Mode Logic (CML) Approach. In Proceedings of the 2018 3rd International Conference for Convergence in Technology (I2CT), Pune, India, 6–8 April 2018; pp. 1–6. [CrossRef]
27. Palumbo, G.; Pennisi, S. *Feedback Amplifiers: Theory and Design*; Springer: Berlin/Heisenberg, Germany, 2002.

28. Maloberti, F. *Analog Design for CMOS VLSI Systems*; Springer: Berlin/Heisenberg, Germany, 2006; Volume 646. [CrossRef]
29. Afacan, E.; Dündar, G. A mixed domain sizing approach for RF circuit synthesis. In Proceedings of the 2016 IEEE 19th International Symposium on Design and Diagnostics of Electronic Circuits & Systems (DDECS), Kosice, Slovakia, 20–22 April 2016; pp. 1–4.
30. Póvoa, R.; Lourenço, R.; Lourenço, N.; Canelas, A.; Martins, R.; Horta, N. LC-VCO automatic synthesis using multi-objective evolutionary techniques. In Proceedings of the 2014 IEEE International Symposium on Circuits and Systems (ISCAS), Victoria, Australia, 1–5 June 2014; pp. 293–296.
31. Passos, F.; Martins, R.; Lourenço, N.; Roca, E.; Povoa, R.; Canelas, A.; Castro-López, R.; Horta, N.; Fernández, F.V. Enhanced systematic design of a voltage controlled oscillator using a two-step optimization methodology. *Integration* **2018**, *63*, 351–361. [CrossRef]
32. Yang, X.S. *Engineering Optimization: An Introduction with Metaheuristic Applications*; John Wiley & Sons: Hoboken, NJ, USA, 2010. [CrossRef]
33. Talbi, E.G. *Metaheuristics: From Design to Implementation*; John Wiley & Sons: Hoboken, NJ, USA, 2009; Volume 74. [CrossRef]
34. Dasgupta, D.; Michalewicz, Z. Evolutionary algorithms—An overview. In *Evolutionary Algorithms in Engineering Applications*; Springer: Berlin/Heisenberg, Germany, 1997; pp. 3–28. [CrossRef]
35. Coello, C.A.C. An introduction to evolutionary algorithms and their applications. In *International Symposium and School on Advancex Distributed Systems*; Springer: Berlin/Heisenberg, Germany, 2005; pp. 425–442. [CrossRef]
36. Woldesenbet, Y.G.; Yen, G.G.; Tessema, B.G. Constraint handling in multiobjective evolutionary optimization. *IEEE Trans. Evol. Comput.* **2009**, *13*, 514–525. [CrossRef]
37. Yu, X.; Gen, M. *Introduction to Evolutionary Algorithms*; Springer: Berlin/Heisenberg, Germany, 2010. [CrossRef]
38. Elhajjami, I.; Benhala, B.; Bouyghf, H. Optimal Design of RF Integrated Inductors via Differential Evolution Algorithm. In Proceedings of the 2020 1st International Conference on Innovative Research in Applied Science, Engineering and Technology (IRASET), Meknes, Morocco, 16–19 April 2020; pp. 1–6. [CrossRef]
39. Li, J.; Zeng, Y.; Wu, H.; Li, R.; Zhang, J.; Tan, H.Z. Performance optimization for LDO regulator based on the differential evolution. In Proceedings of the 2019 IEEE 13th International Conference on ASIC (ASICON), Chongqing, China, 29 October–1 November 2019; pp. 1–4. [CrossRef]
40. Barik, C.K.; Baksi, R.; Shekhar, H.; Kuanr, B.R.; Lata, M. Effect of parameter tuning of differential evolution on PID controller for automatic generation control of a hybrid power system in deregulated environment. In Proceedings of the 2016 International Conference on Circuit, Power and Computing Technologies (ICCPCT), Nagercoil, India, 18–19 March 2016; pp. 1–6. [CrossRef]
41. Chen, P.; Cheng, H.C.; Widodo, A.; Tsai, W.X. A PVT insensitive field programmable gate array time-to-digital converter. In Proceedings of the 2013 IEEE Nordic-Mediterranean Workshop on Time-to-Digital Converters (NoMe TDC), Perugia, Italy, 3 October 2013; pp. 1–4. [CrossRef]

Publisher's Note: MDPI stays neutral with regard to jurisdictional claims in published maps and institutional affiliations.

© 2020 by the authors. Licensee MDPI, Basel, Switzerland. This article is an open access article distributed under the terms and conditions of the Creative Commons Attribution (CC BY) license (http://creativecommons.org/licenses/by/4.0/).

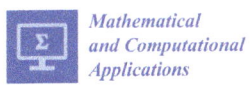

Article

The Pareto Tracer for General Inequality Constrained Multi-Objective Optimization Problems

Fernanda Beltrán [1], Oliver Cuate [1,2] and Oliver Schütze [1,*]

[1] Computer Science Department, Cinvestav-IPN, 07360 Mexico City, Mexico; mbeltran@computacion.cs.cinvestav.mx (F.B.); ocuate@computacion.cs.cinvestav.mx (O.C.)
[2] ESFM, Instituto Politécnico Nacional, 07738 Mexico City, Mexico
* Correspondence: schuetze@cs.cinvestav.mx

Received: 22 October 2020; Accepted: 18 December 2020; Published: 20 December 2020

Abstract: Problems where several incommensurable objectives have to be optimized concurrently arise in many engineering and financial applications. Continuation methods for the treatment of such multi-objective optimization methods (MOPs) are very efficient if all objectives are continuous since in that case one can expect that the solution set forms at least locally a manifold. Recently, the Pareto Tracer (PT) has been proposed, which is such a multi-objective continuation method. While the method works reliably for MOPs with box and equality constraints, no strategy has been proposed yet to adequately treat general inequalities, which we address in this work. We formulate the extension of the PT and present numerical results on some selected benchmark problems. The results indicate that the new method can indeed handle general MOPs, which greatly enhances its applicability.

Keywords: multi-objective optimization; Pareto Tracer; continuation; constraint handling

1. Introduction

In many real-world applications, the problem occurs that several conflicting and incommensurable objectives have to be optimized concurrently. As general example, in the design of basically any product, both cost (to be minimized) and quality (to be maximized) are relevant objectives, among others. Problems of that kind are termed multi-objective optimization problems (MOPs). In the case all of the objectives are continuous and in conflict with each other, it is known that there is not one single solution to be expected (as it is the case for scalar optimization problems, i.e., problems where one objective is considered) but an entire set of solutions. More precisely, one can expect that the solution set—the Pareto set, and, respectively its image, the Pareto front—forms at least locally an object of dimension $k-1$, where k is the number of objectives involved in the problem. Due to this, "curse of dimensionality" problems with more than, e.g., four objectives are also called many objective optimization problems (MaOPs).

In the literature, many different methods for the numerical treatment of MOPs and MaOPs can be found (see also the discussion in the next section). One class of such methods is given by specialized continuation methods that take advantage of the fact that the solution set forms—at least locally and under certain mild assumption on the model as discussed in [1]—a manifold. Continuation methods start with one (approximate) solution of the problem and perform a movement along the Pareto set/front of the given M(a)OP via considering the underdetermined system of equations that is developed out of the Karush–Kuhn–Tucker (KKT) equations of the problem. By construction, continuation methods are of local nature. That is, if the Pareto set consists of different connected components, such methods will have to be fed with several starting points in order to obtain approximations of the entire solution set. On the other hand, continuation methods are probably most effective locally (i.e., within each connected component). Thus far, several multi-objective continuation methods have been proposed. Most of these continuation methods, however, are designed for or restricted to the treatment of bi-objective problems (i.e., MOPs with two objectives). The method of Hillermeier [1] and the Pareto Tracer (PT [2]) have been proposed for general number k of objectives. The method of Hillermeier is applicable to unconstrained and equality constrained MOPs, and the PT in addition to box constrained problems. Thus far, no extensions for these two methods are known for the treatment of general inequalities, which represents a significant shortcoming since such constraints naturally arise in many applications (e.g., [3,4]). In this paper, we extend the PT for the treatment of general inequality constraints. To this end, we utilize and adapt elements from active set methods to decide which of the inequalities have to be treated as equalities at each candidate solution. We demonstrate the strength of the novel algorithm on several benchmark test functions and present comparisons to some other numerical multi-objective solvers. The results indicate that the new method can indeed reliably handle MOPs with general constraints.

The remainder of this paper is organized as follows. In Section 2, we shortly present the required background for the understanding of this work. In Section 3, we adapt the Pareto Tracer for the treatment of general (equality and inequality) constraints. In Section 4, we present some results of the PT as well as some other multi-objective numerical methods on selected benchmark problems. Finally, we draw our conclusions in Section 5 and give possible paths for future research.

2. Background and Related Work

In this section, we briefly state the main concepts and notations that are used for the understanding of this work (for details, we refer to, e.g., [5,6]).

We consider here continuous multi-objective optimization problem (MOPs) that can be defined mathematically as

$$\begin{aligned} \min_{x} \quad & F(x), \\ \text{s.t.} \quad & h_i(x) = 0, \quad i = 1, \ldots, p, \\ & g_i(x) \leq 0, \quad i = 1, \ldots, m, \end{aligned} \quad (1)$$

where $F : Q \subset \mathbb{R}^n \to \mathbb{R}^k$, $F(x) = (f_1(x), \ldots, f_k(x))^T$ is the map of the k individual objectives $f_i : Q \subset \mathbb{R}^n \to \mathbb{R}$. We assume that all objectives and constraint functions are twice continuously differentiable. The domain Q of the functions is defined by the equality and inequality constraints of (1):

$$Q := \{x \in \mathbb{R}^n : h_i(x) = 0, \ i = 1, \ldots, p \text{ and } g_i(x) \leq 0, \ i = 1, \ldots, m\}. \quad (2)$$

If a point $x \in \mathbb{R}^n$ satisfies all constraints of (1), i.e., if $x \in Q$, we call this point feasible. Points $x \notin Q$ are called infeasible. If $k = 2$ objectives are considered, the problem is also termed a bi-objective optimization problem (BOP).

We say that a point $x \in Q$ dominates a point $y \in Q$ (in short: $x \prec y$) if $f_i(x) \leq f_i(y)$ for all $i = 1, \ldots, k$, and there exists an index j such that $f_j(x) < f_j(y)$. A point x^* is called Pareto optimal or simply optimal if there does not exist a vector $y \in Q$ that dominates x^*. A point $x^* \in Q$ is called locally optimal if there does not exist a vector $y \in Q \cap N(x^*)$ that dominates x^*, where $N(x^*)$ is a neighborhood of x^*. The set P_Q of all Pareto optimal solutions is called the Pareto set, and its image $F(P_Q)$ the Pareto front. In [1], it has been shown that one can expect that both Pareto set and front typically form $(k-1)$-dimensional objects under certain (mild) conditions on the problem.

If all objectives and constraint functions are differentiable, local optimal solutions can be characterized by the Karush–Kuhn–Tucker (KKT) equations [7,8]:

Theorem 1. *Suppose that x^* is locally optimal with respect to* (1). *Then, there exist Lagrange multipliers $\alpha \in \mathbb{R}^k$, $\lambda \in \mathbb{R}^p$ and $\gamma \in \mathbb{R}^m$ such that the following conditions are satisfied*

$$\sum_{i=1}^{k} \alpha_i \nabla f_i(x^*) + \sum_{i=1}^{p} \lambda_i \nabla h_i(x^*) + \sum_{i=1}^{m} \gamma_i g_i(x^*) = 0 \tag{3a}$$

$$h_i(x^*) = 0, \quad i = 1 \ldots p, \tag{3b}$$

$$g_i(x^*) \leq 0, \quad i = 1 \ldots m, \tag{3c}$$

$$\alpha_i \geq 0, \quad i = 1 \ldots k, \tag{3d}$$

$$\sum_{i=1}^{k} \alpha_i = 1, \tag{3e}$$

$$\gamma_i \geq 0, \quad i = 1 \ldots m, \tag{3f}$$

$$\gamma_i g_i(x^*) = 0, \quad i = 1 \ldots m. \tag{3g}$$

Multi-objective optimization is an active field of research, and thus far many numerical methods have been proposed for the treatment of such problems. There exist for instance many methods that are designed to compute single solutions such as the weighted sum method [9], the ϵ-constraint method [5,10], the weighted metric and weighted Tchebycheff method [5,11,12], as well as reference point problems [13–15]. All of these methods transform the given MOP into a scalar optimization problem (SOP) that can to a certain extent to include users' preferences. These methods can either be used as standalone algorithm (i.e., for the computation of single solutions) or be used to obtain a finite size approximation of the entire Pareto set/front of the given MOP via utilizing a clever sequence of these SOPs [5,16–19].

Further, there exist set oriented methods such as cell mapping techniques [20–23]), subdivision techniques [24–27], and multi-objective evolutionary algorithms (MOEAs, e.g., [3,28–34]). All of these methods manipulate an entire set of candidate solutions in each iteration and hence yield a finite size approximation of the solution set in one run of the algorithm. Hybridizations of such techniques with mathematical programming techniques can be found in [31,35–41].

Finally, a third class of numerical solvers for MOPs is given by specialized continuation methods that take advantage of the fact that the Pareto set/front of a given problem forms at least locally a manifold of a certain dimension. Methods of this kind start with a given (approximate) solution and perform a movement along the Pareto set/front of the problem. The first such method is proposed in [1], which can be applied to unconstrained and equality constrained MOPs of any number k of objectives, while no strategies are reported on how to treat inequalities. ParCont [42,43] is a rigorous predictor–corrector method that is based on interval analysis and parallelotope domains. The method can deal with equality and inequality constraints, but it is restricted to bi-objective problems. This restriction also holds for the method presented in [44], which has been designed to provide an equispaced approximation of the Pareto front. The Zigzag method [45–47] obtains Pareto front approximations via alternating optimizing one of the objectives. This approach is also limited to the treatment of bi-objective problems.

In [48], a continuation method is presented that is applicable to box-constrained BOPs. In [49], a variant of the method of Hillermeier is presented that is designed for the treatment of high-dimensional problems.

Recently, the Pareto Tracer (PT) was proposed by Martin and Schütze [2]. Similar to the method of Hillermeier, PT addresses the underdetermined nonlinear system of equations that is induced by the KKT equations. However, unlike the method of Hillermeier, the PT aims to separate the decision variables from the associated weight (or Lagrange) vectors whenever possible, leading to significant changes. The latter is due to the fact that the nonlinearity of the equation system can be significantly higher in the compound space compared to the corresponding system that is only defined in decision variable space. As a by-product, the chosen approach allows to compute the tangent space of both

Pareto set and front at every given regular point x. In [50], elements of the PT are used to treat many objective optimization problems (i.e., MOPs with more than, e.g., five objectives). Thus far, PT is only applicable to box and equality constrained problems which limits its application. In the following, we propose and discuss an extension of this method to adequately treat general MOPs, i.e., MOPs that in particular contain general inequalities.

3. Adapting the Pareto Tracer for General Inequality Constrained MOPs

In this section, we adapt the PT so that is can handle general inequality constraints. The core is the predictor–corrector step that generates from a given candidate solution x_i the following candidate x_{i+1} that satisfies the KKT conditions, and so that $F(x_{i+1}) - F(x_i)$ defines a pre-described movement in objective space along the set of KKT points.

Assume we are given a MOP of form (1) and a feasible point x_0 that satisfies the KKT conditions (3), where $\alpha_i > 0, i = 1, \ldots, k$. Let $\epsilon > 0$ and define by

$$I_p(\epsilon) := \{j \in \{1, \ldots, m\} \ : \ g_j(x_0) \geq -\epsilon\} \tag{4}$$

the set of indices corresponding to the nearly active inequalities at x_0. If $I_p(\epsilon) = \{j_1, \ldots, j_s\}, s \leq m$, define

$$G_\epsilon := \begin{pmatrix} \nabla g_{j_1}(x_0)^T \\ \vdots \\ \nabla g_{j_s}(x_0)^T \end{pmatrix} \in \mathbb{R}^{s \times n}. \tag{5}$$

Further, let

$$J := \begin{pmatrix} \nabla f_1(x)^T \\ \vdots \\ \nabla f_k(x)^T \end{pmatrix} \in \mathbb{R}^{k \times n}$$

$$H := \begin{pmatrix} \nabla h_1(x_0)^T \\ \vdots \\ \nabla h_p(x_0)^T \end{pmatrix} \in \mathbb{R}^{p \times n}, \tag{6}$$

and $\alpha \in \mathbb{R}^n$, $\lambda \in \mathbb{R}^p$, and $\gamma \in \mathbb{R}^s$ be the solution of

$$\min_{\tilde\alpha, \tilde\lambda, \tilde\gamma} \left\{ \left\| J^T \tilde\alpha + H^T \tilde\lambda + G_\epsilon^T \tilde\gamma \right\|_2^2 \ : \ \tilde\alpha_i \geq 0, i = 1, \ldots, k, \sum_{i=1}^k \tilde\alpha_i = 1 \right\}. \tag{7}$$

Note that (7) yields the Lagrange multipliers at x_0 for $\epsilon = 0$ if x_0 is a KKT point and if all active inequalities are regarded as equalities. Using α, λ and γ, define the matrix

$$W_{\alpha, \beta, \gamma} := \sum_{i=1}^k \alpha_i \nabla^2 f_i(x) + \sum_{i=1}^p \lambda_i \nabla^2 h_i(x) + \sum_{i=1}^s \gamma_i \nabla^2 g_{j_i}(x) \in \mathbb{R}^{n \times n}. \tag{8}$$

To compute a predictor direction $\nu_\mu \in \mathbb{R}^n$, we solve the the system

$$\begin{pmatrix} W_{\alpha, \lambda, \gamma} & H^T & G_\epsilon^T \\ H & 0 & 0 \\ G_\epsilon & 0 & 0 \end{pmatrix} \begin{pmatrix} \nu_\mu \\ \zeta \\ \sigma \end{pmatrix} = \begin{pmatrix} -J^T \mu \\ 0 \\ 0 \end{pmatrix}. \tag{9}$$

Note that system (9) depends on $\mu \in \mathbb{R}^k$. Before we specify this vector, we first simplify (9). Denote by

$$A := \begin{pmatrix} H \\ G_\epsilon \end{pmatrix} \in \mathbb{R}^{(p+s)\times n}, \quad \xi := \begin{pmatrix} \zeta \\ \sigma \end{pmatrix} \in \mathbb{R}^{p+s}, \qquad (10)$$

then (9) is equivalent to

$$\begin{pmatrix} W_{\alpha,\lambda,\gamma} & A^T \\ A & 0 \end{pmatrix} \begin{pmatrix} \nu_\mu \\ \xi \end{pmatrix} = \begin{pmatrix} -J^T \mu \\ 0 \end{pmatrix}. \qquad (11)$$

Let $d \in \mathbb{R}^k$. It is straightforward to show that for a vector ν_{μ_d} that solves (11), where $\mu_d \in \mathbb{R}^k$ is chosen such that

$$\begin{pmatrix} -JW_{\alpha,\lambda,\gamma}^{-1} J^T \\ 1 \ldots 1 \end{pmatrix} \mu_d = \begin{pmatrix} d \\ 0 \end{pmatrix}, \qquad (12)$$

it holds

$$J\nu_{\mu_d} = d. \qquad (13)$$

That is, (infinitesimal) small steps from x_0 into direction ν_{μ_d} (in decision variable space) will lead to a movement from $F(x_0)$ into direction d (in objective space). It remains to select a suitable choice for d. Since α is orthogonal to the linearized Pareto front at $F(x_0)$ [1], a suggesting choice is hence by (13) to take d orthogonal to α. For this, let

$$\alpha = QR = (q_1, q_2, \ldots, q_k) R, \qquad (14)$$

where $Q \in \mathbb{R}^{k \times k}$ is orthogonal and $R \in \mathbb{R}^{k \times 1}$, be a QR-factorization of α. Then, any vector

$$d \in \text{span}\{q_2, \ldots, q_k\} \qquad (15)$$

can be chosen so that a movement in direction ν_{μ_d} (in decision variable space) leads to a movement from $F(x_0)$ along the Pareto front. Note that the second equation in (12) reads as $\sum_{i=1}^k \mu_i = 0$. Hence, for the special case of a bi-objective optimization problem (i.e., $k = 2$), there are—after normalization—only two choices for μ:

$$\mu^{(1)} = \begin{pmatrix} -1 \\ 1 \end{pmatrix}, \quad \text{and} \quad \mu^{(2)} = \begin{pmatrix} 1 \\ -1 \end{pmatrix}. \qquad (16)$$

Analog to Martin and Schütze [2], one can show that $\mu^{(1)}$ corresponds to a "right down" movement along the Pareto front while $\mu^{(2)}$ corresponds to a "left up" movement along the Pareto front.

After selecting the predictor direction ν_μ, the question is how far to step in this direction. Here, we follow the suggestion made by Hillermeier [1] and use the step size

$$t = \frac{\tau}{\|J\nu_\mu\|_2} \qquad (17)$$

for a (small) value $\tau > 0$ so that

$$\|F(x_0 + t\nu_\mu) - F(x_0)\|_2 \approx \tau. \qquad (18)$$

For the computations presented below, we make the following modifications: instead of $W_{\alpha,\beta,\gamma}$, we use the matrix

$$W_\alpha := \sum_{i=1}^k \alpha_i \nabla^2 f_i(x) \in \mathbb{R}^{n \times n}. \qquad (19)$$

More precisely, for the computation of ν_μ, we use the system

$$\begin{pmatrix} W_\alpha & A^T \\ A & 0 \end{pmatrix} \begin{pmatrix} \nu_\mu \\ \xi \end{pmatrix} = \begin{pmatrix} -J^T \mu \\ 0 \end{pmatrix} \qquad (20)$$

and to obtain μ_d we solve

$$\begin{pmatrix} -JW_\alpha^{-1}J^T \\ 1\ldots 1 \end{pmatrix} \mu_d = \begin{pmatrix} d \\ 0 \end{pmatrix}. \tag{21}$$

We have observed similar performance for both approaches, while the usage of W_α compared to $W_{\alpha,\beta,\gamma}$ comes with the advantage that no Hessians for any of the constraint functions have to be computed.

Given a predictor point

$$\tilde{x}_1 := x_0 + t v_\mu \tag{22}$$

the task of the upcoming corrector step is to find a KKT point x_1 that is ideally near to $\tilde{x}_1$. For this, we suggest to apply the multi-objective Newton method proposed in [51]. In particular, we first compute the solution $(\tilde{v}_1, \tilde{\delta})$ of the following problem

$$\min_{(v,\delta) \in \mathbb{R}^n \times \mathbb{R}} \delta$$
$$\text{s.t. } \nabla f_i(\tilde{x}_1)^T v + \frac{1}{2} v^T \nabla^2 f_i(\tilde{x}_1) v \le \delta, \quad i = 1, \ldots, k, \tag{23}$$
$$h_i(\tilde{x}_1) + \nabla h_i(\tilde{x}_1)^T v = 0, \quad i = 1, \ldots, p.$$

$\tilde{v}_1$ is indeed the Newton direction for equality constrained MOPs as suggested in [2]. To adequately treat the involved inequalities, however, we propose to use the solution of the following problem:

$$\min_{(v,\delta) \in \mathbb{R}^n \times \mathbb{R}} \delta$$
$$\text{s.t. } \nabla f_i(\tilde{x}_1)^T v + \frac{1}{2} v^T \nabla^2 f_i(\tilde{x}_1) v \le \delta, \quad i = 1, \ldots, k, \tag{24}$$
$$h_i(\tilde{x}_1) + \nabla h_i(\tilde{x}_1)^T v = 0, \quad i = 1, \ldots, p.$$
$$g_i(\tilde{x}_1) + \nabla g_i(\tilde{x}_1)^T v = 0, \quad i \in I_c(\epsilon).$$

Note that problem (24) is identical to problem (23) except that $|I_c(\epsilon)|$ inequalities are treated as equalities at $\tilde{x}_1$. In particular, we propose to add an index i to $I_c(\epsilon)$ if

(a) $g_i(\tilde{x}_1) > \epsilon$, i.e., if $\tilde{x}_1$ significantly violates the constraint g_i; or
(b) $g_i(\tilde{x}_1) \in (-\epsilon, \epsilon)$ and $\nabla g(\tilde{x}_1)^T \tilde{v}_1 > 0$, i.e., if x_i is either active but g_i nearly active at x_i or if x_i already slightly violates g_i and a step into direction $\tilde{v}_1$ would lead to (further) violation of this constraint, indicated by $\nabla g(\tilde{x}_1)^T \tilde{v}_1 > 0$.

Algorithm 1 shows the pseudo code to build the index set $I_c(\epsilon)$ at a predictor point $\tilde{x}_i$. Given the Newton direction, the Newton step can then be performed via using the Armijo rule described in [51], as done in our computations. The set $I_c(\epsilon)$ is only computed once, it and remains fixed during the Newton iteration in the corrector step.

Algorithm 2 shows the pseudo code of one predictor–corrector step of the PT for general (equality and inequality constrained) MOPs. For bi-objective problems, μ can be chosen as in (16) leading either to a "left up" or "right down" movement, as discussed above. The algorithm has to be stopped if α is either close enough to $(1,0)^T$ or $(0,1)^T$, depending of course on the chosen search direction. For $k > 2$, one can use the box partition in objective space as described in [2] in order to mark the regions of the Pareto front that have already been "covered" during the run of the algorithm.

For the realization of the predictor–corrector step several linear systems of equations have to be solved, the largest one being (20). The cost is hence $O((n+p+s)^3)$ in terms of flops and $O((n+p+s)^2)$ in terms of storage. Further, for the corrector step the SOP (7) has to be solved that contains $k+p+s$ decision variables. For the computation of the Newton direction, the SOPs (23) and (24) have to be solved for the first Newton iteration that contains both $n+1$ decision variables. For further Newton iterations, only SOP (24) has to be solved since the index set $I_c(\epsilon)$ remains fixed within a corrector step.

Finally, note that, if the method is realized as described above, the Hessians of all individual objectives have to be computed at each candidate solution (including at each Newton iteration). Using ideas from quasi-Newton methods, one can approximate the Hessians so that only gradient information is needed at each candidate solution, as described in [2].

Algorithm 1 Build $I_c(\epsilon)$

Require: $\tilde{x}_i$: predictor, $\tilde{v}_i$: corrector direction for (23), $\epsilon > 0$: tolerance
Ensure: $I_c(\epsilon)$: index set
1: $I := \emptyset$
2: **for** $i = 1, \ldots, m$ **do**
3:     **if** $g_i(\tilde{x}_i) > \epsilon$ **then**
4:         $I := I \cup i$
5:     **else if** $g_i(\tilde{x}_i) \in (-\epsilon, \epsilon) \land \nabla g(\tilde{x}_i)^T \tilde{v}_i > 0$ **then**
6:         $I := I \cup i$
7:     **end if**
8: **end for**
9: **Return** $I_c(\epsilon)$

Algorithm 2 Predictor–corrector step of the Pareto Tracer for general MOPs

---

Require: x_i: current candidate solution, $\tau > 0$: desired distance in objective space, $\epsilon > 0$: tolerance
Ensure: x_{i+1}: new candidate solution
1: Compute $\alpha^{(i)} \in \mathbb{R}^k$ via solving (7)
2: Compute $W_\alpha^{(i)}$ as in (19)
3: Compute A as in (10)
4: Select $\mu^{(i)}$ as in (16) or via (15) and (21)
5: Compute $v_\mu^{(i)}$ via solving (20)
6: $t^{(i)} := \dfrac{\tau}{\|Jv_\mu^{(i)}\|_2}$
7: $\tilde{x}_{i+1} := x_i + t^{(i)} v_\mu^{(i)}$
8: Compute x_{i+1} via a Newton method starting at $\tilde{x}_{i+1}$. For the Newton direction use the solution of (24).
9: **Return** x_{i+1}

As a demonstration example, we consider the problem

$$\min \begin{cases} f_1(x) = (x_1 + 3)^2 + (x_2 - 2)^2, \\ f_2(x) = x_1^2 + (x_2 + 3)^2, \end{cases}$$
$$\text{s.t.} \quad g_1(x) = (x_1 + 1)^2 + x_2^2 \leq 2^2, \quad (25)$$
$$g_2(x) = (x_1 + 2)^2 + (x_2 + 2)^2 \leq 2^2.$$

Figure 1a shows the Pareto set of the above problem where the two inequalities have been left out (i.e., the line segment connecting $(-3, 2)^T$ and $(0, -3)^T$), the sets $g_i(x) = 0, i = 1, 2$, as well as the Pareto set of this problem which is indeed the result of the PT. As starting point, we chose a point which significantly violates both constraints (and, hence, $|I_c(\epsilon)| = 2$ for $\epsilon = 1e - 4$). An application of the above-described Newton method leads to the point on the Pareto set with the smallest x_1-value, which is in fact the initial point for the PT. During the run of PT, first only g_2 is "active" in the corrector step (i.e., $I_c(\epsilon) = \{2\}$), later none of the constraints (in the intersection of the Pareto fronts of the constrained and the unconstrained MOP), and finally only g_1.

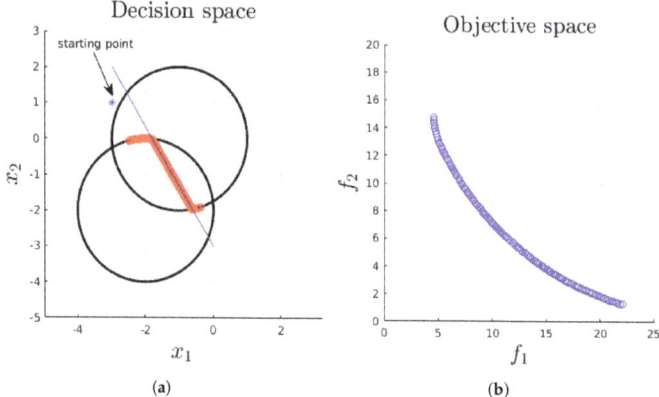

Figure 1. Numerical result of the PT for MOP (25).

4. Numerical Results

In this section, we further demonstrate the behavior of the PT on five benchmark problems that contain inequality constraints. For all problems, we used the quasi-Newton variant of PT that only required function and Jacobian information (and no Hessians). To compare the results, we also show the respective results obtained by the normal boundary intersection (NBI, [16]), the ϵ-constraint method [5], and the multi-objective evolutionary algorithm NSGA-II. For NBI and the ϵ-constraint method, we used the code that is available at [52], and for NSGA-II the implementation of PlatEMO [53]. Regrettably, no comparison to a multi-objective continuation method can be presented since none of the respective codes are publicly available. For a comparison of the PT and the method of Hillermeier on box and equality constrained MOPs, we refer to [2]. We chose also to include a comparison to the famous NSGA-II since it is widely used and state-of-the-art for two- and three-objective problems as we consider here. We stress that the comparisons only show (on the first four test problems) that PT outperforms NSGA-II on these particular cases where the Pareto front consists of one connected component. For highly multi-modal functions where the Pareto set/front falls into several connected components, NSGA-II will certainly outperform the (standalone) PT. A fair comparison can only be obtained when integrating PT into a global heuristic (as, e.g., done in [41]). This is certainly an interesting task, however, beyond the scope of this work.

To compare the results, we compare the total number of function evaluations used for each algorithm on each problem. For this, each Jacobian call is counted as four function calls assuming that the derivative is obtained via automatic differentiation [54]. To measure the quality of the approximations, we used the averaged Hausdorff distance Δ_2 [55–57]. Since NSGA-II has stochastic components, we applied this algorithm for each problem 10 times and present the median result (measured by Δ_2).

4.1. Binh and Korn

Our first test example is a modification of the box-constrained BOP from Binh and Korn [58], where we add two inequality constraints as follows:

$$\min \begin{cases} f_1(x) = 4x_1^2 + 4x_2^2, \\ f_2(x) = (x_1 - 5)^2 + (x_2 - 5)^2, \end{cases}$$
$$\text{s.t.} \quad (x_1 - 2)^2 + (x_2 - 1)^2 \leq 2.3^2,$$
$$(x_1 - 3)^2 + (x_2 - 3)^2 \geq 1.5^2,$$
$$0 \leq x_1 \leq 5,$$
$$0 \leq x_2 \leq 3.$$
(26)

Table 1 shows the design parameters that have been used by NSGA-II for this problem, Table 2 shows the computational efforts and the obtained approximation quality for each algorithm, and Figures 2 and 3 show the obtained Pareto set and front approximations, respectively. For PT, we chose $\tau = 0.6$ leading to 52 solutions along the Pareto set/front in 4.48 s (the computations have been done on a Ubuntu 20.04.1 LTS system with an Intel Core i7-8550U 1.80 GHz x 8 CPU and 12 GB of RAM). We then applied NBI and the ϵ-constraint model using this number of sub-problems. For NSGA-II, we took the population size 100, which is a standard value for this algorithm. The results show nearly perfect Pareto front approximations (at least from the practical point of view) for all algorithms, which is also reflected by the low Δ_2 values that are very close to the optimal value of 0.6 (at least for PT, defined by τ). In terms of function evaluations, PT clearly wins over NBI and the ϵ-constraint method. A comparison to NSGA-II is not possible due to the choice of the population size.

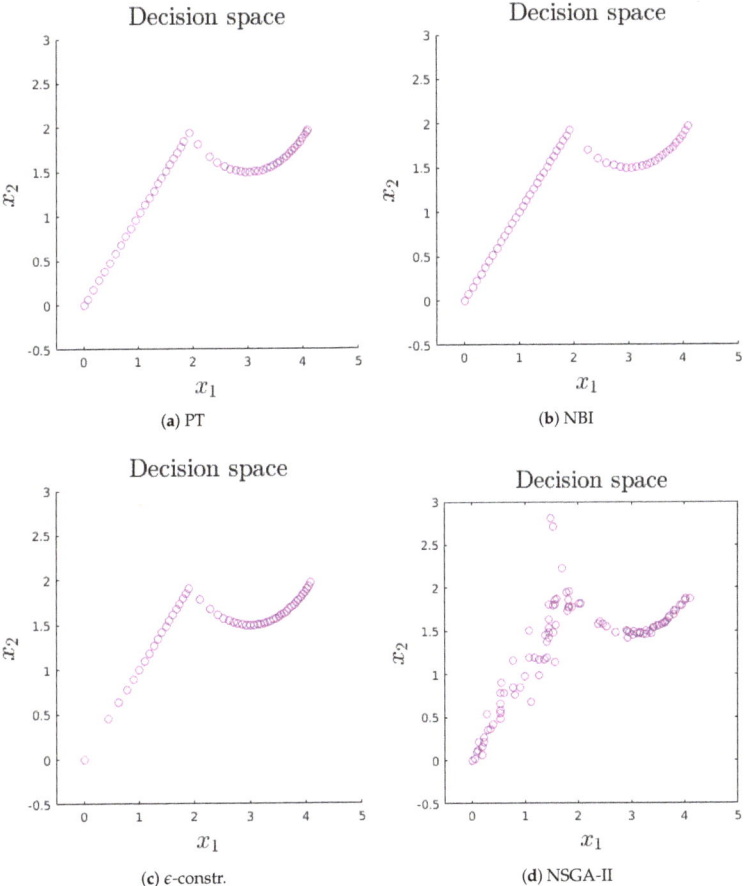

Figure 2. Results in decision space for MOP (26).

Table 1. Parameters used by NSGA-II for MOP (26).

Population Size	100
Number of generations	20
Probability of crossover	0.9
Probability of mutation	0.5

Table 2. Computational efforts and approximation quality of the algorithms for MOP (26).

	PT	NBI	ϵ-Constr.	NSGA-II
Solutions	52	52	52	100
Function Evaluations	151	427	336	2000
Jacobian Evaluations	133	425	336	-
Hessian Evaluations	-	373	284	-
Total of Evaluations	683	8095	6224	2000
Δ_2	0.6050	0.6025	0.9272	0.5626

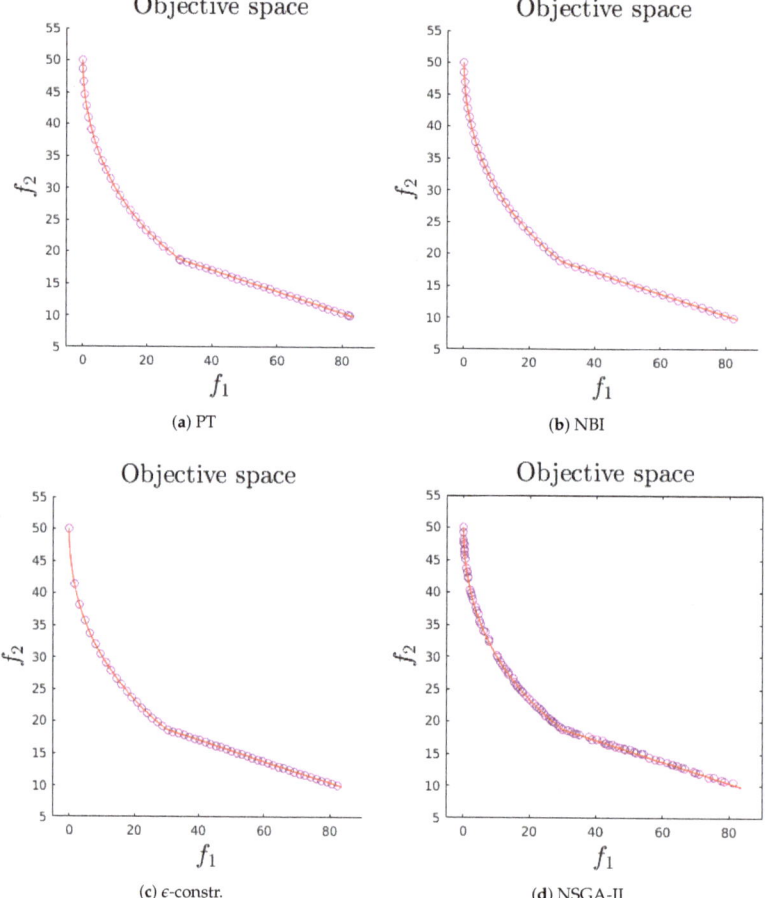

Figure 3. Results in objective space for MOP (26).

4.2. Chakong and Haimes

Next, we consider the bi-objective problem of Chakong and Haimes [59], which contains next to the box constraints one linear and one nonlinear inequality.

$$\min \begin{cases} f_1(x) = 2 + (x_1 - 2)^2 + (x_2 - 1)^2, \\ f_2(x) = 9x_1 - (x_2 - 1)^2, \end{cases}$$
$$\text{s.t.} \quad x_1^2 + x_2^2 \leq 225,$$
$$x_1 - 3x_2 + 10 \leq 0,$$
$$\text{with} \quad -20 \leq x_1, x_2 \leq 20. \tag{27}$$

Table 3 shows the parameter values used for the application of NSGA-II, Table 4 the computational efforts and the approximation qualities, and Figures 4 and 5 the obtained approximations. We used $\tau = 1$ for PT, and proceeded as for the previous example for the other methods. The results are also similar to the previous example: all methods are capable of detecting a nearly perfect Pareto front approximation, and the overall cost is significantly less for PT, in 5.96 s.

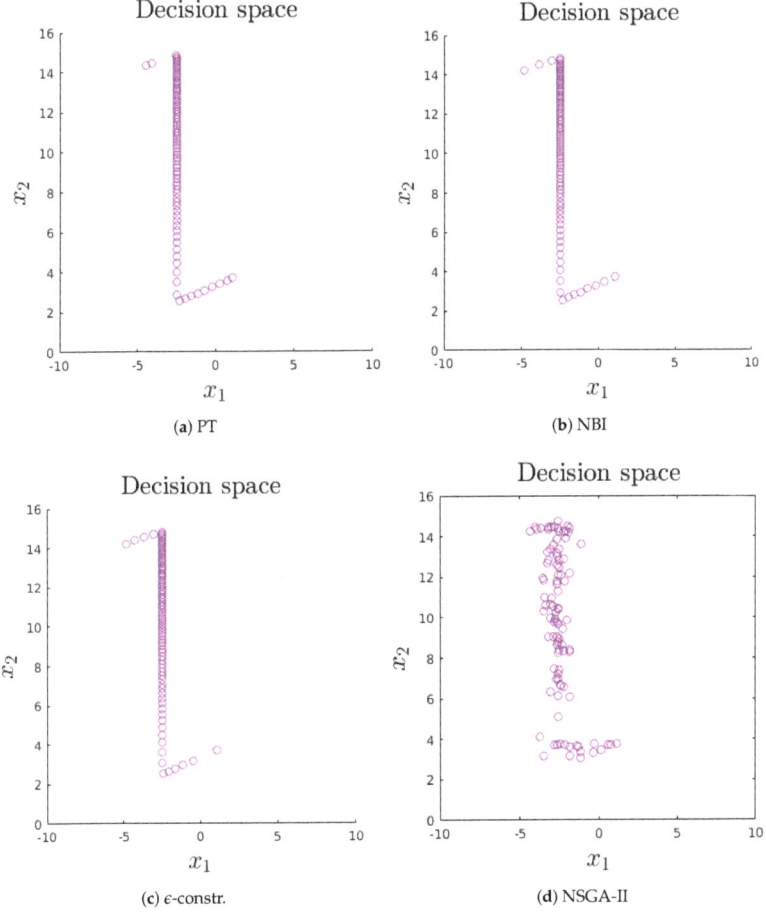

Figure 4. Results in decision space for MOP (27).

Table 3. Parameters used by NSGA-II for problem (27).

Population Size	100
Number of generations	30
Probability of crossover	0.9
probability of mutation	0.5

Table 4. Computational efforts and approximation qualities for problem (27).

	PT	NBI	ϵ-Constr.	NSGA-II
Solutions	80	80	80	100
Function Evaluations	540	678	578	3000
Jacobian Evaluations	499	678	578	-
Hessian Evaluations	-	598	498	-
Total of Evaluations	2536	12,958	10,858	3000
Δ_2	1.1459	1.1457	1.2141	1.1871

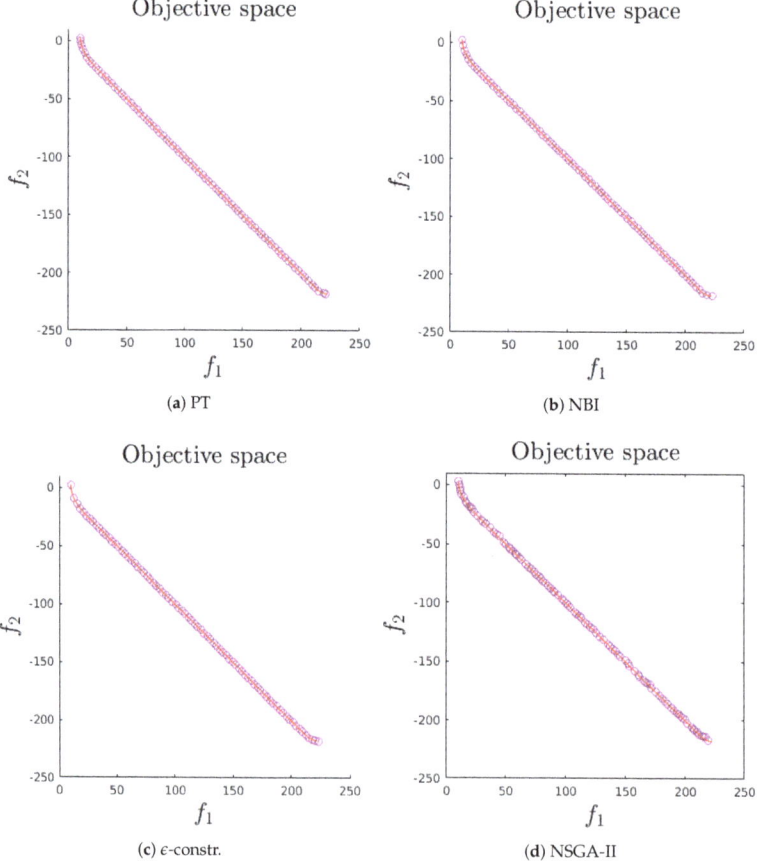

Figure 5. Results in objective space for MOP (27).

4.3. Tamaki

Next, we considered a MOP with three objectives (28):

$$\min \begin{cases} f_1(x) = x_1, \\ f_2(x) = x_2, \\ f_3(x) = x_3, \end{cases}$$
$$\text{s.t.} \quad x_1^2 + x_2^2 + x_3^2 \geq 1,$$
$$0 \leq x_1, x_2, x_3 \leq 4. \tag{28}$$

Both the Pareto set and front for this problem are a part of the unit sphere. Table 5 shows the design parameters for NSGA-II, Table 6 shows the computational effort and the approximation quality for each algorithm, and Figure 6 shows the Pareto front approximations (the respective Pareto set approximations will look identically, albeit in x-space). For this problem, $\tau = 0.05$ was used. The implementation of the ϵ-constrained method did not yield a result. On the Tamaki problem, PT performs better than the other algorithms both in approximation quality and in the overall computational cost.

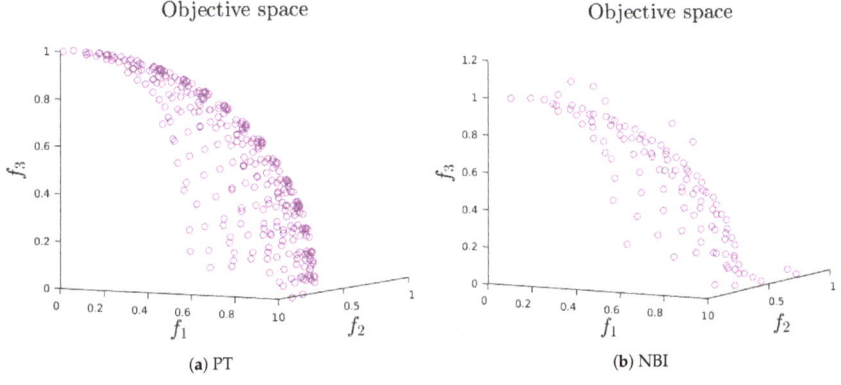

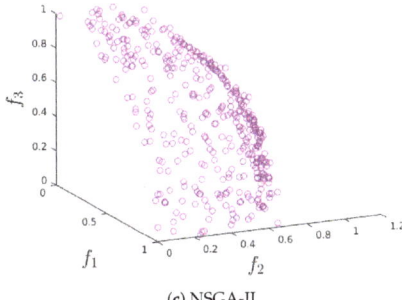

Figure 6. Results in objective space for MOP (28).

Table 5. Parameters used by NSGA-II for MOP (28).

Population Size	300
Number of generations	150
Probability of crossover	0.9
Probability of mutations	0.5

Table 6. Computational efforts and approximation qualities for problem (28).

	PT	NBI	ε-Constr.	NSGA-II
Solutions	305	112	N/A	300
Function Evaluations	2498	3758	N/A	450,000
Jacobian Evaluations	1101	3758	N/A	-
Hessian Evaluations	-	3293	N/A	-
Total of Evaluations	6902	91,236	N/A	450,000
Δ_2	0.0380	0.6353	N/A	0.0390

4.4. BCS

We next considered a second three-objective problem that contains next to one inequality also a linear equality constraint:

$$\min \begin{cases} f_1(x) = (x_1+3)^2 + (x_2+3)^2 + (x_3+3)^2, \\ f_2(x) = (x_1-9)^2 + (x_2+5)^2 + (x_3+5)^2, \\ f_3(x) = (x_1-5)^2 + (x_2-8)^2 + x_3^2, \end{cases} \quad (29)$$

s.t. $x_1 - 2x_2 - 3x_3 = 0$,

$\sin(2x_1) - x_2 \leq 0$.

Table 7 presents the design parameters used by NSGA-II, Table 8 shows the computational effort and the approximation quality for each algorithm, and Figures 7 and 8 present the Pareto front approximation of PT (using $\tau = 2$), which took 16.79 s. For this example, none of the other methods were able to yield feasible solutions, where we counted a solution x to be feasible if $|x_1 - 2x_2 - 3x_3| <$ 1e − 4 and $\sin(2x_1) - x_2 \leq$ 1e − 4.

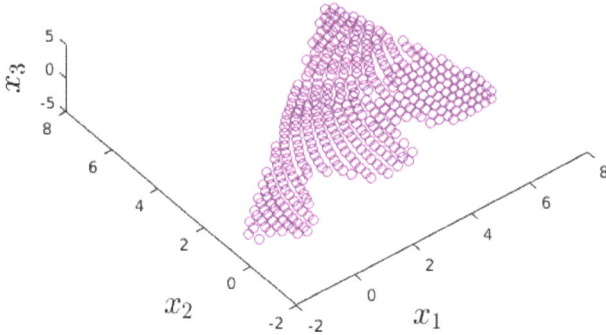

Figure 7. Numerical result of PT in the decision space for MOP (29).

Table 7. Parameters used by NSGA-II for MOP (29).

Population Size	100
Number of generations	500
Probability of crossover	0.9
Probability of mutations	0.5

Table 8. Computation efforts for the proposed test problem (29).

	PT	NBI	ε-Constr.	NSGA-II
Solutions	378	0	N/A	4
Function Evaluations	1923	2290	N/A	50,000
Jacobian Evaluations	756	1641	N/A	-
Hessian Evaluations	-	1431	N/A	-
Total of Evaluations	4947	40,336	N/A	50,000
Δ_2	2.0658	-	N/A	61.7685

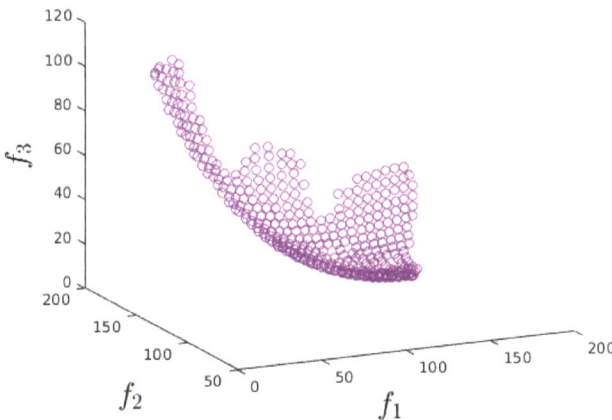

Figure 8. Numerical result of PT in the objective space for MOP (29).

4.5. Osykzka and Kundu

As last example, we considered the bi-objective problem of Osykzka and Kundu [60], which has six decision variables and contains six inequality constraints in addition to the box constraints:

$$\min \begin{cases} f_1(x) = -25(x_1-2)^2 - (x_2-2)^2 - (x_3-1)^2 - (x_4-4)^2 - (x_5-1)^2 \\ f_2(x) = \sum_{i=1}^{6} x_i^2 \end{cases}$$

s.t. $x_1 + x_2 - 2 \geq 0$

$6 - x_1 - x_2 \geq 0$

$2 - x_2 + x_1 \geq 0$

$2 - x_1 + 3x_2 \geq 0$

$4 - (x_3 - 3)^2 - x_4 \geq 0$

$(x_5 - 3)^2 + x_6 - 4 \geq 0$

$0 \leq x_1, x_2, x_6 \leq 10$

$1 \leq x_3, x_5 \leq 5$

$0 \leq x_4 \leq 6$

(30)

While the Pareto front of this problem is connected, its Pareto set consists of three different connected components. Hence, PT is not able to compute an approximation of the entire Pareto front with only one starting point. Figure 9a shows the result of PE for $\tau = 2$ using the three starting points

$$x_{0,1} = (0.60, 1.50, 1.0, 0.00, 1.00, 0.04)^T,$$
$$x_{0,2} = (0.00, 2.00, 2.20, 0.00, 1.00, 0.00)^T, \quad (31)$$
$$x_{0,3} = (5.00, 1.00, 5.00, 0.00, 1.00, 0.01)^T.$$

The computational time to obtain this result was 12.98 s. Figure 9b shows a numerical result of NSGA-II using the design parameters shown in Table 9. The obtained solutions "under" the Pareto front can be explained by the tolerance of 1×10^{-4} that was used to measure feasibility (while 1×10^{-8} was used for PT). Table 10 shows the computational effort for both methods. Needless to say, this represents by no means a comparison of the two methods. Instead, this should be rather seen as a motivation to hybridize PT with a global search strategy in order to obtain a fast and reliable multi-objective solver, which we leave for future studies.

Table 9. Parameters used by NSGA-II for MOP (30).

Population Size	435
Number of generations	50
Probability of crossover	0.9
Probability of mutations	0.5

Table 10. Computational efforts and approximation qualities for problem (30).

	PT	NSGA-II
Solutions	435	428
Function Evaluations	2051	20,000
Jacobian Evaluations	850	-
Hessian Evaluations	-	-
Total of Evaluations	5451	20,000
Δ_2	1.801	2.4819

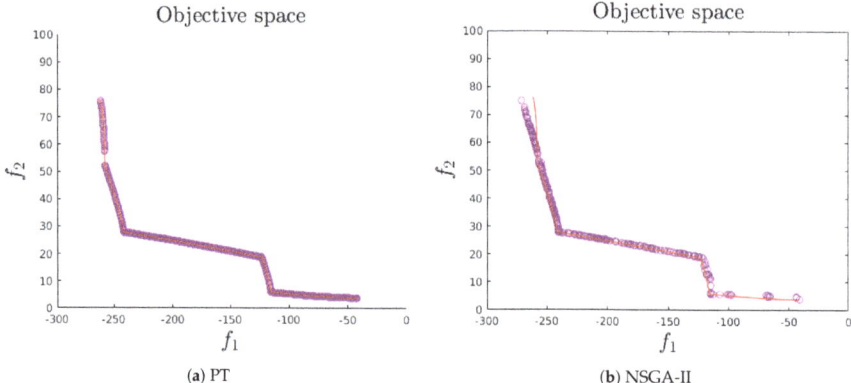

Figure 9. Results in objective space for MOP (30).

5. Conclusions and Future Work

In this paper, we extend the multi-objective continuation method Pareto Tracer (PT) for the treatment of general inequality constraints. To this end, the predictor–corrector step is modified as follows: in the predictor, all nearly active inequalities are treated as equalities. In the following corrector step, the main challenge is to identify the inequalities for which the predictor solution is either nearly active or slightly violates the constraint that has to be considered, namely the equality constraint in the Newton method, and this is done in a bootstrap manner. We formulate the resulting algorithm and show some numerical results on several benchmark problems, indicating that it can reliably handle inequality (and equality) constrained MOPs. We further present comparisons to some other numerical methods. The results show that the extended PT can indeed reliably handle general MOPs (and in particular general inequalities). However, the method is—by construction—of local nature and restricted to the connected component of the solution set for which one initial solution is available. One interesting task is certainly to hybridize PT with a global solver such as a multi-objective evolutionary algorithm and to compare the resulting hybrid against other methods with respect to their ability to compute the entire global Pareto set/front of a given MOP. This is beyond the scope of this work and has been left for future work.

Author Contributions: Conceptualization and formal analysis, O.S.; software, F.B. and O.C.; and writing and editing: F.B., O.C., and O.S. All authors have read and agreed to the published version of the manuscript.

Funding: The authors acknowledge support from Conacyt project No. 285599 and SEP Cinvestav project No. 231.

Conflicts of Interest: The authors declare no conflict of interest.

References

1. Hillermeier, C. *Nonlinear Multiobjective Optimization: A Generalized Homotopy Approach*; Springer: Basel, Switzerland, 2001.
2. Martín, A.; Schütze, O. Pareto Tracer: A predictor–corrector method for multi-objective optimization problems. *Eng. Optim.* **2018**, *50*, 516–536. [CrossRef]
3. Deb, K. *Multi-Objective Optimization Using Evolutionary Algorithms*; John Wiley & Sons: Chichester, UK, 2001.
4. Peitz, S.; Dellnitz, M. A Survey of Recent Trends in Multiobjective Optimal Control—Surrogate Models, Feedback Control and Objective Reduction. *Math. Comput. Appl.* **2018**, *23*, 30. [CrossRef]
5. Miettinen, K. *Nonlinear Multiobjective Optimization*; Springer Science & Business Media: Boston, MA, USA, 2012.
6. Ehrgott, M. *Multicriteria Optimization*; Springer: Berlin/Heidelberg, Germany, 2005.
7. Karush, W. Minima of Functions of Several Variables with Inequalities as Side Constraints. Master's Thesis, Department of Mathematics, University of Chicago, Chicago, IL, USA, 1939.
8. Kuhn, H.W.; Tucker, A.W. Nonlinear programming. In *Proceedings of the Second Berkeley Symposium on Mathematical Statistics and Probability, Berkeley, CA, USA, 31 July–12 August 1950*; University of California Press: Berkeley, CA, USA, 1951; pp. 481–492.
9. Gass, S.; Saaty, T. The computational algorithm for the parametric objective function. *Nav. Res. Logist. Q.* **1955**, *2*, 39–45. [CrossRef]
10. Mavrotas, G. Effective implementation of the ϵ-constraint method in Multi-Objective Mathematical Programming problems. *Appl. Math. Comput.* **2009**, *213*, 455–465.
11. Steuer, R.E.; Choo, E.U. An Interactive Weighted Tchebycheff Prodecure for Multiple Objective Progamming. *Math. Program.* **1983**, *26*, 326–344. [CrossRef]
12. Kim, J.; Kim, S.K. A CHIM-based interactive Tchebycheff procedure for multiple objective decision making. *Comput. Oper. Res.* **2006**, *33*, 1557–1574. [CrossRef]
13. Wierzbicki, A.P. A mathematical basis for satisficing decision making. *Math. Model.* **1982**, *3*, 391–405. [CrossRef]
14. Bogetoft, P.; Hallefjord, A.; Kok, M. On the convergence of reference point methods in multiobjective programming. *Eur. J. Oper. Res.* **1988**, *34*, 56–68. [CrossRef]
15. Hernández Mejá, J.A.; Schütze, O.; Cuate, O.; Lara, A.; Deb, K. RDS-NSGA-II: A Memetic Algorithm for Reference Point Based Multi-objective Optimization. *Eng. Optim.* **2017**, *49*, 828–845. [CrossRef]
16. Das, I.; Dennis, J.E. Normal-boundary intersection: A new method for generating the Pareto surface in nonlinear multicriteria optimization problems. *SIAM J. Optim.* **1998**, *8*, 631–657. [CrossRef]

17. Klamroth, K.; Tind, J.; Wiecek, M. Unbiased Approximation in Multicriteria Optimization. *Math. Methods Oper. Res.* **2002**, *56*, 413–437. [CrossRef]
18. Fliege, J. Gap-free computation of Pareto-points by quadratic scalarizations. *Math. Methods Oper. Res.* **2004**, *59*, 69–89. [CrossRef]
19. Eichfelder, G. *Adaptive Scalarization Methods in Multiobjective Optimization*; Springer: Berlin/Heidelberg, Germany, 2008.
20. Hernández, C.; Naranjani, Y.; Sardahi, Y.; Liang, W.; Schütze, O.; Sun, J.Q. Simple Cell Mapping Method for Multi-objective Optimal Feedback Control Design. *Int. J. Dyn. Control* **2013**, *1*, 231–238. [CrossRef]
21. Xiong, F.R.; Qin, Z.C.; Xue, Y.; Schütze, O.; Ding, Q.; Sun, J.Q. Multi-objective optimal design of feedback controls for dynamical systems with hybrid simple cell mapping algorithm. *Commun. Nonlinear Sci. Numer. Simul.* **2014**, *19*, 1465–1473. [CrossRef]
22. Fernández, J.; Schütze, O.; Hernández, C.; Sun, J.Q.; Xiong, F.R. Parallel simple cell mapping for multi-objective optimization. *Eng. Optim.* **2016**, *48*, 1845–1868. [CrossRef]
23. Sun, J.Q.; Xiong, F.R.; Schütze, O.; Hernández, C. *Cell Mapping Methods—Algorithmic Approaches and Applications*; Springer: Singapore, 2019.
24. Schütze, O.; Mostaghim, S.; Dellnitz, M.; Teich, J. Covering Pareto Sets by Multilevel Evolutionary Subdivision Techniques. In *Proceedings of the International Conference on Evolutionary Multi-Criterion Optimization (EMO 2003), Faro, Portugal, 8–11 April 2003*; Fonseca, C.M., Fleming, P.J., Zitzler, E., Deb, K., Thiele, L., Eds.; Springer: Berlin/Heidelberg, Germany, 2003; pp. 118–132.
25. Dellnitz, M.; Schütze, O.; Hestermeyer, T. Covering Pareto Sets by Multilevel Subdivision Techniques. *J. Optim. Theory Appl.* **2005**, *124*, 113–155. [CrossRef]
26. Jahn, J. Multiobjective search algorithm with subdivision technique. *Comput. Optim. Appl.* **2006**, *35*, 161–175. [CrossRef]
27. Schütze, O.; Vasile, M.; Junge, O.; Dellnitz, M.; Izzo, D. Designing optimal low thrust gravity assist trajectories using space pruning and a multi-objective approach. *Eng. Optim.* **2009**, *41*, 155–181. [CrossRef]
28. Deb, K.; Pratap, A.; Agarwal, S.; Meyarivan, T. A fast and elitist multiobjective genetic algorithm: NSGA-II. *IEEE Trans. Evol. Comput.* **2002**, *6*, 182–197. [CrossRef]
29. Coello Coello, C.A.; Lamont, G.B.; Van Veldhuizen, D.A. *Evolutionary Algorithms for Solving Multi-Objective Problems*, 2nd ed.; Springer: New York, NY, USA, 2007.
30. Beume, N.; Naujoks, B.; Emmerich, M. SMS-EMOA: Multiobjective selection based on dominated hypervolume. *Eur. J. Oper. Res.* **2007**, *181*, 1653–1669. [CrossRef]
31. Lara, A.; Sanchez, G.; Coello Coello, C.A.; Schütze, O. HCS: A new local search strategy for memetic multiobjective evolutionary algorithms. *IEEE Trans. Evol. Comput.* **2009**, *14*, 112–132. [CrossRef]
32. Zhou, A.; Qu, B.Y.; Li, H.; Zhao, S.Z.; Suganthan, P.N.; Zhang, Q. Multiobjective evolutionary algorithms: A survey of the state of the art. *Swarm Evol. Comput.* **2011**, *1*, 32–49. [CrossRef]
33. Cuate, O.; Schütze, O. Variation Rate to Maintain Diversity in Decision Space within Multi-Objective Evolutionary Algorithms. *Math. Comput. Appl.* **2019**, *24*, 82. [CrossRef]
34. Schütze, O.; Hernández, C. *Archiving Strategies for Evolutionary Multi-objective Optimization Algorithms*; Springer: Cham, Switzerland, 2021.
35. Harada, K.; Sakuma, J.; Kobayashi, S. Local search for multiobjective function optimization: Pareto descent method. In *Proceedings of the 8th Annual Conference on Genetic and Evolutionary Computation, Seattle, WA, USA, 8–12 July 2006*; pp. 659–666.
36. Schütze, O.; Coello, C.A.C.; Mostaghim, S.; Dellnitz, M.; Talbi, E.G. Hybridizing Evolutionary Strategies with Continuation Methods for Solving Multi-objective Problems. *IEEE Trans. Evol. Comput.* **2008**, *19*, 762–769. [CrossRef]
37. Zapotecas Martínez, S.; Coello Coello, C.A. A proposal to hybridize multi-objective evolutionary algorithms with non-gradient mathematical programming techniques. In *Proceedings of the 10th International Conference on Parallel Problem Solving From Nature (PPSN '08), Dortmund, Germany, 13–17 September 2008*; pp. 837–846.
38. Bosman, P.A.N. On gradients and hybrid evolutionary algorithms for real-valued multiobjective optimization. *IEEE Trans. Evol. Comput.* **2011**, *16*, 51–69. [CrossRef]
39. Schütze, O.; Martín, A.; Lara, A.; Alvarado, S.; Salinas, E.; Coello, C.A. The Directed Search Method for Multiobjective Memetic Algorithms. *J. Comput. Optim. Appl.* **2016**, *63*, 305–332. [CrossRef]

40. Schütze, O.; Alvarado, S.; Segura, C.; Landa, R. Gradient subspace approximation: A direct search method for memetic computing. *Soft Comput.* **2016**, *21*, 6331–6350. [CrossRef]
41. Cuate, O.; Ponsich, A.; Uribe, L.; Zapotecas, S.; Lara, A.; Schütze, O. A New Hybrid Evolutionary Algorithm for the Treatment of Equality Constrained MOPs. *Mathematics* **2020**, *8*, 7. [CrossRef]
42. Martin, B.; Goldsztejn, A.; Granvilliers, L.; Jermann, C. Certified Parallelotope Continuation for One-Manifolds. *SIAM J. Numer. Anal.* **2013**, *51*, 3373–3401. [CrossRef]
43. Martin, B.; Goldsztejn, A.; Granvilliers, L.; Jermann, C. On continuation methods for non-linear bi-objective optimization: Towards a certified interval-based approach. *J. Glob. Optim.* **2014**, *64*, 3–16. [CrossRef]
44. Pereyra, V.; Saunders, M.; Castillo, J. Equispaced Pareto front construction for constrained bi-objective optimization. *Math. Comput. Model.* **2013**, *57*, 2122–2131. [CrossRef]
45. Wang, H. Zigzag Search for Continuous Multiobjective Optimization. *Inf. J. Comput.* **2013**, *25*, 654–665. [CrossRef]
46. Wang, H. Direct zigzag search for discrete multi-objective optimization. *Comput. Oper. Res.* **2015**, *61*, 100–109. [CrossRef]
47. Zhang, Q.; Li, F.; Wang, H.; Xue, Y. Zigzag search for multi-objective optimization considering generation cost and emission. *Appl. Energy* **2019**, *255*. [CrossRef]
48. Recchioni, M.C. A path following method for box-constrained multiobjective optimization with applications to goal programming problems. *Math. Methods Oper. Res.* **2003**, *58*, 69–85. [CrossRef]
49. Ringkamp, M.; Ober-Blöbaum, S.; Dellnitz, M.; Schütze, O. Handling high dimensional problems with multi-objective continuation methods via successive approximation of the tangent space. *Eng. Optim.* **2012**, *44*, 1117–1146. [CrossRef]
50. Schütze, O.; Cuate, O.; Martín, A.; Peitz, S.; Dellnitz, M. Pareto Explorer: A global/local exploration tool for many-objective optimization problems. *Eng. Optim.* **2020**, *52*, 832–855. [CrossRef]
51. Fliege, J.; Drummond, L.M.G.; Svaiter, B.F. Newton's Method for Multiobjective Optimization. *SIAM J. Optim.* **2009**, *20*, 602–626. [CrossRef]
52. Julia. JuMP—Julia for Mathematical Optimization. Available online: http://www.juliaopt.org/JuMP.jl/v0.14/ (accessed on 17 December 2020).
53. Tian, Y.; Cheng, R.; Zhang, X.; Jin, Y. PlatEMO: A MATLAB platform for evolutionary multi-objective optimization [educational forum]. *IEEE Comput. Intell. Mag.* **2017**, *12*, 73–87. [CrossRef]
54. Griewank, A.; Walther, A. *Evaluating Derivatives: Principles and Techniques of Algorithmic Differentiation*; SIAM: Philadelphia, PA, USA, 2008.
55. Schütze, O.; Esquivel, X.; Lara, A.; Coello, C.A.C. Using the Averaged Hausdorff Distance as a Performance Measure in Evolutionary Multi-Objective Optimization. *IEEE Trans. Evol. Comput.* **2012**, *16*, 504–522. [CrossRef]
56. Bogoya, J.M.; Vargas, A.; Cuate, O.; Schütze, O. A (p,q)-averaged Hausdorff distance for arbitrary measurable sets. *Math. Comput. Appl.* **2018**, *23*, 51. [CrossRef]
57. Bogoya, J.M.; Vargas, A.; Schütze, O. The Averaged Hausdorff Distances in Multi-Objective Optimization: A Review. *Mathematics* **2019**, *7*, 894. [CrossRef]
58. Binh, T.T.; Korn, U. MOBES: A multiobjective evolution strategy for constrained optimization problems. In Proceedings of The Third International Conference on Genetic Algorithms (Mendel 97), Brno, Czech Republic, 25–27 June 1997; Volume 25, pp. 176–182.
59. Chankong, V.; Haimes, Y. *Multiobjective Decision Making: Theory and Methodology*; Dover Publications: Mineola, NY, USA, 2008.
60. Osyczka, A.; Kundu, S. A new method to solve generalized multicriteria optimization problems using the simple genetic algorithm. *Struct. Optim.* **1995**, *10*, 94–99. [CrossRef]

Publisher's Note: MDPI stays neutral with regard to jurisdictional claims in published maps and institutional affiliations.

© 2020 by the authors. Licensee MDPI, Basel, Switzerland. This article is an open access article distributed under the terms and conditions of the Creative Commons Attribution (CC BY) license (http://creativecommons.org/licenses/by/4.0/).

Article

Prediction of Maximum Pressure at the Roofs of Rectangular Water Tanks Subjected to Harmonic Base Excitation Using the Multi-Gene Genetic Programming Method

Iman Bahreini Toussi [1,*], Abdolmajid Mohammadian [1] and Reza Kianoush [2]

1. Department of Civil Engineering, University of Ottawa, 161 Louis Pasteur Private, Ottawa, ON K1N 6N5, Canada; amohamma@uottawa.ca
2. Department of Civil Engineering, Ryerson University, 350 Victoria Street, Toronto, ON M5B 2K3, Canada; kianoush@ryerson.ca
* Correspondence: ibahr094@uottawa.ca; Tel.: +1-(613)-562-5800 (ext. 6159)

Citation: Bahreini Toussi, I.; Mohammadian, A.; Kianoush, R. Prediction of Maximum Pressure at the Roofs of Rectangular Water Tanks Subjected to Harmonic Base Excitation Using the Multi-Gene Genetic Programming Method. *Math. Comput. Appl.* **2021**, *26*, 6. https://doi.org/10.3390/mca26010006

Received: 16 November 2020
Accepted: 29 December 2020
Published: 2 January 2021

Publisher's Note: MDPI stays neutral with regard to jurisdictional claims in published maps and institutional affiliations.

Copyright: © 2021 by the authors. Licensee MDPI, Basel, Switzerland. This article is an open access article distributed under the terms and conditions of the Creative Commons Attribution (CC BY) license (https://creativecommons.org/licenses/by/4.0/).

Abstract: Liquid storage tanks subjected to base excitation can cause large impact forces on the tank roof, which can lead to structural damage as well as economic and environmental losses. The use of artificial intelligence in solving engineering problems is becoming popular in various research fields, and the Genetic Programming (GP) method is receiving more attention in recent years as a regression tool and also as an approach for finding empirical expressions between the data. In this study, an OpenFOAM numerical model that was validated by the authors in a previous study is used to simulate various tank sizes with different liquid heights. The tanks are excited in three different orientations with harmonic sinusoidal loadings. The excitation frequencies are chosen as equal to the tanks' natural frequencies so that they would be subject to a resonance condition. The maximum pressure in each case is recorded and made dimensionless; then, using Multi-Gene Genetic Programming (MGGP) methods, a relationship between the dimensionless maximum pressure and dimensionless liquid height is acquired. Finally, some error measurements are calculated, and the sensitivity and uncertainty of the proposed equation are analyzed.

Keywords: liquid storage tanks; base excitation; artificial intelligence; Multi-Gene Genetic Programming; computational fluid dynamics; finite volume method

1. Introduction

Earthquakes cause damage to various types of structures, and buildings, dams, reservoirs, and liquid storage tanks may be victims of an earthquake excitation. Sloshing in a liquid storage tank can cause irreversible structural failure and spillage of the liquid material into the environment, and this liquid, if toxic or flammable, may affect the area for a long time, even permanently. Thus, protecting liquid storage tanks from damage during an earthquake is crucial. One of the causes is related to the pressure exerted on the roof of the tank due to the sloshing of the liquid. Therefore, it is necessary for a designer to know the maximum pressure caused by such effects on a tank's roof.

Analytical, numerical, and experimental solutions have been introduced by various scholars. Housner [1] provided an analytical solution that is adopted in some design codes and standards such as the ACI 350.3 from the American Concrete Institute [2]. Housner's method divides the liquid into two parts, i.e., impulsive and convective. The former is the lower part of the liquid that moves in unison with the tank walls, while the latter is the upper part of liquid that creates sloshing in a tank. The impulsive mass is assumed to be rigidly connected to the tank's walls, while the convective mass is modeled by a mass–spring system. Figure 1 illustrates Housner's model for ground-supported tanks. Despite attempts at developing analytical solutions other than Housner's method (e.g., Isaacson [3]), most previous studies have concentrated on numerical analyses. The goal of such studies is to provide a solution to the Navier–Stokes equations given in Equations (5)–(8), which are the governing equations in fluid flow. Cho and Cho [4] developed a combined finite element–boundary element (FE–BE) method to predict liquid behavior and its interaction with a structure, and Liu and Lin [5] studied a numerical model to solve 3D non-linear sloshing in a liquid storage tank. Their model adopted the volume of fluid (VOF) method for tracking a free surface in conjunction with the finite difference method (FDM). Chen et al. [6] formulated a numerical model that is based on Reynolds-averaged Navier–Stokes (RANS) fluid motion, which proved to be in good agreement with the experimental data from Daewoo Shipbuilding & Marine Engineering Co., Ltd. (DSME) [7]. The data were obtained from tests on a rectangular tank with plan dimensions of 800 mm × 400 mm and a height of 500 mm that was horizontally excited with different frequencies.

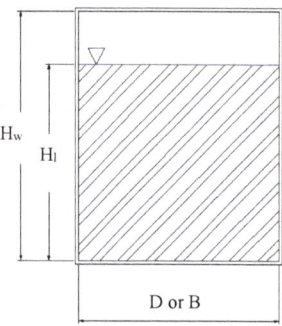 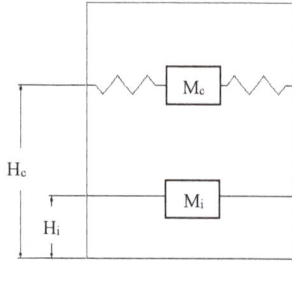

Figure 1. Schematic view of Housner's simplified model.

In recent years, artificial intelligence (AI) has been evolving in all aspects of human life, including engineering problems (Afan et al. [8]). There are several methods for the estimation of a relationship between scattered data based on AI. Among them, the group method of data handling (GMDH; Ivakhnenko and Ivakhnenko [9]) and evolutionary polynomial regression (EPR) can be mentioned. AI techniques such as support vector machine (SVM), artificial neural networks (ANNs), adaptive neuro-fuzzy inference system (ANFIS), Genetic Programming (GP) have recently been used for engineering problems such as water quality index and groundwater level modeling (e.g., Mohammadpour et al. [10]; Ghani and Azamathulla [11]; He et al. [12]; Lallahem et al. [13]; Daliakopoulos et al. [14]; Mirzavand et al. [15]; and Mohammadpour et al. [16]).

Model tree (MT)—a sub-class of the regression tree method—is another regression method in which an equation is generated at each node [17]. In a regression tree, a constant or a relatively simple regression model is used to demonstrate the data [18]. A genetic based method known as GP is also used for the regression of data. In this method, a set of sub-trees is randomly generated based on user-defined specifications using arithmetic operators (i.e., +, −, ×, /), non-linear functions (e.g., sin, cos, log), etc. [19]. The goal is to minimize the errors (e.g., root mean square error (RMSE)) in newer generations until an acceptable error is reached.

Another method for formulating scattered data based on AI is gene expression programming (GEP), which was introduced by Ferreira in 1999 (Sattar and Gharabaghi [20]). This method can be employed to develop relationships between data with minimal error [21]. Azamathulla [22] adopted this method to estimate the scour depth downstream of sills. To do so, he used the following procedure: (1) choose a fitness function; (2) choose a set of terminals (T) and functions (F) to shape chromosomes; (3) choose the chromosome architecture (i.e., head length and the number of genes); (4) choose the linking function (e.g., addition and multiplication operators); and (5) choose the set of genetic operators (e.g., mutation, transportation, etc.). He compared his results with the equation obtained by Chinnarasri and Kositgittiwong [23], which at the time had the lowest error value, and found that the proposed equation using the GEP model had a higher accuracy. Najafzadeh et al. [24] used three methods, i.e., GEP, MT, and EPR, to predict the maximum scour depth near piers with debris accumulation. Gholami et al. [25] used the GEP method to predict the characteristics of stable bank channels. They obtained their own experimental data as well as data from previous experimental studies to complete their GEP modelling. The results were compared with available theoretical and experimental methods. Despite a good agreement and accuracy, the model's complexity was found to be higher in comparison with older analytical methods, and therefore the GEP method was not suggested by the authors. Sheikh et al. [26] applied GEP to analyze shear stress distribution in circular channels with flat beds subject to sediment deposition. They proposed equations for predicting the base shear applied to the bed and the walls of such channels. It was found that the GEP model could lower errors and uncertainties, and hence the model was recommended for the base shear analysis of circular channels with flat beds.

A sub-class of the GP method known as Multi-Gene Genetic Programming (MGGP) can be used in problems with higher complexity. A gene is a weighted linear combination of outputs from a GP tree. In this method, the user has control over the maximum number of genes and the depth of the model tree [27]. In this method, multiple genes are combined to produce an MGGP model. AI techniques have shown to be capable of accurate prediction, and with the development of computing systems, they have become easier to use. However, to the best of the authors' knowledge, they have not been employed in the prediction of pressures and forces in water tanks. Previous studies in engineering applications have shown promising results for MGGP in comparison with other AI techniques such as ANN, ANFIS, traditional GP, etc. (Kaydani et al. [28]; Safari and Mehr [29]; Mehr and Nourani [30]).

The use of GP methods in civil engineering is becoming increasingly popular. Gandomi et al. [31] proposed an empirical model for predicting the ultimate shear strength of reinforced concrete (RC) deep beams using GEP. The results were compared with design codes such as ACI and CSA, and the model was found to give better results than the design codes when compared to the available experimental and numerical data. Gandomi et al. [32] developed a model to find the shear capacity of RC beams without stirrups using the GEP method. To avoid overfitting, they divided the data into three groups of learning, validation, and testing on a random basis. The developed model was tested against the available data and several design codes (e.g., ACI, CSA, NZS, etc.) for various sizes and models of RC beams and was found to give compatible results. GEP can be used in various fields of civil engineering as an optimization method. Zahiri et al. [33] investigated the applications of GEP in hydraulic engineering and found it applicable in different areas, such as estimation of scour depth, discharge rate, and land transport in rivers.

In the present study, data generated by a validated OpenFOAM (Open-Source Field Operation and Manipulation) [34] model are used. The maximum pressure on the roof of a tank is the parameter of interest. Several tank sizes with various liquid heights are excited by a resonance frequency, and the maximum hydrodynamic pressure at the roof of the tank in each case is obtained. Using the GP method in both Single-Gene and Multi-Gene modes, an equation is proposed for predicting the maximum pressure at the roof of the tank. Finally, the proposed equation's reliability is investigated and discussed through error measurements as well as uncertainty and sensibility analyses.

To the best of the authors' knowledge, a study such as this one that predicts the maximum pressure at the roof of a liquid storage tank subjected to base excitation has not been addressed previously. The design codes generally provide a minimum free-board, and if the provided free-board is not sufficient, it is left to the designers to decide how to design the roof. No further data are provided in that manner in the design codes. Furthermore, previous studies have not investigated the pressures at the roof of the tank with the intention of finding a relationship between the tank size and the maximum pressure on the roof. The available codes and standards do not provide details for designing the roof of tanks with insufficient freeboard, and they only recommend designing the roof to resist uplift pressures. Therefore, this study can provide a good estimate of those pressures and help with the design process.

The results from this study can help provide empirical formulations to appropriately estimate the hydrodynamic pressures at the roof of a liquid tank subjected to base excitations. This can be adopted in design codes and standards to better address the uplift forces and hydrodynamic pressures at the roof level. In addition, the artificial intelligence component of this research can significantly reduce computational cost and time.

Although earthquake and harmonic excitations have different characteristics, it was found in a previous study [35] that harmonic resonance excitations can produce higher hydrodynamic pressures on the roof of a tank compared to earthquake excitations, which is the reason this kind of loading was applied in this study instead of earthquake excitations

This paper is organized as follows. Section 2 deals with the details and equations of numerical modeling and MGGP. Section 3 presents the results, discussions, and error measurements, and some concluding remarks complete the study.

2. Materials and Methods
2.1. Numerical Modelling

An OpenFOAM model was previously developed and validated by the authors [35]. The same model was used to generate data for the current study. The maximum hydrodynamic pressure at the roof of rectangular tanks is the parameter of interest in this study. Hence, pressure sensors were distributed on one quarter of the roof for each simulation.

Four different tank sizes were used in the study, the dimensions of which are presented in Table 1. For each tank, a minimum of six different liquid heights were simulated, as discussed later. Since the direction of an earthquake cannot be predicted, four different tank orientations were tested, and among them, the highest roof pressure for each liquid height in each tank was found.

Table 1. Dimensions of tanks used in the study.

	Length (mm)	Width (mm)	Height (mm)
Size 1	755	300	300
Size 2	1978	779	1200
Size 3	1283	327	1200
Size 4	683	342	1200

Many previous studies (e.g., [4,36,37]) have shown that Housner's simplified method [1] predicts resonance frequency accurately, and hence in this study the same method was applied.

Based on Housner's method, the resonance frequency in a rectangular tank can be calculated as follows:

$$M_c = M \frac{\tanh 1.7\, L/h}{1.7\, L/h} \qquad (1)$$

$$k_c = 3 \frac{M_1^2}{M} \frac{gh}{L^2} \qquad (2)$$

$$\omega_c = \sqrt{\frac{k_c}{M_c}} \qquad (3)$$

$$T_c = \frac{2\pi}{\omega_c} \qquad (4)$$

where M_c is the mass of the convective part of the liquid (c = convective), M is the total liquid mass, L is half of the tank length, h is the total liquid height, k_c is the stiffness of the assumed spring that connects the convective mass to the tank's walls in the direction of movement, g is ground acceleration equal to 9.81 m/s², and ω_c and T_c are the resonance frequency and resonance period of the first (fundamental) mode of the oscillating liquid, respectively. In lieu of Housner's method to determine the natural frequency of the tank, Lamb's formula can be used for simplicity [38]. In Table 2, the resonance frequencies that were applied to each tank based on the size and liquid height are presented. Each tank size–liquid height combination was simulated at four different orientations of 0°, 30°, 60°, and 90°. Since the direction of an earthquake is not predictable, the maximum pressure among all orientations was used as the input for the GP section. In other words, the maximum of maximums was found and applied to the GP. The excitation orientations of 0°, 30°, and 60° are presented in Figure 2.

Table 2. Frequency applied to each tank based on the tank size and liquid height.

	Length (mm)	Width (mm)	Tank Height (mm)	Liquid Height (mm)	Dimensionless Liquid Height (h_l/L)	ω_i (rad/s)	T_i (s)
				100	0.265	4.023	1.562
				120	0.318	4.354	1.443
				145	0.384	4.705	1.335
				200	0.53	5.282	1.190
				230	0.609	5.510	1.140
				250	0.662	5.636	1.115
				280	0.742	5.792	1.085
				1100	1.112	3.819	1.645
				1000	1.011	3.777	1.663
Size 2	1978	779	1200	900	0.910	3.721	1.689
				800	0.809	3.644	1.724
				700	0.708	3.540	1.775
				600	0.607	3.400	1.848
				1100	1.714	4.858	1.293
				1000	1.559	4.845	1.297
				900	1.403	4.824	1.303
				800	1.247	4.789	1.312
				700	1.091	4.732	1.328
				600	0.935	4.640	1.354
				1100	3.221	6.686	0.940
				1000	2.928	6.686	0.940
Size 4	683	327	1200	900	2.635	6.685	0.940
				800	2.343	6.682	0.940
				700	2.05	6.677	0.941
				600	1.757	6.662	0.943

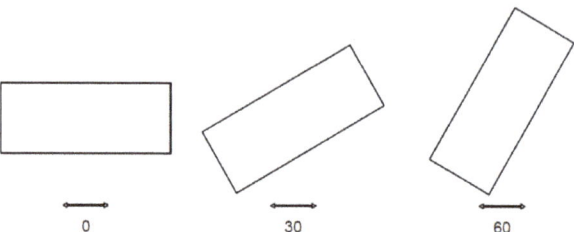

Figure 2. Tank orientations for simulations.

After finding the resonance frequency for each tank size and liquid height, numerical modelling was performed using OpenFOAM software. The OpenFOAM model can provide numerical solutions for various types of engineering problems, such as heat transfer, mass transport, liquid flow, etc. It can also solve fluid–structure interaction problems based on computational fluid dynamics (CFD) modelling [39]. Navier–Stokes equations in Equations (5)–(8) are solved for these types of problems.

$$\frac{\partial u}{\partial x} + \frac{\partial v}{\partial y} + \frac{\partial w}{\partial z} = 0 \tag{5}$$

$$\frac{\partial u}{\partial t} + u\frac{\partial u}{\partial x} + v\frac{\partial u}{\partial y} + w\frac{\partial u}{\partial z} = -\frac{1}{\rho}\frac{\partial p}{\partial x} + \nu\nabla^2 u \tag{6}$$

$$\frac{\partial v}{\partial t} + u\frac{\partial v}{\partial x} + v\frac{\partial v}{\partial y} + w\frac{\partial v}{\partial z} = -\frac{1}{\rho}\frac{\partial p}{\partial y} + \nu\nabla^2 v \tag{7}$$

$$\frac{\partial w}{\partial t} + u\frac{\partial w}{\partial x} + v\frac{\partial w}{\partial y} + w\frac{\partial w}{\partial z} = -\frac{1}{\rho}\frac{\partial p}{\partial z} + \nu\nabla^2 w - g \tag{8}$$

in which

$$\nabla^2 = \frac{\partial^2}{\partial x^2} + \frac{\partial^2}{\partial y^2} + \frac{\partial^2}{\partial z^2} \tag{9}$$

and ρ and p are the liquid density (kg/m^3) and total pressure (Pa) respectively; u, v, and w are the particle speeds in the x, y, and z directions (m/s); t is time (s); and $g = 9.81$ m/s^2 is the gravity acceleration and

$$\rho = \alpha\rho_1 + (1-\alpha)\rho_2 \tag{10}$$

where ρ_1 and ρ_2 are the densities of air and water, respectively, and α indicates the volume of each particle that is filled with each of the fluids. The value of α varies between 0.0 and 1.0, with 1.0 meaning the cell is filled with water and 0.0 indicating air. A value of 0.5 is allocated to the free surface. Any value between 0.0 and 0.5 indicates air, and a value between 0.5 and 1.0 indicates water.

Given the very high momentum of the flow, turbulent stresses have a negligible effect on the flow in comparison with the liquid sloshing forces, and hence, turbulence was not modeled in this study.

2.1.1. Computational Setup

- Mesh

In this study, a structured cubic mesh was used. By running a mesh sensitivity analysis, the optimum mesh size was found. To do so, the pressure at the top corner of the tank was measured with various mesh sizes.

- Initial conditions

For the initial conditions, the velocity, acceleration, and displacement fields were set to zero.

- Wall boundary conditions

The "no flow, frictionless" wall boundary condition is applied to the base and the side walls of the tank. This implicit boundary condition is used when no flow crosses the wall, and the shear stress at the wall and normal gradient of tangent velocity were set to zero. In other words, no fluid enters or exits the boundary where this condition is applied. This boundary condition is applied as follows:

$$U_n = 0 \tag{11}$$

$$\frac{\partial}{\partial n} U_\tau = 0 \tag{12}$$

where U_n and U_τ are the normal and the tangential velocities of the flow, respectively, and n is the normal vector of the boundary.

- Free surface boundary conditions

The pressure at the free surface is set to zero, and the free surface is modelled using the volume of fluid (VoF) method according to the following equation:

$$\frac{\partial \alpha}{\partial t} + \frac{\partial(\alpha u)}{x} + \frac{\partial(\alpha v)}{y} + \frac{\partial(\alpha w)}{z} = 0 \tag{13}$$

2.1.2. CFD Details

In the mesh sensitivity analysis, a mesh size of 6 mm × 6 mm × 6 mm was found to be reasonably accurate. An adjustable scheme was chosen for the time-step, with a maximum step size of 0.05 s. This means each time-step is chosen based on the previous step. This helps with the accuracy of the simulation results; however, it has higher computational costs.

In the validated OpenFOAM model, an eddy viscosity of 2×10^{-4} m^2/s was found to provide the best results compared to the experimental data.

A total of eighteen pressure sensors (probes) are distributed on one quarter of the roof for each of the simulated tanks. The long duration of the simulations is expected that the pressure distribution on a quarter of the domain can be representative of the entire roof. In addition, in this study, the quarter of the roof with the highest pressure was selected for the GP analysis. The placement of sensors on the roof of the tank are presented in Figure 3. Using these sensors, the pressure distribution on the roofs of the tanks can be found. Figure 4 shows a sample of the CFD output; more details on the OpenFOAM model are given by Bahreini et al. [35].

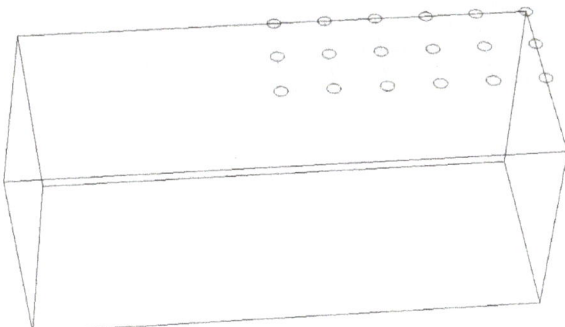

Figure 3. Sensor arrangement at the roof of the tank.

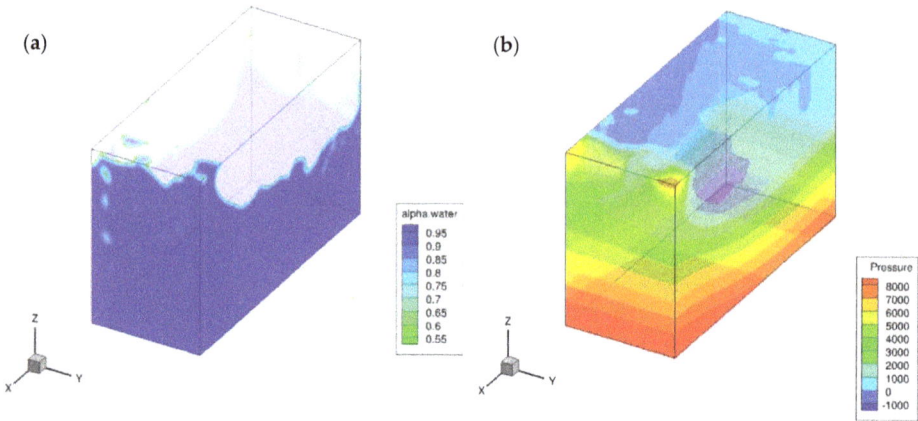

Figure 4. Computational fluid dynamics (CFD) outputs for tank size 2, with 800 mm water depth at 0° orientation and time $t = 9.50$ s; (**a**) liquid surface and (**b**) pressure.

2.2. Genetic Programming

Genetic programming (GP) is a method based on artificial intelligence that can be used in optimization problems. This method can be applied in Single-Gene and Multi-Gene models. In this method, the structure of the solution is not specified at the beginning and is shaped throughout the evolution [40]. Initial chromosomes are created, and during generations of evolutions and mutations, newer chromosomes with optimized characteristics are created. These cycles continue until the maximum number of iterations is reached or until the optimization reaches a point that is close to the solution (i.e., the error is negligible). In the Single-Gene model, mutations occur to one gene, while in the Multi-Gene method, there are mutations and crossovers across several genes.

In this method, the goal is to find the best-fit expression using the fit function (Equation (14)). This function has a value between 0 to 1000, with 1000 being the fittest, i.e., with the minimum error.

$$f_i = 1000 \frac{1}{1 + RRSE_i} \qquad (14)$$

where

$$RRSE_i = \sqrt{\frac{\sum_{j=1}^{n}\left(P_{(ij)} - T_j\right)^2}{\sum_{j=1}^{n}\left(T_j - \overline{T}\right)^2}} \qquad (15)$$

and i is the number of the fit function, j is the number of data, $P_{(ij)}$ is the calculated value for jth data based on ith function, T_j is the actual value for the jth data, and $\overline{T}$ is the average of the T_j values.

In GP-based methods, an initial gene or tree is randomly created, and the process starts. Several reproductions, including mutation (i.e., random changes in a gene and replacing a material with another material) and crossover (i.e., interchange of materials between the parent genes) operations, take place until the termination conditions are fulfilled.

Each gene is in a shape of a tree and consists of two types of nodes: (1) operator nodes, being mathematical operators (e.g., +, −, ×, /, power, sin, cos, log, etc.); and (2) operand nodes, which are the input variables, e.g., x_1, x_2, etc. (Pandey et al. [41]).

Here, an example is presented for further explanation and a better understanding. In a regression problem with two operands of x_1 and x_2 (i.e., $y = f(x_1, x_2)$, y is dependent on two variables of x_1 and x_2), A_1 and B_1 are randomly created parent genes as follows:

$$A_1 = (2.3 \times x_1) - (sinx_2) \qquad (16)$$

$$B_1 = \left(1.1 \times x_1^2\right) + (\log x_2) \tag{17}$$

In a crossover process, a sub-tree of the parent gene A_1 is switched with a sub-tree of the parent gene B_1, resulting in second generation genes, A_2 and B_2:

$$A_2 = (2.3 \times x_1) - \left(1.1 \times x_1^2\right) \tag{18}$$

$$B_2 = (\log x_2) + (\sin x_2) \tag{19}$$

And in a mutation process, a sub-tree of each of the genes A_2 and B_2 is replaced by a new randomly chosen sub-tree, creating the third-generation genes, A_3 and B_3:

$$A_3 = \left(1.3 \times x_2^3\right) - \left(1.1 \times x_1^2\right) \tag{20}$$

$$B_3 = (\log x_2) + \left(\frac{x_1}{x_2}\right) \tag{21}$$

This sequence continues until the termination conditions are fulfilled. At the end, the two genes are combined to form the equation:

$$Y_i = \alpha(A_i) + \beta(B_i) + C \tag{22}$$

which, in this three-generation example, is as follows:

$$y = \alpha\left[\left(1.3 \times x_2^3\right) - \left(1.1 \times x_1^2\right)\right] + \beta\left[(\log x_2) + \left(\frac{x_1}{x_2}\right)\right] + C \tag{23}$$

where α and β are called gene weights, and C is a constant bias term. The gene weights and bias term are calculated by an ordinary least-squared method. Figure 5 shows the procedure of this example in the form of MGGP trees.

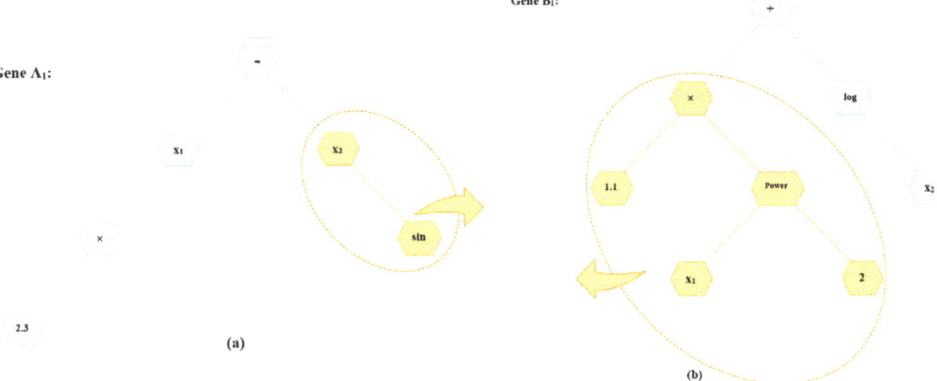

Figure 5. *Cont.*

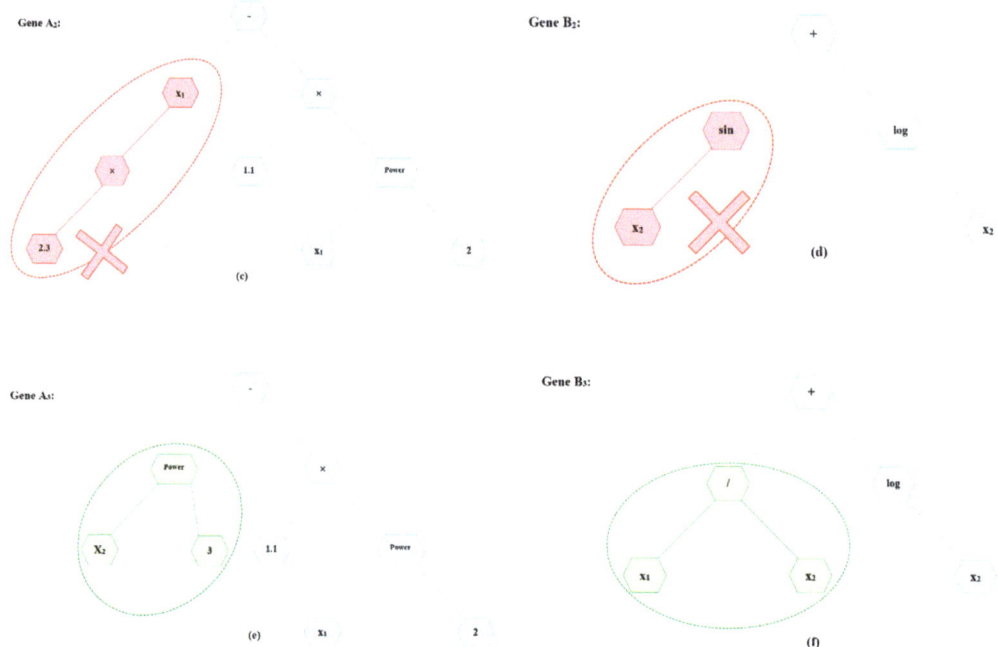

Figure 5. An example of a Multi-Gene Genetic Programming (MGGP) procedure.

In the current study, using MATLAB, an open-source MGGP algorithm (Genetic Programming Toolbox for the Identification of Physical Systems; GPTIPS) [42] is run to provide the general shape of the prediction function. In this algorithm, there is a random initial assumption for the function; then, the function is developed through generations until the error is minimized. Finally, using non-linear least squared optimization, an optimized equation is obtained that can be used for further analysis, as described in the following. This algorithm uses Pareto theory to find a balance between the fitness and complexity of the model in order to select the optimum model.

Figure 6 shows an example output tree of the MGGP algorithm. In this tree, the operators plus (+), minus (−), division (/), and multiplication (×) are used. The tree depth in this example is 12, and it has a total of 35 nodes.

In this method, chromosomes are introduced as computer programs of different shapes and sizes, with each consisting of sub-programs called genes, i.e., each chromosome is composed of genes. A typical GP method procedure is as follows:

1. A set of variables is initiated.
2. The chromosomes' architecture is defined.
3. The chromosomes are randomly formulated.

This cycle continues until the function that best fits the data is found. For this study, from a total of 25 samples, 80% (20 samples) were used to train the model while 20% (5 samples) were used for testing (i.e., for validating the model). The trained data are expected to show higher accuracy and smaller errors since the model is directly obtained from this set of data. The tested and trained data are chosen on a random basis.

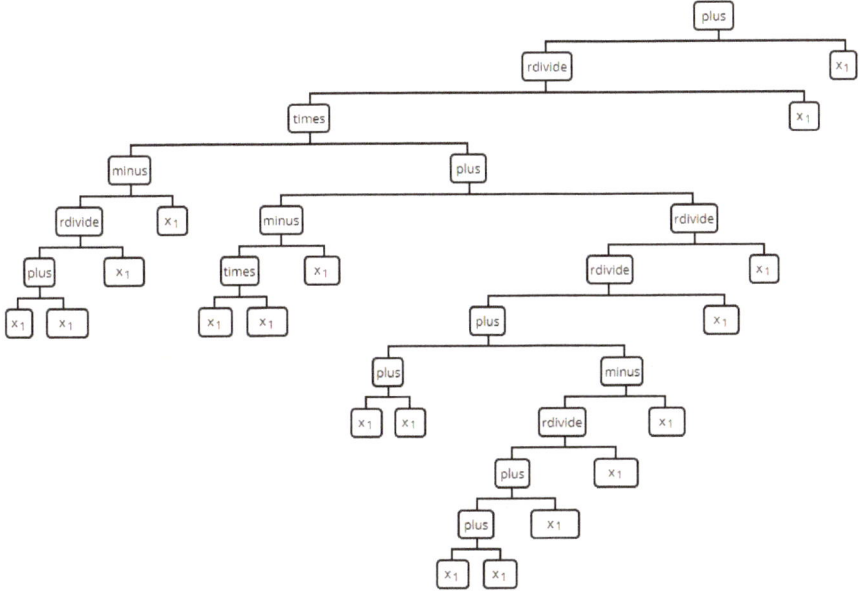

Figure 6. MGGP example output.

3. Results and Discussion

3.1. Numerical Modelling

Following the completion of the simulations, the results were analyzed for each case. At this stage, contours illustrating the maximum pressure distribution (not at a specific timestep but over the simulation time) on the roof are plotted for each simulation. Contours associated with the 755 mm × 300 mm tank are presented in Figures 7–9. In the figures, the bottom left represents the center of the roof with dimension of (0, 0), while the top right shows the corner (375.5, 150). The results from the numerical models show that in 46 out of 67 simulations (67%), the maximum pressure on the roof of the tank occurs at the corner.

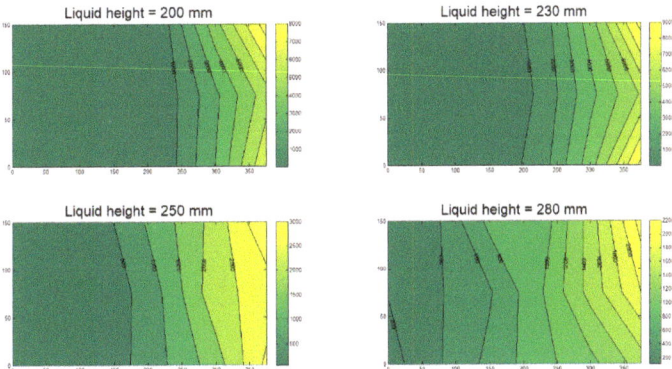

Figure 7. Pressure distribution at the roof of the 755 mm × 300 mm tank, 0° orientation.

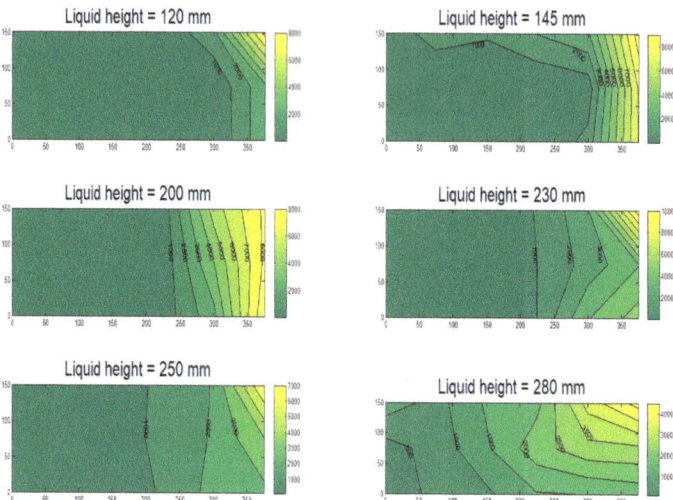

Figure 8. Pressure distribution at the roof of the 755 mm × 300 mm tank, 30° orientation.

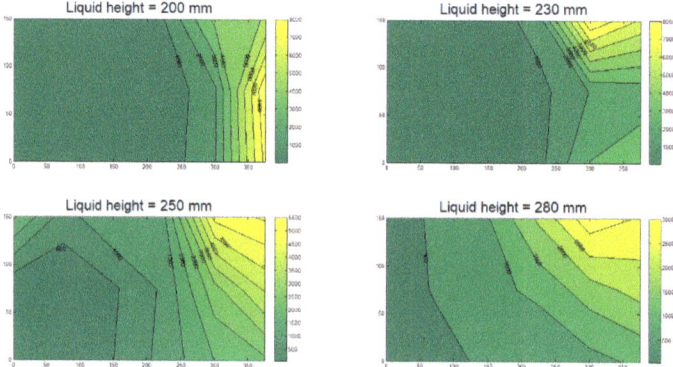

Figure 9. Pressure distribution at the roof of the 755 mm × 300 mm tank, 60° orientation.

To find a relationship to predict the maximum pressure for any tank size with any liquid height, the pressure and liquid height need to be dimensionless. It should be noted that the dimensionless maximum pressure needs to consider all factors that might affect the value of the pressure, and hence, the dimensionless pressure and dimensionless liquid height can be calculated by Equations (24) and (25):

$$P_d = \frac{P_{max}}{\frac{(a.\rho.h.L.H)}{(Fb)^2}} \tag{24}$$

$$h_d = \frac{h}{L} \tag{25}$$

where P_d is the dimensionless pressure, P_{max} is the maximum pressure on the roof, a is the maximum acceleration of the harmonic excitation, ρ is the density of water, h is the liquid height in the tank, H is the height of the tank, L is half of the length of the tank (i.e., the tank's length is 2L), and Fb is the available freeboard. The parameters a and Fb can be calculated by Equations (26) and (27):

$$a = A.\omega_i^2 \qquad (26)$$

$$Fb = H - h \qquad (27)$$

In Equation (26), A is the displacement amplitude of the harmonic motion. In Figure 10, the dimensionless maximum pressure plotted against the dimensionless liquid height are presented in a scatter graph. It should be noted that the results presented in this study are valid for cases when the sloshing height exceeds the wall height, which then generates pressure on the roof of a tank.

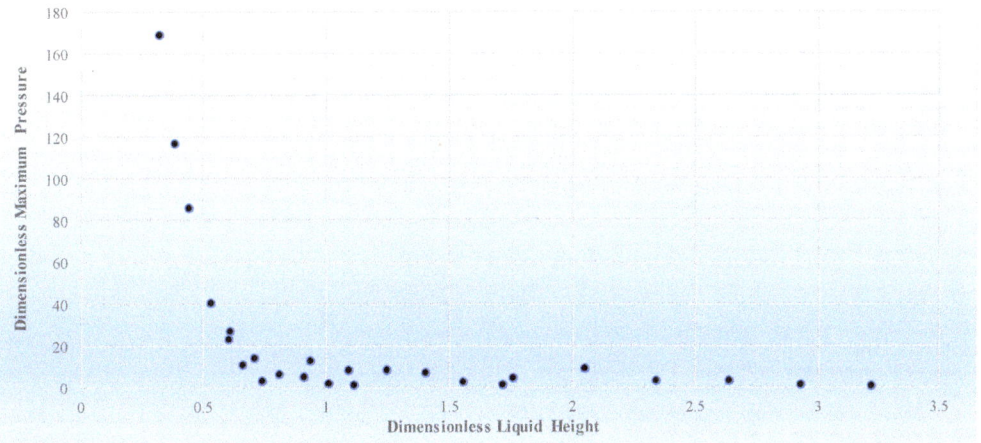

Figure 10. Dimensionless maximum pressure versus dimensionless liquid height for the observed (CFD) data.

3.2. Genetic Programming

The GPTIPS algorithm allows the user to choose between Single-Gene and Multi-Gene solutions. Single-Gene is the more traditional way of GP and results in simpler equations. Although the Multi-Gene process is more complex, it may lead to solutions with higher accuracy. In this study, the default crossover and mutation coefficients were used as follows: probability of Multi-Gene GP tree cross over = 0.85, probability of Multi-Gene GP tree mutation = 0.1, and probability of Multi-Gene GP tree direct copy = 0.05.

In this section, both Single-Gene and Multi-Gene solutions are examined and explained, and the results are presented.

3.2.1. Single-Gene Solution

In the single-Gene solution, the procedure is simple. There is only one gene and a bias term; hence, there is no crossover of sub-trees. Mutations, however, occur in this solution. The equation obtained from the GPTIPS algorithm in the Single-Gene mode is presented in Equation (28):

$$P_{d,S} = 4.6489 - \frac{12.498 \times ln(h_d)}{h_d^3 + 0.0534} \qquad (28)$$

Here, $P_{d,S}$ is the dimensionless maximum pressure obtained by the Single-Gene solution.

To obtain this equation, the algorithm was set to have 200 generations, with a population size of 300. The maximum tree depth was set to 4, and operators plus, minus, multiply, divide, and log (which in MATLAB means the Napierian logarithm, i.e., ln) were used. This equation is obtained in generation 184. It should be noted that for the simulated tanks,

h_d (i.e., dimensionless liquid height) has a value between 0.3179 and 3.2211, and hence the results are valid for tanks with dimensionless liquid height in that range. Since this relationship is obtained based on the maximum pressure in all tank orientations, it is not affected by the angle of tank orientation. Figure 11 presents the complexity of the model plotted against its accuracy level $(1 - R^2)$ for the population on the training set of data. In this figure, green dots represent Pareto models, and blue dots represent non-Pareto models. The green dot with a red circle shows the best model in terms of R^2 on the training data.

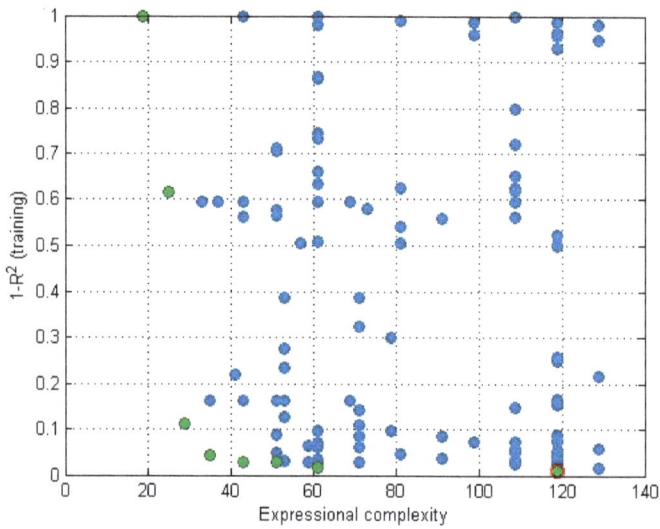

Figure 11. Expressional complexity of the proposed Single-Gene model.

3.2.2. Multi-Gene Solution (MGGP)

In this step, the algorithm is modified to use multiple genes. This mode has both crossover and mutation processes. The following equation (Equation (29)) is obtained from the Multi-Gene procedure.

$$P_{d,M} = 5.1961 + \frac{(2.383h_d^3 - 16.846h_d^2 + 17.484h_d - 3.402)}{h_d^5} \qquad (29)$$

In this equation, $P_{d,M}$ is the dimensionless maximum roof pressure obtained by the Multi-Gene program. The number of generations was set to 500 with a population of 300. Equation (29) was obtained in generation 473. This equation is composed of the following genes:

$$\text{Gene 1}: \quad -\frac{0.920h_d + 3.402}{h_d^5} \qquad (30)$$

$$\text{Gene 2}: \quad \frac{2.383h_d^2 - 16.85h_d + 18.4}{h_d^4} \qquad (31)$$

A bias term equal to 5.196 was obtained. Figure 12 presents the complexity of the model plotted against its accuracy level $(1 - R^2)$ for the population on the training set of data.

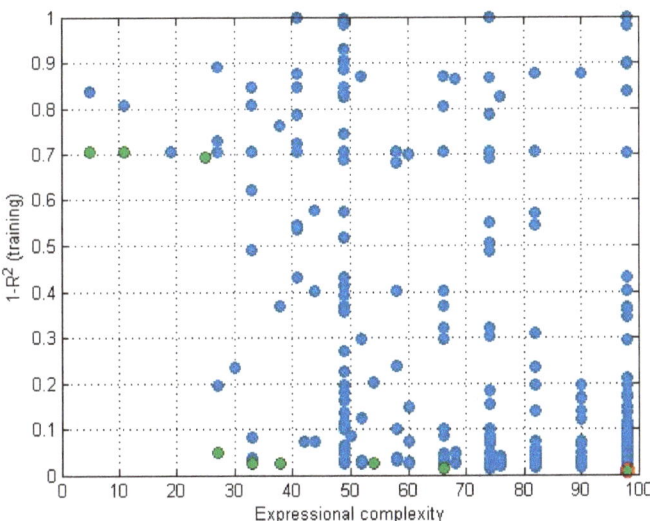

Figure 12. Expressional complexity of the proposed Multi-Gene model.

The reason for having a different number of maximum generations for the GP and MGGP models is that for the GP model, the optimum equation was found in the 184th generation, and for the MGGP model it was in the 473rd generation. Therefore, while the 200 maximum generations sufficed for the GP model, the MGGP model required a higher number of maximum generations. These numbers were chosen on a trial and error basis, starting from 100 generations until the optimum equation was obtained at a generation smaller than the maximum number of generations. This could ensure that the obtained equation was the optimal one.

3.2.3. Error Estimations

In this section, some error measures of the Single-Gene and Multi-Gene models are presented and compared. These measurements can help determine the accuracy of the presented models and the choice of each option. Errors were measured for both Single-Gene and Multi-Gene programs on the trained and tested data and were finally compared against each other.

a. R-Squared (R^2)

In this section, the calculated dimensionless maximum pressure (based on Equations (28) and (29) for Single-Gene and Multi-Gene solutions, respectively) are plotted against the observed dimensionless maximum pressure in Figure 13a,b. The R^2, is calculated as

$$R^2 = 1 - \frac{\sum(P_d - P_{d,GP})^2}{\sum(P_d - \overline{P_d})^2} \tag{32}$$

where $P_{d,GP}$ is the dimensionless maximum pressure obtained by the MGGP, and $\overline{P_d}$ is the average of the observed dimensionless maximum pressures. Table 3 presents the R^2 values for the Single-Gene and Multi-Gene solutions.

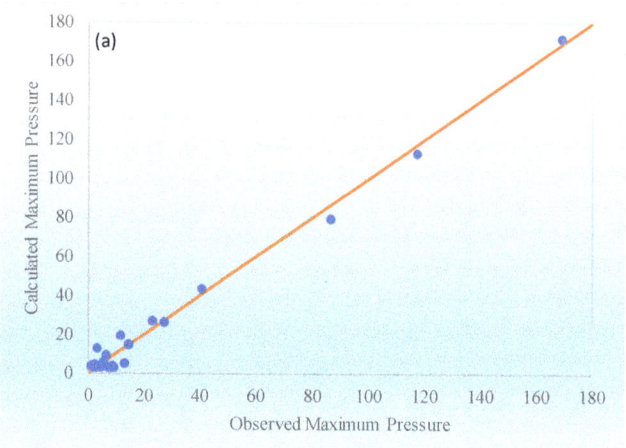

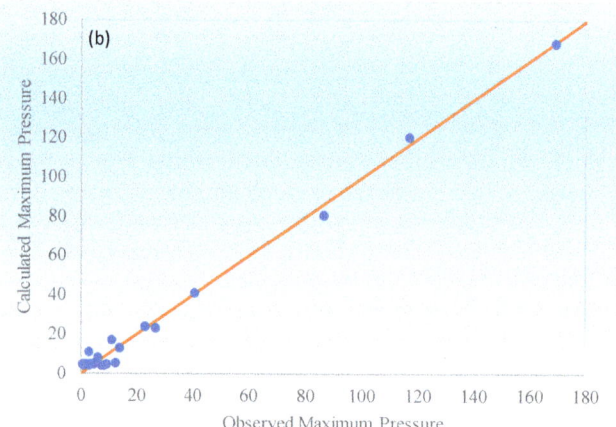

Figure 13. Observed dimensionless maximum pressure plotted against the dimensionless maximum pressure obtained by (**a**) Single-Gene procedure and (**b**) Multi-Gene procedure, for the overall data sets.

Table 3. MAD measurements.

Data Set	MAD		
	Observed Data	Single-Gene Results	Multi-Gene Results
Trained	30.63	30.27	30.44
Test	6.32	17.30	5.90
Overall	26.08	25.90	25.56

b. Root Mean Squared Error (RMSE)

The standard deviation of the residuals, known as root mean squared error (RMSE) is another way of error reporting. It shows the concentration of data near the regression graph. RMSE is calculated based on the following equation:

$$RMSE = \sqrt{\frac{\sum(P_d - P_{d,GP})^2}{N}} \qquad (33)$$

where N is the number of observed data, which in this study is 20 for the trained data set, 5 for the test data set, and 25 for the overall data. RMSE has the same dimensions as the original data. In this case, since the input data set is dimensionless, the RMSE is also dimensionless. RMSE values for each of the data sets are presented in Table 4.

Table 4. Error estimates.

Data Set		R-Squared	RMSE			MAE	MAPE (%)	AIC	PI
			Value	% of Maximum Dimensionless Pressure	% of Mean Dimensionless Pressure				
Single-Gene	Trained	0.989	4.54	2.69	17.09	3.64	68%	21.15	0.086
	Test	0.844	3.23	14.17	46.30	3.03	260%	10.55	0.241
	Overall	0.989	4.31	2.55	19.03	3.52	107%	23.87	0.114
Multi-Gene	Trained	0.992	3.89	2.30	14.63	3.28	76%	21.8	0.073
	Test	0.889	2.73	11.99	39.18	2.19	302%	12.18	0.202
	Overall	0.992	3.69	2.18	16.26	3.06	121%	24.17	0.082

c. Mean Absolute Deviation (MAD)

Mean absolute deviation or MAD is a tool for showing the scatteredness of data around the mean. It can be measured by the following equation:

$$MAD = \frac{\sum |P_d - \overline{P_d}|}{N} \text{ or } MAD = \sum |P_d - \overline{P_d}| \qquad (34)$$

The MAD measurements for each data set are presented in Table 3.

d. Mean Absolute Error (MAE)

Mean absolute error (MAE) is the average of the absolute values of the difference between the observed and measured data. In other words,

$$MAE = \frac{\sum |P_d - P_{d,GP}|}{N} = \sum |P_d - P_{d,GP}| \qquad (35)$$

The MAE values are presented in Table 4.

e. Mean Absolute Percentage Error (MAPE)

This error measures the accuracy of the model as a percentage and is calculated as follows:

$$MAPE = \frac{1}{N}\sum \frac{P_d - P_{d,GP}}{P_d} \times 100\% \qquad (36)$$

The MAPE values found in this study for different data sets of Single-Gene and Multi-Gene modes are presented in Table 4.

f. Akaike Information Criterion (AIC):

The results were also compared using the Akaike information criterion (AIC) using the following equation [43]:

$$\text{AIC} = N \times \log(\sqrt{\text{RMSE}}) + 2k \tag{37}$$

where k is the number of optimized coefficients. The results are presented in Table 4. The value of the AIC can help compare the complexity and the accuracy of the models at the same time [44]. The results show that when combined, the simplicity and accuracy of the two models (i.e., Single-Gene and Multi-Gene methods) are very close, and there is a difference of 3.1%, 13%, and 1.2% between the Single-Gene and Multi-Gene models for the trained, test, and overall data sets.

g. Performance Index (PI):

In addition to error estimates, evaluating the model performance is helpful in the comparison of different models. The performance index (PI) can be used for this purpose as follows [45]:

$$\text{PI} = \frac{\text{RRMSE}}{R+1} \tag{38}$$

$$\text{RRMSE} = \frac{\text{RMSE}}{|\overline{P_d}|} \tag{39}$$

$$R = \frac{\sum (P_d - \overline{P_d})(P_{d,GP} - \overline{P_{d,GP}})}{\sqrt{\sum (P_d - \overline{P_d})^2 \sum (P_{d,GP} - \overline{P_{d,GP}})^2}} \tag{40}$$

where RRMSE is relative root mean square error and R is the correlation coefficient. The lower the PI, the more precise the model. The results of the PI are presented in Table 4. The results show that in all data sets—i.e., test, trained, and overall—the Multi-Gene model has a lower PI, and therefore it is a more precise model than the Single-Gene model.

The error measurements demonstrate that the Multi-Gene method provides a relatively more accurate results compared to the Single-Gene method; however, a rather more complicated formula is required. It is suggested that in the situations where a rough estimate is needed, the Single-Gene method can lead to a reasonable answer in a relatively shorter time with less computational cost, but when a more accurate answer is required, the Multi-Gene formula is recommended.

The error estimates show that the test data sets in both Single-Gene and Multi-Gene models have a lower R^2 and higher MAPE, which can be indicators of higher errors and overfitting of the model. However, the RMSE and MAE values provide comparable results for the test and trained data sets with fewer errors. In other words, two of the four error indicators show better results in test data sets, while the other two may indicate overfitting. Given the circumstances, the results for both Single-Gene and Multi-Gene models are reasonably acceptable.

3.3. Uncertainty Analysis and Confidence Bands

After finding the equation, its credibility needs to be investigated and verified by uncertainty and sensitivity analyses.

A Monte Carlo analysis was also performed for the uncertainty analysis of the resulting equation. The objective of this analysis is to calculate the uncertainty of the final function. To do so, 1,000,000 random inputs of h_d were generated in the range of 0.3179 to 3.2211. Then, the equation was run for each random number. To generate random data with normal-shaped distribution in a specific range, a truncated Gaussian function was used. The histogram of the generated data using the truncated Gaussian function is shown in Figure 14.

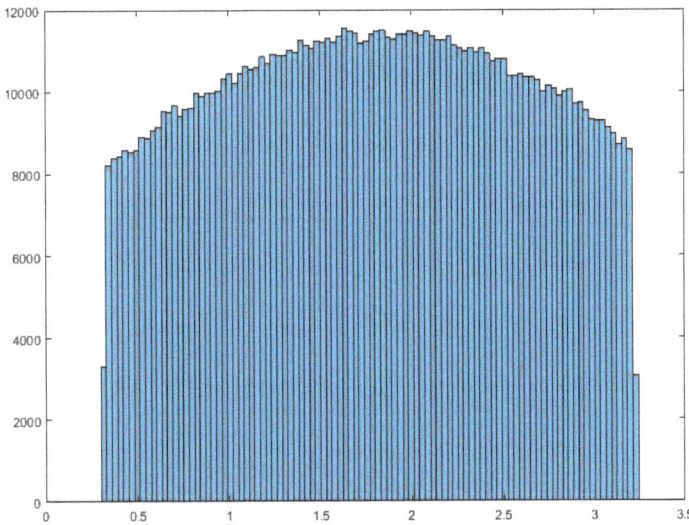

Figure 14. Histogram of generated random inputs created with truncated Gaussian function.

These random numbers were then put into the GP model, and 1,000,000 values for P_d, namely P_{mc}, were calculated. The mean absolute deviation (MAD) was calculated around the average using Equation (27)

$$MAD = \frac{1}{n}\sum_{i=1}^{n}|P_{mc_i} - P_{avg}| \tag{41}$$

where n is the number of samples (i.e., n = 1,000,000 in this case) and P_{avg} is the average of the pressures calculated by the Monte Carlo simulation [20], thus leading to

$$MAD_{SG} = 11.718 \text{ and } MAD_{MG} = 11.4728$$

This can be used to calculate the uncertainty percentage of the function by using the following equation [20]:

$$U = 100 \times \frac{MAD}{P_{avg}} \tag{42}$$

The above leads to

$$U_{SG} = 100 \times \frac{11.718}{10.7485} = 109.02 \text{ and } U_{MG} = 100 \times \frac{11.4728}{11.430} = 100.3738$$

where U_{SG} and U_{MG} are the uncertainty percentages for the Single-Gene and Multi-Gene equations, respectively. Due to the high slope of the graph of the equation in the beginning, these amounts of uncertainty are reasonable.

Confidence bands of the graph are then obtained using a 2nd-order approach in the calculation of the Jacobian Matrix with the central difference scheme. The MATLAB internal function "nlpredci" (non-linear regression prediction confidence intervals) is used. This function can provide the user with 95% confidence band widths of the given equation. According to Dolan et al. [46], this function gives a symmetric confidence interval at each point; hence, the two confidence bands have the same distance from the main equation. The 95% confidence bands for Equations (28) and (29) are plotted in Figure 15a,b, respectively. The average confidence band width for Equation (28) (i.e., Single-Gene mode) is 20.54, and for Equation (29) (i.e., Multi-Gene mode) is 15.27.

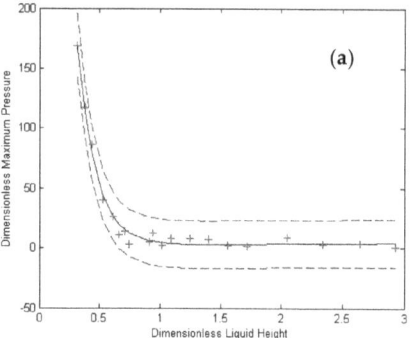
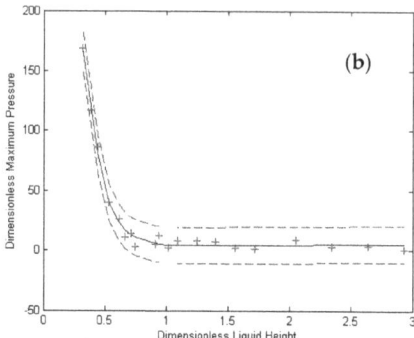

Figure 15. Graph of the proposed equation for dimensionless pressure plotted against dimensionless liquid height with 95% confidence bounds for (**a**) Single-Gene and (**b**) Multi-Gene modes.

3.4. Sensitivity Analysis

For the sensitivity analysis, a 10% perturbation is applied to an input value of the equation (here, the mean), and the perturbation in the outcome is calculated. The calculations are presented in Equations (43)–(45):

$$h_{dp} = 1.1 \times h_{dm} \tag{43}$$

$$\Delta P_d = \frac{|P_{dp} - P_{dm}|}{P_{dm}} \tag{44}$$

$$S_n = \frac{\Delta P_d}{0.1} \tag{45}$$

where h_{dp} is the 10% perturbed mean dimensionless liquid height, h_{dm} is the actual mean dimensionless liquid height, ΔP_d is the perturbation that appears in the dimensionless pressure due to the 10% perturbation in the dimensionless liquid height, P_{dp} is the change in the value of the dimensionless pressure when the dimensionless liquid height changes, P_{dm} is the value of the dimensionless pressure at mean dimensionless liquid height (h_{dm}) calculated based on Equations (28) and (29) for Single-Gene and Multi-Gene modes, and S_n is the normal sensitivity of those equations.

This leads to a sensitivity of $S_{n,SG} = 0.258$, or a 25.8% sensitivity for the Single-Gene solution and $S_{n,MG} = 0.116$ or a 11.6% sensitivity for the Multi-Gene solution.

4. Conclusions

The purpose of this study was to develop an empirical equation for the maximum pressure at the roofs of liquid storage tanks. To do so, a previously validated OpenFOAM model was used to generate the data. The data included the maximum pressure at the roof. Various tank sizes with different liquid heights were modeled, and harmonic sinusoidal base excitations with resonance frequencies were applied to the tanks. To consider the effect of bi-directional excitation, the tanks were shaken in three different orientations. Pressure sensors were distributed on one quarter of the roof, and the maximum pressure at each sensor was recorded.

Using the GP method, a relationship between the dimensionless liquid height and the dimensionless maximum pressure was obtained in both Single-Gene and Multi-Gene modes (Equations (28) and (29)). Using multiple error measures, the two equations were tested, and the results were compared. These results show that the outputs of the equations are in good agreement with the ones obtained by CFD modelling. Uncertainty analyses of the equations were conducted using the Monte Carlo method, leading to reasonable values given that both functions have an ascending shape with a high slope in the beginning of their domains. In addition, the 95% confidence bands for the equation were drawn.

It can be concluded that the use of AI techniques combined with CFD is helpful in predicting the maximum pressure at the roof of a base-excited tank. Further investigation on this aspect is currently in progress by the authors.

Author Contributions: Conceptualization, A.M. and R.K.; data curation, I.B.T.; formal analysis, I.B.T.; funding acquisition, A.M. and R.K.; investigation, I.B.T.; methodology, A.M. and R.K.; project administration, A.M. and R.K.; resources, I.B.T.; software, I.B.T. and A.M.; supervision, A.M. and R.K.; validation, I.B.T.; visualization, I.B.T.; writing—original draft, I.B.T.; writing—review and editing, A.M. and R.K. All authors have read and agreed to the published version of the manuscript.

Funding: This research was funded by Natural Sciences and Engineering Research Council of Canada (NSERC).

Conflicts of Interest: The authors declare no conflict of interest.

References

1. Housner, W.G. The Dynamic Behavior of Water Tanks. *Bull. Seismol. Soc. Am.* **1963**, *53*, 381–387.
2. ACI 350.3. *Seismic Design of Liquid-Containing Concrete Structures and Commentary (ACI 350.3-6)*; American Concrete Institute: Farmington Hills, MI, USA, 2006.
3. Isaacson, M. Earthquake-induced hydrodynamic forces on reservoir roofs. *Can. J. Civ. Eng.* **2010**, *37*, 1107–1115. [CrossRef]
4. Cho, K.H.; Cho, S.Y. Seismic Response of Cylindrical Steel Tanks Considering Fluid-Structure Interaction. *J. Steel Struct.* **2007**, *7*, 147–152.
5. Liu, D.; Lin, P. A numerical study of three-dimensional liquid sloshing in tanks. *J. Comput. Phys.* **2008**, *227*, 3921–3939. [CrossRef]
6. Chen, Y.G.; Djidjeli, K.; Price, W.G. Numerical simulation of liquid sloshing phenomena in partially filled containers. *J. Comput. Fluids* **2009**, *38*, 830–842. [CrossRef]
7. Kang, D.H.; Lee, Y.B. *Summary Report of Sloshing Model Test for Rectangular Model*; Daewoo Shipbuilding & Marine Engineering Co. Ltd.: Geoje, Korea, 2005; Volume 1.
8. Afan, H.A.; El-shafie, A.; Mohtar, W.H.; Yaseen, Z.M. Past, present and prospect of an Artificial Intelligence (AI) based model for sediment transport prediction. *J. Hydrol.* **2016**, *541*, 902–913. [CrossRef]
9. Ivakhnenko, A.G.; Ivakhnenko, G.A. The review of problems solvable by algorithms of the group method of data handling (GMDH). *Pattern Recognit. Image Anal. C/C Raspoznavaniye Obrazov I Anal. Izobrazhenii* **1995**, *5*, 527–535.
10. Mohammadpour, R.; Ghani, A.; Azamathulla, H.M. Estimating time to equilibrium scour at long abutment by using genetic programming. In Proceedings of the 3rd International Conference on Managing Rivers in the 21st Century (Rivers 2011), Penang, Malaysia, 6–9 December 2011.
11. Lallahem, S.; Mania, J.; Hani, A.; Najjar, Y. On the use of neural networks to evaluate groundwater levels in fractured media. *J. Hydrol.* **2005**, *307*, 92–111. [CrossRef]
12. Ghani, A.A.; Azamathulla, H.M. Development of GEP-based functional relationship for sediment transport in tropical rivers. *Neural Comput. Appl.* **2014**, *24*, 271–276. [CrossRef]
13. He, Z.; Wen, X.; Liu, H.; Du, J. A comparative study of artificial neural network, adaptive neuro fuzzy inference system and support vector machine for forecasting river flow in the semiarid mountain region. *J. Hydrol.* **2014**, *509*, 379–386. [CrossRef]
14. Daliakopoulos, I.N.; Coulibaly, P.; Tsanis, I.K. Groundwater level forecasting using artificial neural networks. *J. Hydrol.* **2005**, *309*, 229–240. [CrossRef]
15. Mirzavand, M.; Khoshnevisan, B.; Shamshirband, S.; Kisi, O.; Ahmad, R.; Akib, S. Evaluating groundwater level fluctuation by support vector regression and neuro-fuzzy methods: A comparative study. *Nat. Hazards* **2015**, *1*, 1–15. [CrossRef]
16. Mohammadpour, R.; Shaharuddin, S.; Chang, C.K.; Zakaria, N.A.; Ghani, A.; Chan, N.W. Prediction of water quality index in constructed wetlands using support vector machine. *Environ. Sci. Pollut. Res.* **2015**, *22*, 6208–6219. [CrossRef] [PubMed]
17. Deshpande, N.; Londhe, S.; Kulkarni, S. Modeling compressive strength of recycled aggregate concrete by artificial neural network, model tree and non-linear regression. *Int. J. Sustain. Built Environ.* **2014**, *3*, 187–198. [CrossRef]
18. Loh, W.Y. *Classification and Regression Tree Methods*; Statistics Reference Online; Wiley StatsRef: Hoboken, NJ, USA, 2014.
19. Garg, A.; Garg, A.; Tai, K.J.C.G. A multi-gene genetic programming model for estimating stress-dependent soil water retention curves. *Comput. Geosci.* **2014**, *18*, 45–56. [CrossRef]
20. Sattar, A.M.; Gharabaghi, B. Gene expression models for prediction of longitudinal dispersion coefficient in streams. *J. Hydrol.* **2015**, *524*, 587–596. [CrossRef]
21. Sattar, A.M.A.; Gharabaghi, B.; McBean, E.A. Prediction of Timing of Watermain Failure Using Gene Expression Models. *Water Resour. Manag.* **2016**, *30*, 1635–1651. [CrossRef]
22. Azamathulla, H.M. Gene expression programming for prediction of scour depth downstream of sills. *J. Hydrol.* **2012**, *460*, 156–159. [CrossRef]

23. Chinnarasri, C.; Kositgittiwong, D. Laboratory study of maximum scour depth downstream of sills. In *Proceedings of the Institution of Civil Engineers-Water Management. Vol. 161. No. 5*; Thomas Telford Ltd.: London, UK, 2008.
24. Najafzadeh, M.; Rezaie, M.; Rashedi, E. Prediction of maximum scour depth around piers with debris accumulation using EPR, MT, and GEP models. *J. Hydroinform.* 2016, *18*, 867–884. [CrossRef]
25. Gholami, A.; Bonakdari, H.; Zeynoddin, M.; Ebtehaj, I.; Gharabaghi, B.; Khodashenas, S.R. Reliable method of determining stable threshold channel shape using experimental and gene expression programming techniques. *Neural Comput.* 2019, *31*, 5799–5817. [CrossRef]
26. Khozani, Z.S.; Bonakdari, H.; Ebtehaj, I. An analysis of shear stress distribution in circular channels with sediment deposition based on Gene Expression Programming. *Int. J. Sediment Res.* 2017, *32*, 575–584. [CrossRef]
27. Gandomi, A.H.; Alavi, A.H. A new multi-gene genetic programming approach to nonlinear system modeling. Part I: Materials and structural engineering problems. *Neural Comput. Appl.* 2012, *21*, 171–187. [CrossRef]
28. Kaydani, H.; Mohebbi, A.; Eftekhari, M. Permeability estimation in heterogeneous oil reservoirs by multi-gene genetic programming algorithm. *J. Pet. Sci. Eng.* 2014, *123*, 201–206. [CrossRef]
29. Safari, M.J.S.; Mehr, A.D. Multi-gene genetic programming for sediment transport modeling in sewers for conditions of non-deposition with a bed deposit. *Int. J. Sediment Res.* 2018, *33*, 262–270. [CrossRef]
30. Mehr, A.D.; Nourani, V. Season algorithm-multigene genetic programming: A new approach for rainfall-runoff modelling. *Water Resour. Manag.* 2018, *32*, 2665–2679. [CrossRef]
31. Gandomi, A.H.; Yun, G.J.; Alavi, A.H. An evolutionary approach for modeling of shear strength of RC deep beams. *Mater. Struct.* 2013, *46*, 2109–2119. [CrossRef]
32. Gandomi, A.H.; Alavi, A.H.; Kazemi, S.; Gandomi, M. Formulation of shear strength of slender RC beams using gene expression programming, part I: Without shear reinforcement. *Autom. Constr.* 2014, *42*, 112–121. [CrossRef]
33. Zahiri, A.; Dehghani, A.A.; Azamathulla, H.M. Application of Gene-Expression Programming in Hydraulic Engineering. In *Handbook of Genetic Programming Applications*; Gandomi, A.H., Alavi, A.H., Ryan, C., Eds.; Springer: Cham, Switzerland, 2015; pp. 71–97.
34. OpenFOAM version 2.3.1. Computer Software. Available online: https://openfoam.org/version/2-3-1/ (accessed on 31 December 2020).
35. Bahreini Toussi, I.; Kianoush, R.; Mohammadian, A. Numerical and Experimental Investigation of Rectangular Liquid-Containing Structures under Seismic Excitation. *Infrastructures* 2021, *6*, 1. [CrossRef]
36. Jaiswal, O.R.; Kulkarni, S.; Pathak, P. A Study on Sloshing Frequencies of Fluid-Tank System. In Proceedings of the 14th World Conference on Earthquake Engineering, Beijing, China, 12–17 October 2008.
37. Moslemi, M.; Kianoush, M.R. Parametric study on dynamic behavior of cylindrical ground-supported tanks. *Eng. Struct.* 2012, *42*, 214–230. [CrossRef]
38. Lamb, H. *Hydrodynamics*, 6th ed.; Cambridge University Press: Cambridge, UK, 1932.
39. Greenshields, C.J. *OpenFOAM User Guide*; The OpenFOAM Foundation: London, UK, 2018.
40. Koza, J.R.; Koza, J.R. *Genetic Programming: On the Programming of Computers by Means of Natural Selection (Vol. 1)*; MIT Press: Cambridge, MA, USA, 1992.
41. Pandey, D.S.; Pan, I.; Das, S.; Leahy, J.J.; Kwapinski, W. Multi-gene genetic programming based predictive models for municipal solid waste gasification in a fluidized bed gasifier. *Bioresour. Technol.* 2015, *179*, 524–533. [CrossRef]
42. Searson, D.P.; Leahy, D.E.; Willis, M.J. GPTIPS: An open source genetic programming toolbox for multigene symbolic regression. In Proceedings of the International MultiConference of Engineers and Computer Scientists, Hong Kong, 17–19 March 2010; Volume 1, pp. 77–80.
43. Bonakdari, H.; Moeeni, H.; Ebtehaj, I.; Zeynoddin, M.; Mahoammadian, A.; Gharabaghi, B. New insights into soil temperature time series modeling: Linear or nonlinear? *Theor. Appl. Climatol.* 2019, *135*, 1157–1177. [CrossRef]
44. Azimi, H.; Bonakdari, H.; Ebtehaj, I.; Gharabaghi, B.; Khoshbin, F. Evolutionary design of generalized group method of data handling-type neural network for estimating the hydraulic jump roller length. *Acta Mech.* 2018, *229*, 1197–1214. [CrossRef]
45. Gandomi, A.H.; Roke, D.A. Assessment of artificial neural network and genetic programming as predictive tools. *Adv. Eng. Softw.* 2015, *88*, 63–72. [CrossRef]
46. Dolan, K.D.; Yang, L.; Trampel, C.P. Nonlinear regression technique to estimate kinetic parameters and confidence intervals in unsteady-state conduction-heated foods. *J. Food Eng.* 2007, *80*, 581–593. [CrossRef]

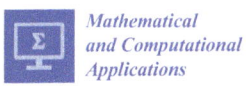

Mathematical and Computational Applications

Article

Chaotic Multi-Objective Simulated Annealing and Threshold Accepting for Job Shop Scheduling Problem

Juan Frausto-Solís [1,*], Leonor Hernández-Ramírez [1], Guadalupe Castilla-Valdez [1], Juan J. González-Barbosa [1] and Juan P. Sánchez-Hernández [2]

1. Graduate Program Division, Tecnológico Nacional de México/Instituto Tecnológico de Ciudad Madero, Cd. Madero 89440, Mexico; iscleo1@gmail.com (L.H.-R.); gpe_cas@yahoo.com.mx (G.C.-V.); jjgonzalezbarbosa@hotmail.com (J.J.G.-B.)
2. Dirección de Informática, Electrónica y Telecomunicaciones, Universidad Politécnica del Estado de Morelos, Boulevard Cuauhnáhuac 566, Jiutepec 62574, Mexico; juan.paulosh@upemor.edu.mx
* Correspondence: juan.frausto@gmail.com

Citation: Frausto-Solis, J.; Hernández-Ramírez, L.; Castilla-Valdez, G.; González-Barbosa, J.J.; Sánchez-Hernández, J.P. Chaotic Multi-Objective Simulated Annealing and Threshold Accepting for Job Shop Scheduling Problem. *Math. Comput. Appl.* **2021**, *26*, 8. https://doi.org/10.3390/mca26010008

Received: 26 September 2020
Accepted: 8 January 2021
Published: 12 January 2021

Publisher's Note: MDPI stays neutral with regard to jurisdictional claims in published maps and institutional affiliations.

Copyright: © 2021 by the authors. Licensee MDPI, Basel, Switzerland. This article is an open access article distributed under the terms and conditions of the Creative Commons Attribution (CC BY) license (https://creativecommons.org/licenses/by/4.0/).

Abstract: The Job Shop Scheduling Problem (JSSP) has enormous industrial applicability. This problem refers to a set of jobs that should be processed in a specific order using a set of machines. For the single-objective optimization JSSP problem, Simulated Annealing is among the best algorithms. However, in Multi-Objective JSSP (MOJSSP), these algorithms have barely been analyzed, and the Threshold Accepting Algorithm has not been published for this problem. It is worth mentioning that the researchers in this area have not reported studies with more than three objectives, and the number of metrics they used to measure their performance is less than two or three. In this paper, we present two MOJSSP metaheuristics based on Simulated Annealing: Chaotic Multi-Objective Simulated Annealing (CMOSA) and Chaotic Multi-Objective Threshold Accepting (CMOTA). We developed these algorithms to minimize three objective functions and compared them using the HV metric with the recently published algorithms, MOMARLA, MOPSO, CMOEA, and SPEA. The best algorithm is CMOSA (HV of 0.76), followed by MOMARLA and CMOTA (with HV of 0.68), and MOPSO (with HV of 0.54). In addition, we show a complexity comparison of these algorithms, showing that CMOSA, CMOTA, and MOMARLA have a similar complexity class, followed by MOPSO.

Keywords: JSSP; CMOSA; CMOTA; chaotic perturbation

1. Introduction

The Job Shop Scheduling Problem (JSSP) has enormous industrial applicability. This problem consists of a set of jobs, formed by operations, which must be processed in a set of machines subject to constraints of precedence and resource capacity. Finding the optimal solution for this problem is too complex, and so it is classified in the NP-hard class [1,2]. On the other hand, the JSSP foundations provide a theoretical background for developing efficient algorithms for other significant sequencing problems, which have many production systems applications [3]. Furthermore, designing and evaluating new algorithms for JSSP is relevant not only because it represents a big challenge but also for its high industrial applicability [4].

There are several JSSP taxonomies; one of which is single-objective and multi-objective optimization. The single-objective optimization version has been widely studied for many years, and the Simulated Annealing (SA) [5] is among the best algorithms. The Threshold Accepting (TA) algorithm from the same family is also very efficient in this area [6]. In contrast, in the case of Multi-Objective Optimization Problems (MOOPs), both algorithms for JSSP and their comparison are scarce.

Published JSSP algorithms for MOOP include only a few objectives, and only a few performance metrics are reported. However, it is common for the industrial scheduling requirements to have several objectives, and then the Multi-Objective JSSP (MOJSSP) becomes an even more significant challenge. Thus, many industrial production areas require the multi-objective approach [7,8].

In single-objective optimization, the goal is to find the optimal feasible solution of an objective function. In other words, to find the best value of the variables which fulfill all the constraints of the problem. On the other hand, for MOJSSP, the problem is to find the optimum of a set of objective functions $f_1(x)$, $f_2(x) \ldots f_n(x)$ depending on a set of variables x and subject to a set of constraints defined by these variables. To find the optimal solution is usually impossible because fulfilling some objective functions may not optimize the other objectives of the problem. In MOOP, a preference relation or Pareto dominance relation produces a set of solutions commonly called the Pareto optimal set [9]. The Decision Makers (DMs) should select from the Pareto set the solution that satisfies their preferences, which can be subjective, based on experience, or will most likely be influenced by the industrial environment's needs [10]. Therefore, the DM needs to have a Pareto front that contains multiple representative compromise solutions, which exhibit both good convergence and diversity [11].

In the study of single-objective JSSP, many algorithms have been applied. Some of the most common are SA, Genetic Algorithms (GAs), Tabu Search (TS), and Ant Systems (ASs) [12]. In addition, as we mention below, few works in the literature solve JSSP instances with more than two objectives and applying more than two metrics to evaluate their performance. Nevertheless, for MOJSSP, the number of objectives and performance metrics remains too small [8,13–15]. The works of Zhao [14] and Mendez [8] are exceptions because the authors have presented implementations with two or three significant objective functions and two performance metrics. Moreover, SA and TA have shown to be very efficient for solving NP-hard problems. Thus, this paper's motivation is to develop new efficient SA algorithms for MOJSSP with two or more objective functions and a larger number of performance metrics.

The first adaptation of SA to MOOP was an algorithm proposed in 1992, also known as MOSA [16]. An essential part of this algorithm is that it applies the Boltzmann criterion for accepting bad solutions, commonly used in single-objective JSSP. MOSA combines several objective functions. The single-objective JSSP optimization with SA algorithm and MOSA algorithm for multi-objective optimization is different in several aspect related to determining the energy functions, using and generating new solutions, and measuring their quality as is well known, these energy functions are required in the acceptance criterion. Multiple versions of MOSA have been proposed in the last few years. One of them, published in 2008, is AMOSA, that surpassed other MOOP algorithms at this time [17]. In this work, we adapt this algorithm for MOJSSP. TA [6] is an algorithm for single-objective JSSP, which is very similar to Simulated Annealing. These two algorithms have the same structure, and both use a temperature parameter, and they accept some bad solutions for escaping from local optima. In addition, these algorithms are among the best JSSP algorithms, and their performance is very similar. Nevertheless, for MOJSSP, a TA algorithm has not been published, and so for obvious reason, it was not compared with the SA multi-objective version.

MOJSSP has been commonly solved using IMOEA/D [14], NSGA-II [18], SPEA [19], MOPSO [20], and CMOEA [21]; the latter was renamed CMEA in [8]. Nevertheless, the number of objectives and performance metrics of these algorithms remains too small. The Evolutionary Algorithm based on decomposition proposed in 2016 by Zhao in [14] was considered the best algorithm [22]. The Multi-Objective Q-Learning algorithm (MOQL) for JSSP was published in 2017 [23]; this approach uses several agents to solve JSSP. An extension of MOQL is MOMARLA, which was proposed in 2019 by Mendez [8]. This MOJSSP algorithm uses two objective functions: makespan and total tardiness. MOMARLA overcomes the classical multi-objective algorithms SPEA [19], CMOEA [21], and MOPSO [20].

The two new algorithms presented in this paper for JSSP are Chaotic Multi-Objective Simulated Annealing (CMOSA) and Chaotic Multi-Objective Threshold Accepting (CMOTA). The first algorithm is inspired by the classic MOSA algorithm [17]. However, CMOSA is different in three aspects: (1) for the first time it is designed specifically for MOJSSP, (2) it uses an analytical tuning of the cooling scheme parameters, and (3) it uses chaotic perturbations for finding new solutions and for escaping from local optima. This process allows the search to continue from a different point in the solution space and it contributes to a better diversity of the generated solutions. Furthermore, CMOTA is based on CMOSA and Threshold Accepting, and it does not require the Boltzmann distribution. Instead, it uses a threshold strategy for accepting bad solutions to escape from local optima. In addition, a chaotic perturbation function is applied.

In this paper, we present two new alternatives for MOJSSP, and we consider three objective functions: makespan, total tardiness, and total flow time. The first objective is very relevant for production management applications [7], while the other two are critical for enhancing client attention service [23]. In addition, we use six metrics for the evaluation of these algorithms, and they are Mean Ideal Distance (MID), Spacing (S), Hypervolume (HV), Spread (Δ), Inverted Generational Distance (IGD), and Coverage (C). We also apply an analytical tuning parameter method to these algorithms. Finally, we compare the achieved results with those obtained with the JSSP algorithm cited below in [8,14].

The rest of the paper is organized as follows. In Section 2, we make a qualitative comparison of related MOJSSP works. In Section 3, we present MOJSSP concepts and the performance metrics that were applied. Section 4 presents the formulation of MOJSSP with three objectives. The proposed algorithms, their tuning method, and the chaotic perturbation are also shown in Section 5. Section 6 shows the application of the proposed algorithms to a set of 70, 58, and 15 instances. Finally, the results are shown and compared with previous works. In Section 7, we present our conclusions.

2. Related Works

As mentioned above, in single-objective optimization, the JSSP community has broadly investigated the performance of the different solution methods. However, the situation is entirely different for MOJSSP, and there is a small number of published works. In 1994, an analysis of SA family algorithms for JSSP was presented [24]; two of them were SA and TA, which we briefly explain in the next paragraph. These algorithms suppose that the solutions define a set of macrostates of a set of particles, while the objective functions' values represent their energy, and both algorithms have a Metropolis cycle where the neighborhood of solutions is explored. In single-objective optimization, for the set of instances used to evaluate JSSP algorithms, SA obtained better results than TA. Furthermore, a better solution than the previous one is always accepted, while a worse solution may be accepted depending on the Boltzmann distribution criterion. This distribution is related to the current temperature value and the increment or decrement of energy (associated with the objective functions) in the current temperature value. In the TA case, a worse solution than the previous one may be accepted using a criterion that tries to emulate the Boltzmann distribution. This criterion establishes a possible acceptance of a worse solution when the decrement of energy is smaller than a threshold value depending on the temperature and a parameter γ that is very close to one. Then at the beginning of the process, the threshold values are enormous because they depend on the temperatures. Subsequently, the temperature parameter is gradually decreased until a value close to zero is achieved, and then this threshold is very small.

In 2001, a Multi-Objective Genetic Algorithm was proposed to minimize the makespan, total tardiness, and the total idle time [25]. The proposed methodology for JSSP was assessed with 28 benchmark problems. In this publication, the authors randomly weighted the different fitness functions to determine their results.

In 2006, SA was used for two objectives: the makespan and the mean flow time [26]. This algorithm was called Pareto Archived Simulated Annealing (PASA), which used the Simulated Annealing algorithm with an overheating strategy to escape from local optima and to improve the quality of the results. The performance of this algorithm was evaluated with 82 instances taken from the literature. Unfortunately, this method has not been updated for three or more objective functions.

In 2011, a two-stage genetic algorithm (2S-GA) was proposed for JSSP with three objectives to minimize the makespan, total weighted earliness, and total weighted tardiness [13]. In the first stage, a parallel GA found the best solution for each objective function. Then, in the second stage, the GA combined the populations, which evolved using the weighted aggregating objective function.

Researchers from the Contemporary Design and Integrated Manufacturing Technology (CDIMT) laboratory proposed an algorithm named Improved Multi-Objective Evolutionary Algorithm based on Decomposition (IMOEA/D) to minimize the makespan, tardiness, and total flow time [14]. The authors experiment with 58 benchmark instances, and they use the performance metrics Coverage [27] and Mean Ideal Distance (MID) [28] to evaluate their algorithm. We notice in Table 1, studies with two or three objectives, but they do not report any metric. On the other hand, IMOEA/D stands out from the rest of the literature, not only because the authors reported good results but also because they considered a more significant number of objectives, and they applied two metrics.

In 2008, the AMOSA algorithm based on SA for several objectives was proposed [17]. In this paper, the authors reported that the AMOSA algorithm performed better than some MOEA algorithms, one of them NSGA-II [29]. They presented the main Boltzmann rules for accepting bad solutions. Unfortunately, a MOJSSP with AMOSA and with more than two objectives has not been published.

In 2017, a hybrid algorithm between an NSGA-II and a linear programming approach was proposed [15]; it was used to solve the FT10 instance of Taillard [30]. This algorithm minimized the weighted tardiness and energy costs. To evaluate the performance, the authors only used the HV metric.

In 2019, MOMARLA was proposed, a new algorithm based on Q-Learning to solve MOJSSP [8]. This work provided flexibility to use decision-maker preferences; each agent represented a specific objective and used two action selection strategies to find a diverse and accurate Pareto front. In Table 1, we present the last related studies for MOJSSP and the proposed algorithms.

This paper analyzes our algorithms CMOSA and CMOTA, as follows: (a) comparing CMOSA and CMOTA versus IMOEA/D [14], (b) comparing our algorithms with the results published for MOMARLA, MOPSO, CMOEA, and SPEA, and (c) comparing CMOSA versus CMOTA.

Table 1. Related Works.

Algorithm	Objectives	Metrics
SA [16]	Makespan	*
SA and TA [24]	Makespan	*
Hybrid GA [25]	Makespan, total tardiness, and total idle time	*
PASA [26]	Makespan, mean flow time	*
2S-GA [13]	Makespan, total weighted earliness, and total weighted tardiness	*
IMOEA/D [14]	Makespan, total flow time, and tardiness time	C, MID
Hybrid GA/LS/LP [15]	Weighted tardiness, and energy costs	HV
MOMARLA [8]	Makespan, total tardiness	HV
CMOSA and CMOTA (This paper)	Makespan, total tardiness, and total flow time	MID, S, HV, Δ, IGD and C

* Not reported.

3. Multi-Objective Optimization

In a single-objective problem, the algorithm finishes its execution when it finds the solution that optimizes the objective function or a very close optimal solution. However, for Multi-Objective Optimization, the situation is more complicated since several objectives must be optimized simultaneously. Then, it is necessary to find a set of solutions optimizing each of the objectives individually. These solutions can be contrasting because we can obtain the best solution for an objective function that is not the best for other objective functions.

3.1. Concepts

Definitions of some concepts of Multi-Objective Optimization are shown below.

Pareto Dominance: In general, for any optimization problem, solution A dominates another solution B if the following conditions are met [31]: A is strictly better than B on at least one objective, and A is not worse than B for any objective function.

Non-dominated set: In a set of P solutions, the non-dominated solutions P1 is integrated by solutions that accomplish the following conditions [31]: any pair of P1 solutions must be non-dominated (one regarding the other), and any solution that does not belong to P1 is dominated by at least one member of P1.

Pareto optimal set: The set of non-dominated solutions of the total search space.

Pareto front: The graphic representation of the non-dominated solutions of the multi-objective optimization problem.

3.2. Performance Metrics

In an experimental comparison of different optimization techniques or algorithms, it is always necessary to have the notion of performance. In the case of Multi-Objective Optimization, the definition of quality is much more complicated than for single-objective optimization problems because the multi-objective optimization criteria itself consists of multiple objectives, of which, the most important are:

1. To minimize the distance of the resulting non-dominated set to the true Pareto front.
2. To achieve an adequate distribution (for instance, uniform) of the solutions is desirable.
3. To maximize the extension of the non-dominated front for each of the objectives. In other words, a wide range of values must be covered by non-dominated solutions.

In general, it is difficult to find a single performance metric that encompasses all of the above criteria. In the literature, a large number of performance metrics can be found. The most popular performance metrics were used in this research and are described below:

Mean Ideal Distance: Evaluates the closeness of the calculated Pareto front (PF_{calc}) solutions with an ideal point, which is usually (0, 0) [28].

$$MID = \frac{\sum_{i=1}^{Q} c_i}{Q} \quad (1)$$

where $c_i = \sqrt{f_{1,i}^2 + f_{2,i}^2 + f_{3,i}^2}$ and $f_{1,i}, f_{2,i}, f_{3,i}$ are the values of the i-th non-dominated solution for their first, second, and third objective function, and Q is the number of solutions in the PF_{calc}.

Spacing: Evaluates the distribution of non-dominated solutions in the PF_{calc}. When several algorithms are evaluated with this metric, the best is that with the smallest S value [32].

$$S = \sqrt{\frac{\sum_{i=1}^{Q}(d_i - \bar{d})^2}{Q}} \quad (2)$$

where d_i measures the distance in the space of the objective functions between the i-th solution and its nearest neighbor; that is the j-th solution in the PF_{calc} of the algorithm, Q is the number of the solutions in the PF_{calc}, $\bar{d}$ is the average of the d_i, that is $\bar{d} = \sum_{i=1}^{Q} \frac{d_i}{Q}$ and $d_i = min_j(|f_1^i(x) - f_1^j(x)| + |f_2^i(x) - f_2^j(x)| + \cdots + |f_M^i(x) - f_M^j(x)|)$, where f_1^i, f_2^i are the values of the i-th non-dominated solution for their first and second objective function, f_1^j, f_2^j are the values of the j-th non-dominated solution for their first and second objective function respectively, M is the number of objective functions and $i, j = 1, \ldots Q$.

Hypervolume: Calculates the volume in the objective space that is covered by all members of the non-dominated set [33]. The HV metric is measured based on a reference point (W), and this can be found simply by constructing a vector with the worst values of the objective function.

$$HV = volume\left(\cup_{i=1}^{|Q|} v_i\right) \quad (3)$$

where v_i is a hypercube and is constructed with a reference point W and the solution i as the diagonal corners of the hypercube [31]. An algorithm that obtains the largest HV value is better. The data should be normalized by transforming the value in the range [0, 1] for each objective separately to perform the calculation.

Spread: This metric was proposed to have a more precise coverage value and considers the distance to the (extreme points) of the true Pareto front (PF_{true}) [29].

$$\Delta = \frac{\sum_{k=1}^{M} d_k^e + \sum_{i=1}^{Q} |d_i - \bar{d}|}{\sum_{k=1}^{M} d_k^e + Q \times \bar{d}} \quad (4)$$

where d_k^e measures the distance between the "extreme" point of the PF_{true} for the k-th objective function, and the nearest point of PF_{calc}, d_i corresponds to the distance between the solution i-th of the PF_{calc}, while its nearest neighbor, $\bar{d}$ corresponds to the average of the d_i and M is the number of objectives.

Inverted Generational Distance: It is an inverted indicator version of the Generational Distance (GD) metric, where all the distances are measured from the PF_{true} to the PF_{calc} [1].

$$IGD(Q) = \frac{\left(\sum_{j=1}^{|T|} \hat{d}_j^p\right)^{1/p}}{|T|} \quad (5)$$

where $T = \{t_1, t_2, \ldots, t_{|T|}\}$ that is, the solutions in the PF_{true} and $|T|$ is the cardinality of T, p is an integer parameter, in this paper $p = 2$ and $\hat{d}_j$ is the Euclidean distance from t_j to its nearest objective vector q in Q, according to (6).

$$d_j = \min_{q=1}^{|Q|} \sqrt{\sum_{m=1}^{M} (fm(t_j) - fm(q))^2} \quad (6)$$

where $fm(t)$ is the m-th objective function value of the t-th member of T and M is the number of objectives.

Coverage: Represents the dominance between set A and set B [27]. It is the ratio of the number of solutions in set B that were dominated by solutions in set A and the total number of solutions in set B. The C metric is defined by (7).

$$C(A, B) = \frac{|\{b \in B | \exists a \in A : a \preceq b\}|}{|B|} \quad (7)$$

When $C(A, B) = 1$, all B solution are dominated or equal to solutions in A. Otherwise, $C(A, B) = 0$, represents situations in which none of the solutions in B is dominated by any solution in A. The higher the value of $C(A, B)$, the more solutions in B are dominated by solutions in A. Both $C(A, B)$ and $C(B, A)$ should be considered, since $C(B, A)$ is not necessarily equal to $1 - C(A, B)$.

4. Multi-Objective Job Shop Scheduling Problem

In JSSP, there are a set of n different jobs consisting of operations that must be processed in m different machines. There are a set of precedence constraints for these operations, and there are also resource capacity constraints for ensuring that each machine should process only one operation at the same time. The processing time of each operation is known in advance. The objective of JSSP is to determine the sequence of the operations in each machine (the start and finish time of each operation) to minimize certain objective functions subject to the constraints mentioned above. The most common objective is the makespan, which is the total time in which all the problem operations are processed. Nevertheless, real scheduling problems are multi-objective, and several objectives should be considered simultaneously.

The three objectives that are addressed in the present paper are:

Makespan: the maximum time of completion of all jobs.

Total tardiness: it is calculated as the total positive differences between the makespan and the due date of each job.

Total flow time: it is the summation of the completion times of all jobs.

The formal MOJSSP model can be formulated as follows [34,35]:

$$Optimize\ F(x) = [f_1(x), f_2(x), \ldots, f_q(x)]\ Subject\ to: x \in S \qquad (8)$$

where q is the number of objectives, x is the vector of decision variables, and S represents the feasible region. Defined by the next precedence and capacity constraints, respectively:

$t_j \geq t_i + p_i$ For all $i, j \in O$ when i precedes j

$t_j \geq t_i + p_i$ or $t_i \geq t_j + p_j$ For all $i, j \in O$ when $M_i = M_j$

where:

t_i, t_j are the starting times for the jobs $i, j \in J$.

p_i and p_j are the processing times for the jobs $i, j \in J$.

$J : \{J_1, J_2, J_3, \ldots, J_n\}$ it is the set of jobs.

$M : \{M_1, M_2, M_3, \ldots M_m\}$ it is the set of machines.

O is the set of operations $O_{j,i}$ (operation i of the job j).

The objective functions of makespan, total tardiness, and total flow time, are defined by Equations (9)–(11), respectively.

$$f_1 = min\left(\max_{j=1}^{n} C_j\right) \qquad (9)$$

where C_j is the makespan of job j.

$$f_2 = min\left(\sum_{j=1}^{n} T_j\right) = min\left(\sum_{j=1}^{n} max(0, C_j - D_j)\right) \qquad (10)$$

where $T_j = max(0, C_j - D_j)$ is the tardiness of job j, and D_j is the due date of job j and is calculated with $D_j = \tau \sum_{i=1}^{m} p_{j,i}$ [36], where $p_{j,i}$ is the time required to process the job j in the machine i. In this case, the due date of the j job is the sum of the processing time of all its operations on all machines, multiplied by a narrowing factor (τ), which is in the range $1.5 \leq \tau \leq 2.0$ [14,36].

$$f_3 = min \sum_{j=1}^{n} C_j \qquad (11)$$

5. Multi-Objective Proposed Algorithms

The two multi-objective algorithms presented in this section for solving JSSP are Chaotic Multi-Objective Simulated Annealing and Chaotic Multi-Objective Threshold Accepting. We describe these algorithms in this section after analyzing the single-objective optimization algorithms for JSSP.

5.1. Simulated Annealing

The algorithm SA proposed by Kirkpatrick et al. comes from a close analogy with the metal annealing process [5]. This process consists of heating and progressively cooling metal. As the temperature decreases, the molecules' movement slows down and tends to adopt a lower energy configuration. Kirkpatrick et al. proposed this algorithm for combinatorial optimization problems and to escape from local minima. It starts with an initial solution and generates a new solution in its neighborhood. If the new solution is better than the old solution, then it is accepted. Otherwise, SA applies the Boltzmann distribution, which determines if a bad solution can be taken as a strategy for escaping from local optima. This process is repeated many times until an equilibrium condition is accomplished.

The SA algorithm is shown in Algorithm 1. Line 1 receives the parameters: the initial ($T_{initial}$) and final (T_{final}) temperatures, the alpha value (α) for decreasing the temperature, and beta (β) for increasing the length of the Metropolis cycle. The current temperature (T_k) is set in line 2. An initial solution ($s_{current}$) is generated randomly in line 3. The stop criterion is evaluated (line 4); this main cycle is repeated while the current temperature (T_k) is higher than the final temperature (T_{final}). The Metropolis cycle starts in line 5, where a neighboring solution (s_{new}) is generated (line 6). In line 7 the increment ΔE of the objective function is determined for the current solution ($s_{current}$) and the new one (s_{new}). When this increment is negative (line 8) the new solution is the best. In this case, the new solution replaces the current solution (line 9). Otherwise, the Boltzmann criterion is applied (lines 11 and 12). This criterion allows the algorithm to escape from local optima depending on the current temperature and delta values. Finally, line 16 increases the number of iterations of the Metropolis cycle, and in line 17, the cooling function is applied to reduce the current temperature.

Algorithm 1 Classic Simulated Annealing algorithm

1: **procedure** SA($T_{initial}, T_{final}, \alpha, \beta, L_k$)
2:    $T_k \leftarrow T_{initial}$
3:    $s_{current} \leftarrow RandomInitialSolution()$
4:    **while** $T_k \geq T_{final}$ **do**
5:       **for** 1 to L_k **do**
6:          $s_{new} \leftarrow perturbation(s_{current})$
7:          $\Delta E \leftarrow E(s_{new}) - E(s_{current})$
8:          **if** $\Delta E < 0$ **then**
9:             $s_{current} \leftarrow s_{new}$
10:         **else**
11:             **if** $(e^{-\Delta E/T_k} > random(0,1))$ **then**
12:                 $s_{current} \leftarrow s_{new}$
13:             **end if**
14:         **end if**
15:       **end for**
16:       $L_k \leftarrow \beta \times L_k$
17:       $T_k \leftarrow \alpha \times T_k$
18:    **end while**
19:    **return** $s_{current}$
20: **end procedure**

5.2. Analytical Tuning for Simulated Annealing

The parameters tuning process for the SA algorithm used in this paper is based on a method proposed in [37]. This method establishes that both the initial and final temperatures are functions of the maximum and minimum energy values E_{max} and E_{min}, respectively. These energies appeared in the Boltzmann distribution criterion that states that a bad solution is accepted in a temperature T when $random(0,1) \leq e^{-\Delta E/T}$. For JSSP, ΔE is obtained with the makespan. For this tuning method, these two functions are obtained from the neighborhood of different solutions randomly generated. A set of previous SA executions must be carried out for obtaining ΔE_{max} and ΔE_{min}. These value are used in the Boltzmann distribution for determining the initial and final temperatures. Then, the other parameters of Metropolis cycle are determined. The process used is detailed in the next paragraph.

Initial temperature ($T_{initial}$): It is the temperature value from which the search process begins. The probability of accepting a new solution is almost 1 at high temperatures so, its cost of deterioration is maximum. The initial temperature is associated with the maximum allowed deterioration and its defined acceptance probability. Let us define s_i as the current solution, s_j a new proposed solution, $E_{(s_i)}$ and $E_{(s_j)}$ are its associated costs, the maximum and minimum deterioration are ΔE_{max} and ΔE_{min}. Then $P(\Delta E_{max})$, is the probability of accepting a solution with the maximum deterioration and it is calculated with (12). Thus the value of the initial temperature ($T_{initial}$) is calculated with (13).

$$P(\Delta E_{max}) = e^{(\Delta E_{max}/T_{initial})} \tag{12}$$

$$T_{initial} = \frac{-\Delta E_{max}}{\ln(P(\Delta E_{max}))} \tag{13}$$

Final temperature (T_{final}): It is the temperature value at which the search stops. In the same way, the final temperature is determined with (14) according to the probability $P(\Delta E_{min})$, which is the probability of accepting a solution with minimum deterioration.

$$T_{final} = \frac{-\Delta E_{min}}{\ln(P(\Delta E_{min}))} \tag{14}$$

Alpha value (α): It is the temperature decrease factor. This parameter determines the speed at which the decrease in temperature will occur, for fast decrements 0.7 it is usually used and for slow decrements 0.99.

Cooling scheme: This function specifies how the temperature is decreased. In this case, the value of the current temperature (T_k) follows the geometric scheme (15).

$$T_{k+1} = \alpha T_k \tag{15}$$

Length of the Markov chain or iterations in Metropolis cycle (L_k): This refers to the number of iterations of the Metropolis cycle that is performed at each temperature k, this number of iterations can be constant or variable. It is well known that at high temperatures, only a few iterations are required since the stochastic equilibrium is rapidly reached [37]. However, at low temperatures, a much more exhaustive level of exploration is required. Thus, a larger L_k value must be used. If L_{min} is the value of L_k at the initial temperature, and L_{max} is the L_k at the final temperature, then the Formula (16) is used.

$$L_{k+1} = \beta L_k \tag{16}$$

where β is the increment coefficient of L_k. Since the Functions (15) and (16) are applied successively in SA from the initial to the final temperature, T_{final} and L_{max} are calculated with (17) and (18).

$$T_{final} = \alpha^n T_{initial} \tag{17}$$

$$L_{max} = \beta^n L_{min} \tag{18}$$

In (17) and (18) n is the number of steps from $T_{initial}$ to T_{final}, then (19) and (20) are obtained.

$$n = \frac{\ln(T_{final}) - \ln(T_{initial})}{\ln(\alpha)} \tag{19}$$

$$\beta = e^{\left(\frac{\ln(L_{max}) - \ln(L_{min})}{n}\right)} \tag{20}$$

The probability of selecting the solution s_j from N random samples in the neighborhood V_{si} is given by (21); and from this equation, the N value is obtained in (22), where the exploration level C is defined in Equation (23).

$$P(S_j) = 1 - e^{\frac{-N}{|V_{si}|}} \tag{21}$$

$$N = -\mid V_{si} \mid \ln(1 - P(S_j)) = C \mid V_{si} \mid \tag{22}$$

$$C = \ln(P(S_j)) \tag{23}$$

The length of the Markov chain or iterations of the Metropolis cycle are defined by (24).

$$L_{max} = N = C \mid V_{si} \mid \tag{24}$$

To guarantee a good exploration level, the C value determined by (23) must be established between $1 \leq C \leq 4.6$ [38].

5.3. Chaotic Multi-Objective Simulated Annealing (CMOSA)

As we previously mentioned, the AMOSA algorithm was proposed in [17]. However, this algorithm is designed for general purposes. In this work, we adapt the AMOSA for JSSP to include the following features: (1) the mathematical constraints of MOJSSP, and (2) the objective functions makespan, total tardiness, and total flow time.

CMOSA has the same features previously described and has the next three elements: (1) a new structure, (2) chaotic perturbation, and (3) apply dominance to select solutions. These elements are described in the next subsections.

5.3.1. CMOSA Structure

The CMOSA algorithm uses a chaotic phase to improve the quality of the solutions considering the three objectives. Algorithm 2 receives its parameters in line 1: initial temperature ($T_{initial}$), final temperature (T_{final}), alpha (α), beta (β), Metropolis iterations in every cycle (L_k), and the initial solution ($s_{current}$) to be improved. In lines 2 and 3, the variables of the algorithm are initialized. In line 4, the $s_{current}$ is processed to obtain the values for each of the three objectives as output. In line 5, the initial temperature is established as the current temperature (T_k). Then the main cycle begins in line 6. This cycle is repeated as long as the current temperature is greater than, or equal to, the final temperature. In line 7, the Metropolis cycle begins. Subsequently, the algorithm verifies if it is stagnant in line 8. If that is the case, lines 9 to 20 are executed. The number of iterations to perform a local search is established in line 10; this value is based on the number of tasks of the instance multiplied by an experimentally tuned parameter (in this case, this parameter is $timesLS = 10$).

In line 11, a local search begins. In the first iteration of this search, a chaotic perturbation (explained in Algorithm 4) is applied to the $s_{current}$ (line 12) to restart the search process from another point in the solution space. In further iterations, a regular perturbation is applied (line 14) that consists only of exchanging the position of two operations in the solution, always verifying that the solution generated is feasible. In line 16, the s_{new} is processed to obtain the values for each of the three objectives. Subsequently, and only if the new solution dominates the current solution of the three objectives, the new solution is used to continue the search process (lines 17 and 18). When the algorithm is not stagnant, a regular perturbation is applied, and the flow continues (line 22). If the current and the new solution are different, we proceed with the dominance verification process to determine which solution is used to continue the search (line 26); this process is explained in Algorithm 5. Finally, from lines 29 to 36, a process is applied to set a limit to the number of times the algorithm is stagnant (See Algorithm 3). The algorithm is determined to be stagnant if, after some iterations, it fails to generate a new, non-dominated solution. In this algorithm, the stagnation is limited to 10 iterations. At the end of the algorithm, in line 37, the number of repetitions of the Metropolis cycle (L_k) is increased by multiplying its previous value by the β parameter value. Additionally, in line 38, the current temperature (T_k) is decreased by multiplying it by the α value. At the end of line 40, the stored solution ($s_{current}$) is generated as the output of the algorithm.

Algorithm 2 Chaotic Multi-Objective Simulated Annealing (CMOSA)

1: **procedure** CMOSA($T_{initial}, T_{final}, \alpha, \beta, L_k, s_{current}$)
2:     $MAXSTAGNANT \leftarrow 10, counterTrapped \leftarrow 0, isCaught \leftarrow FALSE$
3:     $iterationsLocalSearch \leftarrow tasks \times timesLS, verifyCaught \leftarrow TRUE, countCaught \leftarrow 0$
4:     $mks_{current}, tds_{current}, flt_{current} \leftarrow calculateValues(s_{current})$ ▷ mks : makespan, tds : tardiness, flt : flowtime
5:     $T_k \leftarrow T_{initial}$
6:     **while** $T_k \geq T_{final}$ **do**
7:         **for** $i \leftarrow 0$ to L_k **do**
8:             **if** $isCaught = TRUE$ **then**
9:                 $isCaught \leftarrow FALSE$
10:                 **for** $k \leftarrow 0$ to $iterationsLocalSearch$ **do**
11:                     **if** $k = 0$ **then**
12:                         $s_{new} \leftarrow chaoticPerturbation(s_{current})$ ▷ See Algorithm 4
13:                     **else**
14:                         $s_{new} \leftarrow regularPerturbation(s_{current})$ ▷ Exchange of two operations
15:                     **end if**
16:                     $mks_{new}, tds_{new}, flt_{new} \leftarrow calculateValues(s_{new})$
17:                     **if** $(mks_{new} < mks_{current})$ AND $(tds_{new} < tds_{current})$ AND $(flt_{new} < flt_{current})$ **then**
18:                         $s_{current} \leftarrow s_{new}$
19:                     **end if**
20:                 **end for**
21:             **else**
22:                 $s_{new} \leftarrow regularPerturbation(s_{current})$
23:                 $mks_{new}, tds_{new}, flt_{new} \leftarrow calculateValues(s_{new})$
24:             **end if**
25:             **if** $(mks_{new} \neq mks_{current})$ AND $(tds_{new} \neq tds_{current})$ AND $(flt_{new} \neq flt_{current})$ **then**
26:                 $verifyDominanceCMOSA(T_k, s_{new}, s_{current})$ ▷ See Algorithm 5
27:             **end if**
28:         **end for**
29:         **if** $verifyCaught = TRUE$ **then**
30:             **if** $caught(s_{current}, counterTrapped) = TRUE$ **then**   ▷ See Algorithm 3
31:                 $countCaught = countCaught + 1$
32:                 **if** $countCaught = MAXSTAGNANT$ **then**
33:                     $verifyCaught \leftarrow FALSE$
34:                 **end if**
35:             **end if**
36:         **end if**
37:         $L_k \leftarrow \beta \times L_k$
38:         $T_k \leftarrow \alpha \times T_k$
39:     **end while**
40:     **return** $s_{current}$
41: **end procedure**

Algorithm 3 shows the process that is carried out to verify the stagnation mentioned in line 30 of Algorithm 2.

Algorithm 3 Caught

1: **procedure** CAUGHT($s_{current}$, $counterTrapped$)
2:     $isCaught \leftarrow FALSE, timesDominated \leftarrow 0, maxTrapped \leftarrow 10$
3:     $timesDominated \leftarrow countTimesDominated(s_{current})$
4:     **if** $timesDominated = 0$ **then**
5:         $F \leftarrow s_{current}$
6:     **end if**
7:     **if** $timesDominated \geq 1$ **then**
8:         $counterTrapped \leftarrow counterTrapped + 1$
9:     **end if**
10:    **if** $counterTrapped = maxTrapped$ **then**
11:        $isCaught \leftarrow TRUE$
12:        $counterTrapped \leftarrow 0$
13:    **end if**
14:    **return** $isCaught$
15: **end procedure**

In this Algorithm 3 the current solution ($s_{current}$) and the counter of times it has trapped (*counterTrapped*) are received as input. In line 2 the variables used are initialized. Then the times that the current solution is dominated by at least one solution from the non-dominated front are counted (line 3). If the current solution is non-dominated (line 4) it is stored in the front of non-dominated solutions (line 5). If the current solution is dominated by at least one solution (line 7) then the *counterTrapped* is incremented (line 8). When *counterTrapped* equals the maximum number of trapped allowed (line 10), the value of *isCaught* is set to *TRUE* (line 11) and the trap counter is reset to zero in line 12.

5.3.2. Chaotic Perturbation

The logistic equation or logistic map is a well-known mathematical application of the biologist Robert May for a simple demographic model [39]. This application tells us the population in the *n*-th generation based on the size of the previous generation. This value may be found by a popular logistic model mathematically expressed as:

$$x_{n+1} = rx_n(1 - x_n) \tag{25}$$

In Equation (25), the variable x_n takes values ranged between zero and one. This variable represents the fraction of individuals in a specific situation (for instance, into a territory or with a particular feature) in a given instant *n*. The parameter *r* is a positive number representing the combined ratio between reproduction and mortality. Even though we are not interested in this paper in demographic or similar problems, we notice the very fast last variable changes. Then it can be taken as a chaotic variable. Thus, we use this variable for performing a chaotic perturbation function, which may help to escape from local optima for our CMOTA and CMOSA algorithms.

The chaotic function used is very sensitive to changes in the initial conditions, and this characteristic is used to generate a perturbation to the solution for escaping from local optima. Then chaos or chaotic perturbation is a process carried out to restart the search from another point in the space of solutions.

Algorithm 4 can be explained in three steps. Firstly, the feasible operations (operations that can be performed without violating any restrictions) are searched (line 4). Secondly, whether there is only one feasible operation (line 5) means that it is the last operation and selected (line 6). When there is more than one feasible operation, a chaotic function is applied to select the operations. In this case, the logistic function is used (lines 8–19), which applies a threshold in the range [0.5 to 1]. Finally, the selected operation is added to the new solution (line 21). This process is applied until all the operations are selected.

Algorithm 4 Chaotic perturbation

1: **procedure** CHAOTICPERTURBATION($s_{current}$)
2:    $feasibleTasksNumber \leftarrow 0, r \leftarrow 4, repeat \leftarrow TRUE, X_n \leftarrow 0, X_{n1} \leftarrow 0$
3:    **while** $counter < tasks$ **do**
4:       $feasibleTasksNumber \leftarrow searchFeasibleTasks()$
5:       **if** $feasibleTasksNumber = 1$ **then**
6:          $index \leftarrow 0$
7:       **else**
8:          **while** $repeat = TRUE$ **do**
9:             $X_n \leftarrow random(0,1)$
10:            **for** $i \leftarrow 0$ to $feasibleTasksNumber$ **do**
11:                $X_{n1} \leftarrow (r \times X_n) \times (1.0 - X_n)$
12:                **if** $X_{n1} > 0.5$ **then**
13:                    $index \leftarrow i$
14:                    $repeat \leftarrow FALSE$
15:                    break
16:                **end if**
17:                $X_n \leftarrow X_{n1}$
18:            **end for**
19:          **end while**
20:       **end if**
21:       $s_{new} \leftarrow addTask(index)$
22:       $counter \leftarrow counter + 1$
23:    **end while**
24:    **return** s_{new}
25: **end procedure**

5.3.3. Applying Dominance to Select Solutions

In Algorithm 5, the current solution ($s_{current}$) is compared with the new solution (s_{new}) to determine which solution is used to continue the search. In this comparison, there are three cases:

1. If s_{new} dominates $s_{current}$, then s_{new} is used to continue the search (lines 3 to 6).
2. If s_{new} is dominated by $s_{current}$ then the differences of each objective are calculated separately from the two solutions compared to obtain the decreased parameter (Δ) and use it to determine if the s_{new} continues with the search according to the condition in line 12. In this case, $s_{current}$ is added to the non-dominated front (F) and s_{new} replaces $s_{current}$ (lines 13 and 14).
3. If the two solutions are non-dominated by each other, then the current solution $s_{current}$ is added to the non-dominated front (F), and the search continues with s_{new} (lines 18 to 21).

Algorithm 5 Verify dominance CMOSA

```
 1: procedure VERIFYDOMINANCECMOSA(T_k, s_new, s_current, mks_new, tds_new, flt_new, mks_current, tds_current, flt_current)
 2:     newDominateCurrent ← FALSE, currentDominateNew ← FALSE
 3:     if s_new ≺ s_current then
 4:         s_current ← s_new
 5:         newDominateCurrent ← TRUE
 6:     end if
 7:     if s_current ≺ s_new then
 8:         Δ_MKS ← mks_new − mks_current
 9:         Δ_TDS ← tds_new − tds_current
10:         Δ_FLT ← flt_new − flt_current
11:         Δ ← Δ_MKS + Δ_TDS + Δ_FLT
12:         if random(0,1) < e^(−Δ/T_k) then
13:             F ← s_current
14:             s_current ← s_new
15:         end if
16:         currentDominateNew ← TRUE
17:     end if
18:     if (newDominateCurrent = FALSE) AND (currentDominateNew = FALSE) then
19:         F ← s_current
20:         s_current ← s_new
21:     end if
22:     return s_current
23: end procedure
```

5.4. Chaotic Multi-Objective Threshold Accepting (CMOTA)

In 1990, Dueck et al. proposed the TA algorithm as a general-purpose algorithm for the solution of combinatorial optimization problems [6]. This TA algorithm has a simpler structure than SA, and is very efficient for solving many problems but has never been applied for MOJSSP. The difference between SA and TA is basically in the criteria for accepting bad solutions. TA accepts every new configuration, which is not much worse than the old one. In contrast, SA would accept worse solutions only with small probabilities. An apparent advantage of TA is that it is higher simply because it is not necessary to compute probabilities or to make decisions based on a Boltzmann probability distribution.

Algorithm 6 shows CMOTA algorithm, where we observe that it has the same structure as CMOSA algorithm. These two algorithms have a temperature cycle and, within it, a Metropolis cycle. In these algorithms, a perturbation is applied to the current solution. Then, the dominance of the two solutions is verified to determine which of them is used to continue the searching process (Algorithm 7). Finally, the increment of the variable that controls the iterations of the Metropolis cycle, the reduction of the temperature, and the increment of the counter (line 39) for the number of temperatures are performed.

In Algorithm 7, the dominance of the two solutions is verified to determine which continues with the search. It has the same three cases used in CMOSA (Algorithm 5). The main differences are the following:

- In the beginning, while the temperature counter (*counter*) is less than the value of bound (line 4) T has a value equal to T_k (line 5), which is too large, which implies that at high temperature, the new solution (s_{new}) will often be accepted to continue the search. That is, during the processing of 95% temperatures (parameter $limit = 0.95$, whose value is obtained with Equation (19) in the tuning process), the parameter γ is used to obtain the value T (threshold), and since γ is equal to 1, then it means that T has the value of T_k. For the five percent of the remaining temperatures, γ takes the value of $\gamma_{reduced}$ (0.978). This parameter is tuned experimentally (line 12), and it is established to control the acceptance criterion and make it more restrictive as part of the process.

- CMOTA includes a verification process for accepting bad solution lighting different from CMOSA. To determine if the searching process continues using a dominated solution, CMOTA does not use the Boltzmann criterion to accept it as the current solution. Instead, CMOTA uses a threshold defined as the T parameter value (line 19), which is updated in line 29. In other words, it is no longer necessary to calculate the decrement of the objective functions. This modification makes CMOTA much more straightforward than CMOSA or any other AMOSA algorithm. Moreover, because the parameter γ is usually very close to one, it is unnecessary to calculate probabilities for the Boltzmann distribution or make a random decision process for bad solutions.

Algorithm 6 Chaotic Multi-Objective Threshold Accepting (CMOTA)

1: **procedure** CMOTA($T_{initial}, T_{final}, \alpha, \beta, L_k, s_{current}$)
2:   $counter \leftarrow 1, MAXSTAGNANT \leftarrow 10, counterTrapped \leftarrow 0, isCaught \leftarrow FALSE$
3:   $iterationsLocalSearch \leftarrow tasks \times timesLS, verifyCaught \leftarrow TRUE, countCaught \leftarrow 0$
4:   $mks_{current}, tds_{current}, flt_{current} \leftarrow calculateValues(s_{current})$ ▷ mks : makespan, tds : tardiness, flt : flowtime
5:   $T_k \leftarrow T_{initial}$
6:   **while** $T_k \geq T_{final}$ **do**
7:     **for** $i \leftarrow 0$ to L_k **do**
8:       **if** $isCaught = TRUE$ **then**
9:         $isCaught = FALSE$
10:         **for** $k \leftarrow 0$ to $iterationsLocalSearch$ **do**
11:           **if** $k = 0$ **then**
12:             $s_{new} \leftarrow chaoticPerturbation(s_{current})$ ▷ See Algorithm 4
13:           **else**
14:             $s_{new} \leftarrow regularPerturbation(s_{current})$ ▷ Exchange of two operations
15:           **end if**
16:           $mks_{new}, tds_{new}, flt_{new} \leftarrow calculateValues(s_{new})$
17:           **if** ($mks_{new} < mks_{current}$) AND ($tds_{new} < tds_{current}$) AND ($flt_{new} < flt_{current}$) **then**
18:             $s_{current} \leftarrow s_{new}$
19:           **end if**
20:         **end for**
21:       **else**
22:         $s_{new} \leftarrow regularPerturbation(s_{current})$
23:         $mks_{new}, tds_{new}, flt_{new} \leftarrow calculateValues(s_{new})$
24:       **end if**
25:       **if** ($mks_{new} \neq mks_{current}$) AND ($tds_{new} \neq tds_{current}$) AND ($flt_{new} \neq flt_{current}$) **then**
26:         $verifyDominanceCMOTA(counter, T_k, s_{new}, s_{current})$ ▷ See Algorithm 7
27:       **end if**
28:     **end for**
29:     **if** $verifyCaught = TRUE$ **then**
30:       **if** $caught(s_{current}, counterTrapped) = TRUE$ **then**   ▷ See Algorithm 3
31:         $countCaught = countCaught + 1$
32:         **if** $countCaught = MAXSTAGNANT$ **then**
33:           $verifyCaught \leftarrow FALSE$
34:         **end if**
35:       **end if**
36:     **end if**
37:     $L_k \leftarrow \beta \times L_k$
38:     $T_k \leftarrow \alpha \times T_k$
39:     $counter \leftarrow counter + 1$
40:   **end while**
41:   **return** $s_{current}$
42: **end procedure**

Algorithm 7 Verify dominance CMOTA

1: **procedure** VERIFYDOMINANCECMOTA($counter, T_k, s_{new}, s_{current}$)
2:     $\gamma \leftarrow 1, \gamma_{reduced} \leftarrow 0.978, setT \leftarrow 1, bound \leftarrow NumberOfTemperatures \times limit$
3:     $newDominateCurrent \leftarrow FALSE, currentDominateNew \leftarrow FALSE$
4:     **if** $counter < bound$ **then**
5:         $T \leftarrow T_k$
6:     **end if**
7:     **if** $(counter = bound)$ AND $(setT = 1)$ **then**
8:         $setT \leftarrow 0$
9:         $T \leftarrow T_k$
10:     **end if**
11:     **if** $setT = 0$ **then**
12:         $\gamma \leftarrow \gamma_{reduced}$
13:     **end if**
14:     **if** $s_{new} \prec s_{current}$ **then**
15:         $s_{current} \leftarrow s_{new}$
16:         $newDominateCurrent \leftarrow TRUE$
17:     **end if**
18:     **if** $s_{current} \prec s_{new}$ **then**
19:         **if** $random(0,1) < T$ **then**
20:             $F \leftarrow s_{current}$
21:             $s_{current} \leftarrow s_{new}$
22:         **end if**
23:         $currentDominateNew \leftarrow TRUE$
24:     **end if**
25:     **if** $(newDominateCurrent = FALSE)$ AND $(currentDominateNew = FALSE)$ **then**
26:         $F \leftarrow s_{current}$
27:         $s_{current} \leftarrow s_{new}$
28:     **end if**
29:     $T \leftarrow T \times \gamma$
30: **end procedure**

6. Main Methodology for CMOSA and CMOTA

Figure 1 shows the main module for each of the two proposed algorithms CMOSA and CMOTA, which may be considered the main processes in any high-level language.

In this main module, the instance to be solved is read, then the tuning process is performed. The due date is calculated, which is an essential element for calculating the tardiness. The set of initial solutions (S) is generated randomly, as follows. First, a collection of feasible operations are determined, then one of them is randomly selected and added to the solution until all the job operations are added.

Once the set of initial solutions has been generated, an algorithm (CMOSA or CMOTA) is applied to improve each initial solution, and the generated solution is stored in a set of final solutions (F). To obtain the set of non-dominated solutions, also called the zero front (f_0) from the set of final solutions, we applied the fast non-dominated Sorting algorithm [29]. To know the quality of the non-dominated set obtained, the MID, Spacing, HV, Spread, IGD, and Coverage metrics are calculated. To perform the calculation of the spread and IGD, the true Pareto front (PF_{true}) is needed. However, for the instances used in this paper, the PF_{true} has not been published for all the instances. For this reason, the calculation was made using an approximate Pareto front (PF_{approx}), which we obtained from the union of the fronts calculated with previous executions of the two algorithms presented here (CMOSA and CMOTA).

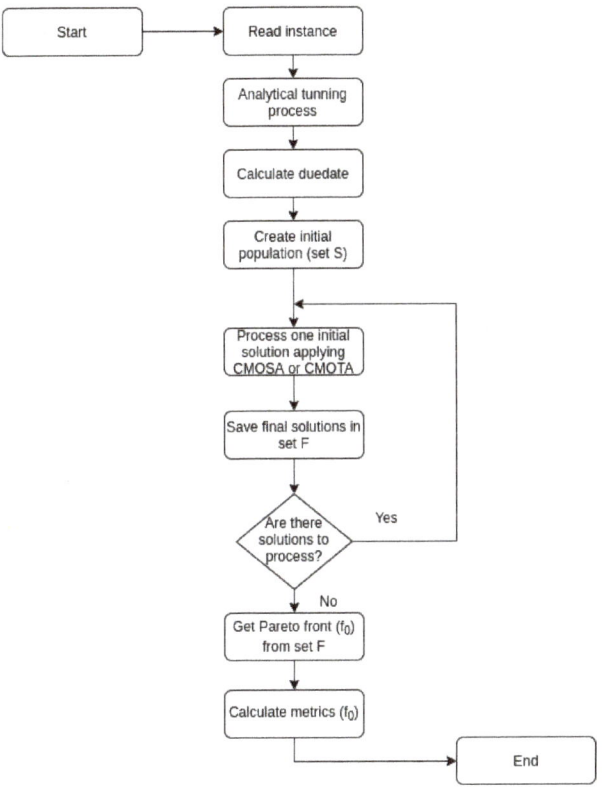

Figure 1. Main module for CMOSA and CMOTA.

6.1. Computational Experimentation

A set of 70 instances of different authors was used to evaluate the performance of the algorithms, including: (1) FT06, FT10, and FT20 proposed by [40]; (2) ORB01 to ORB10 proposed by [41]; (3) LA01 to LA40 proposed by [42]; (4) ABZ5, ABZ6, ABZ7, ABZ8, and ABZ9 proposed by [43]; (5) YN1, YN2, YN3, and YN4 proposed by [44], and (6) TA01, TA11, TA21, TA31, TA41, TA51, TA61, and TA71 proposed by [30].

As already explained, to perform the analytical tuning, some previous executions of the algorithm are necessary. The parameters used for those previous executions are shown in Table 2, and the parameters used in the final experimentation for each instance are shown in Table 3.

Table 2. Tuning parameters for CMOSA/CMOTA.

Number of Executions	Initial Temperature	Final Temperature	Alpha	L_k
50	100	0.1	0.98	100

Table 3. General parameters for CMOSA/CMOTA.

Number of Executions	Initial Solutions	Alpha	Stagnant Number
30	30	0.98	10

The execution of the algorithm was carried out on one of the terminals of the Ehecatl cluster at the TecNM/IT Ciudad Madero, which has the following characteristics:

Intel® Xeon® processor at 2.30 GHz, Memory: 64 GB (4 × 16 GB) ddr4-2133, Linux operating system CentOS, and C language was used for the implementation. We developed CMOSA (https://github.com/DrJuanFraustoSolis/CMOSA-JSSP.git) and CMOTA (https://github.com/DrJuanFraustoSolis/CMOTA-JSSP.git) and we tested the software and using three data sets reported in the paper and taken from the literature.

In the first experiment, the algorithms CMOSA and CMOTA were compared with AMOSA algorithm using the 70 described instances and six performance metrics. In a second experiment, we compared CMOSA and CMOTA with the IMOEA/D algorithm, with the 58 instances used by Zhao [14]. In the second experiment, we used the same MID metric of this publication. The third experiment was based on the 15 instances reported in [8], where the results of the next MOJSSP algorithms are published: SPEA, CMOEA, MOPSO, and MOMARLA. In this publication the authors used two objective functions and two metrics (HV and Coverage); they determined that the best algorithm is MOMARLA followed by MOPSO. We executed CMOSA and CMOTA for the instances of this dataset and we compared our results using the HV metric with those published in [8]. However, a comparison using the coverage metric was impossible because the Pareto fronts of these methods have not been reported [8]. In our case, we show in Appendix A the fronts of non-dominated solutions obtained with 70 instances.

6.2. Results

The average values of 30 runs, for the six metrics obtained by CMOSA and CMOTA for the complete data set of 70 instances are shown in Tables 4 and 5. We observed that CMOSA obtained the best values for MID and IGD metrics. For Spacing and Spread, CMOTA obtained the best results. For the HV metric, both algorithms achieved the same result (0.42). We observed in Table 5 that CMOSA obtained the best coverage result.

A two-tailed Wilcoxon test was performed with a significance level of 5% (last column in Table 4) and this shows that there are no significant differences between the CMOSA and CMOTA except in MID and IGD metrics.

Table 4. Results obtained by the metrics for 70 instances.

Metric	CMOSA	CMOTA	Significant Difference CMOSA-CMOTA
MID	30,680.19 *	31,233.15	Yes
SPACING	28,445.62	28,183.17 *	No
SPREAD	24,969.31	23,401.88 *	No
HV	0.42 *	0.42 *	No
IGD	1666.25 *	1870.94	Yes

* Best result.

Table 5. Results obtained by the coverage metric.

Coverage (CMOSA, CMOTA)	Coverage (CMOTA, CMOSA)
0.854 *	0.063

* Best result.

Table 6 shows the comparison of CMOSA and AMOSA. We observed that CMOSA obtains the best performance in all the metrics evaluated. In addition, the Wilcoxon test indicates that there are significant differences in most of them; thus, CMOSA overtakes AMOSA. We compared CMOTA and AMOSA in Table 7. In this case, CMOTA also obtains the best average results in all the metrics; however, according to the Wilcoxon test, there are significant differences in only two metrics.

Table 6. Comparison among CMOSA with AMOSA.

Metric	CMOSA	AMOSA [17]	Significant Difference CMOSA-AMOSA
MID	30,680.19 *	32,138.19	Yes
SPACING	28,445.62 *	30,129.36	Yes
SPREAD	24,969.31 *	26,625.04	No
HV	0.42 *	0.37	No
IGD	1666.25 *	2209.96	Yes

* Best result.

Table 7. Comparison among CMOTA with AMOSA.

Metric	CMOTA	AMOSA [17]	Significant Difference CMOTA-AMOSA
MID	31,233.15 *	32,138.19	No
SPACING	28,183.17 *	30,129.36	Yes
SPREAD	23,401.88 *	26,625.04	No
HV	0.42 *	0.37	No
IGD	1870.94 *	2209.96	Yes

* Best result.

We compare in Table 8 the CMOSA and CMOTA with the IMOEA/D algorithm using the 58 common instances published in [14] where the MID metric was measured. This table shows the MID average value of this metric for the non-dominated set of solutions of CMOSA and CMOTA. The results showed that CMOSA and CMOTA obtain better performances than IMOEA/D. We notice that both algorithms, CMOSA and CMOTA, achieved smaller MID values than IMOEA/D, which indicates that the Pareto fronts of our algorithms are closer to the reference point (0,0,0). The Wilcoxon test confirms that CMOSA and CMOTA surpassed the IMOEA/D.

Table 8. CMOSA, CMOTA, and IMOEA/D results obtained using MID metric.

CMOSA	CMOTA	IMOEA/D [14]	Significant Difference CMOSA-IMOEA/D	Significant Difference CMOTA-IMOEA/D
15,729.65 *	16,567.07	18,727.04	Yes	Yes

* Best result.

The results of CMOSA and CMOTA were compared with the SPEA, CMOEA, MOPSO, and MOMARLA algorithms [8]. In the last reference, only two objective functions were reported, the makespan and total tardiness. The experimentation was carried out with 15 instances and the average HV values were calculated to perform the analysis of the results, which are shown in Table 9. We notice that MOMARLA surpassed SPEA, CMOEA, and MOPSO. We can observe that CMOSA obtained a better performance than MOMARLA and the other algorithms. Comparing CMOTA and MOMARLA, we notice that both algorithms obtained the same HV average results.

Table 9. Comparison among SPEA, CMOEA, MOPSO, CMOSA, CMOTA, and MOMARLA using HV.

	Instance	SPEA [8]	CMOEA [8]	MOPSO [8]	MOMARLA [8]	CMOSA	CMOTA
1	FT06	0.07	0.07	0.50	0.65	0.64	0.75 *
2	FT10	0.17	0.26	0.87	0.96	0.71	0.69
3	FT20	0.20	0.20	0.21	0.25	0.57 *	0.77 *
4	ABZ5	0.34	0.33	0.36	0.40	0.85 *	0.56 *
5	ABZ6	0.22	0.36	0.31	0.42	0.60 *	0.81 *
6	ABZ7	0.51	0.45	1.00	1.00	0.79	0.51
7	ABZ8	0.88	0.36	0.99	0.99	0.69	0.66
8	LA26	0.33	0.39	0.47	0.47	0.91 *	0.70 *
9	LA27	0.58	0.56	0.41	0.60	0.71 *	0.93 *
10	LA28	0.48	0.42	0.48	0.54	0.92 *	0.44
11	ORB01	0.62	0.74	0.59	0.80	0.87 *	0.63
12	ORB02	0.20	0.04	0.30	0.53	0.88 *	0.77 *
13	ORB03	0.69	0.31	0.85	0.86	0.76	0.80
14	ORB04	0.63	0.28	0.52	0.79	0.76	0.81 *
15	ORB05	0.00	0.023	0.22	0.90	0.74	0.32
	Mean HV	0.39	0.32	0.54	0.68	0.76 *	0.68

* Best result.

6.3. CMOSA-CMOTA Complexity and Run Time Results

In this section, we present the complexity of the algorithms analyzed in this paper. The algorithms' complexity is presented in Table 10, and it was obtained directly when it was explicitly published or determined from the algorithms' pseudocodes. In this table, M is the number of objectives, Γ is the population size, T is the neighborhood size, n is the number of iterations (temperatures for AMOSA, CMOSA, and CMOTA), and p is the problem size. The latter is equal to jm where j and m are the number of jobs and machines, respectively. Because the algorithms with the best quality metrics are CMOSA, CMOTA MOMARLA, and MOPSO, their complexity is compared in this section.

It is well known that the complexity of classical SA is $O(p^2 \log p)$ [45]. However, we notice from Table 10 that CMOSA, and CMOTA have a different complexity even though they are based on SA. This is because these new algorithms applied a different chaotic perturbation and another local search (see Algorithms 2 and 6 in lines 10–20).

The temporal function of MOMARLA, CMOSA, and CMOTA belong to $O(Mnp)$. For MOMARLA, n is the number of iterations, a variable used at the beginning of this algorithm. On the other hand, for CMOSA and CMOTA, n is the number of temperatures used in the algorithm, also at its beginning; in any case, the difference will be only a constant.

We note that AMOSA and MOPSO have a similar complexity class expression, that is $O(n\Gamma^2)$ and $O(M\Gamma^2)$ respectively. However, MOPSO overtakes AMOSA because M is in general lower than n. We observe that CMOSA, CMOTA and MOMARLA belong to $O(Mnp)$ class complexity, while MOPSO belongs to $O(M\Gamma^2)$ [46]. Thus, the relation between them is np/Γ^2 which in general is lower than one. Thus CMOSA, CMOTA and MOMARLA have a lower complexity than MOPSO. Moreover, CMOSA, CMOTA, and MOMARLA have better HV metric quality as is shown in Table 9.

In the next paragraph, we present a comparative analysis of the execution time of the algorithms implemented in this paper.

Table 10. Complexity of the algorithms.

AMOSA	IMOEA/D	SPEA	MOPSO	MOMARLA	CMOSA	CMOTA
$O(n\Gamma^2)$	$O(M\Gamma T)$	$O(M\Gamma)$	$O(M\Gamma^2)$	$O(Mnp)$	$O(Mnp)$	$O(Mnp)$

In Table 11 we show the execution time, expressed in seconds, for the three algorithms (CMOSA, CMOTA, and AMOSA) implemented in this paper for three data sets (70, 58, and 15 instances). In all these cases, we emphasize that the AMOSA algorithm was the base to design the other two algorithms. In fact, all of them have the same structure except that CMOSA and CMOTA apply chaotic perturbations when they detect a possible stagnation. Thus, all of them have similar complexity measures for the worst-case. Table 11 shows the percentage of time saved by these two algorithms concerning AMOSA. For these datasets, we measured that AMOSA saved 2.1, 19.87, and 42.48 percent of the AMOSA run time; on the other hand, these figures of CMOTA versus AMOSA are 55, 68.89, and 46.73 percent. Thus, both of our proposed algorithms CMOSA and CMOTA are significantly more efficient than AMOSA. Unfortunately, we do not have the tools to compare these algorithms versus the other algorithms' execution time in Table 1. Nevertheless, we made the quality comparisons by using the metrics previously published.

Table 11. Runtimes for CMOSA, CMOTA and AMOSA.

Algorithm	CMOSA	CMOTA	AMOSA [17]
Data set of 70 instances			
Average execution time	495.22	229.42 *	505.84
% time saved vs AMOSA	2.1	55 *	0
Data set of 58 instances			
Average execution time	111.68	41.97 *	139.39
% time saved vs AMOSA	19.87	69.89 *	0
Data set of 15 instances			
Average execution time	81.24	75.24 *	141.25
% time saved vs AMOSA	42.48	46.73 *	0

* Best result.

7. Conclusions

This paper presents two multi-objective algorithms for JSSP, named CMOSA and CMOTA, with three objectives and six metrics. The objective functions for these algorithms are makespan, total tardiness, and total flow time. Regarding the results from the comparison of CMOSA and CMOTA with AMOSA, we observe that both algorithms obtained a well-distributed Pareto front, closest to the origin, and closest to the approximate Pareto front as was indicated by Spacing, MID, and IGD metrics, respectively. Thus, using these five metrics, we found that CMOSA and CMOTA surpassed the AMOSA algorithm. Regarding the volume covered by the front calculated by the HV metric, it was observed that both algorithms, CMOSA and CMOTA, have the same performance; however, CMOSA has a higher convergence than CMOTA. In addition, the proposed algorithms surpass IMOEA/D when MID metric was used. Moreover, we use the HV to compare the proposed algorithms with SPEA, CMOEA, MOPSO, and MOMARLA. We found that CMOSA outperforms these algorithms, followed by CMOTA, MOMARLA, and MOPSO.

We observe that CMOSA and CMOTA have similar complexity as the best algorithms in the literature. In addition, we show that CMOSA and CMOTA surpass AMOSA when we compare them using execution time for three data sets. We found CMOTA is, on average, 50 percent faster than AMOSA and CMOSA. Finally, we conclude that CMOSA and CMOTA have similar temporal complexity than the best literature algorithms, and the quality metrics show that the proposed algorithms outperform them.

Author Contributions: Conceptualization: J.F.-S., L.H.-R., G.C.-V.; Methodology: J.F.-S., L.H.-R., G.C.-V., J.J.G.-B.; Investigation: J.F.-S., L.H.-R., G.C.-V., J.J.G.-B.; Software: J.F.-S., L.H.-R., G.C.-V., J.J.G.-B.; Formal Analysis: J.F.-S., G.C.-V.; Writing original draft: J.F.-S., L.H.-R., G.C.-V.; Writing review and editing: J.F.-S., J.J.G.-B., J.P.S.-H. All authors have read and agreed to the published version of the manuscript. All authors have read and agreed to the published version of the manuscript.

Funding: This research received no external funding.

Acknowledgments: The authors would like to express their gratitude to CONACYT and TecNM/IT Ciudad Madero. In addition, the authors acknowledge the support from Laboratorio Nacional de Tecnologías de la Información (LaNTI) for the access to the cluster.

Conflicts of Interest: The authors declare no conflict of interest.

Appendix A. Non-Dominated Front Obtained

The non-dominated solutions obtained by CMOSA algorithm for the 70 instances used are shown in Tables A1–A6, and the non-dominated solutions obtained by CMOTA algorithm for the same instances are shown in Tables A7–A12. In these tables, MKS is the makespan, TDS is the total tardiness and FLT is the total flow time. For each instance, the best value for each objective function is highlighted with an asterisk (*) and in bold type.

Table A1. Non-dominated front obtained by CMOSA for the JSSP instances proposed by [40].

	FT06			FT10			FT20		
	MKS	TDS	FLT	MKS	TDS	FLT	MKS	TDS	FLT
1	**55 ***	30.0	305	**993 ***	1768.5	9234	**1224 ***	8960.0	16614
2	55	38.0	301	994	1609.0	9121	1227	8809.0	16375
3	56	37.0	304	1004	1495.0	9062	1229	8793.0	16359
4	56	29.0	308	1006	1083.0	8584	1235	8774.0	16340
5	57	23.5	305	1036	1053.0	**8406 ***	1243	**8455.5 ***	**16119 ***
6	57	27.0	297	1037	**1009.0 ***	8437			
7	57	26.0	298						
8	58	9.5	280						
9	60	11.0	**279 ***						
10	62	8.5	285						
11	69	**8.0 ***	291						

Table A2. Non-dominated front obtained by CMOSA for the JSSP instances proposed by [41].

	ORB1			ORB2			ORB3			ORB4			ORB5		
	MKS	TDS	FLT	MKS	TDS	FLT	MKS	TDS	FLT	MKS	TDS	FLT	MKS	TDS	FLT
1	**1142 ***	1539.0	9245	**925 ***	767.5	8339	**1104 ***	1874.0	9448	**1063 ***	1186.0	9175	**966 ***	1192.5	8279
2	1143	1517.0	9223	927	781.5	8285	1111	1548.0	9392	1073	1108.5	9270	971	1180.5	8296
3	1144	1522.0	9135	931	722.5	8160	1112	1816.0	9318	1078	1059.5	9128	975	859.5	7648
4	1150	1381.5	9219	951	542.5	8056	1123	1462.0	9306	1107	917.5	9234	978	752.5	8016
5	1161	**1355.5 ***	9469	958	**331.0 ***	7742	1127	1806.0	9288	1111	978.0	9199	980	758.5	8011
6	1172	1508.0	9214	958	339.0	**7730 ***	1162	1579.0	9200	1134	944.5	9221	984	708.5	7961
7	1174	1521.0	**9134 ***				1164	1562.0	9183	1140	795.5	9111	984	706.5	7970
8							1180	1492.5	8984	1156	843.5	9083	998	822.0	7784
9							1187	**1475.5 ***	**8967 ***	1200	**733.5 ***	9049	1001	746.5	7869
10										1230	919.0	8969	1001	834.0	**7620 ***
11										1232	983.5	8813	1013	**689.0 ***	7765
12										1277	995.5	**8735 ***	1017	795.0	7713
13													1032	798.0	7659
14													1049	771.0	7678

Table A2. Cont.

	ORB6			ORB7			ORB8			ORB9			ORB10		
	MKS	TDS	FLT	MKS	TDS	FLT	MKS	TDS	FLT	MKS	TDS	FLT	MKS	TDS	FLT
1	1097 *	1318.0	9573	423 *	207.5	3663	963 *	1804.0	8439	987 *	1193.5	8912	991 *	835.0	8482
2	1100	1199.5	9505	424	167.0	3731	968	1412.5	8204	988	1362.5	8860	993	843.0	8465
3	1100	1267.5	9434	431	161.0 *	3643	970	1387.0	8215	993	1220.0	8898	1020	798.5	8785
4	1105	1225.0	9434	439	295.0	3620	988	1514.5	8099	996	1072.5	8844	1029	742.5	8691
5	1105	1227.0	9412	449	207.5	3625	997	1587.0	8078	1006	1002.0	8538	1043	608.5	8659
6	1110	1255.0	9409	453	230.5	3616	1001	1239.0	7912	1019	1017.5	8523	1044	493.5 *	8522
7	1113	1220.5	9452	455	204.5	3636	1044	1120.0 *	7617 *	1035	1100.5	8493	1072	774.5	8455 *
8	1114	1078.5	9287	459	213.0	3577				1039	1043.5	8430			
9	1141	1153.0	9109 *	461	216.0	3509				1048	887.0 *	8348 *			
10	1171	1097.0	9194	461	203.0	3545									
11	1191	1018.5	9145	461	186.5	3572									
12	1233	988.0 *	9225	466	202.5	3547									
13				466	171.0	3561									
14				470	184.5	3504 *									

Table A3. Non-dominated front obtained by CMOSA for the JSSP instances proposed by [42].

	LA01			LA02			LA03			LA04			LA05		
	MKS	TDS	FLT	MKS	TDS	FLT	MKS	TDS	FLT	MKS	TDS	FLT	MKS	TDS	FLT
1	666 *	1194.0	5436	655 *	1207.0	5123	615 *	1492.5	5000	590 *	1252.0	4900	593 *	1159.5	4451
2	666	1237.5	5362	656	1161.0	5077	622	1400.5	4896	595	1235.0	4948	593	1088.0	4455
3	667	1382.5	5357	665	1222.0	4994	626	1484.5	4881	598	1250.0	4857	594	1053.0	4399
4	668	1068.5	5328	665	1203.0	5050	627	1467.0	4889	598	1226.5	4910	610	1099.5	4386
5	668	1074.0	5309	671	1042.0	4904	628	1343.5	4866	599	1167.0	4915	615	1129.5	4351 *
6	670	1269.5	5300	673	1094.5	4879	630	1357.5	4803	603	1154.5	4895	631	999.5 *	4371
7	672	1152.5	5260	681	938.5	4799	630	1339.5	4850	605	1089.0	4737	648	1036.0	4359
8	688	1145.5	5247	695	927.5	4864	633	1226.5	4750	614	1034.0	4782	659	1032.0	4355
9	700	1120.5	5297	695	930.5	4796	638	1183.0	4649	615	1047.5	4756			
10	706	1081.5	5241	696	910.5	4837	641	1178.5	4713	618	1042.5	4705			
11	706	1179.0	5225	714	997.5	4776	646	1173.0	4718	622	1038.5	4705			
12	713	1065.5	5203	715	936.5	4720	655	1088.5	4482	629	1006.0	4710			
13	718	1025.5	5235	736	925.0	4812	662	1062.0	4595	629	1020.5	4695			
14	727	1056.5	5138	741	993.0	4716 *	662	1081.5	4591	631	982.5	4697			
15	734	1046.0	5184	771	909.5 *	4786	668	1015.0	4522	637	981.0	4576			
16	743	1089.0	5101				669	981.5	4523	638	961.5	4667			
17	751	951.0 *	5115				683	979.5	4516	640	962.0	4566			
18	825	1098.0	5099 *				688	1087.5	4481	643	930.0	4525 *			
19							698	1055.0	4504	648	927.0	4531			
20							741	955.5	4382	650	895.5	4558			
21							744	891.0	4375	655	908.0	4537			
22							744	914.0	4372	663	888.5 *	4551			
23							750	896.5	4323 *	663	906.0	4543			
24							757	867.0 *	4325						

Table A3. Cont.

	LA06				LA07				LA08				LA09				LA10		
	MKS	TDS	FLT	MKS	TDS	FLT	MKS	TDS	FLT	MKS	TDS	FLT	MKS	TDS	FLT
1	**926 ***	4185.5	10,142	**890 ***	4006.5	9554	**863 ***	3717.5	9455	**951 ***	3925.0	10,297	**958 ***	4439.5	10,441
2	927	4183.0	10,171	890	4044.0	9496	863	3792.5	9424	951	3916.5	10,311	969	4476.5	10,437
3	929	4062.0	10,050	894	3974.5	9522	865	3723.5	9387	954	**3908.0 ***	10,280	971	4313.0	10,343
4	931	4122.0	10,041	896	3646.5	9264	870	3685.5	9349	974	3944.5	**10,195 ***	976	4298.0	10,328
5	938	3911.0	9870	904	3684.0	9248	871	3649.5	9284				982	4121.0	10,151
6	940	**3827.0 ***	**9786 ***	906	3615.0	9219	876	3602.5	9340				1052	**4083.0 ***	**10,113 ***
7				910	3652.0	9216	885	3598.5	9309						
8				967	**3595.0 ***	**9199 ***	895	3596.0	9266						
9							896	**3410.5 ***	**9045 ***						

	LA11				LA12				LA13				LA14				LA15		
	MKS	TDS	FLT	MKS	TDS	FLT	MKS	TDS	FLT	MKS	TDS	FLT	MKS	TDS	FLT
1	**1222 ***	9157.5	17,184	**1039 ***	7218.0	14,229	**1150 ***	8436.5	16,208	**1292 ***	10,017.0	18,036	**1207 ***	9447.5	17,581
2	1225	8947.5	16,853	1041	7203.0	14167	1153	8333.5	16,105	1299	9986.0	18,005	1208	9249.5	17,383
3	1241	8879.5	16,785	1043	7198.0	14196	1154	8310.5	16,079	1328	9992.5	17,990	1213	9175.0	17,314
4	1242	8862.5	16,768	1049	7164.0	14162	1155	8247.5	15,953	1352	**9810.5 ***	17,808	1220	9149.0	17,284
5	1243	8860.5	16,766	1050	7126.0	14124	1161	8175.0	15,954	1352	9867.0	**17,797 ***	1229	9014.0	17,149
6	1256	8811.5	16,798	1134	**7114.0 ***	**14,112 ***	1162	8210.5	15,916				1232	9013.0	17,148
7	1257	8725.5	16,712				1182	8057.0	15,836				1234	8991.0	17,126
8	1258	8765.5	16,671				1183	8013.0	15,792				1251	8915.5	17,062
9	1265	**8650.5 ***	**16,637 ***				1184	7994.0	15,773				1271	8947.5	17,040
10							1185	7989.0	15,768				1273	8703.5	16871
11							1189	**7978.0 ***	**15,757 ***				1281	8651.5	16,819
12													1283	8638.5	16,802
13													1289	8603.5	16,767
14													1297	**8601.5 ***	**16,765 ***

	LA16				LA17				LA18				LA19				LA20		
	MKS	TDS	FLT	MKS	TDS	FLT	MKS	TDS	FLT	MKS	TDS	FLT	MKS	TDS	FLT
1	**968 ***	983.5	8777	**796 ***	799.0	7502	**865 ***	488.0	7765	**884 ***	538.0	7950	**934 ***	665.5	8354
2	982	904.0	8754	796	784.0	7509	866	468.5	7743	889	288.0	7945	939	599.5	8409
3	988	898.5	8608	810	855.0	7492	868	439.5	7853	891	495.0	7821	948	631.5	8393
4	992	882.0	8752	811	783.0	7555	873	419.5	7687	900	406.0	7916	957	542.0	8423
5	994	816.5	8669	813	702.0	7458	878	396.5	7755	905	279.0	7846	957	556.0	8302
6	1000	873.0	8570	813	745.0	7450	882	404.5	7732	935	327.0	7730	964	658.0	8232
7	1003	900.0	8565	816	693.0	7458	883	429.5	7648	953	335.5	7726	966	403.0	8032
8	1003	908.0	8545	820	630.0	7395	893	411.0	7671	953	**259.5 ***	7806	967	408.0	8028
9	1003	942.0	8474	823	670.5	7334	923	394.5	7802	979	304.5	**7673 ***	971	408.0	8001
10	1008	493.0	8205	824	633.5	7240	927	368.5	7885				972	419.0	7975
11	1016	553.5	8063	831	623.5	7321	928	351.5	7882				1009	390.5	8094
12	1040	459.5	8232	833	625.5	7320	939	353.0	7691				1067	422.0	7927
13	1050	352.0	7997	835	717.5	7203	939	300.5	7860				1084	424.0	**7908 ***
14	1066	345.5	8285	836	596.5	7291	940	345.0	7827				1100	383.5	8292
15	1071	341.5	8068	836	611.5	7284	945	332.5	7845				1115	382.5	8065
16	1073	401.0	7980	840	597.0	7267	946	305.0	7629				1142	335.5	7915
17	1095	**326.5 ***	**7908 ***	840	612.0	7260	952	**267.0 ***	7778				1142	334.0	7998
18				842	612.0	7194	978	476.0	7614				1148	**262.5 ***	8205
19				849	522.0	7208	982	455.0	**7519 ***				1168	302.5	8204
20				849	521.5	7232	984	439.0	7626						

Table A3. Cont.

21				864	531.0	7135	998	361.5	7603						
22				864	530.5	7159									
23				864	521.5	7169									
24				899	535.0	7114									
25				914	509.0	7034									
26				927	470.0 *	7098									
27				931	475.0	7000 *									

	LA21			LA22			LA23			LA24			LA25		
	MKS	TDS	FLT	MKS	TDS	FLT	MKS	TDS	FLT	MKS	TDS	FLT	MKS	TDS	FLT
1	1124 *	3229.5	15,030	1013 *	2968.5	13,774	1077 *	2292.0	14,222	1000 *	2145.5	13230 *	1071 *	3161.0	14,387
2	1124	3233.5	15,002	1018	2916.5	13,722	1078	2253.5	14,198	1008	2137.5	13,474	1072	3060.0	14,275
3	1127	3180.5	14,883	1020	2906.5	13,712	1078	2249.5	14,238	1008	2120.5	13,606	1089	3002.0	14,096
4	1128	3137.5	14,868	1034	2738.5	13,552	1080	2173.5	14,152	1077	2010.5	13,458	1100	2756.5	13,951
5	1129	3015.5	14,718	1037	2660.0	13,638	1091	2231.5	14,149	1079	1981.5	13,390	1104	2764.5	13,940
6	1137	2998.5	14,400	1038	2774.5	13,548	1095	2243.5	14,147	1088	19,76.5 *	13,385	1118	2721.0	13,962
7	1141	2892.5	14,636	1039	2648.0	13,611	1097	2071.0	14,011				1118	2768.0	13,938
8	1144	2821.5	14,565	1045	2811.0	13,528	1102	1939.0 *	13,867 *				1121	2802.5	13,829
9	1146	2939.0	14,346	1047	2696.5	13,510							1123	2618.5	13,658
10	1150	2543.0	14,344	1050	2614.5	13,445							1131	2584.5	13,845
11	1150	2639.5	14,316	1068	2565.5	13,396							1134	2536.5	13,577
12	1157	2557.5	14,247	1076	2544.5	13,375							1134	2529.0	13,770
13	1158	2545.5	14,222	1082	2462.5	13,253							1154	2517.5	13,535
14	1164	2511.5	14,188	1087	2392.5	13,169							1159	2457.0	13,654
15	1179	2393.5	14,204	1099	2332.5 *	13,109 *							1160	2451.5	13,666
16	1182	2331.5	14,165										1173	2530.0	13,470
17	1182	2355.5	14,153										1175	2445.0	13,385
18	1183	2454.5	14,131										1187	2435.0	13,481
19	1227	2328.0	14,238										1189	2315.0 *	13,255 *
20	1247	2225.0 *	14,161												
21	1258	2561.5	13,967												
22	1272	2527.5	13,963												
23	1285	2465.5	13,871 *												
24	1290	2305.0	14,103												

	LA26			LA27			LA28			LA29			LA30		
	MKS	TDS	FLT	MKS	TDS	FLT	MKS	TDS	FLT	MKS	TDS	FLT	MKS	TDS	FLT
1	1281 *	6921.0	22,576	1332 *	6555.0	22,803	1318 *	7579.0	23,547	1293 *	7971.5	22,802	1434 *	9177.0	25,172
2	1282	6811.0	22,466	1334	6495.0	22,743	1321	7403.0	23,426	1294	7963.5	22,786	1437	8132.0	24,056
3	1304	6708.5	22,434	1340	6399.0	22,647	1329	6603.0	22,626	1317	7799.5	22,693	1445	8064.0	23,991
4	1323	6643.5	22,416	1346	6280.0	22,528	1362	6683.5	22,578	1319	7796.5	22,690	1448	7996.0	23,923 *
5	1325	6629.5	22,402	1358	6228.0 *	22,476 *	1367	6552.0	22,575	1327	7770.5	22,664	1540	7980.0 *	24,000
6	1328	6741.5	22,254				1378	6469.0	22,454	1333	7738.5	22,632			
7	1329	6560.5	22,333				1385	6465.0	22,389	1334	7711.5	22,605			
8	1338	6616.5	22,129				1393	6480.5	22,360	1339	7507.5	22,314			
9	1340	6510.5	22,276				1413	6443.0	22,320	1340	7446.5	22,253			
10	1377	6307.0 *	21,940 *				1416	6439.0	22,316	1368	7411.5	22,218			
11							1454	6429.0	22,298	1375	7398.5	22,289			
12							1476	6239.0	22,013	1376	7464.5	22182			
13							1477	6141.0 *	21,915 *	1376	7374.5	22,268			
14										1379	7018.5	21,912			
15										1389	7011.5 *	21,905 *			

Table A3. Cont.

	LA31			LA32			LA33			LA34			LA35		
	MKS	TDS	FLT	MKS	TDS	FLT	MKS	TDS	FLT	MKS	TDS	FLT	MKS	TDS	FLT
1	**1784** *	20,830.5	43,617	**1850** *	20,861.5	45715	**1719** *	20,933.5	43,387	**1743** *	22,605.5	45,617	**1898** *	24,225.5	47,233
2	1794	20,718.5	43,505	1867	20,860.5	45,714	1721	18,798.5	41,252	1747	21,475.5	44,487	1899	23,434.5	46,652
3	1796	20,390.5	43,177	1871	20,686.5	45,540	1723	18,528.5	40,982	1755	21,271.5	44,283	1900	22,784.5	46,012
4	1797	20,066.5	42,842	1881	20,563.5	45,417	1725	18,137.5	40,591	1756	21,211.5	44,223	1901	22,724.5	45,952
5	1798	20,009.5	42785	1889	20,059.5	44,913	1738	**18,109.5**	***40,563*** *	1759	21041.5	44,037	1903	22,684.5	45,912
6	1800	**19,919.5**	***42,695*** *	1900	**20,049.5**	***44,903*** *				1771	20,916.0	43,916	1920	22,481.5	45,709
7										1774	20,787.0	43,787	1947	22,677.0	45,695
8										1781	20,736.0	43,736	1950	22,442.5	45,670
9										1791	20,693.5	43,705	1953	22,454.0	45,665
10										1801	20,505.5	43,517	1958	22,327.5	45,555
11										1837	20,476.5	43,488	2018	**22,311.5**	***45,539*** *
12										1839	20,356.5	43,368			
13										1840	20,305.5	43,317			
14										1843	20,298.5	43,310			
15										1850	20,072.5	43,084			
16										1906	**19,880.5**	***42,892*** *			

	LA36			LA37			LA38			LA39			LA40		
	MKS	TDS	FLT	MKS	TDS	FLT	MKS	TDS	FLT	MKS	TDS	FLT	MKS	TDS	FLT
1	**1453** *	3131.0	20,575	**1569** *	3065.0	21,444	**1400** *	1586.0	18,171	**1444** *	2371.0	19,447	**1436** *	2617.5	19,260
2	1471	3030.5	20,309	1571	3077.0	21,436	1419	**1578.5** *	18,200	1452	2056.0	19,215	1443	2017.0	18,689
3	1474	2834.5	20,125	1574	3043.0	21,402	1421	2057.5	18,119	1498	1770.5	18,662	1450	1806.0	18,391
4	1475	2936.5	20,085	1574	3025.0	21,404	1439	2092.5	18,067	1499	1731.5	18,607	1458	1719.0	18,303
5	1476	2847.5	20,094	1580	3009.0	21,301	1468	1753.5	18,103	1504	1473.5	18,404	1471	**1433.5** *	18,431
6	1476	2949.5	20,054	1584	3002.0	21,294	1473	1736.5	18,086	1621	1422.5	18,579	1495	1549.5	**18,287** *
7	1487	2633.5	19,889	1590	2331.5	20,755	1496	1744.5	**18,044** *	1817	**1902.0** *	**18,191** *			
8	1498	2474.5	19,694	1593	2289.5	20,748									
9	1505	2492.5	19,675	1608	2247.5	20,585									
10	1521	2604.0	19,671	1614	2384.0	20,153									
11	1521	2379.0	19,840	1614	2414.0	20,101									
12	1529	2459.5	19,679	1618	2374.0	20,143									
13	1530	2420.0	19,668	1621	2418.0	**20,077** *									
14	1534	2335.5	19,812	1649	2234.5	20,600									
15	1534	2472.5	19,650	1650	2237.5	20,587									
16	1548	2278.5	19,755	1650	2241.5	20,557									
17	1563	**2015.5** *	19,237	1700	2222.5	20,453									
18	1573	2532.5	**19,231** *	1700	2205.0	20,517									
19				1707	2187.5	20,418									
20				1781	2012.0	20,554									
21				1781	1964.5	20,634									
22				1790	**1835.5** *	20,309									

Table A4. Non-dominated front obtained by CMOSA for the JSSP instances proposed by [43].

	ABZ5				ABZ6			ABZ7			ABZ8			ABZ9	
	MKS	TDS	FLT	MKS	TDS	FLT	MKS	TDS	FLT	MKS	TDS	FLT	MKS	TDS	FLT
1	1250 *	145.0	11,006	967 *	324.0	8453	746 *	2420.0	13,274	763 *	23,17.0	13,696	805 *	3296.5	14,426
2	1250	134.0 *	11,025	974	256.5	8524	753	2403.0	13,257	763	2332.0	13,688	807	3127.0	14,287
3	1252	139.0	10,998	974	251.5	8550	793	2305.0 *	13,137 *	773	2336.0	13,675	808	2941.0	14,094
4	1289	141.0	10,984	979	204.0	8464				773	2326.0	13,688	822	2846.0	13,820
5	1289	142.0	10,946 *	997	258.5	8357				775	2294.0	13,633	833	2770.0	13,840
6				999	202.0	8553				779	2236.5 *	13,591 *	842	2733.5	13,888
7				1001	172.0	8484							843	2740.5	13,845
8				1009	164.0	8589							845	2727.5	13,832
9				1016	164.5	8532							846	2706.5	13,811
10				1018	134.0	8692							847	2696.5	13,801
11				1019	126.0	8275 *							885	2806.0	13,800
12				1074	35.5	8583							886	2737.0	13,762
13				1077	36.5	8525							889	2726.0	13,720
14				1077	49.5	8459							896	2708.5	13,703
15				1080	25.5	8550							897	2684.5 *	13,679 *
16				1082	29.5	8488									
17				1082	40.5	8472									
18				1085	1.5 *	8423									

Table A5. Non-dominated front obtained by CMOSA for the JSSP instances proposed by [44].

	YN01			YN02			YN03			YN04		
	MKS	TDS	FLT	MKS	TDS	FLT	MKS	TDS	FLT	MKS	TDS	FLT
1	1103 *	2485.0	19,819	1133 *	2178.0	19,429	1083 *	2025.5	19,346	1210 *	2864.5	20,633
2	1105	2442.0	19,776	1137	2205.0	19,424	1084	2015.5	19,336	1221	2814.0 *	20,552
3	1105	2465.5	19,753	1140	2050.0	19,299	1084	2012.5	19,337	1297	2915.5	20,525
4	1106	2418.5	19,706	1140	2067.0	19,286	1089	2003.5	19,328	1300	2910.5	20,520 *
5	1106	2395.0	19,729	1148	2059.0	19,278	1090	1987.5 *	19,308			
6	1108	1901.0	19,129	1150	2023.0 *	19,276 *	1138	2179.5	19,219			
7	1111	1859.0	19,068				1203	2157.5	18,751 *			
8	1117	1867.5	19,013 *									
9	1126	1756.5 *	19,265									
10	1131	1772.5	19,247									

Table A6. Non-dominated front obtained by CMOSA for the JSSP instances proposed by [30].

	TA01			TA11			TA21			TA31		
	MKS	TDS	FLT	MKS	TDS	FLT	MKS	TDS	FLT	MKS	TDS	FLT
1	1412 *	1821.5	18,716	1603 *	6409.5	27,903	2048 *	7261.5	37,039	2083 *	20,557.0	54,457
2	1412	16,41.5	18,749	1607	6365.5	27,859	2050	6184.5	36,322	2091	20,504.0	54,404
3	1414	1809.5	18,704	1619	6051.5	27,722	2051	6184.5	36,290	2096	20,448.0	54,348
4	1433	1753.5	18,648 *	1750	6387.0	27,635	2074	6023.5	36,129	2097	20,112.0	54,012
5	1443	1733.5	18,739	1753	6307.0	27,555 *	2078	6017.5	36,123	2099	20,099.0	53,999
6	1448	1625.0 *	18,765	1766	6293.0	27,572	2091	6031.0	36,050	2106	19,879.0	53,779
7				1859	6088.0 *	27,679	2274	5393.0 *	35,462 *	2109	19,860.0	53,760
8										2119	19,857.0	53,757
9										2121	19,802.0	53,702
10										2125	19,782.0	53,682
11										2132	18,670.5	52,157
12										2139	18,657.5 *	52,144 *

Table A6. Cont.

	TA41 MKS	TA41 TDS	TA41 FLT	TA51 MKS	TA51 TDS	TA51 FLT	TA61 MKS	TA61 TDS	TA61 FLT	TA71 MKS	TA71 TDS	TA71 FLT
1	2530 *	18,610.5	65,529	3121 *	77,760.0	134,637	3437 *	71,924.0	148,370	6050 *	368,519.5	519,856
2	2553	18,589.5	65,508	3124	74,125.0	131,002	3445	71,162.0	147,608	6063	368,491.5	519,828
3	2731	18,298.0	65,157	3125	74,113.0	130,990	3561	70,685.0	147,131	6097	367,933.5	519,270
4	2733	18,257.0	65,116	3127	74,028.0	130,905	3567	70,550.0 *	146,996 *	6098	367,927.5	51,9264
5	2736	18,228.0	65,087	3134	72,636.0	129,513				6129	366,149.5	51,7486
6	2743	18,197.0	65,056	3186	72,624.0	129,501				6165	365,118.5	516,455
7	2832	181,28.5	65,047	3188	71,884.0	128,761				6166	365,116.5	516,453
8	2949	17,853.5 *	64,772 *	3189	71,849.0	128,726				6168	365,090.5	516,427
9				3202	70,643.0	127,520				6215	361,891.5 *	513,228 *
10				3204	70,623.0 *	127,500 *						

Table A7. Non-dominated front obtained by CMOTA for the JSSP instances proposed by [40].

	FT06 MKS	FT06 TDS	FT06 FLT	FT10 MKS	FT10 TDS	FT10 FLT	FT20 MKS	FT20 TDS	FT20 FLT
1	55 *	30.0	305	1021 *	1759.5	9407	1234 *	9571.0	17,132
2	55	38.0	301	1029	1721.0	9122	1240	8914.5	16,578
3	56	29.0	308	1063	1711.0	9358	1243	8934.0	16,526
4	57	23.5	305	1065	1697.0	9280	1249	8898.5	16,562
5	57	26.0	298	1067	1562.5	9226	1258	8959.5	16,480
6	57	27.0	297	1088	1650.5	8859 *	1259	8930.5	16451
7	58	9.5	280	1089	1614.5	9031	1270	8831.5	16,352
8	60	8.5 *	276 *	1091	1619.5	9018	1277	8782.5	16,303
9				1109	1468.0	9046	1327	8768.0	16,365
10				1125	1459.0	8890	1351	8768.5	16,289 *
11				1146	1361.0 *	9003	1359	8738.0 *	16,335

Table A8. Non-dominated front obtained by CMOTA for the JSSP instances proposed by [41].

	ORB1 MKS	ORB1 TDS	ORB1 FLT	ORB2 MKS	ORB2 TDS	ORB2 FLT	ORB3 MKS	ORB3 TDS	ORB3 FLT	ORB4 MKS	ORB4 TDS	ORB4 FLT	ORB5 MKS	ORB5 TDS	ORB5 FLT
1	1180 *	1853.0	9764	964 *	985.5	8421	1124 *	2307.5	10,157	1094 *	1727.5	9897	945 *	1006.0	8032
2	1190	1714.5	9619	983	971.5	8672	1134	1901.0	9579	1104	1720.5	10,062	980	975.0	7992
3	1192	1721.5	9585	985	913.5	8601	1208	1842.5	9770	1109	1695.5	10,117	994	747.0 *	7966
4	1237	1787.5	9440	986	975.5	8593	1212	1795.5	9721	1111	1600.5	9865	999	751.0	7950
5	1238	1714.5	9616	987	1009.0	8347	1217	1829.5	9698	1118	1507.0	9818	1053	979.5	7944 *
6	1249	1799.5	9423	988	980.0	8303	1218	1791.5	9717	1130	1626.0	9704			
7	1253	1771.5	9428	991	857.5	8545	1219	1875.3	9531	1132	1588.5	9768			
8	1255	1582.0	9459	996	918.0	8427	1240	1516.5 *	9349 *	1133	1595.5	9760			
9	1261	1581.0	9387	1011	842.0	8630				1138	1548.5	9713			
10	1336	1415.5	9303	1015	854.5	8526				1143	1487.0	9798			
11	1339	1372.5 *	9260 *	1020	625.5	8251				1153	1626.0	9674			
12				1047	625.0 *	8288				1155	1472.5	9645			
13				1081	753.0	8059 *				1165	1452.5	9625			
14				1209	721.5	8224				1165	1440.0	9645			
15										1166	1428.0	9633			
16										1173	1424.0	9621			
17										1182	1454.0	9404 *			
18										1183	1310.0	9506			

Table A8. Cont.

									1189	1279.0	9481			
19									1189	1279.0	9481			
20									1202	1303.0	9252			
21									1266	1249.5	9639			
22									1284	1198.5 *	9588			

	ORB6			ORB7			ORB8			ORB9			ORB10	
	MKS	TDS	FLT	MKS	TDS	FLT	MKS	TDS	FLT	MKS	TDS	FLT	MKS	TDS	FLT
1	1090 *	1382.5	9489	433 *	226.0	3813	1016 *	1919.5	8465	1009 *	1646.5	9402	1055 *	1366.5	9211
2	1091	1284.5	9341	437	225.0	3770	1025	1635.5	8181 *	1013	1595.0	9331	1065	790.5	8899
3	1134	1078.0	9177	439	271.5	3707	1047	1617.0	8457	1016	1534.0	9251	1108	843.0	8834
4	1153	1059.0	9182	453	220.0	3742	1148	1575.0	8319	1027	1644.0	9187	1114	686.5 *	8810
5	1168	969.0	9030 *	465	236.0	3697	1150	1564.0	8312	1036	1669.0	9130	1115	687.5	8795
6	1204	945.0	9072	471	173.5 *	3620 *	1176	1565.0	8294	1043	1479.0	9206	1246	1080.0	8747 *
7	1221	907.0 *	9034				1184	1502.0 *	8301	1063	1360.0	8975			
8										1064	1355.0 *	8966			
9										1066	1378.0	8942			
10										1073	1358.5	8956			
11										1083	1426.0	8885 *			
12										1092	1417.0	8914			

Table A9. Non-dominated front obtained by CMOTA for the JSSP instances proposed by [42].

	LA01			LA02			LA03			LA04			LA05		
	MKS	TDS	FLT	MKS	TDS	FLT	MKS	TDS	FLT	MKS	TDS	FLT	MKS	TDS	FLT
1	666 *	1416.0	5550	663 *	1327.5	5145	617 *	1807.5	5353	598 *	1396.0	5096	593 *	1241.5	4601
2	666	1367.0	5561	677	1284.0	5053	624	1516.0	4890	598	1414.0	5094	593	1240.5	4604
3	666	1444.0	5500	685	925.0 *	4805 *	630	1444.0	4982	602	1181.0	4842	593	1290.0	4516
4	666	1325.5	5577				630	1511.5	4977	610	1049.0	4730	596	1277.0	4583
5	667	1465.5	5488				633	1383.5	4816	644	1083.5	4726 *	597	1242.0	4537
6	668	1269.0	5403				637	1345.5	4820	660	1014.0 *	4743	600	1233.5	4546
7	672	1245.5	5468				650	1147.5 *	4673	660	1027.5	4737	600	1273.0	4499
8	674	1246.0	5396				673	1164.0	4632 *				600	1190.5	4553
9	676	1313.0	5348										603	1162.0	4571
10	702	1229.5	5438										607	1154.5	4518
11	706	1099.5	5177										607	1185.0	4497
12	726	1072.5	5210										608	1176.5	4502
13	764	1001.0 *	5176 *										610	1133.5	4502
14													613	1093.0 *	4502
15													614	1130.5	4494
16													622	1164.0	4459
17													648	1209.0	4424
18													650	1198.0	4413 *

	LA06			LA07			LA08			LA09			LA10		
	MKS	TDS	FLT	MKS	TDS	FLT	MKS	TDS	FLT	MKS	TDS	FLT	MKS	TDS	FLT
1	926 *	4193.5	10151	890 *	4398.0	10014	863 *	3719.5	9421	951 *	4212.5	10607	958 *	4562.0	10536
2	927	4150.5	10108	893	4494.0	9908	870	3644.5	9346	954	4387.0	10601	958	4558.5	10587
3	943	4104.0	10028	894	4092.5	9651	896	3401.5 *	9139 *	960	4284.5	10586	960	4507.0	10481
4	964	4061.5	9978	904	3890.5 *	9452 *				966	4077.0 *	10411 *	965	4277.0	10251
5	992	4034.5 *	9951 *										988	4271.0 *	10,245 *

Table A9. Cont.

	LA11				LA12				LA13				LA14				LA15		
	MKS	TDS	FLT	MKS	TDS	FLT	MKS	TDS	FLT	MKS	TDS	FLT	MKS	TDS	FLT
1	**1222 ***	9579.5	17,606	**1039 ***	7550.0	14,564	**1150 ***	8618.0	16,397	**1292 ***	9927.5	17,940	**1207 ***	9792.5	17,960
2	1234	9317.5	17,344	1045	7514.0	14,528	1150	8641.5	16,377	1292	9966.0	17,847	1209	9679.5	17,847
3	1238	**9222.5 ***	**17,249 ***	1050	7498.0	14,512	1152	8608.0	16,387	1298	9919.5	17,857	1217	9644.5	17,812
4				1081	**7318.0 ***	**14,332 ***	1153	8459.5	16,160	1321	**9697.0 ***	**17,716 ***	1217	9692.5	17,769
5							1182	7884.0	15,577				1218	9628.5	17,705
6							1189	**7811.0 ***	**15,504 ***				1219	**9312.5 ***	**17,336 ***

	LA16				LA17				LA18				LA19				LA20		
	MKS	TDS	FLT	MKS	TDS	FLT	MKS	TDS	FLT	MKS	TDS	FLT	MKS	TDS	FLT
1	**982 ***	909.5	8738	**825 ***	1045.0	7819	**872 ***	609.5	7920	**901 ***	569.0	8258	**938 ***	749.0	8616
2	1008	771.0	8567	830	1016.0	7782	874	560.5	7836	904	398.0	8071	967	697.0	8549
3	1065	613.5	8503	848	1001.0	7698	905	555.0	8017	916	375.0	8146	967	695.0	8561
4	1082	603.0	8227	850	969.0	7569	908	555.5	7880	916	422.0	7972	969	674.0	8498
5	1091	**490.5 ***	8311	854	983.0	7557	922	549.0	8056	921	342.0	7903	972	645.5	8578
6	1107	524.0	**8130 ***	856	883.5	7656	930	549.0	7866	929	**276.0 ***	7766	972	647.5	8470
7				865	845.5	7612	933	472.0	**7797 ***	931	325.0	7765	978	558.0	8318
8				873	758.0	7517	933	**468.5 ***	7824	953	488.0	**7759 ***	1010	**531.0 ***	8291
9				883	764.5	7500							1025	662.5	8277
10				894	752.0	7539							1041	612.0	**8069 ***
11				911	758.0	7448									
12				918	723.0	7415									
13				927	775.0	**7336 ***									
14				981	760.0	7384									
15				995	770.0	7373									
16				1009	730.0	7368									
17				1176	**720.0 ***	7605									

	LA21				LA22				LA23				LA24				LA25		
	MKS	TDS	FLT	MKS	TDS	FLT	MKS	TDS	FLT	MKS	TDS	FLT	MKS	TDS	FLT
1	**1154 ***	3406.5	15,329	**1041 ***	3315.0	14,265	**1115 ***	2616.5	14,458	**1047 ***	2511.0	14,081	**1073 ***	3252.0	14,388
2	1172	3329.5	15,084	1050	3118.0	14,068	1118	2599.5	14,441	1052	2477.0	14,047	1087	3217.0	14,315
3	1174	3035.5	14,835	1053	3035.0	14,000	1158	2459.0	14,476	1054	2870.5	14,001	1088	3143.0	14,241
4	1177	3059.5	14,607	1070	2994.0	13,975	1160	2457.0	14,436	1060	2613.5	13,860	1110	2638.0	13,761
5	1202	3044.5	14,763	1079	2754.0	13,625	1160	2722.5	14,389	1070	2593.5	13,918	1147	2633.0	13,793
6	1204	3024.5	14,743	1081	**2699.0 ***	**13,562 ***	1163	2437.0	14,416	1073	2598.5	13,874	1148	2682.5	**13,742 ***
7	1220	3032.5	14,609				1172	2761.5	14,370	1079	2547.5	13,859	1148	**2623.5 ***	13,764
8	1238	2881.5	14,783				1178	**2408.0 ***	14,384	1080	2473.0	14,063			
9	1239	2877.5	14,666				1210	2595.5	14,373	1080	2546.5	**13,858 ***			
10	1253	2832.5	14,696				1216	2562.5	**14,340 ***	1087	**2368.0 ***	13,911			
11	1347	2973.5	14,634												
12	1349	2883.0	14,507												
13	1356	2943.0	14,494												
14	1393	2936.0	14,419												
15	1393	2929.5	14,489												
16	1403	**2766.5 ***	**14,412 ***												

	LA26				LA27				LA28				LA29				LA30		
	MKS	TDS	FLT	MKS	TDS	FLT	MKS	TDS	FLT	MKS	TDS	FLT	MKS	TDS	FLT
1	**1300 ***	7356.5	23,129	**1374 ***	8083.0	24,331	**1325 ***	7440.0	23,463	**1328 ***	8518.0	23,291	**1455 ***	9085.0	25,105
2	1336	7171.5	22,944	1377	7946.0	24,194	1326	7315.0	23,338	1337	8513.0	23,286	1457	9071.0	25,091

Table A9. Cont.

3	1337	7077.5	22,850	1378	7660.0	23,875	1340	7233.0	23,256	1345	8501.0	23,274	1465	9211.5	25,064
4	1343	7047.5	22,820	1380	7641.0	23,856	1354	7185.0	23,176	1353	8534.0	23,273	1477	9196.5	25,049
5	1344	6971.5	22,744	1394	7645.5	23,854	1357	7096.0	23,087	1358	8464.0	23,203	1479	8374.5	24,204
6	1353	6947.5 *	22,720	1398	7494.0	23742	1360	7056.0	23,047	1360	8091.5	22,985	1481	8348.5	24,178
7	1396	7083.0	22,666	1401	7438.0	23,686	1375	6997.0	22,885	1363	8064.5	22,958	1519	8280.5	242,20
8	1454	7072.5	22,660 *	1402	7374.0	23,622	1384	6906.0	22,794	1368	8062.5	22,956	1543	8227.5	24167
9				1405	7408.5	23,586	1396	6674.5	22,672	1389	8208.0	22,939	1584	8391.5	24,097
10				1412	7327.0	23,575	1412	6568.5	22,566	1403	7990.5	22,836	1598	8090.5	23,796
11				1446	7265.0	23,513	1417	6518.5	22,509	1432	7971.5	22,865	1657	7980.5 *	23,686 *
12				1454	7367.0	23,500	1436	6491.5 *	22,482 *	1448	7972.0	22,776			
13				1469	7264.5	23,511				1453	7805.0	22,609			
14				1476	7228.0	23,476				1475	7733.5	22,627			
15				1483	7185.0	23,433				1525	7664.5 *	22,558 *			
16				1502	7226.5	23,352									
17				1602	7109.5 *	23,312 *									

	LA31			LA32			LA33			LA34			LA35		
	MKS	TDS	FLT	MKS	TDS	FLT	MKS	TDS	FLT	MKS	TDS	FLT	MKS	TDS	FLT
1	1784 *	219,44.5	44,731	1850 *	22,413.0	47,111	1719	22,284.5	44,738	1768 *	23,263.5	46,275	1899 *	24,702.5	47,930
2	1800	21,424.5	44,211	1850	22,411.5	47,265	1720	21,944.5	44,398	1774	22,903.5	45,915	1908	24,515.5	47,743
3	1807	21,363.5	44,150	1857	22,085.5	46,939	1722	21,802.5	44,256	1775	22,881.5	45,893	1909	23,489.5	46,717
4	1842	20,988.5	43,775	1859	22,074.5	46,928	1723	21,777.5	44,190	1776	22,657.5	45,669	1917	23,481.5	46,709
5	1843	20,814.5 *	43,601 *	1881	21,988.5	46,842	1734	21,723.5	44,177	1792	22,656.5	45,668	1919	23,379.5	46,607
6				1884	21,985.5	46,839	1743	21,447.5	43,901	1796	22,150.5	45,162	1923	23,368.5 *	46,596
7				1896	21,958.5	46,812	1746	21,446.5	43,900	1803	22,109.5	45,121	2029	23,393.5	46,568 *
8				1897	21,509.5	46,363	1750	21,134.5	43,508	1813	21,889.5	44,901			
9				1916	21,481.5	46,335	1755	21,040.5	43,414	1817	21,797.5	44,809			
10				2051	21,401.5	46,255	1771	21,024.5	43,478	1820	21,749.5	44,761			
11				2068	21,362.5	46,216	1776	20,995.5	43,449	1823	21,740.5 *	44,752 *			
12				2084	21,294.5 *	46,148	1777	20,945.5	43,399						
13				2148	21,372.5	46,059 *	1783	20,842.5	43,296						
14							1785	20,778.5	43,232						
15							1787	20,722.5	43,176						
16							1789	20,358.0	42,706						
17							1796	20,310.0	42,658						
18							1800	20,044.0	42,360						
19							1801	19,567.0	41,883						
20							1805	19,558.0 *	41,874 *						

	LA36			LA37			LA38			LA39			LA40		
	MKS	TDS	FLT	MKS	TDS	FLT	MKS	TDS	FLT	MKS	TDS	FLT	MKS	TDS	FLT
1	1467 *	3203.0	20,649	1652 *	2988.5	21,540	1446 *	2646.0	19,043	1474 *	2876.0	20,077	1438 *	2444.0	19,398
2	1503	3180.0	20,626	1653	2988.5	21,536	1472	2601.0	19,159	1494	2872.0	20,073	1531	2369.0	19,333
3	1515	3076.0	20,420	1656	2912.5	21,460	1473	2060.5	18,322	1513	2385.5	19,216	1561	2336.0 *	19,300 *
4	1519	3024.0	20,254	1691	3256.0	21,323	1491	2000.5 *	18,262 *	1597	2396.0	19,175			
5	1596	2988.5	20,597	1692	2894.0	21,493				1603	2362.0	19,101			
6	1616	2948.5	20,557	1696	3233.0	21,300				1605	2254.0 *	18,993 *			
7	1622	2868.5	20,477	1705	2757.0	21,254									
8	1632	2884.5	20,163	1751	2798.5	21,208									
9	1678	2903.5	20,106	1756	2888.5	21,064									
10	1704	2958.0	20,037	1757	2850.0	21,005 *									
11	1709	2869.0	19,948	1839	2670.5	21,086									
12	1735	2654.0	19,510	1883	2578.5 *	21,291									
13	1738	2650.0 *	19,506 *												

Table A10. Non-dominated front obtained by CMOTA for the JSSP instances proposed by [43].

	ABZ5			ABZ6			ABZ7			ABZ8			ABZ9		
	MKS	TDS	FLT	MKS	TDS	FLT	MKS	TDS	FLT	MKS	TDS	FLT	MKS	TDS	FLT
1	1296 *	565.0	11,621	991 *	587.5	8826	796 *	3124.0	14,127	821 *	3504.0	14,883	837 *	3263.0	14,378
2	1306	692.5	11,581	999	460.5	8658	797	2923.5	13,906	823	3447.0	14,826	845	2996.5	14,126
3	1321	683.5	11,572	1013	300.0	8753	803	2805.5	13,826	824	3428.0	14,807	848	2967.5	14,097
4	1322	523.0	11,801	1021	469.5	8543 *	876	2684.5	13,608	825	3423.0	14,802	853	2936.5	14,066
5	1333	507.0	12,016	1037	407.5	8719	890	2636.5 *	13,556 *	835	2786.0 *	14,111	856	2900.5 *	14,030 *
6	1334	407.5	11,786	1037	439.0	8674				847	2817.0	14,086 *			
7	1334	403.0	11,861	1045	235.5	8614									
8	1337	574.0	11,604	1089	197.5 *	8812									
9	1338	566.0	11,534	1115	203.5	8768									
10	1351	533.5	11,768												
11	1356	557.5	11,750												
12	1383	745.0	11,520												
13	1385	759.5	11,401												
14	1386	679.5	11,336												
15	1387	475.0	11,545												
16	1397	468.0	11,538												
17	1409	407.0 *	11,374 *												

Table A11. Non-dominated front obtained by CMOTA for the JSSP instances proposed by [44].

	YN01			YN02			YN03			YN04		
	MKS	TDS	FLT	MKS	TDS	FLT	MKS	TDS	FLT	MKS	TDS	FLT
1	1160 *	3154.5	20,470	1155 *	3592.0	21,112	1138 *	2732.5	19,941	1225 *	4078.0	22,098
2	1166	2654.0	19,808	1159	3545.0	21,105	1154	2543.0	19,839	1228	3780.0	21,449
3	1188	2618.0	19,929	1165	3569.0	21,089	1158	2457.0	19,753	1231	3475.0	21,490
4	1193	2617.0	19,771	1166	3537.0	21,057	1204	2394.5	19,438	1232	3460.0	21,465
5	1197	2399.5	19,912	1169	3491.0	21,011	1223	2370.5	19,414 *	1233	3745.0	21,414
6	1200	2220.5	19,745	1188	3171.5	20,606	1277	2194.0 *	19,462	1245	3530.0	21,431
7	1201	2114.0 *	19,570 *	1211	3068.0	20,216				1247	3254.5	21,188
8				1212	3055.0	20,203 *				1273	3236.5	21,170
9				1280	3024.0 *	20,592				1286	3233.5	21,167
10										1325	3169.0 *	20,977 *

Table A12. Non-dominated front obtained by CMOTA for the JSSP instances proposed by [30].

	TA01			TA11			TA21			TA31		
	MKS	TDS	FLT	MKS	TDS	FLT	MKS	TDS	FLT	MKS	TDS	FLT
1	1469 *	2284.0	19,027	1649 *	7293.0	28,872	2098 *	8414.5	38,534	2126 *	21,558.0	55,423
2	1502	2201.0	19,461	1655	7264.0	28,843	2103	7979.0	38,146	2127	21,553.0	55,453
3	1515	1792.5	18,791	1672	7049.0	28,696	2113	7971.0	38,138	2135	21,552.0	55,417
4	1519	1783.5	18,801	1673	7045.0	28,692	2125	7247.5	37,366	2156	21,540.0	55405
5	1530	1713.0 *	18,750	1677	6903.5	28,431	2128	7153.0	37,398	2161	21,416.0	55,316
6	1532	1725.0	18,714 *	1696	6383.5	28,054	2137	6999.0	37,244	2173	21,109.0	55,009
7				1809	6347.5 *	28,018 *	2139	6974.0	37,209	2177	21052.0	54,952
8							2148	6820.5	37,028	2187	19,966.0	53,866
9							2150	6802.5	37,021	2205	19,963.0 *	53,863 *
10							2214	6550.0	36,679			
11							2238	6539.0	36,668			
12							2372	6316.0	36,317			
13							2373	6190.0 *	36,191 *			

Table A12. Cont.

	TA41			TA51			TA61			TA71		
	MKS	TDS	FLT	MKS	TDS	FLT	MKS	TDS	FLT	MKS	TDS	FLT
1	2632 *	21,027.5	67,904	3128 *	73,001.0	129,878	3420 *	74,932.0	151,378	6094 *	366,221.5	517,558
2	2650	20,910.5	67,829	3132	72,689.0	129,566	3421	73956.0	150,402	6095	365,726.5	517,063
3	2666	20,826.5	67,745	3137	72,651.0	129,528	3423	73884.0	150,330	6098	365,546.5	516,883
4	2672	20,766.5	67,685	3192	70,022.5	126,809	3461	69,778.0	146,224	6174	365,320.5 *	516,657 *
5	2771	20,304.5	67,222	3249	69,935.5 *	126,722 *	3462	69,767.0	146,213			
6	2776	20,265.5 *	67,183 *				3478	69,754.0 *	146,200 *			

References

1. Coello, C.; Cruz, N. Solving Multiobjective Optimization Problems Using an Artificial Immune System. *Genet. Program. Evolvable Mach.* **2005**, *6*, 163–190. [CrossRef]
2. Garey, M.R.; Johnson, D.S.; Sethi, R. PageRank: The complexity of flowshop and jobshop scheduling. *Math. Oper. Res.* **1976**, *1*, 117–129. [CrossRef]
3. Ojstersek, R.; Brezocnik, M.; Buchmeister, B. Multi-objective optimization of production scheduling with evolutionary computation: A review. *Int. J. Ind. Eng. Comput.* **2020**, *11*, 359–376. [CrossRef]
4. Pinedo, M. *Scheduling: Theory, Algorithms, and Systems*; Springer: New York, NY, USA, 2008.
5. Kirkpatrick, S.; Gelatt, C.D.; Vecchi, M.P. Optimization by simulated annealing. *Am. Assoc. Adv. Sci.* **1983**, *220*, 671–680. [CrossRef] [PubMed]
6. Dueck, G.; Scheuer, T. Threshold Accepting: A General Purpose Algorithm Appearing Superior to Simulated Annealing. *J. Comput. Phys.* **1990**, *90*, 161–175. [CrossRef]
7. Scaria, A.; George, K.; Sebastian, J. An artificial bee colony approach for multi-objective job shop scheduling. *Procedia Technol.* **2016**, *25*, 1030–1037. [CrossRef]
8. Méndez-Hernández, B.; Rodriguez Bazan, E.D.; Martinez, Y.; Libin, P.; Nowe, A. A Multi-Objective Reinforcement Learning Algorithm for JSSP. In Proceedings of the 28th International Conference on Artificial Neural Networks, Munich, Germany, 17–19 September 2019; pp. 567–584. [CrossRef]
9. López, A.; Coello, C. Study of Preference Relations in Many-Objective Optimization. In Proceedings of the Genetic and Evolutionary Computation Conference (GECCO' 2009), Montreal, QC, Canada, 8–12 July 2009; pp. 611–618. [CrossRef]
10. Blasco, X.; Herrero, J.; Sanchis, J.; Martínez, M. *Decision Making Graphical Tool for Multiobjective Optimization Problems*; Springer: Berlin/Heidelberg, Germany, 2007; Volume 4527, pp. 568–577. [CrossRef]
11. García-León, A.; Dauzère-Pérès, S.; Mati, Y. An Efficient Pareto Approach for Solving the Multi-Objective Flexible Job-Shop Scheduling Problem with Regular Criteria. *Comput. Oper. Res.* **2019**, *108*. [CrossRef]
12. Qiu, X.; Lau, H.Y.K. An AIS-based hybrid algorithm for static job shop scheduling problem. *J. Intell. Manuf.* **2014**, *25*, 489–503. [CrossRef]
13. Kachitvichyanukul, V.; Sitthitham, S. A two-stage genetic algorithm for multi-objective job shop scheduling problems. *J. Intell. Manuf.* **2011**, *22*, 355–365. [CrossRef]
14. Zhao, F.; Chen, Z.; Wang, J.; Zhang, C. An improved MOEA/D for multi-objective job shop scheduling problem. *Int. J. Comput. Integr. Manuf.* **2016**, *30*, 616–640. [CrossRef]
15. González, M.; Oddi, A.; Rasconi, R. Multi-objective optimization in a job shop with energy costs through hybrid evolutionary techniques. In Proceedings of the Twenty-Seventh International Conference on Automated Planning and Scheduling, Pittsburgh, PA, USA, 18–23 June 2017; pp. 140–148.
16. Serafini, P. Simulated Annealing for Multi Objective Optimization Problems. In Proceedings of the Tenth International Conference on Multiple Criteria Decision Making, Taipei, Taiwan, 19–24 July 1992.
17. Bandyopadhyay, S.; Saha, S.; Maulik, U.; Deb, K. A Simulated Annealing-Based Multiobjective Optimization Algorithm: AMOSA. *Evol. Comput. IEEE Trans.* **2008**, *12*, 269–283. [CrossRef]
18. Liu, Y.; Dong, H.; Lohse, N.; Petrovic, S.; Gindy, N. An Investigation into Minimising Total Energy Consumption and Total Weighted Tardiness in Job Shops. *J. Clean. Prod.* **2013**, *65*, 87–96. [CrossRef]
19. Zitzler, E.; Thiele, L. Multiobjective Evolutionary Algorithms: A Comparative Case Study and the Strength Pareto Approach. *IEEE Trans. Evol. Comput.* **2000**, *3*, 257–271. [CrossRef]
20. Wisittipanich, W.; Kachitvichyanukul, V. An Efficient PSO Algorithm for Finding Pareto-Frontier in Multi-Objective Job Shop Scheduling Problems. *Ind. Eng. Manag. Syst.* **2013**, *12*, 151–160. [CrossRef]
21. Lei, D.; Wu, Z. Crowding-measure-based multiobjective evolutionary algorithm for job shop scheduling. *Int. J. Adv. Manuf. Technol.* **2006**, *30*, 112–117. [CrossRef]
22. Kurdi, M. An Improved Island Model Memetic Algorithm with a New Cooperation Phase for Multi-Objective Job Shop Scheduling Problem. *Comput. Ind. Eng.* **2017**, *111*, 183–201. [CrossRef]

23. Méndez-Hernández, B.; Ortega-Sánchez, L.; Rodriguez Bazan, E.D.; Martinez, Y.; Fonseca-Reyna, Y. Bi-objective Approach Based in Reinforcement Learning to Job Shop Scheduling. *Revista Cubana de Ciencias Informáticas* **2017**, *11*, 175–188.
24. Aarts, E.H.L.; van Laarhoven, P.J.M.; Lenstra, J.K.; Ulder, N.L.J. A Computational Study of Local Search Algorithms for Job Shop Scheduling. *INFORMS J. Comput.* **1994**, *6*, 118–125. [CrossRef]
25. Ponnambalam, S.G.; Ramkumar, V.; Jawahar, N. A multiobjective genetic algorithm for job shop scheduling. *Prod. Plan. Control* **2001**, *12*, 764–774. [CrossRef]
26. Suresh, R.K.; Mohanasundaram, M. Pareto archived simulated annealing for job shop scheduling with multiple objectives. *Int. J. Adv. Manuf. Technol.* **2006**, *29*, 184–196. [CrossRef]
27. Zitzler, E.; Deb, K.; Thiele, L. Comparison of Multiobjective Evolutionary Algorithms: Empirical Results. *Evol. Comput.* **2000**, *8*, 173–195. [CrossRef] [PubMed]
28. Karimi, N.; Zandieh, M.; Karamooz, H. Bi-objective group scheduling in hybrid flexible flowshop: A multi-phase approach. *Expert Syst. Appl.* **2010**, *37*, 4024–4032. [CrossRef]
29. Deb, K.; Agrawal, S.; Pratap, A.; Meyarivan, T. A fast elitist non-dominated sorting genetic algorithm for multi-objective optimization: NSGA-II. In *International Conference on Parallel Problem Solving from Nature*; Spring: Berlin/Heidelberg, Germany, 2000; Volume 1917.
30. Taillard, E. Benchmarks for basic scheduling problems. *Eur. J. Oper. Res.* **1993**, *64*, 278–285. [CrossRef]
31. Deb, K. *Multiobjective Optimization Using Evolutionary Algorithms*; Wiley: New York, NY, USA, 2001.
32. Schott., J.R. Fault Tolerant Design Using Single and Multicriteria Genetic Algorithm Optimization. Master's Thesis, Department of Aeronautics and Astronautics, Massachusetts Institute of Technology, Cambridge, MA, USA, 1995.
33. Veldhuizen, D.A.V. Multiobjective Evolutionary Algorithms: Classifications, Analyses, and New Innovations. Ph.D. Thesis, Air Force Institute of Technology, Wright-Patterson AFB, Dayton, OH, USA, 1999.
34. Sawaragi, Y.; Nakagama, H.; Tanino, T. *Theory of Multi-Objective Optimization*; Springer: Boston, MA, USA, 1985.
35. Bakuli, D.L. A Survey of Multi-Objective Scheduling Techniques Applied to the Job Shop Problem (JSP). In *Applications of Management Science: In Productivity, Finance, and Operations*; Emerald Group Publishing Limited: Bingley, UK, 2015; pp. 51–62.
36. Baker, K.R. Sequencing rules and due-date assignments in job shop. *Manag. Sci.* **1984**, *30*, 1093–1104. [CrossRef]
37. Sanvicente, S.H.; Frausto, J. A method to establish the cooling scheme in simulated annealing like algorithms. In Proceedings of the International Conference on Computational Science and Its Applications, Assisi, Italy, 14–17 May 2004; pp. 755–763.
38. Solís, J.F.; Sánchez, H.S.; Valenzuela, F.I. ANDYMARK: An analytical method to establish dynamically the length of the Markov chain in simulated annealing for the satisfiability problem. *Lect. Notes Comput. Sci.* **2006**, *4247*, 269–276.
39. May, R. Simple Mathematical Models With Very Complicated Dynamics. *Nature* **1976**, *26*, 457. [CrossRef] [PubMed]
40. Fisher, H.; Thompson, G.L. Probabilistic learning combinations of local job-shop scheduling rules. *Ind. Sched.* **1963**, *1*, 225–251.
41. Applegate, D.; Cook, W. A computational study of the job-shop scheduling problem. *ORSA J. Comput.* **1991**, *3*, 149–156. [CrossRef]
42. Lawrence, S. *Resource Constrained Project Scheduling: An Experimental Investigation of Heuristic Scheduling Techniques (Supplement)*; Graduate School of Industrial Administration, Carnegie-Mellon University: Pittsburgh, PA, USA, 1984.
43. Adams, J.; Balas, E.; Zawack, D. The shifting bottleneck procedure for job shop scheduling. *Manag. Sci.* **1988**, *34*, 391–401. [CrossRef]
44. Yamada, T.; Nakano, R. A genetic algorithm applicable to large-scale job-shop problems. In Proceedings of the Second International Conference on Parallel Problem Solving from Nature, Brussels, Belgium, 28–30 September 1992; pp. 281–290.
45. Hansen, P.B. Simulated Annealing. In *Electrical Engineering and Computer Science-Technical Reports*; School of Computer and Information Science, Syracuse University: Syracuse, NY, USA, 1992.
46. Tripathi, P.K.; Bandyopadhyay, S.; Pal, S.K. Multi-Objective Particle Swarm Optimization with time variant inertia and acceleration coefficients. *Inf. Sci.* **2007**, *177*, 5033–5049. [CrossRef]

Mathematical and Computational Applications

Article

Differential Evolution under Fixed Point Arithmetic and FP16 Numbers

Luis Gerardo de la Fraga

Computer Science Department, Center for Research and Advanced Studies of the National Polytechnic Institute (CINVESTAV), Ciudad de Mexico 07360, Mexico; fraga@cs.cinvestav.mx; Tel.: +52-55-57473755

Abstract: In this work, the differential evolution algorithm behavior under a fixed point arithmetic is analyzed also using half-precision floating point (FP) numbers of 16 bits, and these last numbers are known as FP16. In this paper, it is considered that it is important to analyze differential evolution (DE) in these circumstances with the goal of reducing its consumption power, storage size of the variables, and improve its speed behavior. All these aspects become important if one needs to design a dedicated hardware, as an embedded DE within a circuit chip, that performs optimization. With these conditions DE is tested using three common multimodal benchmark functions: Rosenbrock, Rastrigin, and Ackley, in 10 dimensions. Results are obtained in software by simulating all numbers using C programming language.

Keywords: differential evolution; fixed point arithmetic; FP16; pseudo random number generator

Citation: de la Fraga, L.G. Differential Evolution under Fixed Point Arithmetic and FP16 Numbers. *Math. Comput. Appl.* **2021**, *26*, 13. https://doi.org/10.3390/mca26010013

Academic Editor: Leonardo Trujillo

Received: 19 December 2020
Accepted: 2 February 2021
Published: 4 February 2021

Publisher's Note: MDPI stays neutral with regard to jurisdictional claims in published maps and institutional affiliations.

Copyright: © 2021 by the author. Licensee MDPI, Basel, Switzerland. This article is an open access article distributed under the terms and conditions of the Creative Commons Attribution (CC BY) license (https://creativecommons.org/licenses/by/4.0/).

1. Introduction

The use of different number types in machine learning applications has been analyzed extensively in previous years, more specifically in deep learning neural networks [1,2]. These kinds of neural networks use the convolution as the basic function and have thousands of parameters and must be trained first; that is, the network must be optimized by modifying all the parameters to obtain a local minimum of the goal function. The optimization step is called training and it could take hours in modern hardware of general purpose graphics processor units (GPGPUs). A special type of number, Brain Floating Point (bfloat16), which is a half-precision FP format of 16 bits with the same range of the usual single precision FP numbers (float in C programming language, of 32 bits length), has been proposed for training deep learning neural networks [2]. Other FP numbers of 16 bit length are the so-called FP16 numbers, these are an IEEE standard [1,2] for half-precision FP numbers and can be used on ARM processors.

The goal of using different, shorter numbers in machine learning applications is to improve the speed, and as a consequence reduce the power consumption as it would take less time to train a deep learning network, and also reduce the storage memory or disk size for the variables. In [1] it is mentioned that half precision is also attractive for accelerating general purpose scientific computing, such as weather forecasting, climate modeling, and solution of linear systems of equations. The supercomputer Summit (it was in the Top 500 list https://www.top500.org (accessed on 3 February 2021)), has a peak performance of 148.6 petaflops in the LINPACK benchmark, a benchmark that employs only double precision. For a genetics application that uses half precision, the same machine has a peak performance of 2.36 exaflops [1].

In this work it is proposed to analyze the well known heuristic for single objective optimization, the differential evolution (DE) algorithm, under FP16 numbers, and also under fixed point arithmetic that uses integer numbers of different lengths. This analysis is important if we think of embedded optimization algorithms within a chip [3], which performs a dedicated task. One constraint in these kinds of applications must be that the power consumption is as low as possible. Also it is important if one designs a dedicated algorithm in hardware, just as in FPGAs (Field Programmable Gate Arrays), to accelerate its behavior. Also, another possible application is to execute a fast and small DE inside each core in a GPGPU. These three application scenarios justify the analysis of the DE performed in this work.

The rest of this article is organized as: in Section 2 a very brief description of fixed point arithmetic and FP numbers is made. In Section 3 the DE algorithm is analyzed for which parts could be improved by using other different number types. In Section 4 some experiments and their results are described. Finally, in Section 6 some conclusions are presented.

2. Fixed Point Arithmetic and Floating Point Numbers

The notation $a.b$ will be used here to represent a set of integer numbers that uses a bits in the integer part, and b bits in the fractional part. Each number is of size $a + b + 1$ bits (plus the sign bit).

For a number $x \in a.b$, the range of numbers that can be represented is:

$$-2^a \leq x \leq 2^a - 2^{-b} \quad (1)$$

Summing up two numbers $a.b$ results in a number $(a+1).b$ [4]. The multiplication of two numbers $a.b$ results in a number $(2a+1).2b$ [4]. It is possible to verify these results by applying the respective operation to two extreme numbers in (1).

The microprocessors offer the sum and multiplication of two integer numbers and the result is stored in a number of the same size as the operands. In a hardware design for a given application, one must use a big enough number to store the sum of two $a.b$ numbers, and the result to multiply two $a.b$ numbers must be returned to a $a.b$ number. The easiest way to perform this is by truncating the result: the resulted $2a.2b$ is shifted b bits to the right, again the number must be big enough to store the resulted $a.b$ number. In a PC, if one uses 32 bit integer numbers, the first bit is the sign bit, and then one could multiply up two $\sqrt{2^{31}} = 2^{31/2}$ values to keep the result within the used 31 bits. In any application, normally one does not take care if the used numbers can keep the result of the operations applied to them, and one trusts that the numbers are big enough to store the results.

The operations sum and multiplication of two integer numbers are the fastest because each operation is built in the hardware and both take a single clock step.

The sum and multiplication of two FP numbers is totally different. An FP number is composed as $s \cdot 2^e$, where s is the significant and e the exponent. If p bits are used for the significant, it is an integer that could take values from 0 to $2^p - 1$. The exponent e is an integer number too. The sum of two FP numbers is carried on first by expressing both numbers with the same exponent, then summing up both significants. The greater exponent of both numbers is used to express them with the same exponent. The result must be rounded to express the same number of bits used in the significants. Also, the result could be normalized, which means that the exponent will have a single binary precision number.

The multiplication takes more steps because two numbers $s_1 \cdot 2^{e_1}$, and $s_2 \cdot 2^{e_2}$ are multiplied as $s = s_1 \cdot s_2$ and the exponents are summed ($e = e_1 + e_2$), and also both results are rounded and the final result is normalized.

In the IEEE 754 standard [5], an FP number has a sign bit, i, and the represented number is equal to $(-1)^i \cdot s \cdot 2^e$, where $e_{min} \leq p + e - 1 \leq e_{max}$. The values used in common FP numbers are shown in Table 1.

Table 1. Characteristics of floating point (FP) numbers in the IEEE 754 standard.

Precision	Exponent	Significant	e_{min}	e_{max}	Smallest	Biggest
Half	5	10	−14	+15	6.10×10^{-5}	6.55×10^4
Single	8	23	−126	+127	1.17549×10^{-38}	3.40282×10^{38}
Double	11	52	−1022	+1023	2.22507×10^{-308}	1.79769×10^{308}

Floating point operations take more than a clock cycle within a microprocessor.

The IEEE 754 standard [5] gives much more aspects that are necessary to work with FP numbers, such as rounding methods, Not a Number (NaN), infinities, and how to handle exceptions. In [6] all these details about FPs are explained.

3. DE Analysis

DE is a heuristic used for global optimization under continuous spaces. DE solves problems as:

$$\begin{aligned}
\text{minimize: } & f(\mathbf{x}), \\
\text{subject to: } & \mathbf{g}(\mathbf{x}) \geq 0, \text{ and} \\
& \mathbf{h}(\mathbf{x}) = 0, \\
& \mathbf{x} \in S \subset \mathbb{R}^n.
\end{aligned} \quad (2)$$

where $f : \mathbb{R}^n \to \mathbb{R}$ is the function to optimize; $\mathbf{x} \in \mathbb{R}^n$, that is, the problem has n variables; and also we could have $\mathbf{g} : \mathbb{R}^n \to \mathbb{R}^{m_1}$, m_1 inequality constraints; and $\mathbf{h} : \mathbb{R}^n \to \mathbb{R}^{m_2}$, m_2 equality constraints. The solution to the problem $\mathbf{x}$ is in a subset S of the whole search space $\mathbb{R}^n$ and where the constraints are satisfied, this space S is called the *feasible space*.

Also, the *search space* contains the feasible space and is defined by the *box constraints*:

$$x_i \in [l_i, u_i], \text{ for } i = \{1, 2, \ldots, n\}. \quad (3)$$

This is, each variable x_i is searched in the interval defined by the lower bound value l_i, and the upper bound value u_i, for $i = \{1, 2, \ldots, n\}$.

Constraints can be incorporated into the problem (2) by modifying the objective function as:

$$f_1(\mathbf{x}) = f(\mathbf{x}) + \alpha \sum_{i=1}^{m_1} \min[0, g_i(\mathbf{x})]^2 + \beta \sum_{i=1}^{m_2} h_i^2(\mathbf{x}) \quad (4)$$

Now the f_1 will be optimized instead of f in (2). α and β in (4) represent the penalty coefficients that weigh the relative importance of each kind of constraint.

One important point about DE is that the heuristic needs to only evaluate the problem to solve. Classical mathematical optimization methods use the first and perhaps also the second derivative of the given problem. These derivatives are easy to obtain if one has in hand the mathematical expression to the given problem. It is possible to approximate the derivatives numerically but with a very high computational cost [7].

According to the test in the CEC 2005 conference [8], DE is the second best heuristic to solve real parameter optimization problems, when the number of parameters is around 10.

The DE pseudocode is shown in Algorithm 1.

DE works with a population that is composed of a set of individuals, or vectors, of real numbers. All vectors are initialized with random numbers with a uniform distribution within the search bounds of each parameter (line 1 in Algorithm 1). For a certain number of iterations (line 4) the population is modified and this modified population could replace the original individuals. The core of DE is in the loop on lines 8–13: a new individual is generated from three different individuals chosen randomly; each value of the new vector (it represents a new individual) is calculated from the first father, plus the difference of the other two fathers multiplied by F, the difference constant; the new vector value is calculated if a random real number (between zero and one) is less than R, the DE's recombination constant. To prevent the case when the new individual could be equal to the current father i, at least one vector's component (a variable value) is forced to be calculated from their random fathers values: it is in line 9 of the pseudocode, when $j = j_{\text{rand}}$, and j_{rand} is an integer random number between 1 and n. In lines 10–12 it is checked if each combined variable value is within the search space. Then the new individual is evaluated, and if it is better than the father (in lines 11–12), then the child replaces its father. The stop condition used here is: if the number of iterations is greater than a maximum number of iterations or when the difference in the objective function values of the worst and best individuals is less than v. This stop condition is called *diff* criterion in [9], and is recommended for a global optimization task.

Algorithm 1 Differential evolution algorithm (rand/1/bin version)

Require: The search space and the value v for the stop condition. The values for population size, μ; maximum number of generations, g; difference and recombination constants, F and R, respectively.

Ensure: A solution of the minimization problem

1: initialize $(P = \{\mathbf{x}_1, \mathbf{x}_2, \ldots, \mathbf{x}_\mu\})$
2: evaluate (P)
3: $k = 0$
4: **repeat**
5:     **for** $i = 1$ to μ **do**
6:         Let r_1, r_2 and r_3 be three random integers in $[1, \mu]$, such that $r_1 \neq r_2 \neq r_3$
7:         Let j_{rand} be a random integer in $[1, n]$
8:         **for** $j = 1$ to n **do**
9:             $x'_j = \begin{cases} x_{r_3,j} + F(x_{r_1,j} - x_{r_2,j}) & \text{if } U(0,1) < R \text{ or } j = j_{\text{rand}} \\ x_{i,j} & \text{otherwise} \end{cases}$
10:             **if** $x'_j < l_i$ or $x'_j > u_i$ **then**   ▷ Check bounds
11:                 $x'_j = U(0,1)(u_i - l_i) + l_i$
12:             **end if**
13:         **end for**
14:         **if** $f(\mathbf{x}') < f(\mathbf{x}_i)$ **then**
15:             $\mathbf{x}_i = \mathbf{x}'$
16:         **end if**
17:     **end for**
18:     min $= f(\mathbf{x}_1)$, max $= f(\mathbf{x}_1)$
19:     **for** $i = 2$ to μ **do**
20:         **if** $f(\mathbf{x}_i) <$ min **then**
21:             min $= f(\mathbf{x}_i)$
22:         **end if**
23:         **if** $f(\mathbf{x}_i) >$ max **then**
24:             max $= f(\mathbf{x}_i)$
25:         **end if**
26:     **end for**
27:     $k \leftarrow k + 1$
28: **until** (max $-$ min) $< v$ or $k > g$

A general form to set the parameter values for DE is: if d is the number of variables, the population size is set to $10d$, $F \in [0.5, 1.0]$, and $R \in [0.8, 1.0]$ [9].

The DE in Algorithm 1 can be improved by using a random integer number generator as the one described in [10], which does not use divisions or FP numbers. This idea could improve the algorithm in line 6 (to generate three numbers in the interval $[1, \mu]$, and in line 7 where another random integer number is generated in the interval $[1, n]$. Also, the values for F and R are within the interval $[0.5, 1.0]$, and usually no more than one or two decimal values are used for these constants, thus these values are not affected by using half precision numbers (see Table 1). Even more, a totally integer arithmetic could be used in the comparison $U(0,1) < R$ (in line 9 in Algorithm 1), if it is used instead $\text{rand}(1, 2^{31}) < I$, with $I = \lfloor 2^{31} \cdot R \rfloor$.

Two implementations of DE were used in this work: one with fixed point arithmetic, and another one using FP16 numbers. The implementation with fixed point arithmetic uses integer (of 32 bits) numbers for all the variables. The implementation using FP16 numbers uses half precision floats (FP16, 16 bits) for all the variables. In this paper a computer of 64 bits architecture was used, then the multiplication of two integers was stored in a long type variable of 64 bits, shifted and truncated to a integer of 32 bits. The core part of DE (lines 8–13 in Algorithm 1) calculates the selected and mutated vector x' as:

$$x'_j = \begin{cases} x_{r_3,j} + F(x_{r_1,j} - x_{r_2,j}) & \text{if } U(0,1) < R \text{ or } j = j_{rand}, \\ x_{i,j} & \text{otherwise,} \end{cases} \quad (5)$$

for $j = \{1, 2, \ldots, n\}$, this is for each variable of the given problem. Thus, one subtraction $(x_{r_1,j} - x_{r_2,j})$ followed of one multiplication (by constant F) and one summation (with $x_{r_3,j}$) are needed to calculated the new vector x'. The greatest value for F could be 1, if all the search space is equal for all variables, the result in (5) could be the double of the current x'_j value.

Then, the maximum possible values in the search space could be the double of the bound values of the search space. Another problem is to find the maximum possible value in the function space. Also, it is not clear how many bits are necessary in the fractional part for the fixed point arithmetic. These items are solved in the following section.

4. Experiments with Three Multimodal Functions in 10 Dimensions

Three very well known benchmark functions were used: shifted version of Rosenbrock, Rastrigin, and Ackley functions in 10 dimensions. All these functions are multimodal, which justify solving them using the DE heuristic. The used Rosenbrock function is defined as:

$$f_1(\mathbf{x}) = 0.39 + \frac{1}{10} \sum_{i=1}^{n-1} \left\{ \left[(x_i + 1)^2 - (x_{i+1} + 1)\right]^2 + \frac{x_i^2}{100} \right\}, \quad (6)$$

its minimum value is 0.39 with $\mathbf{x} = [0, 0, \ldots, 0]$.

The Rastrigin function is defined as:

$$f_2(\mathbf{x}) = -33 + \sum_{i=1}^{n} \left[\frac{x_i^2}{10} - \cos(2\pi x_i) + 1 \right], \quad (7)$$

its minimum value is -33 for $\mathbf{x} = [0, 0, \ldots, 0]$.

The Ackley function is defined as:

$$f_3(\mathbf{x}) = \frac{1}{20} \left\{ e - \exp\left[\frac{1}{n} \sum_{i=1}^{n} \cos(2\pi x_i)\right] \right\} - 6 - \exp\left[-\frac{1}{5} \sqrt{\frac{1}{n} \sum_{i=1}^{n} x_i^2}\right], \quad (8)$$

its minimum value is -7 with x also equal to $\mathbf{x} = [0, 0, \ldots, 0]$. These three functions are scaled with respect to the three ones defined in [11] in order to keep their amplitudes within the range of half precision FP numbers (see Table 1). A summary of these three functions is described in Table 2.

All functions were programmed in single precision FP (float in C) arithmetic.

Table 2. The three test functions used in this work. The search space was set to $[-10, 10]$, thus the shown values are the extreme possible values that the functions could take, also the minimum value is shown at the optimum solution $x = [0, \ldots, 0]$, and the evaluation at $x = [1, \ldots, 1]$ is shown in the last column.

Function	$x = [10, \ldots, 10]$	$x = [-10, \ldots, -10]$	$x = [0, \ldots, 0]$	$x = [1, \ldots, 1]$
Rosenbrock	10891.29	7291.29	0.39	4.00
Rastrigin	67.00	67.00	−33.00	−32.00
Ackley	−6.14	−6.14	−7.00	−6.82

The number of bits used for the integer and fractional parts for the simulations in fixed point arithmetic is shown in Table 3. The number of bits in the integer part is set according to Table 2 because the maximum number in the third column in Table 3 must be greater than the maximum extreme value shown in Table 2.

Table 3. Calculation of the number of bits in the integer part for the simulations using fixed point arithmetic. Numbers shown here must be greater than the corresponding ones in Table 2 to permit the optimization operations for differential evolution (DE).

Functions	Bits Integer Part	Max. Value	Bits Fractional Part
Rosenbrock	14	$2^{14} = 16384$	1–17
Rastrigin	7	$2^{7} = 128$	1–24
Ackley	5	$2^{5} = 32$	1–26

The resulted statistics for the simulations using 100 runs per bit in the fractional part and FP16 arithmetic are shown in Tables 4–6, for the Rosenbrock, Rastrigin, and Ackley functions, respectively. In those tables the statistics for the number of generations and the obtained function values are shown. The used number of bits in the integer part are shown in Table 3. These number of bits in the integer part were calculated from data in Table 2, for example, for the Rosenbrock function in Table 2 the maximum obtained value function is 10891.29, thus the number of bits for the integer part must be greater than this number, therefore 14 bits were selected because $2^{14} = 16,384 > 10,891.29$. The corresponding variable values for the minimum for each function for the FP16 simulations are shown in Table 7. The obtained mean value for the FP16 simulation for the Rosenbrock function is 0.391538 (see at the end of sixth column in Table 4). The equivalent mean for the fixed point arithmetic is 0.391079 at 11 bits in the fractional part; the associated variable values at this simulation with 11 bits is also shown in Table 7. The same procedure was repeated for the results for the Rastrigin and Ackley functions and are also shown in Table 7.

Table 4. Statistics of the 100 runs per bits used in the fractional part for the fixed point arithmetic and for the Rosenbrock function (14 bits were used for the integer part). Results for 100 runs for the FP16 are also shown. g represents the number of generations.

Bits	$\bar{g}$	$\sigma(g)$	min(g)	max(g)	$\bar{f}_1$	$\sigma(f_1)$	min(f_1)	max(f_1)
1	400.0	0.0	400	400	0.005	0.05	0.000	0.500
2	400.0	0.0	400	400	0.250	0.00	0.250	0.250
3	400.0	0.0	400	400	0.375	0.00	0.375	0.375
4	400.0	0.0	400	400	0.375	0.00	0.375	0.375
5	400.0	0.0	400	400	0.375	0.00	0.375	0.375
6	400.0	0.0	400	400	0.390625	0.00000	0.390625	0.390625
7	400.0	0.0	400	400	0.393360	0.00375	0.390625	0.398438
8	400.0	0.0	400	400	0.394765	0.00145	0.390625	0.398438
9	400.0	0.0	400	400	0.394472	0.00137	0.390625	0.396484
10	400.0	0.0	400	400	0.393555	0.00153	0.390625	0.396484
11	400.0	0.0	400	400	0.391079	0.00098	0.390137	0.395020
12	400.0	0.0	400	400	0.390174	0.00025	0.389893	0.391602
13	400.0	0.0	400	400	0.390064	0.00040	0.390015	0.394043
14	370.02	25.73	298	400	0.390012	2.19×10^{-5}	0.389954	0.390076
15	337.72	25.02	280	400	0.390029	2.17×10^{-5}	0.389984	0.390106
16	333.27	25.73	278	400	0.390040	3.07×10^{-5}	0.389999	0.390167
17	330.18	23.06	259	396	0.390046	2.79×10^{-5}	0.390007	0.390152
FP16	400.0	0.0	400	400	0.391538	0.00040	0.390869	0.392578

Table 5. Simulation results for Rastrigin function. Statistics of the 100 runs per bits used in the fractional part for the fixed point arithmetic (7 bits were used for the integer part). Results for 100 runs for the FP16 are also shown. g is the number of generations.

Bits	$\bar{g}$	$\sigma(g)$	min(g)	max(g)	$\bar{f}_2$	$\sigma(f_2)$	min(f_2)	max(f_2)
1	200.0	0.0	200	200	−33.0	0.0	−33.0	−33.0
2	200.0	0.0	200	200	−33.0	0.0	−33.0	−33.0
3	200.0	0.0	200	200	−33.0	0.0	−33.0	−33.0
4	200.0	0.0	200	200	−33.0	0.0	−33.0	−33.0
5	200.0	0.0	200	200	−33.0	0.0	−33.0	−33.0
6	200.0	0.0	200	200	−32.9917	0.00784	−33.0000	−32.9844
7	200.0	0.0	200	200	−32.9923	0.00136	−33.0000	−32.9844
8	200.0	0.0	200	200	−32.9960	0.00055	−32.9961	−32.9922
9	200.0	0.0	200	200	−32.9979	0.00101	−32.9980	−32.9883
10	200.0	0.0	200	200	−32.9988	0.00113	−32.9990	−32.9883
11	200.0	0.0	200	200	−32.9993	0.00077	−32.9995	−32.9936
12	200.0	0.0	200	200	−32.9996	0.00033	−32.9998	−32.9976
13	200.0	0.0	200	200	−32.9997	0.00031	−32.9999	−32.9971
14	200.0	0.0	200	200	−32.9997	0.00042	−32.9999	−32.9964
15	200.0	0.0	200	200	−32.9998	0.00029	−33.0000	−32.9981
16	200.0	0.0	200	200	−32.9997	0.00090	−33.0000	−32.9915
17	200.0	0.0	200	200	−32.9997	0.00080	−33.0000	−32.9938
18	200.0	0.0	200	200	−32.9997	0.00066	−33.0000	−32.9938
19	200.0	0.0	200	200	−32.9998	0.00066	−33.0000	−32.9938
20	200.0	0.0	200	200	−32.9997	0.00070	−33.0000	−32.9938
21	200.0	0.0	200	200	−32.9997	0.00070	−33.0000	−32.9938
22	200.0	0.0	200	200	−32.9997	0.00071	−33.0000	−32.9938
23	200.0	0.0	200	200	−32.9997	0.00071	−33.0000	−32.9938
24	200.0	0.0	200	200	−32.9997	0.00079	−33.0000	−32.9928
FP16	200.0	0.0	200	200	−32.9997	0.00313	−33.0000	−32.9688

Table 6. Simulation results for Ackley function. Statistics of the 100 runs per bits used in the fractional part for the fixed point arithmetic (5 bits were used for the integer part). Results for 100 runs for the FP16 are also shown. g is the number of generations.

Bits	$\bar{g}$	$\sigma(g)$	$\min(g)$	$\max(g)$	$\tilde{f}_3$	$\sigma(f_3)$	$\min(f_3)$	$\max(f_3)$
1	200.0	0.0	200	200	−7.00000	0.00000	−7.00000	−7.0000
2	200.0	0.0	200	200	−6.95500	0.14381	−7.00000	−6.5000
3	200.0	0.0	200	200	−6.82625	0.06128	−6.87500	−6.75000
4	200.0	0.0	200	200	−6.93750	0.00000	−6.93750	−6.93750
5	200.0	0.0	200	200	−6.96875	0.00000	−6.96875	−6.96875
6	200.0	0.0	200	200	−6.98406	0.00312	−6.98438	−6.95313
7	200.0	0.0	200	200	−6.99219	5.08×10^{-7}	−6.99219	−6.99219
8	200.0	0.0	200	200	−6.99609	8.47×10^{-8}	−6.99609	−6.99609
9	200.0	0.0	200	200	−6.99748	0.00566	−6.99805	−6.94141
10	200.0	0.0	200	200	−6.99900	9.76×10^{-5}	−6.99902	−6.99805
11	200.0	0.0	200	200	−6.99950	9.63×10^{-5}	−6.99951	−6.99902
12	200.0	0.0	200	200	−6.99850	0.00811	−6.99976	−6.94214
13	200.0	0.0	200	200	−6.99990	5.93×10^{-5}	−6.99988	−6.99939
14	108.05	12.28	82	161	−6.99990	3.79×10^{-5}	−6.99994	−6.99963
15	85.25	3.85	76	94	−6.99990	1.99×10^{-4}	−6.99997	−6.99796
16	83.58	3.37	76	91	−6.99993	2.91×10^{-5}	−6.99997	−6.99973
17	82.23	3.26	75	93	−6.99992	4.84×10^{-5}	−6.99996	−6.99961
18	82.06	3.62	75	93	−6.99992	9.82×10^{-5}	−6.99997	−6.99899
19	81.78	3.16	75	88	−6.99990	1.61×10^{-4}	−6.99997	−6.99878
20	81.53	3.14	72	88	−6.99991	1.16×10^{-4}	−6.99996	−6.99887
21	81.31	3.31	75	91	−6.99991	1.00×10^{-4}	−6.99998	−6.99907
22	81.68	3.58	73	90	−6.99991	8.37×10^{-5}	−6.99997	−6.99929
23	81.59	3.41	74	90	−6.99991	8.64×10^{-5}	−6.99996	−6.99927
24	81.49	3.20	73	89	−6.99991	1.10×10^{-4}	−6.99996	−6.99904
25	81.80	3.23	73	93	−6.99991	1.10×10^{-4}	−6.99997	−6.99904
26	81.69	3.26	73	93	−6.99991	1.10×10^{-4}	−6.99997	−6.99904
FP16	66.5	15.54	49	106	−6.99711	0.00172	−7.00000	−6.99609

Table 7. Variables values for the minimum function value for FP16 simulation, and the integer arithmetic simulation. The shown numbers 11, 12, and 11 correspond to the used bits in the fractional part for integer arithmetic, which also correspond to the same mean of FP16 results for each function in Tables 4–6.

	Rosenbrock		Rastrigin		Ackley	
Bits	FP16	11	FP16	12	FP16	11
$\min(f)$	0.39087	0.39111	−33.0000	−32.9998	−7.0000	−6.9995
x_1	−0.003113	−0.000488	−0.000257	−0.000244	0.011742	−0.000488
x_2	−0.014801	−0.006836	−0.004440	−0.000244	−0.008049	−0.000488
x_3	−0.020218	−0.027832	0.017883	−0.001709	−0.009605	0.003418
x_4	−0.048187	−0.071289	0.003246	−0.000244	−0.002329	0.000000
x_5	−0.077759	−0.101562	0.001313	0.001221	−0.001261	0.000977
x_6	−0.147705	−0.153809	−0.002254	0.000000	0.000976	−0.001953
x_7	−0.288574	−0.318359	0.000988	0.000977	0.006023	−0.000977
x_8	−0.471924	−0.544922	−0.014542	−0.001709	0.005493	0.000000
x_9	−0.720215	−0.806641	−0.008965	0.000488	0.004948	0.001953
x_{10}	−0.934082	−0.953613	0.000543	0.000488	−0.001174	−0.001465

5. Discussion

With the simulation results shown in Tables 4–7 it is confirmed that the heuristic DE can be executed in fixed point arithmetic or half precision FP numbers.

As one can see in Tables 4–6 not all the fractional numbers of bits are necessary with a given application. From Table 7 same results for FP16 numbers can be obtained with numbers 14.11, 7.12, and 5.11 for the scaled Rosenbrok, Rastrigin, and Acklen functions.

About the precision obtained in the solution using FP16 or integer arithmetic. The defined machine epsilon value is that such when $\epsilon \neq 1 + \epsilon$. In most of the modern microprocessors (that use two's complement arithmetic) this machine epsilon value for each data type is shown in Table 8.

Table 8. Machine epsilon values for the different floating point numbers, for a general integer number of n bits in the fractional part, and also for the integer arithmetic of results shown in Table 7.

Data Type	Machine Epsilon Value	Precision Bits
double	$2.220446 \cdot 10^{-16} \approx 2^{-52}$	53
float	$1.192093 \cdot 10^{-7} \approx 2^{-23}$	24
FP16	$9.765625 \cdot 10^{-4} \approx 2^{-10}$	11
n bits	2^{-n}	n
fractional part		
11 bits	$4.882813 \cdot 10^{-4} = 2^{-11}$	11
12 bits	$2.441406 \cdot 10^{-4} = 2^{-12}$	12

The *precision bits* is one bit more than the positive exponent of epsilon in floating point types and equal to the number of bits used in the fractional part in integer arithmetic.

Roughly, one cannot expect a result in an optimization problem beyond the precision of the machine epsilon. Thus, using FP16 numbers will give precision in the result at most 9.765625×10^{-4}. Or using an integer number $a.b$, the result will have at most a precision of 2^{-b}. This means also that using FP16 numbers the heuristic, DE in this case, will finish early compared to using single or double precision floating point numbers. In the experiment in this work the DE's stop condition was set equal to 10^{-4}. It is expected that using a smaller stop condition the heuristic will finish in more generations but then is necessary to change to other number types.

One possible application of using FP16 numbers of integer arithmetic could be to obtain first a low precision result within the precision given by the used type numbers (see Table 8). If a bigger precision is required, then a traditional mathematical algorithm, such as the Newton method, could be used. The starting solution for the Newton method will be the previous obtained low resolution solution.

Of course if FP16 numbers of integer arithmetic are used, the application should work at the precision results given by those type numbers. Finally, this behavior must be analyzed in advance for a given application.

For all the simulations the DE's stop condition was set equal to 0.0001. This number in 3.28 notation is equal to 0x000068db (it is a hexadecimal number of 32 bits), and this number can be written by convenience with the binary point as 0x0.00068db. The 13 bits after the binary point are all zeros, thus the stop condition is equal to zero for less than 13 bits used in the fractional part, as one can confirm in Tables 4 and 6 where the simulations show the maximum number of iterations and the stop condition is not taken into account for lesser than and equal to 13 bits.

For the use of fixed point arithmetic in DE, it is critical to know in advance the range of values for the function to optimize. Here the extremes values of the search space were used to know those quantities. In a practical task, it could be tried with the extremes and perhaps other points, on a very coarse grid, to evaluate the function to optimize. The same procedure should be applied to use FP16 numbers.

DE core (in Algorithm 1) uses one difference and one multiplication, thus there is not a numerical problem to be used with fixed point arithmetic or FP16 numbers.

A naive implementation of fixed point arithmetic with a word length of 32 bits is not required, in general. As one can see in Table 4, the same results using 14–17 bits in the fractional part for the Rosenbrock function are obtained. The same applies from results in Table 5 for the Rastringin function for 11–24 bits, and in Table 6 for the Ackley function from 13 to 26 bits in the fractional part.

A future work will be the design in the hardware of DE, which should include the random number generator that can be optimized to use directly the generated bits without FP divisions, as is suggested in [10]. This idea of this design also could be used in software within each core of a GPGPU. Also an interesting idea is to incorporate a random number generator based in chaos [12], which is easy to implement.

6. Conclusions

The DE optimization heuristic was analyzed under its implementation with fixed point arithmetic and half precision floating point arithmetic. Results were shown in software simulation with three multimodal functions: Rosenbrock, Rastrigin, and Ackley in 10 dimensions. To apply these arithmetic representations, it is necessary first to know how to scale the function values to be inside the ranges of FP16 numbers. It is suggested to use the extreme search values to have an idea of those range function values. If this point is solved, DE can be perfectly used in these arithmetics.

Still is possible to optimize the DE algorithm in the pseudo random number generator, without using FP arithmetic. This analysis is required if DE will be embedded in hardware inside a circuit chip or in massive parallel versions in GPGPUs.

Funding: This research received no external funding.

Acknowledgments: The author would like to thank the anonymous reviewers for their valuable comments which have helped to improve the quality of this article.

Conflicts of Interest: The author declares no conflict of interest.

References

1. Higham, N.; Pranesh, S. Simulating Low Precision Floating-Point Arithmetic. *SIAM J. Sci. Comput.* **2019**, *41*, C585–C602. [CrossRef]
2. Kalamkar, D.D.; Mudigere, D.; Mellempudi, N.; Das, D.; Banerjee, K.; Avancha, S.; Vooturi, D.T.; Jammalamadaka, N.; Huang, J.; Yuen, H.; et al. A Study of BFLOAT16 for Deep Learning Training. *arXiv* **2019**, arXiv:1905.12322.
3. Lee, S.; Shi, C.; Wang, J.; Sanabria, A.; Osman, H.; Hu, J.; Sánchez-Sinencio, E. A Built-In Self-Test and In Situ Analog Circuit Optimization Platform. *IEEE Trans. Circuits Syst. I Regul. Pap.* **2018**, *65*, 3445–3458. [CrossRef]
4. Tlelo-Cuautle, E.; Rangel-Magdaleno, J.; de la Fraga, L. *Engineering Applications of FPGAs*; Springer: Berlin/Heidelberg, Germany, 2016. [CrossRef]
5. IEEE Computer Society. *IEEE Standard for Floating-Point Arithmetic*; IEEE Computer Society: Washington, DC, USA, 2008. [CrossRef]
6. Goldberg, D. What Every Computer Scientist Should Know About Floating-Point Arithmetic. *ACM Comput. Surv.* **1991**, *23*, 5–48. [CrossRef]
7. Guerra-Gómez, I.; Tlelo-Cuautle, E.; De la Fraga, L. Richardson extrapolation-based sensitivity analysis in the multi-objective optimization of analog circuits. *Appl. Math. Comput.* **2013**, *222*, 167–176. [CrossRef]
8. Hansen, N. Comparisons Results among the Accepted Papers to the Special Session on Real-Parameter Optimization at CEC-05. 2006. Available online: http://www.ntu.edu.sg/home/epnsugan/index_files/CEC-05/compareresults.pdf (accessed on 3 February 2021).
9. Zielinski, K.; Laur, R. Stopping criteria for differential evolution in Constrained Single-Objective Optimization. In *Advances in Differential Evolution*; Springer: Berlin/Heidelberg, Germany, 2008.
10. Lemire, D. Fast Random Integer Generation in an Interval. *ACM Trans. Model. Comput. Simul.* **2019**, *29*. [CrossRef]
11. Zhang, X.; Kang, Q.; Cheng, J.; Wang, X. A novel hybrid algorithm based on Biogeography-Based Optimization and Grey Wolf Optimizer. *Appl. Soft Comput.* **2018**, *67*, 197–214. [CrossRef]
12. de la Fraga, L.; Torres-Pérez, E.; Tlelo-Cuautle, E.; Mancillas-López, C. Hardware Implementation of pseudo-random number generators based on chaotic maps. *Nonlinear Dyn.* **2017**, *90*, 1661–1670. [CrossRef]

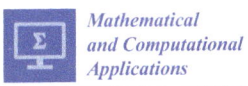

Mathematical and Computational Applications

Article

A Method for Integration of Preferences to a Multi-Objective Evolutionary Algorithm Using Ordinal Multi-Criteria Classification

Alejandro Castellanos-Alvarez [1], Laura Cruz-Reyes [1], Eduardo Fernandez [2], Nelson Rangel-Valdez [3], Claudia Gómez-Santillán [1,*], Hector Fraire [1] and José Alfredo Brambila-Hernández [1]

1. Graduate Program Division, Tecnológico Nacional de México, Instituto Tecnológico de Ciudad Madero, Cd. Madero 89440, Mexico; alex810_castellanos@hotmail.com (A.C.-A.); lauracruzreyes@itcm.edu.mx (L.C.-R.); automatas2002@yahoo.com.mx (H.F.); alfredo.brambila@outlook.com (J.A.B.-H.)
2. Research and Postgraduate Directorate, Universidad Autonoma de Coahuila, Saltillo 26200, Mexico; eddyf171051@gmail.com
3. CONACyT Research Fellow at Graduate Program Division, Tecnológico Nacional de México, Instituto Tecnológico de Ciudad Madero, Cd. Madero 89440, Mexico; nelson.rangel@itcm.edu.mx
* Correspondence: claudia.gomez@itcm.edu.mx

Citation: Castellanos-Alvarez, A.; Cruz-Reyes, L.; Fernandez, E.; Rangel-Valdez, N.; Gómez-Santillán, C.; Fraire, H.; Brambila-Hernández, J.A. A Method for Integration of Preferences to a Multi-Objective Evolutionary Algorithm Using Ordinal Multi-Criteria Classification. *Math. Comput. Appl.* 2021, 26, 27. https://doi.org/10.3390/mca26020027

Academic Editor: Oliver Schütze

Received: 3 March 2021
Accepted: 26 March 2021
Published: 30 March 2021

Publisher's Note: MDPI stays neutral with regard to jurisdictional claims in published maps and institutional affiliations.

Copyright: © 2021 by the authors. Licensee MDPI, Basel, Switzerland. This article is an open access article distributed under the terms and conditions of the Creative Commons Attribution (CC BY) license (https://creativecommons.org/licenses/by/4.0/).

Abstract: Most real-world problems require the optimization of multiple objective functions simultaneously, which can conflict with each other. The environment of these problems usually involves imprecise information derived from inaccurate measurements or the variability in decision-makers' (DMs') judgments and beliefs, which can lead to unsatisfactory solutions. The imperfect knowledge can be present either in objective functions, restrictions, or decision-maker's preferences. These optimization problems have been solved using various techniques such as multi-objective evolutionary algorithms (MOEAs). This paper proposes a new MOEA called NSGA-III-P (non-nominated sorting genetic algorithm III with preferences). The main characteristic of NSGA-III-P is an ordinal multi-criteria classification method for preference integration to guide the algorithm to the region of interest given by the decision-maker's preferences. Besides, the use of interval analysis allows the expression of preferences with imprecision. The experiments contrasted several versions of the proposed method with the original NSGA-III to analyze different selective pressure induced by the DM's preferences. In these experiments, the algorithms solved three-objectives instances of the DTLZ problem. The obtained results showed a better approximation to the region of interest for a DM when its preferences are considered.

Keywords: incorporation of preferences; multi-criteria classification; decision-making process; multi-objective evolutionary optimization; outranking relationships

1. Introduction

Many industrial domains are concerned with multi-objective optimization problems (MOPs), which in general have conflicting objectives to handle [1]. To solve optimally, a MOPs is to find a set of solutions defined as Pareto optimal solutions. They represent the best compromise between the conflicting objectives. A promising alternative is solving MOPs with metaheuristics, like multi-objective evolutionary algorithms (MOEAs); they obtain an approximation of the Pareto optimal set. This approach solves the problem partially. The decision-maker (DM) has to choose the best compromise solution, which satisfies his preferences, from the set of solutions obtained (non-dominated by each other). For practical reasons, the DM needs to choose one solution to implement it.

MOEAs face various problems when dealing with many objectives—exponential growth in the number of non-dominated solutions and high computational cost to maintain population diversity [2–4], among others. In addition to the previous problems, decision-making becomes difficult when the number of objectives increases.

One way to reduce the DM's cognitive effort is to consider the preferences to guide the MOEA to the region of interest (ROI). Incorporating DM's preferences requires considering non-trivial aspects—defining the DM's preferences, determining the ROI and determining the relevance of a solution [5]. The preferences incorporation methods have used the following representation structures [6,7]—weights, ranking of solutions, ranking of objective functions, reference point, trade-offs between objective functions, desirability thresholds, outranking relations. This paper incorporates preferences using outranking relations.

In many real-world situations, the MOPs environment implicates imprecise information derived from inaccurate measurements or the variability in DMs' judgments and beliefs. Not considering these imprecisions can lead to unsatisfactory solutions and, in consequence, to a poor choice between the existing alternatives due to imperfect knowledge of the problem [8]. Imprecise information may be present in different MOP components; for example, it can be either in objective functions, restrictions, or a decision-maker's preferences. Obtaining the preferential model parameters is a difficult task that increases with the objective number, only possible when the handle of imprecision is allowed [9]. The simplest approach to handling imprecise information is to estimate this information's mean value to solve the problem as a deterministic one [10]. The interval numbers are a natural, simple, and effective approach to express imperfect knowledge. This paper incorporates interval analytics to express the parameters of a preferential model.

On the other hand, when we apply MOEAs to solve problems with many objectives, they face challenges such [2–4]:

1. The exponential growth of the number of non-dominated solutions, making it harder to obtain representative samples of the Pareto front.
2. The increase in the number of poor solutions that are difficult to dominate (at least one of your objectives has a value, and the rest are close to optimal).
3. The solutions in the variable space become more distant as more objectives are added to the problem [11]. In such a case, when two distant parent solutions are recombined, the generated offspring solutions likely are also distant [12]; therefore, the efficiency of the genetics operators is questionable.
4. The high computational cost to determine the degree of diversity of the population.

Even though incorporating preferences in MOEAs is a challenging problem, the outranking approach handles it appropriately and aids in reducing the DM's cognitive effort required to choose a final solution [13]. Considering the lack of research devoted to studying the convenience of using the outranking approach in the optimization process, this work proposes a further analysis to observe the performance of a novel strategy of incorporating outranking in a MOEA. Unlike Cruz et al. [6], which requires representative solutions of two classes from the DM, this work proposes to incorporate two classes for internal use to guide the search process and establish greater differentiation between solutions, exerting selective pressure to find the ROI, but with the same cognitive load for the DM.

According to the reviewed literature [2–4,11], and as was mentioned before, MOEAs present difficulties when the number of objectives grows. For example, the classical Non-dominated Sorting Genetic Algorithm II (NSGA-II) [14] presents issues with the diversity-controlling operators [12]; authors extended this algorithm in NSGA-III to replace the crowding distance operator with the generation of well-spread reference point. In this paper, we propose a new method to integrate the DM's preferences to NSGA-III, which can deal with many objectives and is based on non-dominated fronts' ordering.

To the best of our knowledge, few of the previous studies has incorporated the presence of imperfect knowledge, nor have used the INTERCLASS-nC [15] as a classifier in the non-dominated-sorting process or employed more of two of inner classes to guide the search process towards the region of interest, and this work focuses on these issues. This research seeks to evaluate the proposed method's performance when incorporating preferences in the presence of imperfect knowledge with various versions of the proposed algorithm.

The remain of this paper is organized as follows—Section 2 includes reviewing the literature and some definitions of INTERCLASS-nC. Section 3 details the proposed method present. Section 4 specifies the benchmark to be solved, which includes seven problem instances. Section 5 shows and discusses the experimental results. Finally, Section 6 presents the conclusions of this paper and future work.

2. Literature Review

Two main approaches are distinguished in the area of Multi-Criteria Decision-Making (MCDM) [16]:

a The French approach, based on outranking relationships built through comparisons between pairs of solutions to determine, for each pair of solutions, if there is relevant information (preference, indifference, or incompatibility) among them.
b The American Multi-Attribute Utility Theory (MAUT) works based on the formulation of an overall utility function, and an interactive process can obtain this.

In the case of outranking relationship, indicators of dominance or preference are defined given some thresholds. This approach's main criticism is the difficulty to obtain the model parameters [6]; however, there are methods to solve it [17]. On the other hand, MAUT does not work when intransitivity exists between the preferential model [16]. The intransitivity phenomenon occurs in many real cases when exist a looping between the alternatives to select. It is important to consider this property to avoid possible incoherent solutions [18].

The incorporation of *interactive* and *a priori* preferences can reduce the search space because the information is used to guide MOEAs to reach the ROI, which is the region of the Pareto frontier preferred by the DM's. Expressing a DM's preference could be a more difficult cognitive process. According to Cruz et al. [6], the following characteristics are desirable for a preference incorporation method:

1. Easy interaction between the DM and the solution algorithm involves minimizing the cognitive effort of a DM when making a judgment about the solutions.
2. There should be no requirement for comparability and transitivity of preferences.
3. The preference aggregation model must be compatible with the relevant characteristics of the real DMs.
4. There should be techniques to infer the decision model parameters from examples provided by the DM.

In Cruz et al. [6], the multicriteria ordinal classification requires the DM to separate solutions into two categories. In a preference incorporation method with this classifier, the human categorization is the stage with the lowest cognitive demand of the entire process. Assigning solutions to the class "good" or "not good" does not require the DM to worry about the transitivity between them in the same way; the DM only compares the solutions between "good" and "not good".

Using outranking relationships allows handling the characteristics of many DMs facing real-world problems [6]. Being good that used preference incorporation methods meet the desirable characteristics described above, related to interaction with the DM, compatibility between the preferential model and the DM, properties of the preferences, and parameters' inference.

The ordinal multi-criteria classification can be useful to the DM to determine the best solution of a discrete set of alternatives, this is due to the existence of ordinally ordered sets starting with the most preferred alternatives to the least preferred ones [19]. There is a variety of multi-criteria ordinal classification methods, these can be grouped into the following classes [15]:

a Methods based on the objective function value.
b Symbolic methods, mainly those belonging to the theory of rough sets.
c Methods based on outranking relationships.

To our knowledge, the first article that uses multi-criteria ordinal classification based on outranking was Oliveira et al. [20], which uses the popular ELECTRE-TRI method for ordinal classification in a three-objective problem, in which preferences are incorporated *a priori*, directly setting the parameters of the outranking model. Those methods belong to the family ELECTRE (*Elimination Et Choix Traduisant la Realite*) which uses a relation of outranking to identify if a solution x is at least as good as a y.

The hybrid algorithm proposed by Cruz et al. [13] uses a multi-criteria ordinal classification based on outranking. During the first phase, a meta-heuristic algorithm obtains a first approximation to the Pareto frontier. In the second phase, the DM assigns the solutions to two ordered classes and obtains the parameters of the outranking model. In the third phase, the THESEUS classification method applies selective pressure towards "satisfactory" solutions. They test the proposal on project portfolio problems with 4, 9, and 16 objectives; its results surpass the popular NSGA-II and Non-Outranked Ant Colony Optimization (NOACO) proposed in [21].

Cruz et al. [6] proposed the Hybrid Evolutionary Algorithm guided by Preferences (HEAP) algorithm, an extension of their previous work [13]. Where, instead of NSGA-II and NOACO, they use MOEA/D and MOEA/D-DE as metaheuristics for the first phase of the hybrid algorithm. For evaluating the proposed algorithm, they used instances of the portfolio optimization problem and the scalable test DTLZ problem, with three and eight objectives. The DTLZ benchmark are box-constrained continuous n-dimensional multi-objective problems, scalable in fitness dimension. This experimentation aims to analyze different in the activation of classification and the restart of solutions. The use of the DTLZ test suite makes possible assess the closeness to the ROI of a DM and compare the performance with three and eight objectives. The DM's preferences are simulated through an outranking model. In addition to the THESEUS classification method, the popular ELECTRE-TRI is incorporated, and the results of both methods are compared. In most cases, the best results were obtained with ELECTRE-TRI.

Additionally, few of the researches in the state of the art consider the imperfect knowledge in the DM's preferences and its effect in the function's objectives to be optimized. Besides, none has used the classifier INTERCLASS-nC in the non-dominated-sorting process or employed more inner classes to guide the search process towards the ROI. The proposed NSGA-III-P incorporates these characteristics.

2.1. Interval Arithmetic

In [22], Moore et al. formally proposed the interval analysis. An interval number can be viewed as an entity that reflects a quantitative property whose precise value is unknown. Still, the range within the value lies is known [15]. In this work, the imperfect knowledge is represented with interval numbers, Moore et al. [23] describes a number in interval as a range, $\mathbf{E} = [\underline{E}, \overline{E}]$, where $\underline{E}$ represents the lower limit while $\overline{E}$ the upper limit of an interval. Items in bold are numbers in intervals.

Considering two numbers of intervals $\mathbf{D} = [\underline{D}, \overline{D}]$ and $\mathbf{E} = [\underline{E}, \overline{E}]$, the Basic arithmetic operations can be defined for numbers of intervals as follows:

- addition:
$$\mathbf{D} + \mathbf{E} = [\underline{D} + \underline{E}, \overline{D} + \overline{E}] \quad (1)$$

- subtraction:
$$\mathbf{D} - \mathbf{E} = [\underline{D} - \overline{E}, \overline{D} - \underline{E}] \quad (2)$$

- multiplication:
$$\mathbf{D} * \mathbf{E} = [\min\{\underline{DE}, \underline{D}\overline{E}, \overline{D}\underline{E}, \overline{DE}\}, \max\{\underline{DE}, \underline{D}\overline{E}, \overline{D}\underline{E}, \overline{DE}\}] \quad (3)$$

- division:
$$\mathbf{D}/\mathbf{E} = [\underline{D}, \overline{D}] * [\frac{1}{\underline{E}}, \frac{1}{\overline{E}}]. \quad (4)$$

According to Fliedner et al. [24] a *realization* of an interval number is any real number $e \in [\underline{E}, \overline{E}]$. An order relation is defined in the number of intervals as: let e and d be two realizations of **E** and **D** respectively, we say that $\mathbf{E} > \mathbf{D}$ if the preposition "*e is greater than d*" has greater credibility than "*d is greater the an e*".

Fernandez et al. [25] proposes the possibility function:

$$P(\mathbf{E} \leq \mathbf{D}) = \begin{cases} 1 & \text{if } p_{ED} > 1, \\ P_{ED} & \text{if } 0 \leq P_{ED} \leq 1, \\ 0 & \text{if } P_{ED} < 0, \end{cases} \quad (5)$$

where $\mathbf{E} = [\underline{e}, \overline{e}]$ and $\mathbf{D} = [\underline{d}, \overline{d}]$ are numbers of intervals and $P_{ED} = \frac{\overline{e} - \underline{d}}{(\overline{e} - \underline{e}) + (\overline{d} - \underline{d})}$. The order relationship between **D** and **E** is given by:

a   If $\underline{D} = \underline{E}$ and $\overline{D} = \overline{E}$, then $\mathbf{D} = \mathbf{E}$. Therefore $P(\mathbf{E} \geq \mathbf{D}) = 0.5$.
b   If $\underline{E} > \overline{D}$, then $\mathbf{E} > \mathbf{D}$. Therefore $P(\mathbf{E} \geq \mathbf{D}) = 1$.
c   If $\overline{E} < \underline{D}$, then $\mathbf{E} < \mathbf{D}$. Therefore $P(\mathbf{E} \geq \mathbf{D}) = 0$.
d   If $\underline{D} \leq \underline{E} \leq \overline{D} \leq \overline{E}$ or $\underline{D} \leq \underline{E} \leq \overline{E} \leq \overline{D}$, when:

  (a) $P(\mathbf{E} \geq \mathbf{D}) > 0.5$. Therefore, **E** is greater than **D**, $(\mathbf{E} > \mathbf{D})$.
  (b) $P(\mathbf{E} \geq \mathbf{D}) < 0.5$. Therefore, **E** is less than **D**, $(\mathbf{E} < \mathbf{D})$.

2.2. INTERCLASS-nC

Fernandez et al. [15] proposed an ordinal classification method, useful when the DM has a vague idea about the boundaries between adjacent classes but can identify several (even one) representative solutions in each class.

The DM must provide a model of outranking in terms of:

- Weight, $\mathbf{w} = [w^-, w^+]$
- Veto threshold, $\mathbf{v} = [v^-, v^+]$
- Majority threshold $\lambda = [\lambda^-, \lambda^+]$
- Credibility threshold $\beta = [\beta^-, \beta^+]$.

A set of classes $C = \{C_1, ..., C_k, ..., C_m\}$, $(m \geq 2)$ is defined, ordered by increasing preference. Considering a $\delta > 0.5$ and $\lambda > [0.5, 0.5]$. Where, δ corresponds to the maximum probability degree for which the strength of the coalition of agreement exceeds λ.

$R_k = \{r_{kj}, j = 1, ..., card(R_k)\}$ is a subset of reference solutions that characterize C_k, $k = 1, ..., m$ and $\{r_0, R_1, ..., R_m, r_{m+1}\}$ is the set of all reference solutions, in which r_0 and r_{m+1} are the worst and the ideal reference solution respectively. The elements in R_k, $k = 1, ..., m - 1$ must satisfy the conditions defined in Fernandez et al. [15].

Classification is performed using top-down and bottom-up methods jointly. Each method proposes a class for the assignment of x; in case of not coinciding, these rules propose a possible range for the assignment of x.

3. Proposed Method

The Nondominated Sorting Genetic Algorithm III proposed in [12] is a genetic algorithm similar to the original NSGA-II. They search the Pareto optimal set performing a non-dominated sorting. The difference is the maintenance of diversity in the selection stage. The first uses crowding distances, and the second uses reference points. NSGA-III discriminates between the non-dominated solutions using a utility function, which calculates a solution's relevance to approximate a reference point.

To incorporate a DM's preferences, we propose integrating the ordinal classification method INTERCLASS-nC into the NSGA-III, we will call this variant NSGA-III-P. The original work [6] only defines the classes "satisfactory" (Sat) and "unsatisfactory" (Dis); the DM gives a reference set to generate these classes (with one or more representative solutions for each class). This classification complements the non-dominated sorting to increase the capacity to discriminate solutions; this strategy induces a greater selective pressure, focusing the search toward the ROI. In this work, two classes are added internally for giving more precision in the comparison of the solutions:

- The DM is highly satisfied (*HSat*) with an *x* solution, if for each action $w \in R_2$ it is true that $xPr(\beta, \lambda)w$.
- The DM is highly dissatisfied (*HDis*) with an *x*, if for each action $w \in R_1$ it is true that $wPr(\beta, \lambda)x$.

The steps to follow to generate the P_{t+1} of the NSGA-III-P that integrates the INTERCLASS-nC ordinal classification method are shown in the Algorithm 1. Let Q_t the children population of the current generation with equal number of individual N of P_t. The first step is to combine the children and parents tending $R_t = P_t \cup Q_t$ (of size $2N$), the N individuals that will become P_{t+1} will be selected. To do this, R_t will be divided into multiple fronts not dominated by *non-dominated sorting* ($F_1, F_2, ..., F_n$).

The proposed method of integration of preferences works with the set of previously created non-dominated fronts, by classifying all the solutions in F_1 and group the solutions in classes, creating the fronts F'_1, F'_2, F'_3, F'_4 corresponding to classes $HSat, Sat, Dis, HDis$. In the created fronts are joined with the remaining ones in such a way that $F' = \{F'_1, F'_2, F'_3, F'_4\} \cup_{j=2}^{n} F_j$. This process is illustrated in Figure 1 and corresponds to step 7–18 in Algorithm 1.

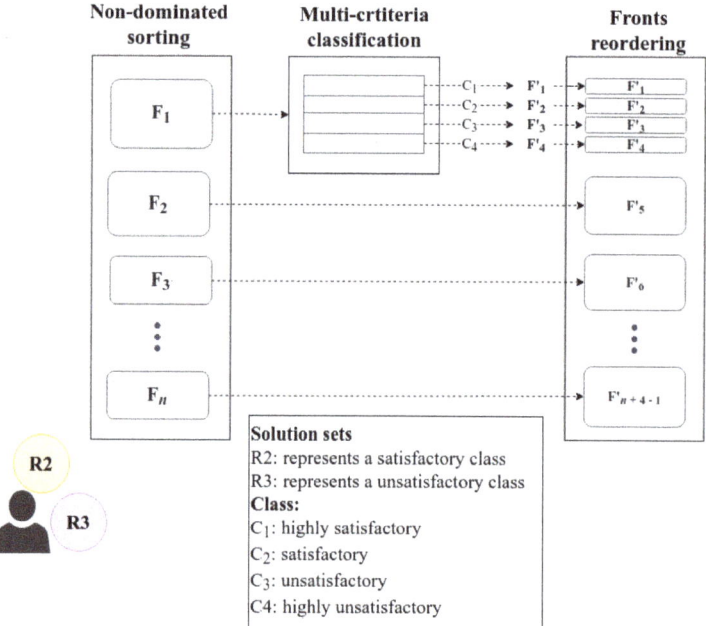

Figure 1. The proposed methodology for classifying the F_1, grouping, and fronts reordering.

After F'_1 the new population is built until the size is N. The last front is called the *l*-th front. Therefore, the front $l + 1$ are rejected; in most situations, l is partially accepted. Only the solutions that maximize the diversity of *l*-th are selected in such a case (steps 21–26).

Algorithm 1 Generation P_t of NSGA-III-P

Input: H structured reference points Z^s or supplied aspiration points Z^a, parent population P_t, Cx iteration where the algorithm applies the classification, Ry solution replacement rate
Output: P_{t+1}

1: $S_t \leftarrow \emptyset, i \leftarrow 1$
2: $Q_t \leftarrow Recombination + Mutation(P_t)$
3: $R_t \leftarrow P_t \cup Q_t$
4: $(F_1, F_2, ..., F_n) \leftarrow Non-dominated-sort(R_t)$
5: // If the rest of the current *iteration* between Cx equals 0, the classification applies
6: **if** $(iteration \bmod Cx) == 0$ **then**
7: $\quad (F'_1, F'_2, F'_3, F'_4) \leftarrow \emptyset$
8: $\quad$ **for** $s \in F_1$ **do** // Classify each member of F_1 and group by class
9: $\quad\quad c \leftarrow classify(s)$
10: $\quad\quad$ **if** $c ==$ "hsat" **then**
11: $\quad\quad\quad F'_1 \leftarrow F'_1 \cup s$
12: $\quad\quad$ **if** $c ==$ "sat" **then**
13: $\quad\quad\quad F'_2 \leftarrow F'_2 \cup s$
14: $\quad\quad$ **if** $c ==$ "dis" **then**
15: $\quad\quad\quad F'_3 \leftarrow F'_3 \cup s$
16: $\quad\quad$ **if** $c ==$ "hdis" **then**
17: $\quad\quad\quad F'_4 \leftarrow F'_4 \cup s$
18: $\quad F' \leftarrow \{F'_1, F'_2, F'_3, F'_4\} \cup_{j=2}^{n} F_j$ // Fronts reordering
19: **else**
20: $\quad F' = (F_1, F_2, ..., F_n)$
21: **while** $|S_t| \leq N$ **do** // Last front to be included $F'_l \leftarrow F'_i$
22: $\quad S_t \leftarrow S_t \cup F'_i$
23: $\quad i \leftarrow i + 1$
24: **if** $|S_t| == N$ **then**
25: $\quad$ **if** $(iteration \bmod Cx) == 0$ **then**
26: $\quad\quad replacement(S_t, Ry)$ // Replace the last Ry random individuals
27: $\quad$ **Return:** S_t
28: **else**
29: $\quad P_{t+1} \leftarrow \cup_{j=1}^{l-1} F_j$
30: $\quad$ Points to be chosen from $F_l : K \leftarrow N - |P_{t+1}|$
31: $\quad$ Normalize objectives & create reference set $Z^r \leftarrow normalize(f^n, S_t, Z^r, Z^s, Z^a)$
32: $\quad$ Associate each member $s \in S_t$ with a reference point:
33: $\quad [\pi(s), d(s)] = associate(S_t, Z^r) \%\pi(s)$
34: $\quad$ Compute niche count of reference point $j \in Z^r : p_j = \sum_{s \in S_t/F_l}((\pi(s) = j)?1 : 0)$
35: $\quad$ Choose K member one at a time from F_l to construct
36: $\quad P_{t+1} : niching(K, p_j, \pi, d, Z^r, F_k, P_{t+1})$
37: $\quad$ **if** $(iteration \bmod Cx) == 0$ **then**
38: $\quad\quad replacement(S_t, Ry)$ // Replace the last Ry random individuals
39: $\quad$ **Return:** P_t

The proposed algorithm has two approaches for controlling the selective pressure generated by the incorporation of preference:

- Apply classification every certain number of iterations (step 6).
- Incorporating a replacement mechanism of Ry individuals from the population (steps 25 and 36), this criterion only applies when classification occurs.

Preference incorporation is, in a certain way, an Intensification approach. The Intensification would be reduced by adding new random solutions and generating a diversification, therefore balancing the search. We analyzed different activation configurations in the experimental section to observe their impact on the algorithm's performance.

4. Experimental Settings

The proposed NSGA-III-P (non-nominated sorting genetic algorithm III with preferences) algorithm's experimentation was carried out to solve the DTLZ1 - DTLZ7 problem's. The algorithm's performance is observed to evaluate the effect of the intensification-diversification mechanism.

All the algorithms used in this experimentation were executed 50 times for each instance on an Intel Core i7-10510U CPU @ 1.80GHz × 8 with 16 GB of RAM. We developed the algorithms in Java using the OpenJDK 11.0.10 64-Bit.

The DTLZ problem's instances configuration is summarized in the Table 1. For his solution, the algorithm has a population size $n = 92$ individuals, the algorithm uses the SBX crossover operator and the polynomial mutation operator. The Table 2 shows the configurations of these operators.

Table 1. Parameters Used for Three-Objective DTLZ Problem's instances.

Problem	Number of Variables	Iterations
DTLZ1	7	400
DTLZ2	12	250
DTLZ3	12	1000
DTLZ4	12	600
DTLZ5	12	500
DTLZ6	12	500
DTLZ7	12	500

Table 2. Crossover and mutation parameters used for NSGA-III-P.

Parameter	Value
Polynomial mutation probability p_m	$\frac{1}{n}$
Polynomial mutation index n_m	20
SBX crossover probability p_c	1
SBX crossover index n_c	30

We analyzed the NSGA-III-P algorithm's versions named $CxRy$, where x is the percentage of iterations to activate the classification. In contrast, y is the percentage of replacement of solutions. Considering the classification increase intensification, less classification reduces the intensification, and restart of solutions increases the diversification; these variants are higher to lower intensification: C100R0, C1R0, C1R2, C10R0, and C0R0 (see Table 3).

Table 3. Experimental configurations carried out.

Name	Description
C0R0	NSGA-III reported in the literature.
C100R0	NSGA-III-P with classification in each iteration with 0% replacement.
C10R0	NSGA-III-P with classification every 10% iterations with 0% replacement.
C1R0	NSGA-III-P with classification every 1% iterations with 0% replacement.
C1R2	NSGA-III-P with classification every 1% iterations with 2% replacement.

4.1. Creation of the ROI

Let T' be a sample of non-dominated solutions taken from a large set T of solutions (≥ 100 thousand) generated analytically at the Pareto frontier of a standard problem. The solutions that integrate the ROI identified with the following sets and measures in T'.

- Outranking weakness of a solution x. A low value of this measure provides positive arguments for selecting x.

$$D_o(x) = \{y | \sigma(y,x) > \beta, \sigma(x,y) < 0.5, y \in T'\{x\}\} \tag{6}$$

- Net score measure used to identify DM preferred solutions.

$$F_n(x) = \sum_{y \in T'} \sigma(x,y) - \sigma(y,x) \tag{7}$$

where $F_n(x) > F_n(y)$ indicates a certain preference of x over y.
- Best compromise solution set more preferred by the DM.

$$x^* = \{x | D(x) = 0, F_n(x) = max_{y \in T'}(F_n(y)), x \in T'\} \tag{8}$$

- Region of interest made up of the best compromise solutions x^*

$$ROI(T') = x^* \cup \{max_{x \in T'}(F_n(x) \geq 0, K)\}, \tag{9}$$

where K are the largest F_n values of x.

4.2. Indicators of Performance

Each algorithm is executed 50 times to the result of a complete run of the NSGA-III-P algorithm configurations, and applying the following indicators:

a Minimum, mean, and maximum Euclidean distance among the obtained non dominated solutions and the ROI (also called Min Euclid, Mean Euclid, Max Euclid)
b Conservation of Dominance: creates a set of non-dominated solutions from the solutions obtained from all configurations. Counting the solutions of each configuration.
c Conservation of Satisfaction: the non-nominated solutions belonging to the HSat and Sat classes (classified by the INTERCLASS-nC) are counted.

4.3. Description of the Instance

The DTLZ problems instance used contains the characterization of the DM preferences (elements 3–6). It has the following elements:

1. objectives number: integer
2. variable number: integer
3. weight vector: *Interval*
4. veto vector: *Interval*
5. lambda: *Interval*
6. references solutions: a vector of solutions is expected.

5. Results

Table 4 shows the reached performance for each algorithm when solving each DTLZ problem. For space reasons, these results are only presented for two performance measures. The first two columns show the result for the original NSGA-III algorithm. The next columns present eight variants of NSGA-III with preferences. The first six columns correspond to variants without activating the solutions restarting strategy. The last two columns correspond to variants that use restarting to reduce the effect of incorporate preferences.

Table 4. Average algorithm performance evaluated with two measures for DTZL problems.

Problem	NSGA-III		NSGA-III-P (with Preferences)							
			without Restart						with Restart	
	C0R0		C100R0		C10R0		C1R0		C1R2	
	%C CHSat	Min Euc	%C CHSat	Min Euc	%C CHSat	Min Euc	%C CHSat	Min Euc	%C CHSat	Min Euc
DTLZ 1	$1.946^{3.5}$	$0.007456^{3.0}$	$\mathbf{92.769^{1.0}}$	$0.001912^{3.0}$	$1.589^{3.5}$	$0.005215^{3.0}$	$1.565^{3.5}$	$0.010437^{3.0}$	$2.131^{3.5}$	$0.011874^{3.0}$
DTLZ 2	$0.843^{3.5}$	$0.007459^{3.0}$	$\mathbf{97.260^{1.0}}$	$0.003802^{3.0}$	$0.625^{3.5}$	$0.008952^{3.0}$	$0.604^{3.5}$	$0.014182^{3.0}$	$0.668^{3.5}$	$0.013754^{3.0}$
DTLZ 3	$8.434^{3.5}$	$0.029905^{5.0}$	$\mathbf{76.477^{1.0}}$	$0.029269^{3.0}$	$5.524^{3.5}$	$0.067064^{3.0}$	$4.481^{3.5}$	$0.049607^{5.0}$	$5.083^{3.5}$	$0.064364^{5.0}$
DTLZ 4	$2.661^{3.5}$	$0.000131^{3.0}$	$\mathbf{78.974^{1.0}}$	$0.000001^{3.0}$	$2.567^{3.5}$	$0.000001^{3.0}$	$11.092^{3.5}$	$0.000796^{3.0}$	$4.706^{3.5}$	$0.000002^{3.0}$
DTLZ 5	$0.365^{3.5}$	$0.001888^{3.0}$	$\mathbf{56.065^{1.0}}$	$0.001635^{3.0}$	$0.852^{3.5}$	$0.005414^{3.0}$	$25.549^{3.5}$	$0.000864^{3.0}$	$17.169^{3.5}$	$0.000819^{3.0}$
DTLZ 6	$1.259^{3.5}$	$0.004893^{3.0}$	$\mathbf{52.887^{1.0}}$	$0.000937^{5.0}$	$1.614^{3.5}$	$0.004585^{3.0}$	$23.793^{3.5}$	$0.001554^{5.0}$	$20.446^{3.5}$	$0.001213^{3.0}$
DTLZ 7	$12.148^{3.5}$	$0.039196^{3.5}$	$\mathbf{42.988^{1.0}}$	$0.006155^{1.0}$	$11.044^{3.5}$	$0.039166^{3.5}$	$17.744^{3.5}$	$0.027163^{3.5}$	$16.075^{3.5}$	$0.028475^{3.5}$
Average	3.95086	0.01299	71.06	0.00624	3.40214	0.01863	12.11829	0.03318	9.46829	0.01827

%C-CHSat: conservation percentage of highly satisfactory solutions; MinEuc: min Euclidean distance.

Table 5 shows the first summary of a statistical comparison of five variants of NSGA-III using the configurations reported in Table 4. We applied the Friedman Test, followed by the Hollman Post-hoc Test. The best and the worst algorithm are identified with the algorithms' ranking considering two measures: the percentage of conservation of highly satisfactory solutions (CHSat) and the minimum Euclidean distance (MinEuc).

Table 5. Best and worst algorithms resulting from their statistical comparison evaluated with two measures.

PROBLEM	Best Variants for		Worst Variants for	
	CHSat	Min	CHSat	Min
DTLZ1	C100R0	C0R0	C1R0	C1R2
DTLZ2	C100R0	C100R0	C1R0	C1R2
DTLZ3	C100R0	C100R0	C1R0	C10R0
DTLZ4	C100R0	C100R0	C10R0	C1R2
DTLZ5	C100R0	C1R2	C0R0	C10R0
DTLZ6	C100R0	C1R2	C0R0	C0R0
DTLZ7	C100R0	C100R0	C10R0	C0R0

In this paper, the main measure to evaluate algorithms is related to the counting of highly satisfactory solutions because preferences elicitation is aligned with this measure. But considering other DM could be interested in the closeness to the ROI, the Euclidean distance is an alternative because it is frequently used in decision-making. For a DM interested in highly satisfactory solutions, the best variant for all DTLZ problems is C100R0. In contrast, if the DM is interested in solutions closer to the ROI, we cannot find a unique variant as the best; They are dependent on the problem. The C100R0 variant offers solutions close to the ROI in four of the seven problems evaluated (DTLZ2–DTLZ4, DTLZ7); For the DTLZ5 and DTLZ6 problems, C1R2 has a better performance. The original NSGA-III algorithm offers solutions closer to the ROI for the DTLZ1 problem. It is noteworthy. that C100R0 is never the worst option; the other variants are the worst at least once.

Table 6 shows the algorithms' average performance for all DTLZ problems. After applying statistical tests to compare algorithms (Friedman aligned and Hollman posthoc). We identify pairwise comparisons with significant differences. Using these pairs, for each algorithm, a set of statistically no better algorithms was obtained. Finally, the algorithms are ranked instead of Hierarchical using the well-known Borda count to accumulate their positioning overall instances for a given measure. The superscript corresponds to ranking Borda.

There are significant statistical differences in 3 of the 5 metrics evaluated (CHSAT, Mean Euclidean, Max Euclidean). For the percentage of conservation of solutions for which the DM is highly satisfied (CHSat), the best algorithm is C100R0. In contrast, the rest of the algorithms have a similar behavior according to Borda's ranking. The indicator of the percentage of solutions for which the DM is satisfied (CSat) does not significantly differ. That is expected because CHSAT gets better well-solutions.

Table 6. The average and standard deviation of the algorithms over 50 independent runs in terms of percentage of conservation and Euclidean distance for the DTLZ family of problems.

	% of Conservation		Euclidean Distance		
Configuration	CHSat	CSat	Min	Mean	Max
C0R0	$4.659^{2.0}_{0.124}$	$4.877^{3.0}_{0.053}$	$0.002289^{2.0}_{0.003}$	$0.779536^{4.0}_{0.396}$	$2.643408^{1.0}_{2.801}$ ↑
C100R0	$62.169^{1.0}_{0.259}$ ↑	$6.736^{3.0}_{0.105}$	$0.000723^{1.0}_{0.001}$ ↑	$0.179397^{1.0}_{0.095}$ ↑	$0.724694^{1.0}_{0.448}$ ↑
C10R0	$4.239^{2.0}_{0.109}$	$7.355^{2.0}_{0.061}$	$0.001157^{2.0}_{0.001}$	$0.790513^{4.0}_{0.403}$	$1.526600^{2.0}_{0.881}$
C1R0	$15.951^{2.0}_{0.279}$	$38.098^{1.0}_{0.356}$ ↑	$0.001337^{3.0}_{0.002}$	$0.676294^{2.0}_{0.410}$	$1.447190^{2.0}_{0.935}$
C1R2	$12.981^{2.0}_{0.230}$	$42.934^{1.0}_{0.424}$ ↑	$0.002135^{2.0}_{0.005}$	$0.697033^{3.0}_{0.422}$	$1.497078^{2.0}_{0.899}$

Statistical test: Friedman of aligned ranks with a significance level of 0.05. The superscript indicates the position in which it was ranked by the Borda method. The subscript indicates the standard deviation of the results. The upper arrow indicates the top-ranked algorithm.

The C100R0 configuration is the one with the greatest contribution of solutions closer to the ROI according to the minimum Euclidean distance indicator. This indicator does not have significant differences. For the average, significant differences were found, and the algorithm C100R0 is the one that provides the closest solutions. The algorithms that provide the least distant solutions are C100R0 and C0R0 based on the maximum of the Euclidean distance.

This global analysis gives the best rank for the C100R0, meaning that it is a good alternative for all analyzed problems. However, C1R2 produces solutions closer to the ROI in some problems. They are extreme variants concerning intensification and diversification, meaning that the balance between them depends on the problem; we need to conduct extensive experimentation to confirm.

To illustrate the superiority of the proposed NSGA-III-P concerning NSGA-III, Figures 2 and 3 shows the non-dominated solutions obtaining when solving the DTLZ3 problem. Figure 2 is for NSGA-III (C0R0) and Figure 3 is for NSGA-III-P with preferences all time and without a restart (C100R0). The variant C100R0 performs a better exploration of the region of interest with highly satisfactory solutions. At the same time, C0R0 scans the entire solution space, but most solutions are highly unsatisfactory. The solutions belonging to the ROI are illustrated in black, the solutions classified as highly satisfactory (HSat) in green, satisfactory solutions (Sat) in blue, unsatisfactory solutions orange (Dis), and highly unsatisfactory solutions (HDis) in red.

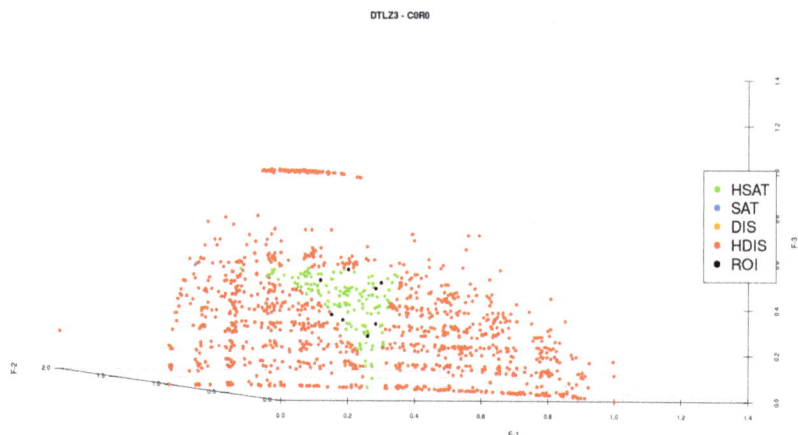

Figure 2. Non-dominated NSGA-III(C0R0) solutions of the DTLZ3 problem.

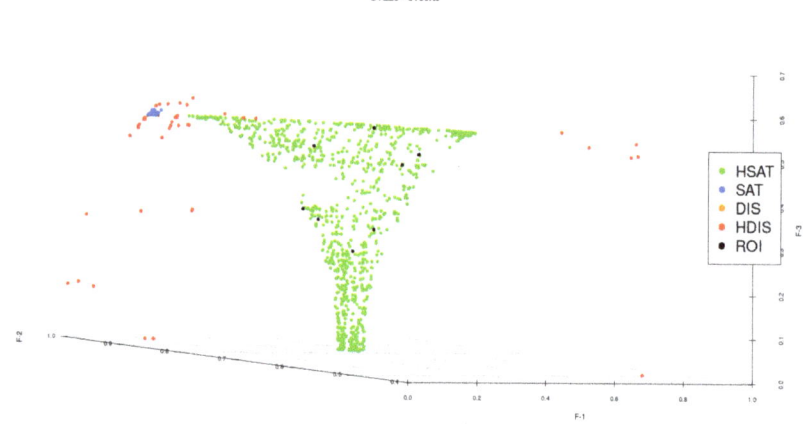

Figure 3. Non-dominated NSGA-III-P(C100R0) solutions of the DTLZ3 problem.

6. Conclusions

This article presents a novel method for incorporating DM's preferences into the NSGA-III algorithm, named NSGA-III-P. INTERCLASS-NC is a multi-criteria and outranking ordinal classifier that allows incorporating preference, giving the algorithm the capacity to improve the discrimination of solutions and intensify the search toward the region of interest. Excessive intensification can diminish the algorithm's effectiveness. To regulate this selective pressure, we add two complementary strategies to the search in NSGA-III-P: control the activations of the classification and control the restarts of solutions.

Experiments with different configurations of NSGA-III-P were proposed to study different levels of intensification and diversification. NSGA-III-P solve the DTLZ test suite, including the preferences of DM with imperfect knowledge.

Based on computational experimentation, the best alternative to the DTLZ problems is the C100R0 (always classify without restarts) when the DM is looking for highly satisfactory solutions. When the DM prefers solutions closer to the ROI, the variants C1R2 (classify and sometimes restart) and C100R0 have the best performance with two and four problems, respectively. In general, the proposed method NSGA-III-P outperforms NSGA-III because it allows obtaining better approximations to the ROI using the principal performance measures; only in one case, the NSGA-III is the best option for the DTLZ1 problem using the Max Euclidean distance.

These preliminary results open a research line to determine the extent to which the selective pressure induced by preferences improves the algorithm performance concerning the closeness to the ROI and the factors that affect it.

As future work, we will evaluate the proposal with a greater number of objectives for the DTLZ problems. Also, the proposal will be integrated into at least one other algorithm representative of the state of the art. We aim to develop a method that dynamically adjusts the diversification and intensification levels required for each problem.

Author Contributions: Conceptualization, A.C.-A., L.C.-R. and E.F.; methodology, L.C.-R., N.R.-V. and A.C.-A.; software, A.C.-A. and N.R.-V.; validation, L.C.-R., N.R.-V., H.F., J.A.B.-H., C.G.-S. and A.C.-A.; formal analysis, L.C.-R.; investigation, L.C.-R., E.F. and A.C.-A.; resources, E.F., L.C.-R. and A.C.-A.; data curation, N.R.-V. and A.C.-A.; writing—original draft preparation, A.C.-A. and L.C.-R., J.A.B.-H.; writing—review and editing, C.G.-S., L.C.-R., H.F., J.A.B.-H., N.R.-V., J.A.B.-H. and A.C.-A.; visualization, L.C.-R.; supervision, L.C.-R.; project administration, L.C.-R.; funding acquisition, L.C.-R., A.C.-A. and H.F. All authors have read and agreed to the published version of the manuscript.

Funding: This research received no external funding.

Data Availability Statement: The instances and other files used here are available at https://www.dropbox.com/sh/5wb8api8zdyjs8y/AAD11EQbI4P0lQgijvgfFC2qa?dl=0 (accessed on 29 March 2021).

Acknowledgments: Authors thanks to CONACYT for supporting the projects from (a) Cátedras CONACYT Program with Number 3058. (b) CONACYT Project with Number A1-S-11012 from Convocatoria de Investigación Científica Básica 2017–2018 and CONACYT Project with Number 312397 from Programa de Apoyo para Actividades Científicas, Tecnológicas y de Innovación (PAACTI), a efecto de participar en la Convocatoria 2020-1 Apoyo para Proyectos de Investigación Científica, Desarrollo Tecnológico e Innovación en Salud ante la Contingencia por COVID-19. (c) Alejandro Castellanos-Alvarez would like to thank CONACYT for the support number 1006467.

Conflicts of Interest: The authors declare no conflict of interest.

Abbreviations

The following abbreviations are used in this manuscript:

DM	Decision-Maker
ROI	Region of Interest
MOP	Multi-objective Optimization Problem
MCDM	Multi-criteria Decision-Making
MAUT	Multi Attribute Utility Theory
HSat	Highly Satisfactory
Sat	Satisfactory
Dis	Unsatisfactory
HDis	Highly Unsatisfactory

References

1. Deb, K.; Kalyanmoy, D. *Multi-Objective Optimization Using Evolutionary Algorithms*; John Wiley & Sons, Inc.: Hoboken, NJ, USA, 2001.
2. Ikeda, K.; Kita, H.; Kobayashi, S. Failure of Pareto-based MOEAs: Does non-dominated really mean near to optimal? In Proceedings of the 2001 Congress on Evolutionary Computation, Seoul, Korea, 27–30 May 2001; Volume 2, pp. 957–962.
3. Bechikh, S.; Elarbi, M.; Said, L.B. Many-objective optimization using evolutionary algorithms: A survey. In *Recent Advances in Evolutionary Multi-Objective Optimization*; Springer: Berlin/Heidelberg, Germany, 2017; pp. 105–137.
4. Sudeng, S.; Wattanapongsakorn, N. Finding Robust Pareto-optimal Solutions Using Geometric Angle-Based Pruning Algorithm. *Studies Comput. Intell.* **2014**, *542*, 277–295. [CrossRef]

5. Goulart, F.; Campelo, F. Preference-guided evolutionary algorithms for many-objective optimization. *Inf. Sci.* **2016**, *329*, 236–255. [CrossRef]
6. Cruz-Reyes, L.; Fernandez, E.; Sanchez-Solis, J.P.; Coello, C.A.C.; Gomez, C. Hybrid evolutionary multi-objective optimization using outranking-based ordinal classification methods. *Swarm Evol. Comput.* **2020**, *54*, 100652. [CrossRef]
7. Bechikh, S. Incorporating Decision Maker's Preference Information in Evolutionary Multi-Objective Optimization. Ph.D. Thesis, University of Tunis, Tunis, Tunisia, 2013.
8. Balderas Jaramillo, F.A. Modelando la Imprecision del Problema de Cartera de Proyectos con Filosofía Gris. Ph.D. Thesis, Instituto Tecnólogico de Tijuana, Tijuana, Mexico, 2018.
9. Balderas, F.; Fernandez, E.; Gomez-Santillan, C.; Rangel-Valdez, N.; Cruz, L. An interval-based approach for evolutionary multi-objective optimization of project portfolios. *Int. J. Inf. Technol. Decis. Mak.* **2019**, *18*, 1317–1358. [CrossRef]
10. Talbi, E.G. *Metaheuristics: From Design to Implementation*; John Wiley & Sons: Hoboken, NJ, USA, 2009; Volume 74.
11. López Jaimes, A.; Coello, C. *Many-Objective Problems: Challenges and Methods*; Springer: Berlin/Heidelberg, Germany, 2005; pp. 1033–1046. [CrossRef]
12. Deb, K.; Jain, H. An Evolutionary Many-Objective Optimization Algorithm Using Reference-Point-Based Nondominated Sorting Approach, Part I: Solving Problems with Box Constraints. *IEEE Trans. Evol. Comput.* **2014**, *18*, 577–601. [CrossRef]
13. Cruz Reyes, L.; Fernandez, E.; Sanchez, P.; Coello, C.; Gomez, C. Incorporation of implicit decision-maker preferences in Multi-Objective Evolutionary Optimization using a multi-criteria classification method. *Appl. Soft Comput.* **2017**, *50*, 48–57. [CrossRef]
14. Deb, K.; Pratap, A.; Agarwal, S.; Meyarivan, T. A fast and elitist multiobjective genetic algorithm: NSGA-II. *IEEE Trans. Evol. Comput.* **2002**, *6*, 182–197. [CrossRef]
15. Fernández, E.; Figueira, J.R.; Navarro, J. Interval-based extensions of two outranking methods for multi-criteria ordinal classification. *Omega* **2020**, *95*, 102065. [CrossRef]
16. Coello, C.A.C. Handling preferences in evolutionary multiobjective optimization: A survey. In Proceedings of the 2000 Congress on Evolutionary Computation, Istanbul, Turkey, 16–19 July 2000; Volume 1, pp. 30–37. [CrossRef]
17. Cruz-Reyes, L.; Fernandez, E.; Rangel-Valdez, N. A metaheuristic optimization-based indirect elicitation of preference parameters for solving many-objective problems. *Int. J. Comput. Intell. Syst.* **2017**, *10*, 56–77. [CrossRef]
18. Collette, Y.; Patrick, S. *Multiobjective Optimization. Principles and Case Studies*; Springer: Berlin/Heidelberg, Germany, 2003. [CrossRef]
19. Zopounidis, C.; Doumpos, M. Multicriteria classification and sorting methods: A literature review. *Eur. J. Oper. Res.* **2002**, *138*, 229–246. [CrossRef]
20. Oliveira, E.; Antunes, C.H.; Gomes, Á. A comparative study of different approaches using an outranking relation in a multi-objective evolutionary algorithm. *Comput. Oper. Res.* **2013**, *40*, 1602–1615. [CrossRef]
21. Cruz, L.; Fernandez, E.; Gomez, C.; Rivera, G.; Perez, F. Many-objective portfolio optimization of interdependent projects with'a priori'incorporation of decision-maker preferences. *Appl. Math. Inf. Sci.* **2014**, *8*, 1517. [CrossRef]
22. Moore, R.E. Interval Arithmetic and Automatic Error Analysis in Digital Computing. Ph.D. Thesis, Stanford University, Stanford, CA, USA, 1963.
23. Moore, R.E. *Methods and Applications of Interval*; Society for Industrial and Applied Mathematics: Philadelphia, PA, USA, 1979.
24. Fliedner, T.; Liesiöb, J. Adjustable robustness for multi-attribute project portfolio selection. *Eur. J. Oper. Res.* **2016**, *252*, 931–946. [CrossRef]
25. Fernandez, E.; Figueira, J.; Navarro, J. An interval extension of the outranking approach and its application to multiple-criteria ordinal classification. *Omega* **2018**, *84*, 189–198. [CrossRef]

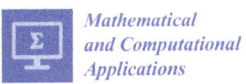

Article

Effect of the Profile of the Decision Maker in the Search for Solutions in the Decision-Making Process

Mercedes Perez-Villafuerte [1,*], Laura Cruz-Reyes [2], Nelson Rangel-Valdez [3], Claudia Gomez-Santillan [2] and Héctor Fraire-Huacuja [2]

1. Department of Computing Science, Tijuana Institute of Technology, Av Castillo de Chapultepec 562, Tomas Aquino, Tijuana 22414, Mexico
2. Graduate Program Division, Tecnológico Nacional de México, Instituto Tecnológico de Ciudad Madero, Cd. Madero 89440, Mexico; lauracruzreyes@itcm.edu.mx (L.C.-R.); claudia.gomez@itcm.edu.mx (C.G.-S.); automatas2002@yahoo.com.mx (H.F.-H.)
3. CONACyT Research Fellow at Graduate Program Division, Tecnológico Nacional de México, Instituto Tecnológico de Ciudad Madero, Cd. Madero 89440, Mexico; nelson.rangel@itcm.edu.mx
* Correspondence: pvmercedes@gmail.com

Citation: Perez-Villafuerte, M.; Cruz-Reyes, L.; Rangel-Valdez, N.; Gomez-Santillan, C.; Fraire-Huacuja, H. Effect of the Profile of the Decision Maker in the Search for Solutions in the Decision-Making Process. *Math. Comput. Appl.* **2021**, *26*, 28. https://doi.org/10.3390/mca26020028

Academic Editor: Oliver Schütze

Received: 1 March 2021
Accepted: 25 March 2021
Published: 31 March 2021

Publisher's Note: MDPI stays neutral with regard to jurisdictional claims in published maps and institutional affiliations.

Copyright: © 2021 by the authors. Licensee MDPI, Basel, Switzerland. This article is an open access article distributed under the terms and conditions of the Creative Commons Attribution (CC BY) license (https://creativecommons.org/licenses/by/4.0/).

Abstract: Many real-world optimization problems involving several conflicting objective functions frequently appear in current scenarios and it is expected they will remain present in the future. However, approaches combining multi-objective optimization with the incorporation of the decision maker's (DM's) preferences through multi-criteria ordinal classification are still scarce. In addition, preferences are rarely associated with a DM's characteristics; the preference selection is arbitrary. This paper proposes a new hybrid multi-objective optimization algorithm called P-HMCSGA (preference hybrid multi-criteria sorting genetic algorithm) that allows the DM's preferences to be incorporated in the optimization process' early phases and updated into the search process. P-HMCSGA incorporates preferences using a multi-criteria ordinal classification to distinguish solutions as good and bad; its parameters are determined with a preference disaggregation method. The main feature of P-HMCSGA is the new method proposed to associate preferences with the characterization profile of a DM and its integration with ordinal classification. This increases the selective pressure towards the desired region of interest more in agreement with the DM's preferences specified in realistic profiles. The method is illustrated by solving real-size multi-objective PPPs (project portfolio problem). The experimentation aims to answer three questions: (i) To what extent does allowing the DM to express their preferences through a characterization profile impact the quality of the solution obtained in the optimization? (ii) How sensible is the proposal to different profiles? (iii) How much does the level of robustness of a profile impact the quality of final solutions (this question is related with the knowledge level that a DM has about his/her preferences)? Concluding, the proposal fulfills several desirable characteristics of a preferences incorporation method concerning these questions.

Keywords: decision maker profile; profile assessment; region of interest approximation; optimization using preferences; hybrid evolutionary approach

1. Introduction

A variety of real-world problems, known as multi-objective optimization problems (MOPs), involve optimizing many objective functions simultaneously [1]. Multi-objective evolutionary algorithms (MOEAs) have been widely used for solving MOPs because of their effectiveness in solving problems in many fields. Nowadays, MOPs solved with metaheuristics like evolutionary algorithms are an important active research field [1,2].

Although the aim in Evolutionary Multi-objective Optimization (EMO) is to find a set of solutions that evenly spread around the Pareto front of a given MOP, it is also equally important to identify the solution to be implemented which best satisfies the preferences of the decision-maker (DM) [3]. Selecting the most preferred Pareto solution requires evaluates many solutions simultaneously, demanding a high cognitive effort, especially in problems with many objectives.

One alternative to reduce the DM's cognitive effort is to incorporate preferences information of the DM into a multi-objective metaheuristic to identify progressively the region of interest (RoI), defined as the set of non-dominated solutions that the DM prefers over the other solutions [4,5]. There is a growing interest in the solution of MOPs with preferences.

The promising variants in the decision-making process are incorporating preferences using the a priori and interactive approaches, which have the advantage of delimiting the search space for searching an optimal solution, avoiding unnecessary exploration of the entire search space. Preferences integration narrows the search space in optimization problems so that the selective pressure directs evolutionary algorithms close to a region of interest [6]. However, the specialized literature starts from arbitrary reference sets, which are examples of random solutions introduced as preference information into the search process of a metaheuristic. In this work, it is proposed that these sets of references are generated from profiles that characterize DMs preferences simpler and realistically.

So far, there is no general definition that associates the mechanisms of incorporation of preferences with the region of interest. Each author captures preferences in different ways, for example, using fuzzy numbers [7], reference points [4,8], weights based [9–11], solution ranking-based [12] and outranking based models [13]. In addition, each captures preferences at different times in the search process, for example, a priori [14,15], a posteriori [16] or interactively [8]. Those differences difficult to make a fair comparison among them. A detailed review on types of approaches for preference incorporation can be seen in [17–19].

In our opinion, a multi-objective optimization metaheuristic proposed for solving MOPs with preferences should satisfy these features: (1) to allow the DM to introduce a priori preferences information with minimum cognitive effort; (2) interactivity, to allow the DM to specify new preference information to adjust his/her preferences. This paper proposes P-HMCSGA (preference hybrid multi-criteria sorting genetic algorithm), a new MOEA that satisfies these requirements; preferences are specified in a preferential profile. The proposed method holds for both multi-objective and many objective problems.

The experimentation was designed to respond to some questions related to the impact of the proposed algorithm in the solution of a real-world problem with nine and sixteen objectives. The results were satisfactory, particularly in the solution quality, sensibility to a profile and robustness.

This paper is organized as follows: Section 2 formalizes the theoretical background of the algorithm proposed. Section 3 contains the description of P-HMCSGA and its phases. Section 4 presents the experimental results that demonstrate the performance of our approach. Finally, Section 5 presents the conclusions and the possible areas of opportunity in the future.

2. Theoretical Background

2.1. Public Portfolio Problem (PPP)

A project is a unique, unrepeatable and temporary process that seeks to achieve a specific set of objectives. A set of projects that can be done in the same period of time is called a portfolio [19]. However, organizations generally do not have sufficient resources to support all proposed projects. In such circumstances, the difficulty is choosing the set of projects that offer the greatest benefit.

The public project portfolio (PPP) problem is defined below [20]:

Consider a set of N projects, where the i-th project is represented by a p-dimensional vector $f(i) = \langle f_1(i), f_2(i), \ldots, f_p(i) \rangle$, where each $f_j(i)$ indicates the contribution of project i to the j-th objective. Each project has an associated cost expressed by c_i. Each objective indicates the number of people benefited who belong to a social category, who will receive a level of benefit from the i-th project.

A portfolio x is a subset of projects generally modeled as a binary vector $x = \langle x_1, x_2, \ldots, x_N \rangle$, where N indicates the number of projects. In this vector, x_i is a binary variable where $x_i = 1$ if the i-th project is supported and $x_i = 0$ otherwise.

There is a total budget that the organization is willing to invest, which is denoted as B. Portfolios are subject to the following budget restriction:

$$\left(\sum_{i=1}^{N} x_i c_i \right) \leq B \tag{1}$$

The i-th project corresponds to an area (health, education, etc.) indicated by a_i. Each area has a budget limit defined by the DM. For each area k, a lower and upper budget limit, L_k and U_k, respectively, is considered. Based on this, the constraint of each area k is

$$L_k \leq \sum_{i=1}^{N} x_i g_i(k) c_i \leq U_k \tag{2}$$

where $g_i(k)$ is defined as

$$g_i(k) = \begin{cases} 1 & \text{if} \quad a_i = k, \\ 0 & \text{otherwise} \end{cases} \tag{3}$$

Each i-th project corresponds to a geographic region indicated by r_i. For each region m, a lower and upper budget limit, L_m and U_m, respectively, is also considered. The restriction by region is defined as follows

$$L_m \leq \sum_{i=1}^{N} x_i h_i(m) c_i \leq U_m \tag{4}$$

where $h_i(m)$ is defined as

$$h_i(m) = \begin{cases} 1 & \text{if} \quad r_i = m. \\ 0 & \text{otherwise} \end{cases} \tag{5}$$

The quality of the portfolio x is determined by the union of the benefits of each one of the projects that compose it. This can be expressed as

$$z(x) = z_1(x), z_2(x), \ldots, z_p(x) \tag{6}$$

where $z_j(x)$ is defined as

$$z_j(x) = \sum_{i=1}^{N} x_i f_j(i) \tag{7}$$

If we denote by R_F the region of feasible portfolios, the project portfolio problem is to identify one or more portfolios that solve

$$max_{x \in R_F} \{z(x)\}. \tag{8}$$

To select a portfolio many conflicting attributes are considered. Due to the nature of the problem, it has been approached by multi-criteria algorithms that generate a set of solutions that presumably are on the Pareto frontier, which would be the set of optimal non-dominated portfolios in PPP. The DM should choose only one portfolio from the set of good solutions, such a decision depends on the DM's preferences.

2.2. Multi-Objective Optimization

In Multi-objective Optimization Problems (MOP), when the objectives are in conflict with each other, the compromise solutions are usually sought rather than a single solution.

A MOP can be defined as a vector of decision variables $\vec{x} = [x_1, x_2, \ldots, x_n]^T$, which optimizes (maximizes or minimizes) a vector function $F(x)$ whose elements represent the objective functions of problem [2], where:

$$F(x) = [f_1(x), f_2(x), \ldots, f_k(x)], \quad f_i : \mathbb{R}^n \to \mathbb{R} \tag{9}$$

subject to:

$$g_i(x) \leq 0; \; i = 1, 2, \ldots, m$$

$$h_j(x) = 0; \; j = 1, 2, \ldots, p$$

where:

n is the number of decision variables,
k is the number of objective functions,
m is the number of inequality constraints,
p is the number of equality constraints.

Therefore, the notion of optimum is different in these cases. The notion of optimum was generalized by Pareto [21]. This notion is commonly known under the term pareto optimality.

In multi-objective algorithms, the concept of Pareto dominance is frequently used when comparing two solutions and determining whether one dominates the other.

One solution $\vec{x_a}$ is said to dominate another $\vec{x_b}$ if the following conditions are met (for the minimization case):

1. The solution $\vec{x_a}$ is no worse than $\vec{x_b}$ in all objectives:

$$f_i(\vec{x_a}) \leq f_j(\vec{x_b}), \quad \forall i \in [1, 2, \ldots, k] \tag{10}$$

2. The solution $\vec{x_a}$ is strictly better than $\vec{x_b}$ in at least one objective:

$$f_i(\vec{x_a}) < f_j(\vec{x_b}), \quad \exists i \in [1, 2, \ldots, k] \tag{11}$$

If any of the conditions (1) or (2) are violated, the solution $\vec{x_a}$ does not dominate the $\vec{x_b}$ solution. That is, for one solution to dominate another, it needs to be strictly better in at least one objective and not worse in any of the rest. Within a set, a non-dominated solution has no other solution that dominates it. When comparing two solutions $\vec{x_a}$ and $\vec{x_b}$, there can only be three possible solutions:

- $\vec{x_a}$ dominates $\vec{x_b}$
- $\vec{x_a}$ is dominated by $\vec{x_b}$
- $\vec{x_a}$ and $\vec{x_b}$ are mutually non-dominated.

Pareto optimal set. For a given MOP, the Pareto optimal set is defined as $P^* = \{x \in S / \nexists x' \in S, F(x') \prec F(x)\}$.

Pareto front. For a given MOP and its Pareto optimal set P^*, the Pareto front is defined as $PF^* = \{F(x), x \in P^*\}$.

2.3. Elitist Non-Dominated Sorting Genetic Algorithm-II (NSGA-II)

Elitist Non-dominated Sorting Genetic Algorithm-II (NSGA-II) [22] is one of the most popular algorithms for solving multi-objective problems due to its simplicity and effectiveness. The algorithm first generates a competitive population of individuals that is then ordered according to the level of dominance that the individual has in the population. This level of dominance generates different fronts, in the first front are the non-dominated solutions. Solutions from this first front, the elite solutions, are passed on to the next generation along with other solutions in such a way that there is diversity.

Like any genetic algorithm, evolutionary operators (cross and mutation, among others) are applied to it. The non-dominated solutions of the last generation will be an approximation to the Pareto front.

2.4. Fernandez's Preference Model

Fernandez et al. [3] assumed that there are methods for assigning a degree of truth $\sigma(x,y)$ in [0, 1] to the predicate xSy "x is at least as good as y". Outranking methods such as ELECTRE-III [23,24] and PROMETHEE [25] can be used for this purpose. This work computes $\sigma(x,y)$ based on ELECTRE-III and it uses the thresholds λ, β and ε to transform the fuzzy preference relations into the crisp preference relations.

The resulting relational system of preference defines five crisp relations. This system considers that: (1) $\varepsilon < \beta < \lambda < 1$; (2) the value $\lambda > 0.5$ is the outranking credibility threshold; (3) the value β is the asymmetry parameter; and (4) the value ε is the symmetry parameter. The formal definition of the relations are the following ones:

Strict Preference: This corresponds to the existence of clear and positive reasons that justify significant preference in favor of one (identified) of the two actions. The statement x is strictly preferred to y is denoted by xPy and exists if at least one of the following conditions holds.

(1) x dominates y
(2) $\sigma(x,y) \geq \lambda \wedge \sigma(y,x) < 0.5$
(3) $\sigma(x,y) \geq \lambda \wedge [0.5 \leq \sigma(y,x) < \lambda] \wedge [\sigma(x,y) - \sigma(y,x)] \geq \beta$

Indifference: This corresponds to the existence of clear and positive reasons that justify equivalence between the two actions. The statement x is indifferent to y is denoted by xIy and it occurs if all the following conditions are met:

(1) $\sigma(x,y) \geq \lambda \wedge \sigma(y,x) \geq \lambda$
(2) $|\sigma(x,y) - \sigma(y,x)| < \varepsilon$

Weak Preference: This arises when indifference and strict preference cannot be distinguished appropriately. The statement x is weakly preferred to y is denoted by xQy and it occurs if all the following conditions are satisfied.

(1) $\sigma(x,y) \geq \lambda \wedge \sigma(x,y) > \sigma(y,x)$
(2) $\neg xPy$
(3) $\neg xIy$

Incomparability: This corresponds to a high heterogeneity among alternatives causing that none of the preceding situations predominates. The statement x is incomparable to y is denoted by xRy and it must satisfy the following condition:

(1) $\sigma(x,y) < 0.5 \wedge \sigma(y,x) < 0.5$.

K-preference: This arises when strict preference and incomparability cannot be distinguished appropriately. The statement x is k-preferred to y is denoted by xKy and it exists if the following conditions are satisfied:

1. $0.5 \leq \sigma(x,y) < \lambda$
2. $\sigma(y,x) < 0.5$
3. $(\sigma(x,y) - \sigma(y,x)) > \beta/2$

Fernandez et al. [3] used the above relations over a feasible set of solutions O of an optimization problem to define the best compromise according to the DM's preferences. The elements to determine the model include the following ones:

- The non-strictly outranked frontier $N_S = \{x \in O \mid card\ (S_O)_x = 0\}$, where $x \in O$ is a feasible solution and $(S_O)_x = \{y \in O \mid yPx\}$ is the set of solutions y that are strictly preferred to x, i.e., the non-strictly outranked solutions;
- The non-weakly outranked frontier $N_W = \{x \in O \mid card\ (W_O)_x = 0\}$, where $x \in O$ is a feasible solution and $(W_O)_x = \{y \in N_S \mid yQx \vee yKx\}$ is the set of non-strict outranked solutions y that have a weak preference or k-preference with x; and,

- The net-flow-score outranked frontier $N_F = \{x \in O \mid card\ (F_O)_x = 0\}$, where $x \in O$ is a feasible solution and $(F_O)_x = card\ \{y \in N_S \mid F_n(y) > F_n(x)\}$ is the set of non-strict outranked solution with larger net flow score than x. The net flow score $F_n(x) = \sum_{y \in NS-\{x\}} [\sigma(x,y) - \sigma(y,x)]$ is a popular measure in the literature and in this work offers a further ranking on the solution inside the non-strictly outranked frontier.

Hence, based on the previous sets, the best compromise for the DM is any solution to the optimization problem defined in Equation (12), with a preemptive priority favoring $card(S_O)$.

$$min_{x \in O}\{\langle |S(O,x)|, |W(O,x)|, |F(O,x)| \rangle\} \quad (12)$$

In summary, the preferences model is the relational system of preferences previously presented. Based on it, the best compromise is any solution in the Pareto frontier of the optimization problem shown in Equation (12).

2.5. Preference-Disaggregation Analysis (PDA)

The parameters of an outranking model (weights and thresholds, etc.) must be elicited, such as the preference model used in the present work. Direct procedures that ask a DM for proper values to be assign are commonly used; however, in such approaches, the DMs reveal difficulties when they are asked to assign values to parameters whose meanings are not understood for them [26]. On the other hand, indirect procedures, which compose the so-called preference-disaggregation analysis (PDA), use regression-like methods for inferring a set of parameters from a battery of decision examples [27]. In [28], a new optimization model for PDA is solved with the NSGA-II algorithm. According to Greco et al. in [29], MCDA approaches based on disaggregation paradigms are of interest because their simplicity and the reduced cognitive effort required from the DM. The use of an ordinal classification on the examples is an easy way for a DM to provides his/her preferences.

2.6. THESEUS

Fernandez proposed in [30] the THESEUS approach that is based on transforming the sorting problem into a particular case of the selection problem. THESEUS assigns new objects to the categories already defined in the set of references, comparing the object with the inconsistencies of the possible assignment and the information of various preference relations that can be strict, weak or indifferent; these are derived from a fuzzy outranking relation, described in Section 2.4. The category assignment is the consequence of comparisons with other objects whose categories are known.

The THESEUS method is based on the following premises:

1. there is a set of ordered categories $Ct = \{C_1, \ldots, C_M\}$, $(M \geq 2)$, where C_M is the preferred category;
2. there is a universe U of objects x which are characterized by a set of N criteria denoted by $G = \{g_1, g_2, \ldots, g_j, \ldots, g_N\}$, where $N \geq 3$;
3. there is a set of reference objects T (also called reference set or training set), which is formed by objects $b_{kh} \in U$ which are assigned to a category C_k, $(k = 1, \ldots, M)$;
4. there is an outranking relation $\sigma(x,y)$ defined in $U \times U$ which models the degree of credibility of the statement "x is at least as good as y" from the DM's perspective.

The Hybrid Multi-Criteria Sorting Genetic Algorithm (H-MCSGA) algorithm presented in [14] uses the THESEUS method to assign solutions to two ordered categories (satisfactory and unsatisfactory). THESEUS is combined with the non-dominated sorting of an evolutionary algorithm to increase the selective pressure towards the RoI.

3. Description of P-HMCSGA

P-HMCSGA is an algorithm designed to solve MOPs, which allows the DM to specify his/her preferences by a realistic profile. Fernandez and Navarro [30] propose an outranking preference model that supports incorporating these preferences, which are regularly obtained by assignment examples. In outranking models, approaches like preference-disaggregation analysis [31,32] reflect preferences into these models' parameters. In this paper, the terms direct and indirect concern the way to determine the outranking model parameters.

P-HMCSGA consists of three phases to perform the multi-objective optimization process. In the first phase, the DM specifies preferences in a profile that characterized her/his, which permits categorize the solutions as good and bad. The second phase transforms the categorized solutions into preference model parameters. Both phases correspond, respectively, with the indirect and direct elicitation of preferences mentioned in [33,34]. Finally, the third phase incorporates preferences in the solution process as the parameters of the preference model, supporting a multi-criteria classifier. Figure 1 illustrates these steps and the next sections explain each one.

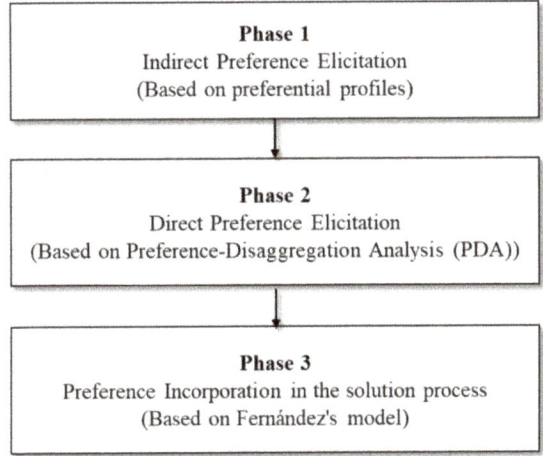

Figure 1. Phases of incorporating preferences in the optimization process.

The profiles are proposed to characterize a DM's preferences expressed in understandable terms, avoiding the cognitive effort involved in selecting, from a solutions sample, the ones as close as possible to his/her preferences. This difficulty increases with the number of objectives.

An example of this characterization would be the profile of a DM who wishes to favor portfolios in which the number of supported projects is maximized. Another DM could be more interested in reducing the consumption of the available budget.

Depending on the selected profile, through profile generators, reference sets are formed to use in different parts of the optimization process. In this algorithm, the following generators are proposed.

- Profile-generator-α: Here, a reference set is formed with solutions selected according to the specified preference profile. It appears in phase 1 (indirect preference obtaining).
- Profile-generator-β: Here, a reference set is formed from solutions with implicit preferences that are inferred using the PDA strategy [35]. It appears in phase 3 (direct obtaining of preferences).

3.1. Phase 1: Indirect Preference Elicitation

In this phase, we start from the idea of presenting solutions to a decision-maker; these solutions can be obtained through a solution generator, a repository, etc. Commonly, it is intended that from these solutions, the DM selects those that are representative for him to be part of the good category and others to consider them in the category of bad solutions. Instead, to reduce the DM's cognitive load, the generator-α method in Figure 2 allows the DM to provide a simple preference profile to emulates him/her in the reference set's construction through this profile. This is a set of classified solutions that serve as training, reflecting the DM's preferences in a categorized way. Similarly, only two categories are considered at this time: good and bad solutions.

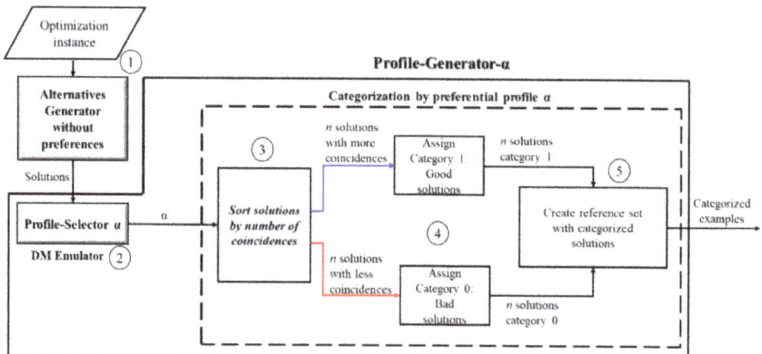

Figure 2. Profile-generator-α: the profiling method to imitate a decision maker in categorizing solutions.

Step 1. In this first part of the optimization process, the optimization instance is introduced to a solution generator without preferential support to generate feasible solutions.

Step 2. The DM selects a profile and, together with the generated solutions, is the input of a categorizer, which separates the good and bad solutions according to the preference profile.

Step 3. For the categorizer, the input is a set of solutions and the selected profile-α. Depending on the profile, the selection of solutions could require additional information. In this step, a coincidence count is made for each solution according to the α profile and, once the coincidence count has been complete, descending ordering is made according to this count's value.

Step 4. The n solutions with the greatest coincidence are selected to form the category of good solutions. In the same way, the n solutions with the lowest coincidences form the category of bad solutions.

Step 5. These two sets form the reference set or categorized examples to use in the next phase.

3.2. Phase 2: Direct Preference Elicitation

For the DM, it is easier to indicate their preferences in profiles (converted a posteriori in categorized solutions) than to perform it directly by assigning weights to objectives, establishing acceptance ranges for each criterion, or giving preferential model parameters. For the Phase 2, the use of a PDA method [31] is proposed to transform the categorized preference information into parameters of a preferential model [30] that is part of the search process; this phase is shown in Figure 3.

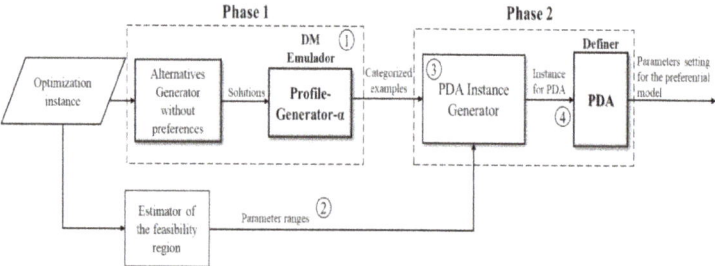

Figure 3. Instance generation process for PDA.

Step 1. For this Phase 2, an instance generator method was developed so that PDA transforms the DM's preferences into parameters of a preferential model. This generator receives as the first input the categorized examples obtained in Phase 1.

Step 2. The second input for the instance generator is the parameter ranges. The estimator of the feasibility region method obtains these approximate reference parameters from the initial optimization instance's objectives. These values are adjusted according to the set of references (categorized examples) also introduced to PDA.

Step 3. Once the approximate reference parameters have been calculated, they are joined with the set of references obtained in Phase 1 to generate an input instance for the PDA.

Step 4. In the PDA procedure, the preferences, expressed in categorized examples, are transformed into preferential model parameters. At the end of Phase 2, a set of preferential model parameters are obtained for its incorporation into the search process of Phase 3.

3.3. Phase 3: Incorporation of Preferences in the Solution Process

Initially, in Phase 1, the preferences are introduced as a profile and converted to a reference set. After, in Phase 2, they are reflected in preference model parameters. Figure 4 shows the process of Phase 3, in which the preferences are incorporated in the optimization process.

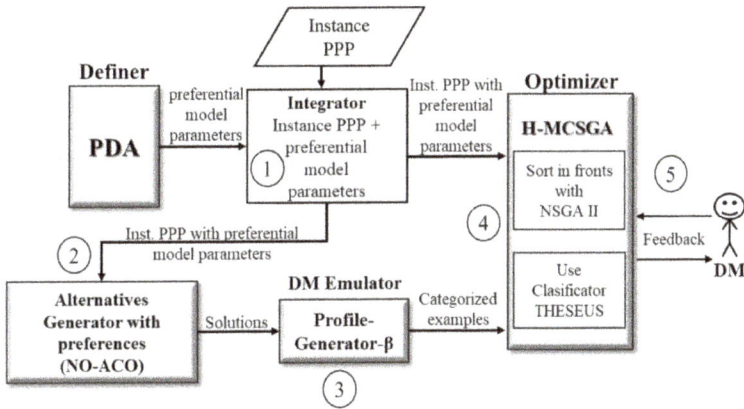

Figure 4. Phase 3: Incorporation of preferences in the solution process.

Step 1. Once the parameters for the preferential model have been generated using PDA, the optimization instance incorporating these parameters is generated so that the preferences are included in the search process.

Step 2. With the instance with preferences, an initial search is conducted with a strategy that approximates the region of interest. For this, an alternatives generator with preferences method, like Non-Outranked Ant Colony Optimization (NO-ACO) proposed in [36] and modified in [14], finds a sample of satisfactory and unsatisfactory solutions, considering net flow, strict-preference and Pareto dominance (see Section 2). In [37], the NO-ACO algorithm uses the three objective Equation (11) as a subrogate model to solve PPP instances.

Step 3. The obtained solutions sample is introduced to the profile-generator-β to form a reference set, considering that the solutions satisfy the DM requested profile and his/her tolerance. The reference set includes good solutions from the satisfactory set and bad solutions from the unsatisfactory ones.

Step 4. After this, the parameterized optimization instance and the reference set obtained with the profile-generator-β are introduced to the H-MCSGA optimizer [14], which uses outranking classification to adds more solutions discrimination capability to the sorting process of NSGA-II. Based on the preference model, this strategy makes a better approximation towards the DM's region of interest.

Step 5. The architecture of the proposed algorithm facilitates the interactive incorporation of preferences to allow the DM to refine them. Every certain number of iterations, the DM can give feedback with a sample of the best solutions obtained for the profile specified, with the possibility of choosing the ones most preferred. This set of solutions can enrich the initial reference set to direct the search more intensively toward the refined region of interest. The evaluation of interactive preference incorporation remains as future work.

Figure 5 shows the proposed P-HMCSGA, in which the intervention of the three phases that have been previously exposed can be observed.

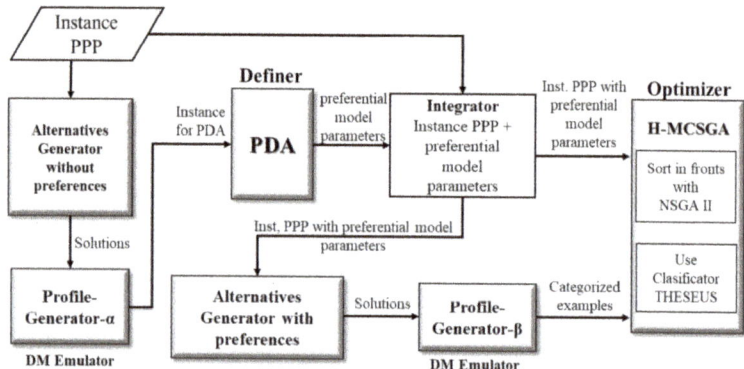

Figure 5. The Preference Hybrid Multi-Criteria Sorting Genetic Algorithm (P-HMCSGA) for incorporating preferences in optimizers.

4. Experimental Design and Results

This section describes the experimental process that evaluates P-HMCSGA. The process analyzes the algorithm in two experiments. The first experiment analyzes the effect of the profile of a decision maker in the search process. The second experiment studies the error variability of initial reference solutions and their impact on final solutions.

The experimental design tested the approach, in each experiment, on three different profiles, one configuration for the involved algorithms and six instances of the project portfolio problem (PPP). The performance of P-HMCSGA was measured using five different indicators that reflect how well it approximates the Pareto front with and without preferences and how well it adjusts the portfolios to the specified profiles.

A summary of the steps followed during the experiment are depicted in Figure 6. The remainder of the section details the elements utilized and the results obtained.

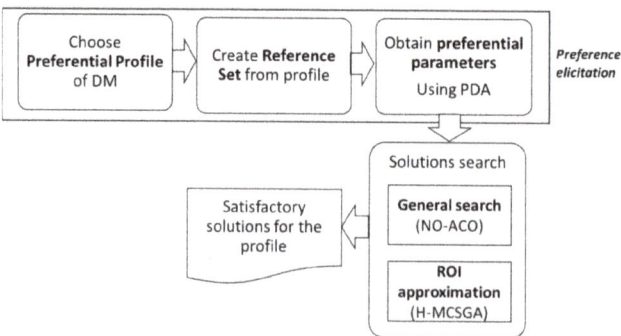

Figure 6. General experimental design with P-HMCSGA.

4.1. DM Profiles

A profile refers to the method used by a DM to make a decision. The evaluation of P-HMCSGA uses the following three preferential profiles:

Established projects: A predefined projects set in the portfolio is considered to be formed and they are defined according to the DM's preferences; one possible reason for this profile is that these projects have been beneficial in the past.

Preference in the area and/or region: For the DMs, a portfolio has more preference with a higher number of supported projects on a pre-specified area or region.

Cardinality: The DM favors portfolios that maximize the number of supported projects.

4.2. Algorithm Configuration

Table 1 shows the algorithms and their parameters' values used for each process involved in the P-HMCSGA. The process is shown in Column 1. Column 2 indicates which strategy was used in each process. Columns 3 to show the configuration of the parameters' values used in each strategy. The used genetic operators were the same as reported in [8,10,17] for each approach.

Table 1. Algorithms used in the proposed P-HMCSGA.

Process	Algorithm	Iterations	Crossover	Mutation	Executions
Generation of alternatives without preferences	A2-NSGA-III [38]	100	1	0.01	30
PDA	NSGA-II [22,28]	1000	0.9	$1/(5*N)$	2
Generation of alternatives based on preferences	NO-ACO [37]	10			30
Optimizer	H-MCSGA [17]	500	1	0.05	30

4.3. Instances of the Project Portfolio Problem

The instances of the PPP proposed in [39] served as a benchmark for the evaluation of P-HMCSGA. Table 2 summarizes the details about the instances. The medium-scale instances have nine objectives and the large-scale instances has 16 objectives.

Table 2. Description of the instances used in the experimentation.

Instance	Description	
	Objectives	Projects
1	9	100
2	9	100
3	9	100
4	9	150
5	9	150
6	16	500

4.4. Quality Indicators to Evaluate Solutions

This work uses five different indicators to evaluate the performance of the proposed P-HMCSGA algorithm. These metrics are detailed in the remainder of this section.

Indicator ND_A measures the non-dominance proportion achieved over an approximated Pareto front (PF) A. Equation (13) computes this indicator as to the quotient of the size of the set of non-dominated solutions F_0 produced by P-HMCSGA and the size of set A.

$$ND_A = \frac{|F_0|}{|A|} \times 100 \qquad (13)$$

Indicator PSO_A measures the proportion between non-strictly outranked solutions (i.e., solutions that are hard to distinguish by preference according to a specific DM (see Section 2) and an approximated PF A. Equation (14) computes this indicator as the quotient of the size of the approximated non-strict-outranked frontier F_{NSO} produced by P-HMCSGA and the size of the set A.

$$PSO_A = \frac{|F_{NSO}|}{|A|} \times 100 \qquad (14)$$

Indicator PC measures the percentage of maximum cardinality achieved by the solutions reported by P-HMCSGA. Equation (15) computes it as the quotient between the number of supported projects in a portfolio, sp, and the estimated maximum projects that could ever be supported, ems.

$$PC = \frac{sp}{ems} \times 100 \qquad (15)$$

Indicator PES (previously established projects) measures the proportion of the DM's previously established projects that are found in a portfolio generated by P-HMCSGA. Equation (16) computed as the quotient between ep, i.e., the number of projects in a portfolio that are wanted by the DM, and EP (established projects), the maximum number of wanted projects.

$$PES = \frac{ep}{EP} \times 100 \qquad (16)$$

Finally, indicator PAR (project in area/region) is the proportion of supported projects that goes in agreement with the area/region desired in the portfolio and established by the DM. Equation (17) measures this proportion as the quotient between EAR, the number of projects in the portfolio constructed by P-HMCSGA that satisfied the area and region conditions of the DM and q, the number of projects in the instance that satisfy the area and region conditions established by the DM.

$$PAR = \frac{EAR}{q} \times 100 \qquad (17)$$

The NDA and PSOA are referred to as general quality indicators because they measure the quality of a strategy based on their closeness to the PF or the RoI, the general metric evaluations for multi-criteria algorithms. The indicators PC, PES and PAR are indicators of specific quality because they measure how well the portfolios constructed have respected the preferences established by a particular preference profile.

4.5. Experiment 1: Effect of the Profile of a Decision Maker in the Search Process

This experiment was carried out based on the idea that if the solutions are presented to two decision makers with different profiles, these may be good for one decision maker and they may not be good for another, or perhaps only some. An example is shown in Figure 7, where, for a DM that seeks to maximize the number of projects included in the portfolio, both solutions satisfy that requirement, but if these same solutions are presented to a DM whose profile establishes that project number 3 must be supported, the first solution is definitely not acceptable because it does not include this.

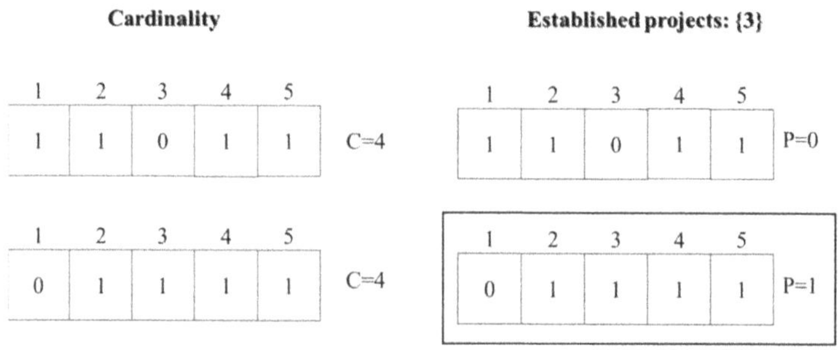

Cardinality

1	2	3	4	5	
1	1	0	1	1	C=4

1	2	3	4	5	
0	1	1	1	1	C=4

Established projects: {3}

1	2	3	4	5	
1	1	0	1	1	P=0

1	2	3	4	5	
0	1	1	1	1	P=1

Figure 7. Solutions evaluated in different profiles.

From the above, an experiment was designed, the process of which is shown in Figure 8. There, it illustrates that P-HMCSGA solves each instance using each of the n profiles (the configurations of the approaches are according to those defined in Section 4.2). With the results, a matrix of size $n \times n$ is formed. The set of solutions produced using each profile i is compared against the other profiles j in order to estimate how well the satisfaction of a profile i by P-HMCSGA behaves in comparison with other profiles j not considered at the moment. Hence, a cell (i,j) contains the number of portfolios that satisfies profiles i and j. Appendices A and B show the complete set of results derived from experimenting with the considered set of instances; the remainder of the sections presents a summary based on selected cases.

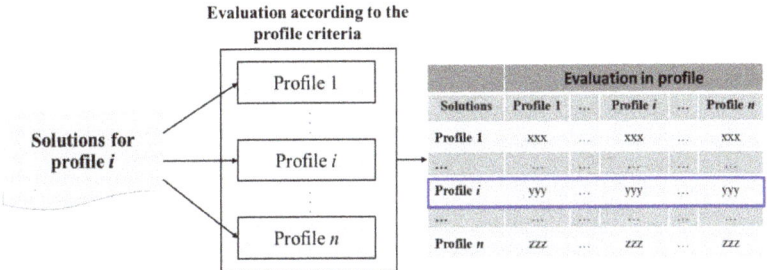

Figure 8. Evaluation of the profile according to the profile criteria.

Table 3 shows the different DM profiles considered in the experiment for all the instances. Each profile defines two values: the expected value, which is the desired amount of elements required to satisfy a DM completely, and the minimum accepted, which is the minimum number of elements necessary to consider a solution as satisfactory. The maximum found shows the best match obtained from a portfolio constructed by P-HMCSGA.

Table 3. DM's profile characterization and maximum found values.

Profile	Expected	Minimum Accepted	Maximum Found
Cardinality	41	38	40
Established projects	15	11	11
Area-Region	22	16	21

Table 4 shows the matrix obtained for the concentration of the results of the evaluations in the profiles. The row leads the profile used by P-HMCSGA to approximate the RoI. The column shows how the best value obtained by fixing the profile behaves in other profiles. The value in parenthesis indicates the best value in the compared profile; the value outside is the number of solutions that obtained that value.

Table 4. Matrix of results of satisfactory solutions evaluated in other preferential profiles using instance o9p100_1.

Parameter Setting	Evaluation in the Profile		
	Cardinality	Established Projects	Area-Region
Cardinality	91 (40)	8 (10)	4 (17)
Established projects	8 (38)	2 (11), 12 (10)	2 (15)
Area-Region	3 (40)	16 (10)	1 (21)

The results from Table 4 show that the highest number of solutions coincide with the main diagonal; this demonstrates that the use of profiles in the search process of P-HMCSGA indeed pursues the construction of portfolios that satisfy such preference conditions.

Table 5 shows the results from the measurements established by the indicators defined in Section 4.4. Again, the highest scores are in the main diagonal and are achieved when the indicator matches the profile used during the search process. These results corroborate the fact that the use of profiles favors the construction of solutions that satisfy a DM's preferences.

Table 5. Specific quality indicators for each profile as established by the DM using instance o9p100_1.

Indicator	Evaluation in the Profile		
	Cardinality	Established Projects	Area-Region
PC	97.56%	66.66%	77.27%
PES	92.68%	73.33%	68.18%
PAR	97.56%	66.66%	95.45%

Figure 9 illustrates the process used to identify the approximate Pareto front and non-strict outranked sets from P-HMCSGA on each profile. There, all the solutions considered satisfactory for each profile were concentrated in bags of satisfactory solutions, sets of non-repeated solutions that satisfy non-dominance or non-strictly outrank conditions.

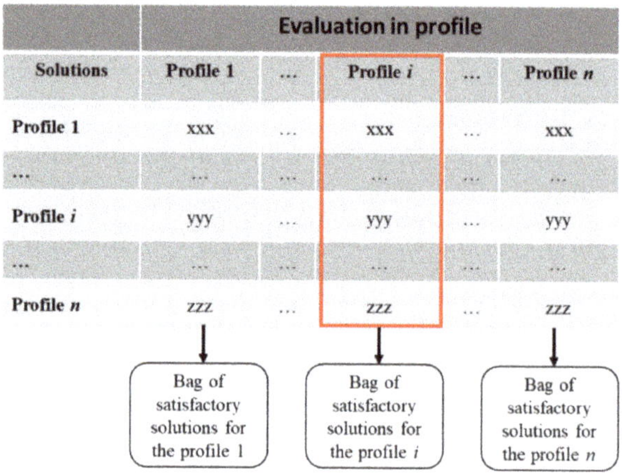

Figure 9. Obtaining bags of satisfactory solutions for each profile evaluated.

Table 6 summarizes the measurements on the *ND* and *NSO* indicators obtained from the cardinality profile. Using P-HMCSGA to approximate the PF and the RoI on instance o9p100_1, under the cardinality profile, the set *A* of reported portfolios was of size 99. The numbers of portfolios that satisfy the cardinality, established projects and area-region profiles are shown in row one and columns 3, 5 and 7, respectively.

Table 6. Dominance and strictly-outranked in cardinality profile using instance o9p100_1.

Bag		Cardinality		Established Projects		Area-Region	
		#Solutions	Percentage	#Solutions	Percentage	#Solutions	Percentage
#Solutions	99	91		8		3	
ND	90	82	90.11	8	100	3	100
NSO	90	90	98.90	0	0	0	0

The proportion of non-dominated solutions on each profile is shown in row 2 and columns 4, 6 and 8. The proportion of non-strictly outranked solution on each profile is shown in row 3 and columns 4, 6 and 8. The results show that if we use cardinality in the profile, the best measures for indicators *ND* and *NSO* are obtained when comparing against the same cardinality.

Table 7 summarizes the measurements on the ND and NSO indicators obtained from the established projects profile. Using P-HMCSGA to approximate the PF and the RoI on instance o9p100_1, under the established projects profile, the set A of reported portfolios was of size 38. The numbers of portfolios that satisfy the cardinality, established projects and area-region profiles are shown in row one and columns 3, 5 and 7, respectively. The proportion of non-dominated solutions on each profile is shown in row 2 and columns 4, 6 and 8. The proportion of non-strictly outranked solution on each profile is shown in row 3 and columns 4, 6 and 8. The results show that if we use established projects in the profile, the best measures for indicators ND and NSO are obtained when comparing against the same established projects.

Table 7. Dominance and strictly-outranked in established profile.

Bag		Cardinality		Established Projects		Area-Region	
		#Solutions	Percentage	#Solutions	Percentage	#Solutions	Percentage
#Solutions	38	8		14		16	
ND	37	8	100	14	100	15	93.75
NSO	37	8	100	14	100	15	93.75

Table 8 summarizes the measurements on the ND and NSO indicators obtained from the area-region profile. Using P-HMCSGA to approximate the PF and the RoI on instance o9p100_1, under the area-region profile, the set A of reported portfolios was of size 56. The numbers of portfolios that satisfy the cardinality, established projects and area-region profiles are shown in row one and columns 3, 5 and 7, respectively. The proportion of non-dominated solutions on each profile is shown in row 2 and columns 4, 6 and 8. The proportion of non-strictly outranked solution on each profile is shown in row 3 and columns 4, 6 and 8. The results show that if we use established projects in the profile, the best measures for indicators ND and NSO are obtained when comparing against the same area-region.

Table 8. Dominance and strictly-outranked in area-region profile.

Bag		Cardinality		Established Projects		Area-Region	
		#Solutions	Percentage	#Solutions	Percentage	#Solutions	Percentage
#Solutions	56	4		2		50	
ND	50	4	100	2	100	44	88
NSO	50	4	100	2	100	44	88

Tables 6–8 show that the percentage of solutions remaining satisfactory (non-dominated and non-strictly outranked) is very high in the solutions obtained from the parameter configuration corresponding to the specified profile. When the search was not configured according to the interesting profile, it obtains few solutions (which were not repeated). Both complementary results show that the search direction depends on the preference profile established by the DM. The solutions obtained from the configuration of specific parameters for the profile are good in dominance and outranking. Besides, using these parameters, it is possible to find a greater number of satisfactory solutions for the profile.

4.6. Experiment 2: Error Variability of Initial Reference Solutions and Its Impact on Final Solutions

The objective of this experiment is to analyze how the quality of an initial reference set affects the performance of P-HMCSGA. For this purpose, the implementation of the algorithm considers the use of two types of reference sets. The low-quality reference set (denoted "Low") has solutions around the minimum value in a profile that is considered satisfactory for a DM. The high-quality reference set (denoted "Good") has solutions close to the maximum value possible of satisfaction for the chosen profile. The experiment compares the final set of solutions produced by P-HMCSGA using each of the reference sets in terms of the level of satisfaction of the profile and the number of solutions produced. The results show that using a robust reference set formed by solutions of high quality improves the performance of P-HMCSGA and allows it to find solutions that better satisfy the preferential profile.

For this experiment, the configuration of P-HMCSGA was in accordance with the values in Table 1, except for the number of executions of the generation of alternatives without preferences that were set to 1 for simplicity. The instance considered for the experiment was o9p100_1. The profile used was established projects and it fixes 15 projects as the desire by the DM (expected column in Table 9); Also, in addition, it considers as satisfactory any solution having a subset of at least 11 of such projects (minimum accepted column in Table 9). The low-quality reference has 20 portfolios or solutions; from them, two contain 12 of the desired 15 projects and the remaining ones contain only 11 projects. The high-quality reference set (or robust reference set) also has 20 portfolios; however, three of them have all the desired projects and 17 of them have 14. Table 9 also shows the maximum number of desired projects that could be found in a solution constructed by P-HMCSGA in the experiment; those solutions could only be found using a reference set of high quality.

Table 9. Values that satisfy the DM with the established projects profile on instance o9p100_1.

	Expected	Minimum Accepted	Maximum Found
Established projects	15	11	14

Table 10 shows the results of this experiment. In row 1, the column "Maximum in RS" shows the composition of the reference sets Low and Good; the column "Finals" shows the composition of the satisfactory solutions found by P-HMCSGA. In both columns, the notation X(Y) indicates that there are X solutions having Y desire projects from the 15 considered in the profile. In row 2, the best value achieved according to the PES indicator is shown, considering the composition of the portfolios reported and 15 as the maximum number of desired projects, EP. It is important to note the contrast of the solutions obtained using reference sets with different qualities. The significant variations in the quality of solutions obtained are evident, favoring the results of the robust reference set; this situation is due to the fact that there are far more solutions with a greater number of desired projects involved in the portfolios and also because those solutions present the highest value in PES, indicating that they are closer to the DM's profile than the others.

Table 10. Error variability of initial reference solutions and its impact on final solutions.

Profile	Quality of Reference Set			
	Low		Good	
	Maximum in RS	Finals	Maximum in RS	Finals
Established projects	2 (12), 18 (11)	6 (13), 1 (12), 3 (11)	3 (15), 17 (14)	14 (14), 206 (13), 686 (12)
PES	80%	86.6%	100%	93%

Finally, Table 11 shows the summary of the dominance comparison of the solutions found using the different referent sets. In the case of the final solutions obtained using the low-quality reference set, of the six of the acceptable solutions according to the preference profile, five remained non-dominated. On the other hand, the use of the high-quality reference set presents a larger number of non-dominated solutions (97.73% of all those reported) all also being satisfactory to the DM.

Table 11. Dominance comparison of solutions with good quality RS and low quality RS.

		Low Quality RS		Good Quality RS	
		#Solutions	Percentage	#Solutions	Percentage
#Solutions	226	6		220	
ND	220	5	83.33%	215	97.73%

5. Conclusions

We present P-HMCSGA, a hybrid evolutionary algorithm for solving multi-objective optimization problems. The algorithm incorporates the DM's preferences to guide the search towards the region of interest that the DM desires the algorithm to approach. The DM gives a preferential profile containing their preferences expressed in understandable terms, which demand less cognitive effort than when he/she selects solutions from a generated sample, which is a common way to elicit preferences. P-HMCSGA reflects this preference profile in the outranking relational parameters of an ordinal multi-criteria ordinal classification method. These strategies add more solutions discriminationcapability to the well-known non-dominated sorting process incorporated in P-HMCSGA, achieving a better approximation towards the DM's region of interest.

The proposed algorithm satisfies some desirable features of a preferences incorporation method: (a) the DM interacts easily with the solutions sample generator method, decreasing the cognitive effort from the DM when the DM gives a simple preferential profile to automatically separate solutions as "good" and "bad" and to the forms reference set for a classifier method; (b) the multi-criteria preferences outranking model is compatible with relevant characteristics of real DMs expressed in preference profiles and preferences are rarely associated with realistic DM's characteristics; (c) it is possible to estimate the preference model parameters from the profile provided by the DM during the interactive process; (d) to a certain extent, the profile generator and the ordinal classification replace the DM during the optimization process, bringing valuable aid to the DM, especially in the presence of a high number of objectives.

Our algorithm obtains, as output, a set of non-dominated solutions which belong to the DM best class. The experiments were carried out to solve a project portfolio optimization problem with instances of nine and sixteen objectives. From these experiments, we can observe that P-HMCSGA has performed as expected and make the following conclusions:

(i) Allowing the DM to express their preferences through a DM characterization profile positively impacts the quality of the solution obtained in the optimization; a reasonable number of the solutions found correspond with the specified profile, being non-dominated and satisfactory for the DM.

(ii) The proposed algorithm is sensible is to different profiles. Our algorithm obtains the greatest number of satisfactory solutions when the preference model parameters correspond to the desired profile. This result confirms that the search direction depends on the preferences profile established by the DM.

(iii) The level of robustness of a profile impacts the quality of final solutions. The result shows that using a robust reference set allows one to find better solutions, satisfying the preferential profile. Therefore, the interactive intervention of the DM is necessary to enrich the reference set, learn from their preferences and learn about the problem itself. Our results were obtained with a single run of the preference elicitation step; we hope that even better results can be obtained through several preference elicitation executions.

The P-HMCSGA running time only doubles the time spent by the slower inner strategy. The latter can be observed from the results when analyzing instances with nine and 16 objectives, separately. In nine objective instances, A2-NSGA-III was the most time-consuming strategy, requiring at least four times the amount of time of any other. In sixteen objective strategies, NO-ACO was the slowest and needed at least five times longer than any other. Hence, the accumulated consumed time would be, at most, twice the slower strategy.

We have not included a comparison with other algorithms because our preference representation requires conversion methods to make a fair and comparable evaluation. Another possible analysis is to implement our preference incorporation method into several state-of-the-art multi-objective optimization metaheuristics to determine the advantages and limits of our proposal. However, this is beyond the scope of this paper.

Future work is proposed to verify the algorithm's interactive capacity, which can enrich the initial reference set with new solutions to intensity the search toward the region of interest. In addition to interactivity, a DM might be interested in specifying their profile with more than one preference. For example, in the project portfolio problem, a DM has particular ideal preferences on portfolios with a small number of projects and their cost is at a most certain quantity. Some voting strategies could be useful to deal with profiles that include several preferences. Pareto Explorer is a recent tool that incorporates user's preferences, articulated either in decision variables, objectives, weight space, or toward knee solutions, in the computation of the "ideal" solution of a given MaOP is the Pareto Explorer [40].

Author Contributions: Conceptualization: M.P.-V., L.C.-R., N.R.-V.; Methodology: H.F.-H., C.G.-S.; Investigation: M.P.-V., L.C.-R., N.R.-V.; Software: M.P.-V., C.G.-S., N.R.-V.; Formal Analysis: M.P.-V., L.C.-R., N.R.-V.; Writing original draft: M.P.-V.; Writing review and editing: M.P.-V., L.C.-R., N.R.-V., H.F.-H. All authors have read and agreed to the published version of the manuscript.

Funding: This research received no external funding.

Acknowledgments: The authors thank CONACYT for supporting the projects from (a) Cátedras CONACYT Program with Number 3058. (b) Project CONACYT A1-S-11012 from Convocatoria de Investigación Científica Básica 2017–2018 and CONACYT Project with Number 312397 from Programa de Apoyo para Actividades Científicas, Tecnológicas y de Innovación (PAACTI), a efecto de participar en la Convocatoria 2020-1 Apoyo para Proyectos de Investigación Científica, Desarrollo Tecnológico e Innovación en Salud ante la Contingencia por COVID-19. (c) M. Pérez-Villafuerte would like to thank CONACYT for the support number 293813.

Conflicts of Interest: The authors declare no conflict of interest.

Abbreviations

The following abbreviations are used in this manuscript:

DM	Decision Maker
H-MCSGA	Hybrid Multi-Criteria Sorting Genetic Algorithm
ND	Non dominated
NO-ACO	Non-Outranked Ant Colony Optimization
NSO	Non-strictly-outranked
PDA	Preference Disaggregation Analysis
P-HMCSGA	Preference Hybrid Multi-Criteria Sorting Genetic Algorithm
PPP	Project Portfolio Problem
RoI	Region of Interest
RS	Reference Set

Appendix A

Tables A1–A7 show matrix of results of satisfactory solutions evaluated in other preferential profiles for instances o9p100_1, o9p100_2, o9p100_3, o9p150_1, o9p150_2 and o16p500_1.

Table A1. Matrix of results of satisfactory solutions evaluated in other preferential profiles. Instance o9p100_1.

Parameter Setting	Evaluation in the Profile		
	Cardinality	Established Projects	Area-Region
Cardinality	91 (40)	8 (10)	4 (17)
Established projects	8 (38)	2 (11), 12 (10)	2 (15)
Area-Region	3 (40)	16 (10)	1 (20)

Table A2. Matrix of results of satisfactory solutions evaluated in other preferential profiles. Instance o9p100_2.

Parameter Setting	Evaluation in the Profile		
	Cardinality	Established Projects	Area-Region
Cardinality	92 (40)	4 (10)	2 (18)
Established projects	1 (40)	1 (13), 21 (12)	1 (20), 5(19)
Area-Region	1 (39)	1 (10)	1(21),1(20)

Table A3. Matrix of results of satisfactory solutions evaluated in other preferential profiles. Instance o9p100_3.

Parameter Setting	Evaluation in the Profile		
	Cardinality	Established Projects	Area-Region
Cardinality	516 (40)	33(15)	5 (20)
Established projects	2(41), 67 (40)	77(15)	6(19)
Area-Region	6 (40)	6(15)	8(20)

Table A4. Matrix of results of satisfactory solutions evaluated in other preferential profiles. Instance o9p150_1.

Parameter Setting	Evaluation in the Profile		
	Cardinality	Established Projects	Area-Region
Cardinality	55 (77)	10(13)	7 (28)
Established projects	1 (76)	5(14), 10 (13)	3 (25)
Area-Region	44 (75)	4 (13)	3(34), 1(33),2(32), 12(31), 24 (30)

Table A5. Matrix of results of satisfactory solutions evaluated in other preferential profiles. Instance o9p150_2.

Parameter Setting	Evaluation in the Profile		
	Cardinality	Established Projects	Area-Region
Cardinality	314 (77)	32 (15)	5 (32)
Established projects	22 (77)	136 (15)	2 (32), 13(31)
Area-Region	179 (77)	0 (15), 32 (11)	1(34), 5(33),35(32)

Table A6. Matrix of results of satisfactory solutions evaluated in other preferential profiles. Instance o16p500_1.

Parameter Setting	Evaluation in the Profile		
	Cardinality	Established Projects	Area-Region
Cardinality	197 (161)	4(15)	2 (61)
Established projects	11 (161)	3 (16), 10 (15)	1 (58), 4 (57)
Area-Region	3 (149)	2 (13)	2 (67), 5(66)

Appendix B

Table A7 shows the average running time for each instance that was part of the experimentation, expressed in seconds; the time in each algorithm that participates in P-HMCSGA is detailed. The average times shown occurred during the execution of P-HMCSGA with the settings indicated in Table 1. The strongest part is in PDA, used to discover the preferential parameters that will guide the search going forward.

Table A7. Average running time in all the process.

Instance	Average Running Time			
	A2-NSGAIII	PDA	NO-ACO	H-MCSGA
9o100p_1	29.665	30.982	0.489	13.551
9o100p_2	29.995	37.185	0.617	17.01
9o100p_3	37.42	61.285	0.491	27.919
9o150p_1	34.003	40.645	0.82	19.447
9o150p_2	36.046	40.518	0.761	32.966
16o500p_1	49.268	52.924	27.802	32.299

References

1. Coello, C.A.C.; Van Veldhuizen, D.A.; Lamont, G.B. *Evolutionary Algorithms for Solving Multi-Objective Problems*, 2nd ed.; Springer: New York, NY, USA, 2007.
2. Deb, K. *Multi-Objective Optimization Using Evolutionary Algorithms*; Wiley: Chichester, UK, 2001.
3. Fernández, E.; Copez, E.; López, F.; Coello, C.A.C. Increasing selective pressure towards the best compromise in evolutionary multiobjective optimization: The extended NOSGA method. *Inf. Sci.* **2011**, *181*, 44–56. [CrossRef]
4. Deb, K.; Sundar, J.; Rao, N.U.B.; Chaudhuri, S. Reference point based multi-objective optimization using evolutionary algorithms. *Int. J. Comput. Intell. Res.* **2006**, *2*, 273–286.
5. Adra, S.F.; Griffin, I.; Fleming, P.J. *A Comparative Study of Progressive Preference Articulation Techniques for Multiobjective Optimisation, Evolutionary Multi-Criterion Optimization*; Springer: Berlin/Heidelberg, Germany, 2007; pp. 908–921.
6. Branke, J.; Corrente, S.; Greco, S.; Słowiński, R.; Zielniewicz, P. Using Choquet integral as preference model in interactive evolutionary multiobjective optimization. *Eur. J. Oper. Res.* **2016**, *250*, 884–901. [CrossRef]
7. Fu, S.; Fan, G.-B. A Multiple Attribute Decision-Making Method Based on Exponential Fuzzy Numbers. *Math. Comput. Appl.* **2016**, *21*, 19. [CrossRef]
8. Nebro, A.J.; Ruiz, A.B.; Barba-González, C.; García-Nieto, J.; Luque, M.; Aldana-Montes, J.F. InDM2: Interactive Dynamic Multi-Objective Decision Making Using Evolutionary Algorithms. *Swarm Evol. Comput.* **2018**, *40*, 184–195. [CrossRef]
9. Eyvindson, K.; Hujala, T.; Kurttila, M.; Kangas, A. Interactive preference elicitation incorporating a priori and a posteriori methods. *Ann. Oper. Res.* **2015**, *232*, 99–113. [CrossRef]
10. Branke, J.; Corrente, S.; Greco, S.; Gutjahr, W. Efficient pairwise preference elicitation allowing for indifference. *Comput. Oper. Res.* **2017**, *88*, 175–186. [CrossRef]
11. Deb, K. *Multi-Objective Evolutionary Algorithms: Introducing Biasamong Pareto Optimal Solutions: KanGAL Report 99002*; Indian Institute of Technology: Kanpur, India, 1999.
12. Branke, J.; Greco, S.; Slowinski, R.; Zielniewicz, P. Interactive evolutionary multiobjective optimization driven by robust ordinal regression. *Bull. Pol. Acad. Sci. Tech. Sci.* **2010**, *58*, 347–358. [CrossRef]
13. Fernandez, E.; Lopez, E.; Bernal, S.; Coello, C.A.C.; Navarro, J. Evolutionary multiobjective optimization using an out-ranking-based dominance generalization. *Comput. Oper. Res.* **2010**, *37*, 390–395.
14. Cruz-Reyes, L.; Fernandez, E.; Sanchez-Solis, J.P.; Coello, C.A.C.; Gomez, C. Hybrid evolutionary multi-objective optimisation using outranking-based ordinal classification methods. *Swarm Evol. Comput.* **2020**, *54*, 100652. [CrossRef]
15. Gong, D.; Wang, G.; Sun, X. Set-based genetic algorithms for solving many-objective optimization problems. In Proceedings of the 2013 13th UK Workshop on Computational Intelligence (UKCI), Guildford, UK, 9–11 September 2013; pp. 96–103.
16. Wang, R.; Purshouse, R.C.; Fleming, P.J. Preference-inspired co-evolutionary algorithm using weights for many-objective optimization. In Proceedings of the 15th Annual Conference Companion on Genetic and Evolutionary Computation, Amsterdam, The Netherland, 6–10 June 2013; pp. 101–102.
17. Cruz-Reyes, L.; Fernandez, E.; Sanchez, P.; Coello, C.A.C.; Gomez, C. Incorporation of implicit decision-maker preferences in multi-objective evolutionary optimization using a multi-criteria classification method. *Appl. Soft Comput.* **2017**, *50*, 48–57. [CrossRef]
18. Wang, H.; Olhofer, M.; Jin, Y. A mini-review on preference modeling and articulation in multi-objective optimization: Current status and challenges. *Complex. Intell. Syst.* **2017**, *3*, 233–245. [CrossRef]

19. Emmerich, M.T.M.; Deutz, A.H. A tutorial on multiobjective optimization: Fundamentals and evolutionary methods. *Nat. Comput.* **2018**, *17*, 585–609. [CrossRef]
20. Carazo, A.F.; Contreras, I.; Gómez, T.; Pérez, F. A project portfolio selection problem in a group decision-making context. *J. Ind. Manag. Optim.* **2012**, *8*, 243–261. [CrossRef]
21. Kleinmuntz, D.N. *Portfolio Decision Analysis: Improved Methods for Resource Allocation, Chapter Foreword*; Springer: New York, NY, USA, 2011; pp. v–vii.
22. Pareto, V. *Cours d'Économie Politique*; Librairie Droz: Geneve, Switzerland, 1964; Volume 1.
23. Deb, K.; Agrawal, S.; Pratap, A.; Meyarivan, T. *A Fast Elitist Non-Dominated Sorting Genetic Algorithm for Multi-Objective Optimization: NSGA-II*; Metzler, J.B., Ed.; Springer: Berlin/Heidelberg, Germany, 2000; pp. 849–858.
24. Roy, B. *Multicriteria Methodology for Decision Aiding*; Springer: New York, NY, USA, 1996. [CrossRef]
25. Roy, B. The outranking approach and the foundations of ELECTRE methods. In *Reading in Multiple Criteria Decision Aid*; Bana e Costa, C.A., Ed.; Springer-Verlag: Berlin, Germany, 1990; pp. 155–183. [CrossRef]
26. Brans, J.P.; Mareschal, B. PROMETHEE methods. In *Multiple Criteria Decision Analysis: State of the Art Surveys*; Figueira, J., Greco, S., Erghott, M., Eds.; Springer Science + Business Media: New York, NY, USA, 2005; pp. 163–190. [CrossRef]
27. Fernández, E.; Navarro, J.; Mazcorro, G. Evolutionary multi-objective optimization for inferring outranking model's parameters under scarce reference information and effects of reinforced preference. *Found. Comput. Decis. Sci.* **2012**, *37*, 163–197. [CrossRef]
28. Rangel-Valdez, N.; Fernández, E.; Cruz-Reyes, L.; Santillán, C.G.; Hernández-López, R.I. Multiobjective optimization approach for preference-disaggregation analysis under effects of intensity. In *Mexican International Conference on Artificial Intelligence*; Springer: Cham, Switzerland, 2015; pp. 451–462.
29. Doumpos, M.; Marinakis, Y.; Marinaki, M.; Zopounidis, C. An evolutionary approach to construction of outranking models for multicriteria classification: The case of the ELECTRE TRI method. *Eur. J. Oper. Res.* **2009**, *199*, 496–505. [CrossRef]
30. Greco, S.; Mousseau, V.; Słowiński, R. Ordinal regression revisited: Multiple criteria ranking using a set of additive value functions. *Eur. J. Oper. Res.* **2008**, *191*, 416–436. [CrossRef]
31. Fernandez, E.; Navarro, J. A new approach to multi-criteria sorting based on fuzzy outranking relations: The THESEUS method. *Eur. J. Oper. Res.* **2011**, *213*, 405–413. [CrossRef]
32. Cruz-Reyes, L.; Fernandez, E.; Rangel-Valdez, N. A metaheuristic optimization-based indirect elicitation of preference parameters for solving many-objective problems. *Int. J. Comput. Intell. Syst.* **2017**, *10*, 56–77.
33. Corazza, M.; Funari, S.; Gusso, R. An evolutionary approach to preference disaggregation in a MURAME-based creditworthiness problem. *Appl. Soft Comput.* **2015**, *29*, 110–121. [CrossRef]
34. Kadziński, M.; Tomczyk, M.K. Interactive evolutionary multiple objective optimization for group decision incorporating value-based preference disaggregation methods. *Group Decis. Negot.* **2017**, *26*, 693–728.
35. Tomczyk, M.K.; Kadzinski, M. Decomposition-Based Interactive Evolutionary Algorithm for Multiple Objective Optimization. *IEEE Trans. Evol. Comput.* **2020**, *24*, 320–334. [CrossRef]
36. Doumpos, M.; Zopounidis, C. *Optimization in Science and Engineering, Chapter the Robustness Concern in Preference Dis-Aggregation Approaches for Decision Aiding: An Overview*; Springer: New York, NY, USA, 2014; pp. 157–177.
37. Fernandez, E.; Gomez, C.; Rivera, G.; Cruz-Reyes, L. Hybrid metaheuristic approach for handling many objectives and decisions on partial support in project portfolio optimisation. *Inf. Sci.* **2015**, *315*, 102–122. [CrossRef]
38. Jain, H.; Deb, K. An Improved Adaptive Approach for Elitist Nondominated Sorting Genetic algorithm for Many-Objective Optimization (A2-NSGA-III). Available online: https://www.egr.msu.edu/~{}kdeb/papers/c2013014.pdf (accessed on 28 March 2021).
39. Rivera, G. Solución a Gran Escala del Problema de Cartera de Proyectos Caracterizados con Múltiples Criterios. Tesis de Doctorado, Instituto Tecnológico de Cd Madero, Tamaulipas, México, 2015.
40. Schütze, O.; Cuate, O.; Martín, A.; Peitz, S.; Dellnitz, M. Pareto Explorer: A global/local exploration tool for many-objective optimization problems. *Eng. Optim.* **2021**, *52*, 832–855.

Article

Convolutional Neural Network–Component Transformation (CNN–CT) for Confirmed COVID-19 Cases

Juan Frausto-Solís [1,*,†], Lucía J. Hernández-González [1,†], Juan J. González-Barbosa [1,*,†], Juan Paulo Sánchez-Hernández [2] and Edgar Román-Rangel [3]

1. Graduate Program Division, Tecnológico Nacional de México/Instituto Tecnológico de Ciudad Madero, Cd. Madero 89440, Mexico; luciajaneth.hernandez@gmail.com
2. Dirección de Informática, Electrónica y Telecomunicaciones, Universidad Politécnica del Estado de Morelos, Boulevard Cuauhnáhuac 566, Jiutepec 62574, Mexico; juan.paulosh@upemor.edu.mx
3. Digital Systems Department, Instituto Tecnologico Autonomo de Mexico, Mexico City 01080, Mexico; edgar.roman@itam.mx
* Correspondence: juan.frausto@gmail.com or juan.frausto@itcm.edu.mx (J.F.-S.); jjgonzalezbarbosa@hotmail.com (J.J.G.-B.)
† These authors contributed equally to this work.

Citation: Frausto-Solís, J.; Hernández-González, L.J.; González-Barbosa, J.J.; Sánchez-Hernández, J.P.; Román-Rangel, E. Convolutional Neural Network–Component Transformation (CNN–CT) for Confirmed COVID-19 Cases. *Math. Comput. Appl.* **2021**, *26*, 29. https://doi.org/10.3390/mca26020029

Academic Editor: Oliver Schütze

Received: 28 February 2021
Accepted: 8 April 2021
Published: 12 April 2021

Publisher's Note: MDPI stays neutral with regard to jurisdictional claims in published maps and institutional affiliations.

Copyright: © 2021 by the authors. Licensee MDPI, Basel, Switzerland. This article is an open access article distributed under the terms and conditions of the Creative Commons Attribution (CC BY) license (https://creativecommons.org/licenses/by/4.0/).

Abstract: The COVID-19 disease constitutes a global health contingency. This disease has left millions people infected, and its spread has dramatically increased. This study proposes a new method based on a Convolutional Neural Network (CNN) and temporal Component Transformation (CT) called CNN–CT. This method is applied to confirmed cases of COVID-19 in the United States, Mexico, Brazil, and Colombia. The CT changes daily predictions and observations to weekly components and vice versa. In addition, CNN–CT adjusts the predictions made by CNN using AutoRegressive Integrated Moving Average (ARIMA) and Exponential Smoothing (ES) methods. This combination of strategies provides better predictions than most of the individual methods by themselves. In this paper, we present the mathematical formulation for this strategy. Our experiments encompass the fine-tuning of the parameters of the algorithms. We compared the best hybrid methods obtained with CNN–CT versus the individual CNN, Long Short-Term Memory (LSTM), ARIMA, and ES methods. Our results show that our hybrid method surpasses the performance of LSTM, and that it consistently achieves competitive results in terms of the MAPE metric, as opposed to the individual CNN and ARIMA methods, whose performance varies largely for different scenarios.

Keywords: forecasting; Convolutional Neural Network; LSTM; COVID-19; deep learning

1. Introduction

Coronaviruses are a large family of viruses characterized by having crown-shaped spikes on their surface. Nowadays, there are seven identified types of coronaviruses that can be transmitted among humans. The most dangerous coronaviruses known until recent years are MERS-CoV and SARS-CoV, and they have caused severe diseases, such as MERS and SARS, in 2003 and 2012, respectively, [1]. However, at the end of 2019, in Wuhan, China, the new epidemiological outbreak of COVID-19 emerged; it was caused by the new coronavirus called SARS-CoV2.

The importance of mathematical models and algorithms to analyze this disease has grown because they allow one to find patterns, make predictions, and understand fluctuations. Epidemiological models can be classified into two groups [2]:

- Dynamic Models. These are old models that usually divide the population into several subsets known as compartments, for instance, the Susceptible, Infectious, Recovered or SIR model. The SIR model was proposed in 1902 by Sir Roland Ross and then expanded by Kermack and McKendrick in 1927 [3].

- Forecasting models using time series. Here, we find classical methods such as ARIMA and Exponential Smoothing (ES) [4]. Furthermore, Machine Learning methods like Support Vector Machines [5] and Deep Learning [6] are also in this group.

This work presents a new method of the second group, based on Convolutional Neural Network (CNN) [7] and a proposed Component Transformation (CT), which we named CNN–CT, whose mathematical formulation is presented. The CNN–CT method is applied to forecast the number of COVID-19 confirmed cases for the United States (US), Mexico, Brazil, and Colombia [8]. The CT changes daily observations into weekly data and back. The forecast made by our hybrid CNN–CT method is further adjusted either with ARIMA or ES methods. We compared the proposed hybrid method versus the individual methods. Our results show that the combined method consistently achieves competitive results in terms of the MAPE metric, as opposed to any of its elements—CNN, ARIMA, or ES—whose performance as individual methods varies largely for different countries. Moreover, the proposed CNN–CT method also outperforms the Long Short-Term Memory (LSTM) [9], which is among the most used methods for dealing with time-series.

Both CNN and LSTM are Deep Learning methods, the first of which is equipped with convolutional filters while the second with recurrent operations, but in both cases with parameters that are learned though gradient-descent-like methods in a scenarios where data are used for training as they become available. In contrast, ARIMA and ES are traditional regression methods that consider a full set of training data at once, thus having the potential of better approximating such a training set, but losing the ability to adjust to newly available data as CNN and LSTM can. The proposed CNN–CT method exploits both the potential of incorporating newly available data as well as the strength of looking at a complete set at once, which results in an enriched forecast method.

We chose to use CNNs, given that the signal processing literature states that convolutional filters are more stable than recurrent operations like LSTM [10]. Moreover, the superior performance of CNNs over traditional methods, like ARIMA, has been confirmed by previous work focused on text classification [11] and sequence modeling [12], where convolutions obtained higher performance with respect to other methods.

The rest of this paper is organized as follows. In Section 2, we discuss works related to the forecast of confirmed cases of COVID-19. In Section 3, we show the proposed forecasting method for daily confirmed cases of COVID-19, highlighting the application of Deep Learning, ARIMA, and ES methods. In Section 4, we present details about the data and tools used to validate our method. Finally, Sections 5 and 6 present results and conclusions of this work.

2. Related Works

COVID-19 is a disease with a high rate of spread, which has led to an interest in estimation and forecasting the number of cases of infected people. Recently, several works have been presented with traditional epidemiological models or Dynamic Models. The Susceptible, Exposed, Infectious, Recovered (SEIR) model [13] was used to forecast confirmed cases in the United Kingdom, and the SIR and SEIR models were applied to forecast cumulative infected and recovered cases in Santiago de Cuba [14]. The Susceptible, Exposed, Infectious, Recovered, Dead (SEIRD) model [15] was used to forecast confirmed and death cases in Mexico. At Chen [16], comparative work was conducted to predict 11 days of confirmed cases in some regions of Canada and the United States. They use SIR, Neural Network, and ARIMA models.

The ARIMA and ES were used as adjusting methods to improve the results obtained for other models such as those obtained for SIR models, Neural Networks, and Support Vector Regression algorithms [2,17]. However, in most cases, the number of days forecast is too short. For instance, the authors of [18] used ARMA to forecast confirmed cases for three days in Chinese provinces, Asian countries, and a few occidental countries (Germany, US, Italy, and Spain). Parvez et al. compared an Adaptive Neuro-fuzzy Inference System versus ARIMA to predict ten days of COVID-19 confirmed cases in Bangladesh [19].

Furthermore, Petropoulus et al. [20], used the ES method known as Holt-Winter to forecast ten days of globally accumulated COVID-19 confirmed cases. Hussain et al. [21], used an ES to estimate twelve days of confirmed cases, and the R_0 parameter known as the basic reproduction number.

ARIMA and Deep Learning methods have been used alone to forecast COVID-19 cases. Chimmula [22] used LSTM to predict daily cases, obtaining with this method an error of eight percent using MAPE. In Chandraa [23], LSTM, BiLSTM, and EDLSTM were used to forecast the spread of COVID-19 infections among selected states in India. The work presented by Zeroul et al. [24] used deep learning to predict 10 days of number of infected people, obtaining a MAPE error between 1.28% and 59%. Saba et al. [25] compared polynomial regression, Holt-Winter, ARIMA, and SARIMA models, to predict the confirmed and deaths cases. Parbat et al. [26] proposed using an SVR-Radial model to forecast total deaths and recovered, daily confirmed cumulative, and confirmed daily deaths in India; this method obtained around thirteen percent MAPE error for the entire country.

Moreover, classical forecast methods have been combined with Machine Learning techniques [2,17,27]. Katris [27] used ARIMA, ES, Neural Network, and MARS models, where the combined methods performed better than the individual methods.

In general, ARIMA and ES methods are used to forecast cases with short-term periods, while Machine Learning and Deep Learning models are able to predict cases over more extended periods. However, the latter do not always obtain good results when used as individual methods.

3. CNN–CT Method

We show the proposed CNN–CT method in Figure 1, where a Convolutional Neural Network is used as primary forecasting method for daily confirmed cases of COVID-19, and it is complemented by ARIMA or ES, which are used as adjusting methods against daily errors.

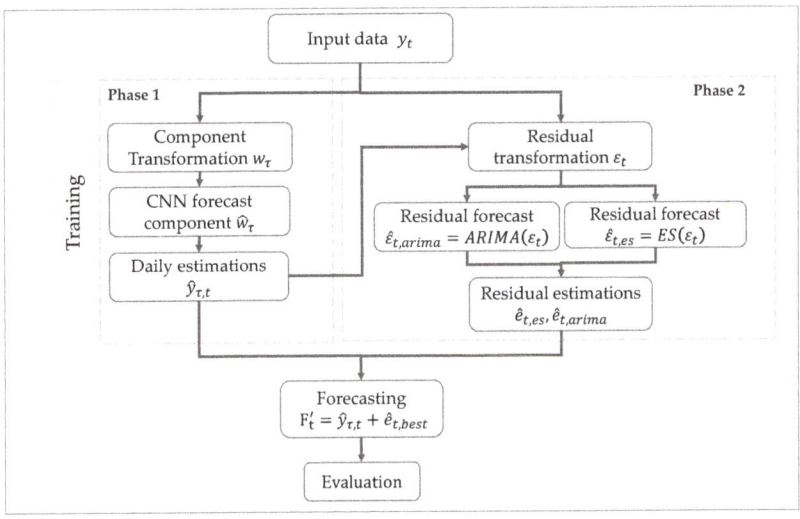

Figure 1. Proposed Convolutional Neural Network (CNN) and temporal Component Transformation (CT) (CNN–CT) method. Training with two phases: the first phase corresponds to forecast method using component values, and the second phase used residual values with a residual forecast method.

Firstly, our method's training stage is composed of two phases, each of which is formed by three internal sub-processes plus one global integration sub-process, as is shown in Figure 1.

In the first sub-process of phase 1, we start by transforming daily values y_t into weekly components w_τ, where t is a day index and τ is a component index. These w_τ components represent average weekly forecast estimations. In the second sub-process, a CNN is used to forecast the component $\hat{w}_\tau$. Finally, in the third sub-process, we convert the component estimation w_τ back into daily estimations $\hat{y}_{t,\tau}$.

In phase 2, the adjusting methods are trained. First, we obtain the residual ε_t from the difference between the daily prediction and its corresponding ground truth value, i.e., $\hat{y}_{\tau,t} - y_t$. We scale these residual values to be in the range $[1,10]$, as required by the Holt-Winter methods.

In the second sub-process of phase 2, we use the residuals ε_t to train an autoregressive model using either ARIMA or ES, which is used to forecast residual values $\hat{e}_t$ (concretely, $\hat{e}_{t,es}$ and $\hat{e}_{t,arima}$ for ES and ARIMA, respectively).

Later, in the third sub-process of phase 2, residual forecasts $e_{t,es}$ or $e_{t,arima}$ are obtained from the previously computed residual forecast values. Finally, this residual forecast $e_{t,X}$ is added to the daily estimation $\hat{y_{\tau,t}}$ obtained from the CNN, resulting in the final prediction value F'_t.

3.1. Data Transformation

Prediction models reflect an increased error as the number of forecasting periods increases. We chose to forecast more cases by transforming daily records into weekly components with the CT module, which maps the daily cases y_t into components w_τ that represent a weighted average of the daily cases obtained within a week. The values w_τ are calculated with Equation (1).

$$w_\tau = \frac{\sum_{t=7\tau-6}^{7\tau} y_t}{7}, \tag{1}$$

where w_τ is the weekly average of week τ and $w_1, w_2, \ldots, w_\tau$ is a set of transformed observation into components. For instance, $w_2 = \frac{y_8 + y_9 + \ldots + y_{14}}{7}$.

3.2. CNN Forecast Component

We used a CNN as a component forecasting method. The training and validation stages are composed of w_τ values. The CNN architecture contains an input layer with 50 convolutional neurons, a maxpooling layer of size equals 2. A complete MLP layer of 50 neurons, and one output layer with a single neuron. The convolutional layers use the ReLU activation function. The training configuration parameters is as follows: Adam optimizer [28], mean absolute error as loss function, 100 epochs, and batch size equal to 10. The above configuration is used to forecast weekly components $\hat{w}_\tau$.

3.3. Daily Estimations

The reverse transformation or daily estimations involves converting the weekly components w_τ back into daily values. For this, it is necessary to calculate the subcomponents of a component, which we define as shown in Table 1.

Table 1. Component segmentation into subcomponents.

			Week w_τ			
	subcomponent $\delta_{\tau,1}$				subcomponent $\delta_{\tau,2}$	
Monday	Tuesday	Wednesday	Thursday	Friday	Saturday	Sunday

The segmentation of the week into two subcomponents provides insights about the social behavior of countries separately into beginning and end of a week. The distribution of the daily cases with respect to their subcomponents can be obtained by Equations (2) and (3).

$$\delta_{\tau,1} = \frac{\sum_{t=1,\tau}^{4,\tau} y_{t,\tau}}{4}, \tag{2}$$

$$\delta_{\tau,2} = \frac{\sum_{t=5,\tau}^{7,\tau} y_{t,\tau}}{3}, \tag{3}$$

where $\delta_{\tau,1}, \delta_{\tau,2}$ are subcomponents ADS-1 (Monday to Thursday) and ADS-2 (Friday to Sunday) for the component τ. We determine that the daily ratio $\mu_{\tau,t}$ represents the proportion of the original daily values for subcomponent 1 and 2 for the component τ (Equation (4)). The daily ratio $\mu_{\tau,t}$ lets us to determine weekday normalized cases x_t (Equation (5)) of the training phase. In other words, $x_1 = mondeys_{avg}, \ldots, x_7 = sundays_{avg}$ are average confirmed cases of each day of the week throughout the time series.

$$\mu_{\tau,t} = \begin{cases} \frac{y_{\tau,t}}{\delta_{\tau,1}}, & \text{if } 1 \leq t \leq 4, \\ \frac{y_{\tau,t}}{\delta_{\tau,2}}, & \text{if } 5 \leq t \leq 7, \end{cases} \tag{4}$$

$$x_t = \frac{\sum_{i=1}^{\tau} \mu_i}{\tau}. \tag{5}$$

The weighting of the daily cases obtained with the ratio $\mu_{\tau,t}$ allows obtaining a statistical estimation on the relevance of persons infected in the first and second subcomponent τ, j of each component τ throughout the training period. The inverse transformation determines the daily cases predicted from the components using Equations (6) and (7).

$$\hat{\delta}_{\tau,i} = \hat{w}_\tau \frac{w_\tau}{\delta_{\tau,i}}, \tag{6}$$

$$\hat{y}_{\tau,t} = \begin{cases} x_t \hat{\delta}_{\tau,1}, & \text{if } 1 \leq t \leq 4, \\ x_t \hat{\delta}_{\tau,2}, & \text{if } 5 \leq t \leq 7, \end{cases} \tag{7}$$

where $\hat{y}_{\tau,t}$ represents the forecasting case values of the component τ at time t, and $\hat{\delta}_{\tau,i}$ is the forecast of the average number of infected sub-component i in the τ component. The data for the learning of the adjustment methods are obtained from the daily prediction values of the validation phase of components $y_{\tau,t}$.

3.4. Residual Transformation

A residual value is given by the difference in the ground truth and the predicted value, as shown in Equation (8).

$$e_t = y_t - \hat{y}_t = y_t - y_{t-1}, \tag{8}$$

where y_t is the ground truth in time t, $\hat{y}_t$ is the forecast value in time t. Using Equation (8), the residuals e_t are obtained by subtraction of y_t and $y_{\tau,t}$, as shown in Equation (9).

$$e_t = y_{\tau,t} - y_t, \tag{9}$$

where $y_{\tau,t}$ is the forecasting value in time t of component τ. ARIMA and ES methods used positive numbers; because of this, the residuals were normalized as shown in Equation (10).

$$\varepsilon_t = |y_{\tau,t} - y_t|, \tag{10}$$

where $|.|$ represents normalization of e_t in the range of values $[1, 10]$.

3.5. Residual Forecast

We used ARIMA and ES forecasting methods as forecasting adjustments methods. The training and validation sets are composed by ε_t values.

The configuration of the ARIMA method is as follows: start_p = 0, d = 0, start_q = 0, max_p = 5, max_q = 5, max_d = 5, start_Q = 0, max_P = 5, max_D = 5, max_Q = 5, m = 4, seasonal = True, error_action = 'warn', trace = True, suppress_warnings = True, stepwise = True, random_state = 20, n_fits = 50, information_criterion = 'aic', and alpha = 0.05.

Furthermore, ES obtained a configuration that used the Holt–Winter (HW) method. The variants of HW used are: additive, multiplicative, additive damped, multiplicative damped. These variants were trained with a norm residuals ε_t.

3.6. Residual Estimations

We use residual transformations ε_t to train ARIMA and ES, from which we obtained four hybrid methods, CNN-ARIMA, CNN-ES, LSTM-ARIMA, and LSTM-ES. The forecasts $\varepsilon_{t,es}$ and $\varepsilon_{t,arima}$ from these hybrid methods are transformed into residuals $e_{t,es}, e_{t,arima}$, which are in the non-normalized domain.

3.7. Forecasting

Finally, we evaluated the forecast values of the validation phase F'_t, which is composed of the daily forecasts $y_{\tau,t}$ of CNN and adjustment forecasts $e_{t,best}$, as is shown in Equation (11).

$$F'_t = y_{\tau,t} + e_{t,best}. \tag{11}$$

4. Experimental Setup

The source of the data, the pre-processing applied, the data separation criterion in training, validation, and testing are described below. Finally, the evaluation metrics are described.

4.1. Data

The COVID-19 database used in this work is the Novel Coronavirus 2019 dataset [8], whose records report the number of infected, recovered, and deceased people in each country of the world. From this database, we used a time series starting from 22 January 2020, and that is called Time_Series_Covid_19_confirmed. We selected the records corresponding to the US, Mexico, Brazil, and Colombia.

We used data records from 2 March 2020 until 28 June 2020 for training (17 weeks); from 29 June 2020 to 19 July 2020 for validation (3 weeks); and from 20 July 2020 to 9 August 2020 for test (3 weeks). Figure 2 shows a scheme for this split of data.

With this split, the training of the CNN–CT method for the US was carried out with 17 weekly components w_τ, as explained in Section 3.1. In the case of Mexico, Brazil, and Colombia, we used only 15 weekly components since the data corresponding to the first week were discarded due to the lack of significant information; that is, the values of the first week were considerably low with respect to the rest of the series. We noticed that processing this first week results in underestimation of the forecast values.

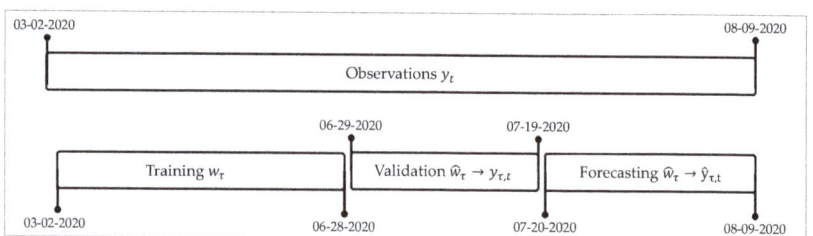

Figure 2. Split of the observations in training and validation set by CNN method.

Although training is conducted using weekly components w_τ, the forecast for the validation and test stages happens in daily values $y_{\tau,t}$, as explained in Section 3.3.

Residual forecasts allow adjusting daily forecast with ARIMA and ES. In addition, it trained with the residuals of forecast daily validation means, and w_τ forecasts obtained in the validation phase were transformed into daily estimations $y_{\tau,t}$ to be used in the training and validation phase of the adjustment methods. Figure 3 shows a scheme for this split of data for the adjusting methods.

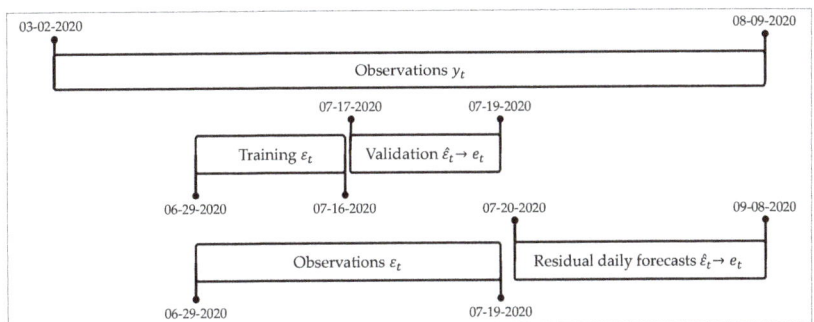

Figure 3. Split of the observations in training and validation set by adjusting methods.

Given that the problem we address corresponds to a scenario of auto-regression, the actual structure of the data is such that each output variable y_t depends on a vector of past values $\mathbf{x} = [y_{t-1}, y_{t-2}, \ldots, y_{t-T}]$. For this work, we used lags of up to three past values, $t-3$, $t-2$, and $t-1$.

4.2. Metrics

The proposed hybridized CNN–CT method and its individual composing methods are evaluated by the MAPE [29], as it has been widely used in the works discussed in Section 2. The MAPE computes the percentage of accuracy in the predicted value with respect to the ground truth. The closer to zero, the more accurate it is. Another common metric is RMSPE [4] which is also used in part of this paper.

$$MAPE = \frac{100}{n} \sum_{t=1}^{n} \frac{|y_t - \hat{y}_t|}{y_t}, \qquad (12)$$

$$RMSPE = \sqrt{\frac{\sum_{t=1}^{n}(y_t - \hat{y}_t)^2}{n}} * 100, \qquad (13)$$

where, y_t is the ground truth, $\hat{y}_t$ is the predicted value, and n indicates the total number of samples.

4.3. Tools

This work was developed with a computer with an iOS operating system, 8 GB, and a 2.3 GHz Dual-Core Intel Core i5 processor. We used Python 3.7.1, and the CNN model was built using Tensorflow and Keras libraries [30].

5. Results

This section shows the results of the CNN–CT method proposed for daily forecasting cases of COVID-19 in the US, Mexico, Brazil, and Colombia. First, we compare the performance of using CNN and LSTM as the main forecasting methods with ARIMA and ES (Holt-Winter, HW) as adjusting methods. Then, we present the comparison of the CNN–CT model versus the individual CNN, LSTM, ARIMA, and Holt-Winters models for each country.

We can see in Figure 4 the comparison of best-performing forecast models for the countries of The United States, Mexico, Brazil, and Colombia. In the US, Figure 4a, the forecasts of LSTM-ARIMA manage to maintain the trend and seasonality patterns with respect to the ground truth. However, the CNN-HW prognosis is well below the actual data. We can see in Table 2 that LSTM-ARIMA achieves the lowest MAPE for the US.

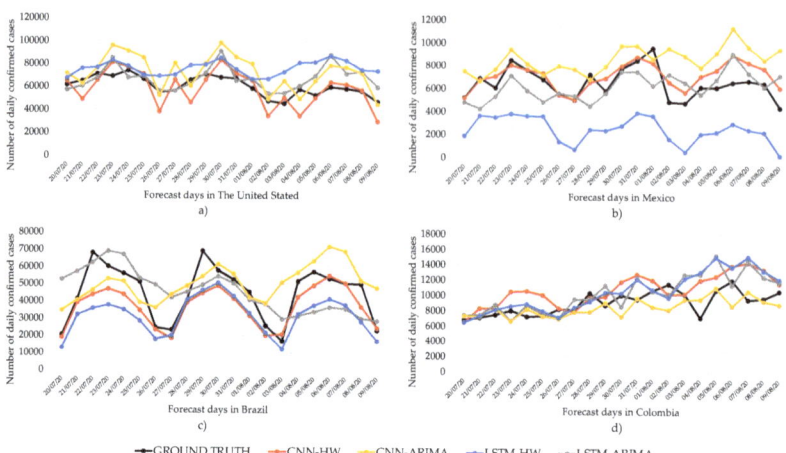

Figure 4. Daily forecast with CNN–CT method using CNN and Long Short-Term Memory (LSTM) as main forecast methods.

Likewise, Figure 4b shows the behavior of the forecasts for daily cases of COVID-19 in Mexico. We can see that all four models are able to maintain trend and seasonality patterns with respect to ground truth. However, LSTM–ARIMA shows a high error rate because of the difference with respect to the actual data. On the other hand, the forecast of CNN-HW is very close to the real data, which allows us to obtain a better performance with respect to the other methods. The average MAPE and its standard deviation are shown in Table 2, where we can see that CNN-HW achieves the best average performance among the four models.

Similarly, Figure 4c shows the comparative Brazil forecast for all the models. We can see that LSTM-ARIMA manages to maintain seasonality patterns concerning the ground truth. In the case of CNN-HW, it follows the trend and seasonality patterns with respect to the ground truth. The average MAPE and its standard deviation are shown in Table 2. However, as we noticed before with the average MAPE and its standard deviation, CNN–HW has the best performance.

We can see in Figure 4d that LSTM–ARIMA manages to maintain seasonality patterns concerning the ground truth for Colombia. In the case of CNN–HW, it follows the trend and seasonality patterns with respect to the ground truth. According to Table 2 CNN-ARIMA shows the best MAPE performance, as its curve is the closest to the ground truth.

In general, our experiments show that smoothing with ARIMA or ES helps obtain lower MAPE in the case of CNN. This is not the case with LSTM. Table 2 shows a summary of the MAPE and RMSPE daily forecasting values of the CNN–CT and LSTM–CT for US, Mexico, Brazil, and Colombia. In the case of US, the method with the best performance is LSTM-ARIMA, having a $MAPE \approx 14\%$. In the case of Mexico and Brazil, CNN–HW is better with MAPE 14.18% and 29.3%. It is possible to see that LSTM–ARIMA and CNN–HW obtain better results in different countries. In Colombia, CNN-ARIMA obtains the best MAPE and RMSPE.

We averaged the MAPE of all the countries for each method in Table 2. We observed that CNN–CT methods have better performance than that of LSTM–CT. Furthermore, for each country, we determined the standard deviation of the error metrics. We noticed that CNN–CT has the lower deviation, which indicates that its best performance is consistent across countries.

Table 2. CNN–CT methods performance. Best MAPE results are marked in bold.

Country	CNN-HW		CNN-ARIMA		LSTM-HW		LSTM-ARIMA	
	MAPE	RMSPE	MAPE	RMSPE	MAPE	RMSPE	MAPE	RMSPE
United States	15.53	19.35	22.64	26.57	38.57	43.64	**13.35**	16.70
Mexico	14.19	18.78	36.82	47.37	71.66	73.32	25.73	31.53
Brazil	**29.30**	31.27	39.69	62.58	62.63	70.75	44.26	54.59
Colombia	21.76	28.46	**13.39**	16.84	24.56	32.48	20.00	26.07
Average	20.19	24.47	28.14	38.34	49.36	55.05	25.84	32.22
Standar Desv	5.98	5.50	10.68	17.82	18.74	17.46	11.51	13.96

Finally, in Figure 5, we show a comparison of the MAPE for the CNN-HW model versus the individual CNN, LSTM, ARIMA, and Holt–Winters models for each country.

Although ARIMA obtained good performance for the US (11.18) and Mexico (16.31), first and third place, respectively, it provides high MAPE for Brazil (50.99) and Colombia (29.75), with the last and second-last places, respectively. Similarly, pure CNN is a good method for Mexico (14.04) and Colombia (14.96) but not so good for US (42.75) and Brazil (38.19).

In contrast, CNN–CT (CNN-HW) is consistently competitive for all cases, obtaining second place for US (15.53), Mexico (14.18, as good as the best-performing CNN alone), and Colombia (21.75), and first for Brazil (29.30).

Figure 5. Daily forecast with CNN–CT (using Holt–Winters (HW)) versus the individual methods CNN, LSTM, ARIMA, and HW.

We show the comparison of CNN–HW versus the four individual methods in Table 3. We can see that CNN–HW surpasses all of these individual methods for Brazil and Colombia. For the case of Mexico, CNN–HW is below the best performing method (CNN) only by 0.14 MAPE points. Furthermore, CNN–HW achieves competitive results for the US.

Table 3. The performance of the CNN–CT vs. individual methods. Best MAPE results are marked in bold.

Country	MAPE Metric				
	CNN-HW	CNN	LSTM	ARIMA	HW
United States	15.53	42.75	23.96	**11.18**	23.65
Mexico	14.18	**14.04**	39.07	16.31	17.71
Brazil	**29.30**	38.19	42.34	50.99	33.76
Colombia	21.75	**14.96**	38.59	29.75	29.29
MAPE Average	20.19	27.49	35.99	27.06	26.10
Standard Desv	5.98	13.09	7.09	15.39	6.03

6. Conclusions

This paper investigates the problem of forecasting confirmed daily cases of COVID-19 in Mexico, Brazil, Colombia, and the US. Given the limited number of data available at the time of conducting our experiments, several limitations of the prediction methods became evident. These limitations were even more obvious due to the presence of noise in the daily data, which might very well be a consequence of the restrictions on the flow of data imposed by the sanitary crisis related to COVID-19 worldwide.

In particular, most prediction methods decrease their accuracy as the periods for forecast become larger. To mitigate this issue, we proposed a component transformation that converts daily values into weekly components for correct prediction in those cases.

We present a hybrid forecasting method termed Convolutional Neural Network–Component Transformation (CNN–CT), which uses CNN and LSTM as the main prediction method and ES and ARIMA as adjusting methods for daily error correction. As a result, there are two variants of the proposed method: CNN–CT with Holt–Winters, and LSTM–CT with ARIMA.

We compared the prediction performance of the individual methods that compose the proposed CNN–CT using the MAPE metric. We noticed that CNN and LSTM are very good with learning trend and seasonality of the time series; however, LSTM forecasts tends to generate increasing and decreasing trend, which causes the error to increase. Our experiments show that smoothing with ARIMA or ES helps obtain lower MAPE in the case of CNN. This is not the case with LSTM.

As future works, we propose applying this methodology to other popular forecasting methods such as SVR, Recurrent Neural Network, and so on; measuring the performance quality in more countries; and applying powerful data cleaning as a preprocessing stage. Furthermore, it could be interesting to use different adjusting methods. Finally, we propose testing if the proposed methodology is completely general or determines which strategy applies in different forecast scenarios.

Author Contributions: Conceptualization L.J.H.-G., J.F.-S., and J.J.G.-B.; methodology L.J.H.-G., J.F.-S., E.R.-R., and J.J.G.-B.; investigation L.J.H.-G., J.F.-S., and J.J.G.-B.; Software L.J.H.-G., J.F.-S., and J.J.G.-B.; validation, J.F.-S., J.P.S.-H., and E.R.-R.; formal analysis J.F.-S., J.P.S.-H., and E.R.-R.; writing—original draft L.J.H.-G. and J.F.-S.; writing—review and editing, J.F.-S., J.J.G.-B., E.R.-R., and J.P.S.-H. All authors have read and agreed to the published version of the manuscript.

Funding: This research received no external funding.

Acknowledgments: The authors would like to acknowledge with appreciation and gratitude CONACYT, TecNM/Instituto Tecnológico de Ciudad Madero, and Asociación Maxicana de Cultura A.C. In addition, the authors acknowledge the support from Laboratorio Nacional de Tecnologías de la Información (LaNTI) for the access to the cluster.

Conflicts of Interest: The authors declare no conflict of interest.

References

1. Sahu, K.K.; Mishra, A.K.; Lal, A. Coronavirus disease-2019: An update on third coronavirus outbreak of 21st century. *QJM Int. J. Med.* **2020**, *113*, 384–386. [CrossRef]
2. Frausto Solis, J.; Olvera Vazquez, J.E.; González-Barbosa, J.J. The Hybrid Forecasting Method SVR-ESAR for COVID-19 Background. *Int. J. Comb. Optim. Probl. Inform.* **2021**, *12*, 42–48.
3. Kermack, W.O.; McKendrick, A.G. A contribution to the mathematical theory of epidemics. *Proc. R. Soc. Lond. Ser. A Contain. Pap. A Math. Phys. Character* **1927**, *115*, 700–721. [CrossRef]
4. Hyndman, R.J.; Athanasopoulos, G. *Forecasting: Principles and Practice*; Monash University: Melbourne, Australia, 2018.
5. Cortes, C.; Vapnik, V. Support-vector networks. *Mach. Learn.* **1995**, *20*, 273–297. [CrossRef]
6. Goodfellow, I.; Bengio, Y.; Courville, A. *Deep Learning*; MIT Press: Cambridge, MA, USA, 2016; Volume 1, p. 692.
7. LeCun, Y.; Bengio, Y. Convolutional networks for images, speech, and time series. *Handb. Brain Theory Neural Netw.* **1995**, *3361*, 255–258.
8. SRK. *Novel CoronaVirus 2019 Dataset*; Kaggle: San Francisco, CA, USA, 2020.
9. Hochreiter, S.; Schmidhuber, J. Long short-term memory. *Neural Comput.* **1997**, *8*, 1735–1780. [CrossRef]

10. Roberts, M.J. *Signals and Systems: Analysis Using Transform Methods and MATLAB*, 3rd ed.; McGraw-Hill: New York, NY, USA, 2018.
11. Zhang, X.; Zhao, J.; LeCun, Y. Character-level Convolutional Networks for Text Classification. In Proceedings of the Advances in Neural Information Processing Systems: Annual Conference on Neural Information Processing Systems 2015, Montreal, QC, Canada, 7–12 December 2015.
12. Bai, S.; Kolter, J.Z.; Koltun, V. An Empirical Evaluation of Generic Convolutional and Recurrent Networks for Sequence Modeling. *arXiv* **2018**, arXiv:1803.01271.
13. Keeling, M.J.; Hill, E.M.; Gorsich, E.E.; Penman, B.; Guyver-Fletcher, G.; Holmes, A.; Leng, T.; McKimm, H.; Tamborrino, M.; Dyson, L.; et al. Predictions of COVID-19 dynamics in the UK: Short-term forecasting and analysis of potential exit strategies. *PLoS Comput. Biol.* **2021**, *17*, e1008619. [CrossRef] [PubMed]
14. Ramirez-Torres, E.E.; Selva Castañeda, A.R.; Rodríguez-Aldana, Y.; Sánchez Domínguez, S.; Valdés García, L.E.; Palú-Orozco, A.; Oliveros-Domínguez, E.; Zamora-Matamoros, L.; Labrada-Claro, R.; Cobas-Batista, M.; et al. Mathematical modeling and forecasting of COVID-19: Experience in Santiago de Cuba province. *Rev. Mex. Física* **2021**, *67*, 123. [CrossRef]
15. Capistran, M.A.; Capella, A.; Christen, J.A. Forecasting hospital demand in metropolitan areas during the current COVID-19 pandemic and estimates of lockdown-induced 2nd waves. *PLoS ONE* **2021**, *16*, e0245669. [CrossRef]
16. Chen, L.P.; Zhang, Q.; Yi, G.Y.; He, W. Model-based forecasting for Canadian COVID-19 data. *PLoS ONE* **2021**, *16*, e0244536. [CrossRef]
17. Ala'raj, M.; Majdalawieh, M.; Nizamuddin, N. Modeling and forecasting of COVID-19 using a hybrid dynamic model based on SEIRD with ARIMA corrections. *Infect. Dis. Model.* **2021**, *6*, 98–111. [CrossRef]
18. Deb, S.; Majumdar, M. A time series method to analyze incidence pattern and estimate reproduction number of COVID-19. *arXiv* **2020**, arXiv:abs/2003.10655.
19. Parvez, S.M.; Rakin, S.S.A.; Asadut Zaman, M.; Ahmed, I.; Alif, R.A.; Rahman, R.M. A Comparison Between Adaptive Neuro-fuzzy Inference System and Autoregressive Integrated Moving Average in Predicting COVID-19 Confirmed Cases in Bangladesh. *ICT Anal. Appl.* **2021**, *154*, 741–754. [CrossRef]
20. Petropoulos, F.; Makridakis, S. Forecasting the novel coronavirus COVID-19. *PLoS ONE* **2020**, *15*, e0231236. [CrossRef]
21. Hussain, Z.; Dutta Borah, M. *Forecasting Probable Spread Estimation of COVID-19 Using Exponential Smoothing Technique and Basic Reproduction Number in Indian Context*; Springer: Berlin/Heidelberg, Germany, 2021; pp. 183–196. [CrossRef]
22. Chimmula, V.K.R.; Zhang, L. Time series forecasting of COVID-19 transmission in Canada using LSTM networks. *Chaos Solitons Fractals* **2020**, *135*, 109864. [CrossRef]
23. Chandraa, R.; Jainb, A.; Chauhanc, D.S. Deep learning via LSTM models for COVID-19 infection forecasting in India. *arXiv* **2021**, arXiv:2101.11881.
24. Zeroual, A.; Harrou, F.; Dairi, A.; Sun, Y. Deep learning methods for forecasting COVID-19 time-series data: A comparative study. *Chaos Solitons Fractals* **2020**, *140*. [CrossRef] [PubMed]
25. Saba, T.; Abunadi, I.; Shahzad, M.N.; Khan, A.R. Machine learning techniques to detect and forecast the daily total COVID-19 infected and deaths cases under different lockdown types. *Microsc. Res. Tech.* **2021**, jemt.23702. [CrossRef] [PubMed]
26. Parbat, D.; Chakraborty, M. A python based support vector regression model for prediction of COVID19 cases in India. *Chaos Solitons Fractals* **2020**, *138*, 3–7. [CrossRef]
27. Katris, C. A time series-based statistical approach for outbreak spread forecasting: Application of COVID-19 in Greece. *Expert Syst. Appl.* **2021**, *166*, 114077. [CrossRef]
28. Kingma, D.P.; Ba, J. Adam: A Method for Stochastic Optimization. In Proceedings of the 3rd International Conference on Learning Representations, ICLR, San Diego, CA, USA, 7–9 May 2015.
29. Makridakis, S.; Armstrong, J.S.; Carbone, R.; Fildes, R. An editorial statement. *J. Forecast.* **1982**, *1*, 1–2. [CrossRef]
30. Raschka, S.; Mirjalili, V. *Python Machine Learning: Machine Learning and Deep Learning with Python, Scikit-Learn, and TensorFlow*, 2nd ed.; Packt Publishing: Birmingham, UK, 2017.

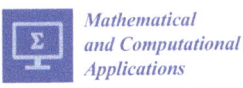

Mathematical and Computational Applications

Article

Derivative-Free Multiobjective Trust Region Descent Method Using Radial Basis Function Surrogate Models

Manuel Berkemeier [1,*] and Sebastian Peitz [2]

[1] Chair of Applied Mathematics, Faculty for Computer Science, Electrical Engineering and Mathematics, Paderborn University, Warburger Str. 100, 33098 Paderborn, Germany
[2] Department of Computer Science, Faculty for Computer Science, Electrical Engineering and Mathematics, Paderborn University, Warburger Str. 100, 33098 Paderborn, Germany; sebastian.peitz@upb.de
* Correspondence: manuelbb@math.upb.de

Citation: Berkemeier, M.; Peitz, S. Derivative-Free Multiobjective Trust Region Descent Method Using Radial Basis Function Surrogate Models. *Math. Comput. Appl.* **2021**, *26*, 31. https://doi.org/10.3390/mca26020031

Academic Editors: Marcela Quiroz, Juan Gabriel Ruiz, Luis Gerardo de la Fraga and Oliver Schütze

Received: 26 February 2021
Accepted: 7 April 2021
Published: 15 April 2021

Publisher's Note: MDPI stays neutral with regard to jurisdictional claims in published maps and institutional affiliations.

Copyright: © 2021 by the authors. Licensee MDPI, Basel, Switzerland. This article is an open access article distributed under the terms and conditions of the Creative Commons Attribution (CC BY) license (https://creativecommons.org/licenses/by/4.0/).

Abstract: We present a local trust region descent algorithm for unconstrained and convexly constrained multiobjective optimization problems. It is targeted at heterogeneous and expensive problems, i.e., problems that have at least one objective function that is computationally expensive. Convergence to a Pareto critical point is proven. The method is derivative-free in the sense that derivative information need not be available for the expensive objectives. Instead, a multiobjective trust region approach is used that works similarly to its well-known scalar counterparts and complements multiobjective line-search algorithms. Local surrogate models constructed from evaluation data of the true objective functions are employed to compute possible descent directions. In contrast to existing multiobjective trust region algorithms, these surrogates are not polynomial but carefully constructed radial basis function networks. This has the important advantage that the number of data points needed per iteration scales linearly with the decision space dimension. The local models qualify as *fully linear* and the corresponding general scalar framework is adapted for problems with multiple objectives.

Keywords: multiobjective optimization; trust region methods; multiobjective descent; derivative-free optimization; radial basis functions; fully linear models

1. Introduction

Optimization problems arise in a multitude of applications in mathematics, computer science, engineering and the natural sciences. In many real-life scenarios, there are multiple, equally important objectives that need to be optimized. Such problems are then called *Multiobjective Optimization Problems* (MOP). In contrast to the single objective case, an MOP often does not have a single solution but an entire set of optimal trade-offs between the different objectives, which we call *Pareto optimal*. They constitute the *Pareto Set* and their image is the *Pareto Frontier*. The goal in the numerical treatment of an MOP is to either approximate these sets or to find single points within these sets. In applications, the problem can become more difficult when some of the objectives require computationally expensive or time consuming evaluations. For instance, the objectives could depend on a computer simulation or some other *black-box*. It is then of primary interest to reduce the overall number of function evaluations. Consequently, it can become infeasible to approximate derivative information of the true objectives using, e.g., finite differences. This holds true especially if higher order derivatives are required. In this work, optimization methods that do not use the true objective gradients (which nonetheless are assumed to exist) are referred to as *derivative-free*.

There is a variety of methods to deal with MOPs, some of which are also derivative-free or try to constrain the number of expensive function evaluations. A broad overview of different problems and techniques concerning multiobjective optimization can be found, e.g., in [1–4]. One popular approach for calculating Pareto optimal solutions is scalarization, i.e., the transformation of an MOP into a single objective problem, cf. [5] for an overview. Alternatively, classical (single objective) descent algorithms can be adapted for the multiobjective case [6–11]. What is more, the structure of the Pareto Set can be exploited to find multiple solutions [12,13]. There are also methods for non-smooth problems [14,15] and multiobjective direct-search variants [16,17]. Both scalarization and descent techniques may be included in Evolutionary Algorithms (EA) [18–22]. To address computationally expensive objectives or missing derivative information, there are algorithms that use surrogate models (see the surveys [23–25]) or borrow from ideas from scalar trust region methods, e.g., [26].

In single objective optimization, trust region methods are well suited for derivative-free optimization [27,28]. Our work is based on the recent development of multiobjective trust region methods:

- In [29], a trust region method using Newton steps for functions with positive definite Hessians on an open domain is proposed.
- In [30], quadratic Taylor polynomials are used to compute the steepest descent direction which is used in a backtracking manner to find solutions for unconstrained problems.
- In [31], polynomial regression models are used to solve an augmented MOP based on the scalarization in [17]. The algorithm is designed unconstrained bi-objective problems, but the general idea has been formulated for more objectives in [32].
- In [33], quadratic Lagrange polynomials are used and the Pascoletti–Serafini scalarization is employed for the descent step calculation.

Our contribution is the extension of the above-mentioned methods to general fully linear models (and in particular Radial Basis Function (RBF) surrogates as in [34]), which is related to the scalar framework in [35]. Most importantly, this reduces surrogate construction complexity, in terms of objective evaluations per iteration, to linear with respect to the number of decision variables, in contrast to the quadratically increasing number of function evaluations for methods using second degree polynomials. We further prove convergence to critical points when the problem is constrained to a convex and compact set by using an analogous argumentation as in [36]. To this end, we extend the theory in [6] to provide new results concerning the continuity of the solutions of the projected steepest descent direction problem, which is based on the alternative formulation by Fliege and Svaiter [7]. We also show how to keep the convergence properties for constrained problems when the Pascoletti–Serafini scalarization is employed (like in [33]).

The remainder of the paper is structured as follows: Section 2 provides a brief introduction to multiobjective optimality and criticality concepts. In Section 3 the fundamentals of the algorithm are explained. In Section 4 we introduce fully linear surrogate models and describe the construction of suitable polynomial models and RBF models for unconstrained and box-constrained problems. We also formalize the main algorithm in this section. Section 5 deals with the descent step calculation so that a sufficient decrease is achieved in each iteration. Convergence is proven in Section 6 and a few numerical examples for unconstrained and finitely box-constrained problems are shown in Section 7. In Section 7 we also compare the RBF models against linear polynomial models that have the same linear construction complexity. We conclude with a brief discussion in Section 8.

2. Optimality and Criticality in Multiobjective Optimization

We consider the following (real-valued) multiobjective optimization problem:

$$\min_{\mathbf{x} \in \mathcal{X}} \mathbf{f}(\mathbf{x}) := \min_{\mathbf{x} \in \mathcal{X}} \begin{bmatrix} f_1(\mathbf{x}) \\ \vdots \\ f_k(\mathbf{x}) \end{bmatrix} \in \mathbb{R}^k, \qquad \text{(MOP)}$$

with a feasible set $\mathcal{X} \subseteq \mathbb{R}^n$ and k objective functions $f_\ell \colon \mathbb{R}^n \to \mathbb{R}$, $\ell = 1,\ldots,k$. We further assume (MOP) to be *heterogeneous*. That is, there is a non-empty subset $I_{\text{ex}} \subseteq \{1,\ldots,k\}$ of indices so that the gradients of $f_\ell, \ell \in I_{\text{ex}}$, are unknown and cannot be approximated, e.g., via finite differences. The (possibly empty) index set $I_{\text{cheap}} = \{1,\ldots,k\} \setminus I_{\text{ex}}$ indicates functions whose gradients are available.

Solutions for (MOP) consist of optimal trade-offs $\mathbf{x}^* \in \mathcal{X}$ between the different objectives and are called non-dominated or Pareto optimal. That is, there is no $\mathbf{x} \in \mathcal{X}$ with $\mathbf{f}(\mathbf{x}) \prec \mathbf{f}(\mathbf{x}^*)$ (i.e., $\mathbf{f}(\mathbf{x}) \le \mathbf{f}(\mathbf{x}^*)$ and $f_\ell(\mathbf{x}) < f_\ell(\mathbf{x}^*)$ for some index $\ell \in \{1,\ldots,k\}$). The subset $\mathcal{P}_S \subseteq \mathcal{X}$ of non-dominated points is then called the *Pareto Set* and its image $\mathcal{P}_F := \mathbf{f}(\mathcal{P}_S) \subseteq \mathbb{R}^k$ is called the *Pareto Frontier*. All concepts can be defined in a local fashion in an analogous way.

Similar to scalar optimization, there is a necessary condition for local optima using the gradients of the objective function. We therefore implicitly assume all objective functions $f_\ell, \ell = 1,\ldots,k$, to be continuously differentiable on $\mathcal{X}$. Moreover, the following assumption allows for an easier treatment of tangent cones in the constrained case:

Assumption 1. *Either the problem is unconstrained, i.e., $\mathcal{X} = \mathbb{R}^n$ or the feasible set $\mathcal{X} \subseteq \mathbb{R}^n$ is compact and convex. All functions are defined on $\mathcal{X}$.*

The second case is a standard assumption in the MO literature for constrained problems [6,7]. Now let $\nabla f_\ell(\mathbf{x})$ denote the gradient of f_ℓ and $\mathbf{Df}(\mathbf{x}) \in \mathbb{R}^{k \times n}$ the Jacobian of $\mathbf{f}$ at $\mathbf{x} \in \mathcal{X}$.

Definition 1. *We call a vector $\mathbf{d} \in \mathcal{X} - \mathbf{x}$ a multi-descent direction for $\mathbf{f}$ in $\mathbf{x}$ if $\langle \nabla f_\ell(\mathbf{x}), \mathbf{d} \rangle < 0$ for all $\ell \in \{1,\ldots,k\}$, or equivalently if*

$$\max_{\ell=1,\ldots,k} \langle \nabla f_\ell(\mathbf{x}^*), \mathbf{d} \rangle < 0 \tag{1}$$

where $\langle \bullet, \bullet \rangle$ is the standard inner product on $\mathbb{R}^n$ and we consider $\mathcal{X} - \mathbf{x} = \mathcal{X}$ in the unconstrained case $\mathcal{X} = \mathbb{R}^n$.

A point $\mathbf{x}^* \in \mathcal{X}$ is called *critical* for (MOP) iff there is no descent direction $\mathbf{d} \in \mathcal{X} - \mathbf{x}^*$ with (1). As all Pareto optimal points are also critical (cf. [6,37] or [2] [Ch. 17]), it is viable to search for optimal points by calculating points from the superset $\mathcal{P}_{\text{crit}} \supseteq \mathcal{P}_S$ of critical points for (MOP). Similar to single objective optimization, using such a first order condition makes sense especially in combination with some global method or when exploring the structure of the critical set. We discuss promising approaches in Section 8. Note, that due the above restrictions, our method is not a general replacement for other methods, e.g., scalarization approaches, but rather an additional tool for situations where those are not applicable.

One intuitive way to approach the critical set is by iteratively performing descent steps. Fliege and Svaiter [7] propose several ways to compute suitable descent directions. The minimizer $\mathbf{d}^*$ of the following problem is known as the multiobjective steepest-descent direction.

$$\min_{\mathbf{d} \in \mathcal{X} - \mathbf{x}} \max_{\ell=1,\ldots,k} \langle \nabla f_\ell(\mathbf{x}), \mathbf{d} \rangle \quad \text{s.t.} \quad \|\mathbf{d}\| \le 1. \tag{P1}$$

Problem (P1) has an equivalent reformulation as

$$\min_{\mathbf{d} \in \mathcal{X} - \mathbf{x}} \beta \quad \text{s.t.} \quad \|\mathbf{d}\| \le 1 \quad \text{and} \quad \langle \nabla f_\ell(\mathbf{x}), \mathbf{d} \rangle \le \beta \; \forall \, \ell = 1,\ldots,k, \tag{P2}$$

which is a linear program, if $\mathcal{X}$ is defined by linear constraints and the maximum-norm $\|\bullet\| = \|\bullet\|_\infty$ is used [7]. We thus stick with this choice because it facilitates implementation, but note that other choices are possible (see for example [33]).

Motivated by the next theorem we can use the optimal value of either problem as a measure of criticality, i.e., as a multiobjective pendant for the gradient norm. As is standard in most multiobjective trust region works (cf. [29,30,33]), we flip the sign so that the values are non-negative.

Theorem 1. *For $\mathbf{x} \in \mathcal{X}$ let $\mathbf{d}^*(\mathbf{x})$ be the minimizer of* (P1) *and $\omega(\mathbf{x})$ be the negative optimal value, that is*

$$\omega(\mathbf{x}) := -\max_{\ell=1,\ldots,k} \langle \boldsymbol{\nabla} f_\ell(\mathbf{x}), \mathbf{d}^*(\mathbf{x}) \rangle.$$

Then the following statements hold:
1. *$\omega(\mathbf{x}) \geq 0$ for all $\mathbf{x} \in \mathcal{X}$.*
2. *The function $\omega \colon \mathbb{R}^n \to \mathbb{R}$ is continuous.*
3. *The following statements are equivalent:*
    (a) *The point $\mathbf{x} \in \mathcal{X}$ is not critical.*
    (b) *$\omega(\mathbf{x}) > 0$.*
    (c) *$\mathbf{d}^*(\mathbf{x}) \neq \mathbf{0}$.*

Consequently, the point $\mathbf{x}$ is critical iff $\omega(\mathbf{x}) = 0$.

Proof. For the unconstrained case all statements are proven in [7] (Lemma 3).
The first and the third statement hold true for $\mathcal{X}$ convex and compact by definition. The continuity of ω can be shown similarly as in [6], see Appendix A.1. □

With further conditions on $\mathbf{f}$ and $\mathcal{X}$ the criticality measure $\omega(\mathbf{x})$ is even Lipschitz continuous and subsequently uniformly and Cauchy continuous:

Theorem 2. *If $\boldsymbol{\nabla} f_\ell, \ell = 1, \ldots, k$, are Lipschitz continuous and Assumption 1 holds, then the map $\omega(\bullet)$ as defined in Theorem 1 is uniformly continuous.*

Proof. The proof for $\mathcal{X} = \mathbb{R}^n$ is given by Thomann [38]. A proof for the constrained case can be found in Appendix A.1 as to not clutter this introductory section. □

Together with Theorem 1 this hints at $\omega(\bullet)$ being a criticality measure as defined for scalar trust region methods in [36] ([Ch. 8]):

Definition 2. *We call $\pi \colon \mathbb{N}_0 \times \mathbb{R}^n \to \mathbb{R}$, a criticality measure for* (MOP) *if π is Cauchy continuous with respect to its second argument and if*

$$\lim_{t \to \infty} \pi(t, \mathbf{x}^{(t)}) = 0$$

implies that the sequence $\left\{\mathbf{x}^{(t)}\right\}$ asymptotically approaches a Pareto critical point.

3. Trust Region Ideas

Multiobjective trust region algorithms closely follow the design of scalar approaches (see [36] for an extensive treatment) and provide an alternative to (approximate) line-search algorithms (e.g., [7]). Consequently, the requirements and convergence proofs in [29,30,33] for the unconstrained multiobjective case are fairly similar to those in [36]. We will reexamine the core concepts to provide a clear understanding and point out the similarities to the single objective case.

The main idea is to iteratively compute multi-descent steps $\mathbf{s}^{(t)}$ in every iteration $t \in \mathbb{N}_0$. We could, for example, use the steepest descent direction given by (P1). This would require knowledge of the true objective gradients, which need not be available for objective functions with indices in I_{ex}. Hence, benevolent surrogate model functions

$$\mathbf{m}^{(t)} \colon \mathbb{R}^n \to \mathbb{R}^k, \quad \mathbf{x} \mapsto \mathbf{m}^{(t)}(\mathbf{x}) = \left[m_1^{(t)}(\mathbf{x}), \ldots, m_k^{(t)}(\mathbf{x})\right]^T,$$

are employed (at least for the expensive objectives).

The surrogate models are constructed to be sufficiently accurate within a trust region

$$B^{(t)} := B\left(\mathbf{x}^{(t)}; \Delta^{(t)}\right) = \left\{\mathbf{x} \in \mathcal{X} : \left\|\mathbf{x} - \mathbf{x}^{(t)}\right\| \leq \Delta^{(t)}\right\}, \quad \text{with } \|\bullet\| = \|\bullet\|_\infty, \quad (2)$$

around the current iterate $\mathbf{x}^{(t)}$. To be precise, the models are made fully linear as described in Section 4.1. This ensures that the model error and the model gradient error are uniformly bounded within the trust region.

The *model* steepest descent direction $\mathbf{d}_m^{(t)}$ can then computed as the optimizer of the surrogate problem

$$\omega_m^{(t)}\left(\mathbf{x}^{(t)}\right) := -\min_{\mathbf{d} \in \mathcal{X} - \mathbf{x}} \beta \quad \text{(Pm)}$$

s.t. $\|\mathbf{d}\| \leq 1$, and $\langle \nabla m_\ell^{(t)}(\mathbf{x}), \mathbf{d} \rangle \leq \beta \quad \forall \ell = 1, \ldots, k$.

Now let $\sigma^{(t)} > 0$ be a step size. The direction $\mathbf{d}_m^{(t)}$ need not be a descent direction for the true objectives $\mathbf{f}$ and the trial point $\mathbf{x}_+^{(t)} = \mathbf{x}^{(t)} + \sigma^{(t)} \mathbf{d}_m^{(t)}$ is only accepted if a measure $\rho^{(t)}$ of improvement and model quality surpasses a positive threshold ν_+. As in [30,33], we scalarize the multiobjective problems by defining

$$\Phi(\mathbf{x}) := \max_{\ell=1,\ldots,k} f_\ell(\mathbf{x}), \quad \Phi_m^{(t)}(\mathbf{x}) := \max_{\ell=1,\ldots,k} m_\ell^{(t)}(\mathbf{x}).$$

Whenever $\Phi(\mathbf{x}^{(t)}) - \Phi(\mathbf{x}_+^{(t)}) > 0$, there is a reduction in at least one objective function of $\mathbf{f}$ because of

$$0 < \Phi(\mathbf{x}^{(t)}) - \Phi(\mathbf{x}_+^{(t)}) = f_\ell(\mathbf{x}^{(t)}) - f_q(\mathbf{x}_+^{(t)}) \overset{\text{df.}}{\leq} f_\ell(\mathbf{x}^{(t)}) - f_\ell(\mathbf{x}_+^{(t)}),$$

where we denoted by ℓ the (not necessarily unique) maximizing index in $\Phi(\mathbf{x}^{(t)})$ and by q the (neither necessarily unique) maximizing index in $\Phi(\mathbf{x}_+^{(t)})$. (The abbreviation "df." above the inequality symbol stands for "(by) definition" and is used throughout this document when appropriate.) Of course, the same property holds for $\Phi_m^{(t)}(\bullet)$ and $\mathbf{m}^{(t)}$.

Thus, the step size $\sigma^{(t)} > 0$ is chosen so that the step $\mathbf{s}^{(t)} = \sigma^{(t)} \mathbf{d}_m^{(t)}$ satisfies both $\mathbf{x}^{(t)} + \mathbf{s}^{(t)} \in B^{(t)}$ and a "sufficient decrease condition" of the form

$$\Phi_m^{(t)}\left(\mathbf{x}^{(t)}\right) - \Phi_m^{(t)}\left(\mathbf{x}^{(t)} + \mathbf{s}^{(t)}\right) \geq \kappa^{sd} \omega\left(\mathbf{x}^{(t)}\right) \min\left\{C \cdot \omega\left(\mathbf{x}^{(t)}\right), 1, \Delta^{(t)}\right\} \geq 0,$$

with constants $\kappa^{sd} \in (0,1)$ and $C > 0$, see Section 5. Such a condition is also required in the scalar case [35,36] and essential for the convergence proof in Section 6, where we show $\lim_{t \to \infty} \omega\left(\mathbf{x}^{(t)}\right) = 0$.

Due to the decrease condition, the denominator in the ratio of actual versus predicted reduction

$$\rho^{(t)} = \begin{cases} \dfrac{\Phi(\mathbf{x}^{(t)}) - \Phi(\mathbf{x}_+^{(t)})}{\Phi_m^{(t)}(\mathbf{x}^{(t)}) - \Phi_m^{(t)}(\mathbf{x}_+^{(t)})} & \text{if } \mathbf{x}^{(t)} \neq \mathbf{x}_+^{(t)}, \\ 0 & \text{if } \mathbf{x}^{(t)} = \mathbf{x}_+^{(t)} \Leftrightarrow \mathbf{s}^{(t)} = 0, \end{cases} \quad (3)$$

is non-negative. A positive $\rho^{(t)}$ implies a decrease in at least one objective f_ℓ, so we accept $\mathbf{x}_+^{(t)}$ as the next iterate if $\rho^{(t)} > \nu_+ > 0$. If $\rho^{(t)}$ is sufficiently large, say $\rho^{(t)} \geq \nu_{++} > \nu_+ > 0$, the next trust region might have a larger radius $\Delta^{(t+1)} \geq \Delta^{(t)}$. If in contrast $\rho < \nu_{++}$, the next trust region radius should be smaller and the surrogates improved.

This encompasses the case $\mathbf{s}^{(t)} = \mathbf{0}$, when the iterate $\mathbf{x}^{(t)}$ is critical for

$$\min_{\mathbf{x} \in B^{(t)}} \mathbf{m}^{(t)}(\mathbf{x}) \in \mathbb{R}^k. \tag{MOPm}$$

Roughly speaking, we suppose that $\mathbf{x}^{(t)}$ is near a critical point for the original problem (MOP) if $\mathbf{m}^{(t)}$ is sufficiently accurate. If we truly are near a critical point, then the trust region radius will approach 0. For further details concerning the acceptance ratio $\rho^{(t)}$, see [33] (Section 2.2).

Remark 1. *We can modify $\rho^{(t)}$ in (3) to obtain a descent in all objectives, i.e., if $\mathbf{x}^{(t)} \neq \mathbf{x}_+^{(t)}$ we test*

$$\rho^{(t)} = \frac{f_\ell(\mathbf{x}^{(t)}) - f_\ell(\mathbf{x}_+^{(t)})}{m_\ell^{(t)}(\mathbf{x}^{(t)}) - m_\ell^{(t)}(\mathbf{x}_+^{(t)})} > \nu_+ \text{ for all } \ell = 1, \ldots, k. \text{ This is the strict acceptance test.}$$

4. Surrogate Models and the Final Algorithm

Until now, we have not discussed the actual choice of surrogate models used for $\mathbf{m}^{(t)}$. As is shown in Section 5, the models should be twice continuously differentiable with uniformly bounded hessians. To prove convergence of our algorithm, we have to impose further requirements on the (uniform) approximation qualities of the surrogates $\mathbf{m}^{(t)}$. We can meet these requirements using so-called fully linear models. Moreover, fully linear models intrinsically allow for modifications of the basic trust region method that are aimed at reducing the total number of expensive objective evaluations. Finally, we briefly recapitulate how radial basis functions and multivariate Lagrange polynomials can be made fully linear.

Remark 2. *Although the trust region framework is suitable for general convexly constrained compact sets, we will discuss the construction of fully linear polynomial and RBF models for unconstrained and box-constrained problems only.*

In the constrained case, we treat the constraints as unrelaxable, *that is, we do not allow for evaluations of the true objectives outside $\mathcal{X}$, see the definition of $B^{(t)} \subseteq \mathcal{X}$ in (2). We also ensure to only select training data in $\mathcal{X}$ during the construction of surrogate models.*

To the best of our knowledge there are no construction procedures for the above model types for general (unrelaxable) constraints. A discussion of how some model based algorithms deal with constraints can be found in [28] (Section 7). The issue is also addressed in [27] (Ch. 13). If the constraints are treated as relaxable, then techniques from [39] (Ch. 15) might be applicable such as merit functions or filter methods, but this is left for future research.

4.1. Fully Linear Models

We start by reciting the abstract definition of full linearity as given in [27,35]:

Definition 3. *Let $\Delta^{ub} > 0$ be given and let $f \colon \mathbb{R} \to \mathbb{R}$ be a function that is continuously differentiable in an open domain containing $\mathcal{X}$ and has a Lipschitz continuous gradient on $\mathcal{X}$. A set of model functions $\mathcal{M} = \{m \colon \mathbb{R}^n \to \mathbb{R}\} \subseteq C^1(\mathbb{R}^n, \mathbb{R})$ is called a fully linear class of models w.r.t. f if the following hold:*

1. *There are positive constants $\epsilon, \dot{\epsilon}$ and L_m such that for any given $\Delta \in (0, \Delta^{ub})$ and for any $\mathbf{x} \in \mathcal{X}$ there is a model function $m \in \mathcal{M}$ with Lipschitz continuous gradient and corresponding Lipschitz constant bounded by L_m and such that*
   - *the error between the gradient of the model and the gradient of the function satisfies*

$$\|\nabla f(\xi) - \nabla m(\xi)\| \leq \dot{\epsilon}\Delta, \quad \forall \xi \in B(\mathbf{x}; \Delta),$$

   - *the error between the model and the function satisfies*

$$|f(\xi) - m(\xi)| \leq \epsilon\Delta^2, \quad \forall \xi \in B(\mathbf{x}; \Delta).$$

2. For this class $\mathcal{M}$ there exists "model-improvement" algorithm that, in a finite, uniformly bounded (w.r.t. $\mathbf{x}$ and Δ) number of steps, can:
   - either establish that a given model $m \in \mathcal{M}$ is fully linear on $B(\mathbf{x}; \Delta)$, i.e., it satisfies the error bounds in 1,
   - or find a model $\tilde{m}$ that is fully linear on $B(\mathbf{x}; \Delta)$.

Remark 3. *In the unconstrained case, the requirements in Definition 3 can be relaxed a bit, at least when using the strict acceptance test with $\mathbf{f}(\mathbf{x}^{(T)}) \leq \mathbf{f}(\mathbf{x}^{(t)})$ for all $T \geq t \geq 0$. We can then restrict ourselves to the set*

$$\mathcal{X}' := \bigcup_{\mathbf{x} \in L(\mathbf{x}^{(0)})} B\left(\mathbf{x}; \Delta^{\mathrm{ub}}\right), \quad \text{where } L(\mathbf{x}^{(0)}) := \left\{\mathbf{x} \in \mathbb{R}^n : \mathbf{f}(\mathbf{x}) \leq \mathbf{f}(\mathbf{x}^{(0)})\right\}.$$

For the convergence analysis in Section 6, we further cite [27] ([Lemma 10.25]). The lemma states that a fully linear model is also fully linear in enlarged regions if the error constants are chosen appropriately:

Lemma 1. *For $\mathbf{x} \in \mathcal{X}$ and $\Delta \leq \Delta^{\mathrm{ub}}$ consider a function f and a fully-linear model m as in Definition 3 with constants $\epsilon, \dot{\epsilon}, L_m > 0$. Let $L_f > 0$ be a Lipschitz constant of ∇f. Assume w.l.o.g. that*

$$L_m + L_f \leq \epsilon \quad \text{and} \quad \frac{\dot{\epsilon}}{2} \leq \epsilon.$$

Then m is fully linear on $B(\mathbf{x}; \tilde{\Delta})$ for any $\tilde{\Delta} \in [\Delta, \Delta^{\mathrm{ub}}]$ with respect to the same constants $\epsilon, \dot{\epsilon}, L_m$.

Finally, we generalize the definition to a *vector* of real valued functions.

Definition 4. *Let $\Delta^{\mathrm{ub}} > 0$ be given and let $\mathbf{f} = [f_1, \ldots, f_k]^T$ be a vector of functions satisfying the requirements of Definition 3. Then $\mathbf{m} = [m_1, \ldots, m_k]^T$, with $m_\ell : \mathbb{R}^n \to \mathbb{R}, \ell \in \{1, \ldots, k\}$, belongs to a collection of fully linear classes w.r.t. $\mathbf{f}$ if for each ℓ the function m_ℓ belongs to a fully linear class w.r.t. f_ℓ, with error constants ϵ_ℓ and $\dot{\epsilon}_\ell$.*

The model-improvement algorithm of $\mathbf{m}$ consists in applying the individual improvement algorithms for all indices $\ell \in \{1, \ldots, k\}$ and $\mathbf{m}$ is deemed fully linear iff all m_ℓ are fully linear with constants ϵ_ℓ and $\dot{\epsilon}_\ell$.

Definition 4 is stated in a way that allows for different model types for the different objectives. Most importantly, we can use $m_\ell = f_\ell$ and $\nabla m_\ell = \nabla f_\ell$ if the objective is cheap, i.e., $\ell \in I_{\text{cheap}}$, and if f_ℓ not only has Lipschitz gradients but also has a Hessian that is uniformly bounded in terms of its norm. The latter requirement is formalized in Assumption 3 and needed for the convergence analysis.

Algorithm Modifications

With Definitions 3 and 4 we have formalized our assumption that the surrogates become more accurate when we decrease the trust region radius. This motivates the following modifications to the basic procedure:

- "Relaxing" the (finite) surrogate construction process to try for a possible descent even if the surrogates are not fully linear.
- A criticality test depending on $\omega_{\mathbf{m}}^{(t)}\left(\mathbf{x}^{(t)}\right)$. If this value is very small at the current iterate, then $\mathbf{x}^{(t)}$ could lie near a Pareto critical point. With the criticality test and Algorithm 1 we ensure that the next model is fully linear and the trust region is not too large. This allows for a more accurate criticality measure and descent step calculation.

- A trust region update that also takes into consideration $\omega_m^{(t)}\left(\mathbf{x}^{(t)}\right)$. The radius should be enlarged if we have a large acceptance ratio $\rho^{(t)}$ and the $\Delta^{(t)}$ is small as measured against $\beta\omega_m^{(t)}\left(\mathbf{x}^{(t)}\right)$ for a constant $\beta > 0$.

These changes are implemented in Algorithm 2. For more detailed explanations we refer to [27] (Ch. 10).

Algorithm 1: Criticality Routine.

Configuration: A backtracking constant $\alpha \in (0,1)$, $\mu > 0$ from Algorithm 2;
Input: Current trust region radius $\Delta^{(t)}$, current models $\mathbf{m}^{(t)}$;
Output: Fully linear models $\mathbf{m}^{(t)}$ and the (possibly shrunken) radius $\Delta^{(t)}$;
Set $\Delta_0 \leftarrow \Delta^{(t)}$;
for $j = 1, 2, \ldots$ do
    Set radius: $\Delta^{(t)} \leftarrow \alpha^{j-1}\Delta_0$;
    Make models $\mathbf{m}^{(t)}$ fully linear on $B^{(t)}$;   /* can change $\omega_m^{(t)}\left(\mathbf{x}^{(t)}\right)$ */
    if $\Delta^{(t)} \leq \mu\omega_m^{(t)}\left(\mathbf{x}^{(t)}\right)$ then
        Break;
    end
end

From Algorithm 2 we see that we can classify the iterations based on $\rho^{(t)}$ as in Definition 5.

Definition 5. *For given constants $0 \leq \nu_+ \leq \nu_{++} < 1, \nu_{++} \neq 0$, we call the iteration with index $t \in \mathbb{N}_0$ of Algorithm* 2.

- …successful *if $\rho^{(t)} \geq \nu_{++}$. The set of successful indices is $\mathcal{S} = \{t \in \mathbb{N}_0 : \rho^{(t)} \geq \nu_{++}\} \subseteq \mathbb{N}_0$. The trial point is accepted and the trust region radius can be increased.*
- …model-improving *if $\rho^{(t)} < \nu_{++}$ and the models $\mathbf{m}^{(t)} = [m_1^{(t)}, \ldots, m_k^{(t)}]^T$ are not fully linear. In these iterations the trial point is rejected and the trust region radius is not changed.*
- …acceptable *if $\nu_{++} > \rho^{(t)} \geq \nu_+$ and the models $\mathbf{m}^{(t)}$ are fully linear. If $\nu_{++} = \nu_+ \in (0,1)$, then there are no acceptable indices. The trial point is accepted but the trust region radius is decreased.*
- …inacceptable *otherwise, i.e., if $\rho^{(t)} < \nu_{++}$ and $\mathbf{m}^{(t)}$ are fully linear. The trial point is rejected and the radius decreased.*

Algorithm 2: General Trust Region Method (TRM) for (MOP).

Configuration: Criticality parameters $\varepsilon_{\text{crit}} > 0$ and $\mu > \beta > 0$, acceptance parameters $1 > \nu_{++} \geq \nu_{+} \geq 0, \nu_{++} \neq 0$, update factors $\gamma_{\uparrow} \geq 1 > \gamma_{\downarrow} \geq \gamma_{\downdownarrows} > 0$ and $\Delta^{\text{ub}} > 0$;

Input: The initial site $\mathbf{x}^{(0)} \in \mathbb{R}^n$;

for $t = 0, 1, \ldots$ **do**

    if $t > 0$ *and iteration* $(t-1)$ *was model-improving (cf. Definition 5)* **then**

        Perform at least one improvement step on $\mathbf{m}^{(t-1)}$ and then let

        $\mathbf{m}^{(t)} \leftarrow \mathbf{m}^{(t-1)}$;

    else

        Construct surrogate models $\mathbf{m}^{(t)}$ on $B^{(t)}$;

    end

    /* Criticality Step: */

    if $\omega_{\mathbf{m}}^{(t)}\left(\mathbf{x}^{(t)}\right) < \varepsilon_{\text{crit}}$ **and** ($\mathbf{m}^{(t)}$ not fully linear or $\Delta^{(t)} > \mu \omega_{\mathbf{m}}^{(t)}\left(\mathbf{x}^{(t)}\right)$) **then**

        Set $\Delta_*^{(t)} \leftarrow \Delta^{(t)}$;

        Call Algorithm 1 so that $\mathbf{m}^{(t)}$ is fully linear on $B^{(t)}$ with

        $\Delta^{(t)} \in \left(0, \mu \omega_{\mathbf{m}}^{(t)}\left(\mathbf{x}^{(t)}\right)\right]$;

        Then set $\Delta^{(t)} \leftarrow \min\left\{\max\left\{\Delta^{(t)}, \beta \omega_{\mathbf{m}}^{(t)}\left(\mathbf{x}^{(t)}\right)\right\}, \Delta_*^{(t)}\right\}$;

    end

    Compute a suitable descent step $\mathbf{s}^{(t)}$;

    Set $\mathbf{x}_+^{(t)} \leftarrow \mathbf{x}^{(t)} + \mathbf{s}^{(t)}$, evaluate $\mathbf{f}(\mathbf{x}_+^{(t)})$ and compute $\rho^{(t)}$ with (3);

    Perform the following updates:

$$\mathbf{x}^{(t+1)} \leftarrow \begin{cases} \mathbf{x}^{(t)} & \text{if } \rho^{(t)} < \nu_+ \text{ or } \nu_+ \leq \rho^{(t)} < \nu_{++} \text{ \& } \mathbf{m}^{(t)} \text{ is not fully linear,} \\ \mathbf{x}_+^{(t)} & \text{if } \rho^{(t)} \geq \nu_{++} \text{ or } \nu_+ \leq \rho^{(t)} < \nu_{++} \text{ \& } \mathbf{m}^{(t)} \text{ is fully linear,} \end{cases}$$

$\Delta^{(t+1)} \leftarrow \Delta_+$, where

$$\Delta_+ \begin{cases} = \Delta^{(t)} & \text{if } \rho^{(t)} < \nu_{++} \text{ \& } \mathbf{m}^{(t)} \text{ is not fully linear,} \\ \in [\gamma_{\downdownarrows}\Delta^{(t)}, \gamma_{\downarrow}\Delta^{(t)}] & \text{if } \rho^{(t)} < \nu_{++} \text{ \& } \mathbf{m}^{(t)} \text{ is fully linear,} \\ \in [\Delta^{(t)}, \min\{\gamma_{\uparrow}\Delta^{(t)}, \Delta^{\text{ub}}\}] & \text{if } \nu_{++} \leq \rho^{(t)} \text{ and } \Delta^{(t)} \geq \beta \omega_{\mathbf{m}}^{(t)}\left(\mathbf{x}^{(t)}\right), \\ = \min\{\gamma_{\uparrow}\Delta^{(t)}, \Delta^{\text{ub}}\} & \text{if } \nu_{++} \leq \rho^{(t)} \text{ and } \Delta^{(t)} < \beta \omega_{\mathbf{m}}^{(t)}\left(\mathbf{x}^{(t)}\right). \end{cases}$$

end

4.2. Fully Linear Lagrange Polynomials

Quadratic Taylor polynomial models are used very frequently. As explained in [27] we can alternatively use multivariate interpolating Lagrange polynomial models when derivative information is not available. We will consider first and second degree Lagrange models. Even though the latter require $\mathcal{O}(n^2)$ function evaluations they are still cheaper than second degree finite difference models. For this reason, these models are also used in [33,38].

To construct an interpolating polynomial model we have to provide p data sites, where p is the dimension of the space Π_n^d of real-valued n-variate polynomials with degree d. For $d = 1$ we have $p = n + 1$ and for $d = 2$ it is $p = \frac{(n+1)(n+2)}{2}$. If $n \geq 2$, the Mairhuber–Curtis theorem [40] applies and the data sites must form a so-called *poised* set in $\mathcal{X}$. The set $\Xi = \{\xi_1, \ldots, \xi_p\} \subset \mathbb{R}^n$ is poised if for any basis $\{\psi_i\}_i$ of Π_n^d the matrix $\mathbf{M}_\psi := [\psi_i(\xi_j)]_{1 \leq i,j \leq p}$ is non-singular. Then for any function $f \colon \mathbb{R}^n \to \mathbb{R}$ there is a unique interpolating polynomial $m(\mathbf{x}) = \sum_{i=1}^p \lambda_i \psi_i(\mathbf{x})$ with $m(\xi_j) = f(\xi_j)$ for all $j = 1, \ldots, p$.

Given a poised set Ξ the associated Lagrange basis $\{l_i\}_i$ of Π_n^d is defined by $l_i(\xi_j) = \delta_{i,j}$. The model coefficients then simply are the data values, i.e., $\lambda_i = f(\xi_i)$.

Same as in [38], we implement Algorithm 6.2 from [27] to ensure poisedness. It selects training sites Ξ from the current (slightly enlarged) trust region of radius $\theta_1 \Delta^{(t)}, \theta_1 \geq 1$, and calculates the associated lagrange basis. We can then separately evaluate the true objectives f_ℓ on Ξ to easily build the surrogates $m_\ell^{(t)}$, $\ell \in \{1, \ldots, k\}$. Our implementation always includes $\xi_1 = x^{(t)}$ and tries to select points from a database of prior evaluations first.

We employ an additional algorithm (Algorithm 6.3 in [27]) to ensure that the set Ξ is even Λ-poised, see [27] ([Definition 3.6]). The procedure is still finite and ensures the models are actually *fully linear*. The quality of the surrogate models can be improved by choosing a small algorithm parameter $\Lambda > 1$. Our implementation tries again to recycle points from a database. Different to before, interpolation at $x^{(t)}$ can no longer be guaranteed. This second step can also be omitted first and then used as a model-improvement step in a subsequent iteration.

4.3. Fully Linear Radial Basis Function Models

The main drawback of quadratic Lagrange models is that we still need $\mathcal{O}(n^2)$ function evaluations in each iteration of Algorithm 2. A possible fix is to use under-determined regression polynomials instead [27,31,41]. Motivated by the findings in [34] we chose so-called Radial Basis Function (RBF) models as an alternative. RBF are well-known for their approximation capabilities on irregular data [40]. In our implementation they have the form

$$m(x) = \sum_{i=1}^{N} c_i \varphi(\|x - \xi_i\|_2) + \pi(x), \text{ with } \pi = \sum_{j=1}^{n+1} \lambda_j \psi_j \in \Pi_n^1 \text{ and } N \geq n+1, \quad (4)$$

which conforms to the construction by Wild et al. [34]. Here, φ is a function from a domain containing $\mathbb{R}_{\geq 0}$ to $\mathbb{R}$. For a fixed φ the mapping $\varphi(\|\bullet\|)$ from $\mathbb{R}^n \to \mathbb{R}$ is radially symmetric with respect to its argument and the mapping $(x, \xi) \mapsto \varphi(\|x - \xi\|_2)$ is called a *kernel*.

We will describe the procedure only briefly and refer to [34,42] and the dissertation [41] for more details. To conform to the algorithmic framework the models must have Hessians of uniformly bounded norm. Additionally, we want them to be twice differentiable due to the following, very general result:

Theorem 3 (Th 4.1 in [41]). *Suppose that f and m are continuously differentiable in an open domain containing $B^{(t)}$ and that ∇f and ∇m are Lipschitz in $B^{(t)}$. Further suppose that m interpolates f on a Λ-poised set $\Xi = \{\xi_1, \ldots, \xi_{n+1}\}$ (for a fixed $\Lambda < \infty$). Then m is fully linear for f as in Definition 3.*

The Λ-poised set is determined using pivotal algorithms from [34,41] in an enlarged trust region of radius $\theta_1 \Delta^{(t)}, \theta_1 \geq 1$. If we restrict ourselves to functions φ that are conditionally positive definite (c.p.d.—see [34] for the definition) of order $D \leq 2$, then for any $f \colon \mathbb{R}^n \to \mathbb{R}$ an interpolating model m of form (4) is uniquely determined by solving a linear equation system. If further φ is either twice continuously differentiable on an open domain containing $[0, \infty)$ with $\varphi'(0) = 0$, then m from (4) is twice continuously differentiable and has Lipschitz gradients exactly if its Hessian stays bounded. This is the case for all φ we consider (see Table 1). The hessian norm is determined by the magnitudes of the coefficients c_i and by $|\varphi'(r)/r|$ and $|\varphi''(r)|$.

Table 1. Some radial functions $\varphi: \mathbb{R}_{\geq 0} \to \mathbb{R}$ that are c.p.d. of order $D \leq 2$, cf. [34].

Name	$\varphi(r)$	c.p.d. order D
Cubic	r^3	2
Multiquadric	$-\sqrt{1+(\alpha r)^2}, \alpha > 0$	1
Gaussian	$\exp(-(\alpha r)^2), \alpha > 0$	0

If there are exactly $N = n+1$ points from a poised set Ξ, then the coefficients c_i vanish and the model (4) is a linear polynomial. The values $|\varphi'(r)/r|$ and $|\varphi''(r)|$ are bounded because of $r \in [0, \Delta^{ub}]$ and $\varphi'(0) = 0$. To exploit the nonlinear modeling capabilities of RBF and perform exploration, there is a procedure in [34] to select additional (database) points from within a region of maximum radius $\theta_2 \Delta^{ub}$, $\theta_2 \geq \theta_1 \geq 1$, so that the values $|c_i|$ stay bounded. Modifications for box constraints can be found in [41] ([Sec. 6.3.1]) and [43].

Table 1 shows the RBF we are using and of which order they are. Both the Gaussian and the Multiquadric allow for fine-tuning with a shape parameter $\alpha > 0$. This can potentially improve the conditioning of the interpolation system.

Figure 1b illustrates the effect of the shape parameter. As can be seen, the radial functions become narrower for larger shape parameters. Hence, we do not only use a constant shape parameter $\alpha = 1$ like [34] do, but we also use an α that is (within lower and upper bounds) inversely proportional to $\Delta^{(t)}$.

Figure 1a shows interpolation of a nonlinear function by a surrogate based on the Multiquadric with a linear tail.

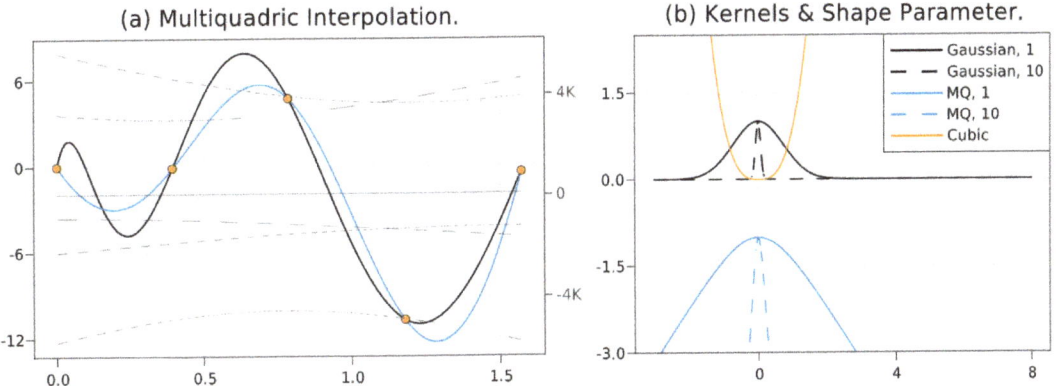

Figure 1. (a) Interpolation of a nonlinear function (black) by a Multiquadric surrogate (blue) based on 5 discrete training points (orange). Dashed lines show the kernels and the polynomial tail. (b) Different kernels in 1D with varying shape parameter (1 or 10), see also Table 1.

5. Descent Steps

In this section we introduce some possible steps $s^{(t)}$ to use in Algorithm 2. We begin by defining the best step along the steepest descent direction as given by (Pm). Subsequently, backtracking variants are defined that use a multiobjective variant of Armijo's rule.

5.1. Pareto–Cauchy Step

Both the *Pareto–Cauchy point* as well as a backtracking variant, the *modified Pareto–Cauchy point*, are points along the descent direction $d_m^{(t)}$ within $B^{(t)}$ so that a sufficient decrease measured by $\Phi_m^{(t)}(\bullet)$ and $\omega_m^{(t)}(\bullet)$ is achieved. Under mild assumptions we can then derive a decrease in terms of $\omega(\bullet)$.

Definition 6. For $t \in \mathbb{N}_0$ let $\mathbf{d}_m^{(t)}$ be a minimizer for (Pm). The best attainable trial point $\mathbf{x}_{PC}^{(t)}$ along $\mathbf{d}_m^{(t)}$ is called the *Pareto–Cauchy point* and given by

$$\mathbf{x}_{PC}^{(t)} := \mathbf{x}^{(t)} + \sigma^{(t)} \cdot \mathbf{d}_m^{(t)},$$

$$\sigma^{(t)} = \arg\min_{0 \leq \sigma} \Phi_m^{(t)}\left(\mathbf{x}^{(t)} + \sigma \cdot \mathbf{d}_m^{(t)}\right) \quad \text{s.t. } \mathbf{x}_{PC}^{(t)} \in B^{(t)}. \tag{5}$$

Let $\sigma^{(t)}$ be the minimizer in (5). We call $\mathbf{s}_{PC}^{(t)} := \sigma^{(t)} \mathbf{d}_m^{(t)}$ the *Pareto–Cauchy step*.

If we make the following standard assumption, then the Pareto–Cauchy point allows for a lower bound on the improvement in terms of $\Phi_m^{(t)}$.

Assumption 2. For all $t \in \mathbb{N}_0$ the surrogates $\mathbf{m}^{(t)}(\mathbf{x}) = [m_1^{(t)}(\mathbf{x}), \ldots, m_k^{(t)}(\mathbf{x})]^T$ are twice continuously differentiable on an open set containing $\mathcal{X}$. Denote by $\mathbf{H}m_\ell^{(t)}(\mathbf{x})$ the Hessian of $m_\ell^{(t)}$ for $\ell = 1, \ldots, k$.

Theorem 4. *If Assumptions 1 and 2 are satisfied, then for any iterate $\mathbf{x}^{(t)}$ the Pareto–Cauchy point $\mathbf{x}_{PC}^{(t)}$ satisfies*

$$\Phi_m^{(t)}(\mathbf{x}^{(t)}) - \Phi_m^{(t)}(\mathbf{x}_{PC}^{(t)}) \geq \frac{1}{2} \omega_m^{(t)}(\mathbf{x}^{(t)}) \cdot \min\left\{ \frac{\omega_m^{(t)}(\mathbf{x}^{(t)})}{c H_m^{(t)}}, \Delta^{(t)}, 1 \right\}, \tag{6}$$

where

$$H_m^{(t)} = \max_{\ell=1,\ldots,k} \max_{\mathbf{x} \in B^{(t)}} \left\| \mathbf{H}m_\ell^{(t)}(\mathbf{x}) \right\|_F \tag{7}$$

and the constant $c > 0$ relates the trust region norm $\|\bullet\|$ to the Euclidean norm $\|\bullet\|_2$ via

$$\|\mathbf{x}\|_2 \leq \sqrt{c} \|\mathbf{x}\| \quad \forall \mathbf{x} \in \mathbb{R}^n. \tag{8}$$

If $\|\bullet\| = \|\bullet\|_\infty$ is used, then c can be chosen as $c = k$. The proof for Theorem 4 is provided after the next auxiliary lemma.

Lemma 2. *Under Assumptions 1 and 2, let $\mathbf{d}$ be a non-increasing direction at $\mathbf{x}^{(t)} \in \mathbb{R}^n$ for $\mathbf{m}^{(t)}$, i.e.,*

$$\left\langle \nabla m_\ell^{(t)}(\mathbf{x}^{(t)}), \mathbf{d} \right\rangle \leq 0 \quad \forall \ell = 1, \ldots, k.$$

Let $q \in \{1, \ldots, k\}$ be any objective index and $\bar{\sigma} \geq \min\{\Delta^{(t)}, \|\mathbf{d}\|\}$. Then it holds that

$$m_q^{(t)}(\mathbf{x}^{(t)}) - \min_{0 < \sigma < \bar{\sigma}} m_q^{(t)}\left(\mathbf{x}^{(t)} + \sigma \frac{\mathbf{d}}{\|\mathbf{d}\|}\right) \geq \frac{w}{2} \min\left\{ \frac{w}{\|\mathbf{d}\|^2 c H_m^{(t)}}, \frac{\Delta^{(t)}}{\|\mathbf{d}\|}, 1 \right\},$$

where we have used the shorthand notation

$$w = -\max_{\ell=1,\ldots,k} \left\langle \nabla m_\ell^{(t)}(\mathbf{x}^{(t)}), \mathbf{d} \right\rangle \geq 0.$$

Lemma 2 states that a minimizer along any non-increasing direction $\mathbf{d}$ achieves a minimum reduction w.r.t. $\Phi_m^{(t)}$. Similar results can be found in in [30] or [33]. But since we do not use polynomial surrogates $\mathbf{m}^{(t)}$, we have to employ the multivariate version of Taylor's theorem to make the proof work. We can do this because according to Assumption 2, the functions $m_q^{(t)}, q \in \{1, \ldots, k\}$ are twice continuously differentiable in an open domain containing $\mathcal{X}$. Moreover, Assumption 1 ensures that the function is defined on the line from χ to $\mathbf{x}$. As shown in [44] (Ch. 3) a first degree expansion at $\mathbf{x} \in B(\chi, \Delta)$ around $\chi \in \mathcal{X}$ then leads to

$$m_q^{(t)}(\mathbf{x}) = m_q(\chi) + \nabla m_q^{(t)}(\chi)^T \mathbf{h} + \frac{1}{2}\mathbf{h}^T H m_q^{(t)}(\xi_q)\mathbf{h}, \qquad \text{with } \mathbf{h} = (\mathbf{x}-\chi), \quad (9)$$

for some $\xi_q \in \{\mathbf{x} + \theta(\chi - \mathbf{x}) : \theta \in [0,1]\}$, for all $q = 1, \ldots, k$.

Proof of Lemma 2. Let the requirements of Lemma 2 hold and let $\mathbf{d}$ be a non-increasing direction for $\mathbf{m}^{(t)}$. Then:

$$m_q^{(t)}(\mathbf{x}^{(t)}) - \min_{0<\sigma\leq\bar{\sigma}} m_q^{(t)}\left(\mathbf{x}^{(t)} + \sigma \frac{\mathbf{d}}{\|\mathbf{d}\|}\right) = \max_{0\leq\sigma\leq\bar{\sigma}}\left\{m_q^{(t)}(\mathbf{x}^{(t)}) - m_q^{(t)}\left(\mathbf{x}^{(t)} + \sigma \frac{\mathbf{d}}{\|\mathbf{d}\|}\right)\right\}$$

$$\stackrel{(9)}{=} \max_{0\leq\sigma\leq\bar{\sigma}}\left\{m_q^{(t)}(\mathbf{x}^{(t)}) - \left(m_q^{(t)}(\mathbf{x}^{(t)}) + \frac{\sigma}{\|\mathbf{d}\|}\langle\nabla m_q^{(t)}(\mathbf{x}^{(t)}),\mathbf{d}\rangle + \frac{\sigma^2}{2\|\mathbf{d}\|^2}\langle\mathbf{d}, Hm_q^{(t)}(\xi_q)\mathbf{d}\rangle\right)\right\}$$

$$\geq \max_{0\leq\sigma\leq\bar{\sigma}}\left\{-\frac{\sigma}{\|\mathbf{d}\|}\max_{j=1,\ldots,k}\langle\nabla m_j^{(t)}(\mathbf{x}^{(t)}),\mathbf{d}\rangle - \frac{\sigma^2}{2\|\mathbf{d}\|^2}\langle\mathbf{d}, Hm_q^{(t)}(\xi_q)\mathbf{d}\rangle\right\}.$$

We use the shorthand $w = -\max_j\langle\nabla m_j^{(t)}(\mathbf{x}^{(t)}),\mathbf{d}\rangle$ and the Cauchy–Schwartz inequality to get

$$\ldots \geq \max_{0\leq\sigma\leq\bar{\sigma}}\left\{\frac{\sigma}{\|\mathbf{d}\|}w - \frac{\sigma^2}{2\|\mathbf{d}\|^2}\|\mathbf{d}\|_2^2\|Hm_q^{(t)}(\xi)\|_F\right\} \stackrel{(8),(7)}{\geq} \max_{0\leq\sigma\leq\bar{\sigma}}\left\{\frac{\sigma}{\|\mathbf{d}\|}w - \frac{\sigma^2}{2}cH_m^{(t)}\right\}.$$

The RHS is concave and we can thus easily determine the global maximizer σ^*. Similar to [30] (Lemma 4.1) we find

$$m_q^{(t)}(\mathbf{x}^{(t)}) - \min_{0<\sigma<\bar{\sigma}} m_q^{(t)}\left(\mathbf{x}^{(t)} + \sigma\frac{\mathbf{d}}{\|\mathbf{d}\|}\right) \geq \frac{w}{2}\min\left\{\frac{w}{\|\mathbf{d}\|^2 cH_m^{(t)}}, \frac{\Delta^{(t)}}{\|\mathbf{d}\|}, 1\right\},$$

where we have additionally used $\bar{\sigma} \geq \min\{\Delta^{(t)}, 1\}$. □

Proof of Theorem 4. If $\mathbf{x}^{(t)}$ is Pareto critical for (MOPm), then $\mathbf{d}_m^{(t)} = 0$ and $\omega_m^{(t)}(\mathbf{x}^{(t)}) = 0$ and the inequality holds trivially.

Else, let the indices $\ell, q \in \{1, \ldots, k\}$ be such that

$$\Phi_m^{(t)}(\mathbf{x}^{(t)}) - \Phi_m^{(t)}(\mathbf{x}_{\text{PC}}^{(t)}) = m_\ell^{(t)}(\mathbf{x}^{(t)}) - m_q^{(t)}(\mathbf{x}_{\text{PC}}^{(t)}) \geq m_q(\mathbf{x}^{(t)}) - m_q(\mathbf{x}_{\text{PC}}^{(t)})$$

and define

$$\bar{\sigma} := \begin{cases} \min\{\Delta^{(t)}, \|\mathbf{d}_m^{(t)}\|\} & \text{if } \|\mathbf{d}_m^{(t)}\| < 1 \text{ or } \Delta^{(t)} \leq 1, \\ \Delta^{(t)} & \text{else.} \end{cases} \quad (10)$$

Then clearly $\bar{\sigma} \geq \min\{\Delta^{(t)}, \|\mathbf{d}_m^{(t)}\|\}$ and for the Pareto–Cauchy point we have

$$m_q^{(t)}\left(\mathbf{x}_{\text{PC}}^{(t)}\right) = \min_{0\leq\sigma\leq\bar{\sigma}} m_q\left(\mathbf{x}^{(t)} + \frac{\sigma}{\|\mathbf{d}_m^{(t)}\|}\mathbf{d}_m^{(t)}\right).$$

From Lemma 2 and $\|\mathbf{d}_m^{(t)}\|$ the bound (6) immediately follows. □

Remark 4. *Some authors define the Pareto–Cauchy point as the actual minimizer $x_{\min}^{(t)}$ of $\Phi_m^{(t)}$ within the current trust region (instead of the minimizer along the steepest descent direction). For this true minimizer the same bound* (6) *holds. This is due to*

$$\Phi_m^{(t)}(x^{(t)}) - \Phi_m^{(t)}(x_{\min}^{(t)}) = m_\ell(x^{(t)}) - \min_{x \in B^{(t)}} m_q(x) \geq m_q(x^{(t)}) - m_q(x_{PC}^{(t)}).$$

5.2. Modified Pareto–Cauchy Point via Backtracking

A common approach in trust region methods is to find an approximate solution to (5) within the current trust region. Usually a backtracking procedure similar to Armijo's inexact line-search is used for the Pareto–Cauchy subproblem, see [36] (Section 6.3) and [30]. Doing so, we can still guarantee a sufficient decrease.

Before we actually define the backtracking step along $d_m^{(t)}$, we derive a more general lemma. It illustrates that backtracking along any suitable direction is well-defined.

Lemma 3. *Suppose Assumptions* 1 *and* 2 *hold. For $x^{(t)} \in \mathbb{R}^n$, let d be a descent direction for $m^{(t)}$ and let $q \in \{1, \ldots, k\}$ be any objective index and $\bar{\sigma} > 0$. Then, for any fixed constants $a, b \in (0,1)$ there is an integer $j \in \mathbb{N}_0$ such that*

$$\Psi\left(x^{(t)} + \frac{b^j \bar{\sigma}}{\|d\|} d\right) \leq \Psi(x^{(t)}) - \frac{ab^j \bar{\sigma}}{\|d\|} w \tag{11}$$

where, again, we have used the shorthand notation $w = -\max_{\ell=1,\ldots,k} \langle \nabla m_\ell^{(t)}(x^{(t)}), d \rangle > 0$ and Ψ is either some specific model, $\Psi = m_\ell$, or the maximum value, $\Psi = \Phi_m^{(t)}$. Moreover, if we define the step $s^{(t)} = \frac{b^j \bar{\sigma}}{\|d\|} d$ for the smallest $j \in \mathbb{N}_0$ satisfying (11), *then there is a constant $\kappa_m^{sd} \in (0,1)$ such that*

$$\Psi(x^{(t)}) - \Psi\left(x^{(t)} + s^{(t)}\right) \geq \kappa_m^{sd} w \min\left\{\frac{w}{\|d\|^2 c H_m^{(t)}}, \frac{\bar{\sigma}}{\|d\|}\right\}. \tag{12}$$

Proof. The first part can be derived from the fact that d is a descent direction, see e.g., [6]. However, we will use the approach from [30] to also derive the bound (12). With Taylor's Theorem we obtain

$$\Psi\left(x^{(t)} + \frac{b^j \bar{\sigma}}{\|d\|} d\right) = m_\ell\left(x^{(t)} + \frac{b^j \bar{\sigma}}{\|d\|} d\right) \quad \text{(for some } \ell \in \{1, \ldots, k\}\text{)}$$

$$= m_\ell^{(t)}(x^{(t)}) + \frac{b^j \bar{\sigma}}{\|d\|} \langle \nabla m_\ell^{(t)}(x^{(t)}), d \rangle + \frac{(b^j \bar{\sigma})^2}{2\|d\|^2} \langle d, Hm_\ell^{(t)}(\xi_\ell) d \rangle$$

$$\leq \Psi(x^{(t)}) + \max_{q=1,\ldots,k} \frac{b^j \bar{\sigma}}{\|d\|} \langle \nabla m_q^{(t)}(x^{(t)}), d \rangle + \max_{q=1,\ldots,k} \frac{(b^j \bar{\sigma})^2}{2\|d\|^2} \langle d, Hm_q^{(t)}(\xi_q) d \rangle$$

$$\stackrel{(Pm),(7)}{\leq} \Psi(x^{(t)}) - \frac{b^j \bar{\sigma}}{\|d\|} w + \frac{(b^j \bar{\sigma})^2}{2} c H_m^{(t)}. \tag{13}$$

In the last line, we have additionally used the Cauchy–Schwartz inequality. For a constructive proof, suppose now that (11) is violated for some $j \in \mathbb{N}_0$, i.e.,

$$\Psi\left(x^{(t)} + \frac{b^j \bar{\sigma}}{\|d\|} d\right) > \Psi(x^{(t)}) - \frac{ab^j \bar{\sigma}}{\|d\|} w.$$

Plugging in (13) for the LHS and substracting $\Psi(x^{(t)})$ then leads to

$$b^j > \frac{2(1-a)w}{\|d\| \bar{\sigma} c H_m^{(t)}},$$

where the right hand side is positive and completely independent of j. Since $b \in (0,1)$, there must be a $j^* \in \mathbb{N}_0, j^* > j$, for which $b^{j^*} \leq \dfrac{2(1-a)w}{\|d\|\bar{\sigma}cH_m^{(t)}}$ so that (11) must also be fulfilled for this b^{j^*}.

Analogous to the proof of [30] ([Lemma 4.2]) we can now derive the constant κ_m^{sd} from (12) as $\kappa_m^{sd} = \min\{2b(1-a), a\}$. $\square$

Lemma 3 applies naturally to the step along $\mathbf{d}_m^{(t)}$:

Definition 7. *For $\mathbf{x}^{(t)} \in B^{(t)}$ let $\mathbf{d}_m^{(t)}$ be a solution to (Pm) and define the modified Pareto–Cauchy step as*

$$\tilde{\mathbf{s}}_{PC}^{(t)} := b^j \bar{\sigma} \frac{\mathbf{d}_m^{(t)}}{\|\mathbf{d}_m^{(t)}\|},$$

where again $\bar{\sigma}$ as in (10) and $j \in \mathbb{N}_0$ is the smallest integer that satisfies

$$\Phi_m^{(t)}(\mathbf{x}^{(t)} + \tilde{\mathbf{s}}_{PC}^{(t)}) \leq \Phi_m^{(t)}(\mathbf{x}^{(t)}) - \frac{ab^j \bar{\sigma}}{\|\mathbf{d}_m^{(t)}\|} \omega_m^{(t)}(\mathbf{x}^{(t)}) \quad (14)$$

for predefined constants $a, b \in (0, 1)$.

The definition of $\bar{\sigma}$ ensures, that $\mathbf{x}^{(t)} + \tilde{\mathbf{s}}_{PC}^{(t)}$ is contained in the current trust region $B^{(t)}$. Furthermore, these steps provide a sufficient decrease very similar to (6):

Corollary 1. *Suppose Assumptions 1 and 2 hold. For the step $\tilde{\mathbf{s}}_{PC}^{(t)}$ the following statements are true:*

1. *A $j \in \mathbb{N}_0$ as in (14) exists.*
2. *There is a constant $\kappa_m^{sd} \in (0,1)$ such that the modified Pareto–Cauchy step $\tilde{\mathbf{s}}_{PC}^{(t)}$ satisfies*

$$\Phi_m^{(t)}(\mathbf{x}^{(t)}) - \Phi_m^{(t)}(\mathbf{x}^{(t)} + \tilde{\mathbf{s}}_{PC}^{(t)}) \geq \kappa_m^{sd} \omega_m^{(t)}(\mathbf{x}^{(t)}) \min\left\{\frac{\omega_m^{(t)}(\mathbf{x}^{(t)})}{cH_m^{(t)}}, \Delta^{(t)}, 1\right\}.$$

Proof. If $\mathbf{x}^{(t)}$ is critical, then the bound is trivial. Otherwise, the existence of a j satisfying (14) follows from Lemma 3 for $\Psi = \Phi_m^{(t)}$. The lower bound on the decrease follows immediately from $\bar{\sigma} \geq \min\left\{\|\mathbf{d}_m^{(t)}\|, \Delta^{(t)}\right\}$. $\square$

From Lemma 3 it follows that the backtracking condition (14) can be modified to explicitly require a decrease in *every* objective:

Definition 8. *Let $j \in \mathbb{N}_0$ the smallest integer satisfying*

$$\min_{\ell=1,\ldots,k}\left\{m_\ell^{(t)}(\mathbf{x}^{(t)}) - m_\ell^{(t)}\left(\mathbf{x}^{(t)} + b^j \bar{\sigma} \frac{\mathbf{d}_m^{(t)}}{\|\mathbf{d}_m^{(t)}\|}\right)\right\} \geq \frac{ab^j \bar{\sigma}}{\|\mathbf{d}_m^{(t)}\|}\omega_m^{(t)}(\mathbf{x}^{(t)}).$$

We define the strict modified Pareto–Cauchy point as $\hat{\mathbf{x}}_{PC}^{(t)} = \mathbf{x}^{(t)} + \hat{\mathbf{s}}_{PC}^{(t)}$ and the corresponding step as $\hat{\mathbf{s}}_{PC}^{(t)} = b^j \bar{\sigma} \dfrac{\mathbf{d}_m^{(t)}}{\|\mathbf{d}_m^{(t)}\|}$.

Corollary 2. *Suppose Assumptions 1 and 2 hold.*

1. The strict modified Pareto–Cauchy point exists, the backtracking is finite.
2. There is a constant $\kappa_m^{sd} \in (0,1)$ such that

$$\min_{\ell=1,\ldots,k}\left\{m_\ell^{(t)}(\mathbf{x}^{(t)}) - m_\ell^{(t)}(\hat{\mathbf{x}}_{PC}^{(t)})\right\} \geq \kappa_m^{sd}\omega_m^{(t)}(\mathbf{x}^{(t)})\min\left\{\frac{\omega_m^{(t)}(\mathbf{x}^{(t)})}{cH_m^{(t)}}, \Delta^{(t)}, 1\right\}. \quad (15)$$

Remark 5. *In the preceding subsections, we have shown descent steps along the model steepest descent direction. Similar to the single objective case we do not necessarily have to use the steepest descent direction and different step calculation methods are viable. For instance, Thomann and Eichfelder [33] use the well-known Pascoletti–Serafini scalarization to treat the subproblem (MOPm). We refer to their work and Appendix B to see how this method can be related to the steepest descent direction.*

5.3. Sufficient Decrease for the Original Problem

In the previous subsections, we have shown how to compute steps $\mathbf{s}^{(t)}$ to achieve a sufficient decrease in terms of $\Phi_m^{(t)}$ and $\omega_m^{(t)}(\bullet)$. For a descent step $\mathbf{s}^{(t)}$ the bound is of the form

$$\Phi_m^{(t)}(\mathbf{x}^{(t)}) - \Phi_m^{(t)}(\mathbf{x}^{(t)}+\mathbf{s}^{(t)}) \geq \kappa_m^{sd}\omega_m^{(t)}(\mathbf{x}^{(t)})\min\left\{\frac{\omega_m^{(t)}(\mathbf{x}^{(t)})}{cH_m^{(t)}}, \Delta^{(t)}, 1\right\}, \quad \kappa_m^{sd} \in (0,1), \quad (16)$$

and thereby very similar to the bounds for the scalar projected gradient trust region method [36]. By introducing a slightly modified version of $\omega_m^{(t)}(\bullet)$, we can transform (16) into the bound used in [30,33].

Lemma 4. *If $\pi(t,\mathbf{x}^{(t)})$ is a criticality measure for some multiobjective problem, then $\tilde{\pi}(t,\mathbf{x}^{(t)}) = \min\{1,\pi(t,\mathbf{x}^{(t)})\}$ is also a criticality measure for the same problem.*

Proof. We have $0 \leq \tilde{\pi}(t,\mathbf{x}^{(t)}) \leq \pi(t,\mathbf{x}^{(t)})$. Thus, $\tilde{\pi} \to 0$ whenever $\pi \to 0$. The minimum of uniformly continuous functions is again uniformly continuous. □

We next make another standard assumption on the class of surrogate models.

Assumption 3. *The norm of all model hessians is uniformly bounded above on $\mathcal{X}$, i.e., there is a positive constant H_m such that*

$$\left\|Hm_\ell^{(t)}(\mathbf{x})\right\|_F \leq H_m \quad \forall \ell = 1,\ldots,k, \forall \mathbf{x} \in B^{(t)}, \forall t \in \mathbb{N}_0.$$

W.l.o.g., we assume

$$H_m \cdot c > 1, \quad \text{with } c \text{ as in (8)}. \quad (17)$$

Remark 6. *From this assumption it follows that the model gradients are then Lipschitz as well. Together with Theorem 2, we then know that $\omega_m^{(t)}(\bullet)$ is a criticality measure for (MOPm).*

Motivated by the previous remark, we will from now on refer to the following functions

$$\tilde{\omega}(\mathbf{x}) := \min\{\omega(\mathbf{x}),1\} \text{ and } \tilde{\omega}_m^{(t)}(\mathbf{x}) := \min\{\omega_m^{(t)}(\mathbf{x}),1\}\forall t=0,1,\ldots \quad (18)$$

We can thereby derive the sufficient decrease condition in "standard form":

Corollary 3. *Under Assumption 3, suppose that for $\mathbf{x}^{(t)}$ and some descent step $\mathbf{s}^{(t)}$ the bound (16) holds. For the criticality measure $\omega_m^{(t)}(\bullet)$ it follows that*

$$\Phi_m^{(t)}(\mathbf{x}^{(t)}) - \Phi_m^{(t)}(\mathbf{x}^{(t)} + \mathbf{s}^{(t)}) \geq \kappa_m^{sd} \omega_m^{(t)}\left(\mathbf{x}^{(t)}\right) \min\left\{\frac{\omega_m^{(t)}\left(\mathbf{x}^{(t)}\right)}{cH_m}, \Delta^{(t)}\right\}. \tag{19}$$

Proof. $\omega_m^{(t)}(\bullet)$ is a criticality measure due to Assumption 3 and Lemma 4. Further, from (18) and (17) it follows that

$$\frac{\omega_m^{(t)}\left(\mathbf{x}^{(t)}\right)}{cH_m} \leq \frac{1}{cH_m} \leq 1$$

and if we plug this into (16) we obtain (19). □

To relate the RHS of (19) to the criticality $\omega(\bullet)$ of the original problem, we require another assumption.

Assumption 4. *There is a constant $\kappa_\omega > 0$ such that*

$$\left|\omega_m^{(t)}\left(\mathbf{x}^{(t)}\right) - \omega\left(\mathbf{x}^{(t)}\right)\right| \leq \kappa_\omega \omega_m^{(t)}\left(\mathbf{x}^{(t)}\right).$$

This assumption is also made by Thomann and Eichfelder [33] and can easily be justified by using fully linear surrogate models and a bounded trust region radius in combination with a criticality test, see Lemma 7.

Assumption 4 can be used to formulate the next two lemmata relating the model criticality and the true criticality. They are proven in Appendix A.2. From these lemmata and Corollary 3 the final result, Corollary 4, easily follows.

Lemma 5. *If Assumption 4 holds, then it holds for $\omega_m^{(t)}(\bullet)$ and $\omega(\bullet)$ from (18) that*

$$\left|\omega_m^{(t)}\left(\mathbf{x}^{(t)}\right) - \omega\left(\mathbf{x}^{(t)}\right)\right| \leq \kappa_\omega \omega_m^{(t)}\left(\mathbf{x}^{(t)}\right).$$

Lemma 6. *From Assumption 4 it follows that*

$$\omega_m^{(t)}\left(\mathbf{x}^{(t)}\right) \geq \frac{1}{\kappa_\omega + 1} \omega\left(\mathbf{x}^{(t)}\right) \quad \text{with } (\kappa_\omega + 1)^{-1} \in (0, 1).$$

Corollary 4. *Suppose that Assumptions 3 and 4 hold and that $\mathbf{x}^{(t)}$ and $\mathbf{s}^{(t)}$ satisfy (19). Then*

$$\Phi_m^{(t)}(\mathbf{x}^{(t)}) - \Phi_m^{(t)}(\mathbf{x}^{(t)} + \mathbf{s}^{(t)}) \geq \kappa^{sd} \omega\left(\mathbf{x}^{(t)}\right) \min\left\{\frac{\omega\left(\mathbf{x}^{(t)}\right)}{cH_m}, \Delta^{(t)}\right\}, \tag{20}$$

where $\kappa^{sd} = \frac{\kappa_m^{sd}}{1+\kappa_\omega} \in (0, 1)$.

6. Convergence

6.1. Preliminary Assumptions and Definitions

To prove convergence of Algorithm 2 we first have to make sure that at least one of the objectives is bounded from below. This is a weaker requirement than the standard assumption that all objectives are bounded from below:

Assumption 5. *The maximum $\max_{\ell=1,\ldots,k} f_\ell(\mathbf{x})$ of all objective functions is bounded from below on $\mathcal{X}$.*

To be able to use $\omega(\bullet)$ as a criticality measure and to refer to fully linear models, we further require:

Assumption 6. *The objective* $\mathbf{f}\colon \mathbb{R}^n \to \mathbb{R}^k$ *is continuously differentiable in an open domain containing $\mathcal{X}$ and has a Lipschitz continuous gradient on $\mathcal{X}$.*

We summarize the assumptions on the surrogates as follows:

Assumption 7. *The vector of surrogate model functions $m_1^{(t)}, \ldots, m_k^{(t)}$ belongs to a collection of fully linear classes as in Definition 4: For each objective objective index $\ell = 1, \ldots, k$ there are error constants ϵ_ℓ so that $\dot{\epsilon}_\ell$ and $m_\ell^{(t)}$ can be made to satisfy the bounds in Definition 3.*

For the subsequent analysis we define component-wise maximum constants as

$$\epsilon := \max_{\ell=1,\ldots,k} \epsilon_\ell, \quad \dot{\epsilon} := \max_{\ell=1,\ldots,k} \dot{\epsilon}_\ell. \tag{21}$$

We also wish for the descent steps to fulfill a sufficient decrease condition for the surrogate criticality measure as discussed in Section 5.

Assumption 8. *For all $t \in \mathbb{N}_0$ the descent steps $\mathbf{s}^{(t)}$ are assumed to fulfill both $\mathbf{x}^{(t)} + \mathbf{s}^{(t)} \in B^{(t)}$ and* (19).

Finally, to avoid a cluttered notation when dealing with subsequences we define the following shorthand notations:

$$\omega_{\mathrm{m}}^{(t)} := \omega_{\mathrm{m}}^{(t)}\left(\mathbf{x}^{(t)}\right), \quad \omega^{(t)} := \omega\left(\mathbf{x}^{(t)}\right) \quad \forall t \in \mathbb{N}_0.$$

6.2. Convergence Proof

In the following we prove convergence of Algorithm 2 to Pareto critical points. We account for the case that no criticality test is used, i.e., $\varepsilon_{\mathrm{crit}} = 0$. We then require all surrogates to be fully linear in each iteration and need Assumption 4. The proof is an adapted version of the scalar case in [35].

It is also similar to the proofs for the multiobjective algorithms in [30,33]. However, in both cases, no criticality test is employed, there is no distinction between successful and acceptable iterations ($\nu_+ = \nu_{++}$) and interpolation at $\mathbf{x}^{(t)}$ by the surrogates is required. We indicate notable differences when appropriate.

We start with two results concerning the criticality test in Algorithm 2.

Lemma 7. *For each iteration $t \in \mathbb{N}_0$ Assumption 4 is fulfilled if the model $\mathbf{m}^{(t)}$ is fully-linear and the criticality test was performed and—if applicable—Algorithm 1 has finished.*

Proof. Let $\ell, q \in \{1, \ldots, k\}$ and $\mathbf{d}_\ell, \mathbf{d}_q \in \mathcal{X} - \mathbf{x}^{(t)}$ be solutions of (P1) and (Pm), respectively, such that

$$\omega_{\mathrm{m}}^{(t)}\left(\mathbf{x}^{(t)}\right) = -\langle \boldsymbol{\nabla} m_\ell^{(t)}(\mathbf{x}^{(t)}), \mathbf{d}_\ell \rangle, \quad \omega\left(\mathbf{x}^{(t)}\right) = -\langle \boldsymbol{\nabla} f_q(\mathbf{x}^{(t)}), \mathbf{d}_q \rangle.$$

If $\omega_{\mathrm{m}}^{(t)}\left(\mathbf{x}^{(t)}\right) \geq \omega\left(\mathbf{x}^{(t)}\right)$, then, using Cauchy–Schwartz and $\|\mathbf{d}_\ell\| \leq 1$,

$$\left|\omega_{\mathrm{m}}^{(t)}\left(\mathbf{x}^{(t)}\right) - \omega\left(\mathbf{x}^{(t)}\right)\right| = \langle \boldsymbol{\nabla} f_q(\mathbf{x}^{(t)}), \mathbf{d}_q \rangle - \langle \boldsymbol{\nabla} m_\ell^{(t)}(\mathbf{x}^{(t)}), \mathbf{d}_\ell \rangle$$
$$\overset{\mathrm{df.}}{\leq} \langle \boldsymbol{\nabla} f_q(\mathbf{x}^{(t)}), \mathbf{d}_\ell \rangle - \langle \boldsymbol{\nabla} m_q^{(t)}(\mathbf{x}^{(t)}), \mathbf{d}_\ell \rangle$$
$$\leq \left\| \boldsymbol{\nabla} f_q(\mathbf{x}^{(t)}) - \boldsymbol{\nabla} m_q^{(t)}(\mathbf{x}^{(t)}) \right\|_2,$$

and if $\omega_m^{(t)}\left(\mathbf{x}^{(t)}\right) < \omega\left(\mathbf{x}^{(t)}\right)$, we obtain

$$\left|\omega_m^{(t)}\left(\mathbf{x}^{(t)}\right) - \omega\left(\mathbf{x}^{(t)}\right)\right| \leq \left\|\nabla m_\ell^{(t)}(\mathbf{x}^{(t)}) - \nabla f_\ell(\mathbf{x}^{(t)})\right\|_2.$$

Because $\mathbf{m}^{(t)}$ is fully linear, it follows that

$$\left|\omega_m^{(t)}\left(\mathbf{x}^{(t)}\right) - \omega\left(\mathbf{x}^{(t)}\right)\right| \leq \sqrt{c}\dot{\varepsilon}\Delta^{(t)}, \qquad \text{with } \dot{\varepsilon} \text{ from (21)}.$$

If we just left Algorithm 1, then the model is fully linear for $\Delta^{(t)}$ due to Lemma 1 and we have $\Delta^{(t)} \leq \mu\omega_m^{(t)}\left(\mathbf{x}^{(t)}\right) \leq \mu\omega_m^{(t)}\left(\mathbf{x}^{(t)}\right)$. If we otherwise did not enter Algorithm 1 in the first place, it must hold that $\omega_m^{(t)}\left(\mathbf{x}^{(t)}\right) \geq \varepsilon_{\text{crit}}$ and

$$\Delta^{(t)} \leq \Delta^{\text{ub}} = \frac{\Delta^{\text{ub}}}{\varepsilon_{\text{crit}}}\varepsilon_{\text{crit}} \leq \frac{\Delta^{\text{ub}}}{\varepsilon_{\text{crit}}}\omega_m^{(t)}\left(\mathbf{x}^{(t)}\right)$$

and thus

$$\left|\omega_m^{(t)}\left(\mathbf{x}^{(t)}\right) - \omega\left(\mathbf{x}^{(t)}\right)\right| \leq \kappa_\omega \omega_m^{(t)}\left(\mathbf{x}^{(t)}\right), \quad \kappa_\omega = \sqrt{c}\dot{\varepsilon}\max\left\{\mu, \varepsilon_{\text{crit}}^{-1}\Delta^{\text{ub}}\right\} > 0.$$

□

In the subsequent analysis, we require mainly steps with fully linear models to achieve sufficient decrease for the true problem. Due to Lemma 7, we can dispose of Assumption 4 by using the criticality routine:

Assumption 9. *Either $\varepsilon_{\text{crit}} > 0$ or Assumption 4 holds.*

We have also implicitly shown the following property of the criticality measures.

Corollary 5. *If $\mathbf{m}^{(t)}$ is fully linear for $\mathbf{f}$ with $\dot{\varepsilon} > 0$ as in (21) then*

$$\left|\omega_m^{(t)}\left(\mathbf{x}^{(t)}\right) - \omega\left(\mathbf{x}^{(t)}\right)\right| \leq \left|\omega_m^{(t)}\left(\mathbf{x}^{(t)}\right) - \omega\left(\mathbf{x}^{(t)}\right)\right| \leq \sqrt{c}\dot{\varepsilon}\Delta^{(t)}.$$

Lemma 8. *If $\mathbf{x}^{(t)}$ is not critical for the true problem (MOP), i.e., $\omega\left(\mathbf{x}^{(t)}\right) \neq 0$, then Algorithm 1 will terminate after a finite number of iterations.*

Proof. At the start of Algorithm 1, we know that $\mathbf{m}^{(t)}$ is not fully linear or $\Delta^{(t)} > \mu\omega_m^{(t)}\left(\mathbf{x}^{(t)}\right)$. For clarity, we denote the first model by $\mathbf{m}_0^{(t)}$ and define $\Delta_0 = \Delta^{(t)}$. We then ensure that the model is made fully linear on $\Delta_1^{(t)} = \Delta_0$ and denote this fully linear model by $\mathbf{m}_1^{(t)}$. If afterwards $\Delta_1^{(t)} \leq \mu\omega_{m_1}^{(t)}\left(\mathbf{x}^{(t)}\right)$, then Algorithm 1 terminates.

Otherwise, the process is repeated: the radius is multiplied by $\alpha \in (0,1)$ so that in the j-th iteration we have $\Delta_j^{(t)} = \alpha^{j-1}\Delta_0$ and $\mathbf{m}_j^{(t)}$ is made fully linear on $\Delta_j^{(t)}$ until

$$\Delta_j^{(t)} = \alpha^{j-1}\Delta_0 \leq \mu\omega_{m_j}^{(t)}\left(\mathbf{x}^{(t)}\right).$$

The only way for Algorithm 1 to loop infinitely is

$$\omega_{m_j}^{(t)}\left(\mathbf{x}^{(t)}\right) < \frac{\alpha^{j-1}\Delta_0}{\mu} \qquad \forall j \in \mathbb{N}. \tag{22}$$

Because $\mathbf{m}_j^{(t)}$ is fully linear on $\alpha^{j-1}\Delta_0$, we know from Corollary 5 that

$$\left|\omega_{\mathrm{m}_j}^{(t)}\left(\mathbf{x}^{(t)}\right) - \omega\left(\mathbf{x}^{(t)}\right)\right| \leq \sqrt{c}\dot{\epsilon}\alpha^{j-1}\Delta_0 \qquad \forall j \in \mathbb{N}.$$

Using the triangle inequality together with (22) gives us

$$\left|\omega\left(\mathbf{x}^{(t)}\right)\right| \leq \left|\omega_{\mathrm{m}_j}^{(t)}\left(\mathbf{x}^{(t)}\right) - \omega\left(\mathbf{x}^{(t)}\right)\right| + \left|\omega_{\mathrm{m}_j}^{(t)}\left(\mathbf{x}^{(t)}\right)\right| \leq \left(\mu^{-1} + \sqrt{c}\epsilon\right)\alpha^{j-1}\Delta_0 \quad \forall j \in \mathbb{N}.$$

As $\alpha \in (0,1)$, this implies $\omega\left(\mathbf{x}^{(t)}\right) = 0$ and $\mathbf{x}^{(t)}$ is hence critical. □

We next state another auxiliary lemma that we need for the convergence proof.

Lemma 9. *Suppose Assumptions 6 and 7 hold. For the iterate $\mathbf{x}^{(t)}$ let $\mathbf{s}^{(t)} \in \mathbb{R}^n$ be a any step with $\mathbf{x}_+^{(t)} = \mathbf{x}^{(t)} + \mathbf{s}^{(t)} \in B^{(t)}$. If $\mathbf{m}^{(t)}$ is fully linear on $B^{(t)}$ then it holds that*

$$\left|\Phi(\mathbf{x}_+^{(t)}) - \Phi_{\mathrm{m}}^{(t)}(\mathbf{x}_+^{(t)})\right| \leq \epsilon\left(\Delta^{(t)}\right)^2.$$

Proof. The proof follows from the definition of Φ and $\Phi_{\mathrm{m}}^{(t)}$ and the full linearity of $\mathbf{m}^{(t)}$. It can be found in [33] (Lemma 4.16). □

Convergence of Algorithm 2 is proven by showing that in certain situations, the iteration must be acceptable or successful as defined in Definition 5. This is done indirectly and relies on the next two lemmata. They use the preceding result to show that in a (hypothetical) situation where no Pareto critical point is approached, the trust region radius must be bounded from below.

Lemma 10. *Suppose Assumptions 1, 3 and 6 to 8 hold. If $\mathbf{x}^{(t)}$ is not Pareto critical for* (MOPm) *and $\mathbf{m}^{(t)}$ is fully linear on $B^{(t)}$ and*

$$\Delta^{(t)} \leq \frac{\kappa_{\mathrm{m}}^{\mathrm{sd}}(1-\nu_{++})\omega_{\mathrm{m}}^{(t)}\left(\mathbf{x}^{(t)}\right)}{2\lambda}, \quad \text{where } \lambda = \max\{\epsilon, c\mathrm{H_m}\} \text{ and } \kappa_{\mathrm{m}}^{\mathrm{sd}} \text{ as in (19),}$$

then the iteration is successful, that is, $t \in \mathcal{S}$ and $\Delta^{t+1} \geq \Delta^{(t)}$.

Proof. The proof is very similar to [35] (Lemma 5.3) and [33] (Lemma 4.17). In contrast to the latter, we use the surrogate problem and do not require interpolation at $\mathbf{x}^{(t)}$:

By definition we have $\kappa_{\mathrm{m}}^{\mathrm{sd}}(1-\nu_{++}) < 1$ and hence it follows from Assumptions 4 and 8 and Corollary 3 that

$$\Delta^{(t)} \leq \frac{\kappa_{\mathrm{m}}^{\mathrm{sd}}(1-\nu_{++})\omega_{\mathrm{m}}^{(t)}\left(\mathbf{x}^{(t)}\right)}{2\lambda} \tag{23}$$

$$\leq \frac{\omega_{\mathrm{m}}^{(t)}}{2\lambda} \leq \frac{\omega_{\mathrm{m}}^{(t)}}{2c\mathrm{H_m}} \leq \frac{\omega_{\mathrm{m}}^{(t)}}{c\mathrm{H_m}}.$$

With Assumption 8 we can plug this into (19) and obtain

$$\Phi_{\mathrm{m}}^{(t)}(\mathbf{x}^{(t)}) - \Phi_{\mathrm{m}}^{(t)}(\mathbf{x}_+^{(t)}) \geq \kappa_{\mathrm{m}}^{\mathrm{sd}}\omega_{\mathrm{m}}^{(t)}\min\left\{\frac{\omega_{\mathrm{m}}^{(t)}}{c\mathrm{H_m}}, \Delta^{(t)}\right\} \geq \kappa_{\mathrm{m}}^{\mathrm{sd}}\omega_{\mathrm{m}}^{(t)}\Delta^{(t)}. \tag{24}$$

Due to Assumption 7 we can take Definition (3) and estimate

$$\left|\rho^{(t)} - 1\right| = \left|\frac{\Phi(\mathbf{x}^{(t)}) - \Phi(\mathbf{x}_+^{(t)}) - (\Phi_m^{(t)}(\mathbf{x}^{(t)}) - \Phi_m^{(t)}(\mathbf{x}_+^{(t)}))}{\Phi_m^{(t)}(\mathbf{x}^{(t)}) - \Phi_m^{(t)}(\mathbf{x}_+^{(t)})}\right|$$

$$\leq \frac{\left|\Phi(\mathbf{x}^{(t)}) - \Phi_m^{(t)}(\mathbf{x}^{(t)})\right| + \left|\Phi_m^{(t)}(\mathbf{x}_+^{(t)}) - \Phi(\mathbf{x}_+^{(t)})\right|}{\left|\Phi_m^{(t)}(\mathbf{x}^{(t)}) - \Phi_m^{(t)}(\mathbf{x}_+^{(t)})\right|}$$

$$\overset{\text{Lemma 9, (24)}}{\leq} \frac{2\epsilon \left(\Delta^{(t)}\right)^2}{\kappa_m^{\text{sd}} \omega_m^{(t)} \Delta^{(t)}} \leq \frac{2\lambda \Delta^{(t)}}{\kappa_m^{\text{sd}} \omega_m^{(t)}} \overset{(23)}{\leq} 1 - \nu_{++}.$$

Therefore $\rho^{(t)} \geq \nu_{++}$ and the iteration t using step $\mathbf{s}^{(t)}$ is successful. □

The same statement can be made for the true problem and $\omega(\bullet)$:

Corollary 6. *Suppose Assumptions 1, 3 and 6 to 9 hold. If $\mathbf{x}^{(t)}$ is not Pareto critical for* (MOP) *and $\mathbf{m}^{(t)}$ is fully linear on $B^{(t)}$ and*

$$\Delta^{(t)} \leq \frac{\kappa^{\text{sd}}(1 - \nu_{++})\omega\left(\mathbf{x}^{(t)}\right)}{2\lambda}, \quad \text{where } \lambda = \max\{\epsilon, cH_m\}, \kappa_m^{\text{sd}} \text{ as in (20),}$$

then the iteration is successful, that is $t \in \mathcal{S}$ and $\Delta^{t+1} \geq \Delta^{(t)}$.

Proof. The proof works exactly the same as for Lemma 10. But due to Assumption 9 we can use Lemma 7 and employ the sufficient decrease condition (20) for $\omega(\bullet)$ instead. □

As in [35] (Lemma 5.4) and [33] (Lemma 4.18), it is now easy to show that when no Pareto critical point of (MOPm) is approached the trust region radius must be bounded:

Lemma 11. *Suppose Assumptions 1, 3 and 6 to 8 hold and that there exists a constant $\omega_m^{\text{lb}} > 0$ such that $\omega_m^{(t)}\left(\mathbf{x}^{(t)}\right) \geq \omega_m^{\text{lb}}$ for all t. Then there is a constant $\Delta^{\text{lb}} > 0$ with*

$$\Delta^{(t)} \geq \Delta^{\text{lb}} \quad \text{for all } t \in \mathbb{N}_0.$$

Proof. We first investigate the criticality step and assume $\epsilon_{\text{crit}} > \omega_m^{(t)} \geq \omega_m^{\text{lb}}$. After we finish the criticality loop, we get radius $\Delta^{(t)}$ so that $\Delta^{(t)} \geq \min\{\Delta_*^{(t)}, \beta\omega_m^{(t)}\}$ and therefore $\Delta^{(t)} \geq \min\{\beta\omega_m^{\text{lb}}, \Delta_*^{(t)}\}$ for all t.

Outside the criticality step, we know from Lemma 10 that whenever $\Delta^{(t)}$ falls below

$$\tilde{\Delta} := \frac{\kappa_m^{\text{sd}}(1 - \nu_{++})\omega_m^{\text{lb}}}{2\lambda},$$

iteration t must be either model-improving or successful and hence $\Delta^{(t+1)} \geq \Delta^{(t)}$ and the radius cannot decrease until $\Delta^{(k)} > \tilde{\Delta}$ for some $k > t$. Because $\gamma_{\shortparallel} \in (0,1)$ is the severest possible shrinking factor in Algorithm 2, we therefore know that $\Delta^{(t)}$ can never be actively shrunken to a value below $\gamma_{\shortparallel}\tilde{\Delta}$.

Combining both bounds on $\Delta^{(t)}$ results in

$$\Delta^{(t)} \geq \Delta^{\text{lb}} := \min\{\beta\omega_m^{\text{lb}}, \gamma_{\shortparallel}\tilde{\Delta}, \Delta_*^{(0)}\} \quad \forall t \in \mathbb{N}_0,$$

where we have again used the fact that $\Delta_*^{(t)}$ cannot be reduced further if it is less than or equal to $\tilde{\Delta}$ due to the update mechanism in Algorithm 2. □

We can now state the first convergence result:

Theorem 5. *Suppose that Assumptions 1, 3 and 6 to 8 hold. If Algorithm 2 has only a finite number $0 \leq |\mathcal{S}| < \infty$ of successful iterations $\mathcal{S} = \{t \in \mathbb{N}_0 : \rho^{(t)} \geq \nu_{++}\}$ then*

$$\lim_{t \to \infty} \varpi\left(\mathbf{x}^{(t)}\right) = 0.$$

Proof. If the criticality loop runs infinitely, then the result follows from Lemma 8.

Otherwise, let t_0 any index larger than the last successful index (or $t_0 \geq 0$ if $\mathcal{S} = \emptyset$). All $t \geq t_0$ then must be model-improving, acceptable or inacceptable. In all cases, the trust region radius $\Delta^{(t)}$ is never increased. Due to Assumption 7, the number of successive model-improvement steps is bounded above by $M \in \mathbb{N}$. Hence, $\Delta^{(t)}$ is decreased by a factor of $\gamma \in [\gamma_{\Downarrow}, \gamma_{\downarrow}] \subseteq (0,1)$ at least once every M iterations. Thus,

$$\sum_{t > t_0}^{\infty} \Delta^{(t)} \leq N \sum_{i=1}^{\infty} \gamma_{\downarrow}^i \Delta^{(t_0)} = \frac{N \gamma_{\downarrow}}{1 - \gamma_{\downarrow}} \Delta^{(t_0)},$$

and $\Delta^{(t)}$ **must go to zero** for $t \to \infty$.

Clearly, for any $\tau \geq t_0$, the iterates (and trust region centers) $\mathbf{x}^{(\tau)}$ and $\mathbf{x}^{(t_0)}$ cannot be further apart than the sum of all subsequent trust region radii, i.e.,

$$\left\|\mathbf{x}^{(\tau)} - \mathbf{x}^{(t_0)}\right\| \leq \sum_{t \geq t_0}^{\infty} \Delta^{(t)} \leq \frac{N \gamma_{\downarrow}}{1 - \gamma_{\downarrow}} \Delta^{(t_0)}.$$

The RHS goes to zero as we let t_0 go to infinity and so must the norm on the LHS, i.e.,

$$\lim_{t_0 \to \infty} \left\|\mathbf{x}^{(\tau)} - \mathbf{x}^{(t_0)}\right\| = 0. \tag{25}$$

Now let $\tau = \tau(t_0) \geq t_0$ be the first iteration index so that $\mathbf{m}^{(\tau)}$ is fully linear. Then

$$\left|\varpi_m^{(t_0)}\right| \leq \left|\varpi^{(t_0)} - \varpi^{(\tau)}\right| + \left|\varpi^{(\tau)} - \varpi_m^{(\tau)}\right| + \left|\varpi_m^{(\tau)}\right|$$

and for the terms on the right and for $t_0 \to \infty$, we find:

- Because of Assumptions 1 and 6 and Theorem 2 $\varpi(\bullet)$ is Cauchy-continuous and with (25) the first term goes to zero.
- Due to Corollary 5 the second term is in $\mathcal{O}(\Delta^{(\tau)})$ and goes to zero.
- Suppose the third term does not go to zero as well, i.e., $\{\varpi_m^{(t)}\left(\mathbf{x}^{(\tau)}\right)\}$ is bounded below by a positive constant. Due to Assumptions 1 and 7 the iterates $x^{(\tau)}$ are not Pareto critical for (MOPm) and because of $\Delta^{(\tau)} \to 0$ and Lemma 10 there would be a successful iteration, a contradiction. Thus the third term must go to zero as well.

We conclude that the left side, $\varpi\left(\mathbf{x}^{(t_0)}\right)$, goes to zero as well for $t_0 \to \infty$. □

We now address the case of infinitely many successful iterations, first for the surrogate measure $\varpi_m^{(t)}(\bullet)$ and then for $\varpi(\bullet)$. We show that the criticality measures are not bounded away from zero.

We start with the observation that in any case the trust region radius converges to zero:

Lemma 12. *If Assumptions 1, 3 and 6 to 8 hold, then the subsequence of trust region radii generated by Algorithm 2 goes to zero, i.e., $\lim_{t \to \infty} \Delta^{(t)} = 0$.*

Proof. We have shown in the proof of Theorem 5 that this is the case for finitely many successful iterations.

Suppose there are infinitely many successful iterations. Take any successful index $t \in \mathcal{S}$. Then $\rho^{(t)} \geq \nu_{++}$ and from Assumption 8 it follows for $\mathbf{x}^{(t+1)} = \mathbf{x}_+^{(t)} = \mathbf{x}^{(t)} + \mathbf{s}^{(t)}$ that

$$\Phi(\mathbf{x}^{(t)}) - \Phi(\mathbf{x}_+^{(t)}) \geq \nu_{++}\left(\Phi_m^{(t)}(\mathbf{x}^{(t)}) - \Phi_m^{(t)}(\mathbf{x}_+^{(t)})\right) \stackrel{(19)}{\geq} \nu_{++}\kappa_m^{sd}\omega_m^{(t)}\min\left\{\frac{\omega_m^{(t)}}{cH_m}, \Delta^{(t)}\right\}.$$

The criticality step ensures that $\omega_m^{(t)} \geq \min\left\{\varepsilon_{\text{crit}}, \frac{\Delta^{(t)}}{\mu}\right\}$ so that

$$\Phi(\mathbf{x}^{(t)}) - \Phi(\mathbf{x}_+^{(t)}) \geq \nu_{++}\kappa_m^{sd}\min\left\{\varepsilon_{\text{crit}}, \frac{\Delta^{(t)}}{\mu}\right\}\min\left\{\frac{\Delta^{(t)}}{\mu cH_m}, \Delta^{(t)}\right\} \geq 0. \qquad (26)$$

Now the right hand side has to go to zero: Suppose it was bounded below by a positive constant $\varepsilon > 0$. We could then compute a lower bound on the improvement from the first iteration with index 0 up to $t+1$ by summation

$$\Phi(\mathbf{x}^{(0)}) - \Phi(\mathbf{x}^{(t+1)}) \geq \sum_{\tau \in \mathcal{S}_t}\Phi(\mathbf{x}^{(\tau)}) - \Phi(\mathbf{x}^{(\tau+1)}) \geq |\mathcal{S}_t|\varepsilon$$

where $\mathcal{S}_t = \mathcal{S} \cap \{0, \ldots, t\}$ are all successful indices with a maximum index of t. Because $\mathcal{S}$ is unbounded, the right side diverges for $t \to \infty$ and so must the left side in contradiction to Φ being bounded below by Assumption 5. From (26) we see that this implies $\Delta^{(t)} \to 0$ for $t \in \mathcal{S}, t \to \infty$.

Now consider any sequence $\mathcal{T} \subseteq \mathbb{N}$ of indices that are not necessarily successful, i.e., $|\mathcal{T} \setminus \mathcal{S}| \geq 0$. The radius is only ever increased in successful iterations and at most by a factor of $\gamma_\uparrow$. Since $\mathcal{S}$ is unbounded, there is for any $\tau \in \mathcal{T}$ a largest $t_\tau \in \mathcal{S}$ with $t_\tau \leq \tau$. Then $\Delta^{(\tau)} \leq \gamma_\uparrow \Delta^{(t_\tau)}$ and because of $\Delta^{(t_\tau)} \to 0$ it follows that

$$\lim_{\substack{\tau \in \mathcal{T},\\ \tau \to \infty}} \Delta^{(\tau)} = 0,$$

which concludes the proof. □

Lemma 13. *Suppose Assumptions 1, 3 and 5 to 8 hold. For the iterates produced by Algorithm 2 it holds that*

$$\liminf_{t \to \infty} \omega_m^{(t)}\left(\mathbf{x}^{(t)}\right) = 0.$$

Proof. For a contradiction, suppose that $\liminf_{t \to \infty} \omega_m^{(t)}\left(\mathbf{x}^{(t)}\right) \neq 0$. Then there is a constant $\omega_m^{lb} > 0$ with $\omega_m^{(t)} \geq \omega_m^{lb}$ for all $t \in \mathbb{N}_0$. According to Lemma 11, there exists a constant $\Delta^{lb} > 0$ with $\Delta^{(t)} \geq \Delta^{lb}$ for all t. This contradicts Lemma 12. □

The next result allows us to transfer the result to $\omega(\bullet)$.

Lemma 14. *Suppose Assumptions 1, 6 and 7 hold. For any subsequence $\{t_i\}_{i \in \mathbb{N}} \subseteq \mathbb{N}_0$ of iteration indices of Algorithm 2 with*

$$\lim_{i \to \infty} \omega_m^{(t_i)}\left(\mathbf{x}^{(t_i)}\right) = 0, \qquad (27)$$

it also holds that

$$\lim_{i \to \infty} \omega\left(\mathbf{x}^{(t_i)}\right) = 0. \qquad (28)$$

Proof. By (27), $\omega_m^{(t_i)} < \varepsilon_{\text{crit}}$ for sufficiently large i. If $\mathbf{x}^{(t_i)}$ is critical for (MOP), then the result follows from Lemma 8. Otherwise, $\mathbf{m}^{(t_i)}$ is fully linear on $B\left(\mathbf{x}^{(t_i)};\Delta^{(t_i)}\right)$ for some $\Delta^{(t_i)} \leq \mu\omega_m^{(t_i)}$. From Corollary 5 it follows that

$$\left|\omega_m^{(t_i)} - \omega^{(t_i)}\right| \leq \sqrt{c}\dot{\varepsilon}\Delta^{(t_i)} \leq \sqrt{c}\dot{\varepsilon}\mu\omega_m^{(t_i)}.$$

The triangle inequality yields

$$\omega^{(t_i)} \leq \left|\omega^{(t_i)} - \omega_m^{(t_i)}\right| + \omega_m^{(t_i)} \leq (\sqrt{c}\dot{\varepsilon}\mu + 1)\omega_m^{(t_i)}$$

for sufficiently large i and (27) then implies (28). □

The next global convergence result immediately follows from Theorem 5 and Lemmas 13 and 14:

Theorem 6. *Suppose Assumptions 1, 3 and 5 to 8 hold. Then* $\liminf_{t \to \infty} \omega\left(\mathbf{x}^{(t)}\right) = 0$.

This shows that if the iterates are bounded, then there is a subsequence of iterates in $\mathbb{R}^n$ approximating a Pareto critical point. We next show that *all* limit points of a sequence generated by Algorithm 2 are Pareto critical.

Theorem 7. *Suppose Assumptions 1 and 3 to 8 hold. Then* $\lim_{t \to \infty} \omega\left(\mathbf{x}^{(t)}\right) = 0$.

Proof. We have already proven the result for finitely many successful iterations, see Theorem 5. We thus suppose that $\mathcal{S}$ is unbounded.

For the purpose of establishing a contradiction, suppose that there exists a sequence $\{t_j\}_{j \in \mathbb{N}}$ of indices that are successful or acceptable with

$$\omega^{(t_j)} \geq 2\varepsilon > 0 \quad \text{for some } \varepsilon > 0 \text{ and all } j. \tag{29}$$

We can ignore model-improving and inacceptable iterations: During those the iterate does not change, and we find a larger acceptable or successful index with the same criticality value.

From Theorem 6 we obtain that for every such t_j, there exists a first index $\tau_j > t_j$ such that $\omega\left(\mathbf{x}^{(\tau_j)}\right) < \varepsilon$. We thus find another subsequence indexed by $\{\tau_j\}$ such that

$$\omega^{(t)} \geq \varepsilon \text{ for } t_j \leq t < \tau_j \text{ and } \omega^{(\tau_j)} < \varepsilon. \tag{30}$$

Using (29) and (30), it also follows from a triangle inequality that

$$\left|\omega^{(t_j)} - \omega^{(\tau_j)}\right| \geq \omega^{(t_j)} - \omega^{(\tau_j)} > 2\varepsilon - \varepsilon = \varepsilon \quad \forall j \in \mathbb{N}. \tag{31}$$

With $\{t_j\}$ and $\{\tau_j\}$ as in (30), define the following subset set of indices

$$\mathcal{T} = \{t \in \mathbb{N}_0 : \exists j \in \mathbb{N} \text{ such that } t_j \leq t < \tau_j\}.$$

By (30) we have $\omega^{(t)} \geq \varepsilon$ for $t \in \mathcal{T}$, and due to Lemma 14, we also know that then $\omega_m^{(t)}$ cannot go to zero neither, i.e., there is some $\varepsilon_m > 0$ such that

$$\omega_m^{(t)} \geq \varepsilon_m > 0 \quad \forall t \in \mathcal{T}.$$

From Lemma 12 we know that $\Delta^{(t)} \xrightarrow{t \to \infty} 0$ so that by Corollary 6, any sufficiently large $t \in \mathcal{T}$ must be either successful or model-improving (if $\mathbf{m}^{(t)}$ is not fully linear). For $t \in \mathcal{T} \cap \mathcal{S}$, it follows from Assumption 8 that

$$\Phi(\mathbf{x}^{(t)}) - \Phi(\mathbf{x}^{(t+1)}) \geq \nu_{++}\left(\Phi_m(\mathbf{x}^{(t)}) - \Phi_m(\mathbf{x}^{(t+1)})\right) \geq \nu_{++}\kappa_m^{sd}\varepsilon_m \min\left\{\frac{\varepsilon_m}{cH_m}, \Delta^{(t)}\right\} \geq 0.$$

If $t \in \mathcal{T} \cap \mathcal{S}$ is sufficiently large, we have $\Delta^{(t)} \leq \frac{\varepsilon_m}{cH_m}$ and

$$\Delta^{(t)} \leq \frac{1}{\nu_{++} \kappa_m^{sd} \varepsilon_m} \left(\Phi(\mathbf{x}^{(t)}) - \Phi(\mathbf{x}^{(t+1)}) \right).$$

Since the iteration is either successful or model-improving for sufficiently large $t \in \mathcal{T}$, and since $\mathbf{x}^{(t)} = \mathbf{x}^{(t+1)}$ for a model-improving iteration, we deduce from the previous inequality that

$$\left\| \mathbf{x}^{(t_j)} - \mathbf{x}^{(\tau_j)} \right\| \leq \sum_{\substack{t=t_j, \\ t \in \mathcal{T} \cap \mathcal{S}}}^{\tau_j - 1} \left\| \mathbf{x}^{(t)} - \mathbf{x}^{(t+1)} \right\| \leq \sum_{\substack{t=t_j, \\ t \in \mathcal{T} \cap \mathcal{S}}}^{\tau_j - 1} \Delta^{(t)} \leq \frac{1}{\nu_{++} \kappa_m^{sd} \varepsilon_m} \left(\Phi(\mathbf{x}^{(t_j)}) - \Phi(\mathbf{x}^{(\tau_j)}) \right)$$

for $j \in \mathbb{N}$ sufficiently large. The sequence $\left\{ \Phi(\mathbf{x}^{(t)}) \right\}_{t \in \mathbb{N}_0}$ is bounded below (Assumption 5) and monotonically decreasing by construction. Hence, the RHS above must converge to zero for $j \to \infty$. This implies $\lim_{j \to \infty} \left\| \mathbf{x}^{(t_j)} - \mathbf{x}^{(\tau_j)} \right\| = 0$.

Because of Assumptions 1 and 6, $\omega(\bullet)$ is uniformly continuous so that then

$$\lim_{j \to \infty} \omega\left(\mathbf{x}^{(t_j)}\right) - \omega\left(\mathbf{x}^{(\tau_j)}\right) = 0,$$

which is a contradiction to (31). Thus, no subsequence of acceptable or successful indices as in (29) can exist. □

7. Numerical Examples

In this section we provide some more details on the actual implementation of Algorithm 2 and present the results of various experiments. We compare different surrogate model types with regard to their efficacy (in terms of expensive objective evaluations) and their ability to find Pareto critical points.

7.1. Implementation Details

We implemented the framework in the Julia language (the code is available under https://github.com/manuelbb-upb/Morbit.jl, accessed on 15 April 2021) and used the surrogate construction algorithms from Sections 4.2 and 4.3. Concerning the RBF models, the algorithms are thus the same as in [41]. The OSQP solver [45] is used to solve (P_m). For non-linear problems we use the NLopt.jl [46] package. More specifically we use the MMA algorithm [47] in conjunction with DynamicPolynomials.jl [48] to construct the Lagrange polynomials. The Pascoletti–Serafini subproblems is solved using the population based ISRES method [49] with MMA for polishing. The derivatives of cheap objective functions are obtained by means of automatic differentiation [50] and Taylor models use FiniteDiff.jl.

In accordance with Algorithm 2, we perform the shrinking trust region update via

$$\Delta^{(t+1)} \leftarrow \begin{cases} \gamma_{\|} \Delta^{(t)} & \text{if } \rho^{(t)} < \nu_+, \\ \gamma_{\downarrow} \Delta^{(t)} & \text{if } \rho^{(t)} < \nu_{++}. \end{cases}$$

Note that for box-constrained problems we internally scale the feasible set to the unit hypercube $[0, 1]^n$ and all radii are measured with regard to this scaled domain.

For **stopping**, we use a disjunction of different criteria:

- We have an upper bound $N_{it.} \in \mathbb{N}$ on the maximum number of iterations and an upper bound $N_{exp.} \in \mathbb{N}$ on the number of expensive objective evaluations.

- The surrogate criticality naturally allows for a stopping test and due to Lemma 11 the trust region radius can also be used (see also [33] [Sec. 5]). We combine this with a relative tolerance test and stop if

$$\Delta^{(t)} \leq \Delta_{\min} \text{ OR } \left(\Delta^{(t)} \leq \Delta_{\text{crit}} \text{ AND } \omega\left(\mathbf{x}^{(t)}\right) \leq \omega_{\min}\right).$$

- At a truly critical point the criticality loop Algorithm 1 runs infinitely. We stop after a maximum number $N_{\text{loops}} \in \mathbb{N}_0$ of iterations.
- We also employ the common relative stopping criteria

$$\left\|\mathbf{x}^{(t)} - \mathbf{x}^{(t+1)}\right\|_\infty \leq \delta_x \left\|\mathbf{x}^{(t)}\right\|_\infty \text{ and}$$
$$\left\|\mathbf{f}(\mathbf{x}^{(t)}) - \mathbf{f}(\mathbf{x}^{(t+1)})\right\|_\infty \leq \delta_f \left\|\mathbf{f}(\mathbf{x}^{(t)})\right\|_\infty$$

to provoke early stopping.

7.2. A First Example

We ran our method on a multitude of academic test problems with a varying number of decision variables n and objective functions k. We were able to approximate Pareto critical points in both cases, if we treat the problems as heterogeneous and if we declare them as expensive. We benchmarked RBF against polynomial models, because in [33] it was shown that a trust region method using second degree Lagrange polynomials outperforms commercial solvers on scalarized problems. Most often, RBF surrogates outperform other model types with regard to the number of expensive function evaluations.

This is illustrated in Figure 2. It shows two runs of Algorithm 2 on the non-convex problem (T6), taken from [38]:

$$\min_{\mathbf{x} \in \mathcal{X}} \begin{bmatrix} x_1 + \ln(x_1) + x_{2'}^2 \\ x_1^2 + x_2^4 \end{bmatrix}, \mathcal{X} = [\varepsilon, 30] \times [0, 30] \subseteq \mathbb{R}^2, \varepsilon = 10^{-12}. \tag{T6}$$

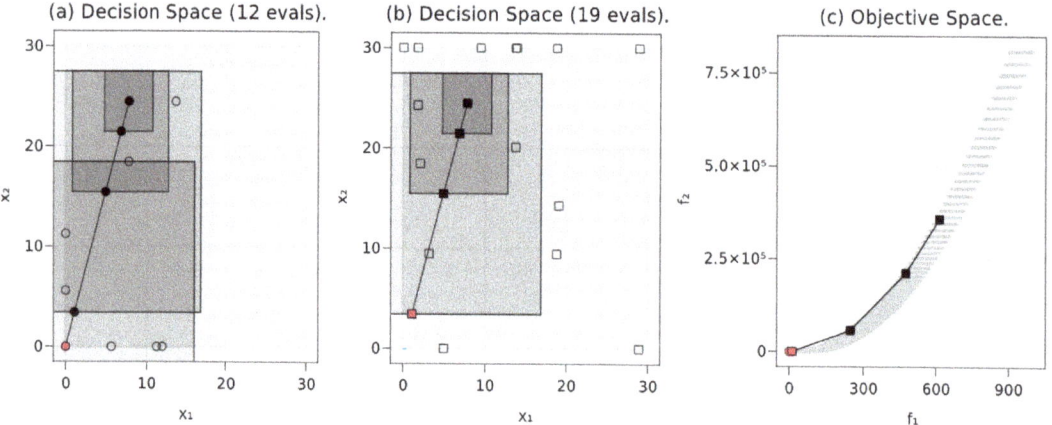

Figure 2. Two runs with maximum number of expensive evaluations set to 20 (soft limit). Test points are light-gray, the iterates are black, final iterate is red, white markers show other points where the objectives are evaluated. The successive trust regions are also shown. (**a**) Using Radial Basis Function (RBF) surrogate models we converge to the optimum using only 12 expensive evaluations. (**b**) Quadratic Lagrange models do not reach the optimum using 19 evaluations. (**c**) Iterations and test points in the objective space.

The first objective function is treated as expensive while the second is cheap. In contrast to most other MOPs, there is only one solution and this Pareto optimal point is $[\varepsilon, 0]^T$. When we set a very restrictive limit of $N_{\exp} = 20$ then we run out of budget with second degree Lagrange surrogates before we reach the optimum, see Figure 2b. As evident in Figure 2a, surrogates based on (cubic) RBF do require significantly less training data. For the RBF models the algorithm stopped after two critical loops and the model refinement during these loops is made clear by the samples on the problem boundary converging to zero. The complete set of relevant parameters for the test runs is given in Table 2. We used a strict acceptance test and the strict Pareto–Cauchy step.

Table 2. Parameters for Figure 2, radii relative to $[0,1]^n$.

Param.	ε_{crit}	$N_{\exp}$	N_{loops}	μ	β	Δ^{ub}	Δ_{min}	$\Delta^{(0)}$	ν_+	ν_{++}	$\gamma_{\downarrow\downarrow}$	$\gamma_{\downarrow}$	$\gamma_{\uparrow}$
Value	10^{-3}	20	2	2×10^3	10^3	0.5	10^{-3}	0.1	0.1	0.4	0.51	0.75	2

7.3. Benchmarks on Scalable Test-Problems

To assess the performance with a growing number of decision variables n, we performed tests on scalable problems of the ZDT and DTLZ family [51,52]. Figure 3 shows results for the bi-objective problems ZDT1-ZDT3 and for the k-objective problems DTLZ1 and DTLZ6 (we used $k = \max\{2, n-4\}$ objectives). All problems are box constrained. Twelve feasible starting points (from the Halton sequence) were generated for each problem setting, i.e., for each combination of n, a test problem and a descent method. The acceptance test and the backtracking were strict.

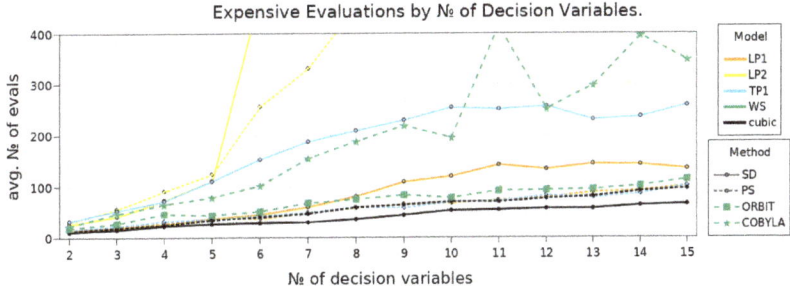

Figure 3. Average number of expensive objective evaluations by number of decision variables n, surrogate type and descent method. "SD" refers to steepest descent and "PS" to Pascoletti–Serafini. "LP1" (orange) are linear Lagrange models, "LP2" (yellow) quadratic Lagrange models, "TP1" (blue) are linear Taylor polynomials based on finite differences and "cubic" (black) refers to cubic RBF models. Additionally the results for weighted sum runs are shown in green, using the COBYLA solver and a single objective variant of the trust region framework, ORBIT.

In all cases the first objective was considered cheap and all other objectives expensive. First and second degree Lagrange models were compared against linear Taylor models and (cubic) RBF surrogates. The Lagrange models were built using a Λ-poised set, with $\Lambda = 1.5$. In the case of quadratic models we used a precomputed set of points for $n \geq 6$. The Taylor models used finite differences and points outside of box constraints were simply projected back onto the boundary. The RBF models were allowed to include up to $(n+1)(n+2)/2$ training points from the database if $n \leq 10$ and else the maximum number of points was $2n+1$. Points were first selected from a box of radius $\theta_1 \Delta^{(t)}$ with $\theta_1 = 2$ and then from a box of radius $\theta_2 \Delta^{ub}$ with $\theta_2 = 2$. All other parameters differing from the parameters in Table 2 are listed in Table 3. The stopping parameters were chosen so as to exit early and save evaluations.

Table 3. Parameters for Figure 3, radii relative to $[0, 1]^n$.

Parameter	$\varepsilon_{\text{crit}}$	$N_{\text{it.}}$	$N_{\text{exp.}}$	N_{loops}	Δ_{crit}	ω_{min}	Δ_{min}	δ_x	δ_f	ν_+	ν_{++}
Value	10^{-2}	100	$n \times 10^3$	3	10^{-2}	10^{-3}	10^{-6}	10^{-3}	10^{-3}	0	0.1

As expected, the second degree Lagrange polynomials require the most objective evaluations and the quadratic dependence on n is clearly visible in Figure 3, and the quadratic growth of the dark-blue line continues for $n \geq 8$. On average, the linear Lagrange models perform better than the linear Taylor polynomials when using the steepest descent steps—also in accordance with our expectations, because only $n + 1$ points are needed for each model (versus $2n$ points). Most models—even the linear ones—profit from using the Pascoletti–Serafini subproblems (see Appendix B) over the steepest descent steps. By far the least evaluations (on average) are needed for the RBF models: The black line consistently stays below all other data points. Note, that the RBF models likely appear to perform slightly better with the steepest descent steps because of the early stopping. In other experiments we noticed that RBF models with Pascoletti–Serafini steps can save evaluations when more precise solutions are required.

For comparison, we also used the weighted sum approach with the single objective $\sum_\ell f_\ell$ on each problem instance. We tested both the derivative-free COBYLA solver (described in [53] and implemented by NLopt.jl) and the trust region method using steepest descent and cubic RBF models, i.e., our own implementation of ORBIT [34]. Both solvers were restricted to the same number of maximum function evaluations. In fact, ORBIT was configured with the exact same parameters as in Table 3 and the relative stopping tolerances for COBYLA were $\delta_x = \delta_f = 10^{-2}$. Although COBYLA also uses linear models it requires significantly more evaluations than most other algorithms. The results of the ORBIT scalarization are more comparable to that of the multiobjective runs.

7.3.1. Solution Quality

Figure 4 illustrates that not only do RBF perform better on average, but also overall. With regard to the final solution criticality, there are a few outliers mostly due to DTLZ1 (see also Figure 5). However, in most cases the solution criticality is acceptable, except for the linear Lagrange models. Moreover, Figure 5 shows that a good percentage of problem instances is solved with RBF, especially when compared to the other linear models. Note, that in cases where the true objectives are not differentiable at the final iterate, ω was set to 0 because the selected problems are non-differentiable only in Pareto optimal points. In Figure 5 it also becomes apparent that the bi-objective DTLZ1 instances were the most challenging for all algorithms. DTLZ1 has many local minima and it is likely to exit early near such a local minimum due to repeated unsuccessful iterations. Likewise, ZDT3 is "flat" towards the true Pareto Front so that it becomes hard to make progress there.

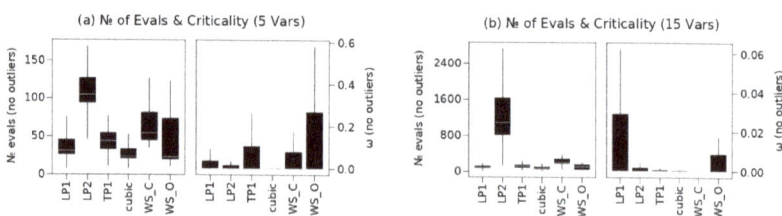

Figure 4. Box-plots of the number of evaluations and the solution criticality for $n = 5$ and $n = 15$ for the runs from Figure 3. Outliers are not shown. "WS_C" and "WS_O" refer to the weighted sum approach using COBYLA and ORBIT, respectively.

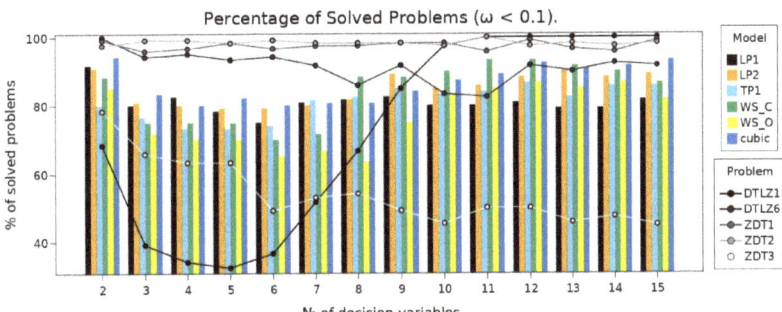

Figure 5. Each group of bars shows the percentage of solved problem instances, i.e., test runs were the final solution criticality has a value below 0.1. From left to right, the bars correspond to the Trust Region Method (TRM) using linear Lagrange polynomials, the TRM with quadratic Lagrange polynomials, TRM with linear Taylor polynomials, weighted sum with COBYLA, weighted sum with ORBIT and TRM with cubic RBF. Per model and n-value there were 60 runs.

Besides criticality, another metric of interest is the spread of solutions for different starting points. Figure 6 shows the final iterates when the algorithm is applied to the bi-objective problems ZDT1 and ZDT2 for 10 different starting points. Additionally, the problems are solved using the weighted sum approach with the derivative-free COBYLA solver. For each starting point the optimizers were allowed 30 objective evaluations and no data were re-used between runs.

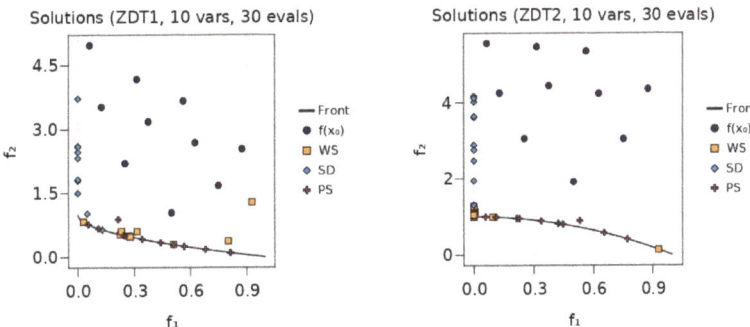

Figure 6. Final iterates in objective space for the bi-objective problems ZDT1 and ZDT2 in 10 variables. The weighted sum method (WS) is compared against the trust region method using steepest descent (DS) and the Pascoletti–Serafini (PS) method.

As can bee seen, for these problems, the trust region method readily reaches the critical set using only 30 evaluations. Here, the steepest descent direction tends to generate solutions on the problem boundary when applied in such a global manner—with relatively large trust region radii ($\Delta^{(0)} = 0.1$ and $\Delta^{ub} = 0.5$). Nonetheless, the method remains applicable for local refinement of approximate solutions, e.g., after a coarse search for good starting points using global methods or as a corrector in continuation frameworks. The Pascoletti–Serafini step can be employed with different reference points/directions to provide a better covering than both the steepest descent steps and the weighted sum approach. For Figure 6, the points $\{[0, -10i], i = 1, \ldots, 10\}$ were used. The weighted sum approach (with fixed weights) tends to produce clustered solutions. Especially for the non-convex problem ZDT2 only the boundary points of the true Pareto Front are reached, as expected [1].

7.3.2. RBF Comparison

Furthermore, we compared the RBF kernels from Table 1. In [34], the cubic kernel performs best on single-objective problems while the Gaussian does worst. As can be seen in Figure 7 this holds for multiple objective functions, too: The Gaussian and the Multiquadric require more function evaluations than the Cubic, especially in higher dimensions. If, however, we use a very simple adaptive strategy to fine-tune the shape parameter, then both kernels can finish significantly faster. In both cases, the shape parameter was set to $\alpha = 20/\Delta^{(t)}$ in each iteration. Nevertheless, the cubic function appears to be a good choice in general.

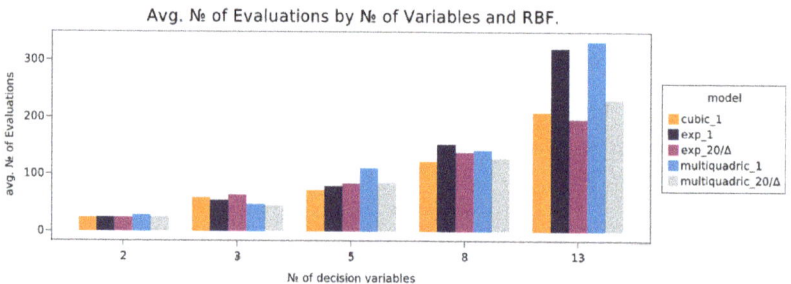

Figure 7. Each group of bars shows the influence of a adaptive shape radius on the performance of different RBF models (tested on ZDT3) for different decision space dimensions. From left to right the bars correspond to the cubic RBF, the Gaussian—with constant shape factor 1 and with adaptive shape factor $20/\Delta^{(t)}$—and the Multiquadric—with shape factors 1 and $20/\Delta^{(t)}$.

8. Conclusions

We have developed a trust region framework for heterogeneous and expensive multiobjective optimization problems. It is based on similar work [29–31,33] and our main contributions are the integration of constraints and of radial basis function surrogates. Subsequently, our method is is provably convergent to first order critical points for unconstrained problems and when the feasible set is convex and compact, while requiring significantly less expensive function evaluations due to a linear scaling of model construction complexity with respect to the number of decision variables.

For future work, several modifications and extensions can likely be transferred from the single-objective to the multiobjective case. For examples, the trust region update can be made step-size-dependent (rather than to depend $\rho^{(t)}$ alone) to allow for a more precise model refinement, see [36] ([Ch. 10]). We have also experimented with the nonlinear CG method [9] for a multiobjective Steihaug–Toint step [36] ([Ch. 7]) and early results look promising.

Going forward, we would like to apply our algorithm to a real world application, similar to what has been done in [54]. Moreover, it would be desirable to obtain not just one but multiple Pareto critical solutions. Because the Pascoletti–Serafini scalarization is still compatible with constraints, the iterations can be guided in image space by providing different global reference points. Furthermore, it is straightforward to use RBF with the heuristic methods from [55] for heterogeneous problems. We believe that it should also be possible to propagate multiple solutions and combine the TRM method with non-dominance testing as has been done in [31] and in [56]. One can think of other globalization strategies as well: RBF models have been used in multiobjective Stochastic Search algorithms [57] and trust region ideas have been included into population based strategies [26]. It will thus be interesting to see whether the theoretical convergence properties can be maintained within these contexts by employing a careful trust-region management. Finally, re-using the data sampled near the final iterate within a continuation framework like in [58] is a promising next step.

Supplementary Materials: Our Julia implementation of the solver is available online at https://github.com/manuelbb-upb/Morbit.jl accessed on 15 April 2021.

Author Contributions: Conceptualization, M.B. and S.P.; methodology, M.B.; software, M.B.; validation, M.B. and S.P.; formal analysis, M.B. and S.P.; investigation, M.B.; writing—original draft preparation, M.B.; writing—review and editing, S.P.; visualization, M.B.; supervision, S.P.; All authors have read and agreed to the published version of the manuscript.

Funding: This research has been funded by the European Union and the German Federal State of North Rhine-Westphalia within the EFRE.NRW project "SET CPS".

Conflicts of Interest: The authors declare no conflict of interest.

Appendix A. Miscellaneous Proofs

Appendix A.1. Continuity of the Constrained Optimal Value

In this subsection we show the continuity of $\omega(\mathbf{x})$ in the constrained case, where $\omega(\mathbf{x})$ is the negative optimal value of (P1), i.e.,

$$\omega(\mathbf{x}) := -\min_{\mathbf{d}\in\mathcal{X}-\mathbf{x}} \max_{\ell=1,\ldots,k} \langle \boldsymbol{\nabla} f_\ell(\mathbf{x}), \mathbf{d}\rangle,$$

$$\text{s.t. } \|\mathbf{d}\| \leq 1.$$

The proof of the continuity of $\omega(\mathbf{x})$, as stated in Theorem 1, follows the reasoning from [6], where continuity is shown for a related constrained descent direction program.

Proof of Item 2 in Theorem 1. Let the requirements of Item 1 be fulfilled, i.e., let **f** be continuously differentiable and let $\mathcal{X} \subset \mathbb{R}^n$ be convex and compact. Further, let **x** be a point in $\mathcal{X}$ and denote the minimizing direction in (P1) by $\mathbf{d}(\mathbf{x})$ and the optimal value by $\theta(\mathbf{x})$. We show that $\theta(\mathbf{x})$ is continuous, by which $\omega(\mathbf{x}) = -\theta(\mathbf{x})$ is continuous as well.

First, note the following properties of the maximum function:

1. $\mathbf{u} \mapsto \max_\ell u_\ell$ is positively homogenous and hence

$$\max_\ell(\langle \boldsymbol{\nabla} f_\ell(\mathbf{x}), \mathbf{d}_1\rangle + \langle \boldsymbol{\nabla} f_\ell(\mathbf{x}), \mathbf{d}_2\rangle) \leq \max_\ell \langle \boldsymbol{\nabla} f_\ell(\mathbf{x}), \mathbf{d}_1\rangle + \max_\ell \langle \boldsymbol{\nabla} f_\ell(\mathbf{x}), \mathbf{d}_2\rangle.$$

2. $\mathbf{u} \mapsto \max_\ell u_\ell$ is Lipschitz with constant 1 so that

$$\left|\max_\ell \langle \boldsymbol{\nabla} f_\ell(\mathbf{x}_1), \mathbf{d}_1\rangle - \max_\ell \langle \boldsymbol{\nabla} f_\ell(\mathbf{x}_2), \mathbf{d}_2\rangle\right| \leq \|\mathbf{Df}(\mathbf{x}_1)\mathbf{d}_1 - \mathbf{Df}(\mathbf{x}_2)\mathbf{d}_2\|,$$

for both the maximum and the Euclidean norm.

Now let $\{\mathbf{x}^{(t)}\} \subseteq \mathcal{X}$ be a sequence with $\mathbf{x}^{(t)} \to \mathbf{x}$. Due to the constraints, we have that $\mathbf{d}(\mathbf{x}) \in \mathcal{X} - \mathbf{x}$ and thereby $\mathbf{d}(\mathbf{x}) + \mathbf{x} - \mathbf{x}^{(t)} \in \mathcal{X} - \mathbf{x}^{(t)}$. Let

$$(0,1] \ni \sigma^{(t)} := \begin{cases} \min\left\{1, \dfrac{1}{\|\mathbf{d}(\mathbf{x}) + \mathbf{x} - \mathbf{x}^{(t)}\|}\right\} & \text{if } \mathbf{d}(\mathbf{x}) \neq \mathbf{x}^{(t)} - \mathbf{x}, \\ 1 & \text{else.} \end{cases}$$

Then $\sigma^{(t)}\left(\mathbf{d}(\mathbf{x}) + \mathbf{x} - \mathbf{x}^{(t)}\right)$ is feasible for (P1) at $\mathbf{x}^{(t)}$:

- $\sigma^{(t)}\left(\mathbf{d}(\mathbf{x}) + \mathbf{x} - \mathbf{x}^{(t)}\right) \in \mathcal{X} - \mathbf{x}^{(t)}$ because $\mathcal{X} - \mathbf{x}^{(t)}$ is convex and $0, \left(\mathbf{d}(\mathbf{x}) + \mathbf{x} - \mathbf{x}^{(t)}\right) \in \mathcal{X} - \mathbf{x}^{(t)}$ as well as $\sigma^{(t)} \in (0, 1]$.
- $\left\|\sigma^{(t)}\left(\mathbf{d}(\mathbf{x}) + \mathbf{x} - \mathbf{x}^{(t)}\right)\right\| \leq 1$ by the definition of $\sigma^{(t)}$.

By the definition of (P1) it follows that

$\max_\ell \langle \nabla f_\ell(\mathbf{x}^{(t)}), \mathbf{d}(\mathbf{x}^{(t)}) \rangle \leq \sigma^{(t)} \max_\ell \langle \nabla f_\ell(\mathbf{x}^{(t)}), \mathbf{d}(\mathbf{x}) + \mathbf{x} - \mathbf{x}^{(t)} \rangle$

and by the maximum property 1

$$\max_\ell \langle \nabla f_\ell(\mathbf{x}^{(t)}), \mathbf{d}(\mathbf{x}^{(t)}) \rangle \leq \sigma^{(t)} \max_\ell \langle \nabla f_\ell(\mathbf{x}^{(t)}), \mathbf{d}(\mathbf{x}) \rangle + \sigma^{(t)} \max_\ell \langle \nabla f_\ell(\mathbf{x}^{(t)}), \mathbf{x} - \mathbf{x}^{(t)} \rangle. \tag{A1}$$

We make the following observations:

- Because of $\|\mathbf{d}(\mathbf{x}) + \mathbf{x} - \mathbf{x}^{(t)}\| \xrightarrow{t \to \infty} \|\mathbf{d}(\mathbf{x})\| \leq 1$, it follows that $\sigma^{(t)} \xrightarrow{t \to \infty} 1$.
- Because all objective gradients are continuous, it holds for all $\ell \in \{1, \ldots, k\}$ that $\nabla f_\ell(\mathbf{x}^{(t)}) \to \nabla f_\ell(\mathbf{x})$ and because $\mathbf{u} \mapsto \max_\ell u_\ell$ is continuous as well, it then follows that

$$\max_\ell \langle \nabla f_\ell(\mathbf{x}^{(t)}), \mathbf{d}(\mathbf{x}) \rangle \to \max_\ell \langle \nabla f_\ell(\mathbf{x}), \mathbf{d}(\mathbf{x}) \rangle \quad \text{for } t \to \infty.$$

- The last term on the RHS of (A1) vanishes for $t \to \infty$.

By taking the limit superior on (A1), we then find that

$$\limsup_{t \to \infty} \theta(\mathbf{x}^{(t)}) = \limsup_{t \to \infty} \max_\ell \langle \nabla f_\ell(\mathbf{x}^{(t)}), \mathbf{d}(\mathbf{x}^{(t)}) \rangle \leq \max_\ell \langle \nabla f_\ell(\mathbf{x}), \mathbf{d}(\mathbf{x}) \rangle = \theta(\mathbf{x}) \tag{A2}$$

Vice versa, we know that because of $\mathbf{d}(\mathbf{x}^{(t)}) \in \mathcal{X} - \mathbf{x}^{(t)}$, it holds that $\mathbf{d}(\mathbf{x}^{(t)}) + \mathbf{x}^{(t)} - \mathbf{x} \in \mathcal{X} - \mathbf{x}$ and as above we find that

$$\max_\ell \langle \nabla f_\ell(\mathbf{x}), \mathbf{d}(\mathbf{x}) \rangle \leq \lambda^{(t)} \max_\ell \langle \nabla f_\ell(\mathbf{x}), \mathbf{d}(\mathbf{x}^{(t)}) \rangle + \lambda^{(t)} \max_\ell \langle \nabla f_\ell(\mathbf{x}), \mathbf{x}^{(t)} - \mathbf{x} \rangle \tag{A3}$$

with

$$\lambda^{(t)} := \begin{cases} \min\left\{1, \dfrac{1}{\|\mathbf{d}(\mathbf{x}) + \mathbf{x}^{(t)} - \mathbf{x}\|}\right\} & \text{if } \mathbf{d}(\mathbf{x}) \neq \mathbf{x}^{(t)} - \mathbf{x}, \\ 1 & \text{else.} \end{cases}$$

Again, the last term of (A3) vanishes in the limit so that by using the properties of the maximum function and the continuity of ∇f_ℓ, as well as $\lambda^{(t)} \xrightarrow{t \to \infty} 1$, in taking the limit inferior on (A3) we find that

$$\begin{aligned}
\theta(\mathbf{x}) &= \max_\ell \langle \nabla f_\ell(\mathbf{x}), \mathbf{d}(\mathbf{x}) \rangle \leq \liminf_{t \to \infty} \max_\ell \langle \nabla f_\ell(\mathbf{x}), \mathbf{d}(\mathbf{x}^{(t)}) \rangle \\
&\leq \liminf_{t \to \infty} \left[\left(\max_\ell \langle \nabla f_\ell(\mathbf{x}), \mathbf{d}(\mathbf{x}^{(t)}) \rangle - \max_\ell \langle \nabla f_\ell(\mathbf{x}^{(t)}), \mathbf{d}(\mathbf{x}^{(t)}) \rangle \right) + \max_\ell \langle \nabla f_\ell(\mathbf{x}^{(t)}), \mathbf{d}(\mathbf{x}^{(t)}) \rangle \right] \\
&\leq \liminf_{t \to \infty} \left[\|\mathbf{Df}(\mathbf{x}) - \mathbf{Df}(\mathbf{x}^{(t)})\| \|\mathbf{d}(\mathbf{x}^{(t)})\| + \max_\ell \langle \nabla f_\ell(\mathbf{x}^{(t)}), \mathbf{d}(\mathbf{x}^{(t)}) \rangle \right] \\
&\leq \liminf_{t \to \infty} \max_\ell \langle \nabla f_\ell(\mathbf{x}^{(t)}), \mathbf{d}(\mathbf{x}^{(t)}) \rangle = \liminf_{t \to \infty} \theta(\mathbf{x}^{(t)}).
\end{aligned} \tag{A4}$$

Combining (A2) and (A4) shows that $\theta(\mathbf{x}^{(t)}) \xrightarrow{t \to \infty} \theta(\mathbf{x})$. □

Theorem 2 claims that $\omega(\mathbf{x})$ is uniformly continuous, provided the objective gradients are Lipschitz. The implied Cauchy continuity is an important property in the convergence proof of the algorithm.

Proof of Theorem 2. We will consider the constrained case only, when $\mathcal{X}$ is convex and compact and show uniform continuity a fortiori by proving that $\omega(\bullet)$ is Lipschitz. Let the objective gradients be Lipschitz continuous. Then $\mathbf{Df}$ is Lipschitz as well with constant $L > 0$. Let $\mathbf{x}, \mathbf{y} \in \mathcal{X}$ with $\mathbf{x} \neq \mathbf{y}$ (the other case is trivial) and let again $\mathbf{d}(\mathbf{x}), \mathbf{d}(\mathbf{y})$ be the respective optimizers.

Suppose w.l.o.g. that

$$\left|\max_\ell \langle \nabla f_\ell(\mathbf{x}), \mathbf{d}(\mathbf{x})\rangle - \max_\ell \langle \nabla f_\ell(\mathbf{y}), \mathbf{d}(\mathbf{y})\rangle\right| = \max_\ell \langle \nabla f_\ell(\mathbf{x}), \mathbf{d}(\mathbf{x})\rangle - \max_\ell \langle \nabla f_\ell(\mathbf{y}), \mathbf{d}(\mathbf{y})\rangle$$

If we define

$$(0,1] \ni \sigma := \begin{cases} \min\left\{1, \frac{1}{\|\mathbf{d}(\mathbf{y})+\mathbf{y}-\mathbf{x}\|}\right\} & \text{if } \mathbf{d}(\mathbf{y}) \neq \mathbf{x} - \mathbf{y}, \\ 1 & \text{else,} \end{cases}$$

then again $\sigma(\mathbf{d}(\mathbf{y}) + \mathbf{y} - \mathbf{x})$ is feasible for (P1) at $\mathbf{y}$. Thus,

$$\begin{aligned}
\max_\ell \langle \nabla f_\ell(\mathbf{x}), \mathbf{d}(\mathbf{x})\rangle &- \max_\ell \langle \nabla f_\ell(\mathbf{y}), \mathbf{d}(\mathbf{y})\rangle \\
&\stackrel{\text{df.}}{\leq} \max_\ell \langle \nabla f_\ell(\mathbf{x}), \sigma(\mathbf{d}(\mathbf{y}) + \mathbf{y} - \mathbf{x})\rangle - \max_\ell \langle \nabla f_\ell(\mathbf{y}), \mathbf{d}(\mathbf{y})\rangle \\
&\leq \|\sigma \mathbf{Df}(\mathbf{x})(\mathbf{d}(\mathbf{y}) + \mathbf{y} - \mathbf{x}) - \mathbf{Df}(\mathbf{y})\mathbf{d}(\mathbf{y})\| \\
&\stackrel{\sigma \leq 1}{\leq} \|\sigma \mathbf{Df}(\mathbf{x}) - \mathbf{Df}(\mathbf{y})\|\|\mathbf{d}(\mathbf{y})\| + \|\mathbf{Df}(\mathbf{x})\|\|\mathbf{x} - \mathbf{y}\|,
\end{aligned} \quad (A5)$$

where we have again used the maximum property 2 for the second inequality. We now investigate the first term on the RHS. Using $\|\mathbf{d}(\mathbf{y})\| \leq 1$ and adding a zero, we find

$$\begin{aligned}
\|\sigma \mathbf{Df}(\mathbf{x}) - \mathbf{Df}(\mathbf{y})\|\|\mathbf{d}(\mathbf{y})\| &\leq \|\mathbf{Df}(\mathbf{x}) - \mathbf{Df}(\mathbf{y}) - (1-\sigma)\mathbf{Df}(\mathbf{x})\| \\
&\leq L\|\mathbf{x} - \mathbf{y}\| + (1-\sigma)\|\mathbf{Df}(\mathbf{x})\|.
\end{aligned} \quad (A6)$$

Furthermore, $\|\mathbf{d}(\mathbf{y}) + \mathbf{y} - \mathbf{x}\| \leq 1 + \|\mathbf{y} - \mathbf{x}\|$ implies $1/(1 + \|\mathbf{y} - \mathbf{x}\|) \leq \sigma$ and

$$1 - \sigma \leq 1 - \frac{1}{1 + \|\mathbf{y} - \mathbf{x}\|} = \frac{\|\mathbf{y} - \mathbf{x}\|}{1 + \|\mathbf{y} - \mathbf{x}\|} \leq \|\mathbf{y} - \mathbf{x}\|.$$

We use this inequality and plug (A6) into (A5) to obtain

$$\begin{aligned}
\max_\ell \langle \nabla f_\ell(\mathbf{x}), \mathbf{d}(\mathbf{x})\rangle - \max_\ell \langle \nabla f_\ell(\mathbf{y}), \mathbf{d}(\mathbf{y})\rangle &\leq L\|\mathbf{x} - \mathbf{y}\| + 2\|\mathbf{Df}(\mathbf{x})\|\|\mathbf{x} - \mathbf{y}\| \\
&\leq (L + 2D)\|\mathbf{x} - \mathbf{y}\|,
\end{aligned}$$

with $D = \max_{\mathbf{x} \in \mathcal{X}} \|\mathbf{Df}(\mathbf{x})\|$ which is well-defined because $\mathcal{X}$ is compact and $\|\mathbf{Df}(\bullet)\|$ is continuous. □

Appendix A.2. Modified Criticality Measures

Proof of Lemma 5. There are two cases to consider:

- If $\omega_m^{(t)}\left(\mathbf{x}^{(t)}\right) \geq \omega\left(\mathbf{x}^{(t)}\right)$ then

$$\left|\omega_m^{(t)}\left(\mathbf{x}^{(t)}\right) - \omega\left(\mathbf{x}^{(t)}\right)\right| = \omega_m^{(t)}\left(\mathbf{x}^{(t)}\right) - \omega\left(\mathbf{x}^{(t)}\right) \leq \kappa_\omega \omega_m^{(t)}\left(\mathbf{x}^{(t)}\right).$$

Now

$$\left|\tilde\omega_m^{(t)}\left(\mathbf{x}^{(t)}\right) - \tilde\omega\left(\mathbf{x}^{(t)}\right)\right| \in \left\{1 - \omega\left(\mathbf{x}^{(t)}\right) \leq \omega_m^{(t)}\left(\mathbf{x}^{(t)}\right) - \omega\left(\mathbf{x}^{(t)}\right) \atop 1 - 1 = 0\right\} \leq \kappa_\omega \omega_m^{(t)}\left(\mathbf{x}^{(t)}\right).$$

- The case $\omega\left(\mathbf{x}^{(t)}\right) < \omega_m^{(t)}\left(\mathbf{x}^{(t)}\right)$ can be shown similarly.

□

Proof of Lemma 6. Use Lemma 5 and then investigate the two possible cases:

- If $\omega_m^{(t)}\left(\mathbf{x}^{(t)}\right) \geq \omega\left(\mathbf{x}^{(t)}\right)$, then the first inequality follows because of $1 \geq 1/(1+\kappa_\omega)$.
- If $\omega_m^{(t)}\left(\mathbf{x}^{(t)}\right) < \omega\left(\mathbf{x}^{(t)}\right)$, then $\omega\left(\mathbf{x}^{(t)}\right) - \omega_m^{(t)}\left(\mathbf{x}^{(t)}\right) \leq \kappa_\omega \omega_m^{(t)}\left(\mathbf{x}^{(t)}\right)$, and again the first inequality follows.

□

Appendix B. Pascoletti–Serafini Step

One example of an alternative descent step $\mathbf{s}^{(t)} \in \mathbb{R}^n$ is given in [33]. Thomann and Eichfelder [33] leverage the Pascoletti–Serafini scalarization to define local subproblems that guide the iterates towards the (local) model ideal point. To be precise, it is shown that the trial point $\mathbf{x}_+^{(t)}$ can be computed as the solution to

$$\min_{\tau \in \mathbb{R}, \mathbf{x} \in B^{(t)}} \tau \quad \text{s.t.} \quad \mathbf{m}^{(t)}(\mathbf{x}^{(t)}) + \tau \mathbf{r}^{(t)} - \mathbf{m}^{(t)}(\mathbf{x}) \geq \mathbf{0}, \tag{A7}$$

where $\mathbf{r}^{(t)} = \mathbf{m}^{(t)}(\mathbf{x}^{(t)}) - \mathbf{i}_m^{(t)} \in \mathbb{R}_{\geq 0}^k$ is the direction vector pointing from the local model ideal point

$$\mathbf{i}_m^{(t)} = \left[i_1^{(t)}, \ldots, i_k^{(t)}\right]^T, \quad \text{with } i_\ell^{(t)} = \min_{\mathbf{x} \in \mathcal{X}} m_\ell^{(t)}(\mathbf{x}) \text{ for } \ell = 1, \ldots, k, \tag{A8}$$

to the current iterate value. If the surrogates are linear or quadratic polynomials and the trust region use a p-norm with $p \in \{1, 2, \infty\}$ these sub-problems are linear or quadratic programs.

A convergence proof for the unconstrained case is given in [33]. It relies on a sufficient decrease bound similar to (20). However, it is not shown that $\kappa^{sd} \in (0, 1)$ exists independent of the iteration index t but stated as an assumption.

Furthermore, constraints (in particular box constraints) are integrated into the definition of $\omega(\bullet)$ and $\omega_m^{(t)}(\bullet)$ using an active set strategy (see [38]). Consequently, both values are no longer Cauchy continuous. We can remedy both drawbacks by relating the (possibly constrained) Pascoletti–Serafini trial point to the strict modified Pareto–Cauchy point in our projection framework. To this end, we allow in (A7) and (A8) any feasible set fulfilling Assumption 1. Moreover, we recite the following assumption:

Assumption A1 (Assumption 4.10 in [33]). *There is a constant* $\mathbf{r} \in (0, 1]$ *so that if* $\mathbf{x}^{(t)}$ *is not Pareto critical, the components* $r_1^{(t)}, \ldots, r_k^{(t)}$, *of* $\mathbf{r}^{(t)}$ *satisfy* $\dfrac{\min_\ell r_\ell^{(t)}}{\max_\ell r_\ell^{(t)}} \geq \mathbf{r}$.

The assumption can be justified because $r_\ell^{(t)} > 0$ if $\mathbf{x}^{(t)}$ is not critical and $r_\ell^{(t)}$ can be bounded above and below by expressions involving $\omega_m^{(t)}(\bullet)$, see Remark 4 and [33] (Lemma 4.9). We can then derive the following lemma:

Lemma A1. *Suppose Assumptions 1 and 2 and Appendix B hold. Let* $(\tau^+, \mathbf{x}_+^{(t)})$ *be the solution to* (A7). *Then there exists a constant* $\tilde{\kappa}_m^{sd} \in (0, 1)$ *such that it holds*

$$\Phi_m^{(t)}(\mathbf{x}^{(t)}) - \Phi_m^{(t)}(\mathbf{x}_+^{(t)}) \geq \tilde{\kappa}_m^{sd} \omega_m^{(t)}\left(\mathbf{x}^{(t)}\right) \min\left\{\frac{\omega_m^{(t)}\left(\mathbf{x}^{(t)}\right)}{cH_m^{(t)}}, \Delta^{(t)}, 1\right\}.$$

Proof. If $\mathbf{x}^{(t)}$ is critical for (MOPm), then $\tau^+ = 0$ and $\mathbf{x}_+^{(t)} = \mathbf{x}^{(t)}$ and the bound is trivial [5]. Otherwise, we can use the same argumentation as in [33] ([Lemma 4.13]) to show that for the strict modified Pareto–Cauchy point $\hat{\mathbf{x}}_{\text{PC}}^{(t)}$ it holds that

$$\Phi_{\text{m}}^{(t)}(\mathbf{x}^{(t)}) - \Phi_{\text{m}}^{(t)}(\mathbf{x}_+^{(t)}) \geq r \min_{\ell} \left\{ m_{\ell}^{(t)}(\mathbf{x}^{(t)}) - m_{\ell}^{(t)}(\hat{\mathbf{x}}_{\text{PC}}^{(t)}) \right\}$$

and the final bound follows from Corollary 2 with the new constant $\tilde{\kappa}_{\text{m}}^{\text{sd}} = r\kappa_{\text{m}}^{\text{sd}}$. □

References

1. Ehrgott, M. *Multicriteria Optimization*, 2nd ed.; Springer: Berlin, Germany, 2005.
2. Jahn, J. *Vector Optimization: Theory, Applications, and Extensions*, 2nd ed.; Springer: Berlin, Germany, 2011; OCLC: 725378304.
3. Miettinen, K. *Nonlinear Multiobjective Optimization*; Springer: Berlin, Germany, 2013; OCLC: 1089790877.
4. Eichfelder, G. Twenty Years of Continuous Multiobjective Optimization. Available online: http://www.optimization-online.org/DB_FILE/2020/12/8161.pdf (accessed on 8 April 2021).
5. Eichfelder, G. *Adaptive Scalarization Methods in Multiobjective Optimization*; Springer: Berlin, Germany, 2008. [CrossRef]
6. Fukuda, E.H.; Drummond, L.M.G. A Survey on Multiobjective Descent Methods. *Pesqui. Oper.* **2014**, *34*, 585–620. [CrossRef]
7. Fliege, J.; Svaiter, B.F. Steepest descent methods for multicriteria optimization. *Math. Method. Operat. Res. (ZOR)* **2000**, *51*, 479–494. [CrossRef]
8. Graña Drummond, L.; Svaiter, B. A steepest descent method for vector optimization. *J. Comput. Appl. Math.* **2005**, *175*, 395–414. [CrossRef]
9. Lucambio Pérez, L.R.; Prudente, L.F. Nonlinear Conjugate Gradient Methods for Vector Optimization. *SIAM J. Optim.* **2018**, *28*, 2690–2720. [CrossRef]
10. Lucambio Pérez, L.R.; Prudente, L.F. A Wolfe Line Search Algorithm for Vector Optimization. *ACM Transact. Math. Softw.* **2019**, *45*, 1–23. [CrossRef]
11. Gebken, B.; Peitz, S.; Dellnitz, M. A Descent Method for Equality and Inequality Constrained Multiobjective Optimization Problems. In *Numerical and Evolutionary Optimization—NEO 2017*; Trujillo, L., Schütze, O., Maldonado, Y., Valle, P., Eds.; Springer: Cham, Switzerland, 2019; pp. 29–61.
12. Hillermeier, C. *Nonlinear Multiobjective Optimization: A Generalized Homotopy Approach*; Springer Basel AG: Basel, Switzerland, 2001; OCLC: 828735498.
13. Gebken, B.; Peitz, S.; Dellnitz, M. On the hierarchical structure of Pareto critical sets. *J. Glob. Optim.* **2019**, *73*, 891–913. [CrossRef]
14. Wilppu, O.; Karmitsa, N.; Mäkelä, M. *New Multiple Subgradient Descent Bundle Method for Nonsmooth Multiobjective Optimization*; Report no. 1126; Turku Centre for Computer Science: Turku, Sweden, 2014.
15. Gebken, B.; Peitz, S. An Efficient Descent Method for Locally Lipschitz Multiobjective Optimization Problems. *J. Optim. Theor. Appl.* **2021**. [CrossRef]
16. Custódio, A.L.; Madeira, J.F.A.; Vaz, A.I.F.; Vicente, L.N. Direct Multisearch for Multiobjective Optimization. *SIAM J. Optim.* **2011**, *21*, 1109–1140. [CrossRef]
17. Audet, C.; Savard, G.; Zghal, W. Multiobjective Optimization Through a Series of Single-Objective Formulations. *SIAM J. Optim.* **2008**, *19*, 188–210. [CrossRef]
18. Deb, K.; Pratap, A.; Agarwal, S.; Meyarivan, T. A fast and elitist multiobjective genetic algorithm: NSGA-II. *IEEE Trans. Evol. Comput.* **2002**, *6*, 182–197. [CrossRef]
19. Deb, K. *Multi-Objective Optimization Using Evolutionary Algorithms*; Wiley: Hoboken, NJ, USA, 2001.
20. Coello, C.A.C.; Lamont, G.B.; Veldhuizen, D.A.V. *Evolutionary Algorithms for Solving Multi-Objective Problems*, 2nd ed.; Springer: New York, NY, USA, 2007.
21. Abraham, A.; Jain, L.C.; Goldberg, R. (Eds.) Evolutionary multiobjective optimization: Theoretical advances and applications. In *Advanced Information and Knowledge Processing*; Springer: New York, NY, USA, 2005.
22. Zitzler, E. Evolutionary Algorithms for Multiobjective Optimization: Methods and Applications. Ph.D. Thesis, ETH, Zurich, Switzerland, 1999.
23. Peitz, S.; Dellnitz, M. A Survey of Recent Trends in Multiobjective Optimal Control—Surrogate Models, Feedback Control and Objective Reduction. *Math. Comput. Appl.* **2018**, *23*, 30. [CrossRef]
24. Chugh, T.; Sindhya, K.; Hakanen, J.; Miettinen, K. A survey on handling computationally expensive multiobjective optimization problems with evolutionary algorithms. *Soft Comput.* **2019**, *23*, 3137–3166. [CrossRef]
25. Deb, K.; Roy, P.C.; Hussein, R. Surrogate Modeling Approaches for Multiobjective Optimization: Methods, Taxonomy, and Results. *Math. Comput. Appl.* **2020**, *26*, 5. [CrossRef]
26. Roy, P.C.; Hussein, R.; Blank, J.; Deb, K. Trust-Region Based Multi-objective Optimization for Low Budget Scenarios. In *Evolutionary Multi-Criterion Optimization*; Series Title: Lecture Notes in Computer Science; Deb, K., Goodman, E., Coello Coello, C.A., Klamroth, K., Miettinen, K., Mostaghim, S., Reed, P., Eds.; Springer International Publishing: Cham, Switzerland, 2019; Volume 11411; pp. 373–385. [CrossRef]

27. Conn, A.R.; Scheinberg, K.; Vicente, L.N. *Introduction to Derivative-Free Optimization*; Number 8 in MPS-SIAM Series on Optimization; Society for Industrial and Applied Mathematics/Mathematical Programming Society: Philadelphia, PA, USA, 2009; OCLC: Ocn244660709.
28. Larson, J.; Menickelly, M.; Wild, S.M. Derivative-free optimization methods. *arXiv* **2019**, arXiv:1904.11585.
29. Qu, S.; Goh, M.; Liang, B. Trust region methods for solving multiobjective optimisation. *Optim. Method. Softw.* **2013**, *28*, 796–811. [CrossRef]
30. Villacorta, K.D.V.; Oliveira, P.R.; Soubeyran, A. A Trust-Region Method for Unconstrained Multiobjective Problems with Applications in Satisficing Processes. *J. Optim. Theor. Appl.* **2014**, *160*, 865–889. [CrossRef]
31. Ryu, J.H.; Kim, S. A Derivative-Free Trust-Region Method for Biobjective Optimization. *SIAM J. Optim.* **2014**, *24*, 334–362. [CrossRef]
32. Audet, C.; Savard, G.; Zghal, W. A mesh adaptive direct search algorithm for multiobjective optimization. *Eur. J. Oper. Res.* **2010**, *204*, 545–556. [CrossRef]
33. Thomann, J.; Eichfelder, G. A Trust-Region Algorithm for Heterogeneous Multiobjective Optimization. *SIAM J. Optim.* **2019**, *29*, 1017–1047. [CrossRef]
34. Wild, S.M.; Regis, R.G.; Shoemaker, C.A. ORBIT: Optimization by Radial Basis Function Interpolation in Trust-Regions. *SIAM J. Sci. Comput.* **2008**, *30*, 3197–3219. [CrossRef]
35. Conn, A.R.; Scheinberg, K.; Vicente, L.N. Global Convergence of General Derivative-Free Trust-Region Algorithms to First- and Second-Order Critical Points. *SIAM J. Optim.* **2009**, *20*, 387–415. [CrossRef]
36. Conn, A.R.; Gould, N.I.M.; Toint, P.L. *Trust-Region Methods*; MPS-SIAM series on optimization; Society for Industrial and Applied Mathematics: Harrisburg, PA, USA, 2000.
37. Luc, D.T. *Theory of Vector Optimization*; Lecture Notes in Economics and Mathematical Systems; Springer: Berlin, Heidelberg, 1989; Volume 319. [CrossRef]
38. Thomann, J. A Trust Region Approach for Multi-Objective Heterogeneous Optimization. Ph.D. Thesis, TU Ilmenau, Ilmenau, Germany, 2018.
39. Nocedal, J.; Wright, S.J. *Numerical Optimization*, 2nd ed.; Springer Series in Operations Research; Springer: Berlin, Germany, 2006; OCLC: Ocm68629100.
40. Wendland, H. *Scattered Data Approximation*, 1st ed.; Cambridge University Press: Cambridge, UK, 2004. [CrossRef]
41. Wild, S.M. *Derivative-Free Optimization Algorithms for Computationally Expensive Functions*; Cornell University: Ithaca, NY, USA, 2009.
42. Wild, S.M.; Shoemaker, C. Global Convergence of Radial Basis Function Trust Region Derivative-Free Algorithms. *SIAM J. Optim.* **2011**, *21*, 761–781. [CrossRef]
43. Regis, R.G.; Wild, S.M. CONORBIT: Constrained optimization by radial basis function interpolation in trust regions. *Optim. Methods Softw.* **2017**, *32*, 552–580. [CrossRef]
44. Fleming, W. *Functions of Several Variables*; Undergraduate Texts in Mathematics; Springer: New York, NY, USA, 1977. [CrossRef]
45. Stellato, B.; Banjac, G.; Goulart, P.; Bemporad, A.; Boyd, S. OSQP: An operator splitting solver for quadratic programs. *Math. Program. Comput.* **2020**, *12*, 637–672. [CrossRef]
46. Johnson, S.G. The NLopt Nonlinear-Optimization Package. Available online: https://nlopt.readthedocs.io/en/latest/ (accessed on 8 April 2021).
47. Svanberg, K. A class of globally convergent optimization methods based on conservative convex separable approximations. *SIAM J. Optim.* **2002**, *12*, 555–573. [CrossRef]
48. Legat, B.; Timme, S.; Weisser, T.; Kapelevich, L.; Rackauckas, C.; TagBot, J. JuliaAlgebra/DynamicPolynomials.jl: V0.3.15. 2020. Available online: https://zenodo.org/record/4153432#.YG5wjj8RVPY (accessed on 8 April 2021).
49. Runarsson, T.P.; Yao, X. Search biases in constrained evolutionary optimization. *IEEE Trans. Syst. Man Cybern. C Appl. Rev.* **2005**, *35*, 233–243. [CrossRef]
50. Revels, J.; Lubin, M.; Papamarkou, T. Forward-Mode Automatic Differentiation in Julia. *arXiv* **2016**, arXiv:1607.07892.
51. Zitzler, E.; Deb, K.; Thiele, L. Comparison of Multiobjective Evolutionary Algorithms: Empirical Results. *Evol. Comput.* **2000**, *8*, 173–195. [CrossRef]
52. Deb, K.; Thiele, L.; Laumanns, M.; Zitzler, E. Scalable Test Problems for Evolutionary Multiobjective Optimization. In *Evolutionary Multiobjective Optimization*; Series Title: Advanced Information and Knowledge Processing; Abraham, A., Jain, L., Goldberg, R., Eds.; Springer: London, UK, 2005; pp. 105–145. [CrossRef]
53. Powell, M.J. A direct search optimization method that models the objective and constraint functions by linear interpolation. In *Advances in Optimization and Numerical Analysis*; Gomez, S., Hennart, J.P., Eds.; Springer: Dordrecht, The Netherlands, 1994; pp. 51–67.
54. Prinz, S.; Thomann, J.; Eichfelder, G.; Boeck, T.; Schumacher, J. Expensive multi-objective optimization of electromagnetic mixing in a liquid metal. *Optim. Eng.* **2020**. [CrossRef]
55. Thomann, J.; Eichfelder, G. Representation of the Pareto front for heterogeneous multi-objective optimization. *J. Appl. Numer. Optim.* **2019**, *1*, 293–323.
56. Deshpande, S.; Watson, L.T.; Canfield, R.A. Multiobjective optimization using an adaptive weighting scheme. *Optim. Methods Softw.* **2016**, *31*, 110–133. [CrossRef]

57. Regis, R.G. Multi-objective constrained black-box optimization using radial basis function surrogates. *J. Comput. Sci.* **2016**, *16*, 140–155. [CrossRef]
58. Schütze, O.; Cuate, O.; Martín, A.; Peitz, S.; Dellnitz, M. Pareto Explorer: A global/local exploration tool for many-objective optimization problems. *Eng. Optim.* **2020**, *52*, 832–855. [CrossRef]

Article

An Interactive Recommendation System for Decision Making Based on the Characterization of Cognitive Tasks

Teodoro Macias-Escobar [1,2,*,†], Laura Cruz-Reyes [3,†], César Medina-Trejo [3,†], Claudia Gómez-Santillán [3,†], Nelson Rangel-Valdez [4,†] and Héctor Fraire-Huacuja [3,†]

1. Department of Computing Science, Tijuana Institute of Technology, Av Castillo de Chapultepec 562, Tomas Aquino, Tijuana 22414, Mexico
2. Departamento de Ingeniería Informática, Universidad de Cádiz, 11519 Puerto Real, Spain
3. Graduate Program Division, Tecnológico Nacional de México, Instituto Tecnológico de Ciudad Madero, Cd. Madero 89440, Mexico; lauracruzreyes@itcm.edu.mx (L.C.-R.); cesarmedinatrejo@gmail.com (C.M.-T.); Claudia.gomez@itcm.edu.mx (C.G.-S.); automatas2002@yahoo.com.mx (H.F.-H.)
4. CONACyT Research Fellow at Graduate Program Division, Tecnológico Nacional de México, Instituto Tecnológico de Ciudad Madero, Cd. Madero 89440, Mexico; nelson.rangel@itcm.edu.mx
* Correspondence: teodoro_macias@hotmail.com or teodoro.maciasescobar@alum.uca.es
† These authors contributed equally to this work.

Citation: Macias-Escobar, T.; Cruz-Reyes, L.; Medina-Trejo, C.; Gómez-Santillán, C.; Rangel-Valdez, N.; Fraire-Huacuja, H. An Interactive Recommendation System for Decision Making Based on the Characterization of Cognitive Tasks. *Math. Comput. Appl.* **2021**, *26*, 35. https://doi.org/10.3390/mca26020035

Academic Editors: Marcela Quiroz, Juan Gabriel Ruiz, Luis Gerardo de la Fraga and Oliver Schütze

Received: 28 February 2021
Accepted: 20 April 2021
Published: 21 April 2021

Publisher's Note: MDPI stays neutral with regard to jurisdictional claims in published maps and institutional affiliations.

Copyright: © 2021 by the authors. Licensee MDPI, Basel, Switzerland. This article is an open access article distributed under the terms and conditions of the Creative Commons Attribution (CC BY) license (https:// creativecommons.org/licenses/by/ 4.0/).

Abstract: The decision-making process can be complex and underestimated, where mismanagement could lead to poor results and excessive spending. This situation appears in highly complex multi-criteria problems such as the project portfolio selection (PPS) problem. Therefore, a recommender system becomes crucial to guide the solution search process. To our knowledge, most recommender systems that use argumentation theory are not proposed for multi-criteria optimization problems. Besides, most of the current recommender systems focused on PPS problems do not attempt to justify their recommendations. This work studies the characterization of cognitive tasks involved in the decision-aiding process to propose a framework for the Decision Aid Interactive Recommender System (DAIRS). The proposed system focuses on a user-system interaction that guides the search towards the best solution considering a decision-maker's preferences. The developed framework uses argumentation theory supported by argumentation schemes, dialogue games, proof standards, and two state transition diagrams (STD) to generate and explain its recommendations to the user. This work presents a prototype of DAIRS to evaluate the user experience on multiple real-life case simulations through a usability measurement. The prototype and both STDs received a satisfying score and mostly overall acceptance by the test users.

Keywords: decision making process; cognitive tasks; recommender system; project portfolio selection problem; usability evaluation

1. Introduction

The decision-making process consists of selecting the best solution among a set of possible alternatives, considering difficult and complicated decisions [1]. Finding efficient strategies or techniques to aid this process is challenging due to the complexity of the problems.

In decision-making processes, such as the solution of optimization problems, the decision-maker (DM) is the person or group whose preferences are decisive for choosing an adequate solution to problems with multiple objectives (which are sometimes in conflict) and multiple efficient solutions [2]. The DM is the one who makes the final decision and chooses the solution that seems more appropriate from the preferences previously established.

There is a recent growing interest in using various techniques to incorporate the DM's preferences within a methodology, heuristic, or meta-heuristic to solve an optimization problem [3]. Among the different preference incorporation techniques available, using a weight vector that defines the importance of each objective is one of the most commonly used and accepted approaches.

The project portfolio selection (PPS) problem is a challenging optimization problem that presents several conditions to consider. First, these problems are usually multi-objective, searching for the best possible outcome for each objective. However, these objectives usually face conflicts between them based on the constraints that the problem sets. Second, the number of constraints that a PPS problem presents can make the decision-making process difficult since many possible solutions within the solution search space may not be feasible.

Usually, PPS problems define a limited number of resources to be distributed to improve each of the objectives while considering a maximum and minimum threshold of said resources for each of the elements defined in the constraints, limiting each objective's gain. Under these circumstances, it is most likely that it will not be possible to determine an optimal single solution, but instead, a set of optimal solutions that define a balance between the objectives of the problem and the DM's preferences, identified by using different strategies [4]. Therefore, it is crucial to select the most suitable solution that reflects the preferences of the DM. Multi-criteria decision analysis (MCDA) methods are among the most widely used tools for solving PPS problems because of their capacity to handle complex problems with multiple objectives (usually in conflict) to satisfy [5].

A practical methodology to solve PPS problems is the decision support system (DSS), which allows the DM to analyze a PPS problem under the current set of preferences and facilitate the decision-making process. However, choosing the best solution is a complex task because of the problem's subjective nature and the DM's preferences, which could be specific to a person or group and might change during the solution process. An interactive DSS allows the DM to show the best solutions based on the current preferences and receive new information from the DM and update its search to adapt to changes. As the name infers, this system can establish a user-system interaction during the solution process.

This paper proposes the Decision Aid Interactive Recommender System (DAIRS), a multi-criteria DSS (MCDSS) framework that considers integrating cognitive tasks to the user-system interaction. DAIRS is able to perform several tasks aiming to aid the DM during the decision-making process, such as evaluating alternatives, interacting with the DM, and recommending a solution while presenting arguments to justify this selection. The most relevant and novel feature DAIRS provides is that it not only is able to obtain information from the DM and adapt it to present an appropriate recommendation. This proposal can also present new information to DM or defend its current recommendation. In other words, DAIRS establishes a dialogue game with the user instead of only being a system that receives information.

This paper addresses the characterization of cognitive tasks involved in the decision support process and its integration in recommender systems to develop more robust DSS. These systems should allow the precise analysis of possible solutions, provide solutions that optimize the results, and at the same time, satisfy the preferences established by a DM. DAIRS includes on its MCDSS framework different MCDA methods supported by argumentation theory in the form of argumentation schemes and proof standards.

This proposal intends to present a recommender system that is able to provide a bidirectional interaction. Both the user and system provide and obtain new information based on the knowledge obtained during a dialogue. For this purpose, this work uses concepts related to argumentation theory, which allow both participants (user and system) to establish a well-structured dialogue.

DAIRS uses a bidirectional interaction under the assumption that the user will satisfactorily carry out a decision-making process even without extensive knowledge of the problem. DAIRS provides information to the DM through the dialogue game, seeking to enhance and accelerate learning about the problem to aid in selecting a suitable solution.

This work seeks to meet three main objectives. First, develop a recommender system, called DAIRS, which suggests a solution to a multi-objective optimization problem (MOP), precisely a PPS problem, with a deep interaction between the decision-maker (DM) and the system. Second, this work seeks to simplify the DM interaction with the proposed recommender system. Lastly, DAIRS endeavors to achieve high-level satisfaction of a DM. For the last objective, this proposal seeks to validate the developed recommender system, evaluating the effects of using argumentation theory and a bidirectional dialogue concerning several properties related to the usability of an MCDSS.

The main contributions of this work, proposed to meet the above objectives, can be summarized in three elements, whose originality is shown in Section 2 :

1. The development of an interactive MCDSS framework prototype, called DAIRS, supported by argumentation theory to perform a study of the effects of the proposed state transition diagrams (STDs), which regulates the flow of interaction with real users when solving a real-life optimization problem. For this paper, this work focuses on PPS problems.
2. The incorporation of argumentation schemes (reasoning patterns) and proof standards (MCDA methods to compare solutions) in an interactive MCDSS to evaluate and analyze their effects on the decision-making process.
3. The proposal, design, and implementation of two STDs, which determine the evolution of a dialogue game established between the DM and DAIRS.

The remaining part of this paper is structured as follows: Section 2 shows a brief review of works related to the proposal in this paper. Section 3 presents the necessary concepts on recommender systems employed in this work. Section 4 describes the proposed methodology and the developed prototype. Section 5 presents the experimental design and the results and analysis regarding the proposed prototype's performance when used to solve a test case study, which simulates a real-life scenario of a PPS problem. Finally, Section 6 addresses conclusions regarding the usability and effectiveness of the proposal and possible future work.

2. Related Work

This section reviews some of the most relevant works related to three topics in particular: (i) DSS frameworks used to solve PPS problems, (ii) interactive systems used for optimization problems, and (iii) proposals that use the characterization of cognitive tools to improve the interaction between the user and the recommender system.

2.1. DSS Frameworks Used to Solve PPS Problems

There are multiple DSS proposed focused on solving PPS problems. These works consider different strategies to incorporate the preferences established by the DM and select the most appropriate solution based on the current preference set or a preference weight vector.

While the proposal presented on this paper focuses on the development of a system that performs a project portfolio selection reflecting the DM's preferences in the best possible form and is able to interact with the user by entering in a dialogue, this bidirectional interaction feature, to the best of the authors' knowledge, has not been considered for solving PPS problems. It is important to understand some of the most relevant approaches to solve this problem.

Chu et al. [6] presents one of the first DSS proposed to solve PPS problems. Their DSS presents an approach based on a cost/benefit model for research and development (R&D) project management. Their work considers monetary and time cost, as well as the probability of success of each project to determine the optimal sequence of R&D projects to execute. The impact of each element when performing a selection of a solution is defined by a pair of weight variables that allowed to define how relevant is for the user to save money or time. More recently, Hummel et al. proposed a DSS framework based on the *Measuring*

Attractiveness by a Categorical Based Evaluation Technique (MACBETH) approach [7] to solve R&D project portfolio management problems interactively [8].

Archer and Ghasemzadeh [9] propose a framework to design decision support systems to solve PPS problems. In their work, they attempt to simplify the PPS process in three main phases: strategic consideration, individual project evaluation, and portfolio selection. At each phase the users are free to select the techniques that they find the most suitable. This framework is used to develop a DSS named Project Analysis and Selection System (PASS) [10] which is able to perform tasks such as data entry, pre-screening, project evaluation, screening and optimization models without the involvement of the DM. PASS is used to solve successfully solve a single-objective PSS problem.

DSS frameworks have proven to be suitable alternatives for solving multi-objective PPS problems. Hu et al. [11] proposes a multi-criteria DSS (MCDSS) framework to solve PPS problems implementing the Lean and Six Sigma concepts [12] and considering the cost and benefit of each project. Their framework considers flexible weight vectors that can be modified during the solution process and the output is a Pareto optimal portfolio set which allows the DM to select the most adequate to their preferences.

Khalili-Damghani's work [13] shows how flexible frameworks developed to solve PPS problems can be. In this case, an evolutionary algorithm (EA) is combined with a data envelope analysis model (DEA) to create the structure of a fuzzy rule-based (FRB) system that measures the suitability of all available candidate project portfolios.

Mira et al. [14] evaluates the performance of a DSS framework by solving a real-life simulation of a PPS problem and comparing the cumulative controlled risk value obtained by the DSS with respect to the controlled risk value obtained by a manual-based portfolio selection method. The results show a 10% improvement of the DSS framework over manual-based selection.

Mohammed [15] proposes the use of various strategies to find appropriate solutions to PPS problems within fuzzy environments. For this purpose, his work relies on the Analytic Hierarchy Process (AHP) [16] and TOPSIS [17] adapted to work using fuzzy strategies, which use a set of vectors of relative criteria weights. In this case, the used strategies incorporate preferences in the decision-making process before the system proceeds to generate a recommendation.

Recently, DSS frameworks have proven to be an adequate alternative to solve PPS problems focused on sustainability. Dobrovolskiene and Tamosiuniene [18] propose integrating the analysis of a sustainability index of each project within a Markowitz risk-return scheme [19]. This incorporation aims to find better portfolios based on a risk-return assessment that at the same time considers the DM's responsibility towards the surrounding environment with a long-term focus on the well-being of society.

Debnath et al. [20] propose a DSS framework supported by a hybrid multi-criteria decision support method. This hybrid system combines strategies such as sensitivity analysis with grey-based Decision-Making Trial and Evaluation Laboratory [21] and Multi-Attributive Border Approximation area Comparison [22] to solve PPS problems focused on the development, quality, and distribution of genetically modified agricultural products considering sustainability under social, beneficial, and differential criteria.

Verdecho et al. [23] present another proposal focused on sustainability. In this case, an AHP is used to solve a PPS problem related to supply chains, whose objectives are focused on financial, environmental, and social sustainability. Their framework also seeks to optimize supply-related processes and customer satisfaction.

2.2. Interactive Systems for Optimization Problems

A common scenario when using DSS frameworks to solve any optimization problem, such as the PPS problem, is that while they present a solution based on preferences defined by a DM, the next step in the decision-making process is not considered. This step consists on determining the acceptance (or rejection) of the recommended solution by the DM, as well as updating the DM's preferences. The preferences of the DM may change during solution process. It must be considered that the DM may be a single agent or group whose preferences are susceptible to social, political or economical-related changes surrounding the problem to be solved. Therefore, it is desirable that the framework is able to adapt to a new preferences.

For this situation, it is advisable to use an interactive process between the DM and the recommender system for decision-making support. The proposal of this work focuses on a bidirectional interaction. This feature is not present in the PPS problem nor in the optimization problems mentioned in this subsection.

Miettinen et al. [24] present a study that focuses on solving multi-objective optimization problems (MOPs) while using an interactive system that allows the system and the user to exchange information. Their study mentions that there are three main stopping criteria for these systems: the DM accepts the solution, the DM stops the process manually or an algorithmic stopping criterion is reached. Also, according to their work and [25] the interactive process can be divided in two phases. First, a learning phase where the DM obtains knowledge regarding the problem. The second phase is the decision phase, where the system identifies the most suitable solution according to the current information and DM must accept or reject it.

The *Flexible and Interactive Tradeoff* method [26] is a proposed approach implemented into a DSS to solve MOPs. This proposal considers that it is easier for the DM to compare results from multiple alternatives based on a definition of strict preferences between criteria rather than on indifference. This approach considers that the DM needs to establish a preferential lexicographic order for all criteria.

The InDM2 algorithm [27] is a recent work that allows interaction between the DM and the recommender system. The DM initially establishes a reference point which reflects to reflect his/her preferences. During the solution process, InDM2 shows the user the best candidate solutions it has found that match the current preferences. The DM is able to accept the solutions obtained, wait for the system to provide new solutions or stop the process at any time. InDM2 also allows the DM to update the current reference point or propose a new one, allowing the system to obtain new information based on the DM's new preferences.

Azabi et al. [28] propose an interactive optimization framework supported by a low fidelity flow resolver and an interactive Multi-objective Particle Swarm Optimization (MOPSO) for the optimization of the aerodynamic shape design of aerial vehicle platforms. As InDM2, the DM can incorporate preferences before and during the solution process. This interaction allows their framework to define and update a region of interest, accelerating the process. The results of their experiments show that the interactive MOPSO outperforms a non-interactive MOPSO, proving that a constant user-system interaction can provide better results.

There are also interactive framework proposals focused on solving PPS problems. Strummer et al. [29] proposes an interactive framework using a strategy based on identifying Pareto optimal solutions to determine a set of optimal portfolios to present to the DM. The system first solves a PPS problem and presents the best solutions under the current preferences and constraints defined by to the DM. The DM can then interact with the system to determine its preference for a particular criterion or set new constraints.

A study in Nowak et al. [30] states that several frameworks presented in the literature assume that the DM has a high-level knowledge of the problem, the methods used to solve, and has a well-defined set of preferences. These assumptions are obviously not always true. Therefore, the recommender system has to be as user-friendly as possible and understand that the user might have little knowledge of the problem prior using the system. Their study also notes a lack of consideration of dynamic elements, such as changes in preferences or the problem environment. The authors propose a general structure for the development of frameworks to solve PPS problems. This structure considers the criteria to be evaluated, the data needed to evaluate the projects, an analysis and evaluation of the projects, as well as the construction of project portfolios. The proposed structure also is capable of obtaining new information from the DM during each iteration, allowing the DSS to adapt to every change and focusing their search towards the new preferences.

Interactive systems can use graphical visualization to support the decision-making process of optimization problems. The work of Haara et al. [31] performs a study to evaluate several interactive data visualization techniques to support the solution of multi-objective forest planning problems. The DM uses visual elements to ease the process of correctly identifying and defining his/her preferences. The authors mention that these interactive systems can be used for proposal management problems. PPS problems are management problems. Therefore, it possible to think that these proposals could work successfully for PPS problems.

The *Your Own Decision Aid* (YODA) framework is an interactive recommender system proposed in Kurttila et al. [32] to solve PPS problems. YODA focuses on working with DMs composed of multiple people, where each user defines his/her preferences and acceptable candidate projects. All available projects are separated in subsets based on the level of group acceptance that each project has. The projects with the highest level of acceptance will have priority when the system defines a candidate project portfolio. Each user is able to update their preferences or define a project acceptance threshold to allow rejected projects that are close enough to their acceptance standards to be considered to be acceptable alternatives.

2.3. Characterization of Cognitive Tools to Improve User-System Interaction

The interactive process between the user and the DSS should not be limited to a series of commands simulating a master-slave structure. The interaction requires the characterization of cognitive tasks to become an entity that not only receives information but also provides new knowledge of the problem to the user.

The problem of characterizing cognitive tasks in the decision support process has been addressed using different approaches. Some representative works on providing explanations to accompany a recommended solution in each interaction are shown in this section. Some works, described below, are based on argumentation to model human argumentation and dialogue processes. Their description includes limitations.

The proposals using artificial intelligence provide a recommendation by learning the user preferences for particular products. They do not seek to recommend a solution for an optimization problem. Instead, they use the AI methods to optimize the recommender systems (e.g., identify similar users). Other related works use queries to obtain information from the DM related to the currently presented solution, but they do not explain the result [33].

Labreuche [34] describes how to use the argumentation theory to perform a pairwise comparison between alternatives, using an MCDA method based on a weight vector. It establishes four different situations, which involve two candidate solutions x and y and a weight vector w for six different criteria representing the DM preferences. These situations use pairwise evaluations based on criteria weights to present an argument in favor or against the statement "x is preferred over y".

Ouerdane [35] extends Labreuche's work, presenting an approach to provide underlying reasons for supporting an alternative selected by a recommendation system. For the process of justification, the argumentation theory and decision support are combined with an established language to enable communication. It also proposed a hierarchical structure of argument schemes to decompose the decision process into steps whose underlying premises are made explicit, allowing identifying when the dialogue should incorporate the information into the dialogue with the DM. This structure has only been tested for a low-dimensional choice problem (CHP), where the decision options are known from the beginning. Said proposal analyzed the required elements to perform a dialogue game with the user, not only to defend an established recommendation by the system but also to obtain new preferences and statements provided by the DM. The new information obtained could change dialogue-related elements, leading the system to provide a new recommendation if necessary.

The work presented in Cruz-Reyes et al. [36] proposes a framework design for generating DSSs focused on a PPS problem by characterizing arguments and dialogue using argumentation theory and rough sets theory. The framework has a justification module for the recommended solution shown to the user; the justification is supported by argument schemes and decision rules generated with rough sets. The process starts by obtaining available preferential information provided by the DM and selecting the appropriate multi-criteria method to evaluate the available portfolios. After, it generates a recommendation and its justification interactively. This work focuses more on the decision rules generated through rough sets. The argumentation theory is a complementing element of the architectural design, and it is presented only in a conceptual form.

Sassoon et al. [37] use argumentation theory by using argumentation schemes within a chatbot. Their chatbot establishes a dialogue between the user and a DSS focused on medical consultation. It considers the user's symptoms, medical history, and a list of available treatments to recommend the most appropriate medication. This DSS can attempt to justify its response through arguments. This system only considers current feasible information and does not use the user's preferences.

The studies conducted by Morveli-Espinoza et al. [38–40] focus on the solution of goal selection problems. Their research uses artificial intelligence and argumentation semantics to select goals that are not in conflict and produce the best results considering a set of premises added before carrying out the solution process. The interface developed in their study is able to answer the "Why?" and "Why not?" questions for each goal, generating arguments based on the semantics used.

Recommender systems for e-commerce often rely on artificial intelligence (AI). The use of advanced AI related methods allow the system to ease the user-system interaction and recommend higher quality e-services and online products more closely related to the DM's preferences [33].

Recently, interactive DSS frameworks that accept arguments from the DM have been proposed to solve PPS problems. Vayanos et al. [41] presents a framework that focuses on obtaining the preferences of the DM before and during the solution of the problem. The system generates a set of preferences based on a moderate number of queries presented to the DM. Each query provides a pairwise comparisons between two solutions. The system is based on weak-preference concept. This means that even if the user shows a preference on a certain criterion, this is not considered to be an absolute factor to determine dominance between solutions and is instead taken as a support by the framework when performing a portfolio project selection.

The previous query-based interactive system research extends in another study [42]. This investigation considers two and multi-stage robust optimization problems, including R&D PPS problems. The DSS framework interacts with the user before making a recommendation by performing a series of queries where the DM must define a value that reflects the level of attractiveness towards a particular item. The system uses these values to elicit preferences considering one of two possible models: maximize worst-case utility or minimize the worst-case regret of the item recommended.

Another DSS interactive framework has been recently proposed in Nowak & Trzaskalik [43]. Their work presents a MCDSS which interacts with the DM during each interaction and allows the user to redefine his/her preferences and constraints to solve dynamic PPS problems. Their DSS considers two possible sources that lead to a change in the problem environment: a time-dependent variable and a change in the DM's preferences and constraints.

These last three proposals allow the user to provide new preferences by using queries. The proposal presented in this paper aims to provide an interactive recommender system that receives new preferential information from the DM and adapts its recommendation. The proposed system is also able to provide the DM with new information based on the knowledge obtained. In addition, the system can argue and defend its proposed project portfolio selection through arguments, with the objective that the DM understands, through dialogue, that the recommendation presented by the system is the most appropriate based on the current information.

The intention of allowing the proposed DSS framework to defend its recommendation through arguments is to allow the user to learn in detail the characteristics and properties of the problem to solve. This also allows the DM to see thoroughly the reasons for the portfolio selection made by the DSS. This paper focuses on the use of argumentation theory to not only support the solution process for a PPS problem, but also to allow the system to defend the recommended solution. Additionally, this paper incorporates two newly proposed STDs, argumentation schemes and a proof standard (TOPSIS [17]) different from those proposed by Ouerdane [35].

3. Background

This section reviews the most relevant concepts related to the proposed work, necessary to understand the said proposal and how it operates. For this, the revised concepts focus on the decision-making problem, several of the most relevant approaches, and recommendation systems, and the argumentation theory.

3.1. Multi-Objective Optimization Problem

As mentioned in Section 1, many cases in which decision problems arise involve multiple objectives to be satisfied and usually in conflict with each other. Equation (1) presents the definition of a multi-objective optimization problem (MOP). This particular example presents a maximization MOP, looking to obtain the variable decision vector $\vec{x}$ that obtains the highest possible value for the M objectives within the function set F. However, it is also necessary to mention that it is possible to define minimization MOPs or combine both maximization and minimization for a subset of objectives.

$$\max F(\vec{x}) = f_1(\vec{x}), f_2(\vec{x}), ..., f_M(\vec{x}) \quad \text{s.t.} \quad g(\vec{x}) > 0, h(\vec{x}) = 0 \ . \tag{1}$$

Each MOP has a set of inequality (g) and equality (h) constraints that define the solutions' feasibility. Based on the above scenario, it is understandable to believe that there are cases in which defining a single solution as optimal over all the other candidates is impossible. At this point, it falls to the decision-maker to carry out the selection of the most appropriate solution (or set of solutions) based on his preferences.

3.1.1. The Decision Making Problem

In real-life situations, the DM may be represented by a person or group which seeks to improve their profits. However, the DM might not have enough resources to support all available alternatives simultaneously. This leads to what can be defined as a decision-making problem. It is necessary to search for actions that meet the current goals in the best way possible, using the available resources and maximizing profit.

Decision-making problems present four basic elements [44]: A set of one or several objectives to solve; a set of candidate solutions to achieve all objectives within the set; a set of factors that define the environment that surrounds the problem; and a set of utility values associated with each solution when they interact with the current environment.

In these cases, DMs might use multi-criteria decision support systems (MCDSS) to support their decisions. MCDSS uses computational techniques used to analyze highly complex decision problems in a reasonable computational time [45]. The multi-criteria decision analysis (MCDA) is a collection of concepts, methods, and techniques that seek to help individuals or groups make decisions involving conflicting points of view and multiple stakeholders [46]. MCDA methods are relevant components of MCDSS. Five elements are involved in these methods: Goal, decision-maker, alternatives or actions, preferences, and a solution set based on preferences.

3.1.2. Project Portfolio Selection Problem

An example of a decision-making problem can be seen in the project portfolio selection (PPS) problem. A project is defined as a temporary, unique, and unrepeatable process that pursues a specific set of objectives [47]. A project portfolio is a set of projects selected for future implementation.

In this case, a person or organization has a set of projects to carry out. These projects share the resources currently available, and there is the possibility that several of those projects complement each other, as they are effective in the same area. Therefore, it is necessary to know which project portfolio meets an organization's demands, maximizing its profit.

Equations (2)–(4) present a formal definition of the PPS problem. Let N be the number of available projects. A project portfolio $\vec{x}$ is an N sized binary vector. The projects that have been selected are given a value of 1, while the non-selected projects are given a value of 0. The value of a project portfolio for an objective i is defined by the sum of each selected portfolio's profit towards the said objective. The profit matrix p contains the respective profit obtained by the jth project for the ith objective.

Two main constraints restrict the PPS problem. First, the budget threshold, which is presented in Equation (3). The cost vector c defines how much each project costs, while B defines the maximum available current budget. The sum of all the selected projects' costs must be equal to or lower than B.

The second constraint refers to all the areas involved in the problem. Thus, it is necessary to consider several A areas and a binary project-area matrix a, which defines which projects are assigned on each area. Each area has lower and upper investment thresholds L_k and U_k, respectively. The sum of all selected projects' costs involved in each area must be between those two thresholds to be considered a feasible portfolio.

$$\max f_i(\vec{x}) = \sum_{j=1}^{N} x_j p_{i,j}. \qquad (2)$$

Such as

$$\sum_{i=1}^{N} x_i c_i \leq B, \qquad (3)$$

$$L_k \leq \sum_{i=1}^{N} x_i c_i a_{k,i} \leq U_k \quad k = 1, 2, \ldots, A. \qquad (4)$$

3.2. Recommender System

By solving a PPS problem using a method such as genetic or exact algorithms, it is possible to generate a set of good quality candidate solutions. However, a prevalent issue at this step lies in presenting the DM too many potential solutions, which may be too many to carry out an analysis using only the human capability. It is also necessary to consider that the DM's preferences might have changed during the problem's solution, making the decision-making process even more difficult.

A recommender system is a potential alternative for this situation. This system relies on the DM's preferences and a set of various heuristics to direct its search and define which solutions from the set may be more attractive to the DM [48]. Specifically, in the PPS problem, a set of solutions, global and area budget constraints, and DM preferences can be used to determine the most appropriate project portfolios.

However, there is a possibility that DM is not entirely convinced and needs to know the reasons behind the decision made by the recommender system. Other possible situations that the system might face when presenting a solution to the DM are related to the human factor. For example, the DM may not know how to express his preferences correctly, may not fully know the details of the problem, and may even directly reject the system's recommendation without waiting for a justification. For these reasons, it is desirable to establish a quick relationship with the DM. The theory of argumentation offers an alternative to carry out this relationship.

3.3. Argumentation Theory in Decision Making

The argumentation theory is within the field of artificial intelligence. It can be defined as the process of constructing and evaluating arguments to justify conclusions. This allows decision-making to be carried out in a justified manner. This theory is based on non-monotonic reasoning. This means that the conclusions obtained may be modified and even rejected when new information is presented [35].

The most relevant elements to consider within the argumentation theory are cognitive artifacts, proof standards, and argumentation schemes.

3.3.1. Cognitive Artifact

Cognitive artifacts human-made objects that seek to help or enhance cognition. Its use is not only focused on supporting memory but also to set reasoning towards classifications and comparisons among several alternatives [49]. The support to the decision-making process presented by the argumentation theory can be seen as a set of cognitive artifacts used sequentially. This sequence occurs through an interaction between an expert and a client. According to [50], this process uses four cognitive artifacts: a representation of the problem, a formulation of the problem, a model of evaluation, and a final recommendation. This work addresses these last two artifacts.

3.3.2. Proof Standard

In argumentation theory, all statements must be analyzed to determine their truthfulness and their effect on a possible conclusion the DM desires to reach [35]. Proof standards are methods and techniques that allow the unification of a set of arguments for and against a certain conclusion. These proof standards analyze and determine each argument's strength and value to solve the conflict between them by accepting or rejecting the established conclusion.

A basic example of a proof standard is the simple majority. This standard takes a statement such as "project x is better than project y". For this case, the M objectives are considered, and the values obtained by each one for both projects are analyzed. If x has more objectives with better value than y, then the conclusion is true. This expression can be formally defined as presented in the following Equation (5), where S_i represent the dominance factor for objective i

$$x \succeq y \leftrightarrow |\{i \in M : xS_iy\}| \geq |\{i \in M : yS_ix\}|. \tag{5}$$

3.3.3. Argumentation Scheme

Argumentation schemes can be defined as argumentative structures capable of detecting common and stereotypical patterns of human reasoning [51]. They are based on a set of inference rules in which the existence of certain premises can lead to a conclusion. The structure of the schemes is based on non-monotonic reasoning, allowing the entry of new information, altering the state of the conclusion.

An argumentation scheme is composed of three main elements:

1. Premises: arguments for or against the conclusion. The status of each premise can be considered to be true or false until proven otherwise or to require further evidence for consideration;
2. Conclusion: statement to be confirmed or rejected based on the premises and a proof standard;
3. Critical questions: questions related to the structure of the argumentation scheme that, if not answered adequately, can falsify the veracity of an argument within it.

Argumentation schemes are not necessarily complex. For example, the cause to effect scheme [52] is based on two premises: If event A occurs, event B occurs as a consequence, and A has occurred. Therefore, the conclusion defines that B will occur. Critical questions focus on the strength of the relationship between A and B, whether if it is strong enough evidence to warrant this event, and if there exist other relevant factors that also provoke B to occur.

3.4. Dialogue Game

One possible form to represent argumentation theory within decision-making problems is through the use of dialogue games. These games model verbally or in-writing the interaction between two or more individuals, called players. The dialogue game intends to exchange arguments both for and against a statement between the players to reach a satisfactory conclusion [53].

Multiple elements must be considered for the dialogue game, such as the players and their respective roles, objectives, limitations, etc. Like any game, a set of rules must be established that defines which actions are acceptable or not during the dialogue. Also, it is necessary to define a system to determine the movements that each participant is allowed to perform at the different stages of the dialogue game.

3.4.1. Dialogue Game Rules

The dialogue game rules establish how the game is performed, defining criteria such as the starting and ending points of the game, the movements allowed for each player. These rules also define the criteria necessary to allow a coherent dialogue between the players. Each one can provide statements, arguments, and premises considered acceptable by the other participants, avoiding fallacies and dialogue loops that would stall the dialogue at a certain point [53].

There are four different types of dialogue game rules.

1. Locution rules: define the set of movements allowed for the entire dialogue game;
2. Compromise rules: define the set of statements and arguments each player is compromised to defend until proven right or wrong;
3. Dialogue rules: define the set of available movements a player has during the current state of the dialogue;
4. Termination rules: define the scenario or state that needs to be reached for the dialogue game to end.

3.4.2. State Transition Diagram

Based on the defined dialogue game rules, it is possible to identify which movements are allowed for each player and when he/she can use them. A state transition diagram (STD) can represent the evolution of the dialogue game graphically. An STD allows the players to visualize each of the different states where the dialogue can be located and the player currently in turn and what their available movements are. Similarly, an STD represents the starting and ending points of the game. With this, the four different types of rules of the dialogue game are effectively represented.

4. Proposed Work

This section describes the methodology and the different cognitive components defined for DAIRS. Afterward, a prototype proposed in this paper implements this methodology, which allows a user-system interaction through a dialogue game. This work focuses on two cognitive tasks: the evaluation model of the alternatives based on proof standards and the construction of arguments for the proposed recommender system's recommendation using argumentation schemes and a dialogue game.

4.1. Dairs Methodology

The evaluation of alternatives is the process of evaluating a set of alternatives based on their attributes, indicators, or dimensions of those alternatives [50]. In this case, the alternatives are the feasible project portfolios for the PPS problem. Each portfolio is evaluated considering its performance on each objective and set of constraints. A criteria weight vector or a criteria hierarchy order is commonly used to solve evaluate alternatives. Therefore, DAIRS also considers these two elements when evaluating portfolios to create a recommendation

Using the previous information regarding the properties of the problem provided by the DM, a proof standard is selected considering said properties and used to evaluate all the feasible portfolios. Then, the recommender system defines an initial recommendation supported by the information provided by the DM and an abductive inference argumentation scheme based on the information obtained by the proof standard used. Therefore, before the dialogue game has begun, the system already has an initial portfolio recommendation to present to the user according to his/her preferences and arguments to defend said recommendation.

The recommendation system presented in this work requires defining a set of crucial elements for its operation: A set of proof standards, argumentation schemes, and a dialogue structure that defines how both user and system will perform a bidirectional interaction using a dialogue game.

4.1.1. Proof Standards

To carry out a proper dialogue game between the user and the system, it is necessary to define methods that allow correctly collecting and analyzing the arguments for and against the current statement to reach a reasonable conclusion. Proof standards allow performing such collection and analysis.

The recommender system is capable of using a large number of proof standards. For this work, the orientation of the set of proof standards selected aims towards defining a solution for the PPS problem and is based on Ouerdane's work [35].

DAIRS considers proof standards that use a criteria preference hierarchy. These standards allow the user to define strict preferences between objectives. The recommender system focuses its search on the criteria defined as most relevant by the DM.

Simple majority: As explained in Section 3.3.2 and presented in Equation (5), this standard evaluates the truth of the statement "x is better than y" based on the number of objectives this statement holds.

Lexicographic order: This proof standard uses a hierarchical order established in the criteria. A project x is better than a project y if, and only if, x has a better value on a criterion of higher priority than y. The criteria hierarchy establishes that a higher-order criterion is infinitely more important than those in a lower position. Therefore, this method disregards the value of any other criterion of lower priority.

There are cases where even when the DM has a higher preference over specific criteria, this preference might not be strict. Instead, there is a certain threshold of acceptance for criteria with lower priority if their improvement is significant in these cases. Therefore, DAIRS considers proof standards that analyze each project portfolio supported by a criteria weight vector, determining each objective's relevance. These standards allow the system to identify possible significant improvements in criteria with different levels of importance for the DM.

Weighted majority: This method follows a similar strategy than simple majority. However, it relies on the weights of each criterion to evaluate. In this case, a criteria weight vector w assigns a weight to each criterion i (w_i). Portfolio x has a preference over portfolio y if the sum of the weights of the criteria where x is better than y is greater than the sum of the weights of the criteria where y is better than x.

$$x \succeq y \leftrightarrow W_{xy} = \sum_{xS_iy} w_i \geq W_{yx} = \sum_{yS_ix} w_i. \qquad (6)$$

Weighted sum: This method defines a single fitness value S_x for each portfolio based on w and the fitness value f obtained on each objective i ($f_i(x)$). Let N be the number of criteria for the current problem. Equation (7) presents a formal definition of the previous statement. Portfolio x is preferred over portfolio y if, and only if, the sum of x is greater than the sum of y ($S_x > S_y$).

$$S_x = \sum_{i=1}^{N} w_i f_i(x).\tag{7}$$

TOPSIS: This proof standard is based on a method proposed in [17], which considers both the distance to the ideal solution, also known as utopia point, and the distance towards the negative ideal solution or nadir point. The solution that is closer to the former and furthest from the latter is the one that takes precedence.

The selection of the proper proof standard is essential to obtain a successful recommendation that follows both the DM's preferences and the quality of the solution itself. This process has a very relevant impact on the dialogue game. Each proof standard can have a set of properties defined, making them unique compared to the other set standards. During the dialogue game, both the user and system can define which properties are suitable to be considered or not in the discussion to obtain better recommendations or enhance the dialogue game's quality, based on the information provided by both players. The properties considered for the proof standard selection are:

1. Ordinality: Only the ordinal information about the performance is relevant.
2. Anonymity: There is no specific preference order for the criteria.
3. Additivity with respect to coalitions: It is possible to formulate additive values regarding the importance of a criteria subset.
4. Additivity with respect to values: The value of a solution is obtained by the sum of each criterion's values.
5. Veto: A solution must improve another over a certain veto threshold to be accepted.
6. Distance to the worst solution. The best solution is determined not only by its closeness towards the best possible solution but also by how far it is from the worst possible solution

This set of properties is based on the recommendations provided multiple works in the literature [35,52]. Table 1 shows the properties belonging to each proof standard. It should be noted that both simple majority and weighted majority methods can be used with or without a veto threshold.

Table 1. Proof Standards used for DAIRS and their properties.

Proof Standard	Ordinality	Anonymity	Add. w.r.t Coalitions	Add. w.r.t Values	Veto	Distance
Simple majority	✓	✓	✓		✓*	
Lexicographic	✓		✓			
Weighted majority	✓		✓		✓*	
Weighted sum				✓		
TOPSIS				✓		✓

* These proof standards can be used with or without using a veto threshold.

4.1.2. Argumentation Schemes

In addition to determining the proof standards to be used, it is necessary to define which human behavior patterns to consider for a dialogue within the system. The intention of defining the patterns to be identified is to regulate the system responses based on these patterns and establish boundaries in the dialogue to avoid situations such as infinite dialogue loops or loss of focus. For this reason, it is necessary to establish a set of argumentation schemes, which allow the process of identifying behavioral patterns to be carried out.

This work seeks to incorporate the proof standards selected in the previous subsection to strengthen and facilitate premise analysis and to define a conclusion for the current statement in the dialogue through argumentation schemes. These schemes are chosen considering proposals provided in previous related works [35,52]:

Abductive reasoning argument: This argumentation scheme allows the system to select the most suitable proof standard according to the current properties identified based on the information provided by user and the system.

Argument from position to know: The system performs an initial recommendation using this argumentation scheme after the system chooses a proof standard. This scheme also provides recommendations for the dialogue game's first cycles. With this, the system does not consider itself an expert yet as it has only obtained the initial information given by the list of available projects, DM's preferences, and budget threshold.

Argument from an expert opinion: After several cycles have passed in the dialogue game, surpassing a certain number of cycles, defined as *cycle threshold*, the system considers that it has obtained enough information from the user to position itself as an expert for the problem analyzed. Under this scheme, the system is more assertive in its arguments, as it has more information to defend them instead of just expecting to obtain new data from the user.

Multi-criteria pairwise comparison: The system compares the current recommendation against other alternatives, as well as solutions picked by the user that might attract his/her interest. The proof standard currently being used supports this scheme to form arguments to either defend the recommendation or select the user-picked solution if the new information provided proves that the DM's selection outperforms the system's recommendation under the current proof standard.

Practical argument from analogy: Sometimes, two solutions might be similar to a high degree. Therefore, it is necessary to consider if the previous solutions considered by either the system or the user can be considered recommendations for the dialogue game's current stage.

Ad ignorantiam: The current state of the system is unable to make inferences. All the information known by the system is considered valid by it. Meanwhile, all unknown information is considered false. The user can provide the system with new information regarding the problem in discussion at any point during the dialogue game.

Cause to effect: A change in the state of a proof standard property or the value of a criterion affects the current state of the system's recommendation. Whenever a change is detected, the system performs a reevaluation of the current solutions based on the new information. Then, it provides the user with a new recommendation, and the dialogue game continues.

From bias: The system considers this fallacy as the user might be biased towards a particular solution. While one of the recommender system's objectives is to provide the most suitable solution, user satisfaction is also a very relevant factor that a system must consider. Therefore, the system allows the user to set the recommended solution as the alternative the user picks. However, the system constantly reminds the DM that his/her choice might be biased and not the best available.

During the dialogue game, the system uses an argumentation scheme selected depending on the activities carried out in its current state by either the system or the user. Therefore, it is necessary to properly establish the dialogue game structure to use the correct argumentation scheme to characterize the arguments and premises used in the dialogue's current state.

The system relies on argumentation schemes to accept or reject a statement and obtain information, leading to changes in the problem's criteria values or the state of the proof standard properties. As previously mentioned, argumentation schemes can define the most suitable proof standard according to the current information provided.

4.1.3. Dialogue Game Rules

DAIRS aims to use a dialogue game to establish a two-dimensional interaction between the user and the system. This interaction allows both participants to provide statements to strengthen the information to ease the decision-making process.

Before carrying out a dialogue game between the user and the system, it is necessary to define the set of rules that the players will follow in the game. As previously mentioned in Section 3.4, there are four types of dialogue game rules: locution, compromise, dialogue, and termination.

The compromise, dialogue, and termination rules followed in this work are established in [35]. However, the locution rules provide two main additions. First, the system can reject an argument presented by the user if it does not satisfy the current evaluation criteria. Second, the user is allowed to reject the system's recommendation at multiple points during the dialogue. These additions focus on the system's capability to defend its recommendation and user's satisfaction. Table 2 presents the locution rules used in this work. Let ϕ be the current statement, C a critical question, and "type" refers to C being an assumption or exception.

Table 2. Locution rules for the dialogue game used in this work.

Movement	Replies	Surrenders	Status
assert(ϕ)	challenge(ϕ) which proof standard? pose(C, type, ϕ, scheme)	accept(ϕ) reject(ϕ)	stated
challenge(ϕ)	argue(ϕ, premises, scheme)	retract(ϕ)	questioned
argue(ϕ, premises, scheme)	challenge(premise) pose(C, type, ϕ, scheme) assert(ϕ) which proof standard?	accept(ϕ) accept(premise) reject(ϕ)	accepted rejected
pose(C, type, ϕ, scheme)	challenge(not C) assert(C) assert(not C)	retract(ϕ)	rejected
accept(ϕ) retract(ϕ)			accepted rejected
which proof standard?	current proof standard		

4.1.4. State Transition Diagrams

Once the dialogue game rules are defined, it is possible to design state transition diagrams (STDs). An STD can graphically represent how the dialogue flow will carry out. A noticeable advantage in using STDs is that they offer an easy method to identify and regulate how the dialogue transpires. Also, STDs show the movements available to both players at each stage of the interaction.

The recommender system proposed uses two STDs. Before a dialogue game begins, the system will select one of these diagrams to establish a user-system interaction for the current instance. The factor considered to define which STD to use is whether the DM establishes criteria preference hierarchy before the dialogue game begins. Depending on which scenario occurs, the system will use a particular STD and a different proof standard according to which properties are considered active.

The reasoning for using different STDs based on the DM's preferences is to take advantage of the amount of information and knowledge the user has regarding the problem. DAIRS provides a learning-focused dialogue if the DM has little knowledge of the problem. Meanwhile, the system provides a more assertive and portfolio selection-driven dialogue if the DM has an acceptable level of knowledge and it is possible to skip or shorten the learning phase.

State Transition Diagram 1 (STD1): This diagram is chosen whenever the initial information available about the problem does not provide an explicit preference hierarchy regarding the problem criteria. This STD follows the structure defined in [35] while adding the additional locution rules mentioned previously. In particular, it adds a move that allows the system to reject the user's suggestion if there are no additional reasons for supporting his or her statement after a certain number of dialogue cycles have passed. A *dialogue cycle* can be defined as the point in the dialogue game when it reaches the initial state (1) once again. This system explains to the user that the reason for this rejection is to avoid a dialogue loop and continue the recommendation process. Figure 1 shows the structure of STD1.

State Transition Diagram 2 (STD2): The second STD is used when there is an explicit user-defined preference hierarchy for the criteria before the dialogue game begins. The system seeks to exploit this situation to use and obtain as much information as possible from the early state of the dialogue game. Also, it allows the user to present critical questions from the beginning, which is not allowed when using STD1. STD2 provides more flexibility for the user by allowing him/her to reject the recommendation since the initial states of the dialogue. Figure 2 shows the structure of STD2.

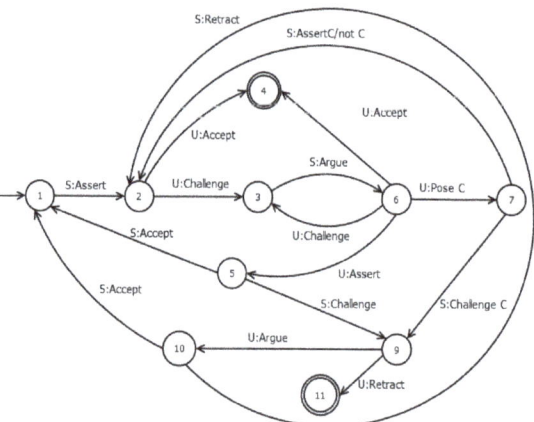

Figure 1. State Transition Diagram 1, used when there is not an explicit criteria preference hierarchy defined on the initial information.

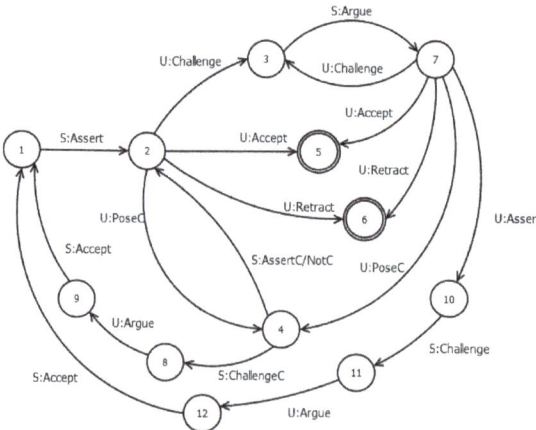

Figure 2. State Transition Diagram 2, used when there is an explicit criteria preference hierarchy defined on the initial information.

4.1.5. System Modules

The next step is to incorporate the dialogue game and all its necessary procedures to be carried out properly within DAIRS. Previously, four main processes were identified as necessary to be implemented in the system to execute a recommendation process properly [36]. Figure 3 presents the structure of these models.

Load instance module: Reads the information concerning an instance to be solved by the recommender system. The DM uploads a file containing initial instance data to the system. This file contains information such as the number of candidate solutions and criteria, a criteria weight vector, a solution/objective matrix, budget threshold, veto threshold (if required), and criteria hierarchy. For the PPS problem, it is also necessary to insert additional data, such as the project portfolio matrix, representing the projects selected by each portfolio.

Configuration module: The system analyzes the information from the instance obtained in the load instance module to determine the initial configuration of all the elements required to start a dialogue game, such as the dialogue game rules, the state transition diagram, and the initial proof standard. This setup will allow the system to provide an initial recommendation to start the dialogue with the user.

Dialogue module: The user and the system start the dialogue game. The system's main objective is to convince the user to accept the recommendation provided by it. However, the user can reject the current recommendation or add new information and modify the initial configuration. This process will provide new information to the system, which the system will use to generate a new recommendation.

Recommendation acceptance/rejection module: The user can accept or reject the system's recommendation. This module determines a final step in the dialogue. The proposed recommender system attempts to consider the human factor by allowing the user to reject the solution at several stages of the dialogue, even if the solution recommended is the most suitable according to the current information provided by both the instance and the user. This option aims towards the user's satisfaction. As previously mentioned, while the recommender system's objective is to provide a high-quality recommendation, it is also desirable that the user feels satisfied with his/her final decision. User satisfaction is also an objective that any recommender system must pursue.

These modules adequately represent a recommender system's structure supported by concepts related to argumentation theory, such as argumentation schemes. For this reason, the development of the recommender system presented in this paper uses the previously mentioned structure.

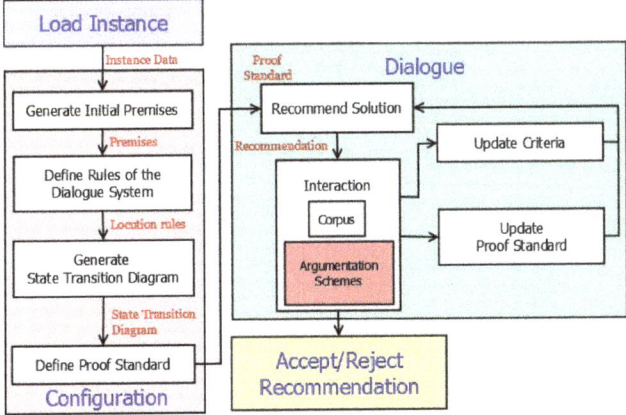

Figure 3. Diagram module of the proposed recommender system, argumentation scheme are used within the dialogue module.

4.2. Interactive Prototype

The next step in developing the proposed recommender system is the implementation of a prototype, which incorporates all the previously mentioned elements (argumentation schemes, proof standards, dialogue games, and STDs). The proposed methodology intends to properly carry out a dialogue game, following the dialogue structures defined and represented in the STDs. The development of this prototype allows a user to directly contact the recommender system and to evaluate the usability of the framework designed in the previous subsection.

Figure 4 shows a dialogue game carried out between two users following the proposed structure. This dialogue shows an interaction between a recommender system (which plays the role of an expert) and the DM (who plays the role of the user). While the system presents recommendations, the user can question them, challenge them, or argue. The end of the dialogue relies on the user's final decision to accept or reject the system's recommendations. Note that the system can evolve its recommendation into a new one when the information provided presents valid arguments to justify the change.

```
1.  Expert: I recommend Portfolio 1 as the best choice. (S: Assert).
2.  User: Why? (U: Challenge).
3.  Expert: Portfolio 1 is globally better than the other alternatives. (S: Argue).
4.  User: Are the reasons that support the recommendation strong enough? (U: PoseC).
5.  Expert: They are strong enough under the current proof standard. (S: AssertC).
6.  User: Why is Portfolio 1 better than Portfolio 2? (U: Challenge).
7.  Expert: Portfolio 1 is better than Portfolio 2 for the criteria 1 and 3. (S: Argue).
8.  User: Does the system have enough information to define a proof standard? (U: PoseC).
9.  Expert: Yes, however, you can modify the status of a property if you want. (S: ChallengeC).
10. User: I want to use a threshold. (Veto threshold activated). (U: Argue).
11. Expert: Veto threshold has been activated. (S: Accept).
12. Expert: With this property modification, the proof standard currently on use is Simple Majority
    + veto. This proof standard, a veto threshold is used during the Simple Majority evaluation.
    According to the new information provided. I recommend Portfolio 6 (S: Assert).
13. User: Why is Portfolio 6 the best option? (U: Challenge).
14. Expert: Portfolio 6 is globally better than the other alternatives. (S: Argue).
15. User: But I prefer the Portfolio 2 over the recommended solution. (U: Assert).
16. Expert: Why? (S: Challenge).
17. User: The budget of the recommended portfolio is close to the maximum budget limit. So, I
    prefer Portfolio 2 (U: Argue).
18. Expert: Portfolio 2 has less than a 10% budget difference from its value to Portfolio 6. There
    is not a significant difference to justify this. (S: Reject).
19. USER ACCEPTS THE RECOMMENDATION (U: Accept).
```

Figure 4. Example of a dialogue game between user and system following the defined STDs.

4.2.1. Bidirectional Interaction Algorithm

Algorithm 1 corresponds to the proposed method for bidirectional interaction between the user and DAIRS. The objective is to present the user with recommended solutions and an explanation of the recommendation while receiving the DM's preferences. The system must define several argumentation elements before the user-system interaction within the prototype may begin: A set of proof standards PS and its properties $PSProperties$, the initial set of premises $Premises$, the argumentation scheme set used for the dialogue game $Schemes$, the dialogue game rules D, and the set of available state transition diagrams STD. The output of this algorithm is a portfolio recommendation r_p

This algorithm also requires a file of the instance (*file*). This file must contain a set of elements as part of the initial input: An alternative/criteria value matrix (C), a criteria preference hierarchy ($PrefC$), a criteria weight vector (W), a veto threshold vector for all criteria (V), a set of available project portfolios (P), its respective cost ($Pcost$), and the maximum allowed budget (B). Appendix A shows in more detail the information that this file should contain.

The algorithm begins using the *Load instance* module to load an instance in step 1, obtaining all the data necessary to proceed to the *Configuration* module. From steps 2 to 7, this module defines each element's values for the cognitive decision tasks and dialogue game, according to the information provided by the instance.

Then, the *Dialogue* module is used from step 8 to step 18, establishing an interaction with the user in step 9, which could result in a possible modification of the values of the alternative/criterion value matrix, the active set of the proof standard properties, or the selected proof standard, as well as an update on the set of premises according to with the new information given by the user during that step.

Algorithm 1 Bidirectional interaction of DAIRS

1: $\{C, PrefC, W, V, P, Pcost, B\} \leftarrow$ load_instance$(file)$
2: $Schemes' \leftarrow$ select_schemes$(PrefC, Premises, Schemes)$
3: $D' \leftarrow$ select_locution_rule_subset$(D, PrefC)$
4: $std \leftarrow$ select_std(STD, D')
5: $PSProperties' \leftarrow$ set_properties$(PSProperties, PrefC, W, V, Premises)$
6: $ps \leftarrow$ proof_standard_selection$(PSProperties', PS)$
7: $r_p \leftarrow$ recommend_portfolio$(ps, P, C, PrefC, W, V)$
8: **do**
9: $\quad \{Premises, C, PSProperties', ps\} \leftarrow$ interaction$(std, D, Schemes', Premises)$
10: $\quad$ **if** modified(C) **then**
11: $\quad\quad$ update_criteria(C)
12: $\quad\quad r_p \leftarrow$ recommend_portfolio$(ps, P, C, PrefC, W, V)$
13: $\quad$ **else if** modified$(PSProperties')$ **then**
14: $\quad\quad PSProperties' \leftarrow$ set_properties$(PSProperties', PrefC, W, V, Premises)$
15: $\quad\quad ps \leftarrow$ proof_standard_selection$(PSProperties', PS)$
16: $\quad\quad r_p \leftarrow$ recommend_portfolio$(ps, P, C, PrefC, W, V)$
17: $\quad$ **else if** modified(ps) **then**
18: $\quad\quad r_p \leftarrow$ recommend_portfolio$(ps, P, C, PrefC, W, V)$
19: $\quad$ **end if**
20: **while** !accept_reject(r_p)

Then, the system checks whether there was a change that could affect the current recommendation. Steps 11 and 12 are executed if there is a change in the alternative/criterion matrix values. These steps update the matrix and use the current proof standard to evaluate all the available portfolios again. Steps 14 to 16 are performed if either the user or the system has modified the proof standard's properties. These steps update the set of active proof standard properties, select the most appropriate proof standard and reevaluate the set of portfolios. The system can directly change the proof standard to offer the user a more flexible system if the user desires. If so, then step 18 is executed, using the chosen proof standard to generate a new recommendation.

The algorithm repeats this process until the user reaches a final state of acceptance or rejection of the system's recommendation. When that happens, DAIRS reaches the *Recommendation acceptance/rejection* module, considering the dialogue game finished and ending the interaction.

4.2.2. Graphical User Interface

The graphical user interface of the proposed prototype seeks to allow the user to interact with the system in multiple ways. From the definition of the instance to work with, establish a dialogue with the system, edit values of the profit obtained by each available project, and manipulate the status of the proof standard properties considered by the system to match the user's preferences better. This interface is composed of a set of windows that allow the user to perform the activities previously mentioned.

Figure 5 presents the graphical user interface (GUI) of DAIRS; the primary areas in this interface are:

1. The menu bar. A set of menus that allow the user to perform actions related to the instance and its properties. It contains two sub-menus. The first sub-menu,

named *Instance*, allows the user to read, start and restart instances. The second submenu, named *Recommendation Options*, lets the user update criteria values, visualize information regarding all available portfolios, the current state of the dialogue game, and even provides the user a Help window with any necessary additional information regarding the GUI.
2. The dialogue area. Displays the recommendations and arguments presented by DAIRS, questions posed, or changes in the user's information. This section of the windows presents the arguments provided by both players during the current and previous steps in the dialogue game.
3. The interaction area. This area allows the user to perform a dialogue with the system. The user can determine his next move within the dialogue game, the statement or question that follows that movement, and, if necessary, the chance to select an alternative portfolio that accompanies the presented statement.
4. The portfolio composition area. Shows information about the portfolios and their selected projects by presenting a portfolio/alternative binary matrix.
5. The evaluation criteria area. Shows the information regarding each criterion's values for every portfolio by presenting a portfolio/criteria matrix.

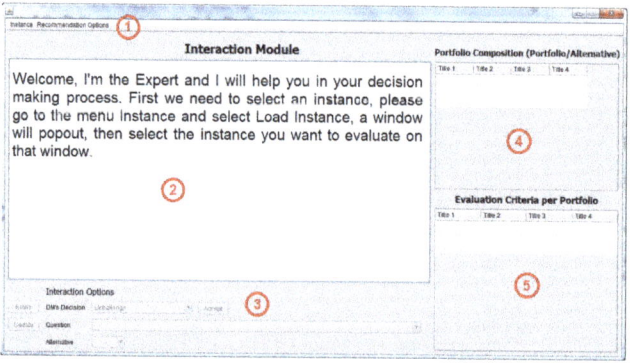

Figure 5. Main window of the DAIRS GUI. The GUI allows the user to read the dialogue, perform actions and see the available portfolios.

As previously mentioned, the recommender system prototype proposed in this work focuses on the PPS problem. As previously mentioned, the GUI intends to allow the user to interact with a recommender system using the proposed structure. The *Load instance* module reads the information about a PPS problem instance from a file. This file includes all the required information necessary to initiate a dialogue game between the user and system in DAIRS, as explained in Algorithm 1.

The *Configuration* module allows the user to select proper parameters to start the dialogue game seeking to aid the DM in his/her decision for the uploaded PPS problem. The initial premises and arguments that both the user and system are available to select from are determined based on the information. The dialogue game rules are defined. Then, DAIRS generates an STD following the structure of said rules. In this case, if there is not a criteria hierarchy defined on the instance file, then STD1 is used. However, if there is a preference order defined in the file, then STD2 is used. Finally, a proof standard is selected based on the information provided by said instance.

After this, the *Dialogue* module is reached. In the first step, the system provides an initial recommendation to the user based on the selected proof standard and all available information regarding the candidate portfolios. Figure 6 shows this process. From this point, the dialogue game begins, the user can accept or reject the said recommendation, provide his arguments to counter the system's proposal, or even introduce additional information which affects weights or veto thresholds of the criteria, the impact of an alternative in a criterion, or the proof standard. Figure 7 presents a screenshot reflecting these movements.

During the dialogue game, it is expected that the prototype's interface allows changes within the instance. The user can change the value of any criterion for each available project. The user can do so until the process reaches the *Recommendation acceptance/rejection* module when the DM accepts or rejects the current recommendation and considers it a final decision. By doing so, the dialogue game reaches its end.

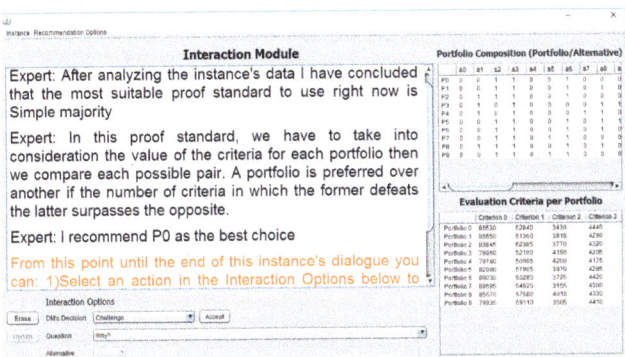

Figure 6. Initial recommendation from the system. DAIRS analyzes all the information provided by the instance file and provides a recommendation.

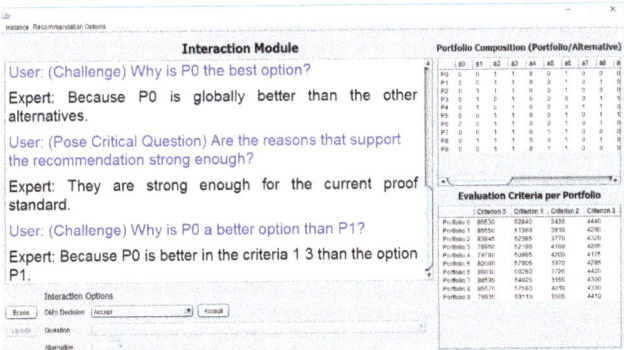

Figure 7. Advanced stage of the dialogue game. The user is questioning reasoning behind the system's recommendation and the system is able to respond.

4.2.3. Definition of the Dialogue Game Rules

Within the prototype, once the instance to read containing the PPS problem's information has been defined, it is necessary to determine how DAIRS will carry out the dialogue game between the user and the system. For this purpose, the system must define the dialogue game rules.

For this prototype, the compromise, dialogue, and termination rules are identical in all possible scenarios where an interaction between the players occurs to aid the decision-making process of a PPS problem, as shown in Section 4.1.3. However, it is necessary to define the locution rules that each dialogue game will use, based on whether or not there is a hierarchy order established for the criteria.

As mentioned in Section 4.1.4, DAIRS uses two STDs. The first one, STD1, does not require an initial preference hierarchy and focuses on obtaining information regarding the PPS problem on the dialogue game's initial cycles. The second diagram, STD2, is used when the DM defines preferences before the dialogue game begins. In this case, the system is more flexible to the user since DAIRS considers that both players have a better understanding of the problem as there is enough information to determine a hierarchy.

Once the dialogue game rules and STD are defined, the user can communicate with the system through the main window's interaction area after the system has presented an initial recommendation. Considering the structure presented by Figure 5, the user has at his disposal a set of available actions that allow him to interact with the system before and during the dialogue game. These actions are the ones that allow the creation of bidirectional interactions between the user and the system:

a. DM's Decision. Dialogue move performed by the DM.
b. Question. Statement related to the decision taken by the DM.
c. Alternative. This option will active to allow the user to select a portfolio from the available candidates if the statement selected requires selecting an alternative (for example, comparing the recommendation and another portfolio).
d. Accept button. Executes the DM's decision.
e. Erase button. Deletes the text from the dialogue text box.
f. Update button. Allows the user to update the values of the project/criteria matrix.

The options available for *DM's decision* depend on the current state of the dialogue within the STD and the locution rules defined. The user can accept the current recommendation (Accept) or reject it (Retract), ending the dialogue game. He/She can also present an argument to challenge the system's actions (Challenge), create an argument for or against the recommendation (Argue), suggest a recommendation for the system to analyze (Assert), or present a critical question that can modify the current proof standard used and its properties (Pose Critical Question).

4.2.4. Use of Argumentation Schemes

DAIRS uses an argumentation scheme based on the current state of the STD and the DM's action in the interaction area. The argumentation schemes used in this prototype are those reviewed in Section 4.1.2. This subsection briefly explains the conditions and events that trigger the use of each scheme.

The *abductive reasoning argument* scheme is used in the prototype when the system reads an instance before generating an initial recommendation, the user uses the GUI to start a dialogue game, after posing a critical question, and when the user argues to have a preference towards a particular criterion.

DAIRS uses the *argument from position to know* scheme after setting the initial proof standard, when the dialogue game starts using the GUI, when the system provides a new recommendation and the dialogues cycles have not surpassed the *cycle threshold*. The system also uses this scheme if the user challenges a system's argument and when the user poses a critical question.

Meanwhile, the recommender system uses the *argument from an expert opinion* scheme under the same scenarios as *argument from position to know*. However, it is only used when the number of dialogue cycles has surpassed the *cycle threshold*, which implies that the system has a more profound knowledge about the instance.

Whenever the user wishes to compare the profit or budget of two portfolios, DAIRS uses the *multi-criteria pairwise comparison* scheme. When the difference between two compared portfolios has no significant difference, DAIRS uses the *practical argument from analogy* argumentation scheme to support its decision.

For the fallacy-based argumentation schemes, the system uses the *ad ignorantiam* scheme at all times, as all information not introduced into the system is considered false by it. Meanwhile, DAIRS uses the *from bias* scheme when there is a criteria hierarchy defined or if the user decides to define a hierarchy.

Lastly, the prototype uses the *cause to effect* argumentation scheme when the user poses a critical question, asserts a preference towards a specific portfolio, or defines a preference towards a particular criterion as an argument to justify his/her preference for a specific portfolio.

4.2.5. Proof Standard Selection

The last step in the *configuration* module before presenting an initial recommendation is to select the initial proof standard. To do the system performs a two-stage method. The first stage corresponds to the definition of the proof standard properties before starting the dialogue game.

In DAIRS, different considerations determine if a property is set as active or inactive. Ordinality is always active unless the value of one of the weight vector values is equal to or exceeds 0.6 under a normalized value. Anonymity is active when there is not an explicit criteria preference hierarchy order defined. Additivity with respect to coalitions and with respect to values are only active if ordinality is active as well. Veto and distance to the worst solution are inactive by default.

The veto property is defined as inactive by default for the definition of the initial proof standard since the simple majority and weighted majority proof standards can have both veto and non-veto versions. Therefore, the user has the choice to activate this property during the dialogue game. Distance to the worst solution is set as inactive as the system seeks to use basic comparisons between all portfolios during the initial recommendation. The user is allowed to activate this property and access more complex proof standards during the dialogue.

After the proof standard properties setup, the system selects the most suitable standard based on the active properties. The DAIRS prototype analyses each proof standard, choosing the one with the most significant number of related properties active at that time in the system.

Following the proof standard selection, the process moves towards the *dialogue* module and performs an interaction between the user and the system using the DAIRS prototype. In this module, the user can modify the current state of all properties during the argument exchange between him/her and the system. Providing new information can also cause said properties to become active or inactive. There are three conditions in which the system can modify the status of each proof standard property:

1. If the user explicitly indicates he/she wishes to modify the state of a property (see steps 9 to 11 in Figure 4).
2. If the user indicates that he/she has a preference for a particular criterion.
3. If the user directly selects the proof standard by posing a critical question asking if the current proof standard is the best available option, in which the system responds by allowing the user to edit the status of a property or choose a new standard directly.

If any previous scenarios occur, the recommender system selects the new proof standard to use by considering the active properties or using the standard that the user directly chose. After doing so, the system analyses the available portfolios under the selected proof standard and presents a new recommendation. This process is what the system considers a *dialogue loop*.

5. Experimentation and Analysis

This section defines an experimental design to evaluate the effect of the developed prototype on various users. Generally, the measurement of recommender systems comes through quantitative measures. However, human factors affect the acceptance of the recommendation that must be evaluated in interactive systems [54], such as user satisfaction and confidence in the results.

This experiment seeks to analyze the usability of the recommender system under a real-life simulation of a PPS problem in a controlled environment, where users interact with the system. Under these considerations, this work performs a usability test to evaluate the proposed prototype.

The analysis presented in this section will allow a study of the effects on user overall satisfaction by using argumentation theory concepts, such as argumentation schemes, proof standards, and dialogue games on an MCDSS. This study will also compare the effects on user satisfaction under the two STDs presented in this proposal.

5.1. Experimental Design

A study is conducted on two groups of seven individuals to evaluate the performance of the DAIRS prototype built; each group includes people with different degrees of computational and mathematical knowledge, from people that have a basic level of computer knowledge to master degree and Ph.D. students.

Each member plays the role of a user and interacts with the system. in a dialogue game. The interaction period given to the users to work with the prototype has a maximum limit set to 50 min. The experimentation process performed by each group consists of the following steps:

(1) Introduction to the system: Users are shown the recommender system prototype and explained how it works. The users receive a detailed explanation about the different components DAIRS has, the possible actions they can perform on the system at any given time, and how the system reacts to each of the user's movements (maximum time length: 5 min).

(2) Initial use of the system to solve a sample PPS problem: In this step, the user directly interacts with the DAIRS prototype for the first time. Users face a real-life simulation of a small-sized PPS problem in terms of the number of available projects. Then, the evaluator asks each user to carry out a set of steps: Create a project/profit matrix of the PPS problem presented, analyze a set of previously made project portfolios to solve this problem, manually select the portfolio he/she believes is the best choice. After that, the users create a file of this PPS problem using the structure mentioned in Section 4.2 and upload it to the recommender system in its GUI. Finally, each user analyzes and compares their decision against the system's recommendation and engages in a brief dialogue game (maximum time length: 10 min).

The introductory PPS problem for this step is a simple example that presents the following scenario: *"You have got $20,000 in savings, and there are some necessities of life and work that you want to cover which have the following costs:"*

- Laptop—$9000.
- Desktop computer—$7000.
- Air conditioner for your room—$3000.
- Car repairs—$10,000.
- New smartphone—$2000.

"However, your savings do not allow you to buy everything, so you must select a subset. You must select which of them to choose taking into account four equally important criteria:"

- Study support
- Personal satisfaction
- Recreation outside of study
- Comfort

(3) Simulation of a complex real-life PPS problem: To fully evaluate the prototype's capabilities, both groups perform a simulation of a real-life PPS under a different environment. The first group works with an instance without a criteria preference hierarchy order defined. Meanwhile, the second group uses an instance with a criteria hierarchy. The PPS problem to solve presents the following scenario:

Four neighboring cities are planning to apply 25 social projects to improve the citizens' quality of life. However, before these projects were budgeted, a natural disaster severely depleted these towns' funds. Because of this, the cities can implement only a subset of the projects. Each city provided a list defining a level of satisfaction provided to the city by each project. Meanwhile, an analyst was hired, who generated a set of possible combinations of the projects that the cities could execute.

The first group users, which manage an instance without a criteria hierarchy, are given the objective: *Determine which project portfolio is the most adequate to best satisfy the four cities.*

The second group users, which manages an instance *with* criteria preference hierarchy, are given the objective: *Determine which project portfolio is the most adequate. The user must* consider that a council composed of members from all four cities has decided to satisfy mainly one of the four cities as it is the one that generates the most income for all of them.

At the beginning of this problem's study, each user expresses preferences through a criteria weight vector. The group supervisor makes a consensus using Borda counting [55,56], obtaining a weight vector that characterizes the group. Appendix A presents the information of the PPS problem file.

Each user receives a file containing the initial information of the PPS problem. The file follows their respective group's structure. The user must upload the file into the recommender system's GUI and engage in a dialogue game to obtain the most suitable solution to satisfy their respective objectives. Since the first group's problem setup does not include a criteria hierarchy, their dialogue game will follow the structure defined in STD1. Meanwhile, the second group will follow the structure of STD2 as there is a predefined criteria ranking (maximum time length: 30 min).

(4) Application of an evaluation to measure the usability of the prototype and to obtain user feedback for potential future work (maximum time length: 5 min).

5.2. Usability Evaluation

This work uses a usability test to evaluate the performance of DAIRS based on the user's opinion and satisfaction. The usability test analyses six critical elements related to a recommender system's quality: Design, functionality, ease of use, learning capacity, user satisfaction, and result and potential future use. The designed usability evaluation questions and structure are based on the models presented by Lewis and Zins et al.'s works [57,58]. This test uses a score between 0 and 10 as a measure, where 0 means complete disagreement and 10 means complete agreement. Each of the analyzed elements features a subset of questions to evaluate it:

Design:
1. I am pleased with the system's GUI.
2. The organization of the information provided by the system was clear.
3. The interface was simple to use.

Functionality:
4. The system has all the functions and capabilities I expect.
5. The information collected by the system helped me complete my activities.
6. The projects recommended by the system are suitable for my investment.
7. Being able to select my solution, disregarding the recommendation presented by the system, was helpful.

Ease of use:
8. The system was simple to use.
9. It was easy to find the information I needed.
10. The Help window provided clear information.
11. Overall, the system is easy to use.

Learning:
12. It was easy learning to use this system.
13. The information provided by the system was easy to understand.
14. The reasoning provided by the system in the dialogue eases my decision-making.
15. I consider that previous system information is required to use it.

Satisfaction:
16. I felt comfortable using this system.
17. I enjoy building my investment plan using this system.
18. Overall, I am satisfied with this system.

Result and future use:
19. I was able to complete the tasks using this system.
20. I was able to complete the tasks quickly using this system.

21. I was able to complete the tasks efficiently using this system.
22. I think that I could become more productive quickly using this system.
23. The system was able to convince me that the recommendations had value.
24. With my experience using the system, I think I would use it regularly.

5.3. Results and Analysis

The results obtained in the usability evaluation for each user were added to a total value per group. Then, the average values were obtained per question and for each of the question subsets representing the elements considered relevant for a recommender system as mentioned in the previous subsection.

Table 3 presents the results obtained on average for each element of the recommendation system considered. A Wilcoxon statistical test [59] was performed to determine whether there is a significant difference between the values obtained by the groups. The greatest difference is found within the satisfaction criterion, while the learning section shows the smallest difference between the two groups.

Figure 8 shows graphically the average values obtained in each section by each of the groups. As mentioned above, the satisfaction section shows the most remarkable difference between the two groups, while the least remarkable difference is in the learning section. Another observation that this figure presents is that the average value for all sections is higher than 8.

Table 4 presents the average value obtained by question for each group and the difference between them. The results presented in this table allow a specific visualization of the main strengths of each STD based on the users' evaluation. Figures 9 and 10 graphically show the results for each question in STD1 and STD2, respectively. These resources allow seeing which elements had a more relevant impact on user satisfaction in each of the analyzed sections of the prototype for each STD and compare them.

Table 3. Difference between the average value obtained per section for both groups. A statistical test is used to find if there is a significant difference between both groups.

Section	Group 1	Group 2	Difference
Design	9.09524	8.80952	0.28571
Functionality	9.28571	8.96429	0.32143
Ease of use	8.46429	8.89286	0.42857
Learning	8.92857	8.85714	0.07143
Satisfaction	9.52381	8.71429	0.80952 *
Result and future use	9.52381	8.73810	0.78571 *

* indicates there is a significant difference between values using Wilcoxon Test.

Based on this, it is possible to assume that STD1, which is selected if the instance does not have a defined criteria hierarchy before establishing a user-system interaction, used in a dialogue game provides better functionality and satisfaction for the users. Also, according to the values obtained for the questions related to the results and future use, it could be implied that test users would prefer to conduct a dialogue game using the structure in STD1 over the structure in STD2.

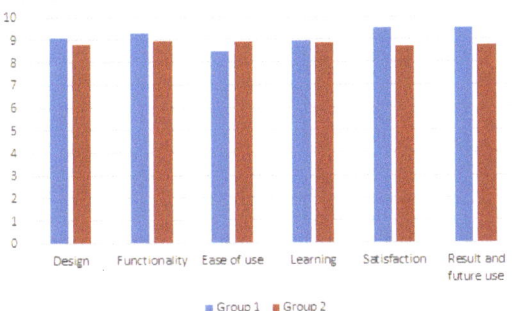

Figure 8. Bar graph comparison of the average value obtained per section by both groups.

Table 4. Difference between the average per question for both groups. This comparison allows analyzing and understanding the specific elements in which users were most satisfied.

Question	Group 1	Group 2	Difference
1	9.00000	8.42857	0.57143
2	9.28571	9.00000	0.28571
3	9.00000	9.00000	0.00000
4	9.42857	8.85714	0.57143
5	9.14286	9.00000	0.14286
6	9.14286	9.28571	0.14286
7	9.42857	8.71429	0.71429
8	7.85714	9.00000	1.14286
9	8.42857	8.71429	0.28571
10	9.00000	8.71429	0.28571
11	8.57143	9.14286	0.57143
12	8.57143	9.42857	0.85714
13	9.28571	9.00000	0.28571
14	9.42857	9.00000	0.42857
15	8.42857	8.00000	0.42857
16	9.28571	8.71429	0.57143
17	9.57143	8.57143	1.00000
18	9.71429	8.85714	0.85714
19	9.85714	8.71429	1.14286
20	9.57143	9.14286	0.42857
21	9.42857	8.85714	0.57143
22	9.71429	8.42857	1.28571
23	9.28571	9.00000	0.28571
24	9.28571	8.28571	1.00000

However, the overall user satisfaction while using STD2, which is used if there is a defined criterion preference hierarchy defined from the initial step of the dialogue game, is also acceptable. STD2 presents advantages over STD1 over certain aspects based on the results obtained, specifically regarding the ease of use, which is one of the main objectives of the STD2 design. Therefore, neither can be discarded as both have potential utility within the prototype and can provide new relevant information to the user during the dialogue.

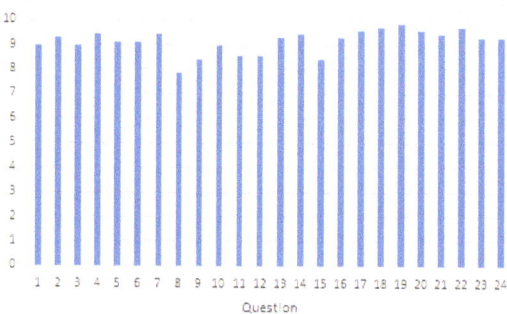

Figure 9. Bar graph showing the average obtained per question by the first group (STD1).

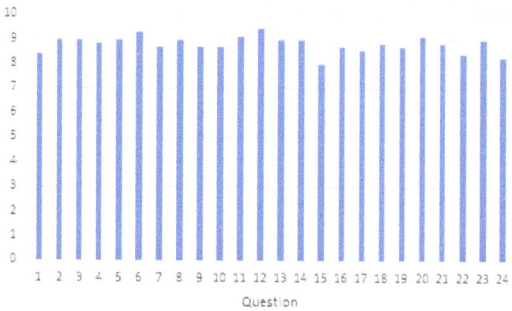

Figure 10. Bar graph showing the average obtained per question by the second group (STD2).

Analyzing the values obtained concerning design, users generally felt comfortable using the GUI presented. According to the answers obtained by the questions made regarding this section, this comfort is because each of the main window parts and the available options and windows given by the menus provide the necessary content without saturating the user with too much unnecessary information. The most common observation regarding the prototype's design is the need to add more colored details to make the relevant elements of the dialogue more noticeable. With this, it is possible to consider that the DAIRS GUI design is easy and straightforward to use. These graphical advantages are intended to favor the flow of the dialogue and thus obtain a better recommendation.

Both groups were also satisfied with the prototype's functionality, as shown from the values in Table 3. Most users think that the system can adequately support the decision-making process for PPS problems and that it has the necessary tools to execute this task. For this analyzed section, the most significant difference between the groups focuses on the users' ability to select their solution. This result suggests that users prefer an assertive but learning-focused interface. Another observation from the users is again focused on graphical aspects since both groups proposed the use of graphs to represent the criteria profit and budgets.

The results regarding ease of use imply that some users in the first group had difficulty adapting to the prototype's operation at the beginning of the test. In fact, concerning the questions related to this section, the most notable difference is presented for the users' opinion regarding the system's simplicity. Although the interface is considered to be simple and accessible for most users, some users from the first group believe that starting a dialogue game can be complicated. The obtained results can conclude that the prototype, though easy to use, requires a certain degree of prior knowledge for proper usage. Users with more previous knowledge of the problem (STD2) quickly adapted to the use of DAIRS. However, the overall results are satisfactory for both groups. As a relevant observation, the users would desire to have access to a user manual that explains each of the prototype components' operations in detail.

An interesting fact that should be mentioned is that, although some users reported issues adapting at the beginning of the test, the results concerning learning, in general, show that the conveniences and information offered by the system allow them to learn how to use it properly quickly.

Most users in both groups conclude that the prototype offers easy and simple ways to learn how to use the system, although the initial impact can present a steep learning curve at the beginning. Similarly, users generally feel that DAIRS adequately supports them in obtaining information and learning quickly and effectively about the PPS problem. Based on the learning section results, it is possible to believe that DAIRS offers the user an advantage to solve a problem, as it offers an effective problem-learning methodology supported by argumentation theory.

The two sections of questions in which there was a statistically significant difference between the two groups were "satisfaction" and "results and future use". Although mentioning the difficulty of adapting at the beginning of using the prototype in general, the first group felt largely satisfied and comfortable using the system by the end of the test. On the other hand, although the users from the second group of users were satisfied with the prototype, they consider it advisable to reduce the system's dialogue game duration. Although users are satisfied with the system's functionality and interface, they feel that the time needed for the user and the system to reach an agreement on a portfolio recommendation could be improved.

Based on the information previously presented, it is possible to say that the definition of bidirectional interaction between the user and DAIRS is effective since users feel generally satisfied with the recommendation obtained to solve a problem by using an interactive recommender system supported by MCDA methods and argumentation theory, using argumentation schemes, proof standards, and dialogue games.

Also, the results obtained in the "satisfaction" and "results and future use" sections can assume that the learning-oriented approach, given by STD1, offers higher user satisfaction in the results obtained compared to a recommendation-oriented approach, as presented by STD2. This assumption agrees with the conclusions obtained by the results in the other analyzed sections, where users using STD2 feel more comfortable using DAIRS when carrying out a dialogue following this diagram but preferred that the system would focus more on continuing the learning process of the problem.

In general, there is a better overall evaluation by the first group, being only the ease of use question subset the only exception. However, there is only a significant difference in the satisfaction and results and future use sections.

All analyzed sections obtained an average value higher than 8, and, except for the analysis for the ease of use on the first group, these values were never lower than 8.5. Based on this, it is possible to consider that the prototype had a satisfactory degree of acceptance by both groups and that the future implementation of all the presented observations could further improve its quality.

The system received an average score of 89.91%. Therefore, it is possible to conclude that this evaluation is satisfactory enough to consider DAIRS as a promising alternative. However, the results and observations from the users evidence the necessity to introduce visual resources; although the plain text could be enough for some people, others prefer a representation using images and graphs.

Most state-of-the-art works presented in Section 2 propose MCDSS frameworks to solve optimization problems and establish an interaction between the user and the system. However, this interaction only allows users to incorporate new information, and the system does not establish a deep interaction with the DM that goes beyond receiving such information and generating new recommendations. Experimentation with DAIRS shows that it is possible to generate an MCDSS to solve PPS problems capable of establishing a bidirectional interaction. In this interaction, both participants generate and obtain new information. The system's defense of the recommendation and the user's statements use argumentation theory in a dialogue game supported by argumentation schemes and proof standards.

6. Conclusions and Future Work

This work studied the characterization of cognitive tasks involved in the decision-aiding process. The cognitive tasks involved in the process were defined, identifying those that could generate an interaction between the user and the system. This paper addressed two cognitive tasks to create a final recommendation: the evaluation model for the alternatives and the argument construction. For the first cognitive task, the proposed recommender system used proof standards to define a method to evaluate and select the best fitting alternative. For the second cognitive task, the system used argumentation schemes and a dialogue game to support the preferred alternative and establish a possible user-system interaction.

One of this work's main contributions is the development of the Decision Aid Interactive Recommender System (DAIRS), an MCDSS framework focused on solving PPS multi-objective problems. The framework is based on the characterization of cognitive tasks through argumentation schemes, dialogue game rules, state transition diagrams, and proof standards. These elements are incorporated into DAIRS to allow the recommender system to perform a bidirectional interaction between it and a user. This work proposed and developed a DAIRS experimental prototype that provides an environment to aid the decision-making to validate the proposed system.

Another contribution is the proposal and design of two state transition diagrams (STDs) to determine the flow of a dialogue game between the DM and DAIRS. These STDs allow two-way interaction between both participants, meaning that both can obtain and provide information. Also, the proposed STDs have two relevant components. First, the user can reject the proposal; this defines a new dialogue stopping criterion aiming towards the user's satisfaction. Second, the system is able to defend its arguments and reject the user's statements if there is not enough information to support them. The first STD, STD1, focuses on a more learning-oriented dialogue. Meanwhile, the second STD, named STD2, assumes that the user has an acceptable degree of knowledge about the problem to solve and focuses on providing recommendations to the user and engaging in a dialogue game focused on said recommendations.

Some of the most relevant features in the DAIRS prototype are designing and implementing several concepts related to argumentation theory within an MCDSS. The first of these concepts is a set of proof standards based on several known MCDA methods. Also, DAIRS incorporates multiple argumentation schemes from the literature on its process, supported by proof standards. Another relevant feature in DAIRS is the use of these elements by employing a dialogue game that uses one of the STDs proposed in this paper to direct the flow of the user-system interaction. DAIRS consider the three standard stopping criteria for a DSS interaction: user acceptance, manual stop, and algorithmic stop. The user can accept or reject the final decision; this considers user acceptance and manual stop. For the last stopping criterion, DAIRS implements a method to avoid loops in a dialogue game using multiple argumentation schemes.

Considering the strategies used by several state-of-the-art works, DAIRS uses proof standards based on a criteria hierarchy and a criteria weight vector. These considerations positively impacted users' overall satisfaction when using the proposed prototype since it considers their preferences using methods focused on qualitative (hierarchy) and quantitative (vector of weights) strategies, which allowed for a more flexible dialogue.

A usability evaluation analyzed the proposed system in this work to measure the quality of the developed DAIRS based on the experience of multiple test users after using it to solve a PPS problem that simulated a real-life situation. This evaluation studied the user experience regarding DAIRS by considering human factors that affect the acceptance or rejection of a recommendation. The results obtained were satisfactory enough as the system received an average approval of 89.91% and an overall acceptance in several critical elements such as design, functionality, ease of use, learning capability, satisfaction, and future use. Users were satisfied using the proposed GUI due to its simple design, ease to learn, use, interaction, and capability to obtain problem information.

On the other hand, the results for users using STD1 were often better than STD2. However, in both cases, the conclusions were primarily positive. These observations allow understanding that users are looking for an interactive system that assertively establishes recommendations, but with a focus directed towards learning about the problem with the objective that both the user and the system gain new knowledge to find a better solution.

The results show that the design of a bidirectional interactive recommender system allows users to successfully and effectively select a suitable recommendation for PPS problems. DAIRS presents a novel approach to the generation of recommendations for this type of problem not previously explored in the literature, to the authors' knowledge.

Considering the research area related to this work and all the observations and comments provided by the test users, multiple areas offer potential future work. First, the use of the proposed system on real-life problems different than the PPS problem. Second, adding new elements that make the recommender system capable of receiving new user-made portfolios during the dialogue game. Currently, the system uses only one STD per dialogue. Therefore, future work could focus on using more than one STD per dialogue game, looking to improve the dialogue game's quality. Also, there exists a wide variety of MCDA methods in the state-of-the-art, opening the possibility of using different methods as proof standards. Finally, the following versions of the prototype could provide the user with a more friendly looking GUI, featuring graphs and a more colorful environment.

Author Contributions: Conceptualization: T.M.-E., L.C.-R. and C.M.-T.; methodology: T.M.-E., C.M.-T. and N.R.-V.; software: T.M.-E. and N.R.-V.; validation: T.M.-E., L.C.-R. and C.G.-S.; formal analysis: T.M.-E., C.M.-T. and H.F.-H.; investigation: T.M.-E., L.C.-R., C.M.-T. and C.G.-S.; resources: T.M.-E., L.C.-R. and H.F.-H.; data curation: T.M.-E.; writing—original draft preparation: T.M.-E. and C.M.-T.; writing—review and editing: T.M.-E., L.C.-R., C.M.-T. and C.G.-S.; visualization: L.C.-R.; supervision: L.C.-R.; project administration: L.C.-R.; funding acquisition: T.M.-E., L.C.-R., C.M.-T. and H.F.-H. All authors have read and agreed to the published version of the manuscript.

Funding: This research received no external funding.

Institutional Review Board Statement: Ethical review and approval were waived for this study due to a completely voluntary and conscientious acceptance by each of the users to participate in the tests carried out to perform the usability evaluation. All users only interacted with the system during the test periods established in advance notice.

Informed Consent Statement: Informed consent was obtained from all subjects involved in the study.

Data Availability Statement: A DAIRS prototype is available at: https://www.dropbox.com/sh/j1yfblg011a7m0w/AABYrgbKBDWEFBg_vRcGE6dja?dl=0 (accessed on 20 April 2021).

Acknowledgments: Authors thank to CONACYT for supporting the projects from (a) Cátedras CONACYT Program with Number 3058. (b) Project CONACyT A1-S-11012 from Convocatoria de Investigación Científica Básica 2017–2018 and CONACYT Project with Number 312397 from Programa de Apoyo para Actividades Científicas, Tecnológicas y de Innovación (PAACTI), a efecto de participar en la Convocatoria 2020-1 Apoyo para Proyectos de Investigación Científica, Desarrollo Tecnológico e Innovación en Salud ante la Contingencia por COVID-19. (c) T. Macias-Escobar would like to acknowledge CONACYT, Mexico National Grant System, Grant 465554.

Conflicts of Interest: The authors declare no conflict of interest.

Abbreviations

The following abbreviations are used in this manuscript:

MCDA   Multi-criteria Decision Analysis
DAIRS Decision Aid Interactive Recommender System
DM   Decision Maker
PPS   Project Portfolio Selection
DSS   Decision Support Systems
CHP   Choice Problem
MOP   Multi-objective Optimization Problem
MCDSS Multi-Criteria Decision Support Systems
STD   State Transition Diagram
GUI   Graphical User Interface

Appendix A. PPS Problem Test Case

This appendix presents the information in the PPS problem file required for the *load instance module*. This information is also used to perform step 3 of the experimental design.

- Problem type: Maximization
- Number of available projects: 25
- Number of available project portfolios: 10
- Criteria size: 4
- Criteria hierarchy (for the second group): {2,3,1,4}
- Criteria weight vector (for the second group): {0.20 0.39 0.36 0.05}
- Budget threshold: 80,000
- Veto threshold per criterion {1500,1200,75,75}

Table A1. Criteria-profit matrix.

Project	Criterion 1	Criterion 2	Criterion 3	Criterion 4
Project 1	3200	2000	165	300
Project 2	6255	1640	385	390
Project 3	5680	6940	270	445
Project 4	8965	4195	355	415
Project 5	6550	6560	315	440
Project 6	6740	6290	150	350
Project 7	9055	7165	375	485
Project 8	4170	3015	410	285
Project 9	9735	2860	480	330
Project 10	3350	4210	400	315
Project 11	8595	7270	150	265
Project 12	9070	2430	455	360
Project 13	9930	5825	420	385
Project 14	4675	4505	425	490
Project 15	8065	4030	165	425
Project 16	7910	7665	240	320
Project 17	9860	6265	415	350
Project 18	3175	6240	225	445
Project 19	9660	655	320	475
Project 20	1150	4500	415	400
Project 21	3245	5950	105	275
Project 22	5350	6750	480	460
Project 23	6050	2505	285	305
Project 24	9190	2395	160	290
Project 25	9615	4340	100	480

List of available project portfolios and required budget (0 indicates that a project has not been included by the portfolio, 1 indicates that a project has been included):

- Portfolio 1 {0,0,1,1,0,0,1,0,0,0,1,1,1,1,0,1,1,1,0,0,0,0,0,0,1} Total cost: 79,290
- Portfolio 2 {0,0,1,1,0,0,1,0,1,0,1,1,1,1,0,1,1,1,0,0,0,0,0,0,0} Total cost: 79,575
- Portfolio 3 {0,1,1,1,0,0,1,0,0,0,1,1,1,0,0,1,1,1,0,0,0,1,0,0,0} Total cost: 79,875
- Portfolio 4 {0,1,0,1,0,0,0,0,1,1,1,1,1,1,0,0,1,1,0,0,0,1,0,0,0} Total cost: 79,525
- Portfolio 5 {0,1,0,1,0,0,0,1,1,0,1,1,1,1,0,0,1,1,0,0,0,1,0,0,0} Total cost: 79,905
- Portfolio 6 {0,0,1,1,0,0,1,0,1,1,1,1,1,1,0,0,1,1,0,0,0,0,0,0,0} Total cost: 79,885
- Portfolio 7 {0,0,1,1,0,0,1,0,1,1,1,1,0,0,0,1,1,0,0,0,0,1,0,0,1} Total cost: 79,410
- Portfolio 8 {0,0,1,1,0,1,1,0,0,0,1,1,1,0,0,1,1,1,0,0,0,0,0,0,1} Total cost: 79,585
- Portfolio 9 {0,1,1,1,0,0,0,1,0,1,0,1,1,1,0,0,0,1,1,0,0,0,1,0,0,0} Total cost: 79,230
- Portfolio 10 {0,0,1,1,0,1,1,0,0,0,1,0,1,1,0,1,1,1,0,0,0,1,0,0,0} Total cost: 79,825

References

1. Keeney, R.L.; Raiffa, H.; Meyer, R.F. *Decisions with Multiple Objectives: Preferences and Value Trade-Offs*; Cambridge University Press: Cambridge, UK, 1993.
2. Fernández González, E.; López Cervantes, E.; Navarro Castillo, J.; Vega López, I. Aplicación de metaheurísticas multiobjetivo a la solución de problemas de cartera de proyectos públicos con una valoración multidimensional de su impacto. *Gestión Política Pública* **2011**, *20*, 381–432.
3. Bechikh, S.; Kessentini, M.; Said, L.B.; Ghédira, K. Preference incorporation in evolutionary multiobjective optimization: A survey of the state-of-the-art. In *Advances in Computers*; Elsevier: Amsterdam, The Netherlands, 2015; Volume 98, pp. 141–207.
4. Fernandez, E.; Lopez, E.; Lopez, F.; Coello, C.A.C. Increasing selective pressure towards the best compromise in evolutionary multiobjective optimization: The extended NOSGA method. *Inf. Sci.* **2011**, *181*, 44–56. [CrossRef]
5. Ishizaka, A.; Nemery, P. *Multi-Criteria Decision Analysis: Methods and Software*; John Wiley & Sons: Hoboken, NJ, USA, 2013.
6. Chu, P.Y.V.; Hsu, Y.L.; Fehling, M. A decision support system for project portfolio selection. *Comput. Ind.* **1996**, *32*, 141–149. [CrossRef]
7. Bana e Costa, C.A.; De Corte, J.M.; Vansnick, J.C. On the mathematical foundations of MACBETH. In *Multiple Criteria Decision Analysis*; Springer: New York, NY, USA, 2016; pp. 421–463.
8. Hummel, J.; Oliveira, M.D.; Bana e Costa, C.A.; IJzerman, M.J. Supporting the project portfolio selection decision of research and development investments by means of multi-criteria resource allocation modelling. In *Multi-Criteria Decision Analysis to Support Healthcare Decisions*; Springer: Cham, Switzerland, 2017; pp. 89–103.
9. Archer, N.P.; Ghasemzadeh, F. An integrated framework for project portfolio selection. *Int. J. Proj. Manag.* **1999**, *17*, 207–216. [CrossRef]
10. Ghasemzadeh, F.; Archer, N.P. Project portfolio selection through decision support. *Decis. Support Syst.* **2000**, *29*, 73–88. [CrossRef]
11. Hu, G.; Wang, L.; Fetch, S.; Bidanda, B. A multi-objective model for project portfolio selection to implement lean and Six Sigma concepts. *Int. J. Prod. Res.* **2008**, *46*, 6611–6625. [CrossRef]
12. Smith, B. Lean and Six Sigma–a one-two punch. *Qual. Prog.* **2003**, *36*, 37.
13. Khalili-Damghani, K.; Sadi-Nezhad, S.; Lotfi, F.H.; Tavana, M. A hybrid fuzzy rule-based multi-criteria framework for sustainable project portfolio selection. *Inf. Sci.* **2013**, *220*, 442–462. [CrossRef]
14. Mira, C.; Feijão, P.; Souza, M.A.; Moura, A.; Meidanis, J.; Lima, G.; Bossolan, R.P.; Freitas, Ì.T. A project portfolio selection decision support system. In Proceedings of the 2013 10th International Conference on Service Systems and Service Management, Hong Kong, China, 17–19 July 2013; pp. 725–730.
15. Mohammed, H.J. The optimal project selection in portfolio management using fuzzy multi-criteria decision-making methodology. *J. Sustain. Financ. Investig.* **2021**, 1–17. [CrossRef]
16. Saaty, R.W. The analytic hierarchy process—What it is and how it is used. *Math. Model.* **1987**, *9*, 161–176. [CrossRef]
17. Hwang, C.L.; Yoon, K. Methods for multiple attribute decision making. In *Multiple Attribute Decision Making*; Springer: Berlin/Heidelberg, Germany, 1981; pp. 58–191.
18. Dobrovolskienė, N.; Tamošiūnienė, R. Sustainability-oriented financial resource allocation in a project portfolio through multi-criteria decision-making. *Sustainability* **2016**, *8*, 485. [CrossRef]
19. Markowitz, H. *Portfolio Selection: Efficient Diversification of Investments*; Yale University Press: New Haven, CT, USA, 1959.
20. Debnath, A.; Roy, J.; Kar, S.; Zavadskas, E.K.; Antucheviciene, J. A hybrid MCDM approach for strategic project portfolio selection of agro by-products. *Sustainability* **2017**, *9*, 1302. [CrossRef]
21. Bai, C.; Sarkis, J. A grey-based DEMATEL model for evaluating business process management critical success factors. *Int. J. Prod. Econ.* **2013**, *146*, 281–292. [CrossRef]
22. Pamučar, D.; Ćirović, G. The selection of transport and handling resources in logistics centers using Multi-Attributive Border Approximation area Comparison (MABAC). *Expert Syst. Appl.* **2015**, *42*, 3016–3028. [CrossRef]

23. Verdecho, M.J.; Pérez-Perales, D.; Alarcón-Valero, F. Project portfolio selection for increasing sustainability in supply chains. *Econ. Bus. Lett.* **2020**, *9*, 317–325. [CrossRef]
24. Miettinen, K.; Hakanen, J.; Podkopaev, D. Interactive nonlinear multiobjective optimization methods. In *Multiple Criteria Decision Analysis*; Springer: New York, NY, USA, 2016; pp. 927–976.
25. Miettinen, K.; Ruiz, F.; Wierzbicki, A.P. Introduction to multiobjective optimization: Interactive approaches. In *Multiobjective Optimization*; Springer: Berlin/Heidelberg, Germany, 2008; pp. 27–57.
26. De Almeida, A.T.; de Almeida, J.A.; Costa, A.P.C.S.; de Almeida-Filho, A.T. A new method for elicitation of criteria weights in additive models: Flexible and interactive tradeoff. *Eur. J. Oper. Res.* **2016**, *250*, 179–191. [CrossRef]
27. Nebro, A.J.; Ruiz, A.B.; Barba-González, C.; García-Nieto, J.; Luque, M.; Aldana-Montes, J.F. InDM2: Interactive dynamic multi-objective decision making using evolutionary algorithms. *Swarm Evol. Comput.* **2018**, *40*, 184–195. [CrossRef]
28. Azabi, Y.; Savvaris, A.; Kipouros, T. The interactive design approach for aerodynamic shape design optimisation of the aegis UAV. *Aerospace* **2019**, *6*, 42. [CrossRef]
29. Stummer, C.; Kiesling, E.; Gutjahr, W.J. A multicriteria decision support system for competence-driven project portfolio selection. *Int. J. Inf. Technol. Decis. Mak.* **2009**, *8*, 379–401. [CrossRef]
30. Nowak, M. Project portfolio selection using interactive approach. *Procedia Eng.* **2013**, *57*, 814–822. [CrossRef]
31. Haara, A.; Pykäläinen, J.; Tolvanen, A.; Kurttila, M. Use of interactive data visualization in multi-objective forest planning. *J. Environ. Manag.* **2018**, *210*, 71–86. [CrossRef]
32. Kurttila, M.; Haara, A.; Juutinen, A.; Karhu, J.; Ojanen, P.; Pykäläinen, J.; Saarimaa, M.; Tarvainen, O.; Sarkkola, S.; Tolvanen, A. Applying a multi-criteria project portfolio tool in selecting energy peat production areas. *Sustainability* **2020**, *12*, 1705. [CrossRef]
33. Zhang, Q.; Lu, J.; Jin, Y. Artificial intelligence in recommender systems. *Complex Intell. Syst.* **2021**, *7*, 439–457. [CrossRef]
34. Labreuche, C. Argumentation of the decision made by several aggregation operators based on weights. In Proceedings of the 11th International Conference on Information Processing and Management of Uncertainty in Knowledge-Based Systems (IPMU'06), Paris, France, 2–7 July 2006; pp. 683–690.
35. Ouerdane, W. Multiple Criteria Decision Aiding: A Dialectical Perspective. Ph.D. Thesis, University of Paris-Dauphine, Paris, France, 2011.
36. Cruz-Reyes, L.; Medina-Trejo, C.; Morales-Rodríguez, M.L.; Gómez-Santillan, C.G.; Macias-Escobar, T.E.; Guerrero-Nava, C.A.; Pérez-Villafuerte, M. A Dialogue Interaction Module for a Decision Support System Based on Argumentation Schemes to Public Project Portfolio. In *Nature-Inspired Design of Hybrid Intelligent Systems*; Springer: Cham, Switzerland, 2017; pp. 741–756.
37. Sassoon, I.; Kökciyan, N.; Sklar, E.; Parsons, S. Explainable argumentation for wellness consultation. In *International Workshop on Explainable, Transparent Autonomous Agents and Multi-Agent Systems*; Springer: Cham, Switzerland, 2019; pp. 186–202.
38. Morveli-Espinoza, M.; Nieves, J.C.; Possebom, A.; Puyol-Gruart, J.; Tacla, C.A. An argumentation-based approach for identifying and dealing with incompatibilities among procedural goals. *Int. J. Approx. Reason.* **2019**, *105*, 1–26. [CrossRef]
39. Espinoza, M.M.; Possebom, A.T.; Tacla, C.A. Argumentation-based agents that explain their decisions. In Proceedings of the 2019 8th Brazilian Conference on Intelligent Systems (BRACIS), Salvador, Brazil, 15–18 October 2019; pp. 467–472.
40. Morveli-Espinoza, M.; Tacla, C.A.; Jasinski, H.M. An Argumentation-Based Approach for Explaining Goals Selection in Intelligent Agents. In *Brazilian Conference on Intelligent Systems*; Springer: Cham, Switzerland, 2020; pp. 47–62.
41. Vayanos, P.; McElfresh, D.; Ye, Y.; Dickerson, J.; Rice, E. Active preference elicitation via adjustable robust optimization. *arXiv* **2020**, arXiv:2003.01899.
42. Vayanos, P.; Georghiou, A.; Yu, H. Robust optimization with decision-dependent information discovery. *arXiv* **2020**, arXiv:2004.08490.
43. Nowak, M.; Trzaskalik, T. A trade-off multiobjective dynamic programming procedure and its application to project portfolio selection. *Ann. Oper. Res.* **2021**, 1–27. [CrossRef]
44. Chernoff, H.; Moses, L.E. *Elementary Decision Theory*; Courier Corporation: Chelmsford, MA, USA, 2012.
45. López, J.C.L.; González, E.F.; Alvarado, M.T. Special Issue on Multicriteria Decision Support Systems. *Computación y Sistemas* **2008**, *12*. Available online: http://www.scielo.org.mx/pdf/cys/v12n2/v12n2a1.pdf (accessed on 20 April 2021).
46. Belton, V.; Stewart, T. *Multiple Criteria Decision Analysis: An Integrated Approach*; Springer Science & Business Media: Berlin, Germany, 2002.
47. Carazo, A.F.; Gómez, T.; Molina, J.; Hernández-Díaz, A.G.; Guerrero, F.M.; Caballero, R. Solving a comprehensive model for multiobjective project portfolio selection. *Comput. Oper. Res.* **2010**, *37*, 630–639. [CrossRef]
48. Resnick, P.; Varian, H.R. Recommender systems. *Commun. ACM* **1997**, *40*, 56–58. [CrossRef]
49. Wilson, R.A.; Keil, F.C. *The MIT Encyclopedia of the Cognitive Sciences*; MIT Press: Cambridge, MA, USA, 2001.
50. Tsoukiàs, A. On the concept of decision aiding process: An operational perspective. *Ann. Oper. Res.* **2007**, *154*, 3–27. [CrossRef]
51. Walton, D.N. *Argumentation Schemes for Presumptive Reasoning*; Psychology Press: New York, NY, USA, 1996.
52. Walton, D.; Reed, C.; Macagno, F. *Argumentation Schemes*; Cambridge University Press: Cambridge, UK, 2008.
53. Walton, D.N. *Logical Dialogue—Games and Fallacies*; University Press of America: Lanham, MD, USA, 1984.
54. He, C.; Parra, D.; Verbert, K. Interactive recommender systems: A survey of the state of the art and future research challenges and opportunities. *Expert Syst. Appl.* **2016**, *56*, 9–27. [CrossRef]
55. Van Newenhizen, J. The Borda method is most likely to respect the Condorcet principle. *Econ. Theory* **1992**, *2*, 69–83. [CrossRef]
56. Orouskhani, M.; Shi, D.; Cheng, X. A Fuzzy Adaptive Dynamic NSGA-II With Fuzzy-Based Borda Ranking Method and Its Application to Multimedia Data Analysis. *IEEE Trans. Fuzzy Syst.* **2020**, *29*, 118–128. [CrossRef]

57. Lewis, J.R. IBM computer usability satisfaction questionnaires: Psychometric evaluation and instructions for use. *Int. J. Hum. Comput. Interact.* **1995**, *7*, 57–78. [CrossRef]
58. Zins, A.H.; Bauernfeind, U.; Del Missier, F.; Venturini, A.; Rumetshofer, H.; Frew, A. *An Experimental Usability Test for Different Destination Recommender Systems*; Springer-Verlag New York Inc.: New York, NY, USA, 2004; pp. 228–238.
59. Wilcoxon, F. Individual comparisons by ranking methods. In *Breakthroughs in Statistics*; Springer: New York, NY, USA, 1992; pp. 196–202.

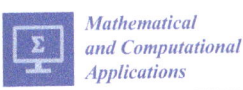

Mathematical and Computational Applications

Article

Modeling and Optimizing the Multi-Objective Portfolio Optimization Problem with Trapezoidal Fuzzy Parameters

Alejandro Estrada-Padilla, Daniela Lopez-Garcia, Claudia Gómez-Santillán, Héctor Joaquín Fraire-Huacuja, Laura Cruz-Reyes, Nelson Rangel-Valdez * and María Lucila Morales-Rodríguez

Graduate Program Division, Tecnológico Nacional de México/Instituto Tecnológico de Ciudad Madero, Ciudad Madero 89440, Mexico; aestrada1993@hotmail.com (A.E.-P.); dann.loga@gmail.com (D.L.-G.); claudia.gs@cdmadero.tecnm.mx (C.G.-S.); hector.fh@cdmadero.tecnm.mx (H.J.F.-H.); laura.cr@cdmadero.tecnm.mx (L.C.-R.); lucila.mr@cdmadero.tecnm.mx (M.L.M.-R.)
* Correspondence: nelson.rv@cdmadero.tecnm.mx

Abstract: A common issue in the Multi-Objective Portfolio Optimization Problem (MOPOP) is the presence of uncertainty that affects individual decisions, e.g., variations on resources or benefits of projects. Fuzzy numbers are successful in dealing with imprecise numerical quantities, and they found numerous applications in optimization. However, so far, they have not been used to tackle uncertainty in MOPOP. Hence, this work proposes to tackle MOPOP's uncertainty with a new optimization model based on fuzzy trapezoidal parameters. Additionally, it proposes three novel steady-state algorithms as the model's solution process. One approach integrates the Fuzzy Adaptive Multi-objective Evolutionary (FAME) methodology; the other two apply the Non-Dominated Genetic Algorithm (NSGA-II) methodology. One steady-state algorithm uses the Spatial Spread Deviation as a density estimator to improve the Pareto fronts' distribution. This research work's final contribution is developing a new defuzzification mapping that allows measuring algorithms' performance using widely known metrics. The results show a significant difference in performance favoring the proposed steady-state algorithm based on the FAME methodology.

Citation: Estrada-Padilla, A.; Lopez-Garcia, D.; Gómez-Santillán, C.; Fraire-Huacuja, H.J.; Cruz-Reyes, L.; Rangel-Valdez, N.; Morales-Rodríguez, M.L. Modeling and Optimizing the Multi-Objective Portfolio Optimization Problem with Trapezoidal Fuzzy Parameters. *Math. Comput. Appl.* **2021**, *26*, 36. https://doi.org/10.3390/mca26020036

Keywords: multi-objective optimization; multi-objective portfolio optimization problem; trapezoidal fuzzy numbers; density estimators; steady state algorithms

Academic Editor: Leonardo Trujillo

Received: 28 February 2021
Accepted: 22 April 2021
Published: 24 April 2021

Publisher's Note: MDPI stays neutral with regard to jurisdictional claims in published maps and institutional affiliations.

Copyright: © 2021 by the authors. Licensee MDPI, Basel, Switzerland. This article is an open access article distributed under the terms and conditions of the Creative Commons Attribution (CC BY) license (https://creativecommons.org/licenses/by/4.0/).

1. Introduction

The Portfolio Optimization Problem (POP) is always present in organizations. One key issue in POP's decision process is the uncertainty caused by the variability in the project benefits and resources. The latter situation arises the necessity of a tool for describing and representing uncertainty associated with real-life decision-making situations. The POP searches a subset of projects under a predefined set of resources that maximizes the produced benefits; its formal definition is as follows.

Let A be a finite set of N projects, each characterized by estimates of its impacts and resource consumption. A portfolio is a subset of A that can be represented by a binary vector $x = x_1, x_2, \ldots, x_n$ that assigns $x_i = 1$ for every financed project i, and $x_i = 0$ otherwise. Let $\vec{z}(x) = z_1(x), z_2(x), \ldots, z_p(x)$ be the vector of impacts resulting from the linear sum of the attribute values of each financed project in x, i.e., the vector of size p representing multiple attributes related to organizational goals that describe the consequences of a portfolio x. Assume w.l.o.g. that the higher an attribute's value is, the better. Then, Problem (1) formally defines POP.

$$Maximize\{z_1(x), z_2(x), \ldots, z_p(x)\}, \ x \in R_F \qquad (1)$$

In Problem (1), R_F is the space of feasible portfolios, usually determined by the available budget and other constraints that the *Decision Maker* (DM) wants to impose (e.g., budget limits on types, geographic areas, social roles of projects, etc.).

Different scientific research works address POP's variant in Problem (1), considering precise values on the available resources and the projects' impacts [1–6]. Moreover, there is an area called Portfolio Decision Analysis (PDA) dedicated to studying mathematical models to solve POP. There are theories, methods, and practices developed within this area to help decision-makers select projects from a very large set of them, taking into account relevant constraints, preferences, uncertainty, or imprecision [7]. PDA-related problems' difficulty comes from a combination of factors such as (1) large entry space; (2) consequences of multidimensionality in portfolio construction and selection; or (3) qualitative, imprecise or uncertain information.

A large entry space requires a solution process with exponential complexity for decision-making problems, even with simple decisions on allocating resources for candidate projects.

The consequences of multidimensionality in portfolio construction and selection relate conflicting attributes with difficulty in the decision process. Usually, the larger the number of dimensions, the more complex the solution space is. The latter causes a situation with so many solutions that it easily exceeds the human cognitive capabilities for evaluating and selecting the best candidate solutions [8].

The qualitative, imprecise, or uncertain information exists because of the varying nature of the distinct attributes and resources considered in the construction of portfolios. Such information can sometimes occur from different circumstances as a DM needs to use non-numerical data to describe the effects of a project instead of a quantitative measure. Other cases might indicate that there is lack of knowledge about future states of specific criteria, vagueness in the provided information, the values used to describe attributes or resources are not accurately known beforehand, or vague approximations and areas of ignorance. All the previous situations, denoted hereafter as *uncertainty*, limit the scientific approach in Operational Research-Decision Aiding [9], and modeling them using probability distributions can be a challenge [9].

Several optimization problems use fuzzy numbers to model the uncertainty in parameters' values from arbitrariness, imprecision, and poor determination [10]. Among the most recent and works related to the Multi-objective Portfolio Optimization Problem are the following: García [11] solved the Multi-objective and Static Portfolio Optimization Problem (MOSPOP) with real parameters using the generational algorithms HHGA-SPPv1 and HHGA-SPPv2 and considering the preferences of a DM. Rivera-Zarate [12] uses the Non-Outranked Ant Colony Optimization (NO-ACO) to address a variant of MOSPOP that includes interdependency among objectives and that has partial support with real parameters. Bastiani [13] solves the MOSPOP variant that includes synergy using ACO-SPRI, ACO-SOP, and ACO-SOP, three strategies based on the ACO that incorporate in their search process priority ranking, preferences, and synergy, respectively. Sánchez [14] proposes using classification methods on the generational algorithms H-MCSGA and I-MCSGA to approximate the Region of Interest (ROI) in MOSPOP. The first algorithm adds the preferences at the beginning of the process, while the second algorithm adds them during the process (while interacting with the DM). Balderas addresses the MOSPOP with uncertainty using intervals; it proposes the generational algorithm I-NOSGA based on NSGAII but incorporates interval numbers. I-NOSGA includes preferences "a priori" and uses Crowding Distance as its density estimator. Martínez [15] addresses the Dynamic Multi-objective Portfolio Optimization Problem (DMOPOP) with real parameters; the proposed approach introduces dynamism by changing the problem definition at the end of each period. Martínez presents three new multi-objective algorithms that also incorporate "a priori" preferences: the generational D-NSGA-II-FF, a new version of a classic genetic algorithm of no-dominance; the D-AbYSS-FF, a modified version of scatter search; and the D-MOEA\D-FF, a new variant of a state-of-the-art algorithm based on decomposition.

Table 1 summarizes the main features of the previously described works. Column 1 cites the research work and the studied POP variant. Columns 2 to 7 show the considered features in the research works: the solution algorithms it proposed, the type of instances it solved, the performance metrics it used, if it integrated preferences in the search process, if it considered a static or dynamic POP's version, the type of parameters it used, and if it used a steady-state selection scheme or not.

Table 1. Related works.

Work	Algorithm	Instances	Metrics	Preferences	E/D	Parameters	Steady State
[11] Social projects	HHGA-SPPv1 HHGA-SPPv2	(3,4,20) (3,9,100)	No-dominated Solutions	Yes	E	Real	NA
[12] Interdependent social projects, several objectives	NO-ACO	(10,4,25) (10,9,100)	No-dominated Solutions, ROI solutions	Yes	E	Real	NA
[13] Social projects with priorities and sinergy	ACO-SPRI ACO-SOP ACO-SOP sinergy	(1,ND,25) (1,ND,40) (1,ND,100)	No-dominated Solutions	Yes	E	Real	NA
[14] Social projects, several objectives	H-MCSGA I-MCSGA	(3,9,100) (2,9,150) (1,16,500)	No-dominated solutions, higher net flow	Yes	E	Real	No
[10] Portfolio selection with interval parameters	I-NSGA-II-CD	(1,2,100) (1,9,100)	Cardinality	Yes	E	Intervals	No
[15] Dynamic portfolio selection and several objectives	D-NSGA-II-FF AbYSS-FF D-MOEA\D–FF	(30,2,100) (30,3,100) (30,9,100)	Hypervolume modified, Spread modified, inverted generational distance modified	Yes	D	Real	No
This work Portfolio selection with trapezoidal fuzzy numbers	T-NSGA-II-CD T-NSGA-II-SSD T-FAME	(12,2,25) (9,2,100)	Hypervolume, Generalized Spread	No	E	Trapezoidal fuzzy numbers	Yes

It is worth nothing that, from the information in Table 1, only approaches based on intervals address POP's variant with uncertainty, and none of them utilized a steady-state selection scheme. The Fuzzy Adaptive Multi-objective Evolutionary solution methodology (FAME) has had great success in many optimization problems; however, there is a lack of studies about its performance on the POP. The previous situations open an area of opportunity, addressed in this work, consisting of studying optimization approaches' performance derived from fuzzy numbers and steady-state selection schemes on their search process to solve the Multi-objective POP with uncertainty (MOPOP).

Evolutionary algorithms commonly use a generational selection scheme to update each generation's population; the process creates several offspring through genetic operators and combines them with the parents to form the next generation of individuals [10,14,15]. On the other hand, an algorithm using a steaty-state selection scheme produces a single offspring during the reproduction process to combine with the parents. The efficiency of the population's update process achieved by the latter method is advantageous for any research [16]. Hence, this work proposes a new method based on FAME and fuzzy numbers to handling uncertainty and obtaining more robust solutions in MOPOP; the approach mainly uses fuzzy trapezoidal sets to reflect a magnitude's imprecision.

This work's main contributions are: (1) a new mathematical model for MOPOP that considers fuzzy trapezoidal parameters; (2) a new algorithm based on FAME to solve the proposed model; (3) two novel steady-state NSGA-II to solve this MOPOP's variant; and

(4) a novel strategy to measure the performance of the fuzzy multi-objective algorithms with the commonly used real metrics.

The remaining structure of this paper is as follows. Section 2 includes some elements of the fuzzy theory used in this work. Section 3 describes a new mathematical model of the Portfolio Optimization Problem with Trapezoidal Fuzzy Parameters. Sections 4 and 5 contain the proposed steady-state algorithms: T-NSGA-II and T-FAME, respectively. Section 6 describes the computational experiments done to assess the performance of the algorithms. Finally, Section 7 presents the conclusions.

2. Elements of Fuzzy Theory

This section contains the main concepts of fuzzy theory used in this work.

2.1. Fuzzy Sets

Let X be a collection of objects x, then a fuzzy set A defined over X is a set of ordered pairs $A = \{(x, \mu_A(x))/x \in X\}$ where $\mu_A(x)$ is called the membership function or grade of membership of x in A which maps X to the real membership subspace M [17]. The range of the membership function is a subset of the nonnegative real numbers whose supremum is finite. Elements with a zero degree of membership usually are not listed.

2.2. Generalized Fuzzy Numbers

A generalized fuzzy number A is any fuzzy subset of the real line R, whose membership function $\mu_A(x)$ satisfies the following conditions [18]:

1. $\mu_A(x)$ is a continuous function from R to the closed interval [0, 1]
2. $\mu_A(x) = 0, -\infty < x < a$
3. $\mu_A(x) = L(x)$, is strictly increasing on [a, b]
4. $\mu_A(x) = w$, for $b < x < \alpha$
5. $\mu_A(x) = R(x)$ is strictly decreasing on $[\alpha, \beta]$
6. $\mu_A(x) = 0$, for $\beta < x < \infty$

where $0 < w < 1$, a, b, α, β are real numbers.

We denote this type of generalized fuzzy number as $A = (a, b, \alpha, \beta, w)_{LR}$. When $w = 1$, the generalized fuzzy number is denoted as $A = (a, b, \alpha, \beta)_{LR}$. When $L(x)$ and $R(x)$ are straight lines, then A is a trapezoidal fuzzy number, and denoted as $A = (a, b, \alpha, \beta)$. When $b = \alpha$, then A is a triangular fuzzy number, and denoted as $A = (a, b, \beta)$.

A triangular membership function definition is as:

$$\mu_A(x) = \begin{cases} 0 & x < a \\ \dfrac{x-a}{b-a} & x \in (a, b) \\ \dfrac{\beta - x}{\beta - b} & x \in (b, \beta) \\ 0 & x > \beta \end{cases} \qquad (2)$$

A trapezoidal membership function definition is as:

$$\mu_A(x) = \begin{cases} 0 & x < a \\ \dfrac{x-a}{b-a} & x \in (a, b) \\ 1 & x \in (b, \alpha) \\ \dfrac{\beta - x}{\beta - \alpha} & x \in (\alpha, \beta) \\ 0 & x > \beta \end{cases} \qquad (3)$$

2.3. Trapezoidal Addition Operator

Given two trapezoidal numbers $A_1 = (a_1, b_1, \alpha_1, \beta_1)$ and $A_2 = (a_2, b_2, \alpha_2, \beta_2)$, then [19]:

$$A_1 + A_2 = (a_1 + a_2, b_1 + b_2, \alpha_1 + \alpha_2, \beta_1 + \beta_2) \tag{4}$$

2.4. Graded Mean Integration (GMI)

Graded mean integration [19] is a defuzzification method to compare two generalized fuzzy numbers. We compare the numbers based on their defuzzified values. The number with a higher defuzzified value is larger. The formula to calculate the graded mean integration of a trapezoidal number A is given by:

$$P(A) = \left(\int_0^w h \left(\frac{L^{-1}(h) + R^{-1}(h)}{2} \right) dh \right) / \int_0^w h \, dh \tag{5}$$

For a trapezoidal fuzzy number $A = (a, b, \alpha, \beta)$, there is a more straightforward expression which is $P(A) = (3a + 3b + \beta - \alpha)/6$.

2.5. Order Relation in the Set of the Trapezoidal Fuzzy Numbers

Given the trapezoidal fuzzy numbers A_1 and A_2, then:

- $A_1 < A_2$ if only if $P(A_1) < P(A_2)$
- $A_1 > A_2$ if only if $P(A_1) > P(A_2)$
- $A_1 = A_2$ if only if $P(A_1) = P(A_2)$

2.6. Pareto Dominance

Given the following fuzzy vectors: $\hat{x} = (x_1, x_2, \ldots, x_n)$ and $\hat{y} = (y_1, y_2, \ldots, y_n)$ where x_i and y_i are trapezoidal fuzzy numbers, then we say that $\hat{x}$ dominates $\hat{y}$, if only if $x_i \geq y_i$ for all $i = 1, 2, \ldots, n$ and $x_i > y_i$ for some $i = 1, 2, \ldots, n$ [20].

3. Multi-Objective Portfolio Optimization Problem with Trapezoidal Fuzzy Parameters

This section presents the proposed mathematical model for MOPOP with Fuzzy Trapezoidal Parameters. It offers a detailed description of the construction of the fuzzy trapezoidal instances used in this work to assess the proposed solution algorithms' performance. It also includes a description of how the fuzzy trapezoidal parameter' values participate in evaluating objective functions and the candidate solutions' feasibility when the solution algorithms search across the solution space.

3.1. Mathematical Model

Let n be the number of projects to consider, C the total available budget, O the number of objectives, c_i the cost of the project i, b_{ij} the produced benefit with the execution of the project i in objective j, K the number of areas to consider, M the number of regions, A_k^{min} and A_k^{max} the lower and upper limits in the available budget for the area k, and R_m^{min} and R_m^{max} the lower and upper limits in the available budget for the region m. The arrays a_i and b_i contain the area and region assigned to the project i. $\hat{x} = (x_1, x_2, \ldots, x_n)$ is a binary vector that specifies the selected projects included in the portfolio. If $x_i = 1$ then the project i is selected, otherwise it is not. Now we define the MOPOP with Fuzzy Trapezoidal parameters as follows:

$$\text{Maximize } \hat{z} = (z_1, z_2, \ldots, z_O) \tag{6}$$

where

$$z_j = \sum_{i=1}^{n} b_{ij} x_i \quad j = 1, 2, \ldots O \tag{7}$$

Subject to the following constraints:

$$\sum_{i=1}^{n} c_i x_i \leq C \tag{8}$$

$$A_k^{min} \leq \sum_{i=1, a_i=k}^{n} c_i x_i \leq A_k^{max} \quad k = 1, 2, \ldots, K \quad (9)$$

$$R_k^{min} \leq \sum_{i=1, b_i=k}^{n} c_i x_i \leq R_k^{max} \quad k = 1, 2, \ldots, M \quad (10)$$

$$x_i \in \{0, 1\} \text{ for all. } i = 1, 2, \ldots, n \quad (11)$$

In this model, all the parameters and variables in **bold** and *italic* are trapezoidal fuzzy numbers.

The objective function tries to maximize the contributions of each objective (6). We calculate each objective by adding all the selected projects' contributions in the binary vector (7). The constraint (8) makes sure that the sum of the costs required for all the selected projects does not exceed the available budget. The set of constraints (9) makes sure that the sum of the projects' costs is in the range of the involved areas' available budget. The set of constraints (10) makes sure that the sum of the projects' costs is in the range of the available budgets for the corresponding regions. The final set of constraints (11) makes sure that the binary variables x_i can only have values of 0 or 1.

We should note that the problem definition is over the space defined by the binary vectors whose size is 2^n. Then the solution algorithms must search across this space to find the Pareto optimal solutions. On the other hand, given that the well-known NP-hard Knapsack problem can be easily reduced to MOPOP, the latter is also NP-hard [21].

3.2. Strategy to Generate the Fuzzy Trapezoidal Instances

This work uses instances initially designed for the POP with interval parameters, where the fuzzy representation of the parameters of the problem uses fuzzy interval type numbers (for example, the interval [76,800, 83,200]) [10]. Fixing the values of α, β to 0.5, and adding them to any interval in the original POP's instances allowed the creation of MOPOP's instances with Trapezoidal Fuzzy Parameters. Following this way, an interval value such as [76800, 83200] would be seen as [76800, 83200, 0.5, 0.5] in the new set of instances.

To create a random fuzzy interval type instance the following real parameters are considered: budget (B), number of objectives (m), projects (p), areas (a) and regions (r), and ranges of costs (c_1, c_2), and objectives (m_1, m_2). Then to generate a fuzzy interval instance the following interval type values must be determined:

$[B, B'] \leftarrow$ Budget as interval
$[a_i, a'_i] \leftarrow$ Limits of each area $I = 1, 2, \ldots, a$
$[r_i, r'_i] \leftarrow$ Limits of each region $r = 1, 2, \ldots, r$
$[b_{ij}, b'_{ij}] \leftarrow$ Benefit from the objective $I = 1, 2, \ldots, m$ and for each project $j = 1, 2, \ldots, p$
$\{C_i, A_i, R_i\} \leftarrow$ Real values of the cost, area and region for each project $i = 1, 2, \ldots, p$.

Implementing MOPOP's instances generator combines the previous parameters along with Equations (12)–(24) to create random instances [10].

$$B = 0.58B \quad B' = 1.3B \quad (12)$$

$$a_l = (0.7 * B)/(1.7^a + 0.1a^2), \; a'_l = (1.27 * B)/(1.7^a + 0.1a^2)] \quad (13)$$

$$a_u = ((1.02 + 0.06r) * B)/r, \; a'_u = ((2.635 + 0.155a) * B)/a \quad (14)$$

$$a_i = a_l + \text{Random}(a'_l - a_l) \text{ for } i = 1, 2, \ldots, a \quad (15)$$

$$a'_i = a_u + \text{Random}(a'_u - a_l) \text{ for } i = 1, 2, \ldots, a \quad (16)$$

$$r_l = (0.7 * B)/(1.7a + 0.1a^2), \; r'_l = (1.27 * B)/(1.7a + 0.1a^2)] \quad (17)$$

$$r_u = ((1.02 + 0.06r) * B)/r, \; r'_u = ((2.635 + 0.155a) * B)/a \quad (18)$$

$$r_i = r_l + \text{Random}(r'_l - r_l) \text{ for } i = 1, 2, \ldots, r \quad (19)$$

$$r'_I = r_u + \text{Random}(r'_u - r_l) \text{ for } i = 1, 2, \ldots, r \quad (20)$$

$$A_i = \text{Random}(a) \; i = 1, 2, \ldots, p \qquad (21)$$

$$R_i = \text{Random}(r) \; i = 1, 2, \ldots, p \qquad (22)$$

$$o = m_1 + \text{Random}(m_2 - m_1), \; b_{ij} = 0.8*o, \qquad (23)$$

$$b'_{ij} = 1.1*o \text{ for } i = 1, 2, \ldots, p \text{ and } i = 1, 2, \ldots, m \qquad (24)$$

The interval instances, built with the instances generator, have names under the following format ompn_idI, where m is the number of objectives the instance has, n is the number of projects, id is a consecutive number, and I indicate that the instance is of interval type. An example of this would be the instance o2p100_1I, meaning that it is the instance number 1 with 2 and 100 projects.

The Algorithm 1 details the structure of a fuzzy interval type instance.

Algorithm 1. o2p25_0I fuzzy interval type instance

// Fuzzy interval type value of the total available budget
[76800, 83200]
// Number of objectives
2
// Number of areas
3
// Fuzzy interval type values of the upper and lower bounds of the available budget
// in each area, a row for each area.
[13060, 16560] [46245, 49745]
[13810, 15810] [47895, 48095]
[13210, 16410] [46545, 49445]
// Number of regions.
2
// Fuzzy interval type values of the upper and lower bounds of the available budget // in each region, a row for each region.
[22775, 24275] [67950, 68050]
[23325, 23725] [67900, 68100]
// Number of projects
25
// For each project, there is a row that includes the following: fuzzy interval type
// value of the project cost, project area, project region, and the fuzzy interval type
// value of the benefits obtained with each objective. (only 5 of the 25 projects are
// showed)
[9308, 10082] [1] [1] [7642, 8278] [231, 249]
[8290, 8980] [2] [1] [8506, 9214] [404, 436]
[5895, 6385] [3] [1] [3831, 4149] [111, 119]
[9053, 9807] [1] [2] [3908, 4232] [399, 431]
[6058, 6562] [1] [2] [5760, 6240] [418, 452]

In order to transform a given fuzzy interval type instance into a fuzzy trapezoidal instance, all the interval values [a, b] are changed to fuzzy trapezoidal values [a, b, a, b] with a = 0.5 and b = 0.5. The Algorithm 2 shows the result of converting the fuzzy interval type instance o2p25_0I to the fuzzy trapezoidal instance o2p25_0T.

Algorithm 2. o2p25_0T fuzzy trapezoidal instance

// Fuzzy trapezoidal value of the total available budget
[76800, 83200, 0.5, 0.5]
// Number of objectives
2
// Number of areas
3
// Fuzzy trapezoidal values of the upper and lower bounds for the available budget
// in each area, a row for each area.
[13060, 16560, 0.5, 0.5] [46245, 49745, 0.5, 0.5]
[13810, 15810, 0.5, 0.5] [47895, 48095, 0.5, 0.5]
[13210, 16410, 0.5, 0.5] [46545, 49445, 0.5, 0.5]
// Number of regions.
2
// Fuzzy trapezoidal values of the upper and lower bounds for the available budget
// in each region, a row for each region.
[22775, 24275, 0.5, 0.5] [67950, 68050, 0.5, 0.5]
[23325, 23725, 0.5, 0.5] [67900, 68100, 0.5, 0.5]
// Number of projects
25
// For each project, there is a row that includes the following: fuzzy trapezoidal value // of the project cost, project area, project region, and the fuzzy trapezoidal values of
// the benefits obtained with each objective. (only 5 of the 25 projects are showed)
[9308, 10082, 0.5, 0.5] [1] [1] [7642, 8278, 0.5, 0.5] [231, 249, 0.5, 0.5]
[8290, 8980, 0.5, 0.5] [2] [1] [8506, 9214, 0.5, 0.5] [404, 436, 0.5, 0.5]
[5895, 6385, 0.5, 0.5] [3] [1] [3831, 4149, 0.5, 0.5] [111, 119, 0.5, 0.5]
[9053, 9807, 0.5, 0.5] [1] [2] [3908, 4232, 0.5, 0.5] [399, 431, 0.5, 0.5]
[6058, 6562, 0.5, 0.5] [1] [2] [5760, 6240, 0.5, 0.5] [418, 452, 0.5, 0.5]

3.3. Evaluating the Solutions and Verifying the Feasibility

This section describes how to calculate the objective values of a solution and how to determine its feasibility. To explain this process, let F the trapezoidal fuzzy numbers set, and R the set of real numbers. Now it is described how to apply the map $\delta : F \to R$ such that $\delta(A) = P(A)$. The map associates the GMI value to each trapezoidal fuzzy number. A remarkable property of this map is that if $X \subset F^n$, then $\delta(X) \subset R^n$, hence, the computation of a vector solution for a MOPOP's instance with two objectives is transformed into a vector of *two* trapezoidal fuzzy numbers, which in turn is transformed into a vector of *two* real numbers. As this process is consistently applied to all the solutions, the algorithms will be performed considering that the binary vector objectives space is the real vector space. The transformation must also be applied to all the trapezoidal fuzzy numbers in the constraints to validate the solutions' feasibility in the search space process. Equations (25)–(30) shows how evaluate the solution and verify the feasibility.

$$\text{Maximize } \hat{z} = (z_1, z_2, \ldots, z_O) \quad (25)$$

where

$$z_j = P\left(\sum_{i=1}^{n} b_{ij} x_i \right) j = 1, 2, \ldots O \quad (26)$$

Subject to the following constraints:

$$P\left(\sum_{i=1}^{n} c_i x_i\right) \leq P(C) \quad (27)$$

$$P(A_k^{min}) \leq P\left(\sum_{i=1, a_i=k}^{n} c_i x_i\right) \leq P(A_k^{max}) \; k = 1, 2, \ldots, K \quad (28)$$

$$P(R_k^{min}) \leq P\left(\sum_{i=1, b_i=k}^{n} c_i x_i\right) \leq P(R_k^{max}) \; k = 1, 2, \ldots, M \quad (29)$$

$$x_i \in \{0, 1\} \text{ for all. } i = 1, 2, \ldots, n \quad (30)$$

An additional benefit is that this mapping transforms the approximated Pareto front in a set of real vectors. In such a case, standard commonly used metrics can be applied to evaluate the performance of the algorithms.

Example: Consider the following simplified instance:

$$n = 3, \ C = [3, 20, 1, 5], \ o = 2$$

$$\begin{array}{c} c_i \\ \begin{bmatrix} [2, 8, 0.5, 0.8] \\ [10, 13, 0.2, 0.5] \\ [4, 12, 0.5, 0.5] \end{bmatrix} \end{array} \bigg| \begin{array}{c} b_{ij} \\ \begin{bmatrix} [3, 6, 1, 1] & [2, 10, 0.2, 0.4] \\ [1, 5, 0.8, 0.8] & [5, 13, 0.7, 0.5] \\ [10, 15, 1, 0.5] & [4, 9, 0.5, 0.8] \end{bmatrix} \end{array}$$

Then using the model, the problem to solve is:

Maximize:

$$z_1 = [3, 6, 1, 1]x_1 + [1, 5, 0.8, 0.8]x_2 + [10, 15, 1, 0.5]x_3 \tag{31}$$

$$z_2 = [2, 10, 0.2, 0.4]x_1 + [5, 13, 0.7, 0.5]x_2 + [4, 9, 0.5, 0.8]x_3 \tag{32}$$

Subject to:

$$[2, 8, 0.5, 0.8]x_1 + [10, 13, 0.2, 0.5]x_2 + [4, 12, 0.5, 0.5]x_3 \leq [3, 20, 1, 5] \tag{33}$$

The objectives z_1 and z_2 are the benefits generated by the projects selected in the binary vector x. The constraint verifies that the cost of that project is not higher than the available budget (C).

Given the solution $x = [0, 1, 0]$, then the fuzzy trapezoidal values of the two objectives are the following:

$$z_1 = [1, 5, 0.8, 0.8] \tag{34}$$

$$z_2 = [5, 13, 0.7, 0.5] \tag{35}$$

Evaluating the constraint to verify the feasibility of the solution x, we have:

$$[10, 13, 0.2, 0.5] \leq [3, 20, 1, 5] \tag{36}$$

Now the GMI is used to compare the fuzzy trapezoidal numbers. For a trapezoidal fuzzy number $A = (a, b, \alpha, \beta)$, the GMI is:

$$P(A) = (3a + 3b + \beta - \alpha)/6 \tag{37}$$

As $P([10, 13, 0.2, 0.5]) = 11.55 \leq P([3, 20, 1, 5]) = 12.166$, solution x is feasible.

Notice that this process was done in the fuzzy trapezoidal numbers space; only at the end the GMI is used to verify the constraint. To perform the process in the real space, the two fuzzy objectives and the fuzzy costs in the constraint are transformed into real numbers using the GMI. The evaluation of the solution is as follows:

$$z_1 = P([3, 6, 1, 1]x_1 + [1, 5, 0.8, 0.8]x_2 + [10, 15, 1, 0.5]x_3) = P([1, 5, 0.8, 0.8]) \tag{38}$$

$$z_2 = P([5, 13, 0.7, 0.5]) \tag{39}$$

Then $z_1 = 3$ and $z_2 = 8.966$.

Transforming the constraint we have:

$$P([2, 8, 0.5, 0.8]x_1 + [10, 13, 0.2, 0.5]x_2 + [4, 12, 0.5, 0.5]x_3) \leq P([3, 20, 1, 5]) \tag{40}$$

$$P([10, 13, 0.2, 0.5]) \leq P([3, 20, 1, 5]) \tag{41}$$

Hence, the solution x is feasible given that $11.55 \leq 12.166$.

The algorithms proposed in this work use the evaluation and feasibility verification procedures described in this section. The algorithms must call such methods on every new solution generated by them.

4. Steady-State T-NSGA-II Algorithm

This section presents the design of all the components included in the definition of the proposed algorithm. This is an adaptation of the classic Deb algorithm NSGA-II [22] modified to work with the trapezoidal fuzzy numbers. As all the algorithms proposed in this work, T-NSGA-II updates the population, applying in each generation the steady-state approach to include in the population only one of the generated individuals. In generational algorithms, the new set of offsprings are combined with the parents to create individuals' next generation; the input to the algorithm is a MOPOP's instance. The output is an approximate Pareto front for the instance.

4.1. Representation of the Solutions

A MOPOP's solution is represented by binary vector $S = \{0,1\}^n$, where n is the number of projects. This vector is a portfolio, and each value $s_i = 1$ represents the inclusion of project i in the portfolio. The first element in the vector is s_0, and the last is s_{n-1}. Figure 1 shows an example of this representation.

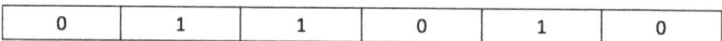

Figure 1. Representation of a solution.

4.2. One-Point Crossover Operator

The one-point crossover operator generates two offsprings from two parents [23]. The process first defines a random cutting point cp in the range $[0, n - 1]$. After this, it split each parent vector into *left* and *right* sections, where for parent i, the $left_i$ contains its values $\{s_0, \ldots, s_{cp}\}$, and the $right_i$ contains its values $\{s_{cp+1}, \ldots, s_{n-1}\}$. Finally, it mixes the split sections to generate two new offsprings h_1, h_2, where h_1 uses $left_1$ and $right_2$, and h_2 uses $left_2$ and $right_1$. The parents are chosen at random. The steady-state approach only utilizes the first offspring h_1. The number of crossovers that are done is a defined parameter. Figure 2 shows an example of this operator.

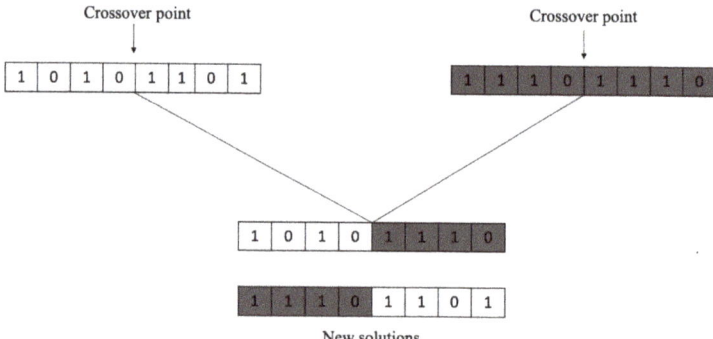

Figure 2. Example of one-point crossover operator at index $cp = 3$.

4.3. Uniform Mutation Operator

The uniform mutation operator generates a new solution for the mutation population from given a solution vector $S = \{s_0, s_1, \ldots, s_{n-1}\}$ [24]. The process generates for each index i, for $0 \leq i \leq n - 1$, a random number u in the range $[0, 1]$, and if $u < mut$ then the value of s_i changes from 1 to 0 or vice versa, otherwise the value s_i remains intact. The parameter *mut* is the mutation probability used by the operator. Figure 3 shows an example of the use of this mutation.

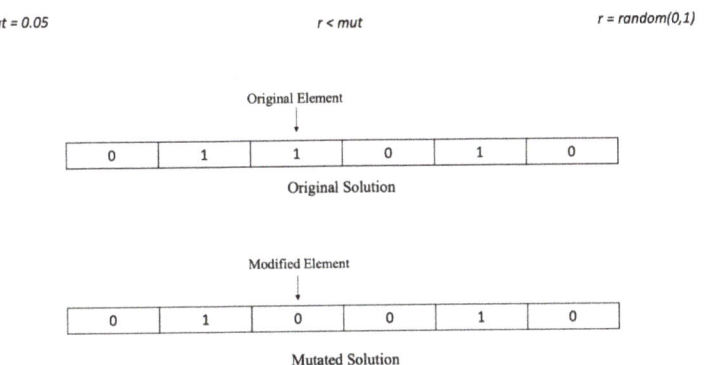

Figure 3. Example of when an element changes its value.

Another parameter of the operator is the number of new mutated solutions that must be generated. Usually, the solutions that undergo this process come from the crossover operator's results; otherwise are randomly chosen.

4.4. Initial Population

A predefined number of randomly generated solutions are created to have an initial population. When a new random solution is generated, the objectives vector for the solution is determined and its feasibility is verified.

4.5. Population Sorting

This process consists of sorting the solutions of the population, and it is composed of two phases: (1) the elitist phase, which keeps the best solutions; and (2) the diversification phase, which ensures that there are solutions different enough to avoid local optima in the search process of the algorithm. The elitist phase is also known as non-dominated sorting. It consists of separating the population in fronts or sets of non-dominated solutions, making sure that the best solutions are always on the first front. The diversification phase sorts the solutions of a front according to the Crowding Distance indicator. The solutions in the best fronts are included in the population, and when a front cannot be completely inserted, the solutions with the worst crowding distances are discarded. Figure 4 shows both phases.

4.6. Non-Dominated Sorting

This process has two parts, and works on a given population. The first part constructs the first front with the set of non-dominated solutions identified from the comparison of vectors of objective values among all the population' solutions. A solution is non-dominated if its vector of objective values is not dominated by any other. Note that the Pareto dominance uses real value vectors in its definition.

The second part builds the remaining fronts one by one. Each new front integrates those solutions that are only dominated by solutions in previously built fronts. The process repeats until no more fronts can be made.

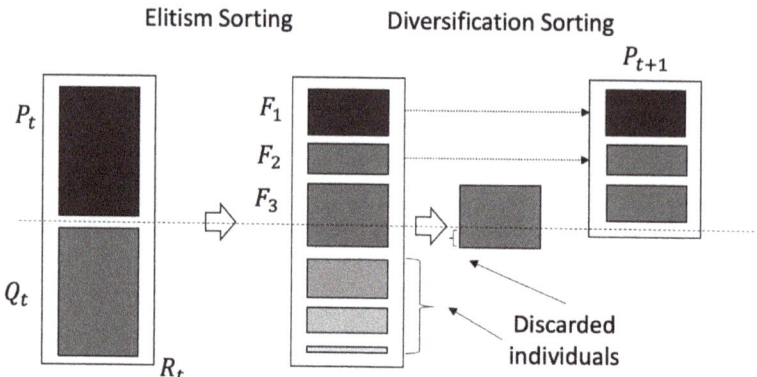

Figure 4. Elitism sorting and diversification phases.

4.7. Calculating the Crowding Distance

According to [22], this process orders the solutions in a front by their Crowding Distance (CD). The distance is a measure of the separation of the solutions, and it is relative to the normalized value of the objectives. The CD identify the solutions with extreme values on the objectives and put it first on the front. After that, the solutions order are according to their accumulated degree of separation per objective, the greatest the separation the better. For each objective, the CD computes the degree of separation using the ordered array of objective values resulting from the front; the solutions with the highest and smallest objective values will have a specific Crowding Distance value d equal to infinite (∞), while the remaining solutions will be calculated by the following formula:

$$d_{I_jm} = d_{I_jm} + \frac{f^{I^m}_{mj+1} - f^{I^m}_{mj-1}}{f^{max}_m - f^{min}_m} \qquad (42)$$

where d is the Crowding Distance, I is the solution position in the whole population in general, j is the solution position after the ordering by objective m within the front, f is the objective value and m is the current objective. The accumulation of Crowding Distance value d of all the objectives results in the final value of CD for each solution I.

4.8. Calculating the Spatial Spread Deviation (SSD)

The Spatial Spread Deviation (SSD) is a density estimator used to rearrange the solutions in a front, so the spread is not by a wide margin [25]. The method calculates for each solution the SSD value using a matrix of normalized distances between the solutions in the approximated front. The solutions are sorted from the lowest to highest SSD value in order to punish solutions according to their standard deviation and their proximity to their closest k-neighbors. The next three equations show how to calculate the SSD values, in the process i is the solution in the front for which the SSD is calculated, and j take values over all the solutions in the front except i.

$$temp1(i) = \frac{1}{n-1}\sqrt{\sum_{j=1}^{n}(D(i,j) - (D_{max} - D_{min}))^2} \forall\, i \neq j \qquad (43)$$

$$temp2(i) = \sum_{j \varepsilon K} \frac{(D_{max} - D_{min})}{D(i,j)} \qquad (44)$$

$$SSD(i) = SSD_0(i) + temp1(i) + temp2(i) \qquad (45)$$

where $D(i,j)$ is the distance from solution i to solution j. D_{max} is the biggest distance between all the solutions and D_{min} is the closest distance between all the solutions. K is the number of k neighbors closest to solution i. SSD_0 is the initial value of SSD, which is $-INF$ if the solution is at one of the ends of the front when the normalized values of the graded mean integration of the objective values are calculated.

4.9. Pseudocode of the T-NSGA-II Algorithm

The T-NSGA-II is based in the structure of the classic multi-objective algorithm NSGA-II proposed by Deb [22]. As previously described, the algorithm had several modifications to work with trapezoidal fuzzy numbers and the proposed MOPOP model. Algorithm 3 shows the detailed pseudocode of the algorithm T-NSGA-II.

Algorithm 3. T-NSGA-II pseudocode

INPUT: Instance with the trapezoidal parameters of the portfolio problem.
OUTPUT: Approximated Pareto Front
NOTE: The algorithm is called T-NSGA-II-CD when the Crowding Distance is used, and T-NSGA-II-SSD when is used the Spatial Spread Deviation.
****

1. Create the initial population *pop*
2. Evaluate all the solutions in *pop*
3. Order *pop* using no-dominated Sorting
4. For all solutions in *pop* calculate Spatial Spread Deviation/Crowding distance
5. *pop* sorting due to fronts and Spatial Spread Deviation/CD
6. **Main loop, until stopping condition is met**
*** Steady state approach: only one generated individual is considered to include in *popc*
7.   Create *popc* using crossover operator
****
8.   Create *popm* using mutation operator
9.   Join *popc* and *popm* to create *popj*
10.   Evaluate solutions in *popj* and put feasibles in *popf*
11.   Add *popf* to *pop*, and calculate objective functions
12.   Order *pop* using no-dominated sorting
13.   Calculate Spatial Spread Deviation/Crowding distance
14.   *pop* sorting due to the front ranking and Spatial Spread Deviation/CD
15.   Truncate *pop* to keep a population of original size
16.   No-dominated sorting
17.   Calculate Spatial Spread Deviation/Crowding distance of the individuals in *pop*
18.   *pop* sorting due to front ranking and Spatial Spread Deviation/CD
19. End **Main loop**
20. Return (Front 0).   ***Approximated Pareto Front

---

5. T-FAME Algorithm

This section presents the design of all the components of the T-FAME algorithm. The algorithm adapts the FAME algorithm to work with the trapezoidal fuzzy numbers [25]. The input to the algorithm is an instance of MOPOP. The output is the approximate Pareto front for that instance. T-FAME updates the population, applying the steady-state approach to include in the population only one of the generated individuals. The following algorithm components are the same described in Section 4: the structure used to represent the solutions, the evaluation of a solution, the construction of the initial population, the sorting of the population, the non-dominated sorting process, and the density SSD estimator. The components described in this section are those not included in the previous description or with significant differences, such as the fuzzy controller, the additional genetic operators, and the structure used to store the approximated Pareto front.

5.1. Fuzzy Controller

This section introduces an intelligent mechanism that allows an MOEA to apply different recombination operators at different search process stages. The use of different operators is dynamically adjusted according to their contribution to the search in the past.

Intuitively, the idea is to favor operators generating higher quality solutions over others. For this purpose, the fuzzy controller dynamically tunes the probability selection of the available recombination operators [25].

The fuzzy controller uses a Mamdani-Type Fuzzy Inference System (FIS) [26] to compute the probability of applying the different operators. Fuzzy sets defined by membership functions represent the linguistic values of the model's input and output variables. Regarding the inference, we use the approach originally proposed by Mamdani based on the "max min" composition: using the minimum operator for implication and maximum operator for aggregation. The aggregation of the consequents from the rules are combined into a single fuzzy set (output), to be defuzzified (mapped to a real value). A widely used defuzzification method is the centroid calculation, which returns the area's center under the curve. We use triangular-shaped membership functions in all inputs and outputs,

$$\mu_A(x) = \begin{cases} 0 & x < a \\ \frac{x-a}{b-a} & x \in (a, b) \\ \frac{c-x}{c-b} & x \in (b, c) \\ 0 & x > c \end{cases} \quad (46)$$

the parameters a and c determine the "corners" of the triangle, and b determines the peak. A membership function $\mu_A(x)$ maps real values of x with a degree of membership $0 \leq \mu_A(x) \leq 1$. The used granularity levels were: Low ($a = -0.4$, $b = 0.0$, $c = 0.4$), Mid ($a = 0.1$, $b = 0.5$, $c = 0.9$) and High ($a = 0.6$, $b = 1.0$, $c = 1.4$).

The interaction of the fuzzy controller with the algorithm works as follows: Let *Operators* the set of genetic operators available. The evolutionary algorithm monitors the search process in a series of time windows, each of size *Window*. At the end of each time window, the algorithm sends to the fuzzy controller the real values of the input variables *Stagnation* and *UseOp*, and receives from the controller the real value of the output variable *ProbOp*.

Each of the fuzzy variables has associated the fuzzy linguistic values: High, Mid and Low. Then the membership functions of the fuzzy variable *Stagnation* are: $\mu_{Stagnation=High}(x)$, $\mu_{Stagnation=Mid}(x)$ and $\mu_{Stagnation=Low}(x)$. In a similar way, the membership functions are defined for the variables *UseOp* and *ProbOp*.

To show how works the fuzzification process consider that the received real values of the input variables are *Stagnation* = 0.7 and *UseOp* = 0.8.

The fuzzified values for the Stagnation variable are the membership degrees: $\mu_{Stagnation=High}(0.7)$, $\mu_{Stagnation=Mid}(0.7)$ y $\mu_{Stagnation=Low}(0.7)$.

For the *UseOp* variable the fuzzified values are the membership degrees: $\mu_{UseOp=High}(0.8)$, $\mu_{UseOp=Mid}(0.8)$ y $\mu_{UseOp=Low}(0.8)$. All the membership degrees are values in the interval (0,1).

Now the FIS includes a set of fuzzy rules which are specified in terms of the fuzzy variables, the linguistic values, and a set of logic operators. To continue with the previous example, consider that the fuzzy rules in the FIS are:

$$R_1: If\ Stagnation = High\ and\ UseOp = High\ then\ ProbOp = High \quad (47)$$

$$R_2: If\ Stagnation = High\ and\ UseOp = Low\ then\ ProbOp = Mid \quad (48)$$

Once the fuzzification of the inputs is done, the next process is to evaluate the antecedents of the rules R_1 and R_2, determining the following values:

$$k_1 = min\left(\mu_{Stagnation=High}(0.7), \mu_{UseOp=High}(0.8)\right) \quad (49)$$

$$k_2 = min\left(\mu_{Stagnation=High}(0.7), \mu_{UseOp=Low}(0.8)\right) \quad (50)$$

In the rule evaluation, the min operator is associated with the logic operator *and*, and the max operator is associated to the logic operator *or*.

Now the membership functions of the consequents of the rules must be determined. For each rule an operator of implication is applied to the antecedent value obtained in the previous process and to the consequent of the rule, to determine the membership function of the conclusion of the rule. The *min* operator is used to implement the implication logic operator, which truncates the membership function of the rule's consequent. For example, the truncated membership functions of the consequents are the following:

$$\mu^*_{ProbOp=High}(z) = \min\left(\mu_{ProbOp=High}(z), k_1\right) z \in (0,1) \quad (51)$$

$$\mu^*_{ProbOp=Mid}(z) = \min\left(\mu_{ProbOp=Mid}(z), k_2\right) z \in (0,1) \quad (52)$$

Now the truncated membership functions are integrated using an aggregation operator to create a new membership function, which is the controller's fuzzy output. The aggregation operators that are frequently used are *max* and *sum*.

For the example, the *max* operator is used to determine the aggregated membership function, which is the following:

$$\mu^{**}(z) = \max(\mu^*_{Z=A}(z), \mu^*_{Z=M}(z)) \; z \in (0,1) \quad (53)$$

Finally, the defuzzification of the fuzzy output obtained is done. In this step a real number is associated to the aggregated membership function, which is the output of the inference process. In the previous example, the center of the area under the curve of the aggregated membership function is used to defuzzify the output of the controller as following:

$$z = \frac{\int \mu^{**}(z) z \, dz}{\int \mu^{**}(z) \, dz} \quad (54)$$

Figure 5 graphically shows the fuzzy inference process for the example described.

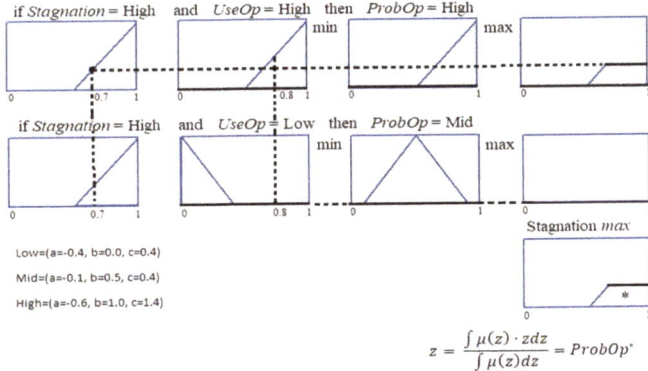

Figure 5. Mamdani Fuzzy Inference System used in the fuzzy controller.

All of the controller rules are of the type: Antecedent AND Antecedent then Consequent. The fuzzy rules were designed to have soft changes in the input variables (*Stagnation* and *UseOp*), to avoid abrupt changes in the output variable (*ProbOp*). The configuration was manually done by observing the surface that these three variables generated [25]. Table 2 shows the rules of the fuzzy controller.

Table 2. Fuzzy controller rules.

AND Antecedents		Consequent
Stagnation	Utilization	ProbOp
High	High	Mid
High	Mid	Low
High	Low	Mid
Mid	High	Mid
Mid	Mid	Low
Mid	Low	Mid
Low	High	High
Low	Mid	Mid
Low	Low	Low

The Algorithm 4 shows the structure of the fuzzy controller used in the fuzzy controller implementation with the Java Library Fuzzy Lite 6.0.

Algorithm 4. Fuzzy controller structure.

[System]
Name='FuzzyController '
Type='mamdani'
Version=2.0
NumInputs=2
NumOutputs=1
NumRules=9
AndMethod='min'
OrMethod='max'
ImpMethod='min'
AggMethod='max'
DefuzzMethod='centroid'
[Input1]
Name='Stagnation'
Range=[0 1]
NumMFs=3
MF1='Low':'trimf',[−0.4 0 0.4]
MF2='Mid':'trimf',[0.1 0.5 0.9]
MF3='High':'trimf',[0.6 1 1.4]
[Input2]
Name='UseOp'
Range=[0 1]
NumMFs=3
MF1='Low':'trimf',[−0.4 0 0.4]
MF2='Mid':'trimf',[0.1 0.5 0.9]
MF3='High':'trimf',[0.6 1 1.4]
[Output1]
Name='ProbOp'
Range=[0 1]
NumMFs=3
MF1='Low':'trimf',[−0.4 0 0.4]
MF2='Mid':'trimf',[0.1 0.5 0.9]
MF3='High':'trimf',[0.6 1 1.4]
[Rules]
3 3, 2 (1) : 1
3 2, 1 (1) : 1
3 1, 2 (1) : 1
2 3, 2 (1) : 1

2 2, 1 (1) : 1
2 1, 2 (1) : 1
1 3, 3 (1) : 1
1 2, 2 (1) : 1
1 1, 1 (1) : 1

In the [Rules] section, the first and second columns contain the linguistic values of the two input variables (1-Low, 2-Mid, 3-High), the third column is the weight of the rules, and the last one indicates the logic operator used in the rule (1-*and*, 2-*or*).

The interaction of the fuzzy controller with the algorithm works as follows: Let *Operators* the set of genetic operators available. The T-FAME algorithm searches in the solutions space in time windows of size *Window*, each time window the algorithm performs *Window* iterations. At the end of each time window, the algorithm sends to the fuzzy controller the values of the input variables *Stagnation* and *UseOp[i]* for all $i \in$ *Operator*. For each pair of input values, a Fuzzy Inference generates *ProbOp[i]* for all $i \in$ *Operator*. This process is done for the T-FAME algorithm with the following pseudocode where v is the windows counter:

If (v == *Window*) then
$$\forall\ i\epsilon\ \{1, 2, \ldots .SizeOP\}$$
38. $ProbOp(i) = FuzzyController(Stagnation, UseOp(i));$

39. v =0; *Stagnation* = 0;
40. Endif

The line numbers are those that appear in the T-FAME algorithm pseudocode included in Section 6.4. Notice that in lines 37 and 38, the algorithm uses the fuzzy controller to update all the available recombination genetic operators' selection probability.

The *Stagnation* value is shared for all the operators, and it is an indicator of the evolution of the search in the current time window. This is a normalized value that is increased by 1.0/*Window* each time the generated solution cannot enter the set where the non-dominated solutions are kept and reset when the time window is over. *UseOp[i]* is a normalized value that is increased by 1.0/*Window* every time the operator *i* is used.

5.2. Additional Genetic Operators

Four operators are used in T-FAME to create new solutions: One-point crossover, Uniform Mutation, Fixed Mutation, and Differential Evolution. Two of these operators (One-point crossover and Uniform Mutation) are the same ones that are used on T-NSGA-II, and they are already described in the previous section.

Differential Evolution: This method was proposed by Rainer [27], and its implementation was based on [28]. It uses the four parents obtained with the tournament method. The first part of the process consists of creating a new solution called Candidate using Parent 1, Parent 2, and Parent 3, this solution is obtained by doing a binary addition of the parents. Figure 6 shows an example of how this operator works.

Once the Candidate is calculated, a binary crossover operator is done between the candidate and Parent 4 to create a new solution called Son, this binary crossover operator is different from the one-point crossover operator described previously, and it uses a parameter called crossover percentage (CP). The binary crossover operator consists of the following: For each array index, a random number between 0 and 1 is generated, if that number has a lesser value than CP, then that index receives the value of the Candidate, if this is not the case, then that index receives the value of Parent 4.

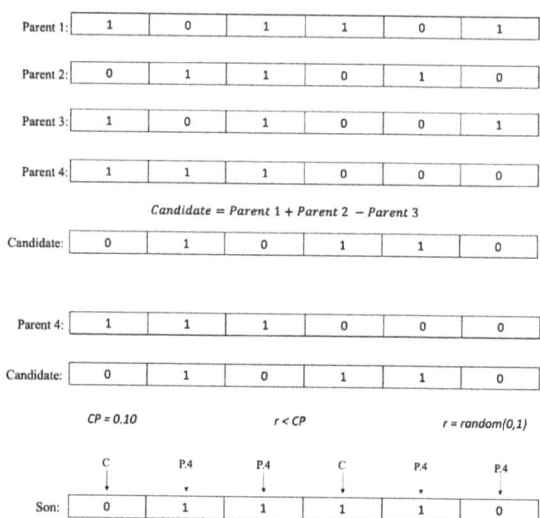

Figure 6. Differential evolution operator example.

Once the new solution Son is completed, a dominance test is done between Son and Parent 4, if the objective values of Parent 4 dominate the objective values of Son, then Parent 4 proceeds to be the new solution, but if this is not the case, then Son proceeds to be the new solution.

Fixed Mutation: This method is very similar to the uniform mutation operator that was described previously. The main difference lies in the fact that the whole process is done in a loop until n mutations are made, where n is a parameter previously defined. This operator also makes sure that no element in the solution is changed twice or more times, this is done by using a fixed array to keep track of the changed elements in the solution. Figure 7 shows an example of the Fixed Mutation operator.

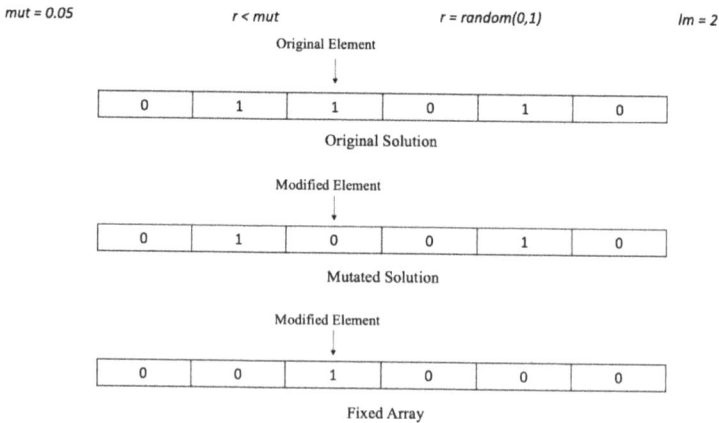

Figure 7. Fixed Mutation operator example.

5.3. Used Structures to Store the Population and the Approximated Pareto Front

The algorithm uses the structure *pop* to maintain a solutions population, which contains the following information for each solution i:

- $V(i)$: vector binary associated to the solution i.

- $O_1(i)$ and $O_2(i)$: values of the two objectives of the solution i, converted to GMI values.
- $r(i)$: ranking of the solution i is the number of the front in which is located.
- Dominated(i): solutions dominated by the solution i.
- Domines(i): solutions that dominates to solution i.
- CD (i): Crowding Distance value of the solution i.
- SSD(i): Spatial Spread Deviation value of solution i.

The structure *Front* is used to store the approximated Pareto front, which contains the following information for each stored solution i:

- $V(i)$: vector binary associated to the solution i.
- $O(i)$: real vector of the graded mean values of the fuzzy triangular objectives of the solution $V(i)$.
- $r(i)$: ranking of the solution i is the number of the front in which is located.
- Dominated(i): solutions dominated by the solution i.
- Domines(i): solutions that dominates to solution i.
- SSD (i): Spatial Spread Deviation value of the solution i.

5.4. T-FAME Algorithm Pseudocode

This section presents the pseudocode for the algorithm T-FAME in Algorithm 5.

Algorithm 5. T-FAME pseudocode

INPUT: Instance with the trapezoidal parameters of the portfolio problem.
OUTPUT: Approximated Pareto front

Variables
pop: Population of solutions (binary vectors)
Front: Limited sized set were no-dominated solutions are kept
Operator: Vector of size *SizeOP* that contains the index of the available operators
Parents: Vector of size *NParents* that contains the chosen parents
ProbOp(i): Probability that operator i has of being chosen, it has values between 0 and 1
UseOp(i): Normalized Indicator of how much operator i has been used, it has values between 0 and 1
Stagnation: Normalized indicator of the number of generated solutions that couldn't be inserted into *Front*, because they were either dominated solutions or there was not space available for them, it can have values between 0 and 1.
MAXEVAL: Maximum number of evaluations of the objective function (stopping criterion)
Window: Size of the time window.
eval: Accumulator of the evaluations of the objective function
v: Counter of the time windows that have elapsed

Functions
CreateaSon(Operator(i), Parents): Generates one solution using the previous chosen operator i with the chosen parents (Steady state)
Evaluate(Son): Calculates the objective values of *Son* and verify feasibility
FuzzyController(Stagnation, UseOp(i)): Function that invokes the fuzzy controller with *Stagnation* and *UseOp(i)* as input values and returns the probability of selection of all the operators
no-dominated_sortingSSD(NewPop): Sorts the fronts of *NewPop* by dominance and uses as ranking the *SSD* values of the solutions.
EliminateWorstSolutionSSD(NewPop): Eliminates from the last front of *NewPop* the solution with the worst *SSD*, and assign *NewPop* to *pop*.
****
1. Create(*pop*) **Create random population
2. *Front*=NoDominated(*pop*) **Insert in Front the no-dominated solutions of *pop*
3. $\forall i \in \{1,2,\ldots,SizeOP\}$ *ProbOp(i)* =1, *UseOp(i)*=0
4. v =0; *Stagnation* = 0; *eval*=0;
5. while (*eval*<*MAXEVAL*) do. **** Stop condition
** Chose |NParents|
** With a probability β each parent is taken from *Front* to intensify) and with 1- β from *pop* to diversify.
6. $\forall i \in \{1,2,..|NParents|\}$ do
7.   if (RandomDouble(0,1) $\leq \beta$) then
**The parent is chosen from *Front*

8. Parents[i] ← TournamentSSD(**Front**)
9. Else
**The parent is chosen from *pop*
10. Parents[i] ← TournamentSSD(***pop***)

*** Roulette to choose an operator with the selection probabilities of the operators
11. sum=0
12. $i = Random(1, 2, \ldots, NParents)$
13. sum=sum+ProbOp(i)
14. while (sum>0) do
15. $i = Random(1, 2, \ldots, NParents)$
16. sum=sum+ProbOp(i)
****
***** The chosen operator is associated with the last value of i
** ***Steady state approach
17. Son ← CreateaSon(Operator(i), Parents)

**** Get the objective vector values corresponding to *Son* and verify feasibility.
18. Evaluate(Son)
19. eval=eval+1
20. UseOp(Operator(i)) = UseOp(Operator(i))+ 1 . 0/ Window
21. v=v+1
****
22. If (*Son* dominates a set S of solutions in *Front*)
23.   then { **Front=Front**\\S; **Front=Front** ∪ *Son*}
24.   else If (∃ s **Front** such that s dominates *Son*)
25.   then (Stagnation= Stagnation+1.0/ Window)
26.   else if (Sizeof(**Front**)<100)
27.   then (**Front=Front** ∪ *Son*)
28.   else {
29.   Front=Front ∪ Son ** Front[1 00]=Son
30.   Calculate SSD for all the solutions in **Front**
31.   Sort the solutions in **Front** in ascending order by SSD
32.   Eliminate the solution in **Front** with worst SSD:**Front**[100]
33.   If (Son **Front**)
34.   then Stagnation= Stagnation+1.0/ Window
35.   }
36. If (v == Window) then
**** The Fuzzy Controller is used to update the selection probability
****of all the operators

37.   ∀ $i∈ \{1, 2, \ldots SizeOP\}$
38. $ProbOp(i) = FuzzyController(Stagnation, UseOp(i))$
39. v =0;   Stagnation = 0;
40.   End if
41. pop=pop ∪ Son
42. NewPop=**pop**
43. no-dominated_sortingSSD(NewPop)
44. **pop** ← EliminateWorstSolutionSSD(NewPop)
45. End while
46. Return(**Front**) *** Approximated Pareto front generated

6. Experimental Results

Two experiments were done in order to evaluate the performance of the proposed algorithms. The tested steady-state algorithms were T-NSGA-II-CD, T-NSGA-II-SSD, and T-FAME. The first experiment was done to make sure the algorithms were implemented correctly, while the second experiment was done to compare the performance between them using performance metrics.

The software and hardware platforms that were used for these experiments include Intel Core i5 1.6GHz processor, RAM 4GB, and IntelliJ IDEA CE IDE.

6.1. Performance Metrics Used

In order to measure the performance of each algorithm, two metrics were used: hypervolume [28] and generalized spread [29].

Hypervolume is the n-dimensional solution space volume that is dominated by the solutions in the reference set. If this space is big, then that means that the set is close to the Pareto Front. It is desirable for the indicator to have large values. Generalized Spread calculates the average of the distances of the points in the reference set to their closest neighbor. If this indicator has small values, then that means the solutions in the reference set are well distributed.

6.2. Experimental Setup

In order to configure the algorithms used in this work, the parameter values reported in the state-of-the-art were considered. The parameter value for the maximum number of evaluations was determined after a preliminary experimental phase. The comparison of all the algorithms, under the same operation conditions, utilizes a steady-state approach, using the dominant son. Tables 3 and 4 show the values of the parameters used in the algorithms. The configuration of algorithm T-NSGA-II-SSD is the same one as T-NSGA-II-CD, however, it uses Spatial Spread Deviation instead of Crowding Distance as its density estimator.

Table 3. T-NSGA-II-SSD parameters.

Parameter	Value
Evaluation of the objective function	5000
Population Size	50
Crossover population %	70
Mutation population %	40
Mutation %	5

Table 4. T-FAME parameters.

Parameter	Value
Evaluation of the objective function	5000
Population Size	25
Front Size	100
Tournament Size	5
Number of parents	4
Window Size	13
Differential Evolution Crossover %	10
Number of mutations in FM	2
Front choice probability (β)	0.9

6.3. Experiment 1. Validating the Implemented Algorithms

For this experiment, an instance named o2p25_rand was used, this instance was originally created for POP with intervals, which was converted in a trapezoidal fuzzy instance by adding two parameters to the intervals. The optimum Pareto Front was obtained using an exhaustive algorithm, and approximate fronts were obtained with T-NSGA-II-CD, T-NSGA-II-SSD, and T-FAME algorithms. All algorithms solve the MOPOP with Fuzzy Parameters and use a steady-state election mechanism, creating one solution from the genetic operators' application. This adaptation from FAME has an advantage over algorithms using the classic generational approach in genetic algorithms.

The purpose of this experiment is to validate the correct operation of the implemented algorithms in the project. In the experiment, the fronts are generated, and they are compared to the optimum front, in order to determine if the algorithms are generating similar fronts. All the fronts that were generated are shown in Table 5. Each front is shown in two columns that contain the values of the two objectives that were originally Trapezoidal Fuzzy numbers, but they were converted into real numbers with the transformation based on GMI. The graph the fronts uses the GMI values obtained from the objectives.

Table 5. Generated fronts of the algorithms with instance o2p25_rand.

Pareto Optimal Front		T-NSGA-II-CD		T-NSGA-II-SSD		T-FAME
O2	O1	O2	O1	O2	O1	O2
3530	78,510	3465	81,155	3425	81,285	3530
3805	62,350	4245	66,240	4400	77,480	3715
3825	76,360	3840	75,650	3860	74,485	3750
3840	70,035	3870	68,610	4240	73,425	3775
3865	77,020	3490			70,350	4005
3965	66,605	4070			66,850	4375
3980	62,755	4090			59,865	4385
4000	77,900	3490				
4025	77,920	3485				
4035						
4060						
4065						
4120						
4150						
4215						
4235						
4240						
4260						
4310						
4375						
4400						
4435						
4460						

It is worth nothing that, in Figure 8, the approximated fronts are relatively close and below the optimum front. Also, observe that the T-NSGA-II-SSD and T-FAME algorithms managed to reach some optimum solutions. Finally, note that the T-FAME algorithm has a good distribution between its solutions.

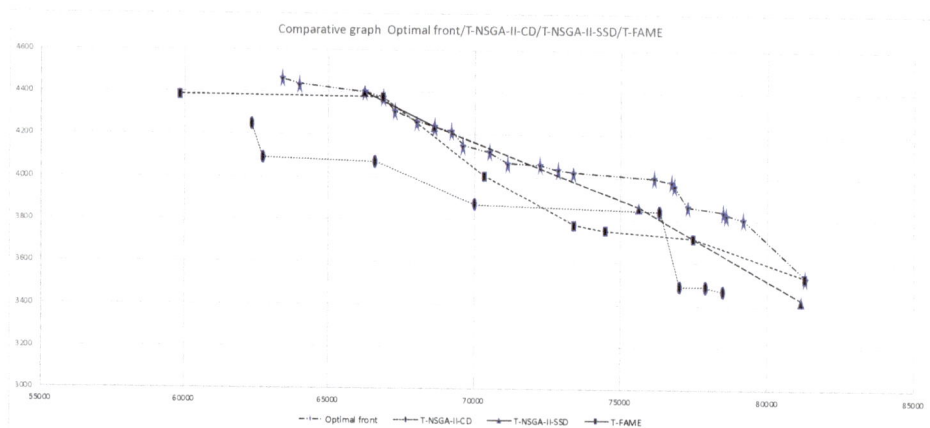

Figure 8. Generated fronts of the algorithms with instance o2p25_rand.

6.4. Experiment 2. Evaluating the Performance of the Algorithms with Instances of 25 Projects

This experiment evaluates the performances of algorithms T-NSGA-II-CD, T-NSGA-II-SSD, and T-FAME, and utilizes 13 instances with 2 objectives and 25 projects. In order to compare the performance between the three algorithms, each algorithm was executed 30 times per instance. The performance metrics used were hypervolume and generalized spread. For each instance, the reference set contains the non-dominated solutions obtained from the combination of the 30 generated fronts. The computation of the metrics uses the reference set as an approximation to the optimum Pareto Front. The computation of the median value and interquartile ranges uses the metric values of the 30 instances sorted in ascending order. With the sorted array, the median value was the average of the metric values from positions 15 and 16. At the same time, the interquartile ranges correspond to those in positions 23 and 8, corresponding to the 75% and 25% of the metrics values, respectively. The median value and the interquartile ranges are used instead of the average and the standard deviation because they are less sensitive to extreme values. The experiment performs a hypothesis test to validate the obtained results. The hypothesis was proven using the parametric t student test on those data sets that passed the normality and homoscedasticity tests and using the non-parametric Wilcoxon signed-rank test on those that do not. Both tests apply a confidence level of 95%, pairing T-FAME with each of the other two algorithms. Tables 6–9 show the results of the normality and homoscedasticity tests done for all the instances used in this work (25 and 100 projects) and the metrics of hypervolume and generalized spread. Tables 6 and 8 show in the last column pairs (i,j), which indicate that the comparison of T-NSGA-II-CD and T-FAME uses test i, and the comparison T-NSGA-II-SSD and T-FAME uses test j. The values t and W in (i, j) stand for t student test and Wilcoxon test. This work tests each instance separately.

Table 6. Hypervolume normality test, the null hypothesis is that the samples follow a normal distribution which is accepted (a) when p-value < 0.05 and rejected (r) otherwise.

Instance	T-NSGA-II-CD Statistic	p-Value	R	T-NSGA-II-SSD Statistic	p-Value	R	T-FAME Statistic	p-Value	R	Tests
o2p25_0T	0.9429	0.1089	a	0.83756	0.00034	r	0.96919	0.51737	a	t,W
o2p25_1T	0.93655	0.07348	a	0.92817	0.04391	r	0.97408	0.65561	a	t,W
o2p25_2T	0.92141	0.02918	r	0.95491	0.22837	a	0.96987	0.53551	a	W,t
o2p25_3T	0.94311	0.11035	a	0.90566	0.01159	r	0.94528	0.12625	a	t,W
o2p25_4T	0.95413	0.21782	a	0.93505	0.06696	a	0.89022	0.00488	r	W,W
o2p25_5T	0.86113	0.00107	r	0.89584	0.00665	r	0.94768	0.14643	a	W,W
o2p25_6T	0.9023	0.00956	r	0.89233	0.00548	r	0.96519	0.41715	a	W,W
o2p25_7T	0.94961	0.16508	a	0.86559	0.00134	r	0.92644	0.03953	r	W,W
o2p25_8T	0.92385	0.0338	r	0.91474	0.01963	r	0.85737	0.00089	r	W,W
o2p25_9T	0.94965	0.16541	a	0.89673	0.00699	r	0.97209	0.59792	a	t,W
o2p25_10T	0.92989	0.04877	r	0.78913	0.00004	r	0.97575	0.70469	a	W,W
o2p25_11T	0.93191	0.05518	a	0.95357	0.21047	a	0.96642	0.44633	a	t,t
o2p25_12T	0.94626	0.13411	a	0.95055	0.17491	a	0.98323	0.9033	a	t,t
o2p100_1T	0.96346	0.37847	a	0.96637	0.44525	a	0.98333	0.90552	a	t,t
o2p100_2T	0.95885	0.28944	a	0.98951	0.98844	a	0.9737	0.64441	a	t,t
o2p100_3T	0.93272	0.05801	a	0.9821	0.87827	a	0.94779	0.14745	a	t,t
o2p100_4T	0.78768	0.00004	r	0.78085	0.00003	r	0.89022	0.00488	r	W,W
o2p100_5T	0.95289	0.20189	a	0.94588	0.13101	a	0.93478	0.06586	a	t,t
o2p100_6T	0.94043	0.09341	a	0.93788	0.07976	a	0.95224	0.194	a	t,t
o2p100_7T	0.97249	0.60937	a	0.99025	0.99229	a	0.94017	0.0919	a	t,t
o2p100_8T	0.96892	0.51019	a	0.98362	0.9115	a	0.96805	0.48728	a	t,t
o2p100_9T	0.57553	0	r	0.52513	0	r	0.71502	0	r	W,W

Table 7. Hypervolume homoscedasticity test, the null hypothesis is that all the input populations come from populations with equal variances, which is accepted (a) when *p*-value < 0.05 and rejected (r) otherwise. We can observe that the null hypothesis is accepted (a) for all the instances. The parametric t student test can be applied for all the instances that accept the null hypothesis in the normality tests.

Instance	Statistic	*p*-Value	R
o2p25_0T	8.46563	0.00044	a
o2p25_1T	17.23159	0	a
o2p25_2T	8.53517	0.00041	a
o2p25_3T	11.87763	0.00003	a
o2p25_4T	7.1698	0.00131	a
o2p25_5T	7.60431	0.0009	a
o2p25_6T	7.19194	0.00129	a
o2p25_7T	2.20562	0.11631	a
o2p25_8T	8.18222	0.00055	a
o2p25_9T	4.45024	0.01445	a
o2p25_10T	3.63843	0.03037	a
o2p25_11T	3.98587	0.02207	a
o2p25_12T	9.90574	0.00013	a
o2p100_1T	0.27401	0.76098	a
o2p100_2T	2.14347	0.1234	a
o2p100_3T	0.29369	0.74624	a
o2p100_4T	1.79147	0.17281	a
o2p100_5T	5.98972	0.00365	a
o2p100_6T	1.09354	0.33959	a
o2p100_7T	2.30064	0.10626	a
o2p100_8T	4.20117	0.01812	a
o2p100_9T	1.39539	0.25322	A

Table 8. Generalized Spread normality test, the null hypothesis is that the samples follow a normal distribution which is accepted (a) when *p*-value < 0.05 and rejected (r) otherwise.

	T-NSGA-II-CD			T-NSGA-II-SSD			T-FAME			
Instance	Statistic	*p*-Value	R	Statistic	*p*-Value	R	Statistic	*p*-Value	R	Tests
o2p25_0T	0.92895	0.04606	r	0.97607	0.71429	a	0.9784	0.78164	a	W,t
o2p25_1T	0.98376	0.91432	a	0.95618	0.24658	a	0.97193	0.59314	a	t,t
o2p25_2T	0.98074	0.84479	a	0.97925	0.8053	a	0.96813	0.48946	a	t,t
o2p25_3T	0.9215	0.02934	r	0.9225	0.03116	r	0.96419	0.39452	a	W,W
o2p25_4T	0.95187	0.18969	a	0.96214	0.35091	a	0.68255	0	r	W,W
o2p25_5T	0.96913	0.51555	a	0.95677	0.25552	a	0.92403	0.03416	r	W,W
o2p25_6T	0.87495	0.00216	r	0.97296	0.62306	a	0.958	0.27513	a	W,t
o2p25_7T	0.94053	0.094	a	0.95631	0.24864	a	0.94784	0.14792	a	t,t
o2p25_8T	0.9648	0.40819	a	0.95561	0.23827	a	0.94282	0.10833	a	t,t
o2p25_9T	0.97001	0.53934	a	0.97168	0.58607	a	0.9686	0.50171	a	t,t
o2p25_10T	0.92765	0.04254	r	0.96999	0.53902	a	0.97623	0.71907	a	W,t
o2p25_11T	0.91446	0.01932	r	0.96986	0.53537	a	0.95816	0.27785	a	W,t
o2p25_12T	0.95492	0.22856	a	0.98402	0.91939	a	0.95432	0.22029	a	t,t
o2p100_1T	0.92495	0.03611	r	0.92054	0.02771	r	0.94295	0.10926	a	W,W
o2p100_2T	0.9812	0.85642	a	0.95454	0.22326	a	0.95353	0.21003	a	t,t
o2p100_3T	0.92278	0.03169	r	0.86033	0.00103	r	0.96482	0.40857	a	W,W
o2p100_4T	0.65395	0	r	0.79925	0.00006	r	0.68255	0	r	W,W
o2p100_5T	0.91266	0.01738	r	0.86347	0.0012	r	0.96541	0.4223	a	W,W
o2p100_6T	0.90797	0.01323	r	0.91912	0.02544	r	0.90857	0.01369	r	W,W
o2p100_7T	0.89328	0.00578	r	0.89889	0.00789	r	0.96516	0.41655	a	W,W
o2p100_8T	0.94824	0.15169	a	0.96578	0.43096	a	0.96071	0.32297	a	t,t
o2p100_9T	0.49141	0	r	0.68971	0	r	0.68313	0	r	W,W

Table 9. Generalized Spread homoscedasticy test, the null hypothesis is that all the input populations come from populations with equal variances, which is accepted (a) when p-value < 0.05 and rejected (r) otherwise. Observe that the null hypothesis is accepted (a) for all the instances. The parametric t student test can be applied for all the instances that accept the null hypothesis in the normality tests.

Instance	Statistic	p-Value	R
o2p25_0T	0.33509	0.71619	a
o2p25_1T	3.11548	0.04934	a
o2p25_2T	5.44373	0.00592	a
o2p25_3T	7.81001	0.00076	a
o2p25_4T	0.38001	0.68498	a
o2p25_5T	3.01271	0.05431	a
o2p25_6T	1.58378	0.21106	a
o2p25_7T	10.87966	0.00006	a
o2p25_8T	1.51668	0.22518	a
o2p25_9T	19.54345	0	a
o2p25_10T	5.78604	0.00437	a
o2p25_11T	7.0285	0.00148	a
o2p25_12T	15.29209	0	a
o2p100_1T	8.48884	0.00043	a
o2p100_2T	9.53401	0.00018	a
o2p100_3T	3.46674	0.0356	a
o2p100_4T	1.42075	0.24708	a
o2p100_5T	3.96176	0.02256	a
o2p100_6T	4.19408	0.01824	a
o2p100_7T	4.62372	0.01235	a
o2p100_8T	5.30008	0.00673	a
o2p100_9T	0.90643	0.40774	a

Table 10 shows the performance results with the hypervolume metric, and Table 11 shows the results with the generalized spread metric. For the hypervolume metric, the algorithm with the largest value is considered to be the one with the best performance. For the generalized spread metric, the best algorithm is considered to be the one with the smallest value. The table's cells show the median value of the metric (M) and the interquartile range (IRQ) in the following format: M_{IRQ}. In the result tables, for each instance the best and second-best values are marked with solid or light black, respectively. In order to indicate if the observed differences in the performance of the algorithms are significant or not, for each algorithm the symbol $\wedge$ indicates that the performance of T-FAME is significantly better that the algorithm which it is being compared. The symbol $\vee$ indicates the opposite, and the symbol $=$ indicates that the difference is not significant. These symbols are marked with an asterisk when the t student test was applied. To confirm the results obtained with the paired tests, a global evaluation is done with the three algorithms. This evaluation was done by applying a Friedman test with 95% confidence.

Table 10. Results with the hypervolume metric.

	Hypervolume		
Instance	T-NSGA-II-CD	T-NSGA-II-SSD	T-FAME
o2p25_0T	$0.4747_{0.0858}\vee*$	$0.3183_{0.3853}\vee$	$0.2024_{0.2491}$
o2p25_1T	$0.3807_{0.0510}\vee*$	$0.2460_{0.2325}\vee$	$0.2003_{0.2876}$
o2p25_2T	$0.3591_{0.0614}\vee$	$0.2467_{0.2042}\vee*$	$0.1613_{0.1526}$
o2p25_3T	$0.2832_{0.0549}\vee*$	$0.2770_{0.2311}\vee$	$0.1345_{0.1646}$
o2p25_4T	$0.3510_{0.0812}\vee$	$0.2836_{0.1489}\vee$	$0.1875_{0.1673}$
o2p25_5T	$0.2635_{0.0383}\vee$	$0.1529_{0.1495}\vee$	$0.1070_{0.1048}$
o2p25_6T	$0.3797_{0.0609}\vee$	$0.2465_{0.1870}\vee$	$0.1380_{0.2060}$
o2p25_7T	$0.2348_{0.2446}\vee$	$0.2816_{0.3644}\vee$	$0.1427_{0.1694}$
o2p25_8T	$0.2574_{0.0664}\vee$	$0.1838_{0.2259}\vee$	$0.1630_{0.1747}$
o2p25_9T	$0.4026_{0.1184}\vee*$	$0.2449_{0.2455}\vee$	$0.1539_{0.1615}$
o2p25_10T	$0.2580_{0.0710}\vee$	$0.1451_{0.1566}\vee$	$0.1126_{0.1070}$
o2p25_11T	$0.3918_{0.0946}\vee*$	$0.2327_{0.1687}=*$	$0.1876_{0.1657}$
o2p25_12T	$0.2934_{0.0708}\vee*$	$0.2621_{0.2174}=*$	$0.2352_{0.1969}$

Table 11. Results with the generalized spread metric.

	Generalized Spread		
Instance	T-NSGA-II-CD	T-NSGA-II-SSD	T-FAME
o2p25_0T	$0.6178_{0.1985}\wedge$	$0.4190_{0.1534}=*$	$0.4154_{0.2064}$
o2p25_1T	$0.7344_{0.1685}\wedge*$	$0.4477_{0.1289}=*$	$0.4661_{0.1128}$
o2p25_2T	$0.6065_{0.2078}\wedge*$	$0.3929_{0.1025}=*$	$0.3983_{0.1047}$
o2p25_3T	$0.7276_{0.2387}\wedge$	$0.5181_{0.1370}=$	$0.5225_{0.0790}$
o2p25_4T	$0.6475_{0.3031}\wedge$	$0.4646_{0.1432}\vee$	$0.5511_{0.1078}$
o2p25_5T	$0.7228_{0.1715}\wedge$	$0.4204_{0.0925}\wedge$	$0.4168_{0.1293}$
o2p25_6T	$0.6258_{0.1539}\wedge$	$0.4026_{0.0982}\vee*$	$0.4629_{0.1703}$
o2p25_7T	$0.8314_{0.5343}\wedge*$	$0.4995_{0.2457}\vee*$	$0.5833_{0.2388}$
o2p25_8T	$0.7546_{0.1739}\wedge*$	$0.4693_{0.1447}=*$	$0.4646_{0.1059}$
o2p25_9T	$0.6534_{0.3432}\wedge*$	$0.4825_{0.1435}=*$	$0.4726_{0.0690}$
o2p25_10T	$0.6542_{0.2697}\wedge$	$0.4793_{0.1031}=*$	$0.4779_{0.0891}$
o2p25_11T	$0.6540_{0.3103}\wedge$	$0.4369_{0.1073}=*$	$0.4784_{0.1629}$
o2p25_12T	$07079_{0.2465}\wedge*$	$0.4684_{0.0953}=*$	$0.4654_{0.0793}$

The information presented in Table 10 shows that T-NSGA-II-CD stands out as the algorithm with the best performance in 12 of 13 cases. The results on Table 11 shows that T-NSGA-II-SSD positions itself as the best algorithm in 10 of 13 cases and T-FAME in 8 of 13 cases. It can also be observed that these differences are significant in all cases, this is due to the fact that when the differences are not significant between the best and second-best algorithms, then that means the algorithms are considered tied. Table 12 confirms the results observed with the t student and Wilcoxon tests. As a result of applying the Friedman test with the three algorithms, the ones with the lowest rank for the hypervolume and generalized spread metrics are T-NSGA-II-CD and T-NSGA-II-SSD, respectively.

Table 12. Friedman ranks of all algorithms with hypervolume and generalized spread.

Hypervolume (p-Value = 5.68 × 10^{-6})		Generalized Spread (p-Value = 5.71 × 10^{-5})	
Algorithm	Ranking	Algorithm	Ranking
T-NSGA-II-CD	14	T-NSGA-II-SSD	19
T-NSGA-II-SSD	25	T-FAME	20
T-FAME	39	T-NSGA-II-CD	39

6.5. Experiment 3. Evaluation of the Algorithm' Perfomances Using Instances with 100 Projects

As indicated previously, the previous experiment was done with instances with 25 projects, for which the algorithms had to navigate in a space of binary vectors of length 25. In that case the size of the solution space was of 2^{25}. For this experiment, 9 instances of 2 objectives and 100 projects were used, these instances represented a greater complexity for the algorithms because the solution space increased to 2^{100}. The experiment conditions were just as in the previous one, using the same metrics but in a scenario of greater complexity scenario. For each instance, the reference set contains the non-dominated solutions obtained from the combination of the 30 generated fronts. The computation of the metrics uses the reference set as an approximation to the optimum Pareto Front. The computation of the median value and interquartile ranges uses the metric values of the 30 instances sorted in ascending order. With the sorted array, the median value was the average of the metric values from positions 15 and 16. At the same time, the interquartile ranges correspond to those in positions 23 and 8, corresponding to the 75% and 25% of the metrics values, respectively. The experiment performs a hypothesis test to validate the obtained results. The hypothesis was proven using the parametric t student test on those data sets that passed the normality and homoscedasticity tests and using the non-parametric Wilcoxon signed-rank test on those that do not. Both tests apply a confidence level of 95%, pairing T-FAME with each of the other two algorithms. Tables 6–9 shows the results of the normality homoscedasticity tests done for all the instances used in this work (25 and 100 projects) and the metrics of hypervolume and generalized spread.

Table 13 shows the results with the hypervolume metric and Table 14 shows the results with the generalized spread metric. For the hypervolume metric, the algorithm with the largest value is considered to be the one with the best performance. For the generalized spread metric, the best algorithm is considered to be the one with the smallest value. The table cells show the median value of the metric (M) and the interquartile range (IRQ) in the following format: M_{IRq}. In the result tables, for each instance the best and second best values are marked with solid or light black, respectively. In order to indicate if the observed differences in the performance of the algorithms are significant or not, for each algorithm the symbol $\wedge$ indicates that the performance of T-FAME is significantly better that the algorithm which it is being compared. The symbol $\vee$ indicates the opposite, and the symbol $=$ indicates that the difference is not significant. These symbols are marked with an asterisk where the t student test was applied. To confirm the results obtained with the paired tests, a global evaluation is done with the three algorithms. This evaluation was done by applying a Friedman test with 95% confidence.

Table 13. Results with the hypervolume metric.

Instance	Hypervolume		
	T-NSGA-II-CD	T-NSGA-II-SSD	T-FAME
o2p100_1T	$0.4681_{0.1948}\wedge*$	$0.5064_{0.1804}\wedge*$	$0.6214_{0.2130}$
o2p100_2T	$0.4094_{0.1613}\wedge*$	$0.5475_{0.2357}=*$	$0.5107_{0.2107}$
o2p100_3T	$0.5524_{0.2781}=*$	$0.6366_{0.3261}=*$	$0.5947_{0.2887}$
o2p100_4T	$0.7738_{0.3543}\wedge$	$0.9261_{0.5476}\wedge$	$0.9395_{0.4006}$
o2p100_5T	$0.2893_{0.1453}\wedge*$	$0.3519_{0.2193}\wedge*$	$0.4611_{0.2668}$
o2p100_6T	$0.5359_{0.3131}=*$	$0.5422_{0.4082}=*$	$0.6163_{0.5234}$
o2p100_7T	$0.2713_{0.1066}\wedge*$	$0.3477_{0.1816}\wedge*$	$0.4896_{0.2093}$
o2p100_8T	$0.3550_{0.1282}=*$	$0.5173_{0.2759}\vee*$	$0.3894_{0.2611}$
o2p100_9T	$0.9142_{0.3142}\wedge$	$1_{0.1428}\vee$	$1_{0.0285}$

Table 14. Results with the generalized spread metric.

Instance	Generalized Spread		
	T-NSGA-II-CD	T-NSGA-II-SSD	T-FAME
o2p100_1T	$0.5209_{0.3128}\wedge$	$0.3210_{0.1922}\wedge$	$0.3039_{0.1152}$
o2p100_2T	$0.5360_{0.2984}\wedge*$	$0.3105_{0.1349}\vee*$	$0.3995_{0.2272}$
o2p100_3T	$0.4849_{0.1753}\wedge$	$0.3791_{0.1171}\wedge$	$0.3777_{0.2171}$
o2p100_4T	$0.2828_{0.0915}\wedge$	$0.2555_{0.0661}\vee$	$0.2651_{0.0746}$
o2p100_5T	$0.6008_{0.2320}\wedge$	$0.3796_{0.2193}\wedge$	$0.2977_{0.1051}$
o2p100_6T	$0.3729_{0.2967}\wedge$	$0.3457_{0.1845}\wedge$	$0.2876_{0.1838}$
o2p100_7T	$0.5056_{0.2843}\wedge$	$0.3221_{0.1803}\wedge$	$0.3185_{0.1463}$
o2p100_8T	$0.5424_{0.2142}\wedge*$	$0.3154_{0.1280}\vee*$	$0.3338_{0.1274}$
o2p100_9T	$0.4084_{0.0670}\wedge$	$0.3681_{0.0604}=$	$0.3718_{0.0489}$

The information presented in Table 13 shows T-FAME stands out as the algorithm with the best performance in 7 of 9 cases and T-NSGA-II-SSD in 5 of 9 cases. The results on Table 14 show that T-FAME stands out as the best algorithm in 6 of 9 cases and T-NSGA-II-SSD in 4 of 9 cases. These differences are significant in all cases, this is due to the fact that when the differences are not significant between the best and second-best algorithms, then that means the algorithms are considered tied. Table 15 confirms the results observed with the t student and Wilcoxon tests. As a result of applying the Friedman test with the three algorithms, the one that has the lowest rank for both metrics is T-FAME.

Table 15. Friedman ranks of all algorithms with hypervolume and generalized spread.

Hypervolume (p-Value = 0.00104)		Generalized Spread (p-Value = 0.00113)	
Algorithm	Ranking	Algorithm	Ranking
T-FAME	12.5	T-FAME	13
T-NSGA-II-SSD	14.5	T-NSGA-II-SSD	14
T-NSGA-II-CD	27	T-NSGA-II-CD	27

7. Conclusions and Future Work

This work approaches the Multi-Objective Portfolio Optimization Problem with Trapezoidal Fuzzy Parameters. To the best of our knowledge, there are no reports of this variant of the problem. This work, for the first time, presents a mathematical model of the problem, and, additionally, contributes with a solution algorithm using the Fuzzy Adaptive Multiobjective Evolutionary (FAME) methodology and two novel steady state algorithms that apply the Non-Dominated Genetic Algorithm (NSGA-II) methodology to solve this variant of the problem. Traditionally, these kinds of algorithms use the Crowding Distance density estimator, so this work proposes substituting this estimator for the Spatial Spread Deviation to improve the distribution of the solutions in the approximated Pareto fronts. This work contributes with a defuzzification process that permits measurements on the algorithms' performances using commonly used real metrics. The computational experiments use a set of problem instances with 25 and 100 projects and hypervolume and generalized spread metrics. The results with the challenging instances of 100 projects show that the algorithm T-FAME has the evaluated algorithms' best performance. Three hypothesis tests supported these results, and this is encouraging because they confirm the feasibility of the proposed solution approach.

The main open works identified in this research are to develop algorithms for solving the problem with many objectives, preferences, and dynamic variants. Currently, we are working to change the fuzzy controller selector for a selector based on a reinforcement learning agent.

Author Contributions: Conceptualization: A.E.-P., D.L.-G., H.J.F.-H., L.C.-R.; Methodology: M.L.M.-R., N.R.-V.; Investigation: H.J.F.-H., L.C.-R.; Software: C.G.-S., N.R.-V.; Formal Analysis: H.J.F.-H.; Writing review and editing: A.E.-P., D.L.-G., H.J.F.-H., C.G.-S. All authors have read and agreed to the published version of the manuscript.

Funding: Authors thanks to CONACYT for supporting the projects from (a) Cátedras CONACYT Program with Number 3058. (b) CONACYT Project with Number A1-S-11012 from Convocatoria de Investigación Científica Básica 2017–2018 and CONACYT Project with Number 312397 from Programa de Apoyo para Actividades Científicas, Tecnológicas y de Innovación (PAACTI), a efecto de participar en la Convocatoria 2020-1 Apoyo para Proyectos de Investigación Científica, Desarrollo Tecnológico e Innovación en Salud ante la Contingencia por COVID-19. (c) A. Estrada and D. López would like to thank CONACYT for the support numbers 740442 and 931846.

Conflicts of Interest: The authors declare no conflict of interest.

References

1. Salo, A.; Keisler, J.; Morton, A. *Portfolio Decision Analysis: Improved Methods for Resource Allocation*; Springer: Berlin/Heidelberg, Germany, 2011; p. 409.
2. Carlsson, C.; Fuller, R.; Heikkila, M.; Majlender, P. A fuzzy approach to R&D portfolio selection. *Int. J. Approx. Reason.* **2007**, *44*, 93–105.
3. Coffin, M.A.; Taylor, B.W. Multiple criteria R&D project selection and scheduling using fuzzy sets. *Comput. Oper.* **1996**, *23*, 207–220.
4. Klapka, J.; Pinos, P. Decision support system for multicriterial R&D and information systems projects selection. *Eur. J. Oper. Res.* **2002**, *140*, 434–446.
5. Ringuest, J.L.; Graves, S.B.; Case, R.H. Mean–Gini analysis in R&D portfolio selection. *Eur. J. Oper. Res.* **2004**, *154*, 157–169.
6. Stummer, C.; Heidemberger, K. Interactive R&D portfolio analysis with project interdependencies and time profiles of multiple objectives. *IEEE Trans. Eng. Manag.* **2003**, *30*, 175–183.
7. Salo, A.; Keisler, J.; Morton, A. *Portfolio Decision Analysis. Improved Methods for Resource Allocation, International Series in Operations Research & Management Science, Chapter An Invitation to Portfolio Decision Analysis*; Springer: New York, NY, USA, 2011; pp. 3–27.
8. Fernandez, E.; Lopez, E.; Lopez, F.; Coello, C. Increasing selective pressure toward the best compromise in Evolutionary Multiobjective Optimization: The extended NOSGA method. *Inf. Sci.* **2011**, *181*, 44–56. [CrossRef]
9. Roy, B. *Robustness for Operations Research and Decision Aiding*; Springer: Berlin/Heidelberg, Germany, 2013.
10. Balderas, F.; Fernandez, E.; Gomez, C.; Rangel, N.; Cruz-Reyes, L. An interval-based approach for evolutionary multi-objective optimization of project portfolios. *Int. J. Inf. Technol. Decis. Mak.* **2019**, *18*, 1317–1358. [CrossRef]
11. García, R.R. Hiper-heurístico para Resolver el Problema de Cartera de Proyectos Sociales. Master's Thesis, Maestro en Ciencias de la Computación, Instituto Tecnológico de Ciudad Madero, Tamps, Mexico, 2010.
12. Rivera, Z.G. Enfoque Metaheurístico Híbrido para el Manejo de Muchos Objetivos en Optimización de Cartera de Proyectos Interdependientes con Decisiones de Apoyo Parcial. Ph.D. Thesis, Doctorado en Ciencias de la Computación, Instituto Tecnológico de Tijuana, Tamps, Mexico, 2015.
13. Bastiani, M.S. Solución de Problemas de Cartera de Proyectos Públicos a partir de Información de Ranking de Prioridades. Ph.D. Thesis, Doctorado en Ciencias de la Computación, Instituto Tecnológico de Tijuana, Tamps, Mexico, 2017.

14. Sánchez, S.P. Incorporación de Preferencias en Metaheurísticas Evolutivas a través de Clasificación Multicriterio. Ph.D. Thesis, Doctorado en Ciencias de la Computación, Instituto Tecnológico de Tijuana, Tamps, Mexico, 2017.
15. Martínez, V.D. Optimización Multiobjetivo de Cartera de Proyectos con Fenómenos de Dependencias Temporales y Decisiones Dinámicas de Financiamiento. Ph.D. Thesis, Doctorado en Ciencias de la Computación, Instituto Tecnológico de Tijuana, Tamps, Mexico, 2020.
16. Durillo, J.J.; Nebro, A.J.; Luna, F.; Alba, E. On the Effect of the Steady-State Selection Scheme in Multi-Objective Genetic Algorithms. In *Evolutionary Multi-Criterion Optimization. EMO 2009. Lecture Notes in Computer Science*; Ehrgott, M., Fonseca, C.M., Gandibleux, X., Hao, J.K., Sevaux, M., Eds.; Springer: Berlin/Heidelberg, Germany, 2009; p. 5467.
17. Zadeth, L.A. Fuzzy Sets. *Inf. Control* **1965**, *8*, 338–353. [CrossRef]
18. Vahidi, J.; Rezvani, S. Arithmetic Operations on Trapezoidal Fuzzy Numbers. *J. Nonlinear Anal. Appl.* **2013**, *2013*, 1–8. [CrossRef]
19. Kumar, V. *Multi-Objective Fuzzy Optimization*; Indian Institute of Technology: Kharagpur, India, 2010.
20. Yao, S.; Jiang, Z.; Li, N.; Zhang, H.; Geng, N. A multi-objective dynamic scheduling approach using multiple attribute decision making in semiconductor manufacturing. *Int. J. Prod. Econ.* **2011**, *130*, 125–133. [CrossRef]
21. Karp, R.M. Reducibility Among Combinatorial Problems. *Complex. Comput. Comput.* **1972**, 85–103. [CrossRef]
22. Deb, K.; Agrawal, S.; Pratap, A.; Meyarivan, T. A Fast Elitist Non-dominated Sorting Genetic Algorithm for Multi-objective Optimization: NSGA-I. In Proceedings of the Proceedings of the Parallel Problem Solving from Nature VI, Paris, France, 18–20 September 2000; pp. 849–858.
23. Umbarkar, A.J.; Sheth, P.D. Crossover operators in genetic algorithms: A review. *ICTAC J. Soft Comput.* **2015**, *6*, 1083–1092.
24. Reeves, C.R. Genetic Algorithms. In *International Series in Operations Research & Management Science, Handbook of Metaheuristics*; Gendreau, M., Potvin, J.Y., Eds.; Springer: Berlin/Heidelberg, Germany, 2010; p. 146.
25. Santiago, A.; Dorronsoro, B.; Nebro, A.J.; Durillo, J.J.; Castillo, O.; Fraire, H.J. A novel multi-objective evolutionary algorithm with fuzzy logic based adaptive selection of operators: FAME. *Inf. Sci.* **2019**, *471*, 233–251. [CrossRef]
26. Roy, S.; Chakraborty, U. *Introduction to Soft Computing: Neurofuzzy and Genetic Algorithms*; Dorling-Kindersley: London, UK, 2013.
27. Rainer, S.; Kenneth, P. Differential Evolution-A Simple and Efficient Heuristic for Global Optimization over Continuous Spaces. *J. Glob. Optim.* **1997**, *11*, 341–359.
28. While, V.; Member, S.; Bradstreet, L.; Barone, V. A Fast Way of Calculating Exact Hypers. *IEEE Trans. Evol. Comput.* **2012**, *16*, 86–95. [CrossRef]
29. Zhou, A.; Jin, Y.; Zhang, Q.; Sendhoff, B.; Tsang, E. Combining Model-based and Genetics-based Offspring Generation for Multi-objective Optimization Using a Convergence Criterion. *IEEE Congr. Evol. Comput.* **2006**, 892–899. [CrossRef]

Mathematical and Computational Applications

Article

A Peptides Prediction Methodology for Tertiary Structure Based on Simulated Annealing

Juan P. Sánchez-Hernández [1,†], Juan Frausto-Solís [2,*,†], Juan J. González-Barbosa [2], Diego A. Soto-Monterrubio [2], Fanny G. Maldonado-Nava [2] and Guadalupe Castilla-Valdez [2]

1. Dirección de Informática, Electrónica y Telecomunicaciones, Universidad Politécnica del Estado de Morelos, Boulevard Cuauhnáhuac 566, Jiutepec 62574, Mexico; juan.paulosh@upemor.edu.mx
2. Graduate Program Division, Tecnológico Nacional de México/Instituto Tecnológico de Ciudad Madero, Cd. Madero 89440, Mexico; jjgonzalezbarbosa@hotmail.com (J.J.G.-B.); diego_060787@hotmail.com (D.A.S.-M.); fanny_mn@hotmail.com (F.G.M.-N.); gpe_cas@yahoo.com.mx (G.C.-V.)
* Correspondence: juan.frausto@gmail.com
† These authors contributed equally to the development of this paper.

Citation: Sánchez-Hernández, J.P.; Frausto-Solís, J.; González-Barbosa, J.J.; Soto-Monterrubio, D.A.; Maldonado-Nava, F.G.; Castilla-Valdez, G. A Peptides Prediction Methodology for Tertiary Structure Based on Simulated Annealing. *Math. Comput. Appl.* **2021**, *26*, 39. https://doi.org/10.3390/mca26020039

Academic Editor: Leonardo Trujillo

Received: 23 February 2021
Accepted: 27 April 2021
Published: 29 April 2021

Publisher's Note: MDPI stays neutral with regard to jurisdictional claims in published maps and institutional affiliations.

Copyright: © 2021 by the authors. Licensee MDPI, Basel, Switzerland. This article is an open access article distributed under the terms and conditions of the Creative Commons Attribution (CC BY) license (https://creativecommons.org/licenses/by/4.0/).

Abstract: The Protein Folding Problem (PFP) is a big challenge that has remained unsolved for more than fifty years. This problem consists of obtaining the tertiary structure or Native Structure (NS) of a protein knowing its amino acid sequence. The computational methodologies applied to this problem are classified into two groups, known as Template-Based Modeling (TBM) and ab initio models. In the latter methodology, only information from the primary structure of the target protein is used. In the literature, Hybrid Simulated Annealing (HSA) algorithms are among the best ab initio algorithms for PFP; Golden Ratio Simulated Annealing (GRSA) is a PFP family of these algorithms designed for peptides. Moreover, for the algorithms designed with TBM, they use information from a target protein's primary structure and information from similar or analog proteins. This paper presents GRSA-SSP methodology that implements a secondary structure prediction to build an initial model and refine it with HSA algorithms. Additionally, we compare the performance of the GRSAX-SSP algorithms versus its corresponding GRSAX. Finally, our best algorithm GRSAX-SSP is compared with PEP-FOLD3, I-TASSER, QUARK, and Rosetta, showing that it competes in small peptides except when predicting the largest peptides.

Keywords: protein structure prediction; Hybrid Simulated Annealing; Template-Based Modeling; structural biology; Metropolis

1. Introduction

Proteins or polypeptides are macromolecules built from amino acids (aa) and are mainly responsible for living beings' functionality. Proteins are essentials elements because every protein has a specific function related to its unique three-dimensional structure named Native Structure (NS). All the proteins consist of a polymer chain of aa; the junctions with a small number of them are named peptides. The peptides have significant importance in the science community because of their multiple applications, for instance, in pharmaceutical research [1–4], drug design [5–7], diagnosis [8–10], and therapy [11,12]. To obtain the NS of proteins from an amino acid sequence could bring benefits to human beings.

The PFP has been identified as an important problem since Kendrew and Perutz's research teams obtained the myoglobin and hemoglobin molecules' tertiary structure, respectively [13,14]. These studies established the relation between function and structure. PFP consists of obtaining the three-dimensional structure of a protein with the lowest Gibbs free energy, thermodynamically stable three-dimensional conformation [15].

The PFP is considered an NP-hard problem [16]. Thus, presumably, none of the known exact algorithms can solve it in polynomial time. In other words, the execution time grows exponentially when using them. In contrast, any protein passes from the aa sequence to its NS three-dimensional structure very rapidly in nature. The latter issue is known as the Levinthal Paradox [17].

Several algorithms have been applied to solve the PFP successfully, and one of the most effective algorithms has been the Simulated Annealing algorithm (SA). The SA is commonly hybridized with other methods; the combination algorithms are called Hybrid Simulated Annealing algorithms (HSA). These algorithms successfully applied to peptides are the following:

(a) The classical Monte Carlo Method, or SA, was applied to the PFP [18,19]. Additionally, an analytical tuning method to SA was proposed [20].
(b) Golden Ratio Simulated Annealing (GRSA) family: Original GRSA proposing a cooling strategy [21], Evolutionary Golden Ratio SA (EGRSA) using genetic operators [22], and GRSA2, which is hybridization with the GRSA and Chemical Reaction Optimization algorithm (CRO) [23].
(c) Metropolis and multiobjective optimization methods were applied in the previous CASP competitions. The approaches that traditionally have obtained the best results were Rossetta [24], QUARK [25], and I-TASSER [26]. However, deep learning applied by the Alphafold algorithm [27] achieved the best score in the CASP13 and CASP14.
(d) PEP-FOLD3 algorithm, which uses secondary structure information and a Monte Carlo method, and is very successful for small peptides (5 to 50 aa) [28].

The HSA algorithms previously mentioned obtained excellent results for small proteins or peptides. However, when the number of aa increases, the variables (torsional angle of aa) are also increased, the computational time for exploring the solution space is considerable. As a result, the PFP area needs new approaches to obtaining better solutions for large peptides or proteins.

This paper proposes the methodology GRSA-SSP that combines GRSA algorithms with the Secondary Structure Prediction (SSP). For a given chain of aa representing a peptide or a protein, the GRSA-SSP performs two processes:

(a) To obtain the first protein prediction from the secondary structure of the aminoacids sequence.
(b) To refine the previous protein prediction by using GRSA family algorithms.

These two processes are performed in several steps described in this paper. The algorithms used in the second phase of GRSA-SSP can be one of the GRSA family algorithms. This paper named these hybrid algorithms GRSAX-SSP, where X is used to distinguish the GRSA algorithm. We evaluate our methodology using RMSD and TM-score metrics [29]. Additionally, experimentation is performed with a set of forty-five instances of peptides and a set of six mini proteins, which are compared with the most popular algorithms in the literature, such as PEP-FOLD3 [28], I-TASSER [30,31], Rosetta [24,32], and QUARK [25,33].

The paper's organization is as follows: first, we present the introduction to PFP and HSA algorithms. Then, in the Background section, we review the Protein Folding Problem definition and some relevant research in the literature, and we explain the GRSA family of algorithms. In the next section, we describe the GRSA-SSP methodology. In the Results section, we present experimentation comparing the GRSA algorithms with those of the literature; also, we analyze the presented methodology's performance. Finally, the conclusions of this research are presented.

2. Background

The PFP is a significant multidisciplinary problem that has been investigated for over half a century [34]. Different scientific areas have been studied, for example, computer science, bioinformatics, and molecular biology, concerning this problem, and three questions in particular need to be answered [34].

- Which is the physical code in which an amino-acids sequence dictates an NS?
- Why in nature do proteins fold very quickly while in silicon they fold relatively slower?

- Is there an algorithm that predicts the protein structure from the amino-acids sequence?

This paper is related to the last question. We propose different strategies to obtain the NS tertiary structure using GRSA family algorithms and secondary structure prediction. As we mentioned before, finding new algorithms for PFP is significant not only because of its potential applications but also because it is an NP-hard problem [16], and the number of combinations that determine which algorithms must be explored in a very large solution space.

2.1. Definition of Ab-Initio and Force Fields

The ab initio modeling can be defined as an optimization problem where the Gibbs free energy is the objective function f(n), and this has to be minimized. Thus, this problem is defined as follows: let there be a sequence of amino acids: n = a1, a2, ..., an; every amino acid has associated with it a set of angles σ1, σ2, ..., σm where m represents a particular dihedral angle; then, minimizing the energy function f(σ|1, σ2, ..., σm) provides the best tertiary structure or NS. The energy functions (force fields) are used for determining the energy of a protein structure [35], and some examples of these are AMBER [36], CHARMM [37], ECEPP/2, and ECEPP/3 [38]. The potential energy of ECEPP/2 is given by Equation (1), which is calculated in vacuo for only intramolecular energies, and this is the energy function to be minimized [39].

$$E_{total} = \sum_{j>i}\left(\frac{A_{ij}}{r_{ij}^{12}} - \frac{B_{ij}}{r_{ij}^6}\right) + 332\sum_{j>i}\frac{q_i q_j}{\varepsilon r_{ij}} + \sum_{j>i}\left(\frac{C_{ij}}{r_{ij}^{12}} - \frac{D_{ij}}{r_{ij}^{10}}\right) + \sum_n U_n(1 \pm \cos(k_n \varphi_n)) \quad (1)$$

where: r_{ij} is the distance in Å (angstroms) between the atoms i and j; A_{ij}, B_{ij}, C_{ij}, and D_{ij} are the parameters of the empirical potentials; q_i and q_j are the partial charges in the atoms i and j, respectively; ε is the dielectric constant; U_n is the energetic torsion barrier of rotation about the bond n; k_n is the multiplicity of the torsion angle φ_n.

In this paper, we use the potential energy of ECEPP/2 as an objective function because we explore the conformational space, and when the energy of the protein structure is minimized, then the protein structure is accepted.

2.2. Computational Approaches for PFP

The CASP organization has classified PFP models into two main groups:

Group 1: Template-based modeling (TBM). In this group, we find algorithms that use biological information obtained from the secondary structure of the target protein, homology, and fragments of other proteins. These algorithms have achieved good results for predicting protein structures in the CASP [32,40,41]. TBM involves several strategies; some of the most common are homology [42,43], threading [44], and fragment assembly [30,45].

Group 2: Ab initio. This prediction approach classically refers to the determination of the NS using only the aa sequence information. Unfortunately, ab initio algorithms have achieved good PFP results but only for small proteins with less than 120 residues [46]. The Ab initio modeling is the most challenging approach because it uses the amino acids' sequence as unique information. Finding an optimal solution with ab initio is very difficult for big proteins because the solution space is enormous.

These two groups can be applied to small proteins or peptides (between 5 to 50 aa) [28,47]. There are successful studies applied to protein prediction using SA [48–50] or Monte Carlo algorithms with Metropolis-Hasting [26,27]. The Monte Carlo algorithms are also applied to the inverse protein folding problem, which objective function is to find a sequence given a structure [51,52]. This paper focuses on the classical PFP that consists of finding the functional structure given a sequence aa.

The Rosetta is a protein structure prediction or de novo approach that performs models for the tertiary structure using the primary and secondary structure predictions. The algorithm generates a local sequence to produce local structures (fragments) that form a target protein template. Additionally, the fragments are then assembled by randomly using a Monte Carlo simulated annealing algorithm. Finally, the fitness of individual conformation interactions is evaluated based on a scoring function derived from known protein structures. However, only peptides longer than 27 aa can be provided as input [32].

Another PFP approach is I-TASSER (Iterative Threading ASSEmbly Refinement). It has four principal parts: generating a template using a multi-threading method, fragments' assembly method, refinement process, final model selection, and annotation tools. The I-TASSER applies an alignment of the target sequence and divides it into aligned using LOMETS [53,54] and nonaligned regions using the Monte Carlo algorithm. In the last step, annotation of functions is performed based on the structural models obtained using the BioLIP [55] database of ligand-protein interactions. Finally, the I-TASSER predicts protein structures from 10 to 1500 amino acids [31].

PEP-FOLD3 has a framework to predict the tertiary structure of peptides using de novo structure modeling. The process of predicting structure consists of three stages. Firstly, for a peptide amino acid sequence, a support vector machine is applied to predict the structural alphabet of fragments. Secondly, several models are generated using series of states and refined by a Monte Carlo algorithm. Finally, the five best conformations are selected [28].

Another approach is QUARK [33], in which an ab initio strategy is used to predict protein structures in ranges of 20 to 200 aa. Additionally, an assembly process of fragments with small structures is carefully selected and applied in the target sequence using a Monte Carlo algorithm.

SAINT2 is a fragment-based de novo structure prediction approach that has been successfully compared with the CASP12 approaches [56], which consists of a sequence-to-structure pipeline divided into four principal sections: (a) the secondary structure prediction where PSI-PRED [57] is applied, (b) the torsion angles prediction using SPINE-X [58], (c) a fragment library with the Flib package, and (d) the residue-residue contact prediction applying metaPSICOV [59]. Finally, the highest-scoring model is selected. In our methodology, sections (a) and (b) are applied, and they are shown in Figure 1.

The GRSA Family Algorithms

The SA algorithm is inspired by the physical annealing process of metals [60,61]. The algorithm has been applied with success in many NP-hard problems [20], including the PFP. SA employs the Metropolis algorithm to efficiently explore the solution space and obtain a good solution to optimization problems. We show the pseudocode of SA in Algorithm 1. T_i and T_f parameters define the initial and final temperatures, respectively; the α parameter represents the cooling factor. In the Metropolis cycle, new solutions are generated by a perturbation function. Finally, to accept or reject a new solution, an acceptance criterion based on Boltzmann distribution is applied (lines 11–14). The SA algorithm is executed until the final temperature, T_f, is reached. The SA algorithm source code is available at https://github.com/DrJuanFraustoSolis/SimulatedAnnealing.git (accessed on 28 April 2021).

Algorithm 1. SA algorithm Procedure.

```
1: Data: T_p, T_f, α
2: T_k = T_p; α = 0.95
3: S_i = generateSolution()
4:     while T_k ≥ T_f do  //Temperature cycle
5:         while Metropolis length do  //Metropolis cycle
6:             S_j = perturbation(S_i)
7:             ΔE = Energy(S_j) – Energy(S_i)
8:             if ΔE ≤ 0 then
9:                 S_i = S_j
10:                E = Energy(S_i)
11:            else if e^(-ΔE/Ti) < random [0-1] then
12:                S_i = S_j
13:                E = Energy(S_i)
14:            end if
15:        end while  //End Metropolis cycle
16:        T_k = T_k * α
17:    end while  //End Temperature cycle
18: end Procedure
```

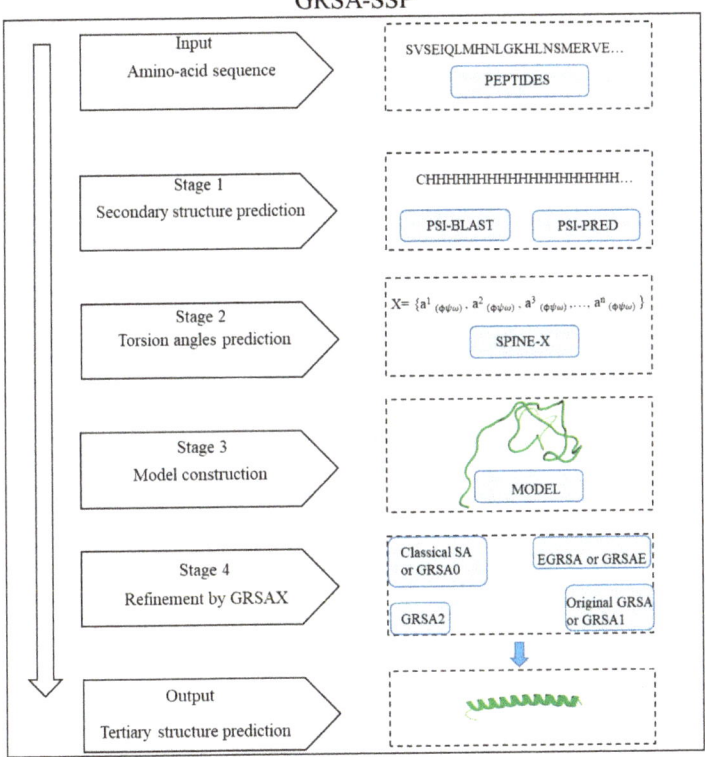

Figure 1. Methodology GRSA-SSP for peptide prediction.

However, when the solution space is very large, the algorithm's exploration takes a long time to obtain optimal solutions. Thus, new algorithms are necessary. The GRSA algorithm was proposed, which has been successfully applied in different NP problems [62,63], including the PFP [18]. The main characteristics of GRSA are the cooling scheme that decreases according to T_{fp} temperature cuts calculated by the golden number (ϕ) and then a stop criterion that reduces the cost of exploration (Algorithm 2). GRSA has a similar structure to the SA algorithm (lines 4 to 16). The difference with SA is that the GRSA calculates T_{fp} temperature cuts (five cuts are recommended), and in each cut, an α parameter in the range [0.7, 1] is associated (the common higher value is 0.95); the intermediate α values in this range are determined with an increment δ which represent the α increment since the lowest until the highest α value (in this case, $\delta = 0.05$). These alpha values are associated with each temperature cut (line 17). The algorithm reduces the temperature cooling speed; thus, the execution time, corresponding to lines 18 to 23, decreases. Finally, to reduce wasting time in low temperatures, where the quality of the result is not improved, a stop criterion was implemented using the least-squares method (lines 24 to 29). This stop criterion detects the stochastic equilibrium for some i Metropolis cycles. We measure the slope (m is a global variable) of the linear regression of the energy of these cycles. In this regression, we used the coordinates (E_i, i); where i is in the range [2, κ_{max}]. In our case, we used $\kappa_{max} = 5$. The equilibrium is found when m is close to zero, calculated by (2).

$$m = \frac{\kappa \sum_{i=2}^{\kappa} iE_i - (\sum_{i=2}^{\kappa} i)(\sum_{i=2}^{\kappa} E_i)}{\kappa \sum_{i=2}^{\kappa} i^2 - (\sum_{i=2}^{\kappa} i)^2} \quad (2)$$

The Equation (2) can be written as follows (3):

$$m = \frac{12 \sum_{i=2}^{\kappa} iE_i - 6(\kappa - 1)(\sum_{i=1}^{\kappa} E_i)}{\kappa^3 - \kappa} \quad (3)$$

where: κ is the number of metropolis cycles for measuring the slope, i is the iteration of every metropolis cycle, and E_i the energy in each iteration.

The evaluation of m in Equation (2) does not imply a significative execution time; the summations on Equation (3) are only cumulative operations in Algorithm 3. This algorithm determines the equilibrium with this Equation (3). The GRSA algorithm source code is available at https://github.com/DrJuanFraustoSolis/GRSA.git (accessed on 28 April 2021).

Algorithm 2. GRSA algorithm Procedure.

```
1: Data: T_i, T_fp, T_f, E, S, α, φ, δ
2:  α=0.70; φ=0.618; δ = 0.05
3:  T_fp = T_i; T_k = T_i; E = 0
4:  S_i=generateSolution()
5:  while T_k ≥ T_f do  //Temperature cycle
6:      while Metropolis length do  //Metropolis cycle
7:          S_j=perturbation(S_i)
8:          ΔE=Energy(S_j) – Energy(S_i)
9:          if ΔE ≤ 0 then
10:             S_i=S_j
11:             E = Energy(S_i)
12:         else if e^-ΔE/Ti < random [0-1] then
13:             S_i=S_j
14:             E = Energy(S_i)
15:         end if
16:     end while  //End Metropolis cycle
17:     T_fp = T_fp*φ  //Golden ratio section (five cuts recommended)
18:     if T_k ≤ T_fp then
19:         α_new =α + δ                ⎫
20:         T_k = α_new * T_k           ⎬ Update cooling speed
21:     else                            ⎪
22:         T_k = T_k*α                 ⎭
23:     end if
24:     if T_k ≤ T_fpn then             ⎫
25:         m= Equilibrium(E)           ⎪
26:         if m ≈ ε then               ⎬ Stop criterion
27:             T_K = T_f               ⎪
28:         end if                      ⎪
29:     end if                          ⎭
30: end while  //End Temperature cycle
31: end Procedure
```

Algorithm 3. Equilibrium Function.

```
1: Equilibrium(E)
2: i = 1; CE=i*E; Kmax=5; SumE=E; m=0
3:    if i < Kmax then
4:        CE=CE+i*E
5:        SumE=SumE+E
6:        i = i+1
7:    end if
8:    if i==Kmax then
9:        m = (((12 * CE)-(6*(i-1)*SumE))/(i³ - i))
10:   end if
11:   return m
12: end Function
```

The EGRSA (Algorithm 4) is an algorithm integrated by the hybridization of GRSA with evolutionary techniques. This algorithm has an evolutionary perturbation (EGRSApert) in the GRSA phase (line 7), where a genetic algorithm is used. The EGRSA algorithm starts with a set of individuals generated for determining the initial solution designed as S_i. Then in the Metropolis Cycle, the S_i is perturbated by EGRSApert to generate new solutions. Next, the best individual generated S_j solution is selected of the population (lines 9 and 10). EGRSA is similar to GRSA, and both applied a stop criterion (see Algorithm 2.1) by the least-squares method [64,65] (lines 24–29). Algorithm 5 presents EGRSApert function, where one individual is a set of dihedral angles $[\phi_1, \Psi_1, X_1, \omega_1, \phi_2, \Psi_2, X_2, \omega_2, \ldots, \phi_n, \Psi_n, X_n, \omega_n]$ and a population is a set of individuals. Then crossover and mutation operators are applied to generate new solutions by the perturbation function. Finally, when the number of generations is reached, the best individual of the population is selected. The EGRSA algorithm source code is available at https://github.com/DrJuanFraustoSolis/EGRSA.git (accessed on 28 April 2021).

Algorithm 4. EGRSA algorithm Procedure.

```
1: Data: T_r, T_fp, T_f, E, S, α, φ
2: α=0.70; φ=0.618; δ = 0.05
3: T_fp = T_i; T_k = T_i; E = 0
4: S_i=generateSolution()
5: while T_k ≥ T_f do //Temperature cycle
6:     while Metropolis length do //Metropolis cycle
7:         S_j = EGRSApert(S_i)
8:         ΔE = Energy(S_j) – Energy(S_i)
9:         if ΔE ≤ 0 then
10:            S_i = S_j
11:            E =Energy(S_i)
12:        else if e^(-ΔE/T) < random [0-1] then
13:            S_i = S_j
14:            E =Energy(S_i)
15:        end if
16:    end while //End Metropolis cycle
17:    T_fp = T_fp*φ //Golden ratio section (five cuts recommended)
18:    if T_k ≤ T_fp then
19:        α_new =α + δ
20:        T_k = α_new * T_k          Update cooling speed
21:    else
22:        T_k = T_k*α
23:    end if
24:    if T_k ≤ T_fpn then
25:        m= Equilibrium(E)
26:        if m ≈ ε then
27:            T_K = T_f            Stop criterion
28:        end if
29:    end if
30: end while //End Temperature cycle
31: end Procedure
```

Algorithm 5. EGRSApert Function.

```
1: EGRSApert(S_i)
2: n= numGen, bestSol[ ], bestEnergy
3: pob=initialPob()
4:    while gen ≤ n do
5:        population = tournament()
6:        population = crossPopulation()
7:        population = mutatePopulation()
8:    end while
9:    pop* = bestIndividual()
10:   return(bestSol[ ], bestEnergy)
11: end Function
```

The GRSA2 algorithm [23] is a hybridization of GRSA with the CRO algorithm [66]. GRSA2 (Algorithm 6) is an enhancement of GRSA. It has the same structure as the previous algorithms revised in this paper. Specifically, GRSA2 has two principal differences in the perturbation phase, applying decomposition and soft collision (line 8) and the acceptance criterion (lines 10 to 14). In Algorithm 7, we show the perturbation process implemented in the GRSA2pert function. In GRSA2, two soft collisions are used (unimolecular, Intermolecular). This algorithm has been applied only in the PFP with a set of 19 peptides and compared with I-TASSER and PEP-FOLD3 approaches obtaining outstanding results in the case of peptides [23]. The GRSA2 algorithm source code is available at https://github.com/DrJuanFraustoSolis/GRSA2.git (accessed on 28 April 2021).

Algorithm 6. GRSA2 algorithm Procedure.

```
1: Data: T_i, T_{fp}, T_f, KE, E, S, α, φ
2: α=0.70; φ=0.618; δ = 0.05
3: KE=0; T_{fp} = T_i; T_k = T_i; E = 0
4: S_i=generateSolution()
5:    while T_k ≥ T_f do   //Temperature cycle
6:        while Metropolis length do   //Metropolis cycle
7:            Eold=Energy(S_i)
8:            S_j = GRSA2pert(S_i)
9:            EP = Energy(S_j)
10:           if (EP ≤ Eold + KE) then
11:               S_i = S_j
12:               E=Energy(S_i)
13:               KE = ((Eold+KE)-EP)*random[0,1]
14:           end if
15:       end while   //End Metropolis cycle
16:       T_{fp} = T_{fp}*φ   //Golden ratio section (five cuts recommended)
17:       if T_k ≤ T_{fp} then
18:           α_{new} = α + δ
19:           T_k = α_{new} * T_k          Update cooling speed
20:       else
21:           T_k = T_k*α
22:       end if
23:       if T_k ≤ T_{fpn} then
24:           m= Equilibrium(E)
25:           if m ≈ ε then                Stop criterion
26:               T_K = T_f
27:           end if
28:       end if
29:   end while   //End Temperature cycle
30: end Procedure
```

Algorithm 7. GRSA2pert Function.

```
1:  GRSA2pert(S_j)
2:  moleColl, b
3:  if b > moleColl then
4:      Randomly select one particle Mw
5:      if Decompositioncriterionmet
6:          S_j = Decomposition(S_j)
7:      else if
8:          S_j = SoftCollition(S_j)
9:      end if
10: end if
11: return S_j
12: end Function
```

3. GRSA-SSP Methodology

In this section, we present the GRSA-SSP methodology (Figure 1). This methodology has two main processes:

(a) The prediction of the torsion angles (initial solution) from the secondary structure; that corresponds to stages 1 to 4 in Figure 1.
(b) The refinement of the solution obtained from the secondary structure. This is performed with GRSA algorithms showed in stage four (Figure 1).

The GRSA-SSP methodology has an input (amino acid sequence), an output (tertiary structure prediction), and four stages: (1) secondary structure prediction, (2) torsion angles prediction, (3) template construction, and (4) refinement by GRSAX algorithms. Next, we explain each of these stages:

Input (Amino acid sequence). The amino acid sequences are taken as input.

(1) Secondary structure prediction. This secondary structure, which corresponds to the amino acid sequence and is predicted using PSI-PRED [57]. This algorithm generates a sequence profile with PSI-BLAST [67] and performs the prediction of the stage, such as the helix (H), strand (E), and coil (C). PSI-PRED calculates the probability of each possible state and defines the most likely structure.

(2) Torsion angles prediction. The secondary structure's prediction is essential for this stage, where SPINE-X is used to obtain the torsion angles (ϕ, Ψ, and ω) of each amino acid. This process is realized through the Position-Specific Score Matrix and Physical Parameters [58]. SPINE-X applies artificial neural networks to obtain the best predictions of the target's proteins.

(3) Model construction. In this stage, the torsion angles or variables are used to construct a template as initial solution $S_i = [\phi_1, \Psi_1, X_1, \omega_1, \phi_2, \Psi_2, X_2, \omega_2, \ldots, \phi_n, \Psi_n, X_n, \omega_n]$ that is represented by amino acids subscript 1 to n and the same form by the following amino acids up to n; n is dependent on the size of an amino acid sequence of the target protein. The torsion angles represent the base column of the peptide on which the refinement will be performed.

(4) Refinement by GRSAX. When the previous stages construct the peptide template, we can apply a GRSAX algorithm such as GRSA (renamed GRSA1), EGRSA (renamed GRSAE), and GRSA2, as well as the classical SA (GRSA0). The GRSAX algorithms are tested individually for comparison, which obtains a better tertiary structure of the target peptide. Moreover, once the energy and three-dimensional structure is obtained, the structure is evaluated with the RMSD and TM-score [29] metrics.

Output. The GRSAX-SSP algorithm obtains the tertiary structure prediction.

4. Results

We performed the next GRSAX-SSP algorithms with the proposed methodology: (a) GRSA0-SSP using classical SA [19], (b) GRSA1-SSP using original GRSA [21], (c) GRSAE-SSP using EGRSA [22], and (d) GRSA2-SSP using GRSA2 [23]. For all of them, we used the methodology presented in Figure 1. The peptides in this experimentation have 9 to 49 amino acids. The number of variables (torsion angles) for each peptide in this data set is in the range [49, 304]. We chose this set because these instances (peptides) were used before in the literature. This set was also useful for comparing the GRSA2-SSP algorithm with the top-performing approaches of the CASP, which can be used for small peptides. We compared the last algorithm with I-TASSER, PEP-FOLD3, QUARK, and Rosetta, which are among the best algorithms in the CASP competition. We noted a difference between the GRSAX-SSP algorithms and the one that only applies ab initio by naming it GRSAX. Table 1 presents the set of 45 instances sorted by the number of variables taken from [23,28,68,69] and a PDB code represents each peptide.

Table 1. Set of instances (peptides).

N°	PDB-Code	aa	Number of Variables (Torsion Angles)	N°	PDB-Code	aa	Number of Variables (Torsion Angles)
1	1uao	10	47	24	1wz4	23	123
2	1egs	9	49	25	1rpv	17	124
3	1eg4	13	61	26	1pef	18	124
4	1l3q	12	62	27	1du1	20	134
5	2evq	12	66	28	1pei	22	143
6	1le1	12	69	29	1yyb	27	160
7	1in3	12	74	30	1t0c	31	163
8	3bu3	14	74	31	1by0	27	193
9	1gjf	14	79	32	2bn6	33	200
10	1rnu	13	81	33	1wr4	36	206
11	1lcx	13	81	34	1yiu	37	206
12	1k43	14	84	35	2ysh	40	213
13	1a13	14	85	36	1bhi	38	216
14	1nkf	16	86	37	1i6c	39	218
15	1le3	16	91	38	1wr7	41	222
16	1pgbF	16	93	39	2dmv	43	229
17	1dep	15	94	40	1bwx	39	242
18	1niz	16	97	41	1f4i	45	276
19	2bta	15	100	42	1dv0	47	279
20	1l2y	20	100	43	1ify	49	290
21	1e0q	17	109	44	2p81	44	295
22	1b03	18	109	45	1pgy	47	304
23	1wbr	17	120	-	-	-	-

In the experimentation, the GRSAX-SSP algorithms were executed 30 times to validate the results. The energy function ECEPP/2 is determined with SMMP framework [38]; it is the objective function of our optimization algorithms. An analytical tuning [20] was performed to obtain the initial and final temperature for each instance. In GRSA0-SSP the α value is 0.95, and the temperature range has zero golden sections. For GRSA1-SSP, GRSAE-SSP, and GRSA2-SSP algorithms, the same cooling scheme was used, using the α parameter with values from 0.75 to 0.95 with five golden ratio sections, which was determined by experimentation [21–23]. The GRSAX-SSP algorithms were executed in one of the terminals of the Ehecatl cluster in TecNM/IT Ciudad Madero, and it has the following characteristics: Intel® Xeon® processor at 2.30 GHz, Memory: 64 GB (4 × 16 GB) ddr4-2133, Linux CentOS operating system, and Fortran language.

We used the minimum energy quality values, the RMSD, and TM-score to evaluate the results, which are two metrics of the structural quality used for PFP algorithms. The RMSD is a structural measure between the native structure and the one predicted by the GRSAX-SSP and classical SA named here as GRSA0:

(a) If the RMSD has a value close to zero, the quality of the structure is considered excellent. On the contrary, the quality is worse.
(b) The TM-score is also used to measure the similarity between two structures. When the TM-score is greater than 0.5, it indicates that there is a good similarity between the two structures, and the tested one has the same fold. Otherwise, as the TM-score is lower than 0.5, the target peptide has a different fold [29].

The TM-score metrics can be calculated using the TM-align [70] (an algorithm to obtain the best structural alignment between two proteins) or in a classical formulation [29]. In this paper, we use the classical formulation of TM-score.

GRSAX-SSP algorithms use a model determined by the secondary structure, and then it is refined for obtaining a better prediction. The results are compared with the GRSAX based on ab initio that only uses the amino acid sequence as information. Figures 2–5 show average results related to energy (kcal/mol), RMSD, and TM-score for each peptide. The numbers in the x-axis, represent the instances or peptides of Table 1, and each instance is a set of torsional angles $X = [\phi_1, \Psi_1, X_1, \omega_1, \phi_2, \Psi_2, X_2, \omega_2, \ldots, \phi_n, \Psi_n, X_n, \omega_n]$ associated to each amino acid. We averaged the results of 30 executions for comparison.

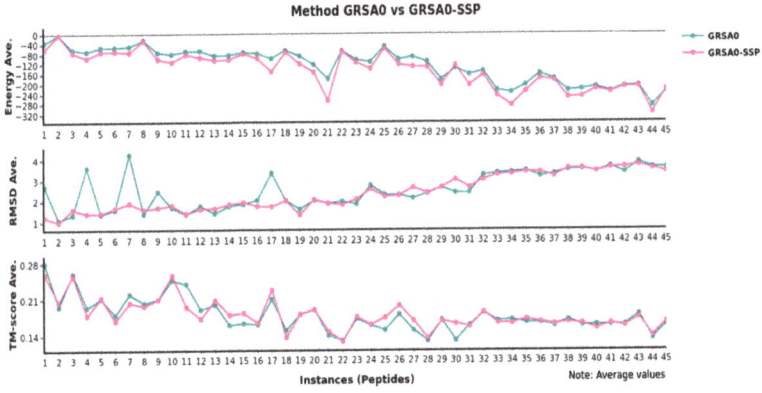

Figure 2. Comparison of GRSA0 versus GRSA0-SSP.

Figure 2 shows that GRSA0-SSP has better behavior than GRSA0 or classical SA. Note that in all the peptides, GRSA0-SSP obtained the lowest energy. In other cases, the RMSD is more stable with small instances (1–16), and in the next instances, the behavior is equal. Additionally, when we compared with TM-score, the behavior, in general, is similar. In conclusion, by implementing this methodology in GRSA0-SSP with these instances, we obtained slightly improved results.

Figure 3 presents the comparison of the GRSA1-SSP versus GRSA1 with the same metrics; we observed the behavior with the 45 instances evaluated. In terms of energy, RMSD, and TM-score, the performance of GRSA1-SSP is equivalent to GRSA1.

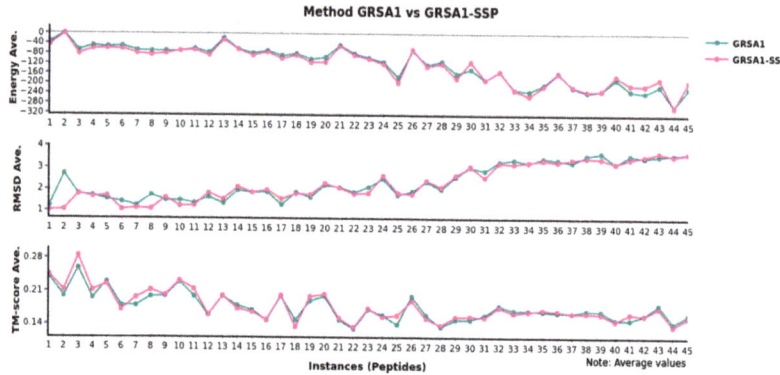

Figure 3. Comparison of GRSA1 versus GRSA1-SSP.

Figure 4 shows the behavior of GRSAE-SSP, and we compared it with the original GRSAE algorithm. In this figure, we can appreciate that the results are equivalent in all cases when energy, RMSD, and TM-score are used for comparison.

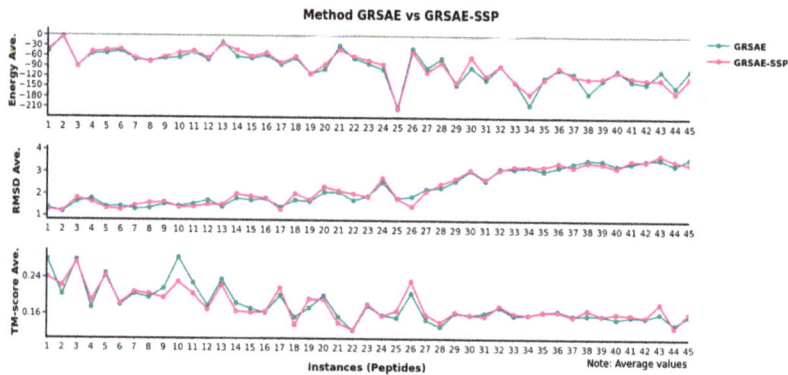

Figure 4. Comparison of GRSAE versus GRSAE-SSP.

In Figure 5, we present the comparison of GRSA2 versus GRSA2-SSP. Note that the results obtained in every instance are very remarkable, and the superiority of GRSA2-SSP uses the metrics of energy, RMSD, and TM-Score. In this case, we applied the methodology GRSA-SSP to improve the behavior of the classical GRSA2 algorithm.

Finally, in Figure 6, we present the comparison of the GRSAX-SSP family algorithms. We observe that GRSA2-SSP has the best values in several instances against the other algorithms, being higher than the others. Therefore, the best behavior of the algorithms with secondary structure prediction is GRSA2-SSP.

Furthermore, Figure 7 presents the computational time of the GRSAX-SSP family algorithms. The GRSA2-SSP has the best behavior in time with low values in most of the instances compared to the other algorithms.

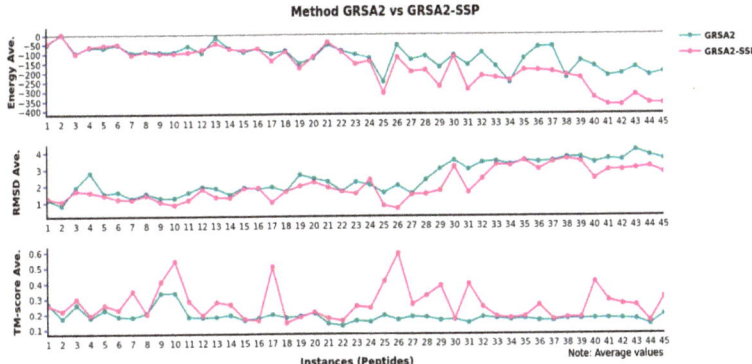

Figure 5. Comparison of GRSA2 versus GRSA2-SSP.

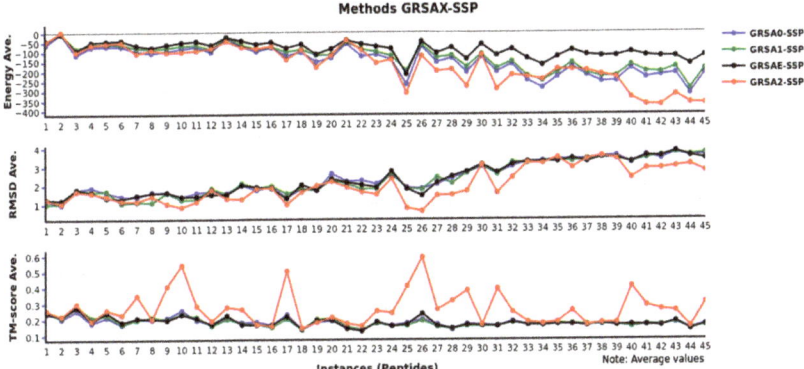

Figure 6. Comparison of GRSAX-SSP algorithms.

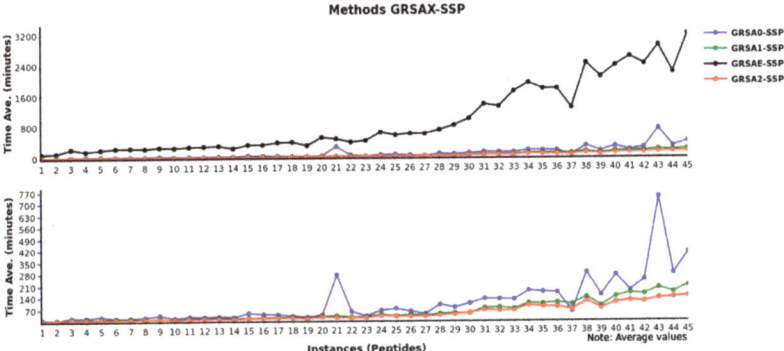

Figure 7. Comparison of the average time of the 30 execution of GRSAX-SSP algorithms.

Table 2 presents the results obtained by GRSA2-SSP. For each instance, we show the best TM-score and their RMSD. Additionally, we calculated the average of the RMSD and TM-score for the five best predictions. Complementing the results, we determined the standard deviation (std) of the RMSD and TM-score for the five best predictions and included the best type of secondary structure: A (mainly alpha), B (mainly beta), and N (mainly none). This classification as A, B, and N is based on the secondary structure predominating in each peptide [27,68,69,71,72]. We sort Table 2 by the number of amino acids for comparing the best results obtained by GRSA2-SSP with the best algorithms of the literature. This comparison is presented in Figures 9–11.

Table 2. Results obtained by GRSA2-SSP.

N°	PDB Code	aa	SS	RMSD	RMSD Ave	RMSD std	TM^1 Best	TM^1 Ave	TM^1 std	N°	PDB Code	aa	SS	RMSD	RMSD Ave	RMSD std	TM^1 Best	TM^1 Ave	TM^1 std
1	1egs	9	N	1.47	0.728	0.737	0.411	0.3630	0.043	24	1pef	18	A	1.5	0.706	0.468	0.686	0.661	0.014
2	1uao	10	B	0.71	1.214	0.828	0.401	0.375	0.022	25	1l2y	20	A	0.77	2.268	0.914	0.258	0.243	0.008
3	1l3q	12	N	1.55	1.486	0.727	0.271	0.252	0.025	26	1du1	20	A	1.13	1.62	0.463	0.266	0.266	0.001
4	2evq	12	B	2.43	1.274	1.020	0.382	0.318	0.031	27	1pei	22	A	2.02	1.43	0.366	0.379	0.364	0.010
5	1le1	12	B	0.38	1.356	1.208	0.316	0.301	0.011	28	1wz4	23	A	2.66	2.66	0.424	0.272	0.265	0.015
6	1in3	12	A	1.07	1.054	0.341	0.395	0.387	0.007	29	1yyb	27	A	1.47	1.75	0.306	0.397	0.395	0.002
7	1eg4	13	N	1.59	1.632	0.397	0.339	0.330	0.006	30	1by0	27	A	1.16	1.44	0.217	0.413	0.408	0.003
8	1rnu	13	A	0.26	0.288	0.033	0.628	0.616	0.010	31	1t0c	31	N	2.73	3.04	0.344	0.216	0.2	0.009
9	1lcx	13	N	1.08	1.412	0.422	0.334	0.323	0.009	32	2bn6	33	A	2.17	2.33	0.22	0.329	0.319	0.010
10	3bu3	14	N	1.02	1.122	0.47	0.294	0.263	0.019	33	1wr4	36	B	3.18	3.09	0.55	0.243	0.21	0.018
11	1gjf	14	A	1.37	0.874	0.461	0.561	0.547	0.040	34	1yiu	37	B	3.01	3.17	0.455	0.221	0.202	0.011
12	1k43	14	B	2.92	1.488	0.916	0.303	0.261	0.027	35	1bhi	38	N	2.76	2.736	0.794	0.306	0.296	0.007
13	1a13	14	N	1.38	1.29	0.126	0.313	0.302	0.007	36	1i6c	39	B	4.29	3.51	0.505	0.205	0.191	0.010
14	1dep	15	A	0.98	0.762	0.352	0.641	0.603	0.023	37	1bwx	39	A	2.98	2.58	0.282	0.451	0.443	0.005
15	2bta	15	N	2.47	1.716	0.455	0.227	0.196	0.018	38	2ysh	40	B	3.21	3.46	0.493	0.243	0.222	0.016
16	1nkf	16	A	3.03	1.838	0.842	0.287	0.278	0.009	39	1wr7	41	B	3.71	3.55	0.146	0.223	0.208	0.011
17	1le3	16	B	1.02	1.25	0.77	0.224	0.215	0.007	40	2dmv	43	B	3.27	3.402	0.6	0.217	0.201	0.013
18	1pgbF	16	B	1.54	2.03	0.409	0.229	0.209	0.018	41	2p81	44	A	3.52	3.21	0.476	0.185	0.178	0.007
19	1niz	16	B	2.4	1.77	0.572	0.235	0.214	0.016	42	1f4i	45	A	3.13	3.46	0.221	0.31	0.302	0.006
20	1e0q	17	B	0.79	1.494	0.536	0.226	0.221	0.008	43	1dv0	47	A	2.65	2.94	0.437	0.303	0.283	0.011
21	1wbr	17	N	1.68	1.31	0.363	0.295	0.2716	0.016	44	1pgy	47	A	3.22	2.62	0.46	0.345	0.336	0.006
22	1rpv	17	A	0.81	0.71	0.096	0.469	0.463	0.005	45	1ify	49	A	2.56	2.77	0.4	0.311	0.297	0.008
23	1b03	18	B	3.04	2.356	0.679	0.2143	0.208	0.004	-	-	-	-	-	-	-	-	-	-

Note: PDB code (Instance), number of amino acids (aa), SS is the predominant secondary structure type: beta strand (B), alpha-helix (A) and none (N), TM^1 = TM-score.

Figure 8 shows the GRSA2-SSP algorithm performance with instances classified by secondary structure. We show that the GRSA2-SSP algorithm has the best behavior in alpha structure instances evaluated with TM-score in Figure 8a and RMSD metrics in Figure 8b. The values in Figure 8 are the best obtained using TM-score and their RMSD. In Figure 8c,d, we present the TM-score average for the five best predictions and their RMSD average.

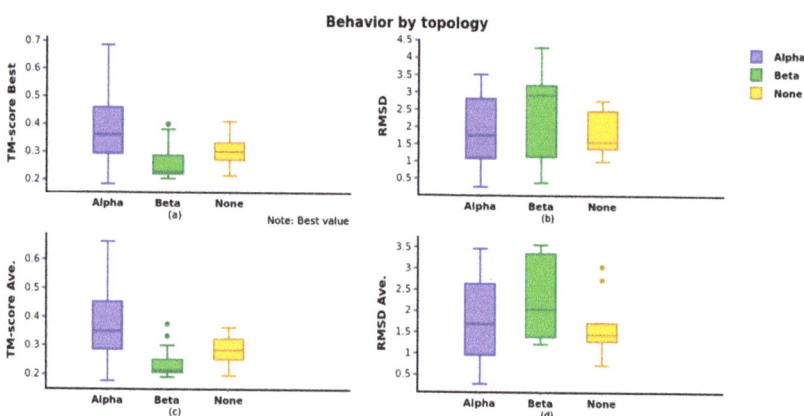

Figure 8. GRSA2-SSP according to the type of secondary structure.

In Figures 9–11, we present the behavior of the GRSA2-SSP algorithm, and we compare it with the results obtained from the approaches PEP-FOLD3, I-TASSER, QUARK, and Rosetta. We divided the dataset of Table 1 into three groups of 15 instances; groups 1, 2, and 3 have instances 1–15, 16–30, and 31–45. We compared these groups using the metrics RMSD, TM-score, GDT-TS [73], and TM-score (classical), and we present the best TM-score, the average of the five best predictions of the TM-score, and their RMSD. Additionally, we present the GDT-TS average and TM-score average.

In Figure 9, we introduced the comparison of the first group, and we observed that GRSA2-SSP behaves similarly to I-TASSER and PEP-FOLD3, but in this group of small peptides, PEP-FOLD3 is slightly better than our algorithm and I-TASSER when GDT-TS is compared (Figure 9e). Furthermore, we observed that our algorithm is competitive in this group. In this comparison, Rossetta and QUARK were not added because the minimal number of amino acids predicted are 27 and 20, respectively.

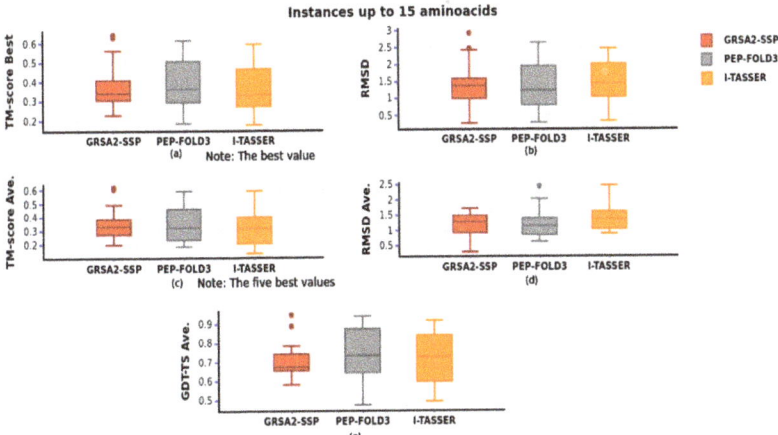

Figure 9. Comparison of GRSA2-SSP, PEP-FOLD3, and I-TASSER by RMSD (up to 15 amino acids). Figure 9 (**a**) best TM-score and (**b**) their RMSD, (**c**) TM-score average of the five best predictions, (**d**) RMSD average of the five best predictions, (**e**) GDT-TS average.

Figure 10 compares the second group of 16 to 30 amino acids with the best and the five best obtained using the TM-score metric and their RMSD, and the GDT-TS average. In this comparison, we added the second group of instances' results of QUARK; Rosetta was omitted because it is unable to predict most of the instances of this group.

In Figure 10a we observe very similar behavior among GRSA2-SSP, PEP-FOLD3, I-TASSER, and Rosetta. Note in this figure, GRSA2-SSP and PEP-FOLD3 obtain the best prediction. In Figure 10c, when the best five predictions are compared, I-TASSER obtains the best results, followed by PEPFOLD3 and GRSA2-SSP. Additionally, when the RMSD average is compared (Figure 10d), I-TASSER is the best, followed by PEP-FOLD3 and GRSA2-SSP. Finally, in Figure 10e, when GDT-TS is compared, GRSA2-SSP has a similar performance to PEP-FOLD3, I-TASSER, and QUARK. According to this figure, GRSA2-SSP and I-TASSER obtained a similar average.

Figure 11 compares the third group of 31 to 49 amino acids with the five best results obtained using the TM-score metric and their RMSD y GDT-TS. This comparison added the Rosetta approach because it can process the number of aa in this group. As we observe, the best algorithm is I-TASSER, followed by Rosetta, QUARK, PEP-FOLD3, and finally GRSA2-SSP.

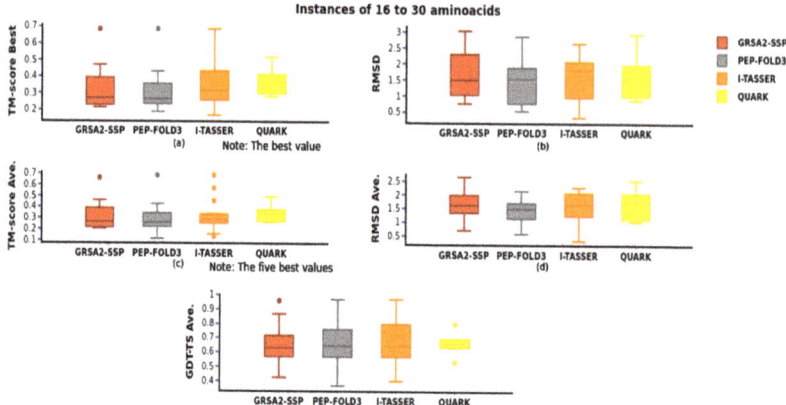

Figure 10. Comparison of GRSA2-TBM, PEP-FOLD3, and I-TASSER by TM-score (16 to 30 amino acids). Figure 10 (**a**) best TM-score, and (**b**) their RMSD, (**c**) TM-score average of the five best predictions, (**d**) RMSD of the five best predictions, and (**e**) GDT-TS average of the five best predictions.

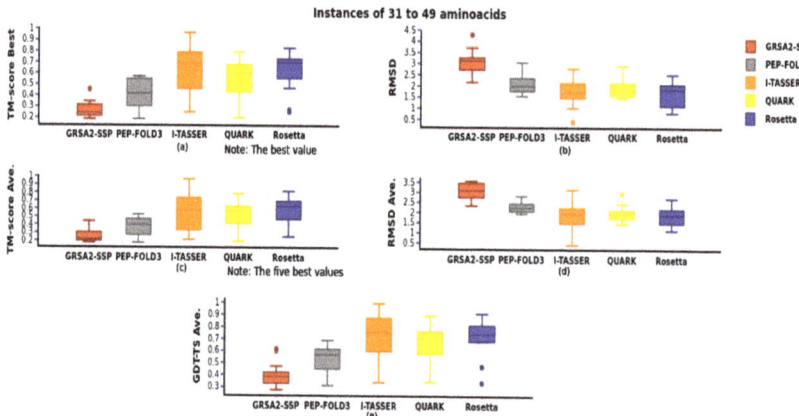

Figure 11. Comparison of GRSA2-SSP, PEP-FOLD3, I-TASSER, QUARK, and Rosetta by TM-Score (31 to 49 amino acids). Figure 11 (**a**) best TM-score, and (**b**) their RMSD, (**c**) TM-score average of the five best predictions, (**d**) RMSD average of the five best predictions, and (**e**) GDT-TS average of the five best predictions.

The 45 instances evaluated in the below experimentation show the application of the secondary structure results and refine them with the GRSAX algorithms, enhancing the performance in energy, RMSD, and TM-score. Specifically, when GRSA2-SSP is compared with PEP-FOLD3, I-TASSER, QUARK, and Rosetta, we observed that our algorithm performs well in small instances (Group 1 and 2). Nevertheless, in the largest instances, our algorithm is not the best, but it is competitive.

We carried out a second experimentation with six mini-proteins (5wll, 5lo2, 5up5, 5uoi, 2ki0, and 2kik) presented in Table 3. The mini-proteins come from the de novo protein design field [74–78]. This data set was proposed to observe the behavior of our best algorithm in these kinds of instances.

Table 3. Mini-proteins.

N°	PDB Code	Instances aa	Number of Variables (Torsion Angles)	SS
1	5wll	26	174	A
2	5lo2	34	192	A
3	2ki0	36	214	N
4	5up5	40	266	N
5	5uoi	43	282	A
6	2kik	48	306	A

Note: alpha-helix (A) and none (N) for secondary structure.

We applied the same evaluation of all the algorithms, as in the first experimentation, using RMSD, TM-score, and GDT-TS metrics. Table 4 shows the results of all the algorithms in this data set. Evaluating them with TM-score and GDT-TS, we observe that the best algorithms were Rosetta, I-TASSER, and GRSA2-SSP, where the number of times the best results were achieved 3, 2, and 1, respectively. Additionally, evaluating with the RMSD, the best algorithms were again Rosseta, I-TASSER, and GRSA2-SSP, but this time they obtained the best results in two instances, which were (5uoi, 2kik), (2ki0, 5up5), and (5wll, 5lo2), respectively. As a result, we can say that Rosetta is the best algorithm, followed by I-TASSER, and GRSA2-SSP.

Table 4. Average metrics results of Mini-proteins.

Approaches	Instances								
	5wll			5lo2			2ki0		
	RMSD	TM-Score	GDT-TS	RMSD	TM-Score	GDT-TS	RMSD	TM-Score	GDT-TS
GRSA2-SSP	0.656 *	0.642 *	0.944 *	1.504 *	0.501	0.649	2.172	0.354	0.504
PEP-FOLD3	1.074	0.526	0.892	1.922	0.532	0.769	2.422	0.466	0.697
I-TASSER	0.823	0.530	0.737	1.734	0.608	0.776	0.620 *	0.899 *	0.986 *
QUARK	0.897	0.565	0.788	1.848	0.527	0.713	2.228	0.450	0.688
Rosetta	N/A	N/A	N/A	1.552	0.694 *	0.849 *	2.146	0.460	0.710

Approaches	Instances								
	5up5			5uoi			2kik		
	RMSD	TM-Score	GDT-TS	RMSD	TM-Score	GDT-TS	RMSD	TM-Score	GDT-TS
GRSA2-SSP	2.234	0.277	0.403	3.194	0.192	0.340	2.756	0.339	0.508
PEP-FOLD3	2.512	0.372	0.541	2.516	0.481	0.629	2.282	0.395	0.597
I-TASSER	1.390 *	0.782 *	0.900 *	2.565	0.512	0.664	2.187	0.448	0.557
QUARK	1.880	0.614	0.778	2.022	0.633	0.777	2.028	0.462	0.627
Rosetta	1.716	0.692	0.838	1.642 *	0.753 *	0.871 *	1.968 *	0.665 *	0.785 *

Note: The asterisk (*) represents the best result in each column.

5. Conclusions

In this paper, we present the methodology GRSA-SSP for Protein Folding Problem applied to peptides. The objective of this problem is to predict the functional tridimensional protein structure. The algorithms developed with this methodology are GRSA0-SSP, GRSA1-SSP, GRSAE-SSP, and GRSA2-SSP. The main relevance of the algorithm GRSA2-SSP, developed with this methodology, is that it produces very good results in the case of peptides; specifically, it is similar or better than the algorithms Rosetta, PEP-FOLD3, QUARK, and I-TASSER for the small and medium peptides, according to the experimentation presented. The last algorithms have traditionally been among the best of the CASP competition; besides, they use modern machine learning techniques like artificial neural networks.

We compared the algorithms developed with the original algorithms GRSA0, GRSA1, GRSAE, and GRSA2; we used a data set of 45 instances for this comparison. We showed that the hybrid algorithms produced with the GRSA-SSP methodology outperform the original ones. For this comparison, we used the metrics Energy, RMSD, TM-score, and execution time. We observed that the best of all these algorithms is GRSA2-SSP formulated with the proposed methodology.

We made a second evaluation comparing the GRSA2-SSP algorithm with the best state-of-the-art algorithms (we used the same data set of 45 instances). We selected for this comparison PEP-FOLD3, I-TASSER, QUARK, and Rosetta. We used a data set of forty-five instances divided into three groups, from small to large peptides. The experimentation shows that for groups 1 and 2, GRSA2-SSP performs as well as these algorithms. We observe that for the first group PEP-FOLD3 was the best, followed by GRSA2-SSP, while in the second group, the best algorithm was I-TASSER followed by GRSA2-SSP and PEP-FOLD3. Finally, in the third group, the best algorithm was Rosseta, followed by I-TASSER. Additionally, we present an analysis of GRSA2-SSP results for each type of secondary structure, obtaining a better behavior with alpha structures.

Furthermore, we assessed GRSA2-SSP with a second data set of six instances named mini proteins. The GRSA2-SSP results were compared with PEP-FOLD3, I-TASSER, QUARK, and Rosetta. The best algorithms in this data set were Rosetta, I-TASSER, and GRSA2-SSP because the number of times the best TM-score and GDT-TS were 3, 2, and 1, respectively. However, each of the three achieved two times the first place when RMSD was evaluated. As a result, the best of these algorithms for this data set is Rosetta, followed by I-TASSER and GRSA2-SSP.

We conclude that GRSAX-SSP algorithms enhance the original GRSA algorithms. The best of them is GRSA2-SSP which achieves very good results, surpassing the best state-of-art for peptides up to thirty amino acids. Finally, we note that the main advantage of our methodology is that it is simpler than the most powerful approaches of the literature.

Author Contributions: J.F.-S. and J.P.S.-H. contributed equally to the development of this paper. Conceptualization, J.P.S.-H., D.A.S.-M. and J.F.-S.; methodology J.F.-S., D.A.S.-M., J.P.S.-H., and J.J.G.-B.; Software J.P.S.-H., D.A.S.-M. and F.G.M.-N.; validation, J.P.S.-H. and J.F.-S.; formal analysis, D.A.S.-M., F.G.M.-N., J.J.G.-B., and G.C.-V.; writing—original draft J.F.-S., J.P.S.-H., and D.A.S.-M.; writing—review and editing, J.F.-S., D.A.S.-M. and J.P.S.-H. All authors have read and agreed to the published version of the manuscript.

Funding: This research received no external funding.

Acknowledgments: The authors would like to acknowledge with appreciation and gratitude CONACYT and TecNM/Instituto Tecnológico de Ciudad Madero. Also, we acknowledge Laboratorio Nacional de Tecnologías de la Información (LaNTI) for the access to the cluster.

Conflicts of Interest: The authors declare that they have no competing interests.

References

1. Uhlig, T.; Kyprianou, T.; Martinelli, F.G.; Oppici, C.A.; Heiligers, D.; Hills, D.; Calvo, X.R.; Verhaert, P. The emergence of peptides in the pharmaceutical business: From exploration to exploitation. *EuPA Open Proteom.* **2014**, *4*, 58–69. [CrossRef]
2. Agyei, D.; Danquah, M.K. Industrial-scale manufacturing of pharmaceutical-grade bioactive peptides. *Biotechnol. Adv.* **2011**, *29*, 272–277. [CrossRef]
3. Patel, L.N.; Zaro, J.L.; Shen, W.-C. Cell Penetrating Peptides: Intracellular Pathways and Pharmaceutical Perspectives. *Pharm. Res.* **2007**, *24*, 1977–1992. [CrossRef]
4. Danquah, M.; Agyei, D. Pharmaceutical applications of bioactive peptides. *OA Biotechnol.* **2012**, *1*. [CrossRef]
5. Fosgerau, K.; Hoffmann, T. Peptide therapeutics: Current status and future directions. *Drug Discov. Today* **2015**, *20*, 122–128. [CrossRef] [PubMed]

6. Vetter, I.; Davis, J.L.; Rash, L.D.; Anangi, R.; Mobli, M.; Alewood, P.F.; Lewis, R.J.; King, G.F. Venomics: A new paradigm for natural products-based drug discovery. *Amino Acids* **2010**, *40*, 15–28. [CrossRef] [PubMed]
7. Craik, D.J.; Fairlie, D.P.; Liras, S.; Price, D. The Future of Peptide-based Drugs. *Chem. Biol. Drug Des.* **2013**, *81*, 136–147. [CrossRef] [PubMed]
8. Stalmach, A.; Johnsson, H.; McInnes, I.B.; Husi, H.; Klein, J.; Dakna, M. Identification of urinary peptide biomarkers associated with rheumatoid arthritis. *PLoS ONE* **2014**, *9*, e104625.
9. Gautam, A.; Kapoor, P.; Chaudhary, K.; Kumar, R.; Raghava, G.P. Tumor homingpeptides as molecular probes for cancer therapeutics, diagnostics and theranostics. *Curr. Med. Chem.* **2014**, *21*, 2367–2391. [CrossRef] [PubMed]
10. Li, Z.J.; Cho, C.H. Peptides as targeting probes against tumor vasculature for diagnosis and drug delivery. *J. Transl. Med.* **2012**, *10* (Suppl. S1). [CrossRef]
11. Lau, J.L.; Dunn, M.K. Therapeutic peptides: Historical perspectives, current development trends, and future directions. *Bioorgan. Med. Chem.* **2018**, *26*, 2700–2707. [CrossRef] [PubMed]
12. Vlieghe, P.; Lisowski, V.; Martinez, J.; Khrestchatisky, M. Synthetic therapeutic peptides: Science and market. *Drug Discov. Today* **2010**, *15*, 40–56. [CrossRef] [PubMed]
13. Kendrew, J.C.; Bodo, G.; Dintzis, H.M.; Parrish, R.G.; Wyckoff, H.; Phillips, D.C. A three-dimensional model of the myoglobin molecule obtained by X-ray analysis. *Nature* **1958**, *181*, 662–666. [CrossRef] [PubMed]
14. Perutz, M.F.; Rossmann, M.G.; Cullis, A.F.; Muirhead, H.I.L.A.R.Y.; Will, G.; North, A.C.T. Structure of hemoglobin. *Brookhaven. Symp. Biol.* **1960**, *13*, 165–183. [PubMed]
15. Anfinsen, C.B. Principles that Govern the Folding of Protein Chains. *Science* **1973**, *181*, 223–230. [CrossRef]
16. Hart, W.E.; Istrail, S. Robust Proofs of NP-Hardness for Protein Folding: General Lattices and Energy Potentials. *J. Comput. Biol.* **1997**, *4*, 1–22. [CrossRef] [PubMed]
17. Levinthal, C. Are There Pathways for Protein Folding. *J. Chim. Phys.* **1968**, *65*, 44–45. [CrossRef]
18. Li, Z.; Scheraga, H.A. Monte Carlo-minimization approach to the multiple-minima problem in protein folding. *Proc. Natl. Acad. Sci. USA* **1987**, *84*, 6611–6615. [CrossRef] [PubMed]
19. Morales, L.B.; Garduño-Juárez, R.; Romero, D. Applications of Simulated Annealing to the Multiple-Minima Problem in Small Peptides. *J. Biomol. Struct. Dyn.* **1991**, *8*, 721–735. [CrossRef]
20. Frausto, J.; Román, E.F.; Romero, D.; Soberon, X.; Liñán, E. Analytically Tuned Simulated Annealing Applied to the Protein Folding Problem. In Proceedings of the 7th International Conference on Computational Science, Beijing, China, 27–30 May 2007; Springer: Berlin/Heidelberg, Germany, 2007; Volume 4488, pp. 370–377.
21. Frausto, J.; Sánchez, J.P.; Sánchez, M.; García, E.L. Golden Ratio Simulated Annealing for Protein Folding Problem. *Int. J. Comput. Methods* **2015**, *12*, 1550037. [CrossRef]
22. Maldonado, F.; Frausto, J.; Sánchez, J.; González, J.; Liñán, E.; Castilla, G. Evolutionary GRSA for Protein Structure Prediction. *Int. J. Comb. Optim. Probl. Inform.* **2016**, *7*, 75–86.
23. Frausto, J.; Sánchez, J.P.; Maldonado, F.; González, J.J. GRSA Enhanced for Protein Folding Problem in the Case of Peptides. *Axioms* **2019**, *8*, 136. [CrossRef]
24. Hiranuma, N.; Park, H.; Baek, M.; Anishchenko, I.; Dauparas, J.; Baker, D. Improved protein structure refinement guided by deep learning based accuracy estimation. *Nat. Commun.* **2021**, *12*, 1–11. [CrossRef]
25. Xu, D.; Zhang, Y. Toward optimal fragment generations for ab initio protein structure assembly. *Proteins* **2012**, *81*, 229–239. [CrossRef] [PubMed]
26. Wang, D.; Geng, L.; Zhao, Y.-J.; Yang, Y.; Huang, Y.; Zhang, Y.; Shen, H.-B. Artificial intelligence-based multi-objective optimization protocol for protein structure refinement. *Bioinformatics* **2020**, *36*, 437–448. [CrossRef] [PubMed]
27. Senior, A.W.; Evans, R.; Jumper, J.; Kirkpatrick, J.; Sifre, L.; Green, T.; Qin, C.; Žídek, A.; Nelson, A.W.R.; Bridgland, A.; et al. Protein structure prediction using multiple deep neural networks in the 13th Critical Assessment of Protein Structure Prediction (CASP13). *Proteins Struct. Funct. Bioinform.* **2019**, *87*, 1141–1148. [CrossRef] [PubMed]
28. Lamiable, A.; Thévenet, P.; Rey, J.; Vavrusa, M.; Derreumaux, P.; Tufféry, P. PEP-FOLD3: Faster de Novo Structure Prediction for Linear Peptides in Solution and in Complex. *Nucleic Acids Res.* **2016**, *44*, W449–W454. [CrossRef]
29. Zhang, Y.; Skolnick, J. Scoring function for automated assessment of protein structure template quality. *Proteins* **2004**, *57*, 702–710. [CrossRef]
30. Yang, J.; Yan, R.; Roy, A.; Xu, D.; Poisson, J.; Zhang, Y. The I-TASSER Suite: Protein structure and function prediction. *Nat. Methods* **2015**, *12*, 7–8. [CrossRef] [PubMed]
31. Yang, J.; Zhang, Y. I-TASSER server: New development for protein structure and function predictions. *Nucleic Acids Res.* **2015**, *43*, W174–W181. [CrossRef] [PubMed]
32. Rohl, C.A.; Strauss, C.E.; Misura, K.M.; Baker, D. Protein Structure Prediction Using Rosetta. *Oncogene Tech.* **2004**, *383*, 66–93. [CrossRef]
33. Xu, D.; Zhang, Y. Ab initio protein structure assembly using continuous structure fragments and optimized knowledge-based force field. *Proteins* **2012**, *80*, 1715–1735. [CrossRef]
34. Dill, K.A.; Maccallum, J.L. The Protein-Folding Problem, 50 Years On. *Science* **2012**, *338*, 1042–1046. [CrossRef] [PubMed]
35. Dill, K.A. Dominant forces in protein folding. *Biochemistry* **1990**, *29*, 7133–7155. [CrossRef] [PubMed]
36. Ponder, J.W.; Case, D.A. Force Fields for Protein Simulations. *Accessory Fold. Proteins* **2003**, *66*, 27–85. [CrossRef]

37. Brooks, B.R.; Bruccoleri, R.E.; Olafson, B.D.; States, D.J.; Swaminathan, S.; Karplus, M. CHARMM: A program for macromolecular energy, minimization, and dynamics calculations. *J. Comput. Chem.* **1983**, *4*, 187–217. [CrossRef]
38. Momany, F.A.; McGuire, R.F.; Burgess, A.W.; Scheraga, H.A. Energy parameters in polypeptides. VII. Geometric parameters, partial atomic charges, nonbonded interactions, hydrogen bond interactions, and intrinsic torsional potentials for the naturally occurring amino acids. *J. Phys. Chem.* **1975**, *79*, 2361–2381. [CrossRef]
39. Eisenmenger, F.; Hansmann, U.H.; Hayryan, S.; Hu, C.-K. [SMMP] A modern package for simulation of proteins. *Comput. Phys. Commun.* **2001**, *138*, 192–212. [CrossRef]
40. Jiang, P.; Xu, J. RaptorX: Exploiting structure information for protein alignment by statistical inference. *Proteins* **2011**, *79*, 161–171.
41. Zhou, H.; Pandit, S.B.; Skolnick, J. Performance of the Pro-sp3-TASSER server in CASP8. *Proteins* **2009**, *77*, 123–127. [CrossRef]
42. Konstantin, A.; Lorenza, B.; Jürgen, K.; Torsten, S. The SWISS-MODEL workspace: A web-based environment for protein structure homology modelling. *Bioinformatics* **2006**, *22*, 195–201.
43. Schmitt, S.; Kuhn, D.; Klebe, G. A New Method to Detect Related Function among Proteins Independent of Sequence and Fold Homology. *J. Mol. Biol.* **2002**, *323*, 387–406. [CrossRef]
44. Lemer, C.M.-R.; Rooman, M.J.; Wodak, S.J. Protein structure prediction by threading methods: Evaluation of current techniques. *Proteins* **1995**, *23*, 337–355. [CrossRef]
45. Dorn, M.; e Silva, M.B.; Buriol, L.S.; Lamb, L.C. Three-dimensional protein structure prediction: Methods and computational strategies. *Comput. Biol. Chem.* **2014**, *53*, 251–276. [CrossRef]
46. Zhang, Y. Interplay of I-TASSER and QUARK for template-based and ab initio protein structure prediction in CASP10. *Proteins* **2013**, *82*, 175–187. [CrossRef]
47. Bhardwaj, G.; Mulligan, V.K.; Bahl, C.D.; Gilmore, J.M.; Harvey, P.J.; Cheneval, O.; Buchko, G.W.; Pulavarti, S.V.S.R.K.; Kaas, Q.; Eletsky, A.; et al. Accurate de novo design of hyperstable constrained peptides. *Nature* **2016**, *538*, 329–335. [CrossRef] [PubMed]
48. Harada, R.; Nakamura, T.; Shigeta, Y. A Fast Convergent Simulated Annealing Algorithm for Protein-Folding: Simulated Annealing Outlier FLOODing (SA-OFLOOD) Method. *Bull. Chem. Soc. Jpn.* **2016**, *89*, 1361–1367. [CrossRef]
49. Zhang, L.; Ma, H.; Qian, W.; Li, H. Protein structure optimization using improved simulated annealing algorithm on a three-dimensional AB off-lattice model. *Comput. Biol. Chem.* **2020**, *85*, 107237. [CrossRef] [PubMed]
50. Zhang, L.; Ma, H.; Qian, W.; Li, H. Sequence-based protein structure optimization using enhanced simulated annealing al-gorithm on a coarse-grained model. *J. Mol. Model.* **2020**, *26*, 1–13. [CrossRef]
51. Mitra, P.; Shultis, D.; Brender, J.R.; Czajka, J.; Marsh, F.; Gray, F.; Cierpicki, T.; Zhang, Y. An Evolution-Based Approach to De Novo Protein Design and Case Study on Mycobacterium tuberculosis. *PLoS Comput. Biol.* **2013**, *9*, e1003298. [CrossRef]
52. Banerjee, A.; Pal, K.; Mitra, P. An evolutionary profile guided greedy parallel replica-exchange Monte Carlo search algorithm for rapid convergence in protein design. *IEEE/ACM Trans. Comput. Biol. Bioinform.* **2019**, *18*, 489–499. [CrossRef] [PubMed]
53. Wu, S.; Zhang, Y. LOMETS: A local meta-threading-server for protein structure prediction. *Nucleic Acids Res.* **2007**, *35*, 3375–3382. [CrossRef]
54. Zheng, W.; Zhang, C.; Wuyun, Q.; Pearce, R.; Li, Y.; Zhang, Y. LOMETS2: Improved meta-threading server for fold-recognition and structure-based function annotation for distant-homology proteins. *Nucleic Acids Res.* **2019**, *47*, W429–W436. [CrossRef] [PubMed]
55. Yang, J.; Roy, A.; Zhang, Y. BioLiP: A semi-manually curated database for biologically relevant ligand–protein interactions. *Nucleic Acids Res.* **2012**, *41*, D1096–D1103. [CrossRef]
56. De Oliveira, S.; Law, E.C.; Shi, J.; Deane, C.M. Sequential search leads to faster, more efficient fragment-based de novo protein structure prediction. *Bioinformatics* **2017**, *34*, 1132–1140. [CrossRef] [PubMed]
57. Jones, D.T. Protein secondary structure prediction based on position-specific scoring matrices. *J. Mol. Biol.* **1999**, *292*, 195–202. [CrossRef] [PubMed]
58. Faraggi, E.; Kloczkowski, A. Accurate Prediction of One-Dimensional Protein Structure Features Using SPINE-X. In *Prediction of Protein Secondary Structure*; Methods in Molecular Biology; Humana Press: New York, NY, USA, 2017; Volume 1484, pp. 45–53.
59. Jones, D.T.; Singh, T.; Kosciolek, T.; Tetchner, S. MetaPSICOV: Combining coevolution methods for accurate prediction of contacts and long range hydrogen bonding in proteins. *Bioinformatics* **2015**, *31*, 999–1006. [CrossRef] [PubMed]
60. Kirkpatrick, S.; Gelatt, C.D.; Vecchi, M.P. Optimization by Simulated Annealing. *Science* **1983**, *220*, 671–680. [CrossRef]
61. Černý, V. Thermodynamical approach to the traveling salesman problem: An efficient simulation algorithm. *J. Optim. Theory Appl.* **1985**, *45*, 41–51. [CrossRef]
62. Frausto, J.; Martinez, F. Golden Ratio Annealing for Satisfiability Problems Using Dynamically Cooling Schemes. In *Foundations of Intelligent Systems*; Springer: Berlin/Heidelberg, Germany, 2008; Volume 4994, pp. 215–224.
63. Frausto, J.; Martinez, F. Golden annealing method for job shop scheduling problem. In *MACMESE'08: Proceedings of the 10th WSEAS International Conference on Mathematical and Computational Methods in Science and Engineering*; World Scientific and Engineering Academy and Society (WSEAS): Stevens Point, WI, USA, 2008; pp. 374–379.
64. Frausto, J.; Liñán, E.; Sánchez, J.P.; González, J.J.; González, C.; Castilla, G. Multiphase Simulated Annealing Based on Boltzmann and Bose–Einstein Distribution Applied to Protein Folding Problem. *Adv. Bioinform.* **2016**, *2016*, 7357123.
65. Martinez, F.; Frausto, J. A simulated annealing algorithm for the satisfiability problem using dynamic Markov chains with linear regression equilibrium. Simulated Annealing. *InTechOpen* **2012**, *21*, 281–285.
66. Lam, A.Y.S.; Li, V.O.K. Chemical Reaction Optimization: A tutorial. *Memetic Comput.* **2012**, *4*, 3–17. [CrossRef]

67. Altschul, S.F.; Madden, T.L.; Schäffer, A.A.; Zhang, J.; Zhang, Z.; Miller, W.; Lipman, D.J. Gapped BLAST and PSI-BLAST: A new generation of protein database search programs. *Nucleic Acids Res.* **1997**, *25*, 3389–3402. [CrossRef]
68. Maupetit, J.; Derreumaux, P.; Tuffery, P. PEP-FOLD: An online resource for de novo peptide structure prediction. *Nucleic Acids Res.* **2009**, *37* (Suppl. S2), W498–W503. [CrossRef]
69. Shen, Y.; Maupetit, J.; Derreumaux, P.; Tufféry, P. Improved PEP-FOLD approach for peptide and miniprotein structure pre-diction. *J. Chem. Theory Comput.* **2014**, *10*, 4745–4758. [CrossRef] [PubMed]
70. Zhang, Y.; Skolnick, J. TM-align: A protein structure alignment algorithm based on the TM-score. *Nucleic Acids Res.* **2005**, *33*, 2302–2309. [CrossRef] [PubMed]
71. Munte, C.E.; Vilela, L.; Kalbitzer, H.R.; Garratt, R.C. Solution structure of human proinsulin C-peptide. *FEBS J.* **2005**, *272*, 4284–4293. [CrossRef]
72. Luitz, M.P.; Bomblies, R.; Zacharias, M. Comparative Molecular Dynamics Analysis of RNase-S Complex Formation. *Biophys. J.* **2017**, *113*, 1466–1474. [CrossRef]
73. Zemla, A.; Moult, J.; Fidelis, K. Processing and evaluation of predictions in CASP4. *Proteins* **2001**, *45*, 13–21. [CrossRef]
74. Lombardi, A.; Pirro, F.; Maglio, O.; Chino, M.; DeGrado, W.F. De Novo Design of Four-Helix Bundle Metalloproteins: One Scaffold, Diverse Reactivities. *Accounts Chem. Res.* **2019**, *52*, 1148–1159. [CrossRef]
75. Liang, H.; Chen, H.; Fan, K.; Wei, P.; Guo, X.; Jin, C.; Zeng, C.; Tang, C.; Lai, L. De novo design of a beta alpha beta motif. *Angew. Chem. Int. Ed. Engl.* **2009**, *48*, 3301–3303. [CrossRef] [PubMed]
76. Baker, E.G.; Bartlett, G.J.; Goff, K.L.P.; Woolfson, D.N. Miniprotein Design: Past, Present, and Prospects. *Accounts Chem. Res.* **2017**, *50*, 2085–2092. [CrossRef] [PubMed]
77. Rocklin, G.J.; Chidyausiku, T.M.; Goreshnik, I.; Ford, A.; Houliston, S.; Lemak, A.; Carter, L.; Ravichandran, R.; Mulligan, V.K.; Chevalier, A.; et al. Global analysis of protein folding using massively parallel design, synthesis, and testing. *Science* **2017**, *357*, 168–175. [CrossRef] [PubMed]
78. Zhang, S.-Q.; Chino, M.; Liu, L.; Tang, Y.; Hu, X.; DeGrado, W.F.; Lombardi, A. De Novo Design of Tetranuclear Transition Metal Clusters Stabilized by Hydrogen-Bonded Networks in Helical Bundles. *J. Am. Chem. Soc.* **2018**, *140*, 1294–1304. [CrossRef] [PubMed]

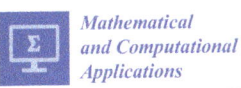

Article

Optimization of Power Generation Grids: A Case of Study in Eastern Mexico

Esmeralda López [1], René F. Domínguez-Cruz [1,*] and Iván Salgado-Tránsito [2,*]

[1] Centro de Innovación Tecnológica en Eléctrica y Electrónica, Universidad Autónoma de Tamaulipas, Carr. a San Fernando, Cruce con Canal Rodhe S/N, Colonia Arcoíris, Reynosa 88779, Mexico; elgarza@docentes.uat.edu.mx

[2] Centro de Investigaciones en Óptica AC, CONACYT, Prol. Constitución 607, Fracc. Reserva Loma Bonita, Aguascalientes 20200, Mexico

* Correspondence: rfdominguez@uat.edu.mx (R.F.D.-C.); isalgadotr@cio.mx (I.S.-T.)

Citation: López, E.; Domínguez-Cruz, R.F.; Salgado-Tránsito, I. Optimization of Power Generation Grids: A Case of Study in Eastern Mexico. *Math. Comput. Appl.* **2021**, *26*, 46. https://doi.org/10.3390/mca26020046

Academic Editors: Marcela Quiroz, Juan Gabriel Ruiz, Luis Gerardo de la Fraga and Oliver Schütze

Received: 5 May 2021
Accepted: 5 June 2021
Published: 8 June 2021

Publisher's Note: MDPI stays neutral with regard to jurisdictional claims in published maps and institutional affiliations.

Copyright: © 2021 by the authors. Licensee MDPI, Basel, Switzerland. This article is an open access article distributed under the terms and conditions of the Creative Commons Attribution (CC BY) license (https://creativecommons.org/licenses/by/4.0/).

Abstract: Optimization of energy resources is a priority issue for our society. An improper imbalance between demand and power generation can lead to inefficient use of installed capacity, waste of fuels, worse effects on the environment, and higher costs. This paper presents the preliminary results of a study of seventeen interconnected power generation plants situated in eastern Mexico. The aim of the research is to apply a linear programming model to find the system-optimal solution by minimizing operating costs for this grid of power plants. The calculations were made taking into account the actual parameters of each plant; the demand and production of energy were analyzed in four time periods of 6 h during a day. The results show the cost-optimal configuration of the current power infrastructure obtained from a simple implementation model in MATLAB® software. The contribution of this paper is to adapt a lineal progamming model for an electrical distribution network formed with different types of power generation technology. The study shows that fossil fuel plants, besides emitting greenhouse gases that affect human health and the environment, incur maintenance expenses even without operation. The results are a helpful instrument for decision-making regarding the rational use of available installed capacity.

Keywords: optimization; linear programming; energy central

1. Introduction

Due to the increase in energy demand, the requirement to reduce its costs, and the need for a transition from a centralized to a distributed power generation system, global integration of energy supply must be planned and managed. Proper management guarantees a more efficient and sustainable delivery. Thus, within the electricity generation sector, different variables and parameters must be considered to enhance its preformance. Some of these considerations are the energy demand, the installed capacity, a plant's ability to ramp up or shut down quickly, and generation costs, among other things [1,2]. Studies based in stochastic techniques have been implemented to forecast the generation or demand for short, medium, and long term analysis [3]. These techniques consider time interval series that allows historical data to be examined to establish the statistical behavior of these variables and predict the values that may occur in the future. [4–6]. These variables delineate the cost-optimal configuration of the power generation grid.

The optimization technique is a mathematical tool that finds the best solution for a modeled system. The solutions are formulated considering system restrictions [7,8], which permits efficient decision-making conditions. Using these optimization models in the energy industry brings benefits such as minimizing costs, increasing utilities, preventing harmful environmental effects, and defining optimal power flow. Thus, this type of tool allows energy generation processes to be more reliable, productive, and cost effective.

Otherwise, neglecting prediction models could impact energy production costs, profit reduction, electrical power losses, and the overuse of non-renewable resources [9].

By means of a mathematical model considering all the system variables and parameters, it is possible to obtain conditions that have an efficient energy system. Each plant's conditions and the optimal distribution of its resources allow the reduction of expenses and losses generated in the power generation process [10,11]. Some of these methods and algorithms are linear programming (LP) [12], quadratic programming (QP) [13], multi-criteria optimization [14], genetic algorithms (GA) [15], particle swarm optimization (PSO) [16], simulated annealing (SA) [17], the ant colony (ACO) [18], Taboo search (TS) [19], bee colony (ABC) [20], and optimal control techniques [21]. These mathematical methods apply to any production system, no matter the nature or application.

Recently, genetic algorithms have been proposed to optimize power plants [22], where the objective is to minimize power losses in the transmission process. Additionally, the particle swarm algorithm [23] minimizes generation costs where it converges to a solution; its advantage is the reduced use of computational resources. However, the drawback of these metaheuristic algorithms is that they are optimal approximation algorithms and search for feasible solutions. Such solutions are close to the optimal and are not the most efficient, generating only local and not absolute optimal results [24].

The economic dispatch technique for optimizing electric power plants has been suggested as an attractive method [25,26]. This linear programming model finds the optimal solution for the generation system according to the parameters concerning minimization or maximization: For example, the minimization of operating costs in the generation of electrical energy [27,28]; the minimization of greenhouse gas emissions [29] from the different fossil fuel plants; and the economic dispatch (ED) problem in fossil fuel power systems including discontinuous prohibited zones, ramp rate limits, and cost functions [30]. Some other studies have addressed solving the economic dispatch problem concerning minimization of losses and costs in a microgrid incorporating renewable energy sources, but not on a large scale [30–34].

This paper presents an optimization study of an electric power generation plant network through the economic dispatch model, which is a linear programming scheme. The proposed model applies to one of the most significant energy production regions in Mexico, called the eastern zone. This region has different types of power generation technologies. Within the analysis presented, actual parameters such as the maximum and minimum powers of each plant, the ramp up and down according to the type of technology, variable costs, fixed costs, and shut-down costs are considered. Fluctuations in energy production by renewable energy plants are estimated based on a probability function according to the historical measured data of each renewable resource in the zone. The study allows a reduction of generation costs during four time perios, without risking the secure supply of energy. The applied model shows a day with 100 percent renewable energy output, 94.90% from hydroelectric plants, 4.32% from wind plants, and 0.78% from geothermal. These three renewable resources show to be profitable options due to their low generation costs and big environmental benefit. Furthermore, the study indicates that plants based on fossil fuels do not significantly contribute to satisfying the demand during the monitored period. This behavior is noticed because the variable costs are directly related to the cost of fuels, which means the operating cost of fossil fuels plants increases.

Power Energy Generation in Mexico

The supply of electrical energy in Mexico is provided through various interconnected transmission networks. Public and private electric utilities compose the national electrification system, and the Federal Electricity Commission, a state-owned electric company, is the institution that supplies electricity to consumers [35]. According to the National Ministry of Energy [36], Mexico has an installed capacity of 75,685.00 MW, of which fossil fuels generate 79.88%; the other 17.08% is generated by renewable energy, and 3.04% by other methods such as nuclear energy. In terms of daily peak demand, it is 48,750 Megawatts, which an increase of around 15% annually due to population growth, economic development, and industrialization.

The energy distribution system in Mexico consists of nine zones, as shown in Figure 1. Each zone has its characteristics of supplying energy according to the requested demand [37].

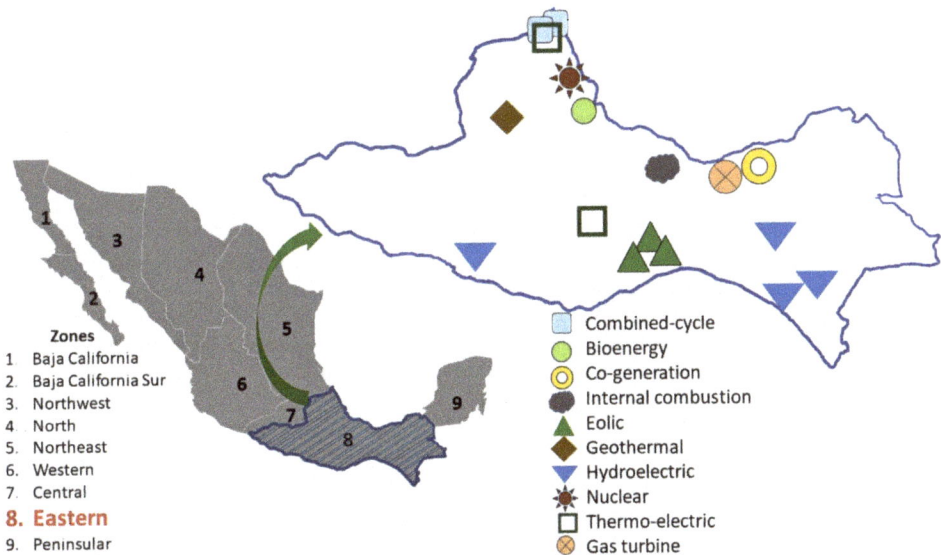

Figure 1. Mexican Electric System denoted by zones. The zone of interest is shaded (zone 8). [34].

The eastern part of Mexico has 110 generation plants, of which the primary source is hydroelectric and wind energy, as shown in Figure 2. This feature is due to its geographical location and high wind potential.

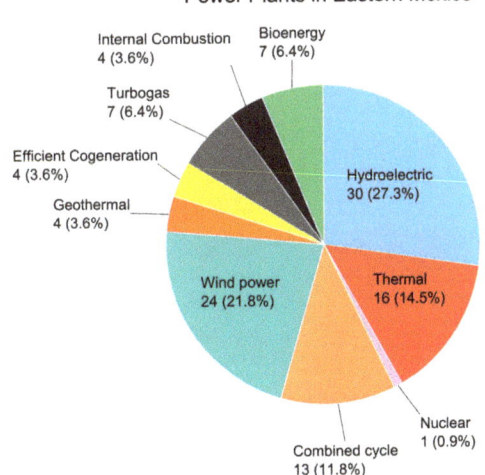

Figure 2. Classification of generation plants in the Eastern Zone of Mexico according to technology used [37].

As shown in Figure 2, the range of generation technologies permits a higher installed capacity in the zone according to the regional demand. This feature allows 22% of energy generation to contribute to the Mexico national requirements [37] and supply other areas such as the Central and Peninsular zones. In the Central Zone, the population density is around 899 inhabitants per km^2. Big corporations established in this zone contribute to 27% of the country's gross domestic product (GDP) [38]. Therefore, the energy demand is much higher compared to the supply capacity in the central zone. On the other hand, there is a high energy demand in the Peninsular Zone because it is a substantial touristic infrastructure [38]. Therefore, it is necessary to promote energy end-use efficiency and optimize energy resources in these zones. The following section describes the implemented model in our case study.

2. Materials and Methods

As we mentioned, economic dispatch is a mathematical model that aims to manage system resources. For our purposes, this model permits efficiently handling all power plant supplies in an interconnected network. The objective is to obtain the optimal combination in each generator's contribution to satisfy the energy demand and minimize its generation costs. The modeling considerations incorporate real characteristic parameters of each of the plants to obtain useful results for decision-making. In the following, the proposed mathematical model is described.

2.1. Modeling for a Certain Time

In an electrical generation system, there are several plants with particular characteristics. These, concerning the central, are denoted by j, that is $j = 1, 2, \ldots, J$. Where J is the total number of generation plants in the system and each one j works under certain limits. No plant can operate below the minimum operating power, which is described as:

$$Pmin_j v_j \leq P_j \tag{1}$$

where $Pmin_j$ is the minimum power of the central and v_j is a binary operating variable. If $v_j = 1$, it means that the central is working. When v_j is multiplied by the minimum power, it will not be below its nominal value and P_j is the optimal power to be generated by each plant. To exemplify these conditions, suppose we have a system of three plants and plant 1 has a minimum power of 45 MW, plant number two is 35 MW and plant 3 is 40 MW. Implementing these parameters in Equation (1), it remains:

$$45v_1 \leq P_1$$
$$35v_2 \leq P_2$$
$$40v_3 \leq P_3$$

On the other hand, no control unit can operate above the maximum operational power $Pmax_j$:

$$P_j \leq Pmax_j \cdot v_j \tag{2}$$

Similarly, if the plant j is working, the power to be generated must not be exceeded. The power generated by each plant must satisfy the demand D requested by the electrical distribution grid; therefore:

$$D = \sum_{j=1}^{J} P_j \tag{3}$$

On the other hand, demand fulfillment generates individual costs which determine the total cost of generation, called R. For this reason, resources must be correctly assigned to minimize them. Thus, the whole cost function R is given as:

$$R = \sum_{j=1}^{J}(A_j \cdot v_j + B_j \cdot p_j + M_j \cdot z_j) \qquad (4)$$

The first term A_j indicates the fixed cost of plant j and v_j is the binary variable described above ($v_j = 1$ is working and $v_j = 0$ is off). The term $B_j\, p_j$ corresponds to the contribution of the cost assumed to be proportional to the production of the plant, where B_j is the variable cost and p_j the production for the plant j. Besides, a plant also generates costs just for being stopped. This contribution is represented by the third term $M_j\, z_j$, where M_j is the cost of having each plant stopped and z_j is also a binary stop variable that takes the value 1 if plant j stops and 0 indicates the opposite case.

This model describes the conditions to satisfy energy demand in a given time, limiting the power plants' administration because it does not allow long-term planning. The following section describes the mathematical considerations in the modeling for time intervals to have a more significant representation in the resources assigned.

2.2. Model for Various Periods

The problem of scheduling power plants by periods consists of determining for the planning horizon both the start-up and shut-down of each power plant and the allocation of energy to be generated. These three parameters must satisfy the demand in each cycle of time, reduce costs, and comply with specific technical and operational safety restrictions in each plant j. These planning horizons are divided into a day by time cycles. These time cycles are denoted by k, so the planning horizon consists of the periods: $k = 1, 2, \ldots, K$, where K is determined by the number of cycles defined in total for the study. Each of the j power plants cannot operate below their minimum energy generation, being established for various periods such as:

$$Emin_j \cdot v_{jk} \leq E_{jk} \qquad (5)$$

where $Emin_j$ is the minimum energy to generate plant j in period k; E_{jk} is the energy that plant j will generate in period k; and v_{jk} is the binary variable described above. Suppose, for example, we have a system of three plants and three established periods, if we talk about the minimum energy to be generated in plant 2 in period 3 it is established as:

$$Emin_2 \cdot v_{2,3} \leq E_{2,3}$$

Similarly, the power plants cannot produce more than the established maximum energy $Emax_j$; then:

$$E_{jk} \leq Emax_j \cdot v_{jk} \qquad (6)$$

The energy to be produced in each plant in one period cannot increase abruptly in the immediately following period above a maximum quantity. This energy is known as the maximum load rise ramp U_j, expressed as:

$$E_{jk+1} - E_{jk} \leq U_j \qquad (7)$$

The difference between energy produced in the immediately following period and the current period's energy must be less than or equal to the maximum rising ramp of U of the plant j. Similarly, no power plant can reduce its energy production under a limit called the maximum load descent ramp F_j. So:

$$E_{jk} - E_{jk+1} \leq F_j \qquad (8)$$

Additionally, it is convenient to define two conditions that allow setting the starting and braking for each plant, in order to have greater control of the costs that may be generated. For the first case, let us consider that a plant that is operating in a period k is established to be in operation and a previous period $k-1$ is also in operation. In this case, it cannot start in period k expressed as:

$$v_{jk} - v_{jk-1} \leq y_{jk} \tag{9}$$

where y_{jk} is also a binary start-up variable, and if $y_{jk} = 1$ indicates the central j is working in a period k and $y_{jk} = 0$ for the opposite case. In the same way, if a plant is in operation, it cannot be stopped and vice versa, therefore:

$$v_{jk} + z_{jk} = 1 \tag{10}$$

where z_{jk} is the stop binary variable that indicates $z_{jk} = 1$ plant j is stopped in period k and $z_{jk} = 0$ when not; thus, it is possible to establish an equation that determines the state and allows these conditions to be fulfilled, given by:

$$v_{jk} - v_{jk-1} + y_{jk} - z_{jk} \leq 0 \tag{11}$$

To verify that the general conditions and any exchange are valid, consider the following particular example. Suppose that control unit 1 is stopped in period 1, but in the following period, it is in operation, which means that in period 2, it is going to start. Therefore it cannot be stopped in the same period 2. The equation for this situation is expressed:

$$v_{1,1} - v_{1,2} + y_{1,2} - z_{1,2} \leq 0 \tag{12}$$

To verify that this last situation is consistent under the proposed model, consider the case that the power plant was off in period 1 and remained off in period 2, which is obtained from Equation (12):

$$0 - 0 + 0 - 1 \leq 0$$
$$-1 \leq 0$$

Thus, employing the example proposed in Equation (12), it is verified that all the variables describe the logic of possible states in the system. On the other hand, the proposed model must supply the demand in each period. In consequence:

$$D_k = \sum_{j=1}^{J} E_{jk} \tag{13}$$

where D_k is the total demand to cover in period k, the proposed Equations (5)–(12) are the restrictions inherent to each power plant in the system, where it is sought to reduce generation scabs by satisfying the demand established in Equation (13).

The cost minimization R now considered in all time intervals must include all the regular electric power production plants' programming. Therefore, it must be expressed in terms of all possible contributions:

$$R = \sum_{k=1}^{K} \sum_{j=1}^{J} \left(A_j \cdot v_{jk} + B_j \cdot E_{jk} + C_j \cdot y_{jk} + M_j \cdot z_{jk} \right) \tag{14}$$

where it is the sum of all the costs of the plants in each of the periods. The first term of Equation (14) incorporates the fixed cost A_j of each generation plant. The second term associates the variable cost B_j, considering that it is proportional to the plant's production and directly related to the cost of fossil fuels. The next cost in this model is considered the start-up C_j of a plant, where it is assumed to be constant throughout the periods. Finally, the fourth term of Equation (14) incorporates the cost M_j, generated when a plant is off. As can be seen, each of the costs described is established according to the state parameters defined by the activation or shut-down binary v_{jk}, p_{jk}, y_{jk}, and z_{jk}, respectively.

The conditions established to satisfy the different energy demands in the time intervals allow long-term planning, maintaining the optimal distribution of resources and minimizing the total cost of generation from the model as shown in Table 1.

Table 1. Model equations.

Minimum Energy
$Emin_j \cdot v_{jk} \leq E_{jk}$
Maximum Energy
$E_{jk} \leq Emax_j \cdot v_{jk}$
Maximum Load Rise Ramp
$E_{jk+1} - E_{jk} \leq U_j$
Maximum Load Descent Ramp
$E_{jk} - E_{jk+1} \leq F_j$
Start
$v_{jk} - v_{jk-1} \leq y_{jk}$
On/Stop
$v_{jk} + z_{jk} = 1$
State
$v_{jk} - v_{jk-1} + y_{jk} - z_{jk} \leq 0$
Demand
$v_{jk} - v_{jk-1} + y_{jk} - z_{jk} \leq 0$

3. Implementation and Discussion of Results

The control area selected to carry out the study consists of 110 power plants that provide 16,992 MW of installed capacity with different technologies. The demand D in the area has a value from 6750 MW to 8500 MW on average per hour, according to the National Center for Energy Control (known by its spanish accronim, CENACE) in Mexico.

From 110 power plants, we select 17 representative power plants which correspond to 57% of the area's installed capacity. This selection maintains the proportionality of the installed capacity of the area by type of technology. These plants have characteristic parameters such as maximum energy ($Emax_j$) and minimum energy ($Emin_j$), variable costs (B_j), fixed cost (A_j), start-up costs (C_j), and shut-down costs (M_j) as is shown in Table 2.

Table 2. Parameters of the Electric Power Plants [39].

Central	$Emin_j$ (MWh)	$Emax_j$ (MWh)	B_j ($/MWh)	A_j ($/h)	C_j ($)	M_j ($/h)
1. Bioenergy	295.14	78.75	3.94	265.524	0	330
2. Combined cycle	2883.9	742.5	2.72	92.28	0	210
3. Combined cycle	5721.06	1474.5	2.69	90.174	0	216
4. Efficient Cogeneration	2138.28	551.1	2.73	93.318	108.3	210
5. Internal Combustion	86.22	23.55	3.16	168.264	108.3	258
6. Wind power	294.9048	246	0	149.778	0	240
7. Wind power	450.4491	375.75	0	149.778	0	240
8. Wind power	420.7788	351	0	149.778	0	240
9. Geothermal	301.98	80.4	0.06	522.708	0	270
10. Hydroelectric	4728.24	1350	0	151.464	0	246
11. Hydroelectric	3152.16	900	0	151.464	0	246
12. Hydroelectric	12,608.64	3600	0	151.464	0	246
13. Hydroelectric	5673.888	1620	0	151.464	0	246
14. Nuclear power plant	8742.9	2265	2.25	588	0	660
15. Thermal	2001.3	525	2.2	170.862	472.86	258
16. Thermal	647.64	172.8	3.94	265.524	468.6	330
17. Turbogas	715.5	181.05	4.19	51.102	216.6	120

For wind power plants, the maximum and minimum energy to be generated are obtained based on the statistics of the historical wind speed data of the place where they are located as reported by the Mexican ministry of energy [36]. The wind statistics are obtained through the Weibull probability density model, and in the same way with respect to hydroelectric plants, but it is a probability function of the flow and level they present.

For the model's implementation, it is necessary to indicate the requested demand in each period of the area, establishing 52% of the total demand for representing the study plants as shown in Figure 3a, and we are assuming 5% additional to compensate for generation losses that could be generated at the time of transmission, which means a total of 57% being established. Therefore, four periods were established in which each period consists of 6 h in duration, as reflected in Figure 3b. It is worth mentioning that these data are real and were provided by CENACE based on monitoring carried out every hour over a three-week interval.

The model established by Equations (5)–(14) and applied to the geographical area described above was implemented using the MATLAB® programming tool, by means of the intlinprog function, which allows solving mixed-integer linear programming problems, and which has the structure as shown in Figure 4.

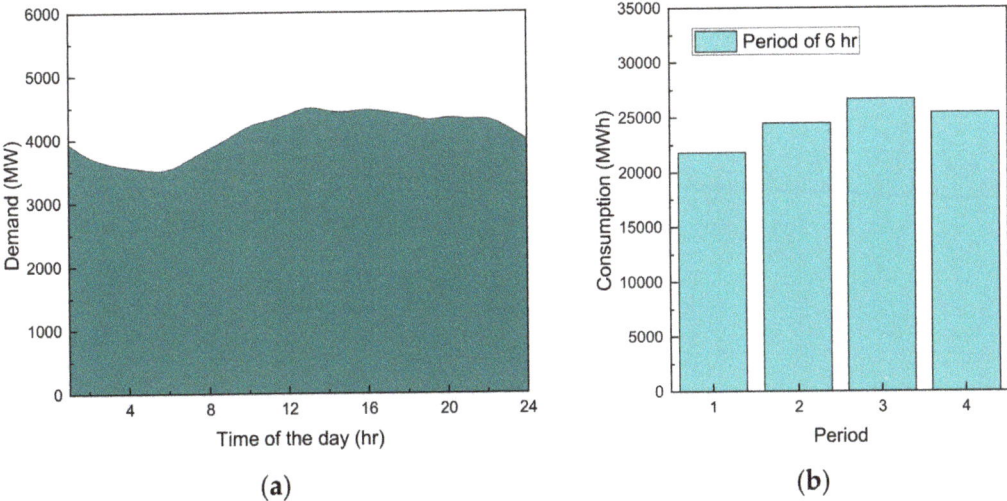

Figure 3. The behavior of demand in the Eastern Zone. (**a**) The corresponding demand in the Eastern Zone per hour. (**b**) Consumption accross periods of 6 h.

$$\min_{x} f^T x \text{ subject to } \begin{cases} x(\text{intcon}) \text{ are integers} \\ A \cdot x \leq b \\ Aeq \cdot x = beq \\ lb \leq x \leq ub. \end{cases}$$

Figure 4. Intlinpro function syntax from MATLAB® [40].

Where f is a vector of the objective function, x is a vector of the binary variables of the problem, A is a matrix, with the values of the left side of the inequalities, and b is the vector of the right side of the inequalities. Aeq is a matrix with the values on the left side of the model equations, beq is the right side of the equations, lb and ub are a vector with the maximum and minimum values of the variables. For the generation of these matrices and vectors, the proper values of each plant established in Table 1 are taken, obtaining the matrices with the following dimensions $F_{272 \times 1}$, $XIntcon_{240 \times 1}$, $A_{190 \times 272}$, $b_{190 \times 1}$, $Aeq_{72 \times 272}$, $beq_{72 \times 1}$, $lb_{272 \times 1}$, and $ub_{272 \times 1}$

Once the matrices of the system were defined, the results presented in Tables 3–6 and Figures 5–8 were obtained. In them, the values for each variable defined in each of the defined periods are indicated.

In the first period, identified from 00:00 to 06:00 h, an energy demand of 21,832.52 MWh was managed. This demand is the lowest of the four periods considered because they are the first hours of the day and, consequently, cover less human activity. The power plants contributing to related demand are from technologies such as internal combustion, wind, geothermal, and hydroelectric, the contributions of which make it optimal, as shown in Table 3 and Figure 5a.

Table 3. Results of Period 1.

Central	Power to Be Generated in 6 h	On V_j	Start Y_j	Stop Z_j
1. Bioenergy	0	0	0	1
2. Combined cycle	0	0	0	1
3. Combined cycle	0	0	0	1
4. Efficient Cogeneration	0	0	0	1
5. Internal Combustion	23.55	1	0	0
6. Wind power	294.9048	1	0	0
7. Wind power	450.4491	1	0	0
8. Wind power	420.7788	1	0	0
9. Geothermal	80.4	1	0	0
10. Hydroelectric	4728.24	1	0	0
11. Hydroelectric	3152.16	1	0	0
12. Hydroelectric	11062.0373	1	0	0
13. Hydroelectric	1620	1	0	0
14. Nuclear power plant	0	0	0	1
15. Thermal	0	0	0	1
16. Thermal	0	0	0	1
17. Turbogas	0	0	0	1

Table 4. Results of Period 2.

Central	Power to Be Generated in 6 h	On V_j	Start Y_j	Stop Z_j
1. Bioenergy	0	0	0	1
2. Combined cycle	0	0	0	1
3. Combined cycle	0	0	0	1
4. Efficient Cogeneration	0	0	0	1
5. Internal Combustion	23.55	1	0	0
6. Wind power	294.91	1	0	0
7. Wind power	450.45	1	0	0
8. Wind power	420.78	1	0	0
9. Geothermal	80.4	1	0	0
10. Hydroelectric	4728.24	1	0	0
11. Hydroelectric	3152.16	1	0	0
12. Hydroelectric	12,608.64	1	0	0
13. Hydroelectric	2708.79	1	0	0
14. Nuclear power plant	0	0	0	1
15. Thermal	0	0	0	1
16. Thermal	0	0	0	1
17. Turbogas	0	0	0	1

Table 5. Results of period 3.

Central	Power to Be Generated in 6 h	On V_j	Start Y_j	Stop Z_j
1. Bioenergy	0	0	0	1
2. Combined cycle	0	0	0	1
3. Combined cycle	0	0	0	1
4. Efficient Cogeneration	0	0	0	1
5. Internal Combustion	23.55	1	0	0
6. Wind power	294.91	1	0	0
7. Wind power	450.45	1	0	0
8. Wind power	420.78	1	0	0
9. Geothermal	80.4	1	0	0
10. Hydroelectric	4728.24	1	0	0
11. Hydroelectric	3152.16	1	0	0
12. Hydroelectric	12,608.64	1	0	0
13. Hydroelectric	4901.96	1	0	0
14. Nuclear power plant	0	0	0	1
15. Thermal	0	0	0	1
16. Thermal	0	0	0	1
17. Turbogas	0	0	0	1

Table 6. Results of period 4.

Central	Power to Be Generated in 6 h	On V_j	Start Y_j	Stop Z_j
1. Bioenergy	0	0	0	1
2. Combined cycle	0	0	0	1
3. Combined cycle	0	0	0	1
4. Efficient Cogeneration	0	0	0	1
5. Internal Combustion	23.55	1	0	0
6. Wind power	294.91	1	0	0
7. Wind power	450.45	1	0	0
8. Wind power	420.78	1	0	0
9. Geothermal	80.4	1	0	0
10. Hydroelectric	4728.24	1	0	0
11. Hydroelectric	3152.16	1	0	0
12. Hydroelectric	12,608.64	1	0	0
13. Hydroelectric	3675.32	1	0	0
14. Nuclear power plant	0	0	0	1
15. Thermal	0	0	0	1
16. Thermal	0	0	0	1
17. Turbogas	0	0	0	1

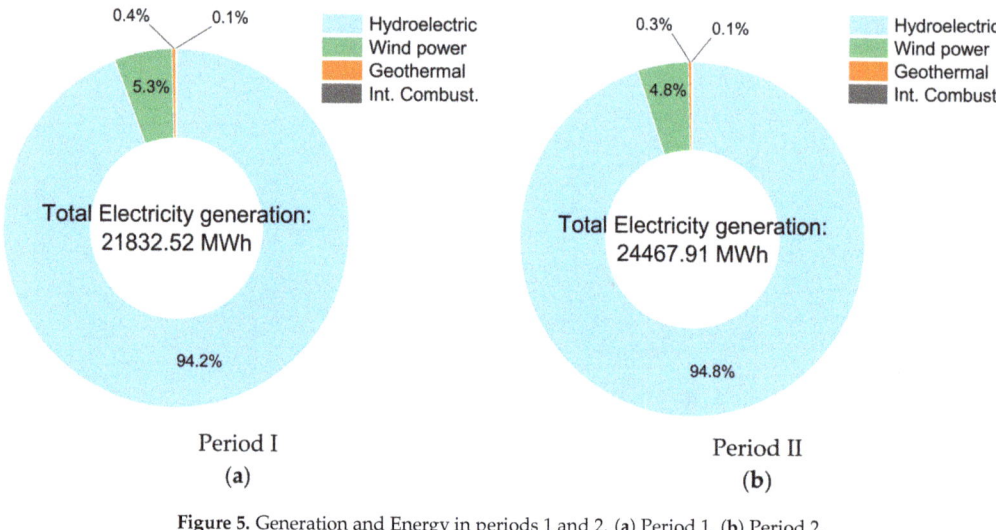

Figure 5. Generation and Energy in periods 1 and 2. (**a**) Period 1. (**b**) Period 2.

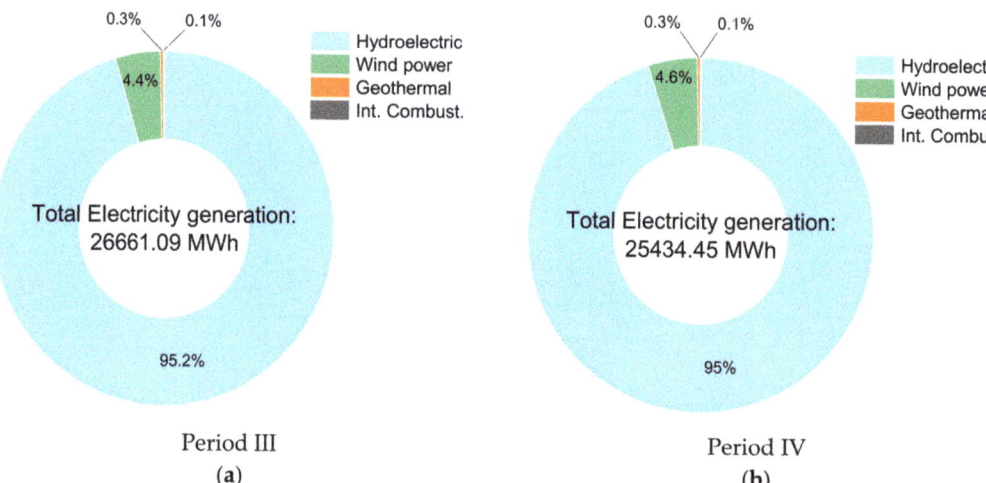

Figure 6. Generation and Energy in periods 3 and 4. (**a**) Period 3. (**b**) Period 4.

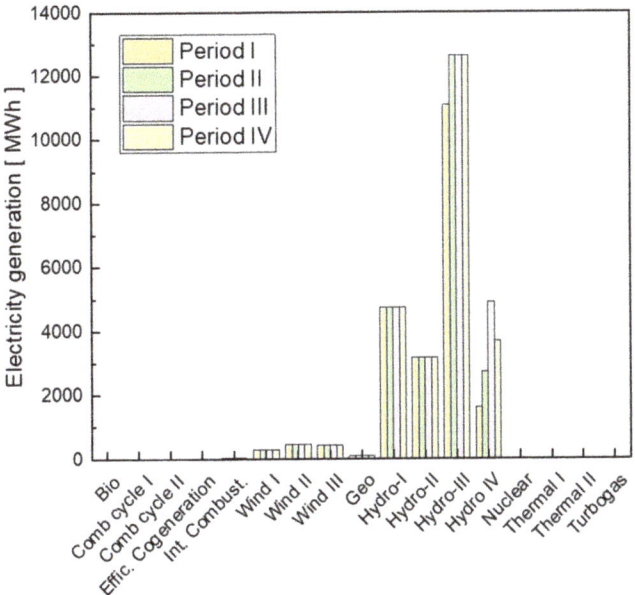

Figure 7. Contribution of energy generation by each plant of the study in the periods.

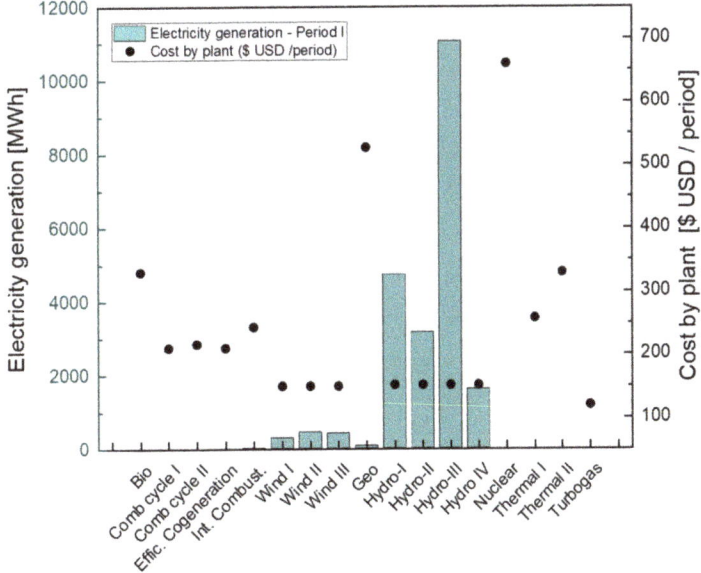

Figure 8. Electricity generation and Energy Costs for period 1.

Table 4 shows the model variables' results in period 2, where the demand to be satisfied is 24,467.92 MWh, as shown in Figure 5b.

Additionally, in Period 3 (see Table 5 and Figure 6a), the demand to be satisfied is the highest of the four periods, corresponding to 26,661.1 MWh. Here, the power plants that contribute to cover most of the demand are wind and hydroelectric. This aspect can be an opportunity to incorporate clean technologies for the generation of energy that satisfies the requested demand.

Finally, in period 4, the demand to satisfy is 25,434.44 MWh; the results of which are produced by the model and are described in Table 6 and Figure 6b. It is in this period where the most significant contribution is observed from renewable energies. In this way, we can observe that the model complies with what is proposed because it satisfies the demand for the established periods.

Figure 7 shows the different plants that comprise the study carried out and the contributions of each one of them in the different periods established to satisfy the demand in each one.

The costs obtained in period 1 are illustrated in Figure 8, which shows the behavior, and this trend continues in the following periods. The highest costs come from fossil fuel technology plants. This is mainly due to the various fossil fuels' high variable costs and the various costs attributed to these technologies. The lowest costs are from clean generation sources because maintenance costs are lower and provide benefits for the ecosystem.

4. Conclusions

In this work, the optimization of an Economic Dispatch model for a power supply network located in Mexico's eastern zone is presented. The established model incorporates real parameters and intrinsic restriction to each plant. The energy production of the renewable energy plants was estimated by means of probability functions according to the historical data of the location. The considerations incorporate the various types of generation costs and seek their minimization. This allows the state logic to be fulfilled at all times, as can be seen in Tables 3–6; this is due to Equations (10)–(12), which do not allow a power plant to be off and on at the same time, as well as also that a plant does not start in a period when it was on in the previous period. In addition, all costs can be better accounted for by relating them to binary variables, such as the shutdown, operation, and start-up of a plant.

The results show a majority participation of clean energy plants during the study time period. The model shows the costs that each of the power plants has in period 1, and it reflects the lower costs of the power generation mix that contribute to satisfying the demand, being in this case a combination of clean energy plants. In contrast, the study shows that some non-operating fossil fuel plants generate even higher costs than renewable plants in operation.

The mathematical model could be an important tool in decision-making in plant planning and a diagnostic mode that allows visualizing those plants with very high costs when incorporating new electricity generation sources. In future works, longer periods of time should be addressed (one year) to obtain more significant results from the most suatiable energy generation mix for the zone. Energy distribution will be incorporated due to the importance of power plants, location, and the loads due to the loss of lines at transmission and their capacities. In this way, there is a broader panorama to analyze the system as a decision-making tool.

Author Contributions: Conceptualization, I.S.-T. and R.F.D.-C.; methodology, E.L.; software, E.L. and R.F.D.-C.; validation, E.L., R.F.D.-C. and I.S.-T.; formal analysis, E.L., R.F.D.-C. and I.S.-T.; investigation, E.L.; resources, R.F.D.-C., data curation, E.L.; writing—original draft preparation, E.L.; writing—review and editing, R.F.D.-C. and I.S.-T.; visualization, E.L. and I.S.-T.; supervision, R.F.D.-C. and I.S.-T. All authors have read and agreed to the published version of the manuscript.

Funding: This research received no external funding.

Conflicts of Interest: The authors declare no conflict of interest.

References

1. Kumar, Y.V.; Sivanagaraju, S.; Suresh, C.V. Analyzing the effect of dynamic loads on economic dispatch in the presence of interline power flow controller using modified BAT algorithm. *J. Electr. Syst. Inf. Technol.* **2016**, *3*, 45–67. [CrossRef]
2. Hadera, H.; Ekström, J.; Sand, G.; Mäntysaari, J.; Harjunkoski, I.; Engell, S. Integration of production scheduling and energy-cost optimization using Mean Value Cross Decomposition. *Comput. Chem. Eng.* **2019**, *129*, 106436. [CrossRef]
3. Ringwood, J.V.; Bofelli, D.; Murray, F.T. Forecasting Electricity Demand on Short, Medium and Long Time Scales Using Neural Networks. *J. Intell. Robot. Syst.* **2001**, *31*, 129–147. [CrossRef]
4. Bruno, S.; Dellino, G.; La Scala, M.; Meloni, C. A Microforecasting Module for Energy Management in Residential and Tertiary Buildings. *Energies* **2019**, *12*, 1006. [CrossRef]
5. Dong, L.; Liu, M.; Fan, S.; Pu, T. A Stochastic Model Predictive Control Based Dynamic Optimization of Distribution Network. In Proceedings of the 2018 IEEE Power & Energy Society General Meeting (PESGM), Portland, OR, USA, 5–10 August 2018; pp. 1–5.
6. Chang, P.-C.; Fan, C.-Y.; Lin, J.-J. Monthly electricity demand forecasting based on a weighted evolving fuzzy neural network approach. *Int. J. Electr. Power Energy Syst.* **2011**, *33*, 17–27. [CrossRef]
7. Kafazi, I.; Bannari, R.; Adib, I.; Nabil, H.; Dragicevic, T. Renewable energies: Modeling and optimization of production cost. *Energy Procedia* **2017**, *136*, 380–387. [CrossRef]
8. Investigación de Operaciones. Available online: https://editorialpatria.com.mx/pdffiles/9786074386967.pdf (accessed on 3 June 2021).
9. Caballero, J.A.; Grossmann, I.E. Una revisión del estado del arte en optimización. *Revista Iberoam. Automática Inf. Ind.* **2007**, *4*, 5–23. [CrossRef]
10. Taha, H.A. *Investigación de Operaciones*, Novena ed.; Pearson Educación: Naucalpan de Juárez, Mexico, 2012; ISBN 978-607-32-0796-6.
11. Somma, M.D.; Yanc, B.; Biancob, N.; Graditia, G.; Luhc, P.B.; Mongibelloa, L.; Naso, V. Design optimization of a distributed energy system through cost and exergy assessments. *Energy Procedia* **2017**, *105*, 2451–2459. [CrossRef]
12. di Pilla, L.; Desogus, G.; Mura, S.; Ricciu, R.; Di Francesco, M. Optimizing the distribution of Italian building energy retrofit incentives with Linear Programming. *Energy Build.* **2016**, *112*, 21–27. [CrossRef]
13. McLarty, D.; Panossian, N.; Jabbari, F.; Traverso, A. Dynamic economic dispatch using complementary quadratic programming. *Energy* **2019**, *166*, 755–764. [CrossRef]
14. Arsuaga-Ríos, M.; Vega-Rodríguez, M.A. Multi-objective energy optimization in grid systems from a brain storming strategy. *Soft Comput.* **2014**, *19*, 3159–3172. [CrossRef]
15. Arabali, A.; Ghofrani, M.B.; Etezadi-Amoli, M.; Fadali, M.S.; Baghzouz, Y. Genetic-Algorithm-Based Optimization Approach for Energy Management. *IEEE Trans. Power Deliv.* **2013**, *28*, 162–170. [CrossRef]
16. He, G.; Yan, H.; Liu, K.; Yu, B.; Cui, G.; Zheng, J.; Pan, Y. An optimization method of multiple energy flows for CCHP based on fuzzy theory and PSO. In Proceedings of the 2017 IEEE Conference on Energy Internet and Energy System Integration (EI2), Beijing, China, 26–28 November 2017; pp. 1–6.
17. Li, Y.; Yao, J.; Yao, D. An efficient composite simulated annealing algorithm for global optimization. In Proceedings of the IEEE 2002 International Conference on Communications, Circuits and Systems and West Sino Expositions, Chengdu, China, 29 June–1 July 2002; Volume 2, pp. 1165–1169.
18. Toksarı, M.D. Ant colony optimization approach to estimate energy demand of Turkey. *Energy Policy* **2007**, *35*, 3984–3990. [CrossRef]
19. Kawaguchi, S.; Fukuyama, Y. Reactive Tabu Search for Job-shop scheduling problems considering peak shift of electric power energy consumption. In Proceedings of the 2016 IEEE Region 10 Conference (TENCON), Singapore, 22–25 November 2016; pp. 3406–3409.
20. Kumar, M.V.L.; Prasanna, H.A.M.; Ananthapadmanabha, T. An Artificial Bee Colony algorithm based distribution system state estimation including Renewable Energy Sources. In Proceedings of the 2014 International Conference on Circuits, Power and Computing Technologies [ICCPCT-2014], Nagercoil, India, 20–21 March 2014; pp. 509–515.
21. Killian, M.; Zauner, M.; Kozek, M. Comprehensive smart home energy management system using mixed-integer quadratic-programming. *Appl. Energy* **2018**, *222*, 662–672. [CrossRef]
22. Zio, E.; Baraldi, P.; Pedroni, N. Optimal power system generation scheduling by multi-objective genetic algorithms with preferences. *Reliab. Eng. Syst. Safety* **2009**, *94*, 432–444. [CrossRef]
23. Rodzin, S.I. Smart Dispatching and Metaheuristic Swarm Flow Algorithm. *J. Comput. Syst. Sci. Int.* **2014**, *53*, 109–115. [CrossRef]
24. Gallego Carrillo, M.; Pantrigo Fernández, J.J.; Duarte Muñoz, A. *Metaheuriísticas*; Dykinson: Madrid, Spain, 2007.
25. Eren, Y.; Küçükdemiral, İ.B.; Üstoğlu, İ. Chapter 2—Introduction to Optimization. In *Optimization in Renewable Energy Systems*; Erdinç, O., Ed.; Butterworth-Heinemann: Oxford, UK, 2017; pp. 27–74. ISBN 9780081010419.
26. Cardona, H.A.; Burgos, M.A.; González, J.W.; Isaac, I.A.; López, G.J. Aplicación en Matlab para la programación del despacho económico hidrotérmico. *Rev. Investig. Aplicadas.* **2012**, *6*, 42–53.
27. Augustine, N.; Suresh, S.; Moghe, P.; Sheikh, K. Economic dispatch for a microgrid considering renewable energy cost functions. In Proceedings of the 2012 IEEE PES Innovative Smart Grid Technologies (ISGT), Washington, DC, USA, 16–20 January 2012; pp. 1–7.
28. Ramanathan, R. Emission constrained economic dispatch. *IEEE Trans. Power Syst.* **1994**, *9*, 1994–2000. [CrossRef]

29. Muslu, M. Economic dispatch with environmental considerations: Tradeoff curves and emission reduction rates. *Electr. Power Syst. Res.* **2004**, *71*, 153–158. [CrossRef]
30. Gaing, Z.-L. Particle swarm optimization to solving the economic dispatch considering the generator constraints. *IEEE Trans. Power Syst.* **2003**, *18*, 1187–1195. [CrossRef]
31. Meiqin, M.; Meihong, J.; Wei, D.; Chang, L. Multi-objective economic dispatch model for a microgrid considering reliability. In Proceedings of the 2nd International Symposium on Power Electronics for Distributed Generation Systems Hefei, Hefei, China, 16–18 June 2010; pp. 993–998. [CrossRef]
32. Wang, Y.; An, Y.; Xi, F.; Yao, J.; Wei, Q. Multi-Objective Optimal Operation of Micro-Grid Based on Demand Side Management. *J. Phys. Conf. Ser.* **2018**, *1087*, 062009. [CrossRef]
33. Zhang, Y.; Gatsis, N.; Giannakis, G. Robust Energy Management for Microgrids With High-Penetration Renewables. *IEEE Trans. Sustain. Energy* **2013**, *4*, 944–953. [CrossRef]
34. Liu, D.; Li, Q.; Yuan, X. Economic and optimal dispatching of power microgrid with renewable energy. In Proceedings of the 2014 China International Conference on Electricity Distribution (CICED), Shenzhen, China, 23–26 September 2014; pp. 16–20.
35. Secretaria de Gobernación. Marco Legal y Regulatorio del Sector Energético en MÉXICO. Available online: https://www.gob.mx/cms/uploads/attachment/file/116455/1665.pdf (accessed on 3 June 2021).
36. Secretaría de Energía. El Gobierno de México Fortalece el Sistema Eléctrico Nacional. Available online: https://www.gob.mx/sener/articulos/el-gobierno-de-mexico-fortalece-el-sistema-electrico-nacional (accessed on 3 June 2021).
37. Centro Nacional de Control de Energía (CENACE). Demandas del Sistema Eléctrico Nacional. Available online: https://www.cenace.gob.mx/Paginas/Publicas/Info/DemandaRegional.aspx (accessed on 3 June 2021).
38. Instituto Nacional de Estadística y Geografía (INEGI). Producto Interno Bruto por Entidad Federativa 2019. Available online: https://www.inegi.org.mx/contenidos/saladeprensa/boletines/2020/OtrTemEcon/PIBEntFed2019.pdf (accessed on 3 June 2021).
39. The Mexican National Institute for the Acess to Information. Ministry of Energy. Application Number: 0001800090519. 2019. Available online: https://buscador.plataformadetransparencia.org.mx/web/guest/buscadornacional?buscador=0001800090519&coleccion=5 (accessed on 3 June 2021).
40. MathWorks. Mixed-Integer Linear Programming (MILP). Available online: https://www.mathworks.com/help/optim/ug/intlinprog.html?s_tid=srchtitle (accessed on 3 June 2021).

MDPI
St. Alban-Anlage 66
4052 Basel
Switzerland
Tel. +41 61 683 77 34
Fax +41 61 302 89 18
www.mdpi.com

Mathematical and Computational Applications Editorial Office
E-mail: mca@mdpi.com
www.mdpi.com/journal/mca

www.ingramcontent.com/pod-product-compliance
Lightning Source LLC
LaVergne TN
LVHW070235100526
838202LV00015B/2130